King James Bible
Built-In
Dictionary

Barry Goddard

© Gail and Bryn Riplinger

ISBN 978-0-9794117-2-4
Printed in the United States of America

Contact the publisher for the following:

- A free catalogue of **King James Bibles** and books, DVDs, CDs, CD-ROMs, and tracts supporting it.

- Additional copies of Barry Goddard's book:

  ❦ *The King James Bible's Built-In Dictionary*

- Other books supporting the **King James Bible**, such as Riplinger's *New Age Bible Versions*, *In Awe of Thy Word*, *The Language of the King James Bible*, *Blind Guides*, and *The Only Authorized Picture of Christ*.

A.V. Publications Corp.
P.O. Box 280
Ararat, VA 24053 USA
❦
To see our online catalogue, research updates,
& to sign-up for Riplinger's newsletter go to:

http://www.avpublications.com

Orders: 1-800-435-4535
Inquiries & Fax: 276-251-1734

Credits: Many thanks to David Jubineau and Christian Mermillod-Poensi for permission to use their photograph of the orchid *Peristeria elata*; Bible photography and cover design by Gail Riplinger with help from Bryn Riplinger and Stephen Shutt.

Reading Through the Holy Bible
with the Holy Ghost Superintending

THE HOLY GHOST orchid, seen on the book's cover, is God's own picture of his superintendence over the Holy Bible. This uncanny image is God's reminder that we are to look at the Bible and study it, "...not in the words which man's wisdom teacheth, but which the Holy Ghost teacheth; comparing spiritual things with spiritual" 1 Cor. 2:13. God's word has provided its own method for comparing spiritual things with spiritual things through its built-in dictionary. Read the Bible along with Barry Goddard, from Genesis to Revelation, and see the definitions for the words in the King James Bible. (Parallelisms also occur in the Greek and Hebrew texts, as well as in all pure vernacular Bibles. They do not occur in corrupt versions such as the NIV, NKJV, NASB, HCSB, ESV, New American Bible, New Jerusalem Bible, New Revised Standard Version, The Message, The Amplified Bible, the New Living Translation, or corrupt foreign editions.)

Robert Loweth (1710-1787) was just one among many who have observed and written about the Bible's own built-in dictionary. As Bishop of London and Professor of poetry at Oxford, Loweth observed that the Bible had parallelisms which reiterated God's thoughts.

Fellow Englishman, Barry Goddard of Nottingham, England, carries on the British tradition. He brings to the Holy Bible his well-trained eye. He admits choosing, as a youth, the English dictionary as his favorite textbook. His reverence for his Saviour, the Lord Jesus Christ, and his awe and trembling at the "holy scriptures" bring a respect for each and every word. This heartfelt love of the Lord and respect for and attention to the Bible's details allowed the abiding Holy Ghost to illuminate to him many marvelous parallelisms seen in this volume. As Mr. Goddard would say, "All the glory goes to the Lord."

Goddard wrote about the Bible's built-in dictionary even before my books, *In Awe of Thy Word* and *The Language of the King James Bible,* taught readers just *how* to find this dictionary for themselves. After reading my books, Goddard changed his methodology. He originally found synonyms by using Wigrim's *The Englishman's Hebrew Concordance of the Old Testament* and *The Englishman's Greek Concordance of the New Testament*. The reader will observe that this edition still retains these various English translations of Greek and Hebrew words. In this much enlarged second edition he limits himself to using *only* the English Bible for all new material. Therefore, in this second edition, the reader will see a mixture of contextual and non-contextual 'definitions.'

Goddard's definitions define words much as a regular dictionary does. For instance: 1.) It defines words using *several* other words, and 2.) It provides words that merely shed *some* light on the term in question, since no two words are absolutely identical in meaning and tone.

God included his own built-in dictionary so that he, not man, would determine just what he *means*. The rich vocabulary of synonyms affords many advantages. 1.) It expands the reader's vocabulary and thereby enhances the reader's ability to 'think,' since words are the tools used for thinking. 2.) Words having parallel meanings bring their own rhythm, pace, emphasis, and rhyming sounds, making them fitly framed together in their given context. The Bible is an orchestra of sounds; its words are music for the mind and spirit. 3.) The huge storehouse in the English vocabulary was built from numerous languages (Latin, Greek, Gothic, Germanic, and Hebrew etc.). (This is why English has become *the* international language of the 21st century. Nearly 2 billion of the 6 billion people in the world can speak English as either a first or second language.) Therefore the Bible's multi-language vocabulary and cross-language built-in dictionary makes it a perfect tool to bring non-native speakers gently from the words they recognizes from their own language on to a full understanding of English and its other language basis.

Begin reading along with Barry Goddard in the New Testament. Go from Matthew to Revelation. Then, begin the longer journey through the Old Testament with him. Seeing the definitions Goddard points to will encourage you to tread more slowly and look more closely at parallelisms in the Bible.

I have learned much from this volume and I trust that you will also. The Bible is an unfathomable mine, showing us the mind of God. We have scarcely touched the surface in demonstrating the riches in God's word. Using other methods, including those demonstrated in the first chapters of *In Awe of Thy Word* and *The Language of the King James Bible*, I continue to proceed in my *own* edition of the Bible's built-in dictionary. I have no anticipated date as yet for its release. Try the methods, described in *In Awe of Thy Word*, for finding the dictionary, and let us know the definitions *you* find, so that we can share them with others. We are truly indebted to Barry Goddard for his untiring labors and for bringing this work forward at this time.

It must always be remembered that we read the Bible to learn of and draw nearer to our beloved Saviour, the Lord Jesus Christ. His name is called, The Word of God. It is not an academic exercise. Only he can open the scriptures to us. "Then opened he their understanding, that they might understand the scriptures..." (Luke 24:45).

Jesus even said, "I thank thee, O Father, Lord of heaven and earth, because thou hast hid these things from the wise and prudent, and hast revealed them unto babes. Even so, Father: for so it seemed good in thy sight" (Matt. 11:25, 26)." The Father will hide God's wisdom from those who esteem themselves "wise and prudent." My books, *In Awe of Thy Word*, chapter 26, and *New Age Bible Versions,* Appendix C, explain the Bible's own criteria for being understood. It is a heart issue, not a head issue.

Fellowservant,
Gail Riplinger
2 Thes. 3:1

PREFACE

I thank God and his Son Jesus Christ our Saviour that the present compilation of his word is now completed. It is alleged that the K.J.V., published in A.D. 1611, is difficult to read. This dictionary is published to disprove this. I have only used the K.J.V. for the meaning of words. I believe the K.J.V. is perfect and that it was translated from the Byzantine text, also called the traditional text, the majority text and Syrian text. The K.J.V. is God's final text; it was translated by learned and pious men believing that the work they were doing was the work of God. The argument today is about two types of texts, that called the majority text and that called the critical text.

I know that God has preserved his word down through centuries and it is the K.J.V.. History resounds with the names of those who sealed their testimony with their own blood, who upheld their belief in the majority text.

To all believers who uphold the K.J.V. Bible — thank God for it and be inspired by it, for it is the sword of the Spirit (Eph. 6:18: Heb. 4:12). Be refreshed anew and drink more deeply of the water of life.

God's word is perfect, I am not, therefore any mistakes are mine. Emphasis is mine throughout. This publication replaces the first edition.

Isaiah 34:16   Seek ye out the book of the LORD, and read:
2 Tim. 3:16   All scripture *is* given by inspiration of God, and *is* profitable
          for doctrine, for reproof, for correction, for instruction in
          righteousness.
    : 17   That the man of God may be perfect, throughly furnished unto all
          good works.

B.R. Goddard   January, 2007
Great Britain

Acknowledgements

I wish to thank Gail Riplinger of A.V. Publications, U.S.A. and Ron Smith of London, England for their invaluable help and encouragement in this work.

GENESIS

GENESIS 1: 1	In the beginning God **created** the heaven and the earth.
: 7	And God **made** the firmament,
2: 7	And the LORD God **formed** man *of* the dust of the ground,

GENESIS 1: 1	In the beginning God created the heaven and the **earth.**
2: 5	there was not a man to till the **ground,**
: 12	And the gold of that **land** *is* good:

GENESIS 1: 6	And God said, Let there be a **firmament** in the midst of the waters,
: 8	And God called the firmament **Heaven.**

GENESIS 1: 10	And God called the dry *land* **Earth;**
: 12	And the gold of that **land** *is* good:

GENESIS 1: 11	and the fruit tree, yielding fruit after his **kind,**
7: 14	and every creeping thing that creepeth upon the earth after his kind, and every fowl after his kind, every bird of every **sort.**

GENESIS 1: 20	and **fowl** *that* may fly above the earth in the open firmament of heaven.
7: 7	and every **fowl** after his kind, every **bird** of every sort.

GENESIS 1: 22	And God blessed them saying, **Be fruitful <u>and</u> multiply,**

N.B. note how the underlined word separates words and phrases having the same meaning.

GENESIS 1: 29	in the which *is* the fruit of a tree yielding seed; to you it shall be for **meat.**
2: 9	and good for **food;**

GENESIS 1: 30	and to every thing that creepeth upon the earth, **wherein** *there is* **life,**
: 29	and every tree, **in** the **which** *is* the fruit of a tree yielding seed,
44: 5	*Is* not this *it* **in which** my lord drinketh,

GENESIS 1: 30	*I have given* every green herb for **meat:**
2: 9	and good for **food;**

GENESIS 2: 3	And God blessed the seventh day and **sanctified** it:
13: 11	and they **separated** themselves the one from the other.

GENESIS 2: 3	because that in it he had rested from all his work from all his work which God **created <u>and</u>** made.

N. B. note how the underlined word separates words and phrases having the same
meaning.

GENESIS 2: 5	and *there was* not a man to **till** the ground.
Deut. 2: 22	Thou shalt not **plow** with an ox and an ass together.

GENESIS 2: 10 And river went out of Eden to water the garden; and from
thence it was parted, and became into four heads.

: 8   and **there** he put the man whom he had formed.

: 14   that *is* it **which** goeth toward the east of Assyria.

GENESIS 2: 11 The name of the first *is* Pison: that *is* it which **compasseth** the whole
land of Havillah,

Exodus 39: 6   And they wrought onyx stones **inclosed** in ouches of gold,

GENESIS 2: 17 thou shalt not eat **of it:** for in the day that thou eatest **thereof**
thou shalt surely die.

GENESIS 2: 18 I will make him a help **meet** for him.

Numbers 27: 7   The daughters of Zelophehad speak **right:**

2 Kings 10: 3   Look even out the **best** and meetest of your master's sons,

GENESIS 3: 1 Now the serpent was more **subtil** than any beast of the field
which the LORD God had made.

Job 5: 12   He disappointeth the devices of the **crafty,**

Psalm 5: 6   the LORD will abhor the bloody and **deceitful** man.

GENESIS 3: 3 But of the fruit of the tree which *is* in the **mid**st of the garden,

Exodus 12: 29   And it came to pass, that at **mid**night the LORD smote all the
firstborn in the land of Egypt,

26: 28   And the **mid**dle bar in the **mid**st of the boards shall reach
from end to end.

GENESIS 3: 5 For God doth know that in the day ye eat **thereof,** then your
eyes shall be opened,

: 3   Ye shall not eat **of it,**

GENESIS 3: 11 Hast thou eaten of the tree, **whereof** I commanded thee thou
shouldest not?

: 17   and hast eaten of the tree, **of which** I commanded thee,

GENESIS 3: 13 And the woman said, The serpent **beguiled** me, and I did eat.

31: 7   And your father hath **deceived** me, and changed my wages ten
times;

GENESIS 3: 15 And I will put **enmity** between thee and the woman,

Ezekiel 25: 15   to destroy *it* for the old **hatred;**

2

	thou shouldest not eat?
: 17	and hast eaten of the tree, **of which** I commanded thee, saying,
	Thou shalt not eat of it:
GENESIS 3: 19	In the sweat of face shalt thou eat **bread,**
2: 9	and good for **food:**
GENESIS 3: 23	to till the ground from **whence** he was taken.
1: 29	in the **which** *is* the fruit of a tree yielding seed,

GENESIS 4: 3   **And in process of time it came to pass,**

N.B. note that the first five of the bold words means the same as the last four, compare ch. 6: 1

GENESIS 4: 4	And Abel, he also brought of the **firstlings** of his flock and of the fat thereof.
10: 15	Canaan begat Sidon his **firstborn,**
GENESIS 4: 6	And the LORD said to Cain, Why are thou **wroth,**
18: 30	And he said *unto him*, O let not the LORD be **angry,**
GENESIS 4: 8	that Cain rose up against Abel his brother, and **slew him.**
37: 31	and they took Joseph's coat, and **killed** a kid of the goats,
GENESIS 4: 12	When thou tillest the ground, it shall not **henceforth** yield her strength;
Psalm 113: 2	Blessed be the name of the LORD **from this time forth** and for evermore.
GENESIS 4: 22	And Zillah, she also bare Tubalcain, an instructor of every **artificer** in brass and iron:
Deut. 27: 15	the work of the **craftsman,**
GENESIS 4: 23	for **I have slain** a man to my wounding, and a young man to my hurt.
1 Samuel 25: 11	and my flesh that **I have killed** for my shearers,
GENESIS 5: 3	and begat *a son* in his own **likeness,** after his **image;**
GENESIS 6: 8	But Noah found **grace** in the eyes of the LORD.
18: 3	And said, My lord, if now I have found **favour** in thy sight,
GENESIS 6: 9	Noah was a **just** man and **perfect** in his generations,
7: 1	thee have I seen **righteous** before me in this generation.
GENESIS 6: 14	and shalt pitch it **within** and without with pitch.
1 Kings 6: 15	*and* he covered *them* on the **inside** with wood,
GENESIS 6: 14	and shalt pitch it within and with**out** with pitch.
1 Kings 7: 9	and *so* on the **outside** toward the great court.

GENESIS 6: 15	the **breadth** of it fifty cubits, and the height of it thirty cubits.
Ezek. 41: 10	And between the chambers *was* the **wideness** of twenty cubits round about the house on every side.
GENESIS 6: 15	the breadth **of it** fifty cubits,
: 16	and the door of the ark shalt thou shalt set in the side **thereof;**
GENESIS 6: 17	to destroy all flesh, **wherein** *is* the breath of life,
1: 29	and every tree, **in the which** *is* the fruit of a tree yielding seed,
GENESIS 6: 18	But with thee will I establish my **covenant;**
Isaiah 28: 15	We have made a **covenant** with death, and with hell are we at **agreement;**
GENESIS 6: 19	And of every living thing of all flesh, two of every *sort* shalt thou bring into the ark,
7: 14	and every fowl after his **kind,** every bird of every **sort.**
GENESIS 7: 14	and every **fowl** after his kind, every **bird** of every sort.
GENESIS 7: 1	for thee have I seen **righteous** before me in this generation.
6: 9	Noah was a **just** man *and* **perfect** in his generations,
Exodus 15: 26	If thou wilt diligently hearken to the voice of the LORD thy God,
	and will do that which is **right** in his sight,
Job 1: 1	and that one was **perfect <u>and</u> upright,** and one that feared God,

N. B. note how the underlined word separates words and phrases having the same meaning.

GENESIS 7: 13	In the self**same day** entered Noah,
: 11	the seventeenth day of the month, the **same day** were all the fountains of the deep broken up,
GENESIS 7: 14	and every fowl after his **kind,** every bird of every **sort.**
GENESIS 7: 19	And the waters **prevailed exceedingly** upon the earth;
7: 18	And the waters prevailed, and were **increased greatly** upon the earth;
GENESIS 7: 23	And **every living substance** was destroyed which was on the face of the ground,
: 21	And **all flesh died** that moved upon the earth,
GENESIS 8: 1	and God made a wind to pass over the earth, and the waters **asswaged;**
: 2	The fountains also of the deep the windows of heaven were **stopped,** and the rain from heaven was **restrained;**
: 3	and after the end of the hundred and fifty days the waters were

	abated.
: 5	And the waters **decreased** continually until the tenth month:

GENESIS 8: 17 and of every creeping thing that creepeth upon the earth; that they may **breed abundantly** in the earth, and **be fruitful, and multiply** upon the earth.

N.B. note how the underlined word separates words and phrases having the same meaning.

GENESIS 8: 21 neither will I again **smite** any more every thing living,
Exodus 12: 7 And they shall take of the blood, and **strike** *it* on the two side posts...

GENESIS 9: 2 And the **fear of you and the dread of you** shall be upon every beast of the earth,

GENESIS 9: 4 But flesh with the life **thereof,** *which is* the blood thereof, shall ye not eat.
3: 17 Thou shalt not eat **of it:**

GENESIS 9: 7 bring forth abundantly in the earth, and multiply **therein.**
2: 3 because that **in it** he had rested from all his work which God created and made.

GENESIS 9: 12 which I make between me and you and every living creature that *is* with you, for **perpetual** generations:
: 16 that I may remember the **everlasting** covenant...

GENESIS 9: 19 These *are* the three sons of Noah: and of them was the whole earth **overspread.**
10: 5 By these were the isles of the Gentiles **divided** in their lands;
: 18 and afterward were the families of the Canaanites **spread abroad.**
11: 4 lest we be **scattered** abroad upon the face of the whole earth.

GENESIS 9: 20 And Noah began *to be* an **husbandman,** and he **planted** a vineyard: but Cain was a **tiller of the ground.**
Isaiah 61: 5 and the sons of the alien *shall be* your **plowmen** and your vine-dressers.

GENESIS 10: 9 **wherefore** it is said, Even as Nimrod the mighty hunter before the LORD.
11: 9 **Therefore** is the name of it is called Babel;

GENESIS 11: 1 And the whole earth was of **one language and one speech.**

N.B. note the underlined word that separates words and phrases having the same meaning.

GENESIS 11: 3 And they said one to another, **Go to,** and let us make brick,

Exodus 1: 10	**Come on,** let us deal wisely with them;
GENESIS 11: 8	So the LORD scattered them abroad **from thence** upon the face of all the earth:
: 2	and they dwelt **there.**
Mark 6: 10	there abide till you depart **from that place.**
GENESIS 11: 28	And Har-an died before his father Te-rah in the land of his **nativity,** in Ur of the Chal-dees.
Exodus 28: 10	according to their **birth.**
GENESIS 11: 30	But Sarai was **barren; she** *had* **no child.**
15: 2	And Abram said, Lord GOD, what wilt thou give me, seeing I go **childless,**
GENESIS 12: 1	Get thee of thy country, and from thy **kin**dred, and from thy **father's house,**
Leviticus 18: 6	None of you shall approach to any that is near of **kin** to him,
20: 5	Then I will set my face against that man, and his **family,**
GENESIS 12: 5	And Abram took Sar-a-I his wife, and Lot **his brother's son,**
Job 18: 19	He shall neither have son nor **nephew** among his people,
GENESIS 12: 8	And he removed **from thence** unto a mountain on the east of Beth-el,
Mark 6: 10	there abide till ye depart **from that place.**
GENESIS 12: 10	And Abram went down into Egypt to **sojourn** there;
13: 6	that they might **dwell** together:
19: 17	neither **stay** thou in all the plain:
19: 2	And they said, Nay; but we will **abide** in the street all night.
GENESIS 12: 15	The princes also of **Pharaoh** saw her,
40: 1	And it came to pass after these things, *that* the butler of the **king of Egypt ...**
GENESIS 12: 16	And he en**treated** Abram well for her sake:
GENESIS 14: 8	and they joined battle with them in the **vale** of Siddim;
: 17	at the **valley** of Shaveh, which *is* the king's **dale.**
GENESIS 14: 11	And they took all the goods of Sodom and Gomorrah, and all their **victuals,** and went their way.
6: 21	And take thou unto thee of all **food** that is eaten,
14: 18	And Melchizedek king of Salem brought forth **bread and wine:**
42: 25	and to give them **provision** for the way:
GENESIS 14: 20	And he gave him **tithes** of all.
28: 22	I will surely give the **tenth** unto thee.

GENESIS 15: 5	and said, Look now toward heaven, and **tell** the stars, if thou be able to **number** them: and he said unto him, So shall thy seed be.
GENESIS 15: 8 26: 9	And he said, Lord GOD, **whereby** shall I that I will inherit it? Behold, of a surety she *is* thy wife: and **how** saidst thou, She *is* my sister?
GENESIS 15: 9 Job 21: 10 Leviticus 22: 28 Genesis 32: 15	And he said unto him, Take me an **heifer of three years old,** their **cow** calveth and casteth not her calf. And *whether it be* **cow** or ewe, thirty milch camels with their colts, forty **kine,**
GENESIS 15: 10 : 11	but the **birds** divided he not. And when the **fowls** came down upon the carcases,
GENESIS 15: 16 16: 13	But in the fourth generation they shall come **hither** again: for she said, Have I also **here** looked after him that seeth me?
GENESIS 16: 8 18: 9	And he said, Ha-gar, Sar-a-i's maid, **whence** camest thou? And they said unto him, **Where** *is* Sarah thy wife? and **whither** wilt thou go?
GENESIS 16: 14 12: 12	**Wherefore** the well was called Beer- la- hai-roi; **Therefore** it shall come to pass,
GENESIS 16: 16 5: 26	And Abram *was* **fourscore** and six years old, And Methuselah lived after he begat Lamech seven hundred **eighty** and seven years,

N.B. The underlined word is a numerical term meaning twenty. To find the value of the 'score' number multiply 4x20=80.

GENESIS 17: 2 19: 3	And I will make my covenant between me and thee, and I will multiply thee **exceedingly.** And he pressed upon them **greatly;**
GENESIS 17: 8 Isaiah 66: 4	the land **wherein** thou art a stranger, all the land of Canaan, and chose *that* **in which** I delighted not.
GENESIS 17: 11 : 10	and it shall be a token of the covenant **betwixt me and you.** This *is* my covenant, which ye shall keep, **between you** and thy seed after thee;
GENESIS 17: 14	And the uncircumcised man child whose flesh of his foreskin is **not** circumcised,

N. B. note the bold lettering which means the same thing.

7

GENESIS 17: 19	And God said, Sarah thy wife shall bear thee a son **indeed;**
18: 10	And he said, I will **certainly** return unto thee according to the time of life;
: 13	Shall I of **a surety** bear a child, which am old?
: 18	Seeing that Abraham **shall surely** become a great and mighty nation,

GENESIS 18: 16	And the men rose up **from thence,** and looked towards Sodom:
: 24	Peradventure **there** be fifty righteous within the city:
Mark 6: 10	There abide till ye depart **from that place.**

| **GENESIS 18: 24** | **Peradventure** there be fifty righteous within the city: |
| : 26 | And the LORD said, **If** I find in Sodom fifty righteous within the city: |

| **GENESIS 18: 24** | wilt thou also **destroy <u>and</u> not spare** the place for the fifty righteous that *are* therein? |

N.B. note how the underlined word separates words and phrases having the same meaning.

| **GENESIS 18: 24** | wilt thou also destroy and not spare the place for the fifty righteous that *are* **therein?** |
| 2: 3 | because that **in it** he had rested from all his work which God created and made. |

N.B. note also that if the two syllables of the first reference are reversed the meaning is clear.

| **GENESIS 18: 26** | And the LORD said, If I find **in** Sodom fifty righteous **within** the city, |
| 1 Kings 6: 15 | *and* he covered *them* on the **inside** with wood, |

| **GENESIS 19: 2** | And he said, Behold now, my lords, turn in, I pray you, into your servant's house, and **tarry** all night, and wash your feet, and ye shall rise early, and go on your ways. And they said, Nay; but we will abide in the street all night. |
| : 17 | look not behind thee, neither **stay** thou in all the plain; |

| **GENESIS 19: 4** | But before they lay down, the men of the city, *even* the men of Sodom **compassed** the house **round,** |
| Psalm 22: 16 | For dogs have **compassed** me: the assembly of the wicked have **inclosed** me: |

N. B. a compass is round so the meaning is clear.

| **GENESIS 19: 19** | Behold now, thy servant hath found **grace** in thy sight, |
| 18: 3 | And said, My Lord, if now I have found **favour** in thy sight, |

| **GENESIS 19: 20** | Behold now, this city *is* near to flee unto, and it *is* a little one: |

	O, let me escape **thither**,
: 1	And **there** two angels to Sodom at even;
2: 8	And the LORD God planted a garden eastward in Eden; and **there** put the man whom he had formed.
18: 24	Peradventure **there** be fifty righteous within the city:

GENESIS 20: 1 And Abraham journeyed from **thence** toward the south country,

21: 31 Wherefore he called that place Beersheba; because **there** they sware both of them.

GENESIS 21: 1 And the LORD visted Sarah **as he had said,** and the LORD did unto Sarah **as he had spoken.**

GENESIS 21: 10 **Wherefore** she said unto Abraham,

: 23 Now **therefore** swear unto me here by God...

GENESIS 21: 12 **hearken** unto her voice; for in Isaac shall thy seed be called.

Isaiah 49: 1 **Listen,** O isles, **hearken,** ye people, from far;

GENESIS 21: 23 thou shalt do unto me, and to the land **wherein** thou hast sojourned.

: 17 for God hath heard the voice of the lad **where** he *is.*

44: 5 *Is* not this *it* **in which** my lord drinketh..?

GENESIS 21: 23 and to the land wherein thou hast **sojourned.**

20: 1 And Abraham journeyed from thence toward the south country, and **dwelled** between Kadesh and Shur,

21: 20 and he grew, and **dwelt** in the wilderness,

GENESIS 21: 26 And Abimelech said, **I wot not** who hath done this thing:

4: 9 And he said, **I know not:** *Am* I my brother's keeper?

GENESIS 22: 1 And it came to pass after these things, that God **did tempt** Abraham,

42: 15 Hereby ye shall be **proved:**

Job 23: 10 *when* he hath **tried** me, I shall come forth as gold.

GENESIS 22: 3 and took two of his young men with him, and Isaac his son, and **clave** the wood for the burnt offering,

Exodus 34: 4 And he **hewed** two tables of stone like unto the first;

2 Chron. 14: 3 and **cut** down the groves:

GENESIS 22: 5 And Abraham said unto his young men, **Abide** ye here with the ass,

19: 17 neither **stay** thou in all the plain;

Exodus 8: 9 to destroy the frogs from thee and thy houses, *that* they may **remain** in the river only?

GENESIS 22: 24 And his **concubine,** whose name *was* Reumah,

Psalm 88: 8 **Lover** and friend hast thou put far from me,

GENESIS 23: 6	none of us shall withhold from thee his **sepulchre,**
: 9	for as much money as it is worth he shall give it to me for a possession of a **buryingplace** amongst you.
35: 20	And Jacob set a pillar upon her **grave:**
Job 21: 32	Yet shall he be brought to the **grave,** and shall remain in the **tomb.**
GENESIS 23: 8	And he **communed with** them saying,
: 3	and **spake** unto the sons of Heth saying,
17: 3	And Abram fell on his face, and God **talked with** him,
GENESIS 23: 11	the field give I thee, and the cave that *is* **therein,** I give it thee;
Genesis 2: 3	because that **in it** he had rested from all his work...
GENESIS 23: 15	what *is* that **betwixt** me and thee?
17: 10	which ye shall keep, **between** me and you...
GENESIS 24: 5	And the servant said unto him, **Peradventure** the woman will not be willing to follow me unto this land:
: 8	And **if** the woman will not be willing to follow thee,
16: 2	**it may be** that I may obtain children by her.
GENESIS 24: 12	I pray thee, **send me good speed this day, <ins>and</ins>** shew **kindness** unto my master Abraham.

N.B. note how the underlined word separates words and phrases having the same meaning.

GENESIS 24: 31	And he said, Come in, thou blessed of the LORD; wherefore standest thou without? for I have **prepared** the house,
43: 25	And they **made ready** the present against Joseph came at noon,
GENESIS 24:14	and **thereby** shall I know that thou hast shewed kindness unto my master.
15: 5	And he said unto him, **So** shall thy seed be.
21: 23	Now **therefore** swear unto me here by God...
Exodus 7: 11	they also did **in like manner** with their enchantments.
12: 11	And **thus** shall ye eat it;
1 Kings 17: 24	Now **by this** I know that thou *art* a man of God,
GENESIS 24: 16	And the **damsel** *was* very fair to look upon, **a virgin, neither had any man known her:**
GENESIS 24: 21	**to wit** wit **whether** the LORD had made his journey prosperous or not.
Deut. 13: 3	**to know whether** ye love the LORD your God with all your heart and with all your soul.
GENESIS 24: 25	She said, moreover unto him, We have both straw and **provender** enough, and room to lodge in.

41: 5	and, behold, seven ears of **corn** came up on one stalk,
Job 6: 5	or loweth the ox over his **fodder?**

GENESIS 24: 25	She said **moreover** unto him,
Exodus 4: 6	And the LORD said **furthermore** unto him,

GENESIS 24: 31	And he said, Come in, thou blessed of the LORD; **wherefore** standest thou without?
27: 45	**why** should I be deprived also of you both in one day?

GENESIS 24: 38	But thou shalt go unto my **father's house,** and to my **kin**dred,
10: 32	These *are* the **families** of Noah, after their generations,

GENESIS 24: 53	And the servant brought forth jewels of silver, and jewels of gold, and **raiment,** and gave *them* to Rebekah:
38: 14	And she put her widow's **garments** off from her,
37: 29	behold, Joseph *was* not in the pit, and he rent his **clothes.**

GENESIS 24: 54	he and the men that *were* with him, and **tarried** all night,
8: 10	And he **stayed** yet another seven days;
32: 13	And he **lodged** there that same night;

GENESIS 24: 63	And Isaac went out to meditate in the field at **eventide:**
29: 23	And it came to pass in the **evening,**

GENESIS 25: 6	But unto the sons of the **concubines,** which Abraham had,
Psalm 38: 11	My **lovers** and my friends stand aloof from my sore,

GENESIS 25: 7	And these *are* the days of the years of Abraham's which he lived, an hundred three**score** and fifteen years.
5: 23	And all the days of Enoch were three hundred and **sixty** and five years:

N.B. The underlined word is a numerical term meaning twenty. To find the value of the score' number multiply 3x20=60.

GENESIS 25: 27	And the boys grew: and Esau was a **cunning** hunter,
1 Chron. 5: 18	able to bear buckler and sword, and to shoot with bow, and **skilful** in war,

GENESIS 25: 29	And Jacob **sod pottage:** and Esau came from the field, and he *was* faint:
1 Kings 19: 21	and slew them, and **boiled** their flesh with the instruments of the oxen,
Genesis 25: 34	Then Jacob gave Esau bread and pottage of **lentiles;**

GENTILES 26: 3	**Sojourn** in this land, and I will be with thee,
: 2	**dwell** in the land which I will tell thee of:
GENESIS 26: 5	Because that Abraham obeyed my voice, and **kept my charge, my commandments, my statutes, and** my laws.

N.B. note how the underlined word separates words and phrases having the same meaning.

GENESIS 26: 9   And Abimelech called Isaac, said, Behold, **of a surety** she *is* thy wife:

: 11   He that toucheth this man or his wife shall **surely** be put to death.

GENESIS 26: 13   And the man **waxed great,** and went forward, and **grew** until he became very great:

GENESIS 26: 15   the Philistines had **stopped them, and filled them with earth.**

N.B. note how the underlined word separates words and phrases having the same meaning.

GENESIS 26: 17   And Isaac departed **thence,** and pitched his tent in the valley of Ge-rar, and dwelt **there.**

GENESIS 26: 28   Let there be now an oath **betwixt** us,
31: 44   and let it be a witness **between** me and thee.

GENESIS 26: 31   And they rose up **betimes** in the morning,
28: 18   And Jacob rose up **early** in the morning,

GENESIS 26: 17   And Isaac departed **thence,** and pitched his tent in the valley of Ge-rar, and dwelt **there.**

GENESIS 26: 27   And Isaac said unto them, **Wherefore** come ye to me, seeing ye hate me, and have sent me away from you?
27: 45   **why** should I be deprived also of you both in one day?

GENESIS 27: 3   Now therefore take, I pray thee, thy **weapons, thy quiver and thy bow,** and go out to the field, and take me *some* venison;

N.B. note how the comma and the underlined word separate words and phrases having the same meaning.

GENESIS 27: 9   Go now to the flock, and fetch me from **thence** two good kids of the goats;
26: 1   And **there** was a famine in the land,

GENESIS 27: 12   My father **peradventure will** feel me,
Acts 8: 22   and pray God, if **perhaps** the thought of thine heart **may** be forgiven thee.
GENESIS 27: 35   And he said, Thy brother came with **subtilty,** and hath taken away thy blessing.
34: 13   And the sons of Jacob answered Shechem and Hamor his

father **deceitfully,**

GENESIS 27: 41	And Esau hated Jacob because of the blessing **wherewith** his father blessed him:
26: 18	and he called their names after the names **by which** his father had called them.

GENESIS 27: 41	The days of mourning for my father are at hand; then will I **slay** my brother Jacob.
: 42	Behold, thy brother Esau, as touching thee, doth comfort himself, *purposing* to **kill** thee.

GENESIS 27: 44	And **tarry** with him a few days,
19: 17	neither **stay** thou in all the plain:
24: 23	is there room *in* thy father's house to **lodge** in?

GENESIS 27: 41	And Esau hated Jacob because of the blessing **wherewith** his father blessed him:
2 Kings 19: 6	Be not afraid of the words **with which** the servants of the king of Assyria have blasphemed me.

GENESIS 27: 44	And **tarry** with him a few days until thy brother's fury turn away;
24 : 23	is there room *in* thy father's house for us to **lodge** in ?
19 : 17	look not behind thee, neither **stay** thou in all the plain;

GENESIS 27: 44	And tarry with him a few days until thy brother's **fury** turn away; until thy brother's **anger** turn away from thee.

GENESIS 28: 1	And Isaac called Jacob, and blessed him, and **charged him,**
21: 4	as God had **commanded him.**

GENESIS 28: 4	and to thee, and to thy seed with thee; that th inherit the land **wherein** thou art a stranger,
44: 5	*Is* not this *it* **in which** my lord drinketh,

GENESIS 28: 6	and sent him away to Pa-dan-ar-am, to take him a wife **thence;** and tarried **tarried** all night,

GENESIS 28: 11	And he lighted upon a certain place, and **tarried** there all night,
31: 21	and himself **lodged** that night in the company.
32:4	I have **sojourned** with Laban, and **stayed** there until now:

GENESIS 28: 13	the land **whereon** thou liest, to thee I will give it,
Leviticus 11: 34	*that* **on which** *such* water cometh shall be unclean.

GENESIS 28: 15	and I will keep thee in all *places* **whither** thou goest,
35: 13	And God went up from him in the place **where** he talked with him.

GENESIS 28: 19	and will give me **bread** to eat, and raiment to put on,
41: 35	and lay up corn under the hand of Pharaoh, and let them keep **food** in the cities.

GENESIS 28: 20	and will give me bread to eat, and **raiment** to put on.
38: 14	And she put her widow's **garments** off from her,
37: 29	behold, Joseph *was* not in the pit; and he rent his **clothes.**
Job 22: 6	and stripped the naked of their **clothing.**

GENESIS 29: 2	And **thither** were all the flocks gathered:
: 3	and, lo, **there** *were* three flocks of sheep lying by it,

GENESIS 29: 15	shouldest thou therefore serve me for **nought?**
26: 29	and as we have done unto thee **nothing** but good,

GENESIS 29: 17	Leah *was* tender eyed; but Rachel was **beautiful and well favoured.**

N.B. note how the underlined word separates words and phrases having the same meaning.

GENESIS 29: 19	than that I should give to another man: **abide** with me.
19: 17	neither **stay** now in all the plain;
27: 40	And by thy sword thou shalt **live,**
30: 20	now will my husband **dwell** with me,
38: 11	**Remain** a widow at thy father's house,

GENESIS 29: 25	What *is* this thou hast done unto me? did not I serve thee for Rachel? **wherefore** then hast thou beguiled me?
27: 45	**why** should I be deprived also of you both in one day?

GENESIS 29: 25	wherefore then hast thou **beguiled** thee?
31: 7	And your father hath **deceived** me,

GENESIS 30: 20	And Leah said, God hath **endued me** *with* a good dowry;
: 27	*for* I have learned by experience that the LORD hath **blessed me** for thy sake.

GENESIS 30: 32	removing from **thence** all the speckled and spotted cattle,
29: 2	and, lo, **there** were three flocks of sheep lying by it;

GENESIS 30: 32	removing from thence all the **speckled and spotted** cattle, and the brown cattle among the sheep, and the **spotted and speckled** among the goats:

N.B. note how the underlined words separates words and phrases having the same meaning. Note also the word order of the two phrases.

GENESIS 30: 36	And he set three days' journey **betwixt** himself and Jacob:
31: 44	and let it be a witness **between** me and thee.

GENESIS 30: 37	and **pilled** white strakes in them, and made the white appear which *was* in the rods.
Isaiah 18: 2	Go, ye swift messengers, to a nation scattered and **peeled,**
GENESIS 30: 41	And it came to pass, **when**soever the stronger cattle did conceive,
31: 49	The LORD watch between me and thee **when** we are absent one from another.
GENESIS 31: 31	Because I was afraid: for I said, **Peradventure** thou wouldest take my daughters by force from me.
16: 2	I pray thee, go in unto my maid; **it may be** that I may obtain children by her.
GENESIS 31: 36	And Jacob was **wroth,** and chode with Laban:
Leviticus 10: 16	and he was **angry** with El-e-azar and Ith-a-mar,
GENESIS 31: 36	And Jacob was wroth, and **chode** with Laban:
1 Samuel 25: 39	Blessed *be* the LORD, that hath **pleaded** the cause of my reproach from the hand of Nabal,
GENESIS 31: 36	What *is* my **trespass**? What *is* my **sin,** that thou hast so hotly pursued after me?
GENESIS 31: 37	**Whereas** thou hast searched all stuff,
12: 11	And it came to pass, **when** he was come near to enter into Egypt,
39: 9	neither hath he kept back any thing from me but thee, **because** thou *art* his wife:
Daniel 2: 47	and a revealer of secrets, **seeing** thou couldst reveal this secret.
GENESIS 31: 40	*Thus* I was; in the day of **drought** consumed me,
1 Kings 8: 35	When heaven is shut up, and there is **no rain,**
Isaiah 53: 2	and as a root out of a **dry** ground:
GENESIS 31: 50	which I have cast **betwixt me and thee.**
: 44	and let it be for a witness **between me and thee.**
GENESIS 31: 51	and behold *this* pillar, which I have cast betwixt **me and thee;**
: 53	the of their father, judge betwixt **us.**
GENESIS 31: 54	and called his brethren to eat **bread:** and they did eat bread,
41: 48	And he gathered up all the **food** of the seven years,
25: 28	And Isaac loved Esau, because he did eat of *his* **venison:**
27: 17	And she gave the savoury **meat** and the **bread,**
GENESIS 31: 54	and **tarried** all night in the mount.
32: 4	I have **sojourned** with Laban, and **stayed** there until now:
: 13	And he **lodged** there that same night;

| 49: 18 | I have **waited** for thy salvation, |

GENESIS 32: 5   and I have sent to tell my lord, that I may find **grace** in thy sight.

| 39: 21 | and gave him **favour** in the sight of the keeper of the prison. |
| 47: 25 | let us find **grace** in the sight of my lord, |

GENESIS 32: 7   then was **greatly afraid <u>and</u> distressed:**

N.B. note how the underlined word separates words and phrases having the same meaning.

GENESIS 32: 8   And said, If Esau come to the one company, and **smite** it,
| 26: 29 | That thou wilt do us no **hurt,** |

GENESIS 32: 9   Return unto thy country, and to thy **kindred,** and I will deal well with thee:
| 12: 1 | and from thy **kindred, <u>and</u> from thy father's house,** |
| Leviticus 25: 10 | and ye shall return every man unto his **family.** |

N.B. note how the underlined word separates words and phrases having the same meaning.

GENESIS 32: 15   Thirty **milch** camels with their colts, forty **kine,**
Leviticus 22: 28	And *whether it be* **cow** or ewe,
1 Samuel 6: 7	and take two **milch kine,** on which there hath come no yoke, and tie the kine to the cart, and bring **there calves** home from them:
Leviticus 22: 28	And *whether it be* **cow** or ewe, ye shall not kill and **her** young both in one day.
1 Samuel 6:7	and take two **milch kine,** on which there hath come no yoke, and tie the **kine** to the cart, and bring their calves home from them:

N.B. note that the word kine refers to the female species of the collective word cattle which is a cow.

GENESIS 32: 16   Pass over before me, and put a space **betwixt** drove and drove.
| 31: 44 | and let it be for a witness **between** me and thee. |

GENESIS 32: 16   Pass over before me, and put a space betwixt **drove and drove.**
| : 7 | and he divided the people that *was* with him, and **the flocks, <u>and</u> the herds,** |

N.B. note how the underlined word separates words and phrases having the meaning.

GENESIS 32: 20   And say ye **moreover,** Behold, thy servant Jacob *is* behind us,
: 6	and **also** he cometh to meet thee,
Exodus 4: 6	And the LORD said **furthermore** unto him,
Deut. 1: 17	*but* ye shall hear the small **as well as** the great;

GENESIS 32: 20	For he said, I will **appease** him with the present that goeth
before me,	
1 Samuel 29: 4	for wherewith should he **reconcile** himself unto his master?
Proverbs 16: 14	but a wise man will **pacify** it.
GENESIS 32: 20	and afterward I will see his face; **peradventure** he will accept of me.
16: 2	**it may be** that I may obtain children by her.
Joshua 14: 12	**if so be** the LORD *will be* with me,
Acts 8: 22	**if perhaps** the thought of thine heart **may be** forgiven thee.
GENESIS 32: 29	**Wherefore** *is* it *that* thou dost ask after my name?
27: 45	**why** should I be deprived also of you both in one day?
GENESIS 33: 2	And he put the handmaids and their children **foremost,** Leah and her children after, and Rachel and Joseph hindermost.
32: 20	I will appease him with the present that goeth **before** me,
GENESIS 33: 2	and Leah and her children **after,** and Rachel and Joseph **hindermost.**
32: 18	it *is* a present sent unto my lord Esau: and, behold also he *is* **behind** us.
GENESIS 33: 10	if now I have found **grace** in thy sight,
18: 3	if now I have found **favour** in thy sight,
GENESIS 34: 2	he took her, and **lay with her, and** defiled her.
Isaiah 13: 16	their houses shall be spoiled, and their wives **ravished.**
GENESIS 34: 3	**And his soul clave unto Dinah** the daughter of Jacob, and **he loved the damsel,** and spake kindly unto the damsel.
24: 16	And the **damsel** *was* very fair to look upon, **a virgin, neither had any man known her:**
GENESIS 34: 7	and the men were grieved, and they were very **wroth,**
45: 5	Now therefore be not grieved, nor **angry** with your selves,
GENESIS 34: 7	because he had **wrought** folly in Israel in lying with Jacob's daughter; which thing ought not to be **done.**
GENESIS 34: 10	and the land shall be before you; and trade **therein,**
30: 35	*and* every one that had *some* white **in it,**

N.B. reverse the syllables in the first reference and the meaning is clear.

GENESIS 34:12	Ask me never so much **dowry and gift,** and I will give according as ye shall ask unto me.

N.B. note how the underlined word separates words and phrases having the same meaning.

| **GENESIS 34: 22** | Only **herein** will the men conset unto us for to dwell with us, |
| : 15 | But **in this** will we consent unto you: |

| **GENESIS 34: 31** | And they said, Should he deal with our sister as with an **harlot**? |
| Leviticus 21: 7 | They shall not take a wife *that is* a **whore**, |

| **GENESIS 35: 8** | But Deborah Rebekah's nurse died, and she was buried **beneath** Beth-el **under** an oak: |
| | A nation and a company of nations **shall be of thee**, and kings shall **come out of** thy loins; |

| **GENESIS 35: 14** | and he poured a drink offering **thereon**, |
| : 20 | And Jacob set a pillar **upon** her grave: |

| **GENESIS 35: 28** | And the days of Isaac were an hundred and four**score** years. |
| 5: 28 | And Lamech lived an hundred **eighty** and two years, |

N.B. The underlined word is a mathematical term meaning twenty. To find the value of the 'score' number multiply 4x20=80.

| **GENESIS 36: 7** | and the land **wherein** they were strangers could not bear them because of their cattle. |
| 44: 5 | *Is* not this *it* **in which** my lord drinketh, |

GENESIS 37: 7	and, behold, your sheaves stood round about, and **made obeisance** to my sheaf.
1 Kings 1: 16	And Bathsheba **bowed, and** did obeisance** unto the king.
: 23	he **bowed** himself before the king **with his face to the ground.**
1 Sam. 9: 6	**he fell on his face and did reverence.**
Lev. 26: 9	For I will have **respect** unto you,

N.B. note how the underlined word separates words and phrases having the same meaning.

| **GENESIS 37: 8** | And his brethren said to him, shalt thou indeed **reign** over us? or shalt thou indeed **have dominion** over? |
| Leviticus 25: 43 | Thou shalt indeed not **rule** over him with vigour; |

| **GENESIS 37: 30** | And he returned unto his brethren, and said, The child *is* not; and I, **whither** shall I go? |
| 38 : 21 | **Where** *is* the harlot, that *was* openly by the way side? |

| **GENESIS 37: 17** | And the man said, They are departed **hence**; |
| Ruth 2: 8 | Go not to glean in another field, neither go **from here**, |

| **GENESIS 37: 20** | Come now therefore, and let us slay **him**, |
| : 21 | and said, Let us not **kill him.** |

| **GENESIS 37: 30** | And he returned unto his brethren, and I, **whither** shall I go? |

: 16	tell me, I pray thee, **where** they feed *their flocks,*
GENESIS 38: 11	for he said, **Lest peradventure** he die also,
16: 2	**it may be** that I may obtain children by her.
18: 26	And the LORD said, **If** I find in Sodom fifty righteous within the city,
GENESIS 38: 15	When Judah saw her *to be* an **harlot:**
Leviticus 21: 7	They shall not take a wife *that is* a **whore,**
GENESIS 38: 26	And Judah acknowledged *them,* and said, She hath been more **right**eous than I;
Job 13: 18	Behold now, I have *ordered* cause; I know that I shall be **justified.**
GENESIS 39: 1	and Potiphar, an officer of **Pharaoh,** captain of the guard,
40: 1	And it came to pass after these things, *that* the butler of the **king of Egypt** and *his* baker had offended their lord…
GENESIS 39: 4	And Joseph found **grace** in his sight, and he served him;
: 21	and shewed him mercy, and gave him **favour** in the sight of the keeper of the prison.
GENESIS 39: 8	Behold, my master **wotteth not** what *is* with me in the house,
33: 13	My lord **knoweth** that the children *are* tender,
GENESIS 40: 1	And it came to after these things, *that* the **butler** of the king of the king of Egypt…
Nehemiah 1: 11	and grant him mercy in the sight of this man. For I was the king's **cupbearer.**
GENESIS 40: 2	And Pharaoh was **wroth** against two *of* his officers,
45: 5	Now therefore be not grieved, nor **angry** with yourselves,
GENESIS 40: 3	And he put them **in ward** in the house of the captain of the guard, into **the prison,** the place where Joseph *was* bound,
GENESIS 40: 7	**Wherefore** look ye *so* sadly to day?
42: 1	Jacob said unto his sons, **Why** do ye look one upon another?
GENESIS 40: 10	and the clusters **thereof** brought forth ripe grapes:
: 8	and *there is* no interpreter **of it.**
GENESIS 40: 17	And in the **uppermost** basket *there was* of all manner of bakements for Pharaoh;
28: 18	and poured oil upon the **top** of it.
GENESIS 41: 2	And behold, there came up out of the river seven **well favoured kine and fatfleshed;** and they fed in a meadow.

N.B. note how the underlined word separates words and phrases having the same

meaning.

GENESIS 41: 3	And, behold, seven other **kine** came up after them out of the river **ill favoured <u>and</u> leanedfleshed;** and stood by the *other* kine upon the brink of the river.
1 Samuel 6: 7	Now therefore make a new cart, and take two **milch kine,** on which there hath come no yoke, and tie the **kine** to the cart, and bring **their calves** home from them.
Job 21: 10	their **cow calveth,** and casteth not **her calf.**
Isaiah 11: 7	And the **cow** and the bear shall feed; **their young ones** shall lie down together.

GENESIS 41: 5	and, behold, seven ears of corn came up on one stalk, **rank <u>and</u> good.**
: 22	and, behold, seven ears came up in one stalk, **full <u>and</u> good:**

N. B. note how the underlined words separate words and phrases having the same meaning.

GENESIS 41: 6	And, behold, **seven thin ears <u>and</u> blasted** with the east wind sprung up after them.

N.B. note how the underlined word separates words and phrases having the same meaning.

GENESIS 41: 8	and all the magicians of Egypt, and all the wise men **thereof:**
: 12	And Joseph said unto him, This *is* the interpretation **of it:**

GENESIS 41: 14	and he shaved *himself,* and changed his **raiment,** and came unto Pharaoh.
49: 11	he **washed his garments in wine, <u>and</u> his clothes in the blood of grapes:**

N.B. note how the underlined word separates words and phrases having the same meaning.

GENESIS 41: 34	and take up the fifth part of the land of Egypt in the seven **plenteous** years.
: 29	Behold, there come seven years of **great plenty** throughout all the land.

GENESIS 41: 35	and lay up **corn** under the hand of Pharaoh, and let them keep **food** in the cities.

GENESIS 41: 39	And Pharaoh said unto Joseph, **For<u>as</u>much as** God hath shewed thee all this,
: 40	Thou shalt be over my house, and **according** unto thy word shall all my people be ruled:
Daniel 2: 47	and a Lord of kings, and a revealer of secrets, **seeing** thou **couldest** reveal this secret.

GENESIS 41: 49	And Joseph gathered corn **as the sand of the sea, very much,** until he left numbering; for *it was* **without number.**
GENESIS 41: 54	And the seven years of **dearth** began to come,
: 56	And the **famine** was all over the face of the earth:
GENESIS 42: 2	And he said, Behold, I have heard that **there** is corn in Egypt: get you down **thither,** and buy for us from **thence; that we** may live and not die.
GENESIS 42: 4	for he said, **Lest peradventure** mischief befall him.
16: 2	**it may be** that I may obtain children by her.
GENESIS 42: 15	**Hereby** ye shall be proved:
34: 15	But **in this** will we consent unto you:
Isaiah 27: 9	**By this** therefore shall the iniquity of Jacob be purged;
GENESIS 42: 15	By the life of Pharaoh ye shall not go forth **hence,** except your youngest brother come **hither.**
19: 12	And the men said unto Lot, Hast thou **here** any besides?
GENESIS 42: 17	And he put them all together **into ward** three days.
: 19	let one of your brethren be bound in the house of your **prison:**
40: 15	and here also have done nothing that they should put me into the **dungeon.**
GENESIS 42: 20	But bring your youngest brother unto me; so shall your words **be verified,** and ye shall not die.
: 15	Hereby ye shall **be proved:**
GENESIS 42: 21	And they said one to another, We *are* **verily** guilty concerning our brother,
17: 19	Sarah thy wife shall bear thee a son **indeed;**
26: 9	Behold, **of a surety** she *is* thy wife:
27: 36	And he said, Is not he **rightly** named Jacob?
29: 14	And Laban said to him, **Surely** thou *art* my bone and my flesh.
29: 32	for she said, Surely the LORD hath looked upon my affliction;
48: 19	but **truly** his younger brother shall be greater than he,
GENESIS 42: 27	And as one of them opened his sack to give his ass **provender** in the inn,
: 26	And they laded their asses with the **corn,**
Job 6: 5	or loweth the ox over his **fodder?**
GENESIS 42: 29	and told him all that **befell** unto them;
Esther 4: 7	And Mordecai told him of all that **had happened** unto him,
GENESIS 42: 33 shall I	And the man, the lord of the country, said unto us, **Hereby**
	know that *ye are* true *men;*

1 Samuel 26: 24	And, behold, as thy life was much set **by this** day in mine eyes,
GENESIS 42: 34	*so* will I deliver you your brother, and ye shall **traffick** in the land.
34: 10	and the land shall be before you; dwell and **trade** ye therein,
GENESIS 42: 38	if mischief **befall** him by the way in the which ye go,
1 Samuel 28: 10	*As* the LORD liveth, there shall no punishment **happen** to thee for this thing.
GENESIS 43: 6	And Israel said, **Wherefore** dealt ye *so* ill with me, *as* to tell the man whether ye had yet a brother?
42: 1	Jacob said unto his sons, **Why** do ye look one upon another?
GENESIS 43: 7	And they said, The man **asked us straitly** of our state,
: 3	The man did **solemnly protest** unto us, saying,
GENESIS 43: 10	For except we had **lingered,** surely now we had returned this second time.
49: 18	I have **waited** for thy salvation, O LORD.
Exodus 32: 1	And when the people saw that Moses **delayed** to come down the mount,
GENESIS 43: 12	carry *it* again in your hand; **peradventure** it *was* an oversight:
16: 2	**it may be** that I may obtain children by her.
Acts 8: 22	if **perhaps** the thought of thine heart **may be** forgiven thee.
GENESIS 43: 16	And when Joseph saw Benjamin with them, he said to **the ruler of his house,**
44: 1	And he commanded **the steward of his house,**
GENESIS 43: 17	And the man did as Joseph **bade;**
44 : 2	And he did according to the word that Joseph **had spoken.**
GENESIS 43: 19	and they **communed with** him at the door of the house,
45 : 15	and after that his brethren **talked with** him.
GENESIS 43: 25	And they made ready the present **against** Joseph came at noon:
45: 5	for God did send me **before** you to preserve life.
GENESIS 43: 28	And they **bowed down their heads, and made obeisance.**

N.B. note how the underlined word separates words and phrases having the same meaning.

GENESIS 44: 4	and when thou dost overtake say unto them, **Wherefore** have ye ewarded evil for good?
42: 1	**Why** do ye look one upon another?
GENESIS 44: 5	*Is* not this *it* in which my lord drinketh, and **whereby** indeed he divineth? ye have done evil in so doing.

26: 18	and he called their names after the names **by which** his father had called them.

GENESIS 44: 6	And they said unto him, **Wherefore** saith my lord these words?
42: 1	Jacob said unto his sons, **Why** do ye look upon another?
Amos 5: 18	Woe unto you that desire the day of the LORD! **to what end** *is* it for you? the day of the LORD *is* darkness, and not light.

GENESIS 44: 11	Then they **speedily** took down every man's sack to the ground,
27: 20	How *is it* that thou hast found *it* so **quickly,** my son?

GENESIS 44:15	And Joseph said unto them, What deed *is* this that ye have done?
	wot ye not that such a man as I can certainly divine?
2 Samuel 3: 38	**Know ye not** that there is a prince and a great man fallen this in Israel?

GENESIS 44: 16	And Judah said, **What shall we say unto my lord? what shall we speak?**

N.B. note how the first question mark separates words and phrases having the same meaning.

GENESIS 44: 34	**Lest peradventure** I see the evil that shall come on my father.
16: 2	**it may be** that I **may** obtain children by her.

GENESIS 45: 1	Then Joseph **could not refrain himself** before all that stood by him; and **he cried,**
Job 4: 2	but who can **withhold himself** from speaking?

GENESIS 45: 5	nor angry with yourselves, that ye sold me **hither:**
42: 33	leave one of your brethren *here* with me,

GENESIS 45: 6	in the which *there shall* neither *be* **earing** nor harvest.
1 Kings 19: 19	Elisha the son of Shaphat, who *was* **plowing**...

GENESIS 45: 8	So now *it was* you *that* sent me **hither,** but God:
40: 15	and **here** also have I done nothing that they should put me into the dungeon.

GENESIS 45: 9	God hath made lord of all Egypt: come down unto me, **tarry not.**
Exodus 22: 29	Thou shall not **delay** *to offer* the first of thy ripe fruits,

GENESIS 45: 15	**Moreover** he kissed all his brethren,
Exodus 4: 6	And the LORD said **furthermore** unto him,

GENESIS 45: 16	An the **fame** thereof was heard in Pharaoh's house,
Exodus 20: 18	and the **noise** of the trumpet,

| GENESIS 45: 16 | And the fame **thereof** was heard in Pharaoh's house, |
| 50: 11 | wherefore the name **of it** was called A-bel-miz-ra-im, |

| GENESIS 45: 21 | and Joseph gave them wagons, according to the commandment of Pharaoh, and gave them **provision** for the way. |
| 45: 23 | and ten she asses laden with **corn and bread and meat** for his father by the way. |

| GENESIS 45: 22 | To all of them he gave each man changes of **raiment;** |
| 49: 11 | he washed his **garments** in wine, and his **clothes** in the blood of the grapes: |

| GENESIS 46: 26 | besides Jacob's son's wives, all the souls *were* **three**score and ten. |
| Exodus 1: 5 | And all the souls that came out of the loins of Jacob were **seventy** souls: |

N.B. The underlined word is a numerical term meaning twenty. To find the value of the 'score' number multiply 3x20=60.

| GENESIS 47: 4 | They said moreover unto Pharaoh, For to **sojourn** in the land are we come; for thy servants have no pasture for their flocks; for the famine *is* sore in the land of Canaan: now therefore, we pray thee, let thy servants **dwell** in the land of Goshen. |

| GENESIS 47: 12 | And Joseph nourished his father, and his brethren, with **bread,** |
| : 24 | for seed of the field, and for your **food,** |

| GENESIS 47: 19 | **Wherefore** shall we die before thine eyes, both we and our land? |
| : 15 | for **why** should we die in thy presence? |

| GENESIS 47: 21 | he removed them to cities from *one* end of the borders of Egypt even to the *other* end **thereof.** |
| 50: 11 | wherefore the name **of it** was called A-bel-miz-ra-im, |

GENESIS 47: 22	and did eat their portion which Pharaoh gave them: **wherefore** they sold not their lands.
: 4	now **therefore,** we pray thee, let thy servants dwell in the land of Goshen.
Numbers 16: 11	**For which cause** *both* thou and all thy company *are* gathered together against the LORD:

| GENESIS 47: 25 | let us find **grace** in the sight of my lord, |
| 39: 21 | and gave him **favour** in the sight of the keeper of the prison. |

| GENESIS 47: 27 | and they had possessions **therein,** |

N.B. Reverse the syllables in the first reference and the meaning is clear.

<u>**GENESIS 47: 27**</u>	and they had possessions therein, and grew, and **multiplied exceedingly.**
24: 35	And the LORD hath blessed my master **greatly,**
Exodus 1: 7	And the children of Israel **were fruitful, and increased abundantly, and multiplied, and waxed exceeding mighty;**

N.B. notice how the underlined words separate words and phrases having the same meaning.

<u>**GENESIS 47: 29**</u>	And the time drew **nigh** that Israel must die:
48: 10	And he he brought them **near** unto him:

<u>**GENESIS 48: 14**</u>	and his left hand upon Manasseh's head, guiding his hands **unwittingly;** for Manasseh *was* the firstborn.
Deut. 4: 42	which should kill his neighbour **unawares.**
19: 4	Whoso killeth his neighbour **ignorantly,**
Job 34: 35	Job hath spoken **without knowledge,**

<u>**GENESIS 48: 16**</u>	and let them grow into a multitude **in the midst of** the earth.
47: 6	and if thou knowest *any* men of activity **among** them,

<u>**GENESIS 49: 7**</u>	Cursed *be* their **anger**, for *it was* fierce; and their **wrath,** for it as cruel:

<u>**GENESIS 49: 9**</u>	Judah *is* a **lion's whelp:**
Lam. 4: 3	they give suck to their **young ones:**

<u>**GENESIS 49: 9**</u>	**he stooped down, he couched as a lion,**

N.B. note how the comma separates words and phrases having the same meaning.

<u>**GENESIS 49: 24**</u>	(from **thence** *is* the shepherd, the stone of Israel:)
: 31	**there** they buried Isaac and Rebekah his wife;

<u>**GENESIS 49: 26**</u>	The blessings of thy father have prevailed above the blessings of my **progenitors** unto the utmost bound of the everlasting hills:
48: 16	and the name of my **fathers** Abraham and Isaac;
Leviticus 26: 45	But I will for their sakes remember the covenant of their **ancestors,**
Jeremiah 11: 10	They are turned back to the iniquities of their **forefathers,**

<u>**GENESIS 49: 27**</u>	Benjamin shall **ravin** *as* a wolf:
22: 27	her princes in the midst thereof *are* like wolves **ravening the prey, to shed blood,**

<u>**GENESIS 49: 32**</u>	The purchase of the field and of the cave that *is* **therein** *was* from the children of Heth.
37: 24	and the pit *was* empty, *there was* no water **in it.**

N.B. Reverse the two syllables of the bold word in the first reference and the meaning is clear.

GENESIS 50: 3 and the Egyptians mourned for him three**score** and ten days.
Exodus 1: 5 And all the souls that came out of the loins of Jacob were **seventy** souls.
Leviticus 27: 7 And if *it be* from **sixty** years old and above.

N.B. The underlined word is a numerical term meaning twenty. To find the value of the 'score' number multiply 30x20=60.

GENESIS 50: 4 Joseph spake unto the house of Pharaoh, saying, If now I have **grace** in your eyes, speak, I pray you,
39: 21 But the LORD was with Joseph, and shewed him mercy, and gave him **favour** in the sight of the keeper of the prison.

GENESIS 50: 11 This *is* a grievous mourning to the Egyptians: **wherefore** the name of it was called A-bel-miz-ra-im, which *is* beyond Jordan.
: 5 Now **therefore** let me go up, I pray thee, and bury my father, and I will come again.

GENESIS 50: 15 Joseph will peradventure hate us, and will certainly **requite** us all the evil which we did unto him.
Job 21: 31 and who shall **repay** him *what* he hath done.

GENESIS 50: 17 So shall ye say unto Joseph, Forgive, I pray thee now, **the trespass of thy brethren, and their sin:**

N.B. note how the underlined word separates words and phrases having the same meaning.

GENESIS 50: 21 I will nourish you, and your little ones. And he **comforted them, and spake kindly unto them.**
N.B. note how the underlined word separates words and phrases having the same meaning.

GENESIS 50: 25 God will surely visit you, and ye shall carry up my bones from **hence.**
19: 12 And the men said unto Lot, Hast thou **here** any besides?
Exodus 13: 3 for by strength of hand the LORD brought you out **from this** *place:*

EXODUS

EXODUS 1: 12 But the more they afflicted them, the more they **multiplied and grew.**

N.B. note how the underlined word separates words and phrases having the same meaning.

<u>EXODUS 1: 13</u>	And the Egyptians made the children of Israel to serve **with rigour:**
: 14	And they made their lives bitter with **hard bondage,**
<u>EXODUS 1: 15</u>	And the **king of Egypt** spake to the Hebrew midwives,
: 22	And **Pharaoh** charged all his people,
<u>EXODUS 1:17</u>	But the midwives feared God, and did not as the king of Egypt **commanded** them, but saved the men children alive.
: 22	And Pharaoh **charged** all his people saying, Every son that is born ye shall cast into the river,
<u>EXODUS 1: 17</u>	But the midwives feared God, and did not as the king of Egypt commanded them, but saved the **men children** alive.
Genesis 50: 13	For his **sons** carried him into the land of Canaan,
34: 25	each man his sword, and slew all the **males.**
<u>EXODUS 1: 19</u>	and are delivered **ere** the midwives come in unto them.
4: 21	see that thou do all those wonders **before** Pharaoh,
<u>EXODUS 2: 3</u>	And when she could not longer hide him, she took for him an ark of **bulrushes,** and daubed it with slime and with pitch, and put the child therein; and she laid *it* in the **flags** by the river's brink.
<u>EXODUS 2: 3</u>	and put the young child therein; and she laid *it* in the flags **by the river's brink.**
: 5	and maidens walked along **by the river's side;**
<u>EXODUS 2: 3</u>	and daubed it with slime and with pitch, and put the child **therein;**
Genesis 37: 24	and the pit *was* empty, *there was* no water **in it.**
<u>EXODUS 2: 4</u>	And his sister stood afar off, to **wit** what would be done to him.
: 7	for I **know** their sorrows;
<u>EXODUS 2: 6</u>	And she had **compassion** on him,
Genesis 39: 21	and shewed him **mercy,**
Deut. 7: 16	thine eye shall have no **pity** upon them:
<u>EXODUS 2: 13</u>	and he said to him that did the wrong, **Wherefore** smitest thou thy fellow?
: 20	And where *is* he? **Why** *is* it *that* ye have left the man?
<u>EXODUS 2: 13</u>	and he said to him that did the wrong, Wherefore **smitest** thou thy fellow?
: 14	intendest thou to kill me, as thou **killest** the Egyptian?
<u>EXODUS 3: 2</u>	And the angel of the LORD appeared unto him in a flame of fire out of the **midst** of a bush:

26: 28	And the **middle** bar in the **midst** of the boards shall reach from end to end.
EXODUS 3: 5	And he said, Draw not **nigh** hither:
Genesis 48:13	and brought *them* **near** unto him.
EXODUS 3: 5	And he said, Draw not nigh **hither:**
Genesis 33: 3	until he came **here** to his brother.
EXODUS 3: 5	for the place **whereon** thou standest is holy ground *is* holy ground.
Lev. 11: 34	*that* **on which** *such* water cometh shall be unclean:
EXODUS 3: 7	I have surely **seen the affliction** of my people which *are* in Egypt,
: 9	and I have also **seen the oppression** wherewith the Egyptians oppress them.
1: 14	And they made their lives bitter with **hard bondage,**
EXODUS 3: 9	and I have also seen the oppression **wherewith** the Egyptians oppress them.
2 Kings 19: 6	Be not afraid of the words **which** thou hast heard, **with which** the servants of the king of Assyria have blasphemed me.
EXODUS 3: 15	And God said **moreover** unto Moses,
4: 6	And the LORD said **furthermore** unto him,
EXODUS 3: 18	and now **let us go, we beseech thee,**
5: 3	**let us go, we pray thee,**
EXODUS 3: 20	And I will stretch out my hand, and **smite** Egypt with all my wonders which I will do in the midst thereof:
12: 7	And they shall take the blood, and **strike** *it* on the two side posts and on the upper door post of the houses,
EXODUS 3: 20	and I will smite Egypt with all my wonders which I will do in
26: 28	And the **middle** bar in the **midst** of the boards shall reach from end to end.
EXODUS 3: 20	and smite Egypt with all my wonders which I will do in the midst **thereof:**
Genesis 3: 3	God hath said, Ye shall not eat **of it,**
: 5	For God doth know that in the day ye eat **thereof,**
EXODUS 3: 22	and jewels of silver, and jewels gold, and **raiment:**
Genesis 49: 11	he washed his **garments** in wine, and his **clothes** in the blood of grapes:
EXODUS 4: 10	O my LORD, I *am* not eloquent, neither **heretofore, nor since**
21: 36	Or if it be known that the ox hath used to push **in time past,**

28

4:21	see that thou do all those wonders **before** Pharaoh,

EXODUS 4: 17	And thou shalt take this rod in thine hand, **wherewith** thou shalt do signs.
2 Kings 19: 6	Be not afraid of the words which thou hast heard **with which** the servants of the king of Assyria have blasphemed me.

EXODUS 4: 31	and that he looked upon their **afflictions,**
5: 4	get you unto your **burdens.**
EXODUS 5: 3	and sacrifice unto the LORD our God, lest he fall upon us with **pestilence**, or with the sword.
11: 1	Yet will I bring one **plague** *more* upon Pharaoh,

EXODUS 5: 4	And the king of Egypt said unto them, **Wherefore** do ye, Moses and Aaron, let the people from their works?
5: 22	And Moses returned unto the LORD, and said, LORD, **Wherefore** hast thou *so* evil entreated this people? **Why** *is* it *that* thou hast sent me?
EXODUS 5: 7	Ye shall no more give the people straw to make brick, **as heretofore:**
Genesis 31: 2	And Jacob beheld the countenance of Laban, and, behold, it *was* not toward him **as before.**

EXODUS 5: 8	And the **tale** of the bricks, which they did make heretofore: ye shall lay upon them;
: 13	Fulfil your works, *your* **daily tasks,** as when there was straw.

EXODUS 5: 8	ye shall not diminish *ought* **thereof:**
Genesis 50: 11	wherefore the name **of it** was called A-bel-miz-ra-im,

EXODUS 5: 21	because ye have made our savour to be **abhorred** in the eyes of Pharaoh,
Genesis 49: 23	and shot *at him,* and **hated** him:

EXODUS 5: 22	And Moses returned unto the LORD, and said, Lord, **wherefore** hast thou *so* evil entreated this people? **why** *is* it thou hast sent?

EXODUS 6: 4	and the land of their pilgrimage, **wherein** they were strangers.
8: 22	And I will sever in that day the land of Goshen, **in which** my people dwell,

EXODUS 6: 6	and I will bring you out from under the **burdens** of the Egyptians, and I will rid you out of their **bondage,**

EXODUS 6: 11	Go in, speak unto **Pharaoh king of Egypt,**

N.B. The first bold word is a title of a ruler and the three successive words give the country over which he rules.

<u>EXODUS 7: 6</u>	And Moses *was* four**score** years old, and Aaron fourscore and three years old,
Genesis 5: 28	And Lamech lived an hundred **eighty** and two years,

N.B. the underlined word ia numerical term meaning twenty. To find the value of the 'score' number multiply 4x20=80.

<u>EXODUS 7: 15</u>	Get thee unto Pharaoh in the morning; **lo,** he goeth out unto the water;
: 16	and, **behold,** hitherto thou wouldest not hear.

<u>EXODUS 7: 15</u>	and thou shall stand by the river's brink **against** he come;
9: 18	such as hath not been in Egypt since the foundation thereof even **until** now.

<u>EXODUS 7: 16</u>	and, behold, **hitherto** thou wouldst not hear.
9: 18	since the foundation thereof **until now.**

<u>EXODUS 7: 20</u>	and he lifted up the rod, and **smote** the waters that *were* in the river,
2 Samuel 12: 15	And the LORD **struck** the child that Uriah's wife bare unto David.

<u>EXODUS 8: 8</u>	Then Pharaoh called for Moses and Aaron, and said, **Intreat** the LORD, that he may take the frogs away from me,
10: 17	Now therefore forgive, I **pray** thee,

<u>EXODUS 8: 17</u>	for Aaron stretched out his hand with his rod, and **smote** the dust of the land,
1 Samuel 2: 14	And he **struck** *it* into the pan,

<u>EXODUS 8: 21</u>	**Else,** if thou wilt not let my people go,
2 Samuel 18: 13	**Otherwise** I should have wrought falsehood against mine own life:

<u>EXODUS 8: 22</u>	And I will **sever** in that day the land of Goshen, in which my people dwell,
: 23	And I will **put a division** between my people and thy people:
Genesis 49: 26	and on the crown of the head of him that was **separate** from his brethren.

<u>EXODUS 8: 24</u>	the land was corrupted **by reason of** the swarms of *flies.*
9: 11	And the magicians could not stand before Moses **because of** the boils;

<u>EXODUS 8: 26</u>	And Moses said, It is not **meet** so to do;
15: 26	and will do that which is **right** in his sight,
18: 17	The thing that thou doest *is* not **good.**
<u>EXODUS 8: 28</u>	only ye shall not go very far away: **intreat** for me.
10: 17	Now therefore forgive, I **pray** thee my sin only this once, and

intreat the LORD your God,

EXODUS 9: 3	and upon the sheep: *there shall be* a very grievous **murrain.**
5: 3	lest he fall upon us with **pestilence,** or with the sword.

EXODUS 9: 4   And the LORD shall **sever** between the cattle of Israel and
the cattle of Egypt:
8: 23   And I will **put a division** between my people and thy people:

EXODUS 9: 14   For I will **at this time** send all my plagues upon thine heart;
: 15   For **now** I will stretch out my hand I may smite thee and
thy people with pestilence;

EXODUS 9: 15   For now I will stretch out my hand I may **smite** thee and
thy people with pestilence;
12: 7   And they shall take of the blood, **and strike** *it* on the two
side posts and on the upper door post of the houses,

EXODUS 9: 18   such as hath not been in Egypt since the foundation
thereof even until now.
12: 9   Eat not **of it** raw, nor sodden at all with water,

EXODUS 9: 24   So there was hail, and fire **m**ingled with the hail,
12: 38   And a **m**ixed multitude went up also with them;

EXODUS 9: 25   And the hail **smote** throughout all the land of Egypt...
1 Samuel 2: 24   And he **struck** *it* into the pan,

EXODUS 9: 30   But as for thee and thy servants, I know that ye will not yet
fear the LORD God.
Leviticus 19: 15   thou shalt not **respect** the person of the poor, nor **honour**
the person of the mighty:
: 30   Ye shall keep my sabbaths, and **reverence** my sanctuary:

EXODUS 9: 32   But the wheat and the rie were not **smitten:**
1 Samuel 2: 24   And he **struck** *it* into the pan,

EXODUS 10: 2   And that thou mayest tell in the ears of thy son, and of thy
son's son, what things **I have wrought in Egypt,** and my
signs which **I have done among them;**

EXODUS 10: 4   **Else,** if thou refuse to let my people go,
2 Samuel 18: 13   **Otherwise** I should have wrought falsehood against mine
own life:

EXODUS 10: 5   and they shall eat **the residue** of **that** which is escaped, **which
remaineth** unto from the hail,

EXODUS 10: 15   or in the herbs of the field, **through all** the land of Egypt.
9: 9   and upon beast, **throughout all** the land of Egypt.

EXODUS 10: 17	Now therefore forgive, I **pray** thee, my sin only this once, and **intreat** the LORD your God,
EXODUS 11: 1	afterwards he will let you go **hence:**
13: 3	the LORD brought you out **from this** *place:*
EXODUS 11: 3	**Moreover** the man Moses *was* very great in the land of Egypt,
4: 6	And the LORD said **furthermore** unto him,
EXODUS 12: 7	on the upper door post of the houses, **wherein** they shall eat it.
13: 3	Remember this day, **in which** ye came out from Egypt,
EXODUS 12: 9	Eat not of it raw, nor **sodden** at all with water,
2 Kings 6: 29	So we **boiled** my son, and did eat him:
EXODUS 12: 9	his head with his legs, and with the **purtenances** thereof.
Leviticus 8: 21	And he washed **the inwards** and the legs in water;
EXODUS 12: 9	but roast *with* fire; his head with his legs, and with the purtenances **thereof.**
: 10	And ye shall let nothing **of it** remain until the morning;
EXODUS 12: 12	and will **smite** all the firstborn in the land of Egypt,
: 7	and **strike** *it* on the two side posts...
EXODUS 12: 14	ye shall keep it a feast by an **ordinance** for ever.
15: 25	there he made for them a **statute and an ordinance,**

N.B. note how the underlined word separates words and phrases having the same meaning.

EXODUS 12: 16	And in the first day *there shall be* an holy **convocation,** and in the seventh day there shall be an holy convocation to you;
13: 6	and in the seventh day *there shall be* a **feast** to the LORD.
EXODUS 12: 18	until the one and twentieth day of the month at **even.**
: 6	the congregation of Israel shall kill it in the **evening.**
EXODUS 12: 22	and strike the **lintel** and the two side posts with the blood that *is* in the bason;
: 7	and on the **upper door post** of the houses,
EXODUS 12: 23	and will not **suffer** the destroyer to come in unto your houses to smite *you.*
: 48	**let** all his males be circumcised,
Luke 11: 48	Truly ye bear witness that ye **allow** the deeds of your fathers:
1 Cor. 16: 7	but I trust to tarry a while with you, if the Lord **permit.**
EXODUS 12: 27	when he **smote** the Egyptians, and delivered our houses.
2 Samuel 12: 15	And the LORD **struck** the child that Uriah's wife bare

unto David,

EXODUS 12: 33   And the Egyptians were **urgent** upon the people, that
they might send them out of the land **in haste;**

EXODUS 12: 34   their kneadingtroughs being bound up in their **clothes**
upon their shoulders.
: 35   and they borrowed of the Egyptians jewels of silver, and
jewels of gold, and **raiment:**

EXODUS 12: 39   and could not **tarry,** neither had they prepared for
themselves any victual.
21: 13   And if a man lie not in **wait,**
22: 29   Thou shalt not **delay** *to offer* the first of thy ripe fruits,

EXODUS 12: 39   neither had they prepared for themselves any **victual.**
21: 10   her **food,** her raiment, and her duty of marriage,
Genesis   45: 21   and gave them **provision** for the way.
: 23   and ten she asses laden with **corn and bread and meat** fo
his father by the way.

EXODUS 12: 43   There shall no stranger eat **thereof:**
10: 9   Eat not **of it** raw, nor sodden at all with water,

EXODUS 12: 46   thou shalt not carry forth **ought** of the flesh abroad out o
the house;
Job 33: 32   If thou hast **any thing** to say answer me:

EXODUS 13: 2   **Sanctify** unto me all the firstborn, whatsoever openeth the
womb among the children of Israel,
: 12   That thou shalt **set apart** unto the LORD all that openeth
the matrix,

EXODUS 13: 12   That thou shalt set apart unto the LORD all that openeth
the **matrix,**
: 2   whatsoever openeth the **womb** among the children of
Israel,

EXODUS 13: 17   God led them not *through* the way of the land of the Philistines,
although that *was* near; for God said, **Lest peradventure**
the people repent when they see war,
Genesis 16: 2   **it may be** that I may obtain children of her.
EXODUS 13: 18   and the children of Israel went up **harnessed** out of the land
of Egypt.
Numbers 31: 5   a thousand of *every* tribe, twelve thousand **armed for war.**

EXODUS 13: 19   God will surely visit you; and ye shall carry up my bones
away **hence** with you.
: 3   for by strength of hand the LORD brought you out **from**
this *place:*

EXODUS 14: 2	Speak unto the children of Israel, that they turn and encamp **before** Pi-ha-hi-roth, between Mig-dol and the sea **over against** Ba-al-ze-phon.
EXODUS 14: 10 12: 48	And when Pharaoh drew **nigh,** and then let him come **near** and keep it:
EXODUS 14: 10 Genesis 32: 7	and they were **sore afraid:** and the children of Israel cried out unto the LORD. Then Jacob was **greatly afraid and distressed:**
EXODUS 14: 11 : 5	**wherefore** hast thou dealt thus with us, to carry us forth out of Egypt? and they said, **why** have we done this, that we have let Israel go from serving us?
EXODUS 14: 16 26: 28	and the children of Israel shall go on dry *ground* through **the midst of** the sea. And the **mid**dle bar in **the midst of** the boards shall reach from end to end.
EXODUS 14: 23	And the Egyptians **pursued, and went in after them** to the midst of the sea, *even* all Pharaoh's horses, his chariots, and his horsemen.

N.B. note how the underlined word separates words and phrases having the same meaning.

EXODUS 15: 1 : 4	the horse and his rider hath he **thrown** into the sea. Pharaoh's chariots and his host hath he **cast** into the sea:
EXODUS 15: 13 : 16	Thou in thy mercy hath led forth the people *which* thou hast **redeemed:** *which* thou hast **purchased.**
EXODUS 15: 16	**Fear and dread** shall fall upon them;

N.B. note how the underlined word separates words and phrases having the same meaning.

EXODUS 15: 25 : 26	there he made for them **a statute and an ordinance,** and wilt give ear to his **commandments,**

N.B. note how the underlined word separates words and phrases having the same meaning.

EXODUS 15: 27 Leviticus 27: 3	And they came to Elim, where *were* twelve wells of water, and three**score** and ten palm trees: And if *it be* from **sixty** years old and above;

N.B. The underlined word is a numerical term meaning twenty. To find the value of the 'score' number multiply 3x20=60.

EXODUS 16: 15	they said one to another, It *is* manna: for they **wist not** what it *was.*
Numbers 22: 34	I have sinned; for I **knew not** that thou stoodest in the way against:

EXODUS 16: 18	And when they did **mete** *it* with an omer,
Numbers 35: 5	And ye shall **measure** from without the city...

EXODUS 16: 20	**Notwithstanding** they hearkened not unto Moses; **but** some of them
	left of it until the morning,
Genesis 47: 26	**except** the land of the priests **only,**
Numbers 13: 28	**Nevertheless** the people *be* strong that dwell in the land,

EXODUS 16: 23	To morrow *is* the rest of the holy sabbath unto the LORD: bake *that* which ye will bake *to day*, and **seethe** that ye will **seethe;**
Leviticus 8: 31	**Boil** the flesh *at* the door of the tabernacle of the congregation:
Deut. 16: 7	And thou shalt **roast** and eat *it* in the place which the LORD thy God shall choose:

EXODUS 16: 24	and it did not stink, neither was there any worm **therein.**
: 26	but on the seventh day, *which is* the sabbath, **in it** there shall be none.

N.B. reverse the syllables of the first bold word and the meaning is clear.

EXODUS 16: 31	And the house of Israel called the name **thereof** Manna: and it *was* like coriander seed, white; and the taste **of it** *was* like wafers *made* with honey.

EXODUS 16: 32	that they may see the bread **wherewith** I have fed you in the wilderness,
2 Kings 19: 6	Be not afraid of the words **which** thou hast heard, **with which** the rvants of the king of Assyria have blasphemed me.

EXODUS 16: 33	Take a pot, and put an omer full of manna **therein,**
: 26	but on the seventh day, *which is* the sabbath, **in it** there shall be none.

N.B. Reverse the syllables of the first reference and the meaning is clear.

EXODUS 17: 2	**Wherefore** the people did chide with Moses,
16: 29	**therefore** he giveth you on the sixth day the bread of two days;

EXODUS 17: 2	Wherefore the people did **chide** with Moses,
Ezekiel 20: 36	so I will **plead** with you, saith the Lord God.

EXODUS 17: 2	**Why** chide ye with me? **wherefore** do ye tempt the LORD?
EXODUS 17: 5	and thy rod, **wherewith** thou smotest the river,
2 Kings 19: 6	Be not afraid of the words **which** thou hast heard, **with which** the servants of the king of Assyria have blasphemed me.
EXODUS 17: 12	and they took a stone, and put *it* under him, and he sat **thereon;**
18: 8	*and* all the travail that had come **upon** the way,
EXODUS 18: 3	for he said, I have been an **alien** in a **strange** land:
EXODUS 18: 7	And Moses went out to meet his father in law, and did **obeisance,** and kissed him;
Genesis 33: 3	and **bowed himself to the ground** seven times,
EXODUS 18: 8	*and* all the **travail** that had come upon them by way,
Deut. 26: 7	and looked on our **affliction,** and our **labour,**
Nehemiah 9: 32	let not all the **trouble** seem little before thee,
EXODUS 19: 3	Thus shalt thou say to **the house of Jacob, and** tell the children of Israel;

N.B. note how the underlined word separates words and phrases having the same meaning.

EXODUS 19: 5	then ye shall be a **peculiar** treasure unto me above all people:
Deut. 7: 6	the LORD thy God hath chosen thee to be a **special** people unto himself,
EXODUS 19: 8	An Moses returned the words **of** the people unto the LORD.
: 12	*that ye* go *not* up into the mount, or touch the border **of it:**
: 18	because the LORD descended upon in fire: and the smoke **thereof** ascended as the smoke of a furnace,
EXODUS 19: 10	And the LORD said unto Moses, Go unto the people, and **sanctify them** to day and to morrow, and let them wash their clothes,
13: 12	That thou shalt **set apart** unto the LORD all that openeth the matrix,
EXODUS 19: 11	And be ready **against** the third day: for the third day the LORD will come down in the sight of all the people...
Genesis 48: 5	which were born unto thee in the land of Egypt **before** I came unto thee into Egypt,
EXODUS 19: 17	and they stood at the **nether** part of the mount.
Deut. 32: 22	and shall burn unto the **lowest** hell,
Nehemiah 4: 13	Therefore set I in the **lower** places behind the wall,

EXODUS 19: 18	And mount **Sinai** was altogether on a smoke, because the
	the LORD descended **upon it** in fire:

EXODUS 19: 18	And mount Sinai was altogether on a smoke, because
	the LORD **descended** upon it in fire:
: 20	And the LORD **came down** upon mount Sinai,
: 25	So Moses **went down** unto the people, and spake unto them.

EXODUS 19: 18	and the smoke **thereof** ascended as the smoke of a furnace,
: 12	*that ye* go *not* up into the mount, or touch the border **of it:**

EXODUS 19: 18	And mount Sinai was altogether on a smoke, because
	the LORD **descended** upon it in fire:
: 20	And the LORD **came down** upon mount Sinai,

EXODUS 19: 19	And when the voice of the trumpet sounded long, and
	waxed louder and louder,
Genesis 47: 27	and they had possessions therein, and **grew,**
2 Chron. 7: 6	and the priests **sounded** trumpets before them,

EXODUS 19: 25	So Moses went down unto **the people, and** spake unto them.

N.B. note how the underlined word separates words and phrases having the same meaning.

EXODUS 20: 4	or that *is* in the earth **beneath,** or that *is* in the water **under**
	the earth.

EXODUS 20: 6	And shewing **mercy** unto thousands of them that love me,
	And keep my commandments.
Genesis 40: 14	But think on me when it shall be well with thee, and shew
	kindness, I pray thee, unto me,

EXODUS 20: 7	Thou shalt not take the name of the LORD **in vain;**
Leviticus 19: 12	And ye shall not **swear by my name falsely,**

EXODUS 20: 11	**wherefore** the LORD blessed the seventh day,
18: 29	**therefore** he giveth you on the sixth day the bread of two days;

EXODUS 20: 13	Thou shalt not **kill.**
Leviticus 24: 17	And he that **killeth any man** shall surely be put to death.

EXODUS 20: 17	Thou shalt not **covet** thy neighbour's house... nor any thing
	that *is* thy neighbour's.
Deut. 5: 21	Neither shalt thou **desire** thy neighbour's wife, neither
	shalt thou **covet** thy neighbour's house, his field...

EXODUS 20: 24	An altar of earth thou shalt make unto me, and shalt
	sacrifice **thereon** thy burnt offerings,
: 25	for if thou lift up thy tool **upon it,**

EXODUS 21: 21	**Notwithstanding**, if he continue a day or two, he shall not be punished: **for he** *is* his money.
: 14	**But** if a man come presumptuously upon his neighbour,
EXODUS 21: 29	But if the ox **were wont to** push with his horn in time past, and it hath been testified to his owner,
: 36	Or if it be known that the ox hath **used to** push in time past,
EXODUS 22: 3	If the sun be risen upon him, *there shall be* blood *shed* for him; *for* he should **make restitution:**
21: 34	The owner of the pit shall **make it good,**
EXODUS 22: 6	If fire break out, and catch in thorns, so that the **stacks of corn,** or the **corn,** or the **standing corn,** or the field,
EXODUS 22: 6	or the field, be consumed *therewith;*
Deut. 16: 3	Thou shalt eat no leavened bread **with it;** seven days shalt thou eat unleavened bread **therewith,**
EXODUS 22: 12	And if it be stolen from him, he shall make restitution unto the owner **thereof.**
19: 12	Take heed to yourselves, *that ye* go *not* up into the mount, or touch the border **of it:**
EXODUS 22: 16	And if a man **entice** a maid that is not betrothed,
2 Chron. 32: 15	Now therefore let not Hezekiah **deceive** you, nor **persuade** you on this manner,
EXODUS 22: 18	Thou shalt not **suffer** a witch to live.
23: 11	But the seventh year thou shalt **let** it rest and lie still;
Luke 11: 48	Truly ye bear witness that ye **allow** the deeds of your fathers:
1 Cor. 16: 7	but I tust to tarry a while with you, ifthe Lord **permit.**
EXODUS 22: 21	Thou shalt neither **vex a stranger, nor** oppress him:
Leviticus 19: 33	And if a stranger sojourn with theein your land, **ye shall not vex him.**
25: 14	or buyest *ought* of thy neighbour's hand, **ye shall not oppress** one another:

N.B. note the underlined word that separates words and phrases having the same meaning.

EXODUS 22: 14	the owner **thereof** *being* not with it,
: 11	the owner **of it** shall accept *thereof,*
EXODUS 22: 27	it *is* his raiment for his skin: **wherein** shall he sleep?
2 Samuel 15: 21	surely **in what** place my lord the king shall be,
EXODUS 23: 1	Thou shalt **not raise a false report:** put not thine hand with the wicked to be **an unrighteous witness.**

EXODUS 23: 2	neither shalt thou speak in a cause to decline after many to **wrest** *judgement:*
Deut. 24: 17	Thou shalt not **pervert** the judgment of a stranger,
Isaiah 10: 2	To **turn aside** the needy from judgment,
EXODUS 23: 5	If thou see the ass **of him** that hateth thee lying under **his** burden,
EXODUS 23: 7	and the innocent and **righteous** slay thou not:
Deut. 32: 4	a God of truth and without iniquity, **just <u>and</u> right** *is* he.
1 Samuel 29: 6	Surely, *as* the LORD liveth thou hast been **upright,**
EXODUS 23: 10	and shalt gather in the fruits **thereof.**
19: 12	or touch the border **of it:**
EXODUS 23: 11	But the seventh *year* thou shalt let it **rest <u>and</u> be still;**

N.B. note how the underlined word separates words and phrases having the same meaning.

EXODUS 23: 13	And in all *things* that I have said unto you be **circumspect:**
: 21	**Beware** of him, and obey his voice,
10: 28	And Pharaoh said unto him, Get thee from me, **take heed** to thyself,
	see thy face no more;
1 Samuel 9: 5	and **take thought** for us.
2 Kings 4: 13	Behold, thou hast been **careful** for us with all this care;
EXODUS 23: 19	Thou shalt not **seethe** a kid in his mother's milk.
Leviticus 8: 31	And Moses said unto Aaron and to his sons, **Boil** the flesh *at* the door of the tabernacle of the congregation:
EXODUS 23: 22	then I will be an **enemy** unto thine enemies, and an **adversary** unto thine adversaries.
EXODUS 23: 24	**but thou shalt utterly overthrow them, <u>and</u> quite break down their images.**

N.B. note how the underlined word separate words and phrases having the same meaning.

EXODUS 24: 2	And Moses alone shall **come near** the LORD: but they shall not **come nigh;**
EXODUS 24: 7	and they said, All that the LORD hath said **will we do, <u>and</u> be obedient.**

N.B. note how the underlined word separates words and phrases having the same meaning.

EXODUS 24: 14	And he said unto the elders, **Tarry** ye here for us,
Numbers 3: 10	and they shall **wait** on their priest's office:
EXODUS 24: 18	And Moses went into the **mid**st of the cloud,
26: 28	And the **mid**dle bar in the **mid**st of the boards shall reach from end to end.
EXODUS 25: 7	Onyx stones, and stones to be set in the **ephod,**
1 Samuel 2: 18	But Samuel ministered before the LORD, *being* a child, girded with a linen **ephod.**
EXODUS 25: 12	And thou shalt cast four rings of gold for it, and put *them* in the four orners **thereof;** and two rings *shall be* in the one side **of it,**
EXODUS 25: 14	that the ark may be **borne** with them.
Genesis 50: 13	For his sons **carried** him into the land of Canaan,
EXODUS 25: 24	and make **thereto** a crown of gold round about.
: 26	And thou shalt make **for it** four rings of gold,
EXODUS 25: 28	and overlay them with gold, that the table may be **borne** with them.
Genesis 50: 13	For his sons **carried** him into the land of Canaan,
EXODUS 25: 29	and covers thereof, and bowls thereof, **to cover withal:**
12: 9	nor sodden at **all with** water,
EXODUS 26: 1	and scarlet: *with* cherubims of **cunning** work shalt thou make them.
1 Chron. 5: 18	and to shoot with bow, and **skilful** in war,
EXODUS 26: 6	And thou shalt make fifty **taches** of gold, and couple the curtains together with the **taches:**
: 19	and all the **pins** thereof, and all the **pins** of the court, *shall* be *of* brass.
EXODUS 26: 9	and the shalt couple five curtains by themselves, and six curtains by themselves, and shalt double the sixth curtain in the **forefront** of the tabernacle.

N.B. The bold word is made up of two words 'fore and front.' and the two words have the same meaning.

EXODUS 26: 28	And the **mid**dle bar in the **mid**st of the boards shall reach from end to end.
EXODUS 26: 31	and fine twined linen of **cunning** work:
2 Chron. 2: 14	and his father *was* a man of Tyre, **skilful to** work in gold,
EXODUS 27: 5	And thou shalt put it **under** the compass of the altar

	beneath, that the net may be even to the midst of the altar.
EXODUS 27: 7	and the staves shall be upon the two sides of the altar to **bear** it.
33: 15	If thy presence go not *with me,* **carry** us not up hence.
EXODUS 28: 3	that they may make Aaron's garment **to consecrate** him,
: 41	and shalt **anoint** them, and sanctify them,
EXODUS 28: 11	thou shalt make them to be **set in ouches** of gold.
: 17	And thou shalt **set it in settings,** *even* four rows of stones:
: 20	they shall be **set in** gold in their **inclosings.**
EXODUS 28: 26	and thou shalt put them upon the two ends of the breast plat in the border **thereof,**
30: 10	And Aaron shall make an atonement upon the horns **of it** once in a year with the blood of the sin offering...
EXODUS 28: 28	that *it* may be above the **curious** girdle of the ephod,
: 39	And thou shalt **embroider** the coat of fine linen...and thou shalt make the girdle *of* **needlework.**
EXODUS 28: 32	as it were the hole of an **habergeon,** that it be not rent.
1 Samuel 17: 5	and he *was* armed with a **coat of mail;**
EXODUS 28: 32	as it were the hole of an habergeon, that it be not **rent.**
22: 13	If it be **torn** in pieces,
EXODUS 29: 1	And this *is* the thing that thou shalt do unto them to **hallow** them,
	to minister unto me in the priest's office:
28: 41	And thou shalt put them upon Aaron thy brother, and his sons with him; and shalt **anoint them, <u>and</u> consecrate them, <u>and</u> consecrate them, <u>and</u> sanctify them,**
13: 12	That thou shalt **set apart** unto the LORD all that openeth the matrix,
Genesis 30: 40	And Jacob did **separate** the lambs,
EXODUS 29: 1	Take one young **bullock,** and two rams **without blemish.**
: 36	And thou shalt offer every day **a bullock** *for* atonement:
Leviticus 9: 2	And he said unto Aaron, Take thee **a young calf** for a sin offering,

N.B. An ox is is a male animal which had been castrated and therrfore was not ' without blemish.' It was a domesticated animal used for pulling wagons and carts.

EXODUS 29: 2	And unleavened bread, and cakes unleavened **tempered with** oil,
12: 38	And a **mixed** multitude went up also with them;

EXODUS 29: 9	and the priest's office shall be theirs for a **perpetual** statute:
: 28	And it shall be Aaron's and his sons' by a statute **for ever** from the children of Israel:
EXODUS 29: 29	And the holy garments of Aaron shall be his sons' after him, to be anointed **therein** and to be consecrated **in them.**
EXODUS 29: 31	And thou shalt take the ram of the consecration, and **seethe** his flesh in the holy place.
Leviticus 8: 31	**Boil** the flesh *at* the door of the tabernacle of the congregation:
EXODUS 29: 33	And they shall eat those things **wherewith** the atonement was made,
2 Kings 19: 6	Be not afraid of the words **with which** the servants of the king of Assyria have blasphemed me.
EXODUS 29: 40	And with the one lamb a tenth deal of flour **mingled** with the fourth part of an hin of beaten oil;
12: 38	And a **mixed** multitude went up also with them;
EXODUS 29: 41	and shalt do **thereto** according to the meat offering of the morning,
30: 4	And two golden rings shalt thou make **to it** under the crown of it,
25: 12	And thou shalt cast four rings of gold **for it,**
EXODUS 30: 4	And two golden rings shalt thou make to it under the crown **of it,** by the two corners **thereof,**
EXODUS 30: 4	and they shall be for places for the staves to **bear** it withal.
33: 15	If thy presence go not *with me,* **carry** us not up hence.
EXODUS 30: 4	and they shall be for the staves to bear it **withal.**
12: 9	nor sodden at **all with** water,
EXODUS 30: 7	And Aaron shall burn **thereon** sweet incense every morning: when he dresseth the lamps **upon it.**
: 10	And Aaron shall make an atonement **upon** the horns of it...
EXODUS 30: 12	When thou **takest the sum of** the children of Israel after their number, then shall they give every man a ransom for his soul unto the LORD, when thou **numberest them:**
EXODUS 30: 18	Thou shalt make **a laver** *of* brass, **to wash** *withal:*
EXODUS 30: 18	and thou shalt put it between the tabernacle of the congregation and the altar, and thou shalt put water **therein.**
28: 17	And thou shalt set **in it** settings of stones,

N. B. reverse the syllables of the bold word in the first reference and the meaning is clear.

EXODUS 30: 18	Thou shalt also make **a laver** *of* brass, and his foot *also of* brass, to **wash** *withal:* and thou shalt put between the tabernacle of the congregation and the altar, and thou shalt **put water therein.**
EXODUS 30: 19	For Aaron and his sons shall wash their hands and their feet **thereat:**
Leviticus 26: 32	and your enemies which dwell therein shall be astonished **at it.**
EXODUS 30: 22	**Moreover** the LORD spake unto Moses, saying,
4: 6	And the LORD said **furthermore** unto him,
30: 23	Take thou **also** unto thee principal spices,
EXODUS 30: 25	an ointment **compound** after the art of the apothecary:
: 32	after the **composition** of it:
: 35	And thou shalt make it a perfume, a **confection** after the art of the apothecary, **tempered together,**
12: 38	And a **mixed** multitude went up also with them;
29: 40	And with the one lamb a tenth deal of flour **mingled** with the fourth part of an hin of beaten oil;
EXODUS 30: 26	And thoushalt anoint the tabernacle of the congregation **therewith,**
22: 14	the owner thereof *being* not **with it,**
EXODUS 30: 35	And thou shalt make it a perfume, **a** confection after the ar of the apothecary,
: 25	an ointment **compound** after the art of the apothecary: it shall be an holy anointing oil.
EXODUS 30: 38	Whosoever shall make like unto that, to smell **thereto,**
: 36	And thou shalt beat *some* **of it** very small,
EXODUS 31: 4	To devise **cunning** works, to work in gold, and in silver, and in brass,
1 Chron. 5: 18	and to shoot with bow, and **skilful** in war,
EXODUS 31: 13	Speak thou also unto the children of Israel, saying, **Verily** my sabbaths ye shall keep:
: 15	whosoever doeth *any* work in the sabbath day, he shall **surely** be put death.
Numbers 14: 21	But *as* **truly** *as* I live, all the earth shall be filled with the glory of the LORD.
EXODUS 31: 14	for whosoever doeth *any* work **therein,** that soul shall be

	cut off from among his people.
39: 10	And they set **in it** four rows of stones:

EXODUS 31: 18   when he had an end of **communing** with him upon mount
Sinai,

34: 33   And *till* Moses had done **speaking** with him,

Genesis 17: 22   And he left **talking** with him, and God went up from
Abraham.

EXODUS 32: 1   the man that brought us up out of the land of Egypt, we **wot
not** what is become of him.

Genesis 4: 9   And he said, I **know not:**

EXODUS 32: 8   and have sacrificed **thereunto,** and said, These *be* thy gods,

30: 4   And two golden rings shalt thou make **to it** under the crown
of it,

EXODUS 32: 10   Now therefore let me alone, that my **wrath** may wax hot
against them,

: 22   And Aaron said, Let not the **anger** of my lord wax hot:

EXODUS 32: 12   **Wherefore** should the Egyptians speak and say,

: 11   **why** doth thy wrath wax hot against thy people,

EXODUS 32: 19   And it came to pass, as soon as he **came nigh** unto the camp,

40: 32   and when they **came near** unto the altar,

EXODUS 32: 30   and now I will go up unto the LORD; **peradventure** I shall
make an atonement for your sin.

Genesis 16: 2   **it may be** that I may obtain children by her.

EXODUS 33: 12   Yet thou hast said, I know thee by name, and thou hast
also found **grace** in my sight.

: 19   and will shew **mercy** on whom I will show mercy.

12: 36   And the LORD gave the people **favour** in the sight of the
Egyptians,

EXODUS 33: 18   And he said, **I beseech thee,** shew me thy glory,

34: 9   let my Lord, **I pray thee,** go among us;

EXODUS 34: 1   And the LORD said unto Moses, **Hew** thee two tables of
stone like unto the first:

: 13   break their images, and **cut down** their groves:

EXODUS 34: 6   The LORD God, merciful and gracious, **longsuffering,**

Psalm 103: 8   The LORD *is* merciful and gracious, **slow to anger,**

Eccl. 7: 8   *and* the **patient** in spirit *is* better than the proud in spirit.

EXODUS 34: 7   Keeping mercy for thousands, forgiving **iniquity and
transgression and sin,**

<u>**EXODUS 34: 12**</u>	lest thou make a covenant with the inhabitants of the land **whither** thou goest,
50: 26	**where** I will meet with thee:
<u>**EXODUS 34: 19**</u>	All that openeth the **matrix** *is* mine;
Numbers 8: 16	instead of such as open every **womb,**
<u>**EXODUS 34: 21**</u>	in **earing** time and in harvest thou shalt rest.
Deut. 22: 10	Thou shalt not **plow** with an ox and an ass together.
Prov. 13: 23	Much food *is in* the **tillage** of the poor:
Genesis 2: 5	and *there was* not a man to **till** the ground.
<u>**EXODUS 34: 23**</u> GOD,	**Thrice** in the year shall all men children appear before the Lord
	the God of Israel.
2: 2	and when she saw him that he *was a* goodly *child*, she hid him **three months.**
Numbers 24: 10	behold, thou hast altogether blessed *them* these **three times.**
Deut. 16: 16	**Three times** in a year shall all thy males appear before the the LORD thy God in the place he shall choose;
2 Kings 13: 19	whereas now thou shalt smite Syria *but* **thrice.**
: 25	**Three times** did Joash beat him,
<u>**EXODUS 34: 23**</u>	Thrice in the year shall all **men children** appear before the Lord GOD, the God of Israel.
Deut. 16: 16	Three times in a year shall all thy **males** appear before the Lord GOD, the God of Israel.
<u>**EXODUS 34: 26**</u>	Thou shall not **seethe** a kid in his mother's milk.
Leviticus 8: 31	**Boil** the flesh *at* the door of the tabernacle of the congregation:
<u>**EXODUS 34: 29**</u>	when he came down from the mount, that Moses **wist not** that the skin of his face shone while he talked with him.
Genesis 42: 8	And Joseph knew his brethren, but they **knew** not him.
<u>**EXODUS 34: 30**</u>	the skin of his face shone; and they were afraid to **come nigh** him.
Numbers 16: 5	and *who is* holy; and will cause *him* to **come near** unto him:
<u>**EXODUS 34: 32**</u>	And afterward all the children of Israel **came nigh:**
40: 32	and when they **came near** unto the altar,
<u>**EXODUS 35: 11**</u>	The **tabernacle,** his **tent,** and his covering,

N.B. note how the two bold words have the same meaning.

EXODUS 35: 11   The tabernacle, his tent, and his covering, his **ta<u>ch</u>es,** and his bars, his pillars, and his sockets,

: 18   the **pins,** of the tabernacle, and the pins of the court, and their cords,

N. B. note the underlined letters are pronounced with a 'k' sound as in the milk word 'milk.'
(Exodus 34: 26.) Note the old way of spelling of milk in Gen. 32:15.

Note therefore that the 'ch' is likewise pronounced with a 'k' sound thus, word is tack and a tack is a pin with a sharp point. This is confirmed in the second reference. The word tack can also mean rough stitching but the word in this cotext is a noun and not a verb.

EXODUS 35: 12   The ark, and the staves **thereof,**

37: 1   and a cubit and a half the height **of it:**

EXODUS 35: 33   And in the cutting of stones, to set *them,* and in carving of wood, to make any manner of **cunning** work.

1 Chron. 5: 18   and to shoot with bow, and **skilful** in war,

EXODUS 36: 4   And all the wise men, that **wrought** all the work of the sanctuary, came every man from his work which they **made;**

EXODUS 36: 13   And he made fifty **taches** of gold,

35: 18   The **pins** of the tabernacle, and the pins of the court,

EXODUS 36: 29   And they were coupled beneath, and coupled together at the head **thereof,** to one ring:

37: 1   and a cubit and a half the breadth **of it,**

EXODUS 36: 36   And he made **thereunto** four pillars *of* shittim *wood,*

37: 27   And he made two rings of gold **for it** under the crown thereof,

EXODUS 36: 38   and he overlaid their **<u>ch</u>apiters** and their fillets with gold:

1 Kings 7: 16   And he made two chapiters *of* molten brass, **to set upon the tops of the pillars:**

N.B. note the underlined letters in the bold word in the first reference if the letters are spelled out in order then the whole word is clear and confirmed in the second reference. There are further references in Kings 7: 17, 18-20 and also 2 Chronicles 3: 15,16 ; and 2 Chronicles 4: 12, 13.

EXODUS 37: 16   and his spoons, and his bowls, and his covers to cover **withal,**

12: 9   Eat not of it raw, nor sodden at **all with** water,

EXODUS 38: 10   Their pillars *were* twenty, and their **brasen sockets** twenty;

: 11   their pillars *were* twenty, and their **sockets of brass** twenty;

EXODUS 38: 25	and a thousand seven hundred and **threescore** and fifteen fifteen shekels,
: 28	And of the thousand seven hundred **seventy** and five *shekels* he made hooks for the pillars,
Leviticus 27: 7	And if *it be* **sixty** years old,

N.B. The underlined word is a numerical term meaning twenty. To find the value of the score' number multiply 3x20=60.

EXODUS 38: 30	And **therewith** he made the sockets to the door of the tabernacle of the congregation,
22: 15	*But* if the owner thereof be **with it;**
2 Kings 19: 6	Be not afraid of the words which thou hast heard, **with which** the servants of the king of Assyria have blasphemed me.

EXODUS 39: 3	and in the scarlet, and in the fine linen, *with* **cunning** work.
1 Chron. 5: 18	and to shoot with bow, and **skilful** in war,

EXODUS 39: 6	And they wrought onyx stones inclosed in **ouches** of gold,
28: 17	And they shalt **set in** it **settings** of stones, *even* four rows of stones:

EXODUS 39: 20	the forepart **of it,** over against the *other* coupling **thereof,**

EXODUS 39: 23	as the hole of an **habergeon,** *with* a band round about the hole,
1 Samuel 17: 5	and he *was* armed with a **coat of mail;**

EXODUS 39: 33	and all his furniture, his **taches,**
: 40	his cords, and his **pins,** and all the vessels of the service of the tabernacle,

EXODUS 40: 3	And thou shalt put **therein** the ark of the testimony, and cover the ark with the vail.
39: 10	And they set **in it** four rows of stones:

N.B. reverse the syllables of the bold word in the first reference and the meaning is clear.

EXODUS 40: 17	And it came to pass in the first month in the second year, on the first *day* of the month, *that* the tabernacle was **reared up.**
: 2	On the first day of the first month shalt thou **set up** the tabernacle of the tent of the congregation.

EXODUS 40: 24	And he put the candlestick in the **tent** of the congregation, over against the table, on the side of the **tabernacle** southward.

EXODUS 40: 27	And he burnt sweet incense **thereon;**

: 29	and offered **upon it** the burnt offering and the meat offering;
EXODUS 40: 33	And he **reared up** the court round about the tabernacle and the altar, and **set up** the hanging of the court gate.

LEVITICUS

LEV. 1 : 17	And he shall **cleave it** with the wings thereof, *but* shall not **divide** *it* asunder:
LEV. 1: 17 2: 6	*but* shall not divide *it* **asunder:** Thou shalt **part it in pieces,**
LEV. 2: 1	and he shall pour oil **upon it,** and put incense **thereon:**
LEV. 2: 2 Ex. 37: 21	and he shall take **thereout** his handful of the flour thereof, according to the six branches go **out of it.**
LEV. 2: 2	with all the frankincense **thereof;** and the priest shall burn the memorial **of it** upon the altar,
LEV. 2: 4 oven, Ex. 23: 8	And if thou bring an **oblation** of a meat **offering** baken in the And thou shalt take no **gift:** for the gift blindeth the wise,
LEV. 2: 4 Ex. 12: 38	*it shall be* unleavened cakes of fine flour **mingled** with oil, And a **mixed** multitude went up also with them;
LEV. 2: 6 : 15	Thou shalt part in pieces, and pour oil **thereon:** And thou shalt put oil **upon it,** and lay frankincense **thereon:**

N. B. note how the underlined words give the meaning of the whole word.

LEV. 2: 13 4: 3	neither shalt thou **suffer** the salt of the covenant of thy God to be lacking from thy meat offering: then **let** him bring for his sin,
LEV. 2: 15	And thou shalt put oil **upon it,** and lay frankincense **thereon:**
LEV. 2: 16	And the priest shall burn shall burn the memorial **of it,** *part* of the beaten corn **thereof,**
LEV. 3: 1	And if his **oblation** *be* a sacrifice of peace **offering,**
LEV. 3: 9 6: 10 9: 5	the fat thereof, *and* the whole rump, it shall be taken off **hard by** the backbone; and he shall put them **beside** the altar. and all the congregation drew **near** and stood before the LORD.

Num.5: 13	and it be hid from the eyes of her husband, and be kept **close,**
LEV.3: 17	It *shall be* a **perpetual** statute for your generations through-out your dwellings,
6: 22	*it is* a statute **for ever** unto the LORD;
16: 3	And this shall be an **everlasting** statute unto you,
LEV. 4: 33	and **slay** it for a sin offering in the place where they **kill** the burnt offering.
LEV. 5: 8	and wring off his head from his neck, but shall not divide *it* **asunder:**
2: 6	Thou shalt **part it in pieces,**
LEV. 5: 11	he shall put no oil **upon it,** neither shall he put *any* frankin-cense **thereon:**
LEV. 5: 16	And he shall **make amends** for the harm that he hath done in the holy thing,
6: 5	he shall even **restore it** in the principal,
LEV. 5: 16	and shall add the fifth part **thereto,**
Ex. 30: 4	And two golden rings shalt thou make **to it** under the crown of it,
LEV. 5: 17	though he **wist *it* not,** yet he is guilty,
Num. 22: 34	I have sinned; for I **knew it not** that thou stoodest in the way...
LEV. 5: 18	and the priest shall make an atonement for him concerning his ignorance **wherein** he erred and wist *it* not,
13: 18	The flesh also **in which,** *even* in the skin thereof,
LEV. 6: 3	and **lieth** concerning it, and **sweareth falsely:**
LEV. 6: 3	in any of all these that a man doeth, sinning **therein:**
: 9	and the fire of the altar shall be burning **in it.**
LEV. 6: 4	or the thing which he hath **deceitfully gotten,** or that which was delivered him to keep,
Exodus 20: 15	Thou shalt not **steal.**
1 Samuel 12: 3	whose ass have I taken? or whom have I **defrauded?**
LEV. 6: 5	*and* give it unto him to whom it **pertaineth.**
Num.8: 24	This *is it* that ***belongeth*** unto the Levites:
LEV. 6: 7	for any thing of all that he hath done **therein.**
: 9	and the fire of the altar shall be burning **in it.**
LEV. 6: 12	and lay the burnt offering in order **upon it;** and he shall and he shall burn **thereon** the fat of the peace offerings.

LEV. 6: 13	The fire shall **ever be burning** upon the altar, it shall **never go out.**
LEV. 6: 15	And he shall take **of it** his handful, of the flour of the meat offering: and of the oil **thereof,**
LEV. 6: 20	for a meat offering **perpetual,** half of it in the morning, and half half thereof at night.
: 18	All the males among the children of Aaron shall eat of it.
LEV. 6: 20	for a meat offering perpetual, half **of it** in the morning, and half **thereof** at night.
LEV. 6: 27	thou shalt wash **that whereon** it was sprinkled in the holy place.
11: 34	**that on which,** *such* cometh shall be unclean:
LEV. 6: 28	But the earthen vessel wherein it is **sodden** shall be broken:
1 Kings 19: 21	and **boiled** their flesh with the instruments of the oxen,
LEV. 6: 30	And no sin offering, **whereof** *any* of the blood is brought into the tabernacle of the congregation...
7: 25	**of which** men offering made by fire unto the LORD,
LEV. 7: 3	And he shall offer **of it** all the fat **thereof;**
LEV. 7: 7	*there is* one law for them: the priest that maketh atonement **therewith** shall have *it.*
Ex. 22: 14	the owner thereof *being* not **with it,**
LEV. 7: 10	And every meat offering, **mingled** with oil, and dry,
Ex. 12: 38	And a **mixed** multitude went up also with them,
LEV. 7: 14	And of it he shall offer one out of the whole **oblation** *for* an heave **offering** unto the LORD,
LEV. 7: 18	neither shall it be **imputed** unto him that offereth it:
Num. 18: 27	And *this* your heave offering shall be **reckoned** unto you,
LEV. 7: 21	**Moreover** the soul that touch any unclean *thing,*
Deut. 4: 21	**Furthermore** the LORD was angry with me for sakes,
Lev. 7: 16	and on the morrow **also** the remainder of it shall be eaten:
LEV. 8: 3	And gather thou all the **congregation** together unto the door of the tabernacle of the congregation.
: 4	and the **assembly** was gathered together unto the door of the tabernacle of the congregation.
LEV. 8: 7	and he girded him with the curious girdle of the ephod, and

	bound *it*
	unto him **therewith.**
Numbers 4: 5	and they shall take down the covering vail, and cover the ark **with it.**

LEV. 8: 10   and anointed the tabernacle and all that *was* **therein,**
6: 9   and the fire of the altar shall be burning **in it.**

LEV. 8: 11   And he sprinkled **thereof** upon the altar seven times,
: 23   And he slew *it;* and Moses put the blood **of it,**

LEV. 8: 34   *so* the LORD hath commanded to do, **to make an atone-ment** for you.
: 15   and sanctified it, **to make reconciliation** upon it.

LEV. 9: 2   And he said unto Aaron, Take thee **a young calf** for a sin offering, **without blemish,** and offer *them* before the LORD.
: 4   Also a **bullock** and a ram for a peace offerings,

LEV. 9: 4   and a meat offering **mingled with** oil:
Ex. 12: 38   And a **mixed** multitude went up also with them;

LEV. 10: 1   And Nadab and A-bi-hu, took **either of them** his censer,
8: 11   and anointed the altar and all his vessels, **both** the laver and his foot,

LEV. 10: 1   took either of them his censer, and put fire **therein,**
6: 12   And the fire upon the altar shall be burning **in it;**

N.B. reverse the syllables of the bold word in the first reference and the meaning is clear.

LEV. 10: 1   and put fire therein, and put strange incense **thereon,**
6: 12   and lay the burnt offering in order **upon it;**

LEV. 10: 3   I will be sanctified in them that come **nigh** me,
: 4   Come **near,** carry your brethren from before the sanctuary out of the camp.

LEV. 10: 17   **Wherefore** have ye not eaten the sin offering in the holy place,
Ex. 32: 11   **why** doth thy wrath wax hot against thy people,

LEV. 11: 32   whether *it be* any vessel of wood, or **raiment,** or skin,
: 25   shall wash his **clothes,**
16: 4   these *are* holy **garments;**

LEV. 11: 33   And every earthen vessel, **whereinto** *any* of them falleth,
Psalm 118: 20   This gate of the LORD, **into which** the righteous shall enter.

LEV. 11: 38	But if *any* water be put **upon** the seed, and *any part* of their carcase fall **thereon**, it *shall be* unclean unto you.
LEV. 11: 43	neither shall ye make yourselves unclean with them, that ye should be defiled **thereby**.
Genesis 29: 2	and, lo, there *were* three flocks of sheep lying **by it;**
LEV. 12: 5	and she shall continue in the blood of her purifying three**score** and six days.
27: 7	And if *it be* from **sixty** years and above;

N.B. The underlined word is a numerical term meaning twenty. To find the value of the 'score' number multiply 3x20=60.

LEV. 13: 10	and *there be* **quick** raw flesh in the rising;
14: 6	As for the **living** bird, he shall take it, and the cedar wood,
LEV. 3: 18	The flesh also, in which, *even* in the skin **thereof,**
: 56	the plague *be* somewhat dark after the washing **of it;**
LEV. 13: 21	and, behold, *there be* no white hairs **therein,**
: 31	and *that there is* no black hair **in it:**
LEV. 13: 24	Or if there be *any* flesh, in the skin **whereof** *there is* a hot burning,
: 18	The flesh also, **in which,** *even* in the skin thereof,
LEV. 13: 30	then the priest shall pronounce him unclean: it *is* a dry **scall,** *even* a **leprosy** upon the head or beard.
LEV. 13: 46	he shall be **defiled;** he *is* **unclean:** he shall dwell alone;
LEV. 14: 13	And **he shall slay the lamb** in the place where **he shall kill the sin offering** and the burnt offering,
LEV. 14: 45	And he shall break down the house, the stones **of it,** and the timber **thereof,**
LEV. 15: 4	Every bed, **whereon** he lieth that hath the issue, is unclean:
16: 9	And Aaron shall bring the goat **upon which** the LORD'S lot fell, and offer him *for* a sin offering.
16: 10	But the goat **on which** the lot fell to be the scapegoat,
LEV. 15: 24	And if any man lie with her at all, and **flowers** be upon him,
: 25	And if a woman have **an issue of blood** many days out of the time of her separation,
Matt. 9: 20	And behold, a woman, which was diseased with **an issue of blood** twelve years,

LEV. 15: 32	and *of him* whose seed goeth from him, and is defiled **there-with;**
Num. 4: 5	and they shall and they shall take down the covering vail, and cover the ark of testimony **with it:**
LEV. 16: 3	Thus shall Aaron come into the holy *place:* with **a young bullock** for a sin offering,
9: 2	Take thee **a young calf** for a sin offering, and a ram for a burnt offering, **without blemish,**
LEV. 16: 4	and shall be girded with a linen girdle and with a linen mitre shall be **attired:**
8: 7	and **clothed** him with the robe, and put the ephod on him,
LEV. 16: 21	And Aaron shall lay both his hands upon the head of the live goat, and confess over him **all the iniquities of the children of Israel,** **and all their transgressions in all their sins,** putting them upon the head of the goat,

N.B. note how the underlined words separates words and phrases having the same meaning.

LEV. 16: 22	And the goat shall bear upon him all their iniquities unto a **land not inhabited;** and he shall let go the goat in the **wilderness.**
LEV. 16: 32	in his father's stead, shall make the atonement, and shall put on the linen **clothes,** *even* the holy **garments:**
LEV. 17: 4	blood shall be **imputed** unto that man; he hath shed blood,
Num. 18: 27	And *this* your heave offering shall be **reckoned** unto you,
LEV. 17: 10	I will even set my face against that eateth blood, and will **cut him off** from among his people.
20: 2	he shall surely **be put to death:**
LEV. 17: 14	For *it is* the life of all flesh: the blood **of it** *is* for the life **thereof:**
LEV. 18: 3	After the doings of the land of Egypt, **wherein** ye dwelt,
14: 40	Then the priest shall command that they take away the stones **in which** ye dwelt,
LEV. 18: 3	and after the doings of the land of Canaan, **whither** I bring you, shall ye not do:
14: 13	And he shall slay the lamb in the place **where** he shall kill the sin offering and the burnt offering,
LEV. 18: 20	**Moreover** thou shalt not lie carnally with thy neighbour's wife,

Deut. 4: 21	**Furthermore** the LORD was angry with me for your sakes.
Lev. 18: 19	**Also** thou shalt not approach unto a woman to uncover her nakedness,

<u>LEV. 18: 23</u>	Neither shalt thou lie with any beast to defile thyself **therewith:**
Num. 4: 5	and they shall take down the covering vail and cover the ark of the testimony **with it:**

<u>LEV. 18: 23</u>	neither shall any woman stand before a beast to lie down **thereto:**
Ex. 37: 2	and made a crown of gold **to it.**
Joshua 10: 18	and set men **by it** for to keep them:

<u>LEV. 18: 25</u>	therefore I do visit the iniquity **thereof** upon it,
17: 14	the blood **of it** *is* for the life thereof:

<u>LEV. 18: 25</u>	and the land itself **vomiteth out** her inhabitants.
: 28	That the land **spue** not you out also,

<u>LEV. 18: 30</u>	which were committed before you, and that ye defile not yourself **therein:**
11: 33	whereinto *any* of them falleth whatsoever *is* **in it** shall be unclean,

<u>LEV. 19: 3</u>	Ye shall **fear** every man his mother, and his father, and keep my sabbaths: I *am* the LORD your God.
: 15	thou shalt not **respect** the person of the poor, nor **honour** the person of the mighty:
: 30	Ye shall keep my sabbaths, and **reverence** my sanctuary:

<u>LEV. 19: 10</u>	And thou shall not **glean** thy vineyard, neither shalt thou **gather** *every* grape of thy vineyard;

<u>LEV. 19: 12</u>	And **ye shall not swear by my name falsely, neither shalt thou profane the name of the LORD thy God:**

N.B. note how the comma separates words and phrases having the same meaning.

<u>LEV. 19: 13</u>	Thou shalt not **defraud** thy neighbour, neither **rob** *him:*

<u>LEV. 19: 14</u>	nor put a stumblingblock before the blind, but shalt **fear** thy God:
: 15	thou shalt not **respect** the person of the poor, nor **honour** the person of the mighty:
: 30	Ye shall keep my sabbaths, and **reverence** my sanctuary:

<u>LEV. 19: 18</u>	Thou shalt **not avenge, nor bear any grudge against** the children,

N.B. note how the comma separates words and phrases having the same meaning.

LEV. 19: 35   Ye shall do no unrighteousness in judgment, **in mete**yard, in weight, or **in measure.**

LEV. 20: 2   he shall surely be **put to death:** the people of the land shall stone him with stones.

       : 3   and will **cut him off** from among his people;

       : 4   when he giveth of his seed unto Molech, and **kill him** not:

LEV. 20: 20   Moreover **thou shalt not lie carnally with thy neighbour's wife,**

     20: 14   **Thou shalt not commit adultery.**

LEV. 20: 26   And ye shall be holy unto me: for I the LORD *am* holy, and have **severed** you from *other* people, that ye should be mine.

       : 24   I *am* the LORD your God, which have **separated** you from *other* people.

LEV. 22: 5   Or whatsoever toucheth any creeping thing, **whereby** he be made unclean,

Joshua 3: 4   that ye know the way **by which** ye must go:

LEV. 22: 8   he shall not eat to defile himself there**with:**

Deut. 16: 3   Thou shalt eat no leavened bread **with it;**

LEV. 22: 13   she shall eat of her father's meat: but there shall no stranger eat **thereof.**

       : 11   he shall eat **of it,** and he that is born in the house:

LEV. 22: 14   And if a man eat *of* the holy thing **unwittingly,**

Num. 15: 28   And the priest shall make an atonement for the soul that sinneth **ignorantly,**

LEV. 23: 2   Speak unto the children of Israel, and say unto them, *Concerning* the **feasts of the LORD,** which ye shall proclaim *to be* **holy convocations,** *even* these *are* my feasts.

LEV. 23: 32   in the ninth *day* of the month at **even, from even unto even,**

     24: 3   shall Aaron order it from the **evening** until the morning...

LEV. 24: 3   shall Aaron order it from the evening unto the morning before the LORD **continually:** *it shall be* a statute **for ever** in your in your generations.

       : 8   *being taken* from the children of Israel by an **everlasting** covenant.

1 Kings 9: 3   I have hallowed this house, to put my name there for ever:

and mine eyes and my heart shall be there **perpetually.**

<u>**LEV. 24: 11**</u>	And the Israelitish woman's son **blasphemed** the name *of the LORD*, and **cursed.**

<u>**LEV. 24: 5**</u> 25: 16	And thou shalt take fine flour, and bake twelve cakes **thereof,** and according to the fewness of years thou shalt diminish the price **of it:**

<u>**LEV. 25: 19**</u> : 11	and ye shall eat your fill, and dwell **therein** in safety. neither reap that which growth of itself **in it,**

<u>**LEV. 25: 27**</u> Num. 3: 49	and restore **the overplus** unto the man who sold; And Moses took the redemption money of them that were **over and above** them that were redeemed by the Levites:

<u>**LEV. 25: 31**</u> : 34	But the **houses of the villages** which have no wall round about them shall be counted as the fields of the country: But the **field of the suburbs** of their cities may not be sold;

<u>**LEV. 25: 32**</u> : 34	**Notwithstanding** the cities of the Levites, **But** the field of the suburbs of their cities may not be sold;

<u>**LEV. 25: 34**</u> Num. 35: 3	But the field of the **suburbs** of their cities may not be sold; and the **suburbs** of them shall be for their **cattle,** and for their goods, and for **all their beasts.**

<u>**LEV. 25: 36**</u>	Take thou no **usury of him, <u>or</u> increase:** but fear thy God;

N.B. note how the underlined word separates words and phrases having the same meaning.

<u>**LEV. 25: 37**</u> 22: 7	Thou shalt not give him thy money upon usury, nor lend him thy **victuals** for increase. and shall afterward eat of the holy things; because it *is* his **food.**

<u>**LEV. 25: 45**</u> Duet. 4: 21 Lev.26: 16	**Moreover** of the children of strangers that do sojourn among you, **Furthermore** the LORD was angry with me for your sakes, I **also** will do this unto you;

<u>**LEV. 25: 49**</u> Ruth 2: 20	Either his uncle, or his uncle's son, may redeem him, or *any* that is **nigh** of kin unto him of his family may redeem him; The man *is* **near** of kin unto us,

<u>**LEV. 26: 1**</u>	neither **rear you up** a standing image, neither shall ye **set up** *any* image of stone in your land,

<u>**LEV. 26: 15**</u>	And if ye shall **despise** my statutes, or if your soul **abhor** my judgments,
: 17	they that **hate** you shall reign over you;
<u>**LEV. 26: 17**</u>	And I will set my face against you, and ye shall **be slain** before your enemies:
14: 5	And the priest shall command that one of the birds **be killed** in an earthern vessel over running water:
<u>**LEV. 26: 25**</u>	and when ye are gathered together within your cities, I will send the **pestilence** among you;
14: 48	and behold, the **plague** hath not spread in the house,
<u>**LEV. 26: 28**</u>	and I, even I, will **chastise you** seven times for your sins.
:18	then I will **punish you** seven times more for your sins.
<u>**LEV. 26: 32**</u>	and your enemies which dwell **therein** shall be astonished at it.
25: 11	neither reap that which growth of itself **in it,**
<u>**LEV. 26: 43**</u>	even **because, they despised my judgments, <u>and</u> bcause their soul abhorred my statutes.**

N.B. note how the underlined word separates words and phrases having the same meaning.

<u>**LEV. 27: 9**</u>	And if *it be* a beast, **whereof** men bring an offering unto the LORD,
: 11	And if *it be* any unclean beast, **of which** they do not offer a sacrifice unto the LORD,
<u>**LEV. 27: 10**</u>	and if he shall at all change beast for beast, then it and the exchange **thereof** shall be holy.
: 27	and shall add a fifth *part* **of it** thereto:
<u>**LEV. 27: 23**</u>	Then the priest shall **reckon** unto him the **worth** of thy **estimation,**
<u>**LEV. 27: 27**</u>	and shall add a fifth *part* of it **thereto:** or if it be not redeemed,
Num. 1: 50	and over all the vessels thereof, and over all things that *belong* **to it:**
<u>**LEV. 27: 30**</u>	And all the **tithe** of the land, *whether* of the seed of the land,
: 32	And concerning the tithe of the herd, or of the flock, *or* whatsoever passeth under the rod, the **tenth** shall be holy unto the LORD.

NUMBERS

<u>**NUM. 1: 2**</u>	with the number of *their* names, every male by their **polls;**
: 16	princes of the tribes of their fathers, **heads** of thousands in

Israel.

NUM. 1: 39	Those that were numbered of them, *even* of the tribe of Dan, *were* three**score** and two thousand and seven hundred.
Lev. 27: 7	And if *it be* from **sixty** years old and above;

N.B. The underlined word is a numerical term meaning twenty. To find the value of the 'score' number multiply 3x20=60.

NUM. 1: 49	Only thou shalt not **number** the tribe of Levi, neither **take the sum** of them among the children of Israel:

NUM. 1: 49	and over all the vessels **thereof,**
3: 26	and the cords **of it** for all the for all the service **thereof.**

NUM. 2: 4	And his host, and those that were numbered of them, *were* three**score** and fourteen thousand and six hundred.
Lev. 27: 7	And if *it be* from **sixty** years old and abov;

N.B. The underlined word is a numerical term meaning twenty. To find the value of the 'score' number multiply 3x20=60.

NUM. 2: 31	They shall go **hindmost** with their standards.
3: 23	The families of the Gershonites shall **behind** the tabernacle westward.
10: 25	*which was* the **rere**ward of all the camps throughout their hosts.

NUM. 3: 12	instead of all the firstborn that openeth the **matrix** among the children of Israel:
: 16	instead of such as open every **womb,**

NUM. 3: 26	and by the altar round about, and the cords **of it** for all the service **thereof.**

NUM. 3: 31	and the vessels of the sanctuary **wherewith** they minister,
2 Kings 19: 6	**with which** the servants of the king of Assyria have blasphemed me.

NUM. 3: 36	And *under* the **custody and charge** of the sons of Me-rar-i *shall be* the boards of the tabernacle,

N. B. note how the underlined word separates words and phrases having the same meaning.

NUM. 3: 38	But those that encamp before the tabernacle **toward the east,** *even* before the tabernacle of the congregation **eastward,**

NUM. 3: 46	And those who are to be redeemed of the two hundred and three**score** and thirteen of the firstborn of the children of Israel,

Leviticus 27: 7   And if *it be* from **sixty** years old and above;

N.B. The underlined word is a numerical term meaning twenty. To find the value of the 'score' number multiply 3x20=60.

NUM. 3: 47   Thou shalt even take five shekels **apiece** by the poll,
   1: 44   and the princes of Israel, *being* twelve men: **each one** was for the house of his fathers.

NUM. 3: 50   a thousand three hundred and **three<u>score</u>** and five *shekels,*
Lev. 27: 7   And if *it be* from **sixty** years old and above;

N.B. The underlined word is a numerical term meaning twenty. To find the value of the 'score' word multiply 3x20=60.

NUM. 4: 6   And shall put **thereon** the covering of badgers's skins,
   : 10   and shall put *it* **upon** a bar.

N.B. reverse the two syllables of the bold word in the first reference and the meaning is clear.

NUM. 4: 6   and shall put **thereon** the covering of badgers' skins,
   : 10   and shall put *it* **upon** a bar.
Gen. 28: 12   and behold the angels of God ascending **on it**.

N.B. Reverse the syllables in the first reference and the meaning is clear.

NUM. 4: 7   and the spoons, and the bowls, and covers to cover **withal:**
Exod. 12: 9   Eat not of it raw, nor sodden at **all with** water,

NUM. 4: 9   and all the oil vessels thereof, **wherewith** they minister unto it:
2 Kings 19: 6   Be not afraid **with which** the servants of the king of Assyria have blasphemed me.

NUM. 4: 10   And they shall put it and all the vessels **thereof** within a covering of badgers' skins,
   : 14   they shall spread upon it a covering of badgers' skins, and put to the staves **of it.**
NUM. 4: 15   the sons of Ko-hath shall come to **bear** *it:*
   11: 12   that thou shouldest say unto me, **Carry** them in thy bosom,

NUM.4: 22   **Take also the sum of** the sons of Gershon,
   : 23   From thirty years old and upward until fifty years old shalt thou **number them;**

NUM. 4: 48   Even those that were numbered of them, were eight thousand and five hundred and four<u>score</u>.
Gen. 5: 25   And Methuselah lived an hundred **eighty** and seven years,

59

N.B. The underlined word is a numerical term meaning twenty. To find the value of the 'score' number multiply 4x20=80.

NUM. 5: 3	that they defile not their camps, in the midst **whereof** I dwell.
10: 29	We are journeying unto the place **of which** the LORD said,
NUM. 5: 7	and he shall **recompense** the trespass unto, his trespass with the
	principal thereof, and **add unto it** the fifth *part* thereof, and **give** *it* unto him against whom he hath trespassed.
Deut. 32: 35	To me *belongeth* vengeance, and **recompence**;
: 41	I will **render** vengeance to mine enemies, and will **reward** them that hate me.
Lev. 5: 16	And he shall **make amends** for the harm that he hath done in the holy thing,
Exodus 22: 3	*for* he should **make full restitution;**
: 14	the owner thereof *being* not with it, he shall surely **make it good.**
NUM. 5: 8	beside the ram of the atonement, **whereby** an atonement shall be made for him.
Josh. 3: 4	that ye may know the way **by which** ye must go:
NUM. 6: 19	And the priest shall take the **sodden** shoulder of the ram,
1 Kings 19: 21	and took a yoke of oxen, and slew them, **boiled** their flesh...
NUM. 7: 13	And his offering *was* one silver charger, the weight **thereof** *was* an hundred and thirty *shekels,*
3: 26	and by the altar round about, and the cords **of it** for all the service **thereof.**
7: 19	He offered *for* his offering one silver charger, the weight **whereof** *was* an hundred and thirty *shekels,*
: 31	His offering *was* one silver charger, the weight **of** an hundred and thirty *shekels,*
10: 29	We are journeying unto the place **of which** the LORD said,
NUM. 7: 13	both of them *were* full of fine flour **mingled** with oil for a meal offering:
Exod. 12: 38	And a **mixed** multitude went up also with them;
NUMBERS 8: 3	And Aaron did so; he lighted the lamps **thereof** over against the candlestick, as the LORD commanded Moses.
9: 3	ye shall keep it in his appointed season: according to all the rites **of it,**
NUM. 8: 17	on the day that I **smote** every firstborn in the land of Egypt I sanctified them for myself.
1 Sam. 2: 14	And he **struck** *it* into the pan,

<u>NUM. 9: 3</u>	according to all the **rites** of it, and according to all the **ceremonies** therof,
<u>NUM. 9: 3</u>	according to all the rites **of it,** and according to all the ceremonies **thereof,**
<u>NUM. 9: 7</u>	**wherefore** are we kept back, that we may not offer an offering of the LORD in his appointed season among the children of Israel?
11: 20	and have wept before him, saying, **Why** came we forth out of Egypt?
<u>NUM. 9: 14</u>	And if a stranger shall sojourn among you, and will keep the passover, unto the LORD; **according to the ordinance of** the pass-over and **according to the manner thereof,** so shall he do:
<u>NUM. 9: 19</u>	And when the cloud **tarried** long upon the tabernacle many days,
16: 48	And he stood between the dead and the living; and the plague was **stayed.**
<u>NUM. 9: 22</u>	that the cloud tarried **upon** the tabernacle, remaining **thereon,**
<u>NUM. 10: 21</u>	and *the other* did set up the tabernacle **against they came.**
: 33	and the ark of the covenant of the LORD went **before them...**
<u>NUM. 10: 25</u>	And the standard of the camp of the children of Dan set for forward, *which was* the **rereward** of all the camps...

N.B. note the bold word, the first syllable gives the meaning of the whole word.

<u>NUM. 11: 7</u>	And the manna *was* as coriander seed, and the colour **thereof** as the colour of bdellium.
: 8	and the taste **of it:**
<u>NUM. 11: 7</u>	and the **colour** thereof as **the colour of bdellium.**
Ex. 16: 31	and it *was* like coriander seed, **white:**
<u>NUM. 11: 11</u>	And Moses said unto the LORD, **Wherefore** hast thou afflicted thy servant?
: 20	**Why** came we forth out of Egypt?
<u>NUM. 11: 13</u>	**Whence** should I have flesh to give unto all this people?
Ex. 2: 20	And he said unto his daughters, And **where** *is* he?
<u>NUM. 11: 22</u>	Shall the flocks and the herds be slain for them, **to suffice** them?

Job 38: 27	**To satisfy** the desolate and waste *ground;*
NUM. 12: 11	Alas, my lord, **I beseech thee,** lay not the sin upon us,
11: 15	kill me, **I pray thee,** out of hand,
NUM. 12: 11	lay not the sin upon us, **wherein** we have done foolishly,
14: 34	After the number of the days **in which** ye searched the land,
NUM. 13: 18	and the people that dwelleth **therein,** whether they *be* strong or weak, few or many;
: 18	and the people that dwelleth **therein,**
: 32	and all the people that we saw **in it** *are* men of a great stature.
2 Kings 2: 21	And he went forth unto the spring of the waters, and cast the salt **in there,**
NUM. 13: 22	And they **ascended** by the south, and came unto He-bron;
: 31	But the men that **went up** with him said,
NUM. 13: 23	and cut down from **thence** a branch with one cluster of grapes,
: 28	and moreover we saw the children of Anak **there.**
NUM. 13: 27	We came unto the land **whither** thou sentest us,
: 22	and came unto He-bron; **where** A-hi-man, She-shai,
NUM. 13: 28	**Nevertheless** the people *be* strong that dwell in the land,
14: 21	**But** *as* truly *as* I live,
NUM. 13: 28	and **moreover** we saw the children of Anak there.
Deut. 4: 21	**Furthermore** the LORD was angry for your sakes,
Num. 12: 2	hath he not spoken **also** by us?
NUM. 13: 32	*is* a land that eateth up the inhabitants **there**of;
: 27	and this *is* the fruit **of it.**
NUM. 13: 32	and all the people that we saw in it *are* men of a great **stature.**
Exod. 38: 18	and the **height** in the breadth *was* five cubits,
NUM. 14: 3	And **wherefore** hath the LORD brought us unto this land,
11: 20	**Why** came we forth out of Egypt?
NUM. 14: 12	I will **smite** them with the pestilence, and disinherit them,
Exodus 12: 7	and **strike** *it* on the two side posts and on the upper door posts of the houses,
NUM. 14: 24	him will I bring into the land **whereinto** he went;
: 16	Because the LORD was not able to bring this **into** the land **which** he sware unto them, :
Psalm 118: 20	This gate of the LORD, **into which** the righteous shall enter.
NUM. 14: 30	*concerning* which I sware to make you dwell **therein,**

13: 32	and all the people that we saw **in it** *are* men of a great stature.

NUM. 14: 36	and made all the congregation to murmur against him by bringing **a slander upon the land,**
: 37	Even those men that did bring up the **evil report upon the land,** died by the plague before the LORD.

NUM. 14: 41	And Moses said, **Wherefore** now do ye transgress the commandment of the LORD?
11: 20	And have wept before him, saying, **Why** came we forth out of Egypt?

NUM. 15: 15	One **ordinance** *shall be both* for you of the congregation,
:16	One **law** and one manner shall be for you,

NUM. 15: 18	When ye come into the land **whither** I bring you,
17: 4	**where** I will meet with you.

NUM. 15: 24	Then it shall be, if *ought* be committed **by ignorance without the knowledge of** the congregation,

N.B. note how the second fourth and fifth bold word mean the same as the first.

NUM. 15: 38	and they put upon the fringe of the borders a rib**band** of blue:

NUM. 16: 2	two hundred and fifty princes of the assembly, **famous** in the congregation, **men of renown;**

NUM. 16: 3	**wherefore** then lift ye up yourselves above the congregation of the LORD?
1: 20	**Why** came we forth out of Egypt?

NUM. 16: 7	And put fire **therein,** and put incense **in them** before the LORD to morrow:

NUM. 16: 14	**Moreover** thou hast not brought us into a land that floweth with milk and honey,
Num. 9: 13	**Furthermore** the LORD spake unto me, saying,
16: 10	and seek ye the priesthood **also?**
NUM. 16: 18	And they took every man his censer, and put fire in them, and laid incense **thereon,**
Genesis 21: 33	And *Abraham* planted a grove in Beer-she-ba; and called **there on** the name of the LORD, the everlasting God.
Lev. 6: 12	and the priest shall burn wood **on it** every morning, and lay the burnt offering in order **upon it;** and he shall burn **thereo** the fat of the peace offerings.
Num. 16: 46	and put **on** incense, and go quickly unto the congregation, and make an atonement for them: for **there** is wrath gone out

from the LORD;

NUM. 16: 22	shall one man sin, and wilt thou be **wroth** with all the congregation?
Deut. 1: 37	And the LORD was **angry** with me for your sakes,
NUM. 16: 25	Get you up from about the **tabernacle** of Kor-ah, Da-than, and A-bi-ram.
: 26	Depart, I pray you, from the **tents** of there wicked men.
NUM. 16: 28	And Moses said, **Hereby** ye shall know that the LORD hath sent me to do all these works;
1 Sam. 26: 24	as thy life was much set **by this** day in mine eyes,
NUM. 16: 30	with all that *appertained* unto them, and they go down **quick** into the pit;
: 33	They, and all that *appertained* to them, went down **alive** into the pit,
NUM. 16: 31	made an end of speaking all these words, that the ground clave **asunder** that *was* under them,
Lev. 15: 19	she shall be put **apart** for seven days:
NUM. 16: 38	and that they put upon the fringe of the borders a rib**band** of blue.
NUM. 16: 39	And El-e-a-zar the priest took the brazen censers, **wherewith** they that were burnt had offered;
: 11	For **which** cause *both* thou and all thy company *are* gathered together against the LORD:
2 Kings 19: 6	Be not afraid of the words **with which** the servants of the king of Assyria have blasphemed me.
NUM. 16: 46	And Moses said unto Aaron, Take a censer, and put fire **therein** from off the altar,
13: 32	and all the people that we saw **in it** *are* men of a great stature.
2 Kings 2: 21	and cast the salt **in there,** and said, Thus saith the LORD,
NUM. 17: 5	and I will make to cease from me the murmurings of the children of Israel, **whereby** they murmur against you.
16: 11	For **which** cause *both* thou and all thy company *are* gathered together against the LORD:
2 Kings 19: 6	Be not afraid of the words **with which** the servants of the king of Assyria have blasphemed me.
NUM. 17: 6	and every one of their princes gave him a rod **apiece, for each** prince one,

N.B. note how the comma separates words and phrases having the same meaning.

NUM. 18: 3	only they shall not **come nigh** vessels of the sanctuary and

	the altar,
16: 40	that no stranger, which *is* not of the seed of Aaron, **come near** to offer incense before the LORD;

NUM. 18: 5 — that there be no **wrath** any more upon the children of Israel.
22: 22 — And God's **anger** was kindled because he went:

NUM. 18: 8 — I also have given thee the charge of mine heave offerings of all the **hallowed** things of the children of Israel;
: 9 — This shall be thine of the most **holy** things,

NUM. 18: 8 — unto thee have I given them by reason of the anointing, and to thy sons, by an **ordinance** for ever.
: 11 — and to thy sons and daughters with thee, by a **statute** for ever:
19: 14 — This *is* the **law,** when a man dieth in a tent:

NUM. 18: 9 — every **oblation** of theirs, every meat **offering** of theirs,
11 — the heave offering of their **gift,**

NUM. 18: 9 — and every trespass offering of theirs, which they shall **render** unto me,
: 28 — and ye shall **give** thereof the LORD'S heave offering to Aaron the priest.

NUM. 18: 26 — When ye take of the children of Israel **tithes** which I have given you from them for your inheritance, then shall ye offer up an heave offering of it for the LORD, *even* **a tenth** *part* of the tithe.

NUM. 18: 27 — And *this* your heave offering shall be **reckoned** unto you,
: 30 — then it shall be **counted** unto the Levites as the increase of the threshingfloor,
NUM. 18: 29 — of all the best **thereof,** *even* the hallowed part thereof out **of it.**

NUM. 19: 2 — Speak unto the children of Israel, that they bring thee **a red heifer** without spot,
Isaiah 7: 21 — *that* a man shall nourish **a young cow,**
15: 5 — My heart shall out for Moab; his fugitives *shall flee* unto Zoar, **an heifer of three years old:**
NUM. 19: 17 — and running water shall he put **thereto** in a vessel:
1: 50 — and over all the vessels thereof, and over all things that *belong* **to it;**

NUM. 19: 26 — I will saddle me an ass, that I may ride **thereon,** and go to the king;
Lev. 6: 12 — and the priest shall burn wood **on it** every morning, and lay the burnt offering in order **upon it;** and he shall burn **thereon** the fat of the peace offerings.

NUM. 20: 3	And the people **chode** with Moses,
21: 7	We have sinned, for we have **spoken against** the LORD,
NUM. 20: 4	And **why** have ye brought up the congregation of the LORD into this wilderness,
: 5	And **wherefore** have ye made us to come up out of Egypt,
NUM. 20: 14	Thus saith thy brother Israel, Thou knowest all the **travail** that hath befallen us:
2 Kings 19: 3	This day *is* a day of **trouble,** and of rebuke,
NUM. 21: 4	by the way of the Red sea, to **compass** the land of Edom:
22: 4	Now shall this company lick up all *that are* **round about** us,
NUM. 21: 5	**Wherefore** have ye brought us up out of Egypt to die in the wilderness?
20: 3	And **why** have ye brought up the congregation of the LORD into this wilderness,
NUM. 21: 12	From **thence** they removed, and pitched in the valley of Zared.
22: 5	Behold, **there** is a people come out from Egypt:
NUM. 21: 14	**Wherefore** it is said in the book of the wars of the LORD,
: 7	**Therefore** the people came to Moses,
NUM. 21: 16	And from thence *they went* to Beer: that *is* the well **whereof** the LORD spake unto Moses,
31: 39	**of which** the LORD'S tribute *was* threescore and one.
NUM. 21: 22	**Let** me pass through thy land:
: 23	And Si-hon would not **suffer** Israel to pass through his border:
Luke 11: 48	Truly ye bear witness that ye **allow** the deeds of your fathers:
1 Cor. 16: 7	but I trust to tarry a while with you, if the Lord **permit**.
NUM. 21: 25	in Heshbon, and in all the villages **thereof.**
18: 32	when ye have heaved from it the best **of it:**
NUM. 22: 3	And Moab was **sore afraid** of the people, because they *were* many: and Moab **was distressed** because of the children of Israel.
NUM. 22: 6	for they *are* too mighty for me: **peradventure** I shall prevail,
Genesis 16: 2	go in unto my maid; **it may be** that I may obtain children by her.
18: 26	And the LORD said, **If** I find in Sodom fifty righteous within the city,
1 Sam. 14: 6	**it may be** that the LORD will work for us:
NUM. 22: 6	for I **wot** that he whom thou blessest *is* blessed,
: 19	that I may **know** what the LORD will say unto me more.

<u>NUM. 22: 19</u>	Now therefore, I pray you, **tarry** ye also here this night,
: 8	And he said unto them, **Lodge** here this night,

<u>NUM. 22: 37</u>	**wherefore** camest thou unto me?
20: 4	And **why** have ye brought the congregation of the LORD into this wilderness,

<u>NUM. 23: 3</u>	and I will go: **peradventure** the LORD will come to meet me:
1 Sam. 14: 6	**it may be** that the LORD will work for us:

<u>NUM. 23: 9</u>	For from the top of the rocks **I see** him, and from the hills **I behold** him, **lo,** the people shall dwell alone,

<u>NUM. 23: 13</u>	from **whence** thou mayest see them:
22: 26	**where** *was* no way to turn either to the right hand or to the left.

<u>NUM. 23: 18</u>	And he took up his parable, and said, Rise up, Balak, and **hear; hearken** unto me, thou son of Zippor:

N.B. note that the word 'hear' and 'ear' are in 'hearken' and thust he meaning is clear.

<u>NUM. 23: 21</u>	**He hath not beheld iniquity in Jacob, neither hath he seen perverseness in Israel:**

N.B. note how the comma separates words and phrases having the same meaning.

<u>NUM. 23: 23</u>	Surely *there is* **no enchantment against Jacob, neither** *is there* **any divination against Israel,**

N.B. note how the first comma separates words and phrases having the same meaning.

<u>NUM. 23: 23</u>	according to this time it shall be said **of Jacob, <u>and</u> of Israel,** What hath God wrought!

N.B. note how the underlined word separates words and phrases having the same meaning.

<u>NUM. 23: 23</u>	according to this time it shall be said of Jacob, and of Israel, What hath God **wrought!**
: 11	What hast thou **done** unto me?

<u>NUM. 23: 27</u>	**peradventure** it will please God that thou mayest curse me them from thence.
1 Sam.14: 6	**it may be** that the LORD will work for us:

<u>NUM. 23: 27</u>	peradventure it will please God that thou mayest curse me

| | them from **thence.** |
| 24: 17 | **there** shall come a Star out of Jacob, |

NUM. 24: 5   **How goodly are thy tents, O Jacob, _and_ thy tabernacles, O Israel!**

N.B. note how the underlined word separates words and phrases having the same meaning.

NUM. 24: 9   He **couched,** he **lay down** as a lion,

N.B. note how the comma separates words and phrases having the same meaning.

| **NUM. 24: 14** | come *therefore,* and I will **advertise** thee what this people what this people shall do to thy people in the latter days. |
| 23: 3 | and whatsoever he sheweth me I will **tell** thee. |

| **NUM. 25: 12** | **Wherefore** say, Behold, I give unto him my covenant of peace: |
| 22: 19 | Now **therefore,** I pray you, tarry ye also here this night, |

| **NUM. 25: 14** | *and* I will **advertise** what this people shall do to thy people in the latter days. |
| 23: 3 | and whatsoever he sheweth me I will **tell** thee. |

| **NUM. 25: 17** | **Vex** the Midianites, and smite them: |
| Joshua 6: 18 | and make the camp of Israel a curse, and **trouble it.** |

| **NUM. 25: 18** | For they vex you with their wiles, **wherewith** they have beguiled you in the matter of Pe-or, |
| 2 Kings 19: 6 | Be not afraid of the words which thou hast heard **with which,** the servants of the king of Assyria have blasphemed me. |

| **NUM. 25: 18** | wherewith they have **beguiled** you in the matter of Pe-or, |
| Deut. 11: 16 | Take heed to yourselves, that your heart be not **deceived,** |

| **NUM. 26: 22** | These *are* the families of Judah according to those that were numbered of them, three**score** and sixteen thousand and five hundred. |
| 7: 88 | the rams **sixty,** the he goats sixty, the lambs of the first year sixty. |

N.B. The underlined word is a numerical term meaning twenty. To find the value of the 'score' number multiply 3x20=60.

| **NUM. 27: 11** | then ye shall give his inheritance unto his unto his **kin**sman that that is next to him of his **family,** |

| **NUM. 28: 5** | **mingled** with the fourth *part* of an hin of beaten oil. |
| Exod. 12: 38 | And a **mixed** multitude went up also with them; |

<u>NUM. 28: 6</u>	*It is* a continual burnt offering, which was **ordained** in mount Sinai for a sweet savour,
9: 13	because he brought not the offering of the LORD in his **appointed** season,
<u>NUM. 28: 7</u>	And the drink offering **thereof** *shall be* the fourth *part* of an hin for the one lamb:
18: 32	when ye have heaved from it the best **of it:**
<u>NUM. 28: 18</u>	In the first day *shall be* an holy **convocation:**
: 17	And in the fifteenth day of this month *is* the **feast:**
Lev. 23: 2	Speak unto the children of Israel, *Concerning* the **feasts** of the LORD,
	which ye shall proclaim *to be* holy **convocations,**
	even these *are* my **feasts.**
<u>NUM. 28: 19</u>	and seven lambs of the first year: they shall be unto you **without blemish:**
: 9	And on the sabbath day two lambs of the first year **without spot,**
Lev. 22: 21	or a freewill offering in beeves or sheep, it shall be **perfect** to be accepted;
<u>NUM. 30: 4</u>	And her father hear her vow, and her bond **wherewith** she hath bound her soul,
2 Kings 19: 6	Be not afraid of the words which thou heard **with which** the servants of the king of Assyria have blasphemed me.
<u>NUM. 30: 8</u>	But if her husband **disallowed** her on the day that he heard *it,* then he shall make her vow which she vowed, **of non effect:**
: 12	or concerning the bond of her soul, **shall not stand:**
<u>NUM. 31: 7</u>	And they warred against the Midianites, as the LORD commanded Moses; and they **slew** all the males.
: 19	whosoever hath **killed,** any person, hath touched any **slain,**
<u>NUM. 31: 10</u>	And they burnt all their cities **wherein** they dwelt,
Deut. 2: 14	And in the space **in which** we came from Ka-desh-bar-ne-a,
<u>NUM. 31: 14</u>	And Moses was **wroth** with the officers of the host,
Deut. 4: 21	Furthermore the LORD was **angry** with me for your sakes,
<u>NUM. 31: 19</u>	whosoever hath **killed** any person, and whosoever hath touched any **slain,**
<u>NUM. 31: 20</u>	And purify all *your* **raiment,** and all that is made of skins,
: 24	And ye shall wash your **clothes** on the seventh day,
20: 28	And Moses stripped Aaron of his **garments,**

<u>NUM. 31: 33</u>	And three**score** and twelve thousand beeves,
7: 88	the rams **sixty**, the he goats sixty,

N.B. The underlined word is a numerical term meaning twenty. To find the value of the 'score' number multiply 3x20=60.

<u>NUM. 31: 50</u>	We have therefore brought an **oblation** for the LORD,
: 52	And all the gold of the **offering** that they offered up to the LORD,

<u>NUM. 32: 5</u>	**Wherefore,** said they, **if** we have found grace in thy sight,
35: 34	Defile not **therefore** the land which ye shall inhabit,

<u>NUM. 32: 5</u>	Wherefore said they, if we have found **grace** in thy sight,
11: 15	if I have found **favour** in thy sight;

<u>NUM. 32: 27</u>	But thy servants will pass over, **every man armed for war,**
: 29	**every man armed to battle,** before the LORD,

<u>NUM. 32: 33</u>	and the kingdom of Og king of Ba-shan, the land, with the cities **thereof** in the coasts,
34: 12	And the border shall go down to Jordan, and the goings out **of it** shall be at the salt sea:

<u>NUM. 32: 40</u>	and he dwelt **therein.**
: 39	and dispossessed the Amorite which *was* **in it.**

<u>NUM. 33: 3</u>	And they **departed** from Ram-e-ses in the first month,
: 5	And the children of Israel **removed** from Ram-e-ses,
: 23	And they **went from** Ke-he-la-thah,

<u>NUM. 33: 6</u>	and **pitched in** E-tham, which *is* in the edge of the wilderness,
: 10	and **encamped** by the Red sea.

<u>NUM. 33: 53</u>	And ye shall dispossess *the inhabitants of* the land, and dwell **therein:**
35: 25	and he shall abide **in it** unto the death of the high priest,

N.B. reverse the syllables in the first reference and the meaning is clear.

<u>NUM. 33: 55</u>	and thorns in your sides, and shall vex you in the land **wherein ye** dwell.
Deut. 2: 14	And the space **in which** we came from Ka-desh-bar-ne-a,

<u>NUM. 34: 4</u>	and the going forth **thereof** shall be from the south to Ka-desh barnea,
: 5	and the goings out **of it** shall be at the sea.

<u>NUM. 34: 5</u>	And the border **shall fetch a compass** from Azmon unto the

	river of Egypt,
2 Sam. 5: 23	*but* fetch a compass **behind them,**
2 Chr. 13: 13	But Jer-o-bo-am caused an ambushment to **come about behind them:**

NUM. 35: 3	And the cities shall they have to dwell in; and the **suburbs** of them shall be **for their cattle,**
Lev. 25: 34	But the **field** of their suburbs of their cities may not be sold;

NUM. 35: 6	which ye shall appoint for the manslayer, that he may flee **thither:**
Deut. 1: 28	and moreover we have seen the sons of Anakims **there.**

NUM. 35: 16	And if he **smite** him with an instrument of iron, so that he die,
Ex. 12: 7	and **strike** *it* on the two side posts...

NUM. 35: 17	And if he **smite** him with throwing a stone, wherewith he may die,
Deut. 21: 4	which is neither eared nor sown, and shall **strike** off the heifer's neck there in the valley:

NUM. 35: 17	And if he smite him with throwing a stone, **wherewith** he may die,
Joshua 22: 17	**from which** we are not cleansed until this day,

NUM. 35: 21	he that **smote** *him* shall surely be put to death;
2 Sam. 12: 15	And the LORD **struck** the child that Uriah's wife bare unto David,

NUM. 35: 25	and the congregation shall restore him to the city of his refuge, **whither** he was fled:
33: 54	every man's *inheritance* shall be in the place **where** his lot falleth;

NUM. 35: 31	**Moreover** ye shall no satisfaction for the life of a murderer,
Deut. 4: 21	**Furthermore** the LORD was angry with me for your sakes,

NUM. 36: 3	and shall be put to the inheritance of the tribe **whereunto** they are received:
Ps. 118: 20	The gate of the LORD, **into which** the righteous shall enter.

DEUTERONOMY

DEUT. 1: 7	and unto all *the places* **nigh** thereunto, in the plain,
: 22	And ye came **near** unto me every one of you,

DEUT. 1: 7	and unto all *the places* nigh **thereunto,** in the plain,
Num. 1: 50	and over all things that *belong* **to it:**

DEUT. 1: 16	and judge **right**eously between *every* man and his brother,

| 6: 18 | and thou shalt do *that which is* **right** and good in the sight of the of the Lord; |
| Psalm 58: 1 | do ye judge up**rightly**, O ye sons of men? |

| **DEUT. 1: 12** | How can I myself alone **bear your cumbrance, <u>and</u> your burden, <u>and</u> your strife?** |

N. B. note how the underlined words separate words and phrases having the same meaning.

| **DEUT. 1: 21** | as the LORD God of thy fathers hath said unto thee, **fear not, neither be discouraged.** |
| : 29 | Then I said unto you, **Dread not, neither be afraid of them.** |

N.B. note how the bold words mean the same even though separated by a comma.

| **DEUT. 1: 28** | **Whither** shall we go up? our brethren have discouraged our |
| : 19 | And **when** we departed from Horeb, |

| **DEUT. 1: 34** | And the LORD heard the voice of your words, and was **wroth,** |
| : 37 | And the LORD was **angry** with me for your sakes, |

DEUT. 1: 39	**Moreover** your little ones,
: 37	**Also** the LORD was angry with me for your sakes,
4: 21	**Furthermore** the LORD was angry with me for your sakes,

| **DEUT. 1: 39** | they shall go in **thither,** and unto them will I give it, |
| : 35 | Surely **there** shall not one of these men of this generation... |

| **DEUT. 1: 45** | And returned and wept before the LORD; but the LORD **would not hearken to your voice, <u>nor</u> give ear unto you.** |
| Isaiah 49: 1 | **Listen, O isles, unto me; <u>and</u> hearken ye people, from far;** |

N.B. note how the underlined words separate words and phrases having the same meaning.

DEUT. 2: 1	as the LORD spake unto me: and we **compassed** mount Seir many days.
Psalm 22:16	For dogs have **compassed** me: the assembly of the wicked **inclosed me:**
: 12	strong *bulls* of Bashan have **beset me round.**

| **DEUT. 2: 9** | And the LORD said unto me, **Distress not** the Moabites, neither contend with them in battle: |
| Joshua 6: 18 | when ye take the accursed thing, and make the camp of Israel a curse, and **trouble** it. |

DEUT. 2: 10	The E-mims dwelt **therein in times past,**
: 20	(giants dwelt **therein in old time...**)
2 Kings 2: 21	and cast the salt **in there,**

<u>**DEUT. 2: 19**</u>	And *when* thou comest nigh over against the children of Ammon, **distress them not, nor meddle with them:**

N.B. note how the underlined word separates words and phrases having the same meaning.

<u>**DEUT. 2: 25**</u>	This day will I begin to put **the fear of thee and the dread of thee** upon the nations *that are* under the whole heaven, who shall report of thee, and **shall tremble, and be in anguish** because of thee.

N.B. note how the underlined word separates words and phrases having the same meaning.

<u>**DEUT. 2: 28**</u>	Thou shalt sell me **meat** for money,
10: 18	in giving him **food** and raiment.

<u>**DEUT. 2: 33**</u>	and we **smote** him, and his sons, and all his people.
: 34	and **utterly destroyed** the men, and the women, and the little ones, of every city, we **left none to remain:**

<u>**DEUT. 3: 4**</u>	there was not a city which we took not from them, three<u>**score**</u> cities, all he region of Argob,
Num. 7: 88	the rams **sixty**, the goats **sixty**, the lambs of the first year **sixty**.

N.B. The underlined word is a numerical term meaning twenty. To find the value of the 'score' number multiply 3x20=60

<u>**DEUT. 3: 11**</u>	nine cubits *was* the length **thereof,** and four cubits breadth **of it,**

<u>**DEUT. 3: 18**</u>	ye shall pass over **armed** before your brethren the children of Israel, all *that are* meet for war.
Josh. 4: 13	About forty thousand **prepared for war** passed over before the LORD unto battle,

<u>**DEUT. 3: 21**</u>	so shall the LORD do unto all the kingdoms **whither** thou passest,
8: 15	**where** *there was* no water;

<u>**DEUT. 3: 26**</u>	But the LORD was **wroth** with me for your sakes,
4: 21	Furthermore the LORD was **angry** with me for your sakes,

<u>**DEUT. 3: 26**</u>	and the LORD said unto me, Let it **suffice** thee;
Job 38: 27	To **satisfy** the desolate and waste *ground;*

<u>**DEUT. 4: 7**</u>	For what nation *is there so* great, who *hath* God *so* **nigh** unto them,
: 11	And ye came **near** and stood under the mountain;

DEUT. 4: 9	Only take heed to thyself, and keep thy soul **diligently,**
15: 5	Only if thou **carefully** hearken unto the voice of the LORD thy God,
DEUT. 4: 14	that ye might do them in the land **whither** ye go over to possess it.
: 19	And lest thou lift up thine eyes unto heaven, and **when** thou seest the sun,
8: 15	and drought, **where** *there was* no water;
DEUT. 4: 16	Lest ye corrupt *there,* and make a graven **image,** the **similitude** of
	any **figure,** the **likeness** of any male or female.
DEUT. 4: 26	that ye shall soon utterly perish from off the land **where**unto ye go over Jordan to possess it;
DEUT. 4: 27	**whither** the LORD shall lead you.
: 30	**When** thou art in tribulation,
DEUT. 4: 34	Or hath God **assayed** to go *and* take him a nation from the midst of *another* nation,
Acts 16: 10	immediately we **endeavoured** to go into Macedonia,
DEUT. 4: 41	Then Moses **severed** three cities on this side Jordan toward the sun rising;
10: 8	At that time the LORD **separated** the tribe of Levi,
DEUT. 4: 42	That the slayer might flee **thither,** which should kill his neighbour unawares, and hated him not in times past;
: 32	whether **there** hath been *any such thing* as this great thing *is,*
DEUT. 4: 42	That the slayer might flee thither, which should kill his neighbour **unawares,**
19: 4	And this *is* the case of the slayer, which shall flee thither, that he may live: Whoso killeth his neighbour **ignorantly,** whom he hated not in time past;
DEUT. 5: 15	and *that* the LORD thy God brought thee out **thence** through a mighty hand and stretched out arm: **there**fore the LORD thy God commandeth thee to keep the sabbath day.
DEUT. 5: 16	Honour thy father and thy mother, as the LORD thy God hath commanded thee, that thy days **may be** prolonged,
Exodus 20: 12	Honour thy father and thy mother: that thy days **may be long** upon the land that the LORD thy God giveth thee.
DEUT. 5: 21	Neither shalt thou **desire** neighbour's wife, neither shalt thou **covet** thy neighbour's house,

<u>DEUT. 5: 33</u>	and *that it may be* well with you, and *that* ye may **prolong** *your*
	days in the land which ye shall possess.
1 Kings 3: 14	And if thou wilt walk in my ways, to keep my statutes and my commandments, as thy father did walk, then I will **lengthen** thy days.
<u>DEUT. 6: 1</u>	that ye might do *them* in the land **whither** ye go to possess it:
8: 15	**where** *there was* no water;
<u>DEUT. 6: 2</u>	and thy son's son, all the days of thy life; and thy life and that thy
	days may be pro**long**ed.
<u>DEUT. 6: 7</u>	and thou shall **diligently** unto thy children,
15: 5	Only if thou **carefully** hearken unto the voice of the LORD thy God,
<u>DEUT. 6: 23</u>	And he brought us out from **thence,**
: 3	Hear **there**fore, O Israel, and observe to do *it;*
<u>DEUT. 7: 2</u>	And when the LORD thy God shall deliver them before thee;
	thou shalt smite them, *and* utterly destroy them;

N.B. note how the underlined word separates words and phrases having the same
meaning.

<u>DEUT. 7: 13</u>	and thine oil, the increase of thy **kine,**
1 Sam. 6: 7	Now therefore make a new cart, and take two **milch kine,** on which there hath come no yoke, and tie the kine to the cart, **and bring their calves** home from them:
Job 21: 10	their **cow** calveth, and casteth not **her calf.**

N.B. Kine is the female animal of the collective word cattle.

<u>DEUT. 7: 19</u>	and the mighty hand, and the outstretched arm, **whereby** the LORD
	thy God brought thee out:
Joshua 3: 4	that ye may know the way **by which** ye must go:
<u>DEUT. 7: 20</u>	**Moreover** the LORD thy God will send the hornet among them,
9: 13	**Furthermore** the LORD spake unto me,
7: 13	he will **also** bless the fruit of thy womb,
<u>DEUT. 7: 21</u>	Thou shalt not be **affrighted** at them:
. 7: 19	so shall the LORD thy God do unto all the people of whom thou art **afraid.**
<u>DEUT. 7: 25</u>	thou shalt not desire the silver or gold *that is* on them, nor

	take *it*
	lest thou be snared **therein:**
16: 3	Thou shalt not eat no leavened bread **with it;**

DEUT. 7: 26   lest thou be a cursed thing like it: *but* **thou shalt utterly detest** it, **and thou shalt utterly abhor it;**

N.B.   note how the underlined word separates words and phrases having the same meaning.

DEUT. 8: 4   Thy **raiment** waxed not old upon thee,

29: 5   your **clothes** are not waxen old upon you,

Num. 20: 28   And Moses stripped Aaron of his **garments,**

DEUT. 8: 9   A land **wherein** thou shalt eat bread without scarceness,

2: 14   And the space **in which** we came from Ka-desh-bar-ne-a,

DEUT. 8: 15   Who led thee through that great and terrible wilderness, *wherein were* fiery serpents,

2: 14   And the space **in which** we came from Ka-desh-bar-ne-a,

DEUT. 8: 15   *wherein were* fiery serpents, and scorpions, and **drought,** where *there was* **no water;**

DEUT. 9: 5   Not for thy **righteousness,** or for the **uprightness** of thine heart,

DEUT. 9: 7   **Remember, and forget not,** how thou provokedst the LORD thy God to wrath in the wilderness:

N.B.   note how the underlined word separates words and phrases having the same meaning.

DEUT. 9: 12   And the LORD said unto me, Arise get thee down quickly from **hence;**

12: 8   Ye shall not do after all *the things* that we do **here** this day,

DEUT. 9: 19   For I was afraid of the **anger and hot displeasure,**

N.B.   note how the underlined word separates words and phrases having the same meaning.

DEUT. 9: 19   wherewith the LORD was **wroth** against you to destroy you.

: 20   And the LORD was **very angry** with Aaron to have destroyed him:

DEUT. 9: 19   For I was afraid of the anger and hot displeasure, **wherewith** the LORD was wroth against you to destroy you.

2 Kings 19: 6   Be not afraid of the words **with which** the servants of the king of Assyria have blasphemed me.

<u>**DEUT. 9: 21**</u>	and I cast the dust **thereof** into the brook that descended out of the mount.
3: 11	the length **thereof,** and four cubits the breadth **of it,**
<u>**DEUT. 9: 21**</u>	and I cast the dust thereof into the brook that **descended** out of the mount.
10: 5	And I turned myself and **came down** from the mount.
<u>**DEUT. 9: 28**</u>	Lest the land **whence** thou broughtest out say, Because the LORD was not able to bring them into the land **which** he promised them,
<u>**DEUT. 10: 7**</u>	From **thence** they journeyed unto Gud-go-dah;
: 5	and **there** they be, as the LORD commanded me.
<u>**DEUT. 10: 9**</u>	**Wherefore** Levi hath no part nor inheritance with his brethren;
11: 1	**Therefore** thou shalt love the LORD thy God,
<u>**DEUT. 10: 14**</u>	Behold, the heaven and the heaven of heavens *is* LORD'S thy God, the earth *also,* with all that **there**in *is.*
8: 9	thou shalt not lack any *thing* **in it;**
<u>**DEUT. 10: 18**</u>	in giving him food and **raiment.**
29: 5	your **clothes** are not waxen old upon you,
Job 22: 6	and stripped the naked of their **clothing.**
<u>**DEUT. 10: 22**</u>	Thy fathers went down into Egypt with three**score** and ten persons;
Exodus 1: 5	And all the souls that came out of the loins of Jacob were **seventy** souls:
Lev. 27: 3	And thy estimation shall be of the male from twenty years old even unto **sixty** years old,

N.B. The underlined word is a numerical term meaning twenty. To find the value of the 'score' number multiply by 3x20=60+10=70

<u>**DEUT. 11: 8**</u>	that ye may be strong, and go in and possess the land, **whither** ye go o possess it;
: 10	*is* not as the land of Egypt, from **whence** ye came out, **where** thou sowedst thy seed,
: 13	if ye shall hearken diligently unto my commands **which** I command you this day,
<u>**DEUT. 11: 10**</u>	For the land, **whither** thou goest in to possess it, *is* not as the land of Egypt, from **whence** ye came out, **where** thou sowedst thy seed,
<u>**DEUT. 11: 13**</u>	if ye shall hearken **diligently** to my commands which I command you this day,
15: 5	Only if thou **carefully** hearken unto the voice of the LORD thy

God,

DEUT. 11: 24	Every place **whereon** the soles of your feet shall tread shall be yours:
Lev. 11: 34	Of all meat **which** may be eaten, *that* **on which** *such* water cometh shall be unclean:
DEUT. 11: 25	*for* the LORD your God shall lay **the fear of you** and **the dread of you** upon all the land that ye shall tread upon,

N.B. note how the underlined word separates words and phrases having the same meaning.

DEUT. 11: 29	And it shall come to pass, when the LORD thy God hath brought in unto the land **whither** thou goest to possess it,
: 30	*Are* they not on the other side Jordan, by the way **where** the sun goeth down, in the land in the land of the Canaanites, **which dwell** in the champaign over against Gilgal,
: 31	For ye shall pass over Jordan to go in to possess the land which the LORD your God giveth you, and ye shall possess it, dwell **therein.**
DEUT. 11: 30	in the **land** of the Canaanites, which dwell in the **champaign** over against Gilgal, beside the **plains** Mo-reh?
DEUT. 12: 2	Ye shall utterly destroy all the places, **wherein** the nations which ye shall possesss served their gods,
DEUT. 12: 6	And **thither** ye shall bring your burnt offerings,
: 14	and **there** thou shalt do all that I command thee.
DEUT. 12: 7	ye and your households, **wherein** the LORD thy God hath blessed thee.
2: 14	And the space **in which** we came from Ka-desh-bar-ne-a,
DEUT. 12: 12	and your maidservants, and the Levite that *is* within your gates; **Forasmuch as** he hath no part nor inheritance with you.

N.B. note the underlined word which gives the meaning of the entire word.

DEUT. 12: 15	**Notwithstanding** thou mayest kill and eat flesh in all thy gates,
: 5	**But** unto the place which the LORD your God shall choose...
DEUT. 12: 32	thou shalt not add **thereto,** nor diminish from it.
Numbers 1: 50	and over all things that *belong* **to it:**
Eccl. 2: 14	nothing can be **put to it,**
DEUT. 12: 32	thou shalt not add thereto, nor **diminish from it.**
Eccl. 2: 14	nothing can be put to it, nor **any thing taken from it:**

DEUT. 13: 13	*Certain* men, the **children of Belial,** are gone out from among you,

N.B. the first syllable of the third bold word spell out the name of a Babylonian god.

DEUT. 13: 16	And thou shalt gather all the spoil **of it…thereof** every whit,
DEUT. 13: 16	and shalt burn with fire the city, and **all** the spoil thereof **every whit,** for the LORD thy God:
DEUT. 13: 17	And there shall cleave **nought** of the cursed thing to thine hand;
20: 16	thou shalt save alive **nothing** that breatheth:
DEUT. 13: 17	and **shew thee mercy, <u>and</u> have compassion upon thee,**

N.B. note how the underlined word separates words and phrases having the same meaning.

DEUT. 14: 2	and the LORD thy God, hath chosen thee to be a **peculiar** people people unto himself, above all the nations that *are* upon the earth.
7:6	the LORD thy God hath chosen thee to be a **special** people unto himself, above all people that *are* upon the face of the earth.
DEUT. 14: 7	**Nevertheless** these ye shall not eat of them that chew the cud.
: 12	**But** these *are they* of which ye shall not eat:
DEUT. 13: 17	And there shall cleave **nought** of the cursed thing to thine hand:
20: 16	thou shalt save alive **nothing** that breatheth:
DEUT. 14: 21	Thou shalt not **seethe** a kid in his mother's milk.
Leviticus 8: 31	**Boil** the flesh *at* the door of the tabernacle of the congregation:
DEUT. 14: 23	Only thou shalt not the blood **thereof;**
13: 16	And thou shalt gather all the spoil **of it** into the midst of the street thereof,
DEUT. 14: 26	And thou shalt bestow that money for whatsoever thy soul **lusteth after…** whatsoever thy soul **desireth:**
DEUT. 15: 14	*of that* **wherewith** the LORD thy God hath blessed thee thou shalt give unto him.
2 Kings 19: 6	Be not afraid of the words **which** thou hast heard, **with which** the servants of the king of Assyria have blasphemed me.
DEUT. 16: 3	Thou shalt not eat no leavened bread **with it;** seven days shalt thou eat unleavened bread **therewith,** *even* the bread of

affliction;

DEUT. 16: 19	Thou shalt not **wrest** judgment; thou shalt not respect persons, **neither take a gift:** for a gift doth blind the eyes of the wise, and **pervert** the words of the righteous.
1 Samuel 12: 3	or of whose hand have I received *any* **bribe** to blind mine eyes therewith?

DEUT. 17: 1	or sheep, **wherein** is blemish, *or* evilfavouredness:
2: 14	And the space **in which** we came from Ka-desh-bar-ne-a,

DEUT. 17: 4	and enquired **diligently**, and, *it be* true,
15: 5	Only if thou **carefully** hearken unto the voice of the LORD thy God,

DEUT. 17: 14	and shalt dwell **therein**, and shalt say,
8: 9	thou shalt not any *thing* **in it;**

N.B. reverse the two syllables in the first reference and the meaning is clear.

DEUT. 17: 16   **forasmuch** as the LORD hath said unto you,

N.B. note how the underlined word gives the meaning of the whole word.

DEUT. 18: 4	and the first of the **fleece** of thy sheep, shalt thou give him.
Judges 6: 37	Behold, I will put a **fleece of wool** in the floor;

DEUT. 18: 8	They shall have like portions to eat, beside that which cometh of his **patrimony.**
: 2	Therefore shall they have no **inheritance,** among their brethren:

DEUT. 19: 7	**Wherefore** I command thee, saying,
18: 2	**Therefore** shall they have no inheritance, among their brethren:

DEUT. 19: 18	And the judges shall make **diligent** inquisition:
2 Kings 4: 13	Behold, thou hast been **careful** for us with all this care:
DEUT. 19: 18	And the judges shall make diligent **inquisition:**
Prov. 20: 25	and after vows to make **inquiry.**

DEUT. 20: 2	And it shall be, when you are **come nigh** unto the battle,
21: 5	And the priests the sons of Levi **come near;**

DEUT. 20: 3	let not your hearts faint, **fear not, and do not tremble,** neither ye terrified because of them;

N.B. note how the underlined word separates words and phrases having the same meaning.

<u>**DEUT. 20: 8**</u>	What man *is there that is* **fearful and fainthearted?**

N.B. note how the underlined word separates words and phrases having the same meaning.

<u>**DEUT. 20: 13**</u>	And when the LORD thy God hath delivered it into thy hands, thou shalt smite every male **thereof** with the edge of the sword:
: 6	let him *also* go and return unto his house, lest he die in the battle, and another man eat **of it.**
<u>**DEUT. 20: 13**</u>	thou shalt **smite** every male thereof with the edge of the sword:
21: 4	and shall **strike** off the heifer's neck there in the valley:
<u>**DEUT. 20: 14**</u>	and all that is in the city, *even* all the spoils **thereof,**
: 6	lest he die in the battle, and another man eat **of it.**
<u>**DEUT. 21: 1**</u>	If *one* be found **slain** in the land which the LORD thy God giveth thee to possess it,
Num. 31: 19	whosoever hath **killed** any person, and whosoever hath touched any **slain,**
<u>**DEUT. 21: 3**</u>	the elders of that city shall take an **heifer,**
Genesis 15: 9	Take me an heifer of **three years old,**
Isaiah 7: 21	*that* a young man shall nourish **a young cow,**
<u>**DEUT. 21: 3**</u>	which hath not been **wrought** with,
Neh. 4: 21	So we **laboured** in the work:
<u>**DEUT. 21: 4**</u>	And the elders of that city shall bring down the heifer unto a rough valley, which is neither **eared** nor sown,
Judges 14: 18	If ye had not **plowed** with my heifer,
<u>**DEUT. 21: 12**</u>	Then thou shalt bring her home to thine house; and she shall shave her head, and **pare** her nails;
20: 20	thou shalt destroy and **cut them** down:
<u>**DEUT. 21: 13**</u>	And she shall put the **raiment** of her captivity from off her,
29: 5	your **clothes** are not waxen old upon you,
<u>**DEUT. 22: 8**</u>	that thou bring not blood upon thine house, if any man fall from **hence.**
21: 4	and shall strike off the heifer's neck **there** in the valley:
<u>**DEUT. 22: 9**</u>	Thou shalt not sow thy vineyard with **divers seeds:**
Lev. 19: 19	Thou shalt not let thy cattle gender with a **diverse** kind:
Num. 31: 30	of the asses, and of the flocks, of **all manner of** beasts,
<u>**DEUT. 22: 11**</u>	Thou shalt not wear a **garment** of divers sorts,
: 12	Thou shalt make thee fringes upon the four corners of the **vesture,**

DEUT. 22: 12	Thy shalt make fringes upon the four quarters of thy vesture, **therewith** thou coverest *thyself.*
2 Kings 19: 6	Be not afraid of the words which thou hast heard, **with which** the servants of the king of Assyria have blasphemed.
DEUT. 22: 17	I found not thy daughter a **maid;**
: 19	and give *them* unto the father of the **damsel,** because he hath brought up an evil name upon a **virgin** of Israel:
DEUT. 23: 5	**Nevertheless** the LORD thy God would not hearken unto Balaam; **but** the LORD thy God turned the curse into a blessing unto thee, blessing unto thee,
DEUT. 23: 12	Thou shalt have a place also without the camp, **whither** thou shalt go abroad:
: 16	shall choose in one of thy gates, **where** it liketh him best:
DEUT. 23: 13	and it shall be, when thou wilt ease thyself abroad, thou shalt dig **therewith,**
16: 3	thou shalt eat no leavened bread **with it;** seven days shalt thou eat unleavened bread **therewith,**
DEUT. 23: 17	There shall be no whore of the daughters of Israel, nor **a sodomite** of the sons of Israel.
: 18	Thou shalt not bring the hire of a whore, or the price of **a dog,**
Rom. 1: 27	And likewise also the men, **leaving the natural use of the woman urned in their lust one toward another; men with men working that which is unseemly,**
1 Cor. 6: 9	Know ye not that the unrighteous shall not inherit the kingdom of God? Be not deceived: neither fornicators, nor idolators, nor adulterers, **nor effeminate, nor abusers of themselves with mankind,**
Rev. 22: 15	For without *are* **dogs,**
DEUT. 24: 6	No man shall take the **nether** or the upper millstone to pledge:
Neh. 4: 13	Therefore set I in the **lower** places behind the wall,
DEUT. 24: 8	Take heed in the plague of leprosy, that tou observe **diligently,**
15: 5	Only if thou **carefully** hearken unto the voice of the LORD thy God,
DEUT. 24: 13	that he may sleep in his own **raiment,** and bless thee:
22: 11	Thou shalt not wear a **garment** of divers sorts,
DEUT. 24: 20	When thou beatest thine olive tree, **though shalt not go over the boughs again:**
: 21	When thou gatherest the grapes of thy vineyard, **thou shalt not glean *it* afterward:** it shall be for the stranger, for the fatherless,

and for the widow.

<u>**DEUT. 25: 18**</u>	How he met thee by the way, and **smote** the hindmost of thee,
1 Sam. 2: 14	And he **struck** *it* into the pan;

<u>**DEUT. 25: 18**</u> How he met thee by the way, and smote the **hindmost** of thee, *even* all *that were* feeble **behind** thee,

<u>**DEUT. 25: 18**</u> *even* all *that were* **feeble** behind thee, when thou *wast* **faint and weary;**

N.B. note how the underlined word separates words and phrases having the same meaning.

<u>**DEUT. 26: 5**</u> And thou shalt **speak and say** before the LORD thy God,

N. B. note how the underlined word separates words and phrases having the same meaning.

<u>**DEUT. 26: 14**</u>	I have not eaten **thereof** in my mourning,
20: 6	and hath not *yet* eaten **of it?**

<u>**DEUT. 26: 17**</u>	Thou hast **avouched** the LORD this day to be thy God,
: 18	as he hath **promised** thee,

<u>**DEUT. 26: 18**</u>	And the LORD hath avouched thee this day to be his **peculiar** people,
7: 6	the LORD thy God thy God hath chosen thee to be a **special** people unto himself,

<u>**DEUT. 27: 9**</u>	And Moses and the priests the Levites spake unto all Israel saying, **Take heed, and hearken,** O Israel;
Isaiah 49: 1	**Listen,** O isles unto me; and **hearken,** ye people, from far;

N.B. note how the underlined word separates words and phrases having the same meaning.

<u>**DEUT. 28: 1**</u>	And it shall come to pass, if thou shalt hearken **diligently** unto the voice of the LORD thy God,
15: 5	Only if thou **carefully** hearken unto the voice of the LORD thy God,

<u>**DEUT. 28: 21**</u>	The LORD shall make the **pestilence** cleave unto thee,
: 59	Then the LORD will make thy **plagues** wonderful,

<u>**DEUT. 28: 24**</u> The LORD shall make the rain of thy land **powder and dust:**

<u>**DEUT. 28: 26**</u> and unto the beasts of the earth, and no man shall **fray** *them*

Isaiah 17: 2	which shall lie down, and none shall **make *them* afraid.**
DEUT. 28: 27	The LORD will **smite** thee with the botch of Egypt,
21: 4	and shall **strike** off the heifer's neck there in the valley:
DEUT. 28: 27	and with the scab, and with the itch, **whereof** thou canst not be healed.
14: 12	But these *are they* **of which** ye shall not eat:
DEUT. 28: 30	thou shalt build an house and not dwell **therein:**
8: 9	thou shalt not lack any *thing* **in it;**
: 30	thou shalt plant a vineyard, and shalt not gather the grapes **thereof.**
17: 4	And it be told thee, and thou hast heard *of it,*
DEUT. 28: 35	The LORD shall **smite** thee in the knees,
21: 4	and shall **strike** off the heifer's neck there in the valley:
DEUT. 28: 35	The LORD shall smite thee in the knees, and in thy legs, with **a sore** that cannot be healed,
Job 2: 7	and smote Job with **sore boils** from the sole of his foot unto his crown.
DEUT. 28: 37	And thou shalt become **an astonishment, a proverb, and a byword,**

N.B. note how the underlined word separates words and phrases having the same meaning,

DEUT. 28: 37	And thou shalt become an astonishment, a proverb, and a byword, among all nations **whither** the LORD shall lead thee.
23: 16	he shall choose in one of thy gates, **where**it liketh him best:
DEUT. 28: 45	**Moreover** all these curses shall come upon thee,
: 61	**Also** every sickness, and every plague,
9: 13	**Furthermore** the LORD spake unto me, saying,
DEUT. 28: 47	Because thou servedst not the LORD thy God **joyfulness, and with gladness of heart,**

N.B. note how the underlined word separates words and phrases having the same meaning.

DEUT. 28: 51	And he shall eat of the fruit of thy cattle, and the fruit of thy land,
	until thou be destroyed: which *also* shall not leave thee *either* corn, wine, or oil, *or* the increase of thy **kine,**
Leviticus 22: 28	And *whether it be* **cow** or ewe,

| DEUT. 28: 52 | until thy high and fenced walls come down, **wherein** thou trustedst, |
| 2: 14 | And the space **in which** we came from Ka-desh-bar-ne-a, |

DEUT. 28: 53	which the LORD thy God hath given thee, in the siege, and in **straitness,** wherewith thine enemies shall **distress** thee,
DEUT. 28: 57	**wherewith** thine enemy shall distress thee in thy gates.
Zech. 13: 6	Then he shall answer, *Those* **with which** I was wounded *in* the house of my friends.

| DEUT. 28: 61 | And **every sickness, and every plague,** which *is* not written in the book of this law, |

N.B. note how the underlined word separates words and phrases having the same meaning.

| DEUT. 28: 63 | and ye shall be plucked from the land **whither** tou goest to possess it. |
| 23: 16 | he shall choose in one of thy gates, **where** it liketh him best. |

| DEUT. 28: 68 | by the way **whereof** I spake unto thee, |
| 14: 12 | But these *are they* **of which** ye shall not eat: |

| DEUT. 29: 23 | which the LORD overthrew in his **anger, and in his wrath:** |

N.B. note how the underlined word separates words and phrases having the same meaning.

| DEUT. 29: 24 | Even all nations shall say, **Wherefore** hath the LORD done thus unto this land? |
| Joshua 7: 25 | And Joshua said, **Why** hast thou troubled us? |

| DEUT. 29: 28 | And the LORD rooted them out of their land **in anger, and in wrath, and in great indignation,** |

N.B. note how the the underlined words sepate words and phrases having the same meaning.

| DEUT. 30: 1 | which I have set before thee, and thou shalt **call to mind** among all the nations, |
| 32: 7 | **Remember** the days of old, |

| DEUT. 31: 17 | and they shall be devoured, and many **evils and troubles** are befallen them, |

N.B. note how the underlined word separates words and phrases having the same meaning.

| DEUT. 31: 18 | And I will surely hide my face in that day for all the evils |

Ruth 3: 3	which they **shall have wrought,** until he **shall have done** eating and drinking.

DEUT. 32: 5   *they are* a **perverse and crooked** generation.

N.B. note how the underlined word separates words and phrases having the same meaning.

DEUT. 32: 6	Do ye thus **requite** the LORD, O foolish people and unwise?
Job 21: 31	and who shall **repay** him *what* he hath done?
Num. 5: 8	But if the man hath no kinsman to **recompense** the trespass unto,
DEUT. 32: 6	Do ye thus requite the LORD, O **foolish people and unwise?**

N.B. note how the underlined word separates words and phrases having the same meaning.

DEUT. 32: 9   For the LORD'S **portion** *is* his people; Jacob *is* the **lot** of his inheritance.

DEUT. 32: 18   Of the Rock *that* begat thee thou art **unmindful, and hast forgotten** God that formed thee.

N.B. note how the underlined word separates words and phrases having the same meaning.

DEUT. 32: 20	I will see what their end *shall be:* for they *are* a very **froward** generation, in whom *is* **no faith.**
4: 25	and shall **corrupt** *yourselves,*
25: 2	And it shall be, if the **wicked** man be worthy to be beaten,

DEUT. 32: 21	they have provoked me to anger with their **vanities:**
Psalm 78: 58	and moved him to jealousy with their **graven images.**
82: 1	he judgeth among the **gods.**
96: 5	For all the **gods** of the nations *are* **idols:**

DEUT. 32: 28   For they *are* nation **void of counsel, neither** *is* **there any understanding in them.**

DEUT. 32: 33   Their wine *is* the **poison** of dragons, and the cruel **venom** of asps.

DEUT. 32: 35	To me *belongeth* vengeance and **recompence;**
: 41	and will **reward** them that hate me.

DEUT. 32: 41	If I **whet** my glittering sword,
1 Sam. 13: 20	But all the Israelites went down to the Philistines, **to sharpen** every man his share, and his coulter, and his axe, and his mattock.
Job 24: 8	They are **wet** with the showers of the mountains,

N.B. note that the word 'wet' is contained in the first bold word.

<u>**DEUT. 33: 1**</u>	And this *is* the blessing, **wherewith** Moses the man of God blessed the children of Israel before his death.
2 Kings 19: 6	Be not afraid of the words which thou hast heard, **with which** the servants of the king of Assyria have blasphemed me.

JOSHUA

<u>**JOSHUA 1: 8**</u>	This book of the LORD shall not depart from out of thy mouth; but thou shalt meditate **therein** day and night,
10: 30	and all the souls that *were* **therein;** he let none remain **in it;**
<u>**JOSHUA 1: 11**</u>	Prepare you **victuals;** for within three days ye shall pass over this Jordan,
Deut. 10: 18	and loveth the stranger, in giving him **food** and raiment.
<u>**JOSHUA 1: 14**</u>	but ye shall pass before your brethren armed, all the mighty men of **valour,** and help them.
2: 11	neither did there remain any more **courage** in any man,
<u>**JOSHUA 2: 1**</u>	And Joshua the son of Nun sent out of Shittim two men **to spy secretly,**
: 2	Behold, there came in men in hither to night of the children of Israel **to search out** the country.
<u>**JOSHUA 2: 2**</u>	Behold, there came men in **hither** to night of the children of Israel to search out the country.
Deut. 29: 15	But with *him* that standeth **here** with us this day before the LORD our God,
<u>**JOSHUA 2: 4**</u>	There came men unto me, but **I wist not** whence they *were:*
Num. 22: 34	for **I knew not** that thou stoodest in the way against me:
<u>**JOSHUA 2: 5**</u>	**whither** the men went I wot not not:
4: 3	out of the place **where** the priest's feet stood firm,
<u>**JOSHUA 2: 5**</u>	whither the men went **I wot not**: pursue after them quickly;
Exodus 5: 2	**I know not** the LORD, neither will I let Israel go.
<u>**JOSHUA 2: 17**</u>	And the men said unto her, We *will be* **blameless** of this thine oath which thou hast made us swear.
: 19	and we *will be* **guiltless:** and whosoever shall be with thee in the house,
<u>**JOSHUA 3: 4**</u>	that ye may know the way by which ye must go: for ye have not passed *this* way **heretofore.**
: 6	And they took up the ark of the covenant, and they went

before the people.

JOSHUA 3: 9	And Joshua said unto the children of Israel, Come **hither,**
Duet. 29: 15	But with *him* that standeth **here** with us this day before the LORD our God,

JOSHUA 3: 10	And Joshua said, **Hereby** ye shall know that the living God *is* among you,
Exodus 12: 26	And it shall come to pass, when your children shall say unto you,
	What mean ye **by this** service?

JOSHUA 4: 3	And command ye them, saying, Take you **hence out of** the midst of Jordan, out of the place where the priest's feet stood firm, twelve stones,

N.B. note how the first bold word means the same as the second and third words.

JOSHUA 4: 16	Command the priests that **bear** the ark of the testimony,
: 18	And it came to pass, when the priests that **bare** the ark of the covenant of the LORD were come up out of the midst of Jordan.

JOSHUA 5: 4	And this *is* the **cause** why Joshua did circumcise:
1 Kings 9: 15	And this *is* the **reason** of the levy which king Solomon raised;

JOSHUA 5: 7	them Joshua circumcised: for they were **un**circumcised, because they
	had **not** circumcised them by the way.

N.B. note how the bold words gives the opposite meaning to the main word.

JOSHUA 5: 8	when they had circumcising all the people, that they **abode** in their places in the camp,
: 10	And the children of Israel **encamped** in Gilgal,

JOSHUA 5: 11	And they did eat of the old corn of the land on the morrow after the
	passover, unleavened cakes, and **parched** *corn* in the selfsame day.
Leviticus 2: 14	thou shalt offer for the meat offering of thy firstfruits green ears of **corn dried by the fire,**

JOSHUA 5: 14	And he said, Nay; but *as* **captain of the host of the LORD** am I now come.
: 15	And the **captain of the LORD'S host** said unto Joshua,

N.B. The bold phrases although slightly worded differently mean the same thing.

JOSHUA 6: 1	Now Jericho was **straitly shut up** because the children of Israel: **none went out, and none came in.**
Jeremiah 52: 5	So the city was **besieged** unto the eleventh year of king Zed-e-ki-ah.
JOSHUA 6: 3	And ye shall **compass the city,** all *ye* men of war, *and* **go round** about the city once.
JOSHUA 6: 5	and the people shall **ascend up** every man straight before him.
: 20	so that the people **went up** into the city,
JOSHUA 6: 9	and the **rereward came after** the ark, *the priests* going on,
8: 14	but he wist not that *there were* liers in ambush against him **behind** the city.
JOSHUA 6: 17	And the city shall be accursed, *even* it, and all that *are* **there**in,
10: 30	and all the souls that *were* **therein;** he let none remain **in it;**
JOSHUA 6: 23	and they brought out all her **kind**red,
: 25	and her **father's household,**
JOSHUA 6: 26	he shall lay the foundation **thereof** in his firstborn, and in his youngest *son* shall he set up the gates **of it.**
JOSHUA 7: 4	So **there** went up **thither** of the people about three thousand men:
JOSHUA 7: 7	And Joshua said, Alas, O Lord GOD, **wherefore** hast thou at all brought this people over Jordan,
: 25	And Joshua said, **Why** hast thou troubled us?
JOSHUA 7: 9	for the Canaanites and all the inhabitants of the land shall hear *of it a*nd shall **environ** us round,
6: 3	And ye shall **compass** the city, all ye men of war, *and* **go round** about the city once.
JOSHUA 7: 11	and have also stolen, and **dissembled** also,
Deut. 11: 16	that ye be not **deceived,**
1 Kings 13: 18	*But* he **lied** unto him.
JOSHUA 7: 15	because he hath transgressed the covenant of the LORD, and because **he hath wrought** folly in Israel.
24: 20	after that **he hath done** you good.
JOSHUA 8: 2	shall ye take for a prey unto yourselves: lay thee an **ambush** foɪ the city behind it.
: 4	ye shall **lie in wait** against the city,
JOSHUA 8: 9	and **abode** between Beth-el and A-i, on the west side of A-i: but Joshua **lodged** that night among the people.

89

| JOSHUA 8: 14 | at a time appointed, before the plain; but **he wist not** tha *there were* liers in ambush against him behind the city. |
| Genesis 39: 6 | And he left all that he had in Joseph's hand; and **he knew not** ought he had, |

| JOSHUA 8: 20 | the smoke of the city **ascended up** to heaven, |

N.B. the first bold word means the same as the second bold word.

| JOSHUA 8: 24 | in the wilderness **where**in they chased them, |
| Judges 4: 14 | for this *is* the day **in which** the LORD hath delivered Sis-e-ra into thine hand: |

| JOSHUA 8: 29 | and raise **thereon** a great heap of stones, |
| Deut. 29: 27 | to bring **upon it** all the curses that are written in this book. |

| JOSHUA 8: 35 | and the strangers that were **conversant among** them. |
| Luke 24: 5 | Why seek ye the **living among** the dead? |

| JOSHUA 9: 4 | They did work **wilily**, and went and **made as if** they had been ambassadors, |
| Exodus 8: 29 | but let not Pharaoh deal **deceitfully** any more... |

JOSHUA 9: 5	And old shoes and **clouted** upon their feet,
Judges 21: 23	and **repaired** the cities, and dwelt in them.
Judges 21: 23	and they went and returned unto their inheritance,
Jer. 38: 12	*these* **old cast clouts <u>and</u> rotten rags** under thine armholes under the cord.

N.B. note how the underlined word separates words and phrases having the same meaning.

| JOSHUA 9: 7 | And the men of Israel said unto the Hivites, **Peradventure** ye dwell among us; and how shall we make a league with you? |
| 1 Samuel 14: 6 | **it may be** that the LORD will work for us: |

JOSHUA 9: 11	Take **victuals** with you for the journey,
: 12	This our **bread** we took hot *for* our provision...
Deut. 10: 18	and loveth the stranger, in giving him **food** and raiment.

| JOSHUA 9: 22 | **Wherefore** have ye beguiled us, We *are* very far from you; |
| 7: 25 | And Joshua said, **Why** hast thou troubled us? |

| JOSHUA 8: 35 | with the women, and the little ones, and the strangers that were **were conversant among** them. |

N.B. note the third bold word in the first reference means the same as the third word

JOSHUA 10: 2	and because it *was* greater than A-i, and all the men **thereof** *were* mighty.
6: 26	and in his youngest *son* shall he set up the gates **of it.**
JOSHUA 10: 3	**Wherefore** Ad-o-ni-ze-dek king of Jerusalem sent unto Ho-ham king of He-bron,
: 5	**Therefore** the five kings of the Amorites,
JOSHUA 10: 7	So Joshua **ascended** from Gilgal,
: 9	*and* **went up** from Gilgal all night.
JOSHUA 10: 27	and they took them down off the trees and cast them into the cave **wherein** they had been hid,
Judges 4: 14	for this is the day **in which** the LORD hath delivered Sis-e-ra into thine hand:
JOSHUA 10: 28	and the king thereof he utterly destroyed them, and all the souls that *were* **there**in;
: 30	and all the souls that *were* **therein; he let none remain in it;**
JOSHUA 11: 4	And they went out, they and all their hosts with them, **much people,** even as the sand that *is* upon the sea shore in **multitude, with** horses and chariots **very many.**
JOSHUA 13: 13	Nevertheless the children of Israel **expelled** not the Ge-shu-rites,
Num. 21: 32	and they took the villages thereof, and **drove out** the Amorites that *were* there.
JOSHUA 14: 10	and now, lo, I *am* this day four**score** and five years old.
Genesis 5: 28	And La-mech lived an hundred **eighty** and nine years:

N.B. The underlined word is a numerical term meaning twenty. To find the value of the 'score number' multiply the number by twenty thus, 4x20=80+5=85

JOSHUA 14: 4	save cities to dwell *in,* with their **suburbs for their cattle** and for their substance.
21: 2	The LORD commanded by the hand of Moses to give us cities to dwell in, with the **suburbs** thereof **for our cattle.**
: 12	But the **fields** of the city, and the villages thereof,
JOSHUA 15: 3	and passed along to Zin, and **ascended up** on the south side unto Ka-desh-bar-ne-a, and passed along to Hezron, and **went up** to A-dar,
JOSHUA 15: 7	and the goings out **thereof** were at En-ro-gel:
17: 9	and the goings out **of it** were at the sea:

JOSHUA 15: 19	And he gave her the upper springs, and the **nether** springs.
Nehemiah 4: 13	Therefore set I in the **lower** places behind the wall,

JOSHUA 17: 9	And the coast **descended** unto the river Ka-nah southward of the river,
18: 16	And the border **came down** to the end of the mountain that *lieth* before the valley of the son of Hinnom,
: 18	and **went down** unto Ar-a-bah:

JOSHUA 17: 14	Why hast thou given me *but* **one lot <u>and</u> one portion** to inherit,

N.B. note how the underlined word separates words and phrases having the same meaning.

JOSHUA 17: 15	if mount E-phra-im be **too narrow** for thee.
: 16	The hill **is not enough** for us:

JOSHUA 18: 5	And they shall **divide** it into seven parts:
: 6	Ye shall therefore **describe** the land *into* seven parts,

JOSHUA 18: 14	and the goings out **thereof** were at Kir-jath-je-a-rim,
: 20	And Jordan was the border **of it.**

JOSHUA 18: 16	And the border **came down** to the end of the mountain that *lieth* before the valley of the son of Hinnom, *and* which *is* in the valley of the giants on the north, and **descended** to the valley of Hinnom,
: 18	and **went down** unto Ar-a-bah northward.

JOSHUA 19: 50	and he built the city, and dwelt **therein.**
10: 30	and all the souls that *were* **therein;** he let none remain **in it;**

JOSHUA 20: 3	That the slayer that killeth *any* person **unawares <u>and</u> unwittingly** may flee thither:
Lev. 4: 2	If a soul shall sin **through ignorance...**
Deut. 19: 4	Whoso killeth his neighbour **ignorantly,**

N.B. note how the underlined word separates words and phrases having the same meaning.

JOSHUA 20: 3	That the slayer that killeth *any* person unawares and unwittingly may flee **thither:**
18: 2	And **there** remained among the children of Israel seven tribes,

JOSHUA 20: 8	And on the other side Jordan by Jericho eastward, **they assigned** Bezer in the wilderness upon the plain out of the tribe of Rueben,
: 9	These were the cities **appointed** for all the children of Israel,

<u>JOSHUA 21: 2</u>	The LORD commanded by the hand of Moses to give us cities to dwell in, with the **suburbs** thereof **for our cattle.**
: 12	But the **fields** of the city, and the villages thereof, gave they to Caleb the son of Je-phun-neh for his possession.
<u>JOSHUA 21: 11</u>	with the suburbs **thereof** round about it.
17: 9	and the outgoings **of it** were at the sea.
<u>JOSHUA 22: 8</u>	and with iron, and with very much **raiment:**
Job 22: 6	and stripped the naked of their **clothing.**
<u>JOSHUA 22: 9</u>	**whereof** they were possessed, according to the word of the
LORD by	
	the hand of Moses.
Judges 20: 31	**of which** one goeth up to the house of God,
<u>JOSHUA 22: 18</u>	that to morrow he will be **wroth** with the whole congregation
of	
	Israel.
Judges 18: 25	lest **angry** fellows run upon thee,
<u>JOSHUA 22: 19</u>	**Notwithstanding, if** the land of your possession *be* unclean,
: 26	**Therefore** we said, Let us now prepare to build us an altar,
: 27	**But** *that it may be* a witness between us, and you,
<u>JOSHUA 22: 19</u>	**wherein** the LORD'S tabernacle dwelleth,
Judges 4: 14	for this *is* the day **in which** the LORD hath delivered Sis-e-ra into thine hand:
<u>JOSHUA 22: 23</u>	or if to offer **thereon** burnt offering or meat offering,
Leviticus 6: 12	and the priest shall burn wood **on it** every morning, and lay the burnt offering in order **upon it;**
<u>JOSHUA 23: 5</u>	And the LORD your God, he shall **expel them from before you, and drive them from out of your sight;**

N.B. note how the underlined word separates words and phrases having the same meaning.

<u>JOSHUA 23: 13</u>	but they shall be **snares <u>and</u> traps** unto you,

N.B. note how the underlined word separates words and phrases having the same meaning.

<u>JOSHUA 24: 14</u>	Now therefore fear the LORD, and serve him **in sincerity <u>and</u> in truth:**

N.B. note how the underlined word separates words and phrases having the same meaning.

| JOSHUA 24: 31 | And Israel served the LORD all the days of Joshua, and all the days of the elders that **overlived** Joshua, |
| Judges 2: 7 | And the people served the LORD all the days of the elders that **over-lived** Joshua, |

JUDGES

| JUDGES 1: 7 | And Ad-o-ni-be-zek said, Three**score** and ten kings, having their
thumbs and their great toes cut off, |
| Leviticus 27: 7 | And if *it be* from **sixty** years old and above; |

N.B. note the underlined word which is mathematical term meaning twenty. To find the value of the 'score' number multiply 3x20=60+10=70

| JUDGES 1: 7 | as I have done, so God hath **requited** me. |
| 1 Sam. 24: 17 | for thou hast **rewarded** me good, |

| JUDGES 1: 11 | And from **thence** he went against the inhabitants of De-bir: |
| : 7 | And they bought him back to Jereusalem, and **there** he died. |

| JUDGES 1:15 | And Caleb gave her the upper and the **nether** springs. |
| Nehemiah 4: 13 | Therefore set I in the **lower** places behind the wall, |

| JUDGES 1: 18 | And Judah took Ga-za with the coast **thereof,** |
| Joshua 22: 12 | And when the children of Israel heard *of it,* |

| JUDGES 1: 23 | And the house of Joseph sent to **descry** Beth-el. |
| Joshua 2: 2 | there came men in hither to night of the children of Israel **to search out** the country. |

JUDGES 1: 33	**but** he dwelt among the Canaanites, the inhabitants of the land: **nevertheless** the inhabitants of Beth-she-mesh and of Beth-a-nath...
JUDGES 1: 34	for they would not **suffer** them to come down to the valley:
: 25	but they **let** go the man and all his family.
JUDGES 2: 22	whether they will keep the way of the LORD to walk **therein,**
19: 11	and let us turn into this city of the Jeb-u-sites, and lodge **in it.**

| JUDGES 3: 19 | But he himself turned again from the **quarries** that *were* by Gilgal, |
| Deut. 7: 25 | The **graven images of their gods** shall ye burn with fire: |

| JUDGES 3: 25 | And they **tarried** till they were ashamed: |
| Genesis 8: 10 | And he **stayed** another seven days; |

| JUDGES 3: 29 | And they **slew** of Moab at that time about ten thousand men, |
| Numbers 31: 19 | whosoever hath **killed** any person, |

| JUDGES 3: 30 | And the land had rest four**score** years. |

Genesis 5: 28	And La-mech lived an hundred **eighty** and two years:

N.B. The underlined word is a numerical term meaning twenty. To find the value of the 'score' number multiply, 4x20=80+2=82.

JUDGES 4: 9	And she said, I will surely go with thee: **notwithstanding** the journey that thou takest shall not be for thine honour;
: 16	**But** Bar-ak pursued after the chariots,

JUDGES 4: 17	**Howbeit** Sis-e-ra fled away on his feet to the tent of Ja-el the wife of He-ber the Ke-nite:
: 9	**notwithstanding** the journey that thou takest shall not be for thine honour;
: 16	**But** Bar-ak pursued after the chariots,

JUDGES 5: 11	there shall they **rehearse** the righteous acts of the LORD,
: 10	**Speak,** ye that ride on white asses,
: 12	Awake, awake, Deborah: awake, awake, **utter** a song:
14: 12	if ye can certainly **declare** it me within the seven days of the feast,
: 16	Behold, I have not told *it* my father nor my mother, and shall I **tell** *it* thee?

JUDGES 5: 11	there shall they rehearse the **right**eous acts of the LORD,
1 Samuel 29: 6	Surely, *as* the LORD liveth, thou hast been up**right,**

JUDGES 5: 18	Ze-bu-lun and Naph-ta-li *were* a people *that* **jeoparded** their lives unto the death in the high places of the field.
9: 17	(For my father fought for you, and **adventured** his life far...)

JUDGES 5: 23	curse ye bitterly the inhabitants **thereof;**
Deut. 20: 6	lest he die in the battle, and another man eat **of it.**
Joshua 22: 12	And when the children of Israel heard *of it,*

JUDGES 5: 26	and with the hammer she **smote** Sis-e-ra, smote off his head,
2 Sam. 12: 15	And the LORD **struck** the child that Uriah's wife bare unto David,

JUDGES 5: 28	Why is his chariot *so* long in coming? Why **tarry** the wheels of his chariots?
Exodus 22: 29	Thou shalt not **delay** *to offer* the first of thy ripe fruits,
Psalm 25: 3	Yea, let none that **wait** on thee be ashamed:

JUDGES 5: 30	to Sis-e-ra a prey of **divers** colours,
7: 2	The people that *are* with thee *are* too **many** for me to give the Midianites into their hands,

JUDGES 6: 4	And they **encamped** against them,
: 33	and went over, and **pitched** in the valley of Jez-reel.

JUDGES 6: 5	and they came as grasshoppers for **multitude;** *for* both they and their camels were **without number:**
JUDGES 6: 6	And Israel was greatly **impoverished** because of the Midianites;
: 15	behold, my family is **poor** in Ma-nas-seh,
JUDGES 6: 11	and his son Gideon **threshed** wheat by the winepress,
Ruth 2: 17	and **beat out** that she had gleaned:
JUDGES 6: 15	**Wherewith** shall I save Israel?
13: 12	**How** shall we order the child?
JUDGES 6: 16	Surely I will be with thee, and thou shalt **smite** the Midianites as one man.
Exodus 12: 7	and **strike** *it* on the two side posts and on the upper door posts of the houses,
JUDGES 6: 18	And he said, I will **tarry** until thou come again.
Psalm 25: 3	Yea, let none that **wait** on thee be ashamed.
JUDGES 6: 22	Alas, O Lord GOD! **for because** I have seen an angel of the LORD face to face.

N.B. note how the two bold words mean the same thing.

JUDGES 6: 25	and **throw down** the altar of Ba-al that thy father hath,
: 28	behold, the altar of Ba-al was **cast down,**
JUDGES 6: 29	And when they **enquired <u>and</u> asked,** they said, Gideon the son of Jo-ash hath done this thing.

N.B. note how the underined word separates words and phrases having the same meaning.

JUDGES 7: 2	lest Israel **vaunt** themselves against me, saying, Mine own hand hath saved me.
1 Kings 20: 11	Let not him that girdeth on *his harness* **boast** himself as he that putteth it off.
JUDGES 7: 3	Whosoever *is* **fearful <u>and</u> afraid,** let him return and depart early from mount Gilead.

N.B. note how the underlined word separates words and phrases having the same meaning.

JUDGES 7: 8	So the people took **victuals** in their hand, and their trumpets:
8: 5	Give, I pray you, **loaves of bread** unto the people that follow me;
Genesis 47: 24	and for your **food,** and for them of your households,

| **JUDGES 7: 25** | and they **slew** Or-eb upon the rock Or-eb, |
| Num. 31: 19 | whosoever hath **killed** any person, |

| **JUDGES 8: 1** | And they did **chide** with him sharply. |
| 1 Sam. 25: 39 | Blessed *be* the LORD, that hath **pleaded** the cause of my reproach from the hand of Na-bal, |

| **JUDGES 8: 3** | Then their anger was **abated** toward him, when he had said that. |

| Genesis 8: 5 | And the waters **decreased** continually until the tenth month: |

| **JUDGES 8: 8** | And he went up **thence** to Pen-u-el, |
| 7: 3 | And **there** returned of the people twenty and two thousand; |

| **JUDGES 8: 14** | and the elders thereof, *even* **three**score and seventeen men. |
| Leviticus 27:7 | And if *it be* from **sixty** years old and above; |

N.B. The underlined word is a mathematical term meaning twenty. To find the value of the 'score' number multiply 3x20=60.

| **JUDGES 8: 25** | And they spread a garment, and did cast **therein** every man the earrings of his prey. |

N.B. reverse the syllables of the bold word in the first reference and the meaning is clear.

| **JUDGES 8: 27** | And Gideon made an ephod **thereof,** |
| Deut. 20: 6 | lest he die in the battle, and another man eat **of it.** |

| **JUDGES 8: 27** | and all Israel went **thither** a whoring after it: |
| 9: 21 | and fled, and went to Beer, and dwelt **there,** |

| **JUDGES 8: 30** | And Gideon had **three**score and ten sons of his body begotten: |
| Lev. 27: 7 | And if *it be* from **sixty** years old and above; |

N.B. The underlined word is a numerical term meaning twenty. To find the value of the 'score' number multiply 3x20=60.

JUDGES 8: 31	And his **concubine** that was in She-chem, she also bare him a son,
	a son, whose name he called A-bim-e-lech.
Psalm 88: 18	**Lover** and friend hast thou put far from me,

| **JUDGES 9: 5** | **notwithstanding yet** Jo-tham the youngest son of Jer-ub-ba-al was left. |

N.B. note the two bold words, how they have the same meaning.

JUDGES 9: 11	Should I **forsake** my sweetness...?
: 13	Should I **leave** my wine...?
JUDGES 9: 38	Then said Ze-bul unto him, Where *is* now thy mouth, **wherewith** thou saidst,
2 Kings 19: 6	Be not afraid of the words **with which** the servants of the king of Assyria have blasphemed me.
JUDGES 9: 45	and slew the people that *was* **there**in,
19: 11	and let us turn in into the city of the Jeb-u-sites, and lodge **in it.**
2 Kings 2: 21	and cast the salt **in there,** and said,
JUDGES 9: 51	But **there** ws a strong tower within the city, and **thither** fled all the men and women,
JUDGES 10: 8	And that year they **vexed** **and** **oppressed** the chidren of Israel:

N.B. note how the underlined word separates words and phrases having the same meaning.

JUDGES 10: 9	**Moreover** the children of Ammon passed over Jordan to fight **also** against Judah,
Deut. 9: 13	**Furthermore** the LORD spake unto me, saying,
JUDGES 10: 13	**wherefore** I will deliver you no more.
11: 8	**Therefore** we turn again to thee now,
JUDGES 11: 1	and he *was* the son of an **harlot:** and Gilead begat Jephthah.
: 2	for thou *art* the son of a **strange woman.**
19: 2	And his concubine played the **whore** against him,
JUDGES 11: 7	Did not ye hate me, and **expel** me out of my father's house?
: 24	So whomsoever our God shall **drive out** from before us, them will we possess.
JUDGES 11: 25	And now *art* thou any thing better than Balak the son of Zippor, king of Moab? did he ever **strive against Israel, or did he ever fight against them.**

N.B. note how the underlined word separates words and phrases having the same meaning.

JUDGES 11: 26	**why** therefore did ye not recover *them* within that time?
: 27	**Wherefore** I have not sinned against thee,
JUDGES 11:27	**but** thou doest me wrong to war against me:
: 28	**Howbeit** the king of the Ammon hearkened not unto the words of Jephthah which he sent him.

JUDGES 11: 34	and she was *his* **only child;** beside her he had **neither son nor daughter.**
JUDGES 11: 36	**for<u>as</u>much as** the LORD hath taken vengeance for thee of thine enemies,

N.B. note the underlined word means the same as the second bold word.

JUDGES 12: 12	**Wherefore** passedst thou over to fight against the children of Ammon, and didst not call us to go with thee?
11: 26	**why** therefore did ye not recover *them* within that time?
JUDGES 13: 2	and his wife *was* **barren <u>and</u> bare not.**

N.B. note how the underlined word separates words and phrases having the same meaning,

JUDGES 13: 6	A man of God came unto me, and his **countenance** *was* like the countenance of an angel of God, very terrible:
6: 22	Alas, O Lord GOD! for because I have seen an angel of the LORD **face** to face.
JUDGES 13: 20	when the flame **went up** toward heaven from off the altar, that the angel of the LORD **ascended** in the flame of the altar.
JUDGES 14: 9	And he took **thereof** in his hands, and went on eating,
Deut. 20: 6	lest he die in the battle, and another man eat **of it.**
JUDGES 14: 14	and they could not in three days **expound** the riddle.
: 15	Entice the thy husband, that he may **declare** unto us the riddle,
: 16	Behold, I have not told *it* my father nor my mother, and shall I **tell** *it* thee?
JUDGES 15: 1	But her father would not **suffer** him to go in.
16: 30	And Samson said, **Let** me die with the Philistines.
JUDGES 15: 2	And her father said, I **verily** thought that thou hadst utterly hated her;
: 13	but **surely** we will not kill thee.
9: 16	if ye have done **truly** and sincerely,
JUDGES 15: 5	he let *them* go into the **standing corn** of the Philistines, and burnt up both the **shocks,**
Exodus 22: 6	so that the **stacks of corn,** or the **standing corn,**
JUDGES 15: 15	and put forth his hand, and took it, and **slew** a thousand men therewith.
Num. 31: 19	whosoever hath **killed** any person,

JUDGES 15: 15	and slew a thousand men **therewith.**
Deut. 16: 3	Thou shalt eat no leavened bread **with it;** seven days shalt thou eat leavened bread **therewith,**
JUDGES 15: 18	And he was sore **athirst,** and called on the LORD,
4: 19	Give me, I pray thee a little water to drink; for I am **thirsty.**
JUDGES 15: 19	and there came water **thereout;** and when he had drunk, his spirit came again,
JUDGES 16: 2	And they **compassed** *him* in,
20: 43	*Thus* they **inclosed** the Benjamites **round about,**
JUDGES 16: 5	and said unto her, **Entice** him, and see wherein his great strength *lieth,*
1 Kings 22: 20	And the LORD said, Who shall **persuade** Ahab,
JUDGES 16: 5	and said unto her, Entice him, and see **where**in his great strength *lieth,*
JUDGES 16: 6	Tell me, I pray thee, wherein thy great strength *lieth,* and **wherewith** thou mightest be bound to afflict thee.
Exodus 10: 26	and we know not **with what** we must serve the LORD,
JUDGES 16: 12	Deliliah therefore took new ropes, and bound him **therewith,**
19: 24	and humble ye them, and do **with them** would seemeth good to you:
JUDGES 16: 16	And it came to pass, when she **pressed him** daily with her words, and
	urged him, *so* that his soul was **vexed** unto death.
Numbers 11: 10	Moses was also **displeased.**
JUDGES 16: 20	And he **wist not** that the LORD was departed from him.
13: 16	For Ma-no-ah **knew not** that he *was* an angel of the LORD.
JUDGES 16: 21	**But** the Philistines took him, and put out his eyes,
: 22	**Howbeit** the hair of his head began to grow again after he was shaven.
JUDGES 16: 26	**Suffer me** that I may feel the pillars whereupon the house standerth,
: 30	And Samson said, **Let me** die with the Philistines.
JUDGES 16: 26	Suffer me that I may feel the pillars **whereupon** the house standeth,
: 29	And Samson took hold of the two middle pillars **upon which** the house stood,
JUDGES 16: 30	and the house fell upon the lords, and upon all the people that

were **therein.**

19: 11   and let us turn into this city of the Jeb-u-sites, and lodge **in it.**

N.B. reverse the two syllables in the first reference and the meaning is clear.

JUDGES 17: 3   to make a **graven image and a molten image:** now therefore
I will restore it unto thee.
    : 5   And the man Micah had an house of **gods,** and made an
ephod, and **terephim,**

N.B. note how the underlined word separates words and phrases having the same
meaning.

JUDGES 17: 9   and I go to **sojourn** where I may find *a place.*
    : 10   And Micah said unto him, **Dwell** with me,

JUDGES 17: 10   and a suit of **apparel,** and thy victuals.
11: 35   and when he saw her, that he rent his **clothes,**

JUDGES 17: 10   and a suit of apparel, and thy **victuals.**
1 Samuel 14: 24   Cursed *be* the man that eateth *any* **food** until evening,

JUDGES 18: 2   and from Esh-ta-ol, **to spy out the land, and to search it;**

N.B. note how the underlined word separates words and phrases having the same
meaning.

JUDGES 18: 3   and they turned in **thither,** and said unto him,
    : 2   they lodged **there.**

JUDGES 18: 3   Who brought thee **hither?** and what makest thou in this
place? and what hast thou **here?**

JUDGES 17: 6   And the priest said unto them, Go in peace: before the
LORD *is* your way **wherein** ye go.
4: 14   for this *is* the day **in which** the LORD hath delivered
Sis-e-ra into thine hand:

JUDGES 18: 7   and saw the the people that *were* **therein,** how they dwelt
careless,

19: 11   and let us turn in into this city of the Jeb-u-sites, and lodge
in it.

N.B. reverse the syllables in the first bold word and the meaning is clear.

JUDGES 18: 9   and *are* ye still? be not **slothful** to go,
Exodus 5: 17   But he said, Ye *are* **idle,** *ye are* idle:

JUDGES 18: 11   And there went from **thence** of the family of the Danites,

: 2	to the house of Micah, they lodged **there.**
JUDGES 19: 8	And they **tarried** until afternoon, and they did eat both of them.
Joshua 10: 13	And the sun stood still, and the moon **stayed,**
Genesis 43: 10	For except we had **lingered,** surely now we had returned this second time.
JUDGES 19: 19	Yet there is both straw and **provender** for our asses;
15: 5	and also the standing **corn,**
Job 6: 5	or loweth the ox over his **fodder?**
JUDGES 20: 1	and the **congregation** was gathered together as one man,
: 2	presented themselves in the **assembly** of the people of God,
JUDGES 20: 7	Behold, ye *are* a children of Israel; give here your **advice <u>and</u> counsel.**

N.B. note how the underlined word separates words and phrases having the same meaning.

JUDGES 20: 21	And the children of Benjamin came forth out Gib-e-ah, and **destroyed down to the ground** of the Israelites that day twenty and two thousand men.
Psalm 137: 7	who said, **Rase** *it,* **rase** *it, even* **to the foundation** thereof.
JUDGES 20: 31	and they began to **smite** of the people, *and* **kill,**
JUDGES 20: 37	And the liers in wait **hasted, <u>and</u> rushed** upon Gib-e-ah,

N.B. note how the underlined word separates words and phrases having the same meaning.

JUDGES 20: 40	and, behold, the flame of the city **ascended up** to heaven.
13: 20	For it came to pass, when the flame **went up** toward heaven from off the altar,
JUDGES 20: 43	*Thus* they **inclosed** the Benjamites **round about,** *and* chased them,
JUDGES 20: 43	*and* chased them, *and* **trode** them down with ease...
Job 28: 8	The lion's whelps have not **trodden** it,
Daniel 8: 7	but he cast him down to the ground, and **stamped** upon him:
JUDGES 21: 9	*there were* none of the inhabitants of Ja-besh-gil-e-ad **there.**
: 10	And the congregation sent **thither** twelve thousand men of the valiantest,
JUDGES 21: 14	and yet so they **sufficed** them not.
Psalm 17: 15	I shall be **satisfied,** when I awake, with thy likeness.

JUDGES 21: 18	**Howbeit** we may not give them wives of our daughters:
16: 21	**But** the Philistines took him,

RUTH

RUTH 1: 1	And there was a certain man of Beth-lehem-judah went to **sojourn** in the country of Moab,
Josh. 9: 21	And the princes said unto them, Let them **live;**
Judges 18: 1	and in those days the tribe of Dan sought them an inheritance to **dwell** in;
1 Sam. 1: 22	he may appear before the LORD, and there **abide** forever.

RUTH 1: 6	how that the LORD had visited his people in giving them **bread.**
1 Sam. 14: 24	Cursed *be* the man that eateth *any* **food** until evening,

RUTH 1: 13	Would ye **tarry** for them till they were grown? Would ye **stay** for them from having husbands:
RUTH 1: 16	for **whither** thou goest, I will go; and **where** thou lodgest,

RUTH 1: 18	When she saw that she was **stedfastly minded** to go with her,
1 Sam. 20: 33	whereby Jonathan knew that it was **determined** of his father,

RUTH 2: 2	and glean ears of corn after *him* in whose sight I shall find **grace.** And she said unto her, Go, my daughter.
: 13	Then she said, Let me find **favour** in thy sight, my lord;

RUTH 2:2	and glean ears of corn after *him* in whose sight I shall find **grace.**
: 13	Then she said, Let me find **favour** in thy sight, lord;

RUTH 2: 3	and her **hap** was to light on a part of the field *belonging* unto Boaz,
1 Sam. 6: 9	it *was* a **chance** *that* happened to us.

RUTH 2: 3	who *was* of the **kin**dred of E-lim-e-lech.
: 20	The man *is* near of **kin** unto us,
1 Sam. 9: 21	and my **family** the least of all the families of the tribe...

RUTH 2: 7	And she said, I pray you, let me **glean and gather** after the reapers among the sheaves:

N.B. note how the underlined word separates words and phrases that have the same meaning.

RUTH 2: 8	neither go from **hence,** but abide **here** fast by my maidens:

RUTH 2: 9	and when thou art **athirst,** go unto the vessels,
Judg. 4: 19	Give me, I pray thee, a little water to drink; for I am **thirsty.**

RUTH 2: 11	and art come unto a people which thou knewest not **heretofore.**
1 Sam. 14: 21	*that* were with the Philistines **before** that time,
RUTH 2: 12	The LORD **recompense** thy work, and a full **reward** be given thee of the LORD God of Israel,
RUTH 2: 14	and he reached her **parched** *corn,* and she did eat,
Lev. 2: 14	green ears of **corn dried by the fire,**
RUTH 2: 14	and she did eat, and was **sufficed,** and left.
Psalm 17: 5	I shall be **satisfied,** when I awake, with thy likeness.
RUTH 2: 15	Let her glean even among the sheaves, and **reproach her not:**
: 16	and leave *them,* that she may glean *them,* and **rebuke her not.**
RUTH 2: 17	So she gleaned in the field until even, and **beat out** that she had gleaned:
Judges 6: 11	and his son Gideon **threshed** wheat by the winepress,
RUTH 2: 18	and gave to her that she had **reserved** after she was sufficed.
1 Sam. 9: 24	for unto this time hath it **been kept** for thee since I said,
RUTH 2: 18	and gave to her that she had reserved after she was **sufficed.**
Deut. 33: 23	And of Naph-ta-li he said, O Naph-e-ta-li **satisfied** with favour,
RUTH 2: 19 thou?	Where hast thou gleaned to day? and where **wroughtest**
Prov. 16: 26	He that **laboureth** laboureth for himself;
RUTH 2: 20	And Naomi said unto her, The man *is* near of **kin** unto us, one of our next **kins**man.
RUTH 2: 20	And Naomi said unto her, The man *is* **near** of kin unto us, one of our **next** kinsman.
RUTH 2: 21	Thou shalt keep **fast** by my young men,
Num. 32: 16	And they came **near** unto him, and said,
RUTH 3: 10	in**as**much **as** thou followedst not young men,

N.B. note the underlined letters which give the meaning of the entire word.

RUTH 3: 12	And now it is true that I *am thy* near kinsman: **howbeit** there is a kinsman nearer than I.
: 13	let him do the kinsman's part: **but** if he will not do the part...
RUTH 4: 4	And I thought to **advertise** thee, ...**tell me,** that I may know:
RUTH 4: 9	Ye *are* witnesses this day, that I have **bought** all that *was* E-lim-e-lech's,

: 10	the wife of Mahlon, have I **purchased** to be my wife,

RUTH 4: 10	**Moreover** Ruth the Moabitess,
3: 15	**Also** he said, Bring the vail that *thou hast* upon thee,
Deut. 9: 13	**Furthermore** the LORD spake unto me,

1 SAMUEL

1 SAM. 1: 10	And she *was* in **bitterness of soul,** and prayed unto the LORD, and wept **sore.**
1 SAM. 1: 15	And Hannah answered and said, No, my lord, I *am* a woman of **a sorrowful spirit:**

1 SAM. 1: 16	Count not thine handmaid for **a daughter of Belial:**
2: 9	and the **wicked** shall be silent in the darkness;
: 12	Now the sons of Eli *were* **sons of Belial: they knew not the LORD.**
Psalm 1: 1	Blessed *is* the man that walketh not in the counsel of the **ungodly,**

N.B. In the first bold word the first syllable refers to 'Bel' a Babylonian god.

1 SAM. 1: 16	for out of the abundance of my complaint and grief have I spoken **hitherto.**
Ruth 2: 7	and hath continued even from the morning **until now,**

1 SAM. 1: 18	And she said, Let thine handmaid find **grace** in thy sight.
Ruth 2: 13	Then she said, Let me find **favour** in thy sight, my lord,

1 SAM. 1: 20	**Wherefore** it came to pass,
: 28	**Therefore** also I lent him to the LORD;

1 SAM. 2: 3	Talk no more so **exceedingly proudly;** let *not* **arrogancy** come out of your mouth:

1 SAM. 2: 12	Now the sons of Eli *were* **sons of Belial; they knew not the LORD.**

N.B. note how the semi- colon separates words and phrases having the same meaning.

1 SAM. 2: 13	the priest's servant came, while the flesh was in **seething,**
Ezekiel 46: 23	and *it was* made with **boiling** places under the rows round about.

1 SAM. 2: 14	So they did in Shi-loh unto all the Israelites that came **thither.**
9: 1	Now **there** was a man of Benjamin,

1 SAM. 2: 15	Give flesh to **roast** for the priest; for he will not have **sodden**

flesh but raw.

1 SAM. 2: 17	**Wherefore** the sin of the young men was very great before the LORD:
1: 28	**Therefore** also I have lent him to the LORD;
1 SAM. 2: 19	**Moreover** his mother made him a little coat,
1: 6	And her adversary **also** provoked her sore,
26: 10	David said **furthermore,** *As* the LORD liveth,
1 SAM. 2: 25	**but** if a man sin against LORD, who shall intreat for him? Notwithstanding they hearkened not unto the voice of their father.
1 SAM. 2: 25	but if a man sin against the LORD, who shall **intreat** for him?
: 36	Put me, I **pray** thee into one of the priests' offices,
1 SAM. 2: 29	**Wherefore** kick ye at my sacrifice and at mine offering,
: 23	And he said unto them, **Why** do ye such things?
1 SAM. 3: 18	And Samuel told him **every whit, and** hid nothing from him.
1 SAM. 4: 1	Now Israel went out against the Philistines to battle, and **pitched** beside Eb-en-zer:
13: 16	but the Philistines **encamped** in Mich-mash.
1 SAM. 4: 2	and when they joined battle, Israel was **smitten** before the Philistines: and they **slew** of the army in the field about about four thousand men.
: 11	and the sons of E-li, Hoph-ni and Phin-e-has, were **slain.**
24: 11	for in that I cut off the skirt of the robe, and **killed** thee not,
1 SAM. 4: 3	the elders of Israel said, **Wherefore** hath the LORD smitten us to day before the Philistines?
2 : 23	And he said unto them, **Why** do ye such things?
1 SAM. 4: 4	that they might bring from **thence** the ark of the covenant of the LORD of hosts,
6: 14	And he cart came into the field of Joshua, a Beth-she –mite, and stood **there,**
1 SAM. 4: 7	And they said, Woe unto us! For there hath not been such a thing **heretofore.**
14: 21	Moreover the Hebrews *that* were with the Philistines **before** that time,
1 SAM. 4: 21	**because** the ark of God **was** taken,
: 22	**for** the ark of God **is** taken,
1 SAM. 5: 6	But the hand of the LORD was **heavy** upon them of Ashdod,

: 9	and destroyed them, of the LORD was **against** the city with a very great destruction:
1 SAM. 5: 6	and **smote** them with emerods, *even* Ashdod and the coasts thereof.
2: 14	And he **struck** *it* into the pan,
1 SAM. 5: 6	and smote them with emerods, *even* Ashdod and the coasts **thereof.**
7: 12	and called the name **of it** Eb-en-e-zer,
1 SAM. 6: 2	What shall we do to the ark of the LORD? tell us **wherewith** we shall send it to his place.
1: 14	And Eli said unto her, **How** long wilt thou be drunken?
1 SAM. 6: 5	**Wherefore** ye shall make images of your emerods,
: 7	Now **therefore** make a new cart,
1 SAM. 6: 5	and images of your mice that **mar** the land;
Ex. 3: 22	and upon your daughters; and ye shall **spoil** the Egyptians.
Psalm 89: 40	thou hast brought his strong holds to **ruin.**
1 SAM. 6: 5	**peradventure** he will lighten his hand from off you,
14: 6	**it may be** that the LORD will work for us:
1 SAM. 6: 6	**Wherefore** then do you harden your hearts, as the Egyptians and Pharaoh hardened their hearts?
2: 23	And he said unto them, **Why** do ye such things?
1 SAM. 6: 6	when he **had wrought** wonderfully among them,
: 9	*then* he hath **done** us this great evil:
1 SAM. 6: 7	Now therefore make a new cart, and take and take two **milch** **kine,** on which there hath come no yoke, and tie the kine to the cart, and bring **their calves** home from them:
Judges 5: 25	He asked water, *and* she gave *him* **milk;**
Num. 18: 17	But the firstling of a **cow,**

N.B. A kine is a female cow as the context clearly states. The word milc is the
(O.E.) for milk.

1 SAM. 6: 15	and the **coffer** that *was* with it, wherein the jewels of gold *were,*
Deut. 25: 14	Thou shalt not have in thine house divers measures, **great and** **small.**
2 Kings 9: 1	Gird up thy loins, and take this **box** of oil in thine hand,
12: 9	But Je-hoi-a-da the priest took **a chest,**

1 SAM. 6: 15	and the coffer that *was* with it, **wherein** the jewels of gold
were,	
Judges 4: 14	for this *is* the day **in which** the LORD hath delivered Sis-e-ra into thine hand:

| 1 SAM. 6: 18 | even unto the great *stone of* Abel, **whereon** they set down the ark of the LORD, |
| : 7 | and take two milch kine, **on which** there hath come no yoke, |

| 1 SAM. 6: 19 | even he smote of the people fifty thousand and three**score** and ten men: |
| Num. 7: 88 | the he goats **sixty**, the lambs of the first year sixty. |

N.B. The underlined word is a numerical term meaning **twenty**. To find the value of the 'score' number multiply by twenty 3x20=60.

1 SAM. 6: 19	and the people lamented **had smitten** *many* of the people with a great slaughter.
22: 21	And A-bi-a-thar, shewed David that Saul **had slain** the LORD'S riests.
2 Chron. 25: 3	that he **slew** his servants that **had killed** the king his father.

| 1 SAM. 7: 12 | and called the name of it Eb-en-e-zer, saying, **Hitherto** hath the LORD helped us. |
| 2 Sam. 5: 2 | Aso **in time past**, when Saul was king over us, |

| 1 SAM. 7: 14 | and the coasts **thereof** did Israel deliver out of the hands of the Philistines. |
| : 12 | and set *it* between Miz-peh and Shen, and called the name **of it** Eb-en-zer, |

1 SAM. 8: 3	And his sons walked not in his ways, but turned aside after **lucre, and** took bribes**, and perverted judgment.
Prov. 15: 27	He that is **greedy of gain** troubleth his own house;
Ezek. 22: 27	to get **dishonest gain.**

1 SAM. 8: 6	**But** the thing displeased Samuel,
: 9	**howbeit** yet protest solemnly unto them,
: 19	**Nevertheless** the people refused to obey the voice of Samuel;

| 1 SAM. 8: 8 | even unto this day, **wherewith** they have forsaken me, |
| Judges 4: 14 | Up; for this *is* the day **in which** the LORD hath delivered Sis-e-ra into thine hand: |

| 1 SAM. 8: 9 | Now therefore hearken unto their voice: **howbeit** yet protest solemnly unto them, |
| : 6 | **But** the thing displeased Samuel, |

| 1 SAM. 8: 12 | and *will set them* to **ear** his ground, and to reap his harvest, |
| Job 1: 14 | and said, The oxen were **plowing**, |

| 1 SAM. 8: 13 | And he will take your daughters *to be* **confectionaries, and** *to be* **cooks, and** *to be* **bakers.** |

N.B. note how the underlined words separate words and phrases having the same meaning.

1 SAM. 8: 21	and **he rehearsed them** in ears of the LORD.
Deut. 4: 13	And he **declared** unto you his covenant,
Jerem. 38: 27	and **he told them** according to all these words that the king had commanded.

| 1 SAM. 9: 1 | the son of A-phi-ah, a Benjamite, a **mighty man of power.** |
| Judges 6: 12 | The LORD *is* with thee thou **mighty man of valour.** |

| 1 SAM. 9: 6 | now let us go **thither;** |
| : 1 | Now **there** was a man of Benjamin, |

1 SAM. 9: 6	**peradventure** he can shew us our way that we should go.
14: 6	**it may be** the LORD will work for us.
Acts 8: 22	and pray God, if **perhaps** the thought of thine heart **may be** for-given thee.

| 1 SAM. 9: 7 | for the **bread** is spent in our vessels, |
| 14: 28 | Cursed *be* the man that eateth *any* **food** this day. |

| 1 SAM. 9: 13 | **As soon as** ye be come into the city, ye shall **straightway** find him. |

| 1 SAM. 9: 14 | Samuel came out **against** them, for to go up to the high place. |
| : 19 | I *am* the seer: go up **before** me unto the high place; |

1 SAM. 9: 21	and my family the least of all the families of the tribe of Benjamin?
	Wherefore then speakest thou so to me?
2: 23	And he said unto them, **Why** do ye such things?

1 SAM. 9: 25	*Samuel* **communed** with Saul upon the top of the house.
: 17	Behold the man whom I **spake** to thee of !
2 Sam. 7: 17	and according to all this vision, so **did** Nathan **speak** unto David.

1 SAM. 10: 5	thou shalt meet a company of prophets coming down from the high
	place with a **psaltery,**
Psalm 33: 2	sing unto him with the **psaltery *and* an instrument of ten strings.**

| 1 SAM. 10: 11 | And it came to pass, when all that knew him **before** time saw that, |

1 SAM. 10: 14	And Saul's uncle said unto him and to his servant, **Whither** went ye?
Ruth 2: 19	**Where** hast thou gleaned to day?
1 SAM. 10: 16	But of the matter of the kingdom, **whereof** Samuel spake,
9: 23	Bring the portion which I gave thee, **of which** I said unto thee,
1 SAM. 10: 19	And ye have this day rejected your God, who himself saved you out of all **adversities and your tribulations;**
Deut. 31: 17	and they shall be devoured, and **many evils and troubles** shall befall them;

N.B. note how the underlined words separate words and phrases having the same meaning.

1 SAM. 10: 27	But the **children of Belial** said, How shall this man save us?
Psalm 1: 4	The **ungodly** *are* not so:
1 Sam. 2: 9	and the **wicked** shall be silent in darkness;
1 SAM. 11: 21	did not a woman cast a piece of a millstone upon him from the wall that he died in The-bez? why went ye **nigh** the wall?
1 SAM. 12: 3	or of whose hand have I received *any* bribe to blind mine eyes there**with?**
1 SAM. 12: 6	*It is* the LORD that **advanced** Moses and Aaron,
Esther 5: 11	and all *the things* wherein the king had **promoted** him,
1 SAM. 12: 7	Now therefore stand still, that I may reason with you before the LORD of all the **right**eous acts of the LORD,
: 23	but I will teach you the good and the **right** way:
1 SAM. 12: 13	Now therefore behold the king whom ye have **chosen,** *and* whom ye have **desired!**
1 SAM. 12; 23	**Moreover** as for me,
26: 10	David said **furthermore,**
1 SAM. 13: 3	And Jonathan **smote** the garrison of the Philistines that *was* Ge-ba,
13: 4	And all Israel heard say *that* Saul had **smitten** a garrison of the Philistines,
14: 13	and his armourbearer **slew** after him.
24: 11	for in that I cut off the skirt of thy robe, and **killed** thee not,
1 SAM. 13: 6	When the men of Israel saw that they were **in a strait, (for the people were distressed,)**
1 SAM. 13: 8	And he **tarried** seven days,

: 16	and the people *there were* present with them, **abode** in Gibeah of Benjamin:
20: 19	And *when* thou hast **stayed** three days,
1 Kings 20: 38	So the prophet departed, and **waited** for the king by the way,

1 SAM. 13: 20	But all the Israelites went down to the Philistines, to sharpen every man his **share,** and his **coulter,** and his **axe,** and his **mattock.**
: 21	Yet they had a **file** for the **mattocks,** and for the **coulters,**
Isaiah 2: 4	and they shall beat there swords into **plowshares,**

1 SAM. 14: 1	Jonathon the son of Saul said unto **the man that bare his armour,**
: 7	And his **armourbearer** said unto him,

1 SAM. 14: 8	and we will **discover** ourselves unto them.
: 12	Come up to us, and we will **shew** you a thing.

1 SAM. 14: 9	If they say thus unto us, **Tarry** until we come to you; then we will **stand still** in our place,

1 SAM. 14: 11	And both of them **discovered** themselves unto the garrison of the Philistines:
3: 7	neither was the word of the LORD yet **revealed** unto him.

1 SAM. 14: 15	and the spoilers, they also **trembled, and** the earth quaked:

N.B. note how the underlined word separates words and phrases having the same meaning.

1 SAM. 14: 18	And Saul said unto A-hi-ah, Bring **hither** the ark of God.
: 34	and slay *them* **here,** and eat;

1 SAM. 14: 24	for Saul had **adjured** the people, saying, Cursed *be* the man that eateth *any* food until evening,
: 27	But Jonathan heard not when his father **charged the people with the oath:**

1 SAM. 14: 30	How much more, **if haply** the people had eaten freely...

N.B. note that the word **if** means haply and also vice-versa.

1 SAM. 14: 34	Bring me **hither** every man his ox, and every man his sheep, and slay *them* **here,** and eat;
: 36	Then said the priest, Let us draw **near hither** unto God.

1 SAM. 14: 38	And know and see **wherein** this sin hath been this day.
2 Kings 19: 10	Let not thy God **in whom** thou trusteth deceive thee,

1 SAM. 14: 45	**there** shall not **one** hair of **his head** fall to the **ground;**

1 Kings 1: 52	there shall not **an** hair of **him** fall to the **earth;**
1 SAM. 15: 3	Now go and **smite** Am-a-lek, and **utterly destroy** all that they have,
	and spare them not; but **slay** both man and woman,
17: 9	If he is able to fight with me, and to **kill** me,
1 SAM. 15: 6	And Saul said unto the Ke-nites, **Go, depart,**
1 SAM. 15: 19	**Wherefore** then didst thou not obey the voice of the LORD
17: 8	**Why** are ye come out to set *your* battle in array?
1 SAM. 15: 32	Then said Samuel, Bring ye **hither** to me Agag the king of the the A-mal-ek-ites,
14: 34	Bring me **hither** every man his ox, and every man his sheep, and slay *them* **here,**
1 SAM. 16: 2	And the LORD said, Take an **heifer** with thee, and say, I am come sacrifice to the LORD.
Num. 18: 17	But the firstling of a **cow,**
Isaiah 7: 21	And it shall come to pass in that day, *that* a man shall nourish **a young cow,**
Isaiah 15: 5	an heifer of **three years old:**
1 SAM. 16: 7	Look not on his countenance, or on the **height** of his **stature;**
1 SAM. 16: 11	And Samuel said unto Jesse, Send and fetch him: for we will not sit down till he come **hither.**
14: 34	Bring me **hither** every man his ox, and every man his sheep, and slay *them* **here.**
1 SAM. 16: 12	Now he *was* ruddy, *and* withal of **a beautiful countenance, and goodly to look to.**

N. B. note how the underlined word separates words and phrases having the same meaning.

1 SAM. 16: 16	to seek out a man, *who is* a **cunning** player on a harp:
: 17	I have seen a son of Jesse the Beth-lehemite, that **can play well,** and bring him to me.
1 Chron. 5: 18	and to shoot with bow, and **skilful** in war,
1 SAM. 16: 20	And Jesse took an ass *laden* with **bread,** and a bottle of wine,
14: 24	Cursed the man that eateth *any* **food** until evening,
1 SAM. 17: 6	and a **target** of brass between his shoulders.
: 45	Thou comest to me with a sword, and with a **shield:**
1 SAM. 17: 11	When Saul and all Israel heard those words of the Philistine, were **dismayed and greatly afraid.**

N.B. note how the underlined word separates words and phrases having the same meaning.

<u>**1 SAM. 17: 17**</u>	Take now for thy brethren an ephah of this **parched *corn*,**
Lev. 2: 14	for the meat offering of thy firstfruits green ears of **corn dried by the fire,**
Jerem. 29: 22	whom the king of Babylon **roasted** in the fire;

<u>**SAM. 17: 21**</u>	For Israel and the Philistines put the **battle in array, army against army.**

N.B. note how the comma separates words and phrases having the same meaning.

<u>**1 SAM. 17: 28**</u>	I know the **naughtiness** of thine heart;
12: 20	ye have done all this **wickedness:**

<u>**1 SAM. 17: 31**</u>	And when the words were heard which David **spake,** they **rehearsed** *them* before Saul:

<u>**1 SAM. 17: 35**</u>	and when he arose against me, I caught *him* by his beard, and **smote him <u>and</u> slew him.**

N. B. note how the underlined word separates words and phrases having the same meaning.

<u>**1 SAM. 17: 37**</u>	David said **moreover,** The LORD that delivered me out of the lion,
26: 10	David said **furthermore,** *As* the lord liveth,

<u>**1 SAM. 17: 39**</u>	And David girded his sword upon his armour, and he **assayed to go;**
Acts 16: 10	immediately we **endeavoured to go** into Macedonia,
2 Sam. 22: 31	*As for* God, his way *is* perfect; the word of the LORD *is* **tried:**
<u>**1 SAM. 17: 40**</u>	and chose him five smooth stones out of the brook, and put them in a **shepherd's bag** which he had, even in **a scrip;**

<u>**1 SAM. 17: 42**</u>	And when the Philistine looked about, and saw David, **he disdained him:**
10: 27	And they **despised** him, and brought him no presents.

<u>**1 SAM. 17: 46**</u>	and I will the **carcases** of the host of the Philistines this day unto the fowls of the air,
2 Kings 19: 35	and when they arose in the morning, behold they *were* all dead **corpses.**

<u>**1 SAM. 17: 48**</u>	and **drew nigh** to meet David,
: 41	And the Philistine came on and **drew near** unto David;

<u>**1 SAM. 17: 48**</u>	that David **hasted, <u>and</u> ran** toward the army to meet the Philistine.

1 SAM. 17: 49	And David put his hand in his bag, and took **thence** a stone,
1 Kings 22: 43	he turned not aside **from it,**
1 SAM. 17: 50	So David **prevailed** over the Philistine with a sling and a stone, and **smote** the Philistine, and **slew him:**
1 SAM. 17: 51	and drew it out of the sheath **thereof,**
7: 12	and called the name **of it** Eb-en-e –zer,
1 SAM. 17: 51	and slew him, and cut off his head **therewith.**
18: 11	for he said, I will smite David even to the wall *with it.*
6: 15	and the coffer that *was* **with it** wherin the jewels of gold *were,*
1 SAM. 17: 56	And the king said, Enquire thou whose son the **stripling** *is.*
: 58	And Saul said to him, Whose son *art* thou, *thou* **young man?**
1 SAM. 18: 6	singing, and dancing, to meet king Saul, with **tabrets,** with and with **instruments of musick.**
1 SAM. 18: 8	And Saul was **very wroth,** and the saying **displeased** him;
1 SAM. 18: 9	And Saul eyed David **from that day <u>and</u> forward.**

1 SAM. 18: 11	And David **avoided out** of his presence twice.
19: 10	And Saul sought to smite David even to the wall with the javelin; but he **slipped away** out of Saul's presence, and he smote the wall: and David **fled, <u>and</u> escaped** that night.

1 SAM. 18: 15	**Wherefore when** Saul saw that he behaved wisely,
: 22	and all his servants love thee: now **therefore** be the king's son in law.
1 SAM. 18: 21	Thou shalt this day be my son in law in *the one of* the **twain.**
14: 49	and the names of his **two** daughters *were these;*
1 SAM. 19: 5	and didst rejoice: **wherefore** then wilt thou sin against innocent blood, to slay David without a cause?
: 17	**why** should I kill thee?

1 SAM. 19: 5	wherefore then wilt thou sin against innocent blood, to slay David
	without **a cause?**
12: 7	Now then stand still
	acts of the LORD,
1 SAM. 19: 21	and they prophesied **likewise.** And Saul sent messengers again the third time **also.**
2 Samuel 6: 19	*even* among the whole multitude of Israel, **as well** to the women as men,
1 SAM. 19: 23	And he went **thither** to Nai-oth in Ramah:
21: 8	And is **there** not here under thine hand spear or sword?
1 SAM. 20: 3	Thy father **certainly** knoweth that I have found grace in thine eyes;
	and he saith, Let not Jonathan know this, lest he be grieved: but **truly** *as* the Lord liveth,
1 SAM. 20: 8	**notwithstanding,** if there be in me any iniquity,
: 15	But *also* thou shalt not cut off thy kindness from my house for ever:
: 26	**Nevertheless** Saul spake not any thing that day:
1 SAM. 20: 20	And I will shoot three arrows on the side *thereof*,
7: 12	and called the name **of it** Eb-en-e-zer,
1 SAM. 20: 27	**Wherefore** cometh not the son of Jesse to meat,
21: 1	**Why** *art* thou alone, and no man with thee?
1 SAM. 20: 31	**Wherefore now** send and fetch him unto me, for he shall die.

N.B. note that the two bold words are interchangeable.

1 SAM. 20: 33	**whereby** Jonathon knew it was determined of his father to slay David.
1 Samuel 26: 24	And, behold, as thy life was much set **by this** day in mine eyes,
1 SAM. 20: 38	And Jonathan cried after the lad, **Make speed, haste, stay not.**

N.B. note how the comma separates words and phrases having the same meaning.

| 1 SAM. 20: 42 | And Jonathan said to David, Go in peace, **for<u>asmuch</u> as** we have sworn both of us in the name of the LORD, |

N.B. note the underlined word which gives the meaning of the whole word.

| 1 SAM. 21: 4 | *There is* no common bread under mine hand, but there is **hallowed** bread; |

<u>**1 SAM. 21: 5**</u>	And David answered the priest, and said unto him, **Of a truth** women *have been* kept from us about these three days,
20: 3	Thy father **certainly** knoweth that I have found grace in thine eyes; and he saith, Let not Jonathan know this, lest he be grieved: but **truly** *as* the LORD liveth,
<u>**1 SAM. 21: 13**</u>	And he **changed his behaviour** before them, and **feigned himself** **mad** in their hands,
: 15	have I need of mad men, that ye have brought this *fellow* **to play the mad man** in my presence?
<u>**1 SAM. 21: 14**</u>	Lo, ye see the man is mad: **wherefore** *then* have ye brought to me?
: 1	**Why** *art* thou alone, and no man with thee?
<u>**1 SAM. 22: 1**</u>	David therefore departed **thence,** and escaped to the cave Adullam: and when his brethren and all his father's house heard *it,* they went down **thither** to him.
: 2	and **there** were with him were about four hundred men.
<u>**1 SAM. 22:10**</u>	and gave him **victuals,** and gave him the sword of Goliath the Philistine.
: 6	for there was no bread but the **shewbread,**
<u>**1 SAM. 22: 15**</u>	be it far from me: let not the king **impute** *any* thing unto his servant,
1: 16	**Count** not thine hand maid for a daughter of Belial:
Num. 4: 32	and by name ye shall **reckon** the instruments of the charge...
<u>**1 SAM. 22: 18**</u>	and **slew** on that day fourscore and five persons that did wear a linen ephod.
: 21	And A-bi-a-thar shewed David that Saul **had slain** the LORD'S priests.
24: 11	for in that I cut off the skirt of thy robe, and **killed** thee not,
<u>**1 SAM. 22: 18**</u>	and slew on that day **fou<u>rscore</u>** and five persons that did wear a linen ephod.
Genesis 5: 28	And La-mech lived an hundred **eighty** and two years,

N.B. note the underlined word which is a numerical term meaning twenty. To find the value of the 'score' number multiply 4x20=80.

<u>**1 SAM. 22: 21**</u>	And A-bi-a-thar shewed David that Saul **had slain** the LORD'S priests.
: 18	and **slew** on that day fourscore and five persons that did wear an ephod.
24: 11	for in that I cut off the skirt of thy robe and **killed** thee not,

1 SAM. 23: 2	Therefore David enquired of the LORD, saying, Shall I go and **smite** these Philistines?
: 10	Saul seeketh to **destroy** the city for my sake.
24: 10	how that the LORD had delivered thee to day into mine hand in the cave: and *some* bade *me* **kill** thee:
22: 17	Turn, and **slay** the priests of the LORD;
1 SAM. 23: 9	And David knew that Saul **secretly practised mischief against him:**
: 15	And David saw that Saul **was come to seek his life:**
1 SAM. 23: 9	and he said to A-bi-a-thar the priest, Bring **hither** the ephod.
21: 8	And is there not **here** under thine spear or sword?
1 SAM. 23: 11	O LORD God of Israel, I **beseech thee,** tell thy servant.
25: 8	for we come in a good day: give, **I pray thee,**
1 SAM. 23: 13	And went **whither**soever they could go.
: 22	and know and see his place **where** his haunt is,
1 SAM. 23: 23	See **therefore,** and take knowledge of all the lurking places where he hideth himself,
: 25	And they told David: **wherefore** he came down into a rock,
1 SAM. 23: 26	for Saul and his men **compassed** David and his men **round about** to take them.
Psalm 22: 16	the assembly of the wicked have **inclosed** me:

N.B. note that a compass has 360 degrees so to compass anything it has to be inclosed.

1 SAM. 23: 28	**Wherefore** Saul returned from pursuing after David, and went against the Philistines: **therefore** they called that place, Se-la-ham- mah-le-koth.
1 SAM. 23: 29	And David went up from **thence,**
27: 5	that I may dwell **there:**
1 SAM. 24: 7	So David stayed his servants with these words, and **suffered** them not to rise against Saul,
25: 8	Ask thy young men, and they will shew thee. Wherefore **let** the young men find favour in thine eyes:
1 SAM. 24: 9	And David said to Saul, **Wherefore** hearest thou men's words saying, Behold, David seeketh thy hurt?
22: 13	And Saul said unto him, **Why** have ye conspired against me?
1 SAM. 24: 11	**Moreover,** my father, see,
26: 10	David said **furthermore,**
1 SAM. 24: 18	**forasmuch** as when the LORD had delivered me into thine hand, thou killedst me not.

N.B. note the underlined word that separates words and phrases having the same meaning.

<u>1 SAM. 24: 19</u>	**wherefore** the LORD reward thee good for that thou hast done unto me this day.
: 15	The LORD **therefore** be judge, between thee, and see,

<u>1 SAM. 24: 21</u>	Swear now therefore unto me by the LORD, that thou wil not **cut off** my seed after me, and that thou wilt not **destroy** my name out of my father's house.

<u>1 SAM. 25: 17</u>	for he *is such* **a son of Belial,** that a *man* speak to him.
: 3	but the man *was* **churlish <u>and</u> evil** in his doings;

N.B. note the name Nabal can be written backwards and it spells Laban, Jacob's father-in-law whose character was the same as Nabal's.

<u>1 SAM. 25: 18</u>	and five sheep ready dressed, and five measures of **parched corn,**
Leviticus 2: 14	thou shalt offer for the meat offering of thy firstfruits green ears of corn **dried by the fire,**

<u>1 SAM. 25: 20</u>	And it was *so, as* she rode on the ass, that she came down by the **covert** of the hill,

N.B. note that the word cover is contained in the bold word which gives another word meaning the same thing.

<u>1 SAM. 25: 20</u>	David and his men **came down against her; <u>and</u> she met them.**

N.B. note how the underlined word separates words and phrases having the same meaning.

<u>1 SAM. 25: 21</u>	and he hath **requited** me evil for good.
24: 17	for thou hast **rewarded** me good, whereas I have **rewarded** thee evil.

<u>1 SAM. 25: 31</u>	either that thou hast shed blood **causeless,** or that my lord hath avenged himself:
19: 5	then wilt thou sin against innocent blood, to slay David **without a cause?**
Job 1: 9	Then Satan answered the LORD, and said, Doth Job fear God **for nothing?**

<u>1 SAM. 25: 34</u>	For **in very deed** *as* the LORD God of Israel liveth,
: 28	for the LORD will **certainly** make my lord a sure house;
20: 3	but **truly** *as* the LORD liveth,
29: 6	**Surely,** *as* the LORD liveth, thou hast been upright,

1 SAM. 25: 36	for he *was* very drunken: **wherefore** she told him nothing, less or more, until the morning light.
: 26	Now **therefore,** my lord, *as* thy soul liveth,
1 SAM. 25: 42	with five **damsels** of hers that went after her,
Genesis 24: 16	And the damsel *was* very fair to look upon, **a virgin, neither had any man known her:**
1 SAM. 26: 15	**wherefore** then hast thou not kept thy lord the king?
27: 5	for **why** should thy servant dwell in the royal palace with thee?
1 SAM. 27: 5	If I have found **grace** in thy eyes, let them give me a place in some town in the country,
25: 8	Wherefore let the young man find **favour** in thine eyes:
1 SAM. 27: 6	**wherefore** Ziglag pertaineth unto the kings of Judah unto this day.
: 12	**therefore** he shall be my servant for ever.
1 SAM. 27: 10	And A-chish said, **Whither** have ye made a road to day?
19: 22	**Where** *are* Samuel and David?
1 SAM. 27: 10	And A-chish said, Whither have ye **made a road** to day?
: 8	And David and his men went up, and **invaded** the Ge-shu-rites, and the Gezrites, and the A-mal-ek-ites:
1 SAM. 27: 12	He hath made his people Israel utterly to **abhor** him;
2: 30	and they that **despise** me shall be lightly esteemed.
Psalm 119: 163	I **hate** **and** **abhor** lying:

N.B. note how the underlined word separates words and phrases having the same meaning.

1 SAM. 28: 1	And A-chish said unto David, Know thou **assuredly,** that thou shalt go out with me to battle, thou and thy men.
: 2	And David said to A-chish, **Surely** thou shalt know what thy servant can do.
25: 28	for the LORD will **certainly** make my lord a sure house;
20: 3	but **truly** *as* the LORD liveth,
1 SAM. 28: 8	And Saul disguised himself, and put on other **raiment,**
18: 4	and his **garments,** even to his sword,
19: 24	And he stripped off his **clothes** also,
Job 22: 6	and stripped the naked of their **clothing.**
1 SAM. 28: 9	**Wherefore** then layest thou a snare for my life,
: 12	**Why** hast thou deceived me? for thou *art* Saul,

<u>**1 SAM. 28: 19**</u>	**Moreover the LORD** will **also** deliver Israel with thee into the Philistines:
26: 10	David said **furthermore,**
<u>**1 SAM. 28: 24**</u>	and took and did bake unleavened bread **thereof:**
2 Samuel 6: 6	and took hold **of it;** for the oxen shook *it.*
<u>**1 SAM. 29: 2**</u>	David and his men passed on in the **rere**ward with A-chish.
Joshua 6: 9	and the **rereward, came after** the ark, *the priests* going on,

N.B. note also that the first syllable of the first bold word gives the meaning and the second bold word in the second reference confirms it.

<u>**1 SAM. 29: 4**</u>	And the princes of the Philistines were **wroth** with him;
2 Sam. 19: 42	wherefore then be ye **angry** for this matter?
<u>**1 SAM. 29: 4**</u>	for **wherewith** should he reconcile himself unto his master?
2 Sam. 1: 4	And David said unto him, **How** went the matter?
<u>**1 SAM. 29: 6**</u>	**nevertheless** the lords favour thee not.
: 8	**But** what have I done?
: 9	**notwithstanding** the princes of the Philistines have said...
<u>**1 SAM. 29: 7**</u>	**Wherefore** now return, and go in peace,
24: 15	The LORD **therefore** be judge,
<u>**1 SAM. 30: 2**</u>	And had taken the women captives, that *were* **therein:**
2 Kings 2: 21	And he went forth unto the spring of the waters and cast the salt **in there ,**
7: 13	(behold, they *are* as all multitude of Israel that are left **in it**...)

N.B. in the first reference reverse the two syllables and the meaning is clear.

<u>**1 SAM. 30: 6**</u>	And David was **greatly distressed:** for the people spake of stoning him, because the soul of all the people **was grieved,**
<u>**1 SAM. 30: 7**</u>	I pray thee, bring me **hither** the ephod.
21: 8	And is there not **here** under thine hand spear or sword?
<u>**1 SAM. 30: 7**</u>	And A-bi-a-thar brought **thither** the ephod to David.
: 19	And **there** was nothing lacking to them.
<u>**1 SAM. 30: 11**</u>	And they found an Egypt in the field, and brought him to David, and gave him **bread,**
1 Kings 5: 9	and thou shalt accomplish my desire, in giving **food** for my household.
<u>**1 SAM. 30: 13**</u>	and my master left me, because three days **ago**ne I fell sick.
<u>**1 SAM. 30: 18**</u>	And David **recovered** all that the A-mal-ek-ites had carried

away: and **rescued** his two wiv

| 1 SAM. 30: 22 | Then answered all the **wicked men and** *men* of Belial, |

N.B. note how the underlined word separates words and phrases having the same meaning.

1 SAM. 30: 31	and to all the places where David himself and his men were **wont to** haunt.
Exodus 21: 36	Or if it be known that the ox hath **used to** push in time past,
Jerem. 13: 23	*then* may ye also do good, that are **accustomed to** do evil.

| **1 SAM. 31: 4** | Then said Saul unto his armourbearer, Draw thy sword, and thrust me through **therewith;** |
| Deut. 16: 3 | Thou shalt eat no leavened bread **with it;** seven days shalt eat unleavened bread **therewith,** |

1 SAM. 31: 7	and that Saul and his sons were **dead,**
: 8	when the Philistines came to strip the **slain,**
28: 24	and she hasted, and **killed** it,

| **1 SAM. 31: 9** | to **publish** *it in* the house of their idols, and among the people. |
| 2 Sam. 1: 20 | **Tell** *it* not in Gath, **publish** *it* not in the streets of As-ke-lon; |

2 SAMUEL

| **2 SAM. 1: 2** | and *so* it was, when he came to David, that **he fell to the earth, and did obeisance.** |
| 9: 6 | he fell on his face, and **did reverence.** |

| **2 SAM. 1: 10** | and have brought them **hither** unto my lord. |
| 1 Sam. 21: 8 | And is there not **here** under thine hand spear or sword? |

| **2 SAM. 1: 13** | And David said unto the young man that told him, **Whence** *art* thou? |
| : 8 | And he said unto me, **Who** *art* thou? |

| **2 SAM. 1: 16** | for thy mouth hath testified against thee, **I have slain** the LORD'S aointed. |
| 1 Sam. 25: 11 | and my flesh that **I have killed** for my shearers, |

| **2 SAM. 1: 20** | **Tell** *it* not in Gath, **publish** *it* not in As-ke-lon; |

| **2 SAM. 2: 1** | And David said, **Whither** shall I go up? And he said, Unto Hebron. |
| 9: 4 | And the king said, **Where** *is* he? |

| **2 SAM. 2: 2** | So David went up **thither,** and his two wives also, |
| : 4 | And the men of Judah came, and **there** anointed David king... |

2 SAM. 2: 6	and I also will **requite** you this kindness,
3: 39	the LORD shall **reward** the doer of evil according to his wickedness.
Deut. 7: 10	he will **repay** him to his face.
2 SAM. 2: 16	**wherefore** that place was called Hel-kath-haz-zu-rim, which *is* in Gibeon.
: 7	**Therefore** now let your hands be strengthened,
2 SAM. 2: 23	**Howbeit** he refused to turn aside:
: 21	**But** As-a-hel would not turn aside from following of him.
2 SAM. 2: 22	**wherefore** should I smite thee to the ground?
3: 24	**why** *is* it *that* thou hast sent him away,
2 SAM. 2: 22	wherefore should I **smite** thee to the ground?
Exodus 12: 7	and **strike** *it* on the two side posts and on the upper door post of the houses,
2 SAM. 2: 31	*so that* three hundred and three**score** men died.
Num. 7: 88	the rams **sixty**,

N.B. the underlined word is a numerical term meaning twenty. To find the value of the 'score number' multiply 3x20=60

2 SAM. 3: 1	but David **waxed** stronger, and the house of Saul waxed weaker and weaker.
5: 10	And David went on and **grew** great,
2 SAM. 3: 7	**Wherefore** hast thou gone in unto my father's concubine?
: 24	**why** *is* it *that* thou hast thou sent him away,
2 SAM. 3: 12	Make thy **league** with me,
Isaiah 28: 18	And your **covenant** with death shall be disannulled, and your **agreement** with hell shall not stand;
2 SAM. 3: 27	and **smote** him there under the fifth *rib,*
12: 15	And the LORD **struck** the child that Uriah's wife bare unto David,
2 SAM. 3: 35	And when all the people came to cause David to eat **meat** while it was yet day, David sware, saying, So do God to me, and more also, if I taste **bread,** or ought else, till the sun be down.
9: 10	that thy master's son may have **food** to eat:
2 SAM. 4: 6	And they came **thither** into the midst of the house,
3: 29	and let **there** not fail from the house one that hath an issue,
2 SAM. 4: 9	*As* the LORD liveth, who hath redeemed my soul out of all

	adversity,
1 Kings 1: 29	*As* the LORD liveth, that hath redeemed my soul out of all **distress,**
2 SAM. 5: 2	**Also** in time past, when Saul was king over us,
1 Chron. 11: 2	And **moreover,** in time past, even when Saul was king,
2 SAM. 5: 2	**Also in time past, when** Saul was king over us,
	Also in time past, when Saul was king over us,
	Also **in time past,** when Saul was king over us,
	Also in time past, **when** Saul was king over us,
2 SAM. 5: 2	Thou shalt be **a captain** over Israel.
1 Chron. 11: 2	and thou shalt be **ruler** over my people Israel.
: 3	and they anointed David **king** over Israel,
2 SAM. 5: 3	and king David made a **league** with them in He-bron before the LORD:
1 Chr. 11: 3	and David made a **covenant** with them in He-bron before the LORD;
Isaiah 28: 15	Because ye have said, We have made a covenant with death, and with hell are we at **agreement;**
2 SAM 5: 6	Except thou take away the blind and the lame, thou shalt not come in **hither:**
11: 12	And David said to Uriah, Tarry **here** to day also,
2 SAM. 5: 7	**Nevertheless** David took the strong hold of Zion:
5: 17	**But** when the Philistines heard that they had anointed David king over Israel,
2 SAM. 5: 7	Nevertheless David took the **strong hold** of Zion:
1 Chr. 11: 5	Nevertheless David took the **castle** of Zion,
2 SAM. 5: 12	and that he had **exalted** his kingdom for his people Israel's sake.
1 Chr. 14: 2	for his kingdom **was lifted up** on high,
2 SAM. 5: 21	And there they left their **images,**
1 Chr. 14: 12	And when they had left their **gods,**
2 SAM. 5: 23	And when David enquired of the LORD, he said, Thou shalt not go up; *but* **fetch a compass behind them,** and come upon them against the mulberry trees.
2 Chron. 13: 13	But Jer-o-bo-am caused an ambushment to **come about them:** so they were before Judah, and the ambushment was **behind them.**
2 SAM. 5: 24	then thou shalt **bestir** thyself:

Exodus 11: 7	But against any of the children of Israel shall not a dog **move** his tongue,
2 SAM. 6: 2	to bring up from **thence** the ark of God,
2: 4	and **there** they anointed David king over the house of Judea.
2 SAM. 6: 5	and on **psalteries,** and on timbrels,
Psalm 33: 2	sing unto him with the **psaltery** *and* **an instrument of ten strings.**
2 SAM. 6: 14	and David *was* **girded with a linen ephod.**
1 Chr. 15: 27	And David was **clothed with a robe of fine linen,** ... David also *had* **upon him an ephod of linen.**
2 SAM. 6: 17	And they brought in the ark of the LORD, and set it in his place, in the midst of the **tabernacle** that David had pitched for it:
1 Chron. 16: 1	So they brought the ark of **God,** and set it in the midst of the **tent** that David had pitched for it:
2 SAM. 7: 2	**See now,** I dwell in an house of cedar but the **ark of God dwelleth within curtains.**
1 Chr. 17: 1	**Lo,** I dwell in an house of cedars, the **ark of the covenant of the LORD** *remaineth* **under curtains.**
2 SAM. 7: 4	that the **word of the LORD** came unto Nathan,
1 Chr. 17: 3	that the **word of God** came **to** Nathan,
2 SAM. 7: 6	**Whereas** I have not dwelt in *any* house since the time that I brought up the children of Israel out of Egypt,
1 Chr. 17: 5	**For** I have not dwelt in an house since the day that I brought up Israel unto this day;
2 SAM. 7: 7	In all *the places* **wherein** I have walked with all the children of Israel spake I a word with any of the tribes of Israel,
Judges 4: 14	Up; for this *is* the day **in which** the LORD hath delivered Sis-e-ra into thine hand:
2 SAM. 7: 7	In all *the places* **wherein** I have walked with all the children of Israel spake I a word with any of the tribes of Israel,
1 Chr. 17: 6	**Wheresoever** I have walked with all Israel,
2 SAM. 7: 9	And **I was** with thee whithersoever thou wentest,
1 Chr. 17: 8	And **I have been** with thee whithersoever thou hast walked,
2 SAM. 7: 9	And I was with thee whithersoever **thou wentest,**
1 Chr. 17: 8	And I have been with thee whithersoever **thou hast walked,**
2 SAM.7: 10	**Moreover** I will appoint a place for my people Israel,

1Sam. 26: 10	David said, **furthermore,** *As* the LORD liveth,
1 Chr. 17: 9	**Also** I will ordain a place for my people Israel,

2 SAM. 7: 10	Moreover I will **appoint** a place for my people Israel,
1 Chron. 17: 9	Also I will **ordain** a place for my people Israel,

2 SAM. 7: 10	neither shall the children of wickedness **afflict** them any more, as beforetime,
1 Chron. 17: 9	neither shall the children of wickedness **waste** them any more, as at the beginning,

2 SAM. 7: 10	neither shall the children of wickedness afflict them any more, **as beforetime,**
1 Chr. 17: 9	neither shall the children of wickedness waste them any more, **as at he beginning,**

Lev. 26: 31	And I will make your cities waste, and bring your sanctuaries unto **desolation,**
Ezekiel 36: 35	And they shall say, This land that was desolate is become like the garden of Eden; and the **waste <u>and</u> desolate...**

N.B. note how the underlined word separates words and phrases having the same meaning.

2 SAM. 7: 14	If he commit iniquity, I will **chasten** him with the rod of men,
Psalm 39: 11	When thou with rebukes dost **correct** man for iniquity,
Prov. 17: 26	Also to **punish** the just *is* not good,

2 SAM. 7: 18	and what *is* my house, that thou hast brought me **hitherto?**
11: 12	And David said to Uriah, Tarry **here to day** also,

2 SAM. 7: 22	**Wherefore** thou art great, O LORD God:
: 29	**Therefore** now let it please thee to bless the house of thy servant,

2 SAM. 8: 5	And when the Syrians of Damascus came **to succour** Had-a-de-zer king of Zo-bah,
1 Chr. 18: 5	And when the Syrians of Damascus came **to help** Had-a-de-zer king of Zob-bah,

2 SAM. 8: 8	king David took **exceeding much** brass.
1 Chron. 18: 8	brought David **very much** brass,

2 SAM. 9: 10	Thou therefore, and thy sons, and thy servants shall **till** the land for him,
Deut. 22: 10	Thou shalt not **plow** with an ox and an ass together.

2 SAM. 10: 3	**And** the princes of the children of Ammon said unto Ha-nun their lord,
1 Chr. 19: 5	**But** the princes of the children of Ammon said **to** Ha-run,

2 SAM. 10: 5	and the king said, **Tarry** at Jericho until your beards be grown,
2 Kings 6: 33	what should I **wait** for the LORD any longer?
2 SAM. 10: 6	And when the children of Ammon saw that they **stank** before
David,	
1 Chron.19: 6	And when the children of Ammon saw that they had made
	themselves **odious** to David,
2 SAM. 10: 15	And when the Syrians saw that they were **smitten** before
	Israel,
1 Chron. 19: 16	And when the Syrians saw that they were **put to the worse**
	before Israel,
2 SAM. 11: 8	and there followed him **a mess *of meat*** from the king.
: 19	and a good **piece *of flesh*,**
2 SAM. 11: 20	And if so that the king's wrath arise, and he say unto thee,
	Wherefore approached ye so nigh unto the city when ye
	did fight?
: 21	**why** went ye nigh the wall?
2 SAM. 11: 20	Wherefore approached ye so **nigh** unto the city when ye did
	fight?
14: 30	See, Jo-ab's field is **near** mine,
2 SAM. 12: 2	The rich *man* had **exceeding** many flocks and herds:
1 Chron. 18: 8	brought David **very** much brass,
2 SAM. 12: 8	I would **moreover** have given unto thee such and such things.
1 Sam.26: 10	David said **furthermore,**
2 Sam. 12: 13	The LORD **also** hath put away thy sin;
2 SAM. 12: 9	**Wherefore** hast thou despised the commandment of the
	LORD, to do evil in his sight?
11: 21	**why** went ye nigh the wall?
2 SAM. 12: 9	thou **hast killed** Uriah the Hittite with the sword, and hast
taken his	
	wife *to be* thy wife, and **hast slain** him with the sword of the
	children of Ammon.
2 SAM. 12: 14	**Howbeit, because** by this deed thou hast given great occasion
	to the to the enemies of the LORD to blaspheme,

N.B. note the two bold words which mean the same thing.

2 SAM. 12: 23	But now he is dead, **wherefore** should I fast?
13: 4	And he said unto him, **Why** *art* thou, *being* the king's son,

2 SAM. 12: 30	And he took the king's crown from off his head, the weight
	whereof *was* a talent of gold with the precious stones:
1 Kings 6: 38	and according to all the fashion **of it.**
2 SAM. 12: 31	And he brought forth the people that *were* **therein,**
1 Chr. 20: 3	And he brought out the people that *were* **in it,**
2 Kings 2: 21	and cast the salt **in there,**
2 SAM. 13: 3	and Jon-a-dab *was* a very **subtil** man.
Job 5: 12	He disappointeth the devices of the **crafty,**
2 SAM. 13: 13	And I, **whither** shall I cause my shame to go?
16: 3	And the king said, And **where** *is* thy master's son?
2 SAM. 13: 14	**Howbeit** he would not hearken unto her voice: **but,** being
	stronger than she, forced her, and lay with her.
2 SAM. 13: 15	so that the hatred **wherewith** he hated her *was* greater than the
	love wherewith he had loved her.
2 Kings 19: 6	Be not afraid of the words which thou hast heard **with which**
	the servants of the king of Assyria have blasphemed me.
2 SAM. 13: 18	And *she had* a garment of **divers** colours upon her:
22: 17	he drew me out of **many** waters;
Esther 1: 7	And they gave *them* drink in vesselsof gold, (the vessels being
	diverse one from another,)
2 SAM. 13: 18	for with such robes were the king's daughters **apparelled.**
1: 24	who **clothed** you in scarlet,
1 Kings 11: 29	and he had **clad** himself with a new garment;
2 SAM. 13: 21	But when king David heard of all these things, he was very
	wroth.
19: 42	wherefore then be ye **angry** for this matter?
2 SAM. 13: 24	let the king, **I beseech thee,** and his servants go with thy
	servant.
: 26	Then said Absalom, If not, **I pray thee,**
2 SAM. 13: 25	And he pressed him: **howbeit** he would not go, **but** blessed
	him.
2 SAM. 13: 28	and when I say unto you, **Smite** Amnon; then **kill him,**
2 SAM. 13: 30	that tidings came to David, saying, Absalom **hath slain** all the
	king's sons.
Num. 31: 19	whosoever **hath killed** any person,
2 SAM. 13: 31	Then the king arose, and tare his **garments,** and lay on the
	earth; and all his servants stood by with their **clothes** rent.

2 SAM. 13: 32	Let not my lord **suppose** *that* they have slain all the young men the king's sons;
: 33	let not my lord the king take the thing to his heart, **to think** that all the the king's sons are dead:
2 SAM. 14: 2	and put on mourning **apparel,** and anoint not thyself with oil,
13: 31	Then the king arose, and tare his **garments,** and lay on the earth; and all his servants stood by with their **clothes** rent.
2 SAM. 14: 2	I pray thee, **feign thyself** to be a mourner, and put on now mourning apparel, and anoint not thyself with oil, but **be as** a woman that had a long time mourned for the dead:
2 SAM. 14: 4	And when the woman of Te-ko-ah spake to the king, **she fell on her face to the ground, <u>and</u> did obeisance,**

N.B. note how the underlined word separates words and phrases having the same meaning.

2 SAM. 14: 13	And the woman said, **Wherefore then** hast thou thought such a thing against the people of God?
13: 26	And the king said unto him, **Why** should he go with thee?
2 SAM. 14: 22	To day thy servant knoweth that I have found **grace** in thy sight,
15: 25	if I shall find **favour** in the eyes of the LORD,
2 SAM. 14: 27	and one daughter, whose name *was* Ta-mar: she was a woman of a fair **countenance.**
: 33	and bowed himself on his **face** to the ground before the king:
2 SAM. 14: 31	**Wherefore** have thy servants set my field on fire?
13: 26	**Why** should he go with thee?
2 SAM 14: 32	Behold, I sent unto thee, Come **hither,**
18: 30	And the king said *unto him,* Turn aside, *and* stand **here.**
2 SAM. 15: 4	Absalom said **moreover,** O that I were made judge in the land,
: 19	Wherefore goest thou **also?**
1 Chron. 17: 10	**Moreover** I will subdue all thine enemies. **Furthermore** I tell thee that the LORD will build thee an house.
2 SAM. 15: 5	And it was *so,* that when any man came nigh *to him* **to do obeisance,** he put forth his hand, and took him, and kissed him.
14: 4	And when the woman of Te-ko-ah spake to the king, she **fell on her face to the ground, <u>and</u> did obeisance,**

| 9: 6 | the son of Saul, was come unto David, he **fell on his face, and did reverence.** |

N.B. note how the underlined verses separate words and phrases having the same meaning.

| **2 SAM. 15: 11** | *that were* called; **and they went in their simplicity, and they knew not any thing.** |

N.B. note how the underlined word separates words and phrases having the same meaning.

2 SAM. 15: 17	And the king went forth, and all his household after him, and **tarried** in a place that was far off.
17: 17	Now Jonathan and A-hi-ma-az **stayed** by En-ro-gel;
1 Kings 20: 38	So the prophet departed, and **waited** for the king by the way,

| **2 SAM. 15: 19** | **Wherefore** goest thou also with us? |
| 16: 9 | **Why** should this dead dog curse my lord the king? |

| **2 SAM. 15: 20** | **Whereas** thou camest *but* yesterday, |

N.B. note how the underlined word gives the meaning of the entire word.

| **2 SAM. 15: 20** | seeing I go **whither** I may, return thou, |
| : 32 | that *when* David was come to the top *of the mount,* **where** he worshipped God, |

2 SAM. 15: 28	See, I will **tarry** in the plain of the wilderness,
: 19	return to thy place, and **abide** with the king:
1 Samuel 22: 8	to lie in **wait,** as at this day?

| **2 SAM. 15: 28** | until they come a word from you to **certify** me. |
| 12: 18 | And the servants of David feared to **tell** him... |

| 2 Sam. 15: 34 | O king; *as I have been* thy father's servant **hitherto,** |
| 19: 7 | and that will be worse unto thee all the evil that befell thee from thy **until now.** |

| **2 SAM. 16: 4** | And Zi-ba said, I humbly **beseech thee** *that* I may find grace in thy sight, my lord, O king. |
| : 9 | let me go over, I **pray thee,** and take off his head. |

| **2 SAM. 16: 4** | And Zi-ba said, I humbly beseech thee *that* I may find **grace** in thy sight, |
| 15: 25 | if I shall find **favour** in the eyes of the LORD, |

| **2 SAM. 16: 5** | behold, **thence** came out a man of the family of the house of Saul, |
| : 14 | came weary, and refreshed themselves **there.** |

2 SAM. 16: 10	Who shall then say, **Wherefore** hast thou done so?
: 9	**Why** should this dead dog curse my lord the king?
2 SAM. 16: 12	and that the LORD will **requite** me good for his cursing this day.
Job 21: 31	and who shall **repay** him *what* he hath done?
2 SAM. 16: 18	his I will be, and with him will I **abide**.
24: 16	It is enough: **stay** now thine hand.
2 SAM. 16: 21	and all Israel shall hear that thou art **abhorred** of thy father:
13: 22	for Absalom **hated** Amnon,
2 SAM. 17: 2	and all the people that *are* with him shall flee; and I will **smite** the king only:
2 Kings 5: 11	and call on the name of the LORD his God, and **strike** his hand upon the place,
2 SAM. 17: 5	Call now Hu-shai the Ar-chite **also**, and let us hear **likewise** what he saith.
2 SAM. 17: 13	**Moreover,** if he be gotten into a city,
1 Sam. 26: 13	David said **furthermore,**
2 Sam. 17: 10	And he **also** *that* is valiant,
2 SAM. 17: 17	and a **wench** went and told them,
14: 19	and he put all these words in the mouth of thine **handmaid:**
2 SAM. 17: 18	**Nevertheless** a lad saw them, and told Absalom: **but** they went both of them away quickly,
2 SAM. 17: 18	which had a well in his court; **whither** they went down.
15: 32	**where** he worshipped God,
2 SAM. 17: 19	and spread ground corn **thereon;** and the thing was not known.
Leviticus 6: 12	and the priest shall burn wood **on it** every morning, and lay the burnt offering in order **upon it;** and he shall burn **thereon** the fat of the peace offerings.
2 SAM. 17: 28	and barley, and flour, and **parched** *corn,* and beans, and parched *pulse,*
Leviticus 2: 14	thy firstfruits green ears of **corn dried by the fire,**
2 Chron. 35: 13	And they **roasted** the passover with fire according to the ordinance:
2 SAM. 17: 29	And honey, and butter, and sheep, and cheese of **kine,**
Leviticus 22: 28	And *whether it be* **cow** or ewe,
2 SAM. 18: 3	therefore *it is* better that thou **succour** us out of the city.

1 Chron. 12: 17	If ye come peaceably unto to me to **help** me,
2 SAM. 18: 25	If he *be* alone *there is* tidings in his mouth. And he **came apace, and drew near.**

N.B. note how the underlined word separates words and phrases having the same meaning.

2 SAM. 19: 12	Ye *are* my brethren, ye *are* my bones and my flesh: **wherefore** then are ye the last to bring the king back?
: 36	and **why** should the king recompense it me with such a reward?
2 SAM. 19: 19	And said unto the king, Let not my lord **impute** iniquity unto me,
24: 1	and he moved David against them to say, Go, number Israel and Judah.
Numbers 4: 32	and by name ye shall **reckon** the instruments of the charge of their burden.
23:10	Who can **count** the dust of Jacob...?
2 SAM. 19: 26	I will saddle me an ass, that I may ride **thereon,** and go to the king;
Leviticus 6: 12	and the priest shall burn wood **on it** every morning, and lay the burnt offering in order **upon it;** and he shall burn **thereon** the fat of the peace offerings.
2 SAM. 19: 32	Now Bar-zil-la-i was a very **aged** man, *even* fourscore years **old:**
2 SAM. 19: 32	Now Bar-zil-la-i was a very aged man, *even* four**score** years old:
Genesis 5: 28	And La-mech lived an hundred **eighty** and two years,

N.B. The underlined word is a numerical term meaning twenty. To find the value of the 'score' number multiply the number by twenty 4x20=80.

2 SAM. 19: 36	and why should the king **recompense** it me with a reward?
1 Sam. 24: 19	wherefore the LORD **reward** thee good for that thou hast done unto me this day.
2 SAM. 19: 42	**wherefore** then be angry for the matter?
: 43	**why** then did you despise us..?
2 SAM. 20: 3	whom he had left to keep the house, and **put them in ward,** and fed them, but went not into them.
Genesis 40: 3	And he **put them in ward** in the house of the captain of the captain of the guard, **into the prison,**

2 SAM. 20: 5	So A-ma-sa went to assemble *the men of* Judah: but he **tarried** longer than the set time which he had appointed.
17: 17	Now Jonathan and A-hi-ma-az **stayed** by En-ro-gel;
Exodus 32: 1	And when the people saw that Moses **delayed** to come down out of the mount,
2 SAM. 20: 10	so he **smote** him therewith in the fifth *rib,* and shed out his bowels to the ground, and **struck** him not again;
2 SAM. 20: 18	Then she spake, saying, They were **wont to speak** in old time,
Exodus 21: 29	But if the ox **were wont to** push with his horn **in time past,**
Jerem. 13: 23	*then* may ye also do good, that are **accustomed** to do evil.
2 SAM. 21: 3	**Wherefore** David said unto the Gibeonites, What shall I do for you? and wherewith shall I make the atonement, that ye may bless he inheritance of the LORD?
22: 50	**Therefore** I will give thanks unto thee, O LORD,
2 SAM. 21: 3	and **wherewith** shall I make the atonement, that ye may bless the inheritance of the LORD?
Ex. 10: 26	and we know not **with what** we must serve the LORD, until we come thither.
2 SAM. 21: 10	and **suffered** neither the birds of the air to rest on them by day,
: 6	**Let** seven men of his sons be delivered unto us,
2 SAM. 21: 13	And he bought up from **thence** the bones of Saul and the bones of Jonathan his son;
: 18	And it came to pass after this, that **there** was again a battle with the Philistines at God:
2 SAM. 21: 15	**Moreover** the Philistines had yet war again with Israel;
1 Sam. 26: 10	David said **furthermore,**
2 SAM. 21: 17	But Ab-i-shai the son of Zer-u-i-ah **succoured him,**
1 Kings 1: 7	and they following Ad-o-ni-jah **helped *him.***
2 SAM. 22: 6	The sorrows of hell **compassed me,** floods of ungodly men made me afraid;
Psalm 22: 12	strong *bulls* of Ba-shan have **beset me round.**
: 16	the assembly of the wicked have **inclosed me:**
2 SAM. 22: 6	the snares of death **prevented me;**
Psalm 68: 25	The singers **went before,** the players,
Psalm 88: 2	Let my prayer **come before thee:**
: 13	and in the morning shall my prayer **prevent thee.**
2 SAM. 22: 8	Then the **earth shook <u>and</u> trembled; the foundations of**

heaven moved <u>and</u> shook,

N.B. note how the underlined words separate words and phrases having the same meaning.

<u>**2 SAM. 22: 21**</u>	The LORD **rewarded me** according to my righteousness: according to the cleanness of my hands hath he **recompensed me.**
<u>**2 SAM. 22: 27**</u>	and with the **froward** thou wilt shew thyself unsavoury.
Deut. 32: 5	*they are* a **perverse and crooked** generation.
1 Kings 8: 32	condemning the **wicked,**
1 Sam. 20: 30	And he said unto him, Thou son of the **perverse rebellious** *women,*
<u>**2 SAM. 22: 28**</u>	but thine eyes *are* upon the **haughty,** *that* thou mayest bring *them* down.
Job 40: 11	and behold every one *that is* **proud,**
<u>**2 SAM. 22: 31**</u>	the word of the LORD *is* tried: he *is* a **buckler** to all them that trust in him.
: 36	Thou hast also given me the **shield** of thy salvation:
<u>**2 SAM. 23: 6**</u>	But *the* **sons** of **Belial** *shall be* all of them as thorns thrust away,
22: 5	the floods of **ungodly men** made me afraid;
<u>**2 SAM. 23: 16**</u>	and took *it,* and brought *it* to David: **nevertheless** he would not drink thereof,
1 Chron. 11: 18	**but** David would not drink *of* it,
<u>**2 SAM. 23: 16**</u>	nevertheless he would not drink **thereof,**
1 Chron. 11: 18	but David would not drink **of it,**
<u>**2 SAM. 24: 3**</u>	how many soever they be, an hundred**fold,**
1 Chron. 21: 3	The LORD make his people and hundred **times** so many as they *be:*
<u>**2 SAM. 24: 10**</u>	And David's heart **smote** him after that he had numbered the people.
20: 10	and **struck** him not again;
<u>**2 SAM. 24: 10**</u>	and now, **I beseech thee,** O LORD, take away the iniquity of thy servant;
: 17	let thine hand, **I pray thee,** be against me,
<u>**2 SAM. 24: 13**</u>	or that there be three days' **pestilence** in thy land?
: 21	that the **plague** may be stayed from the people.
<u>**2 SAM. 24: 14**</u>	And David said unto Gad, I am in a great **strait:**

22: 7	In my **distress** I called upon the LORD,
Job 15: 24	**Trouble and anguish** shall make him afraid;

2 SAM. 24: 17 and said, Lo, **I have sinned, and I have done wickedly:**

N.B. note how the underlined word separates words and phrases having the same meaning.

2 SAM. 24: 21	And A-rau-nah said, **Wherefore** is my lord the king come to his servant?
19: 36	and **why** should the king recompense it me with such a reward?

2 SAM. 24: 24	Nay; but I will **surely** buy*it* of thee at a price:
1 Chron. 21: 24	Nay; but I will **verily** buy it for the full price:
1 Sam. 20: 3	Thy father **certainly**...but **truly** *as* the LORD liveth,

1 KINGS

1 KINGS 1: 2	**Wherefore** his servants said unto him, Let there be sought for my lord the king a young virgin:
: 12	Now **therefore** come, let me, I pray thee, give thee counsel,

1 KINGS 1:2	Wherefore his servants said unto him, Let there be **sought** for my lord the king a young virgin:
2 Sam. 24: 20	And A-rau-nah **looked,** and saw the king and his servants coming on toward him:
Job 5: 27	Lo this, we have **searched** it,

1 KINGS 1: 9	And Ad-o-ni-jah **slew** sheep and oxen and fat cattle by the stone Zo-he-leth,
: 19	And he **hath slain** oxen and fat cattle and sheep in abundance,
16: 7	because he **killed** him.
1 KINGS 1: 16	And Bath-she-ba **bowed, and did obeisance** unto the king.
: 31	Then Bath-she-ba **bowed with *her* face to the earth, and did reverence** to the king,

N.B. note how the underlined words separate words and phrases having the same meaning.

1 KINGS 1: 30 Even as I sware unto thee by the LORD God of Israel, saying, **Assuredly** Solomon thy son shall reign after me, and he shall sit upon my throne in my stead; even so will I **certainly** do this day.

1 KINGS 1: 31 Then Bath-she-ba **bowed with *her* face to the earth, and did reverence to the king,** and said, Let my lord king David live for ever.

N.B. note how the underlined word separates words and phrases having the same

meaning.

1 KINGS 1: 41	**Wherefore** *is this* noise of the city being in an uproar?
: 6	**Why** hast thou done so?

1 KINGS 1: 43	And Jonathan answered and said to Ad-o-ni-jah, **Verily** our lord king
	David hath made Solomon king.
2: 43	and walkest abroad any whither, that thou shalt **surely** die?
1 Sam. 20: 3	Thy father **certainly** knoweth that I have found grace in thine eyes; and he saith, Let not Jonathan know this, lest he be grieved: but **truly** the LORD liveth,

1 KINGS 1: 45	and they are come up from **thence** rejoicing,
: 52	**there** shall not an hair of him fall to the earth:

1 KINGS 1: 45	and they are come up from **thence** rejoicing,
: 14	Behold, while thou yet talkest **there** with the king,

1 KINGS 1: 47	And **moreover** the king's servants came to bless our lord king David,
: 48	And **also** thus said the king,
1 Samuel 26: 10	David said **furthermore,**

1 KINGS 2: 15	that I should reign: **howbeit** the kingdom is turned about,
2: 26	**but** I will not at this time put thee to death,

1 KINGS 2: 36	Build thee an house in Jerusalem, and dwell **there,** and go not forth **thence** any whither.

1 KINGS 2: 36	and go not forth thence any **whither.**
4: 28	brought they unto the place **where** *the officers* were,

1 KINGS 3: 1	And Solomon **made affinity** with Pharaoh king of Egypt,
7: 8	Solomon made also an house for Pharaoh's daughter, whom he **had taken** *to wife*,

1 KINGS 3: 5	according as he walked before thee **in truth, and** in righteous- **and** in uprightness of heart with thee;

N.B. note how the underlined words separate words and phrases having the same meaning.

1 KINGS 3: 8	a great people, that cannot be **numbered nor counted** for multitude.

N.B. note how the comma separates words and phrases having the same meaning.

1 KINGS 3: 27	Then the king answered and said, Give her the living child, and in no wise slay it: she *is* the mother **thereof.**
6: 38	and according to all the fashion **of it.**

1 KINGS 3: 27	Give her the living child, and in no wise **slay it:**
Lev. 22: 28	And *whether it be* cow or ewe, ye shall not **kill it** and her both in one day.
1 KINGS 4: 7	which provided **victuals** for the king and his household:
5: 9	and thou shalt accomplish my desire, in giving **food** for my household.
1 KINGS 4: 13	which *is* in Ba-shan, three**score** great cities with walls and brazen bars.
Genesis 5: 27	And all the days of Methuselah were nine hundred **sixty** and nine years:

N.B. The underlined word is numerical term meaning twenty. To find the value of the 'score' number multiply 3x20=60.

1 KINGS 4: 28	Barley also and straw for the horses and **dromedaries** brought they unto the place where *the offices were,* every man according to his charge.
1 Kings 10: 2	And she came to Jerusalem with a very great train, with **camels** that bare spices,
1 KINGS 5: 4	*so that there is* neither adversary nor evil **occurrant.**
: 5	And, behold, I **purpose** to build an house unto the name of the LORD my God,
Eccl. 9: 11	but time and **chance** happeneth to them all.
1 KINGS 5: 12	and there was peace between Hiram and Solomon; and they two made a **league** together.
Isaiah 28: 15	We have made a **covenant** with death, and with hell we are at **agreement;**
1 KINGS 5: 15	And Solomon had **threescore** and ten thousand that bare burdens,
Lev. 27: 7	And if *it be* from **sixty** years old,

N.B. The underlined word is a numerical term meaning twenty. To find the value of the 'score' number multiply by twenty, 3x20=60.

1 KINGS 5: 15	and four**score** thousand hewers in the mountains;
Genesis 5: 28	And La-mech lived an hundred **eighty** and two years,

N.B. The underlined word is a numerical term meaning twenty. To find the value of the 'score' number multiply by twenty, 4x20=80.

1 KINGS 5: 18	so they **prepared** timber and stones to build the house.
6: 7	was built of stone **made ready** before it was brought thither:
1 KINGS 6: 3	And the porch **before** the temple of the house,

2 Chron. 3: 4	And the porch **that *was* in the front** *of the house,*
1 KINGS 6: 3	And the porch before the temple of the house, twenty cubits *was* the length **thereof,**
2 Chron. 3: 4	And the porch that *was* in the front *of the house,* the length *of it was* according to the breadth of the house,
1 KINGS 6: 6	The **nethermost** chamber *was* five cubits broad,
Isaiah 22: 9	and ye gathered together the waters of the **lower** pool.
Ezekiel 40: 7	and so increased *from* the **lowest** *chamber* to the highest by the midst.
1 KINGS 6: 7	And the house, when it was in building, was built of stone made ready made ready before it was brought **thither:** so that **there** was neither hammer nor axe *nor* any tool of iron heard in the house,
1 KINGS 6: 15	And he built the walls of the house **within** with boards of cedar, both the floor of the house, and the walls of the cieling: *and* he covered *them* on the **inside** with wood,
1 KINGS 6: 15	*and* he **covered** *them* on the inside with wood,
: 21	So Solomon **overlaid** the house within with pure gold:
1 KINGS 6: 15	And he built the walls of the house **within** the boards of cedar, both the floor of the house, and the walls of the cieling: and he covered *them* on the **inside** with wood,
1 KINGS 6: 16	he even built *them* for it within, *even* for the **oracle,** even for **the most holy** *place.*
2 Chron. 3: 8	And he made **the most holy house,**
1 KINGS 6: 20	and twenty cubits in breadth, and twenty cubits in the height **thereof:**
: 38	the house was finished throughout all the parts **thereof,** and according to all the fashion **of it.**
1 KINGS 6: 20	and he **overlaid it** with pure gold; and *so* **covered** the altar *which was* of cedar.
1 KINGS 6: 31	the **lintel** *and* side posts *were* a fifth part *of the wall.*
Exodus 12: 7	and on the **upper door post** of the houses,
1 KINGS 6: 38	which *is* the eighth month, was the house finished throughout
all the	parts **thereof,** and according to all the fashion **of it.**
1 KINGS 7: 9	within and **without,** even from the foundation unto the coping, and *so* on the **outside** toward the great court.

| **1 KINGS 7: 13** | and understanding, and **cunning** to work all works in brass. |
| 2 Chron. 2:14 | and his father *was* a man of Tyre, **skilful** to work in gold, |

1 KINGS 7: 15	For he cast **two** pillars of brass, of eighteen cubits high **apiece:**
6: 5	***both*** of the temple and of the oracle:
: 23	***each*** ten cubits high.

| **1 KINGS 7: 16** | And he made two cha<u>p</u>iters *of* molten brass, to set upon **the tops of the pillars:** |
| : 19 | And the **chapiters that *were* on the top of the pillars** *were* of lily work in the porch, |

N.B. note the underlined letters which form the word **'caps'** thus giving the meaning of the whole word.

| **1 KINGS 7: 26** | and the brim **thereof** was wrought like the brim of a cup, |
| : 27 | and four cubits the breadth thereof, and three cubits the height **of it.** |

| **1 KINGS 7: 26** | and the brim thereof was **wrought** like the brim of a cup, |
| : 27 | And he **made** ten bases of brass; |

| **1 KINGS 7: 31** | And **the mouth of it** within the chapiter and above *was* a cubit: but **the mouth thereof** *was* round *after* the work of the base, |

| **1 KINGS 7: 31** | And the mouth of it **within** the chapiter and above *was* a cubit: |
| 6: 15 | *and* he covered *them* on the **inside** with wood, |

| **1 KINGS 7: 33** | and **their felloes, <u>and</u> their spokes,** *were* all molten. |

N.B. note how the underlined word separates words and phrases having the same meaning.

| **1 KINGS 7: 41** | The two pillars, and the *two* bowls of the cha<u>p</u>iters that *were* **on the top of** the two pillars; |

N.B. note how the bold underlined letters in order spell the meaning of the whole word.

| **1 KINGS 7: 48** | and the table of gold, **whereupon** the showbread *was,* |
| 2 Kings 1: 4 | Thou shalt not come down from that bed **on which** thou art gone up, |

| **1 KINGS 7: 51** | So **was** ended all the work that king Solomon made for the house of the LORD. |
| 2 Chron. 5: 1 | **Thus** all the work that Solomon made for the house of the LORD was finished: |

| **1 KINGS 7: 51** | So **was ended** all the work that king Solomon made for the house of the LORD. |

2 Chron. 5: 1	Thus all the work that king Solomon made for the house of the LORD **was finished.**
1 KINGS 8: 5	that could **be told nor numbered** for multitude.

N.B. note how the underlined word separates words and phrases having the same meaning.

1 KINGS 8: 6	And the priests brought in the ark of the covenant of the LORD unto
	his place, into the oracle of the house, to the most holy place, *even* under the wings of the cherubims.
6: 16	he built *them* for it within, *even* **for the oracle,** *even* **for the most holy** *place.*
2 Chron. 3: 8	And he made **the most holy house,**
1 KINGS 8: 7	For the cherubims spread forth *their* two wings **over** the place of the ark, and the staves thereof **above.**
1 KINGS 8: 7	and the cherubims covered the ark and the staves **thereof** above.
7: 27	and four cubits the breadth **thereof,** and three cubits the height **of it.**
1 KINGS 8: 8	and they were not seen **without:**
7: 9	and *so* on the **outside** toward the great court.
1 KINGS 8: 9	*There was* nothing in the ark save the two tables of stone, which Moses put **there** at Horeb,
2 Chron . 5: 10	*There was* nothing in the ark save the two tables of stone, which Moses *therein* at Horeb,
1 KINGS 8: 12	Then **spake** Solomon, The LORD **said** that he would dwell in the thick darkness.
2 Chron. 6: 1	Then **said** Solomon, The LORD said that he would dwell in the thick darkness.
1 KINGS 8: 13	I have surely built thee an house **to dwell in,** a settled place for thee **to abide in,** for ever.
1 KINGS 8: 16	that my name might be **therein;**
2 Chr. 6: 6	that my name might be **there;**
2 Kings 7: 13	they *are* as all the multitude of Israel that are left **in it:**
2: 21	and cast the salt **in there,**
1 KINGS 8: 18	And the LORD said unto David my father, **Whereas** it was in thine heart to build an house unto my name,
2 Chron. 6: 8	But the LORD said to David my father, **Forasmuch as** it was in thine heart to build an house for my name,

N.B. note the underlined words which gives the meaning of the whole word.

<u>**1 KINGS 8: 19**</u>	**Nevertheless** thou shalt not build the house;
2 Chron. 6: 9	**Notwithstanding** thou shalt not build the house;

<u>**1 KINGS 8: 19**</u>	he shall build the house **unto** my name.
2 Chron. 6: 10	and have built the house **for** the name of the LORD GOD of Israel.

<u>**1 KINGS 8: 20**</u>	And the LORD hath performed his word that **he spake,**
2 Chron. 8: 10	The LORD therefore hath performed his word that **he hath spoken:**

<u>**1 KINGS 8: 21**</u>	And I have set there a place for the ark, **wherein** *is* the covenant of LORD,
Job 3: 3	Let the day perish **wherein** I was born, and the night *in which* it was said, There is a man child conceived.
Isaiah 66: 4	but they did evil before mine eyes, and chose *that* **in which** I delighted not.

<u>**1 KINGS 8: 22**</u>	And **Solomon** stood before the altar of the LORD...
2 Chron. 6: 12	And **he** stood before the altar of the LORD...

<u>**1 KINGS 8: 26**</u>	And now, O God of Israel, let thy word, I pray thee, **be verified,**
Genesis 42: 16	and ye shall be kept in prison, that your words may **be proved,**

<u>**1 KINGS 8: 27**</u>	behold, the heaven and heaven of heavens cannot contain thee; how much less this house **that I have builded?**
2 Chron. 6: 18	behold, the heaven of heavens cannot contain thee; how much less this **which I have built!**

<u>**1 KINGS 8: 28**</u>	Yet have thou respect **unto** the prayer of thy servant,
2 Chron. 6: 19	Have respect therefore **to** the prayer of thy servant,

<u>**1 KINGS 8: 31**</u>	If any man **trespass** against his neighbour,
2 Chron. 6: 22	If a man **sin** against his neighbour,

<u>**1 KINGS 8: 31**</u>	and an oath be laid upon him **to cause** him to swear,
2 Chron. 6: 22	and an oath be laid upon him **to make** him swear,

<u>**1 KINGS 8: 32**</u>	Then hear thou from heaven, and do, and judge thy servants, **condemning** the wicked, to bring his way upon his head;
2 Chron. 6: 23	Then hear thou from heaven, and do, and judge thy servants, by **requiting** the wicked, by **recompensing** his way upon his own head,

<u>**1 KINGS 8: 33**</u>	When thy people Israel **be smitten** down before the enemy,
2 Chron. 6: 24	And if thy people Israel **be put to the worse** before the enemy,

<u>**1 KINGS 8: 33**</u>	and shall turn again to thee, and confess thy name, **pray, <u>and</u> supplication** unto thee in this house:

N.B. note how the underlined word separates words and phrases having the same meaning.

<u>**1 KINGS 8: 37**</u>	If there be in the land famine, if there be **pestilence,** blasting, mildew, locust, *or* if there be caterpillar; if their enemy besiege them in the land of their cities; whatsoever **plague,** whatsoever **sickness** *there be;*

<u>**1 KINGS 8: 41**</u>	**Moreover** concerning a stranger,
9: 21	whom the children of Israel **also** were not able utterly to destroy,
1 Sam. 26: 10	David said **furthermore,** *As* the LORD liveth,

<u>**1 KINGS 8: 44**</u>	If thy people go out to **battle** against their enemy, whithersoever thou shalt send them,
2 Chron. 6: 34	If thy people go out to **war** against their enemies by the way that thou shalt send them,

<u>**1 KINGS 8: 44**</u>	If thy people go out to battle against their enemy, **whithersoever** thou shalt send them,
2 Chron. 6: 34	If thy people go out to war against their enemies **by the way that** thou shalt send them,

<u>**1 KINGS 8: 47**</u>	*Yes* if they shall **bethink** themselves in the land whither they were carried captive, and **repent, and make supplication** unto thee in the land that carried them captive, saying, We have sinned, and have sinned, and have done perversely, we committed wickedness;
: 48	**And** *so* **return unto thee with all their heart, nd with all their soul,**
2 Chron. 6: 37	and turn and pray unto thee in the land of captivity, saying, **We have sinned, we have done amiss, and have dealt wickedly;**

<u>**1 KINGS 8: 47**</u>	*Yes* if they shall bethink themselves in the land **whither** they were carried captive,
7: 7	Then he made a porch for the throne **where** he might judge,

<u>**1 KINGS 8: 49**</u>	Then hear thou **their prayer <u>and</u> their supplication** in heaven thy dwelling place,

N.B. note how the underlined word separates words and phrases having the same meaning.

<u>**1 KINGS 8: 50**</u>	And forgive thy people that have sinned against thee, and all their transgressions **wherein** they have transgressed thee,

Judges 4: 14	for this is the day **in which** the LORD hath delivered Sis-e-ra into into thine hand:
1 KINGS 8: 54	**And it was** *so,* that **when** Solomon had made an end of praying all this prayer and supplication unto the LORD,
2 Chron. 7: 1	Now **when** Solomon had made an end of praying,
1 KINGS 8: 57	The LORD our God be with us, as he was with our fathers: **let him not leave us, nor forsake us:**

N.B. note how the underlined word separates words and phrases having the same meaning.

1 KINGS 8: 59	And let these my words, **wherewith** I have made supplication before the LORD,
2 Kings 19: 6	Be not afraid of the words **with which** the servants of the king of Assyria have blasphemed me.
1 KINGS 9: 3	which thou hast built, to put thy name there **for ever;** and mine eyes and mine heart shall be there **perpetually.**
1 KINGS 9: 14	And Hiram sent to the king **sixscore** talents of gold.
10: 10	And she gave the king an **hundred and twenty** talents of gold,

N.B. The underlined word is a numerical term meaning twenty. To find the value of the 'score' number multiply the number 6x20=120.

1 KINGS 9: 17	And Solomon built Ge-zer, and Beth-hor-on the **nether,**
12: 31	and made priests of the **lowest** of the people,
2 Chron. 9: 27	and cedar made he as the sycamore trees that *are* in the **low** plains in abundance.
1 KINGS 9: 28	And they came to O-phir, and fetched from **thence** gold,
: 3	which thou hast built, to put my name **there** for ever:
1 KINGS 10: 2	And she came to Jerusalem with **a very great train,** with camels that bare spices, and very much gold,
2 Chron. 9: 1	with a **very great company,** and camels that bare spices,
1 KINGS 10: 2	And she came to Jerusalem with a very great train, with camels that bare spices, and **very much gold,**
2 Chron. 9: 1	and camels that bare spices, and **gold in abundance,**
1 KINGS 10: 5	and his **ascent** by which he **went up** into the house of the LORD;
1 KINGS 10: 7	**Howbeit** I believed not the words,

9: 24   **But** Pharaoh's daughter came up out of the city of David...

1 KINGS 10: 14   Now the weight of gold that came to Solomon in one year
                       was sixteen hundred three**score** and six talents of gold,
Lev. 27: 7   And if *it be* from **sixty** years old,

N.B. The underlined word is a numerical term meaning. To find the value of the
'score' number multiply 3x20=60+6=66.

1 KINGS 10: 15   Beside *that he had* of the merchantmen, and of the **traffick**
                       of the spice merchants,
Genesis 34: 10   and the land shall be before you; dwell and **trade** ye therein,

1 KINGS 10: 18   **Moreover** the king made a great throne of ivory,
1 Chron. 17: 10   Moreover I will subdue all thine enemies. **Furthermore** I
                       tell thee that the LORD will build thee an house.

1 KINGS 10: 23   So king Solomon **exceeded** all the kings of the earth for riches
                       and for wisdom.
2 Chron. 9: 22   And king Solomon **passed** all the kings of the earth in riches
                       and wisdom.

1 KINGS 10: 27   made he *to be* as the sycamore trees that *are* in the **vale**,
2 Chron. 9: 27   and cedar trees made he as the sycamore trees that *are* in the
                       low plains in abundance.

1 KINGS 11: 11   **Wherefore** the LORD said unto Solomon, Forasmch as this
                       is done of thee,
            : 12   **Notwithstanding** in thy days I will not do it for David thy
                       father's sake: *but* I will rend it out of the hand of thy son.

            : 13   **Howbeit** I wil l give one tribe to thy son for David my
                       servant's sake,
            : 22   Then Pharaoh said unto him, **But** what hast thou lacked with
                       me,

1 KINGS 11: 15   For it came to pass, David was in Edom, and Jo-ab the captain
                       of the host was gone up to bury **the slain**, after he had smitten
                       every male in Edom,
1 Kings 3: 23   Then said the king, The one saith, This *is* my son that liveth,
                       and thy son *is* **the dead**:

1 KINGS 11: 15   For it came to pass, David was in Edom, and Jo-ab the captain
                       of the captain of the host was gone up to bury the slain, after
                       he **had smitten** every male in Edom,
2 Chron. 25: 3   that he slew his servants that **had killed** the king his father.

1 KINGS 11: 18   which gave him an house, and appointed him **victuals**, and
                       gave him land.
            5 : 9   and thou shalt accomplish my desire, in giving **food** for my

143

household.

1 KINGS 11: 22 Then Pharaoh said unto him, **But** what hast thou lacked with me, that, behold, thou seekest to go to thine own country? And he answered, Nothing: **howbeit** let me go in any wise.

1 KINGS 11: 24 and dwelt **therein,** and reigned in Damascus.
2 Kings 2: 21 and cast the salt **in there,**
7: 13 (behold, they *are* as all the multitude of Israel that are left **in it:** behold…)

1 KINGS 11: 25 and he **abhorred** Israel, and reigned over Syria.
2 Samuel 22: 18 *and* from them that **hated** me:

1 KINGS 11: 34 **Howbeit** I will not take the whole kingdom out of his hand: **but** I will make him prince all the days of his life for David my my servant's sake,

1 KINGS 12: 9 And he said unto them, **What counsel** give ye that we may answer this people,
2 Chron. 10: 9 And he said unto them, **What advice** give ye that we may return an answer to this people,

1 KINGS 12: 9 And he said unto them, What counsel give ye that we may answer this people, **who** have spoken to me saying, Make the yoke **which** thy father did put upon us lighter?
2 Chron. 10: 9 What advice give ye that we may return answer to this people **which** have spoken to me, saying, Ease somewhat the yoke **that** thy father put upon us?

1 KINGS 12: 10 Thus shalt thou **speak** unto this people that spake unto thee,
2 Chron. 10: 10 Thus shalt thou **answer** the people that spake unto thee,

1 KINGS 12: 14 My father made your yoke heavy, and I will add **to** your yoke:
1 Chron. 10: 14 My father made your yoke heavy, but I will add **thereto:**
2 Kings 18: 4 unto those days the children of Israeldid burn incense **to it:**

1 KINGS 12: 15 **Wherefore** the king hearkened not unto the people;
: 24 They hearkened **therefore** to the word of the LORD,
2 Chron. 10: 15 **So** the king hearkened not unto the people:

1 KINGS 12: 15 for the cause was from the LORD, **that** he might perform his saying, **which** the LORD spake by A-hi-jah the Shi-lo-nite unto Jer-o-bo-am the son of Nebat.

1 KINGS 12: 21 And when Re-ho-bo-am was come to Jerusalem, he **assembled all** the house of Judah.
2 Chron. 11: 1 And when Re-ho-bo-am was come to Jerusalem, he **gathered** of the house of Judah…

144

1 KINGS 12: 21	with the tribe of Benjamin, an hundred and **fourscore** thousand men.
Genesis 5: 28	And La-mech lived an hundred **eighty** and two years,

N.B. The underlined word is a mathematical term meaning twenty. To find the value of the 'score' number multiply by 4x20=80.

1 KINGS 12: 25	Then Jer-o-bo-am built She-chem in mount E-phra-im, and dwelt **therein;**
2 Kings 2: 21	and cast the salt **in there,**
1 Chron. 16: 19	When ye were but few, even a few, and strangers **in it.**

1 KINGS 13: 6	And the king answered and said unto the man of God, **Intreat** now the face of the LORD thy God, and **pray for me,**

1 KINGS 13: 13	So they saddle him the ass: and he rode **thereon,**
Lev. 6: 12	and the priest shall burn wood **on it** every morning, and lay the burnt offering in order **upon it;** and he shall burn **thereon** the fat of the peace offerings.

1 KINGS 13: 21	**Forasmuch as** thou hast disobeyed the mouth of the LORD,

N.B. note the underlined word that gives the meaning of the whole word.

1 KINGS 14: 5	thus and thus shalt thou say unto her: for it shall be, when she cometh in, that she shall **feign herself *to be* another *woman.***

1 KINGS 14: 7	Go, tell Jer-o-bo-am, Thus saith the LORD God of Israel, **Forasmuch** as I exalted thee from among the people,

N.B. note how the underlined word gives the meaning of the whole word.

1 KINGS 14: 10	**Therefore, behold,** I will bring evil upon thehouse of Jer-o-bo-am,

N.B. note how the two bold words mean the same thing.

1 KINGS 14: 14	**Moreover** the LORD shall raise him up a king over Israel,
2 Chron. 4: 9	**Furthermore** he made the court of the priests,

1 KINGS 14: 15	For the LORD **shall smite** Israel,
Job 20: 24	*and* the bow of steel **shall strike** him through.

1 KINGS 14: 26	And he **took away** the treasures of the house of the LORD,
2 Chron. 12: 9	he **carried away** also the shields of gold that Solomon had made.

I KINGS 14: 27	And king Re-ho-bo-am made in their stead **brasen shields,**
2 Chron. 12: 10	Instead of which king Re-ho-bo-am made **shields of brass,**

1 KINGS 14: 27	which kept the **door** of the king's house.
2 Chron. 12: 10	that kept the **entrance** of the king's house.

1 KINGS 15: 4	**Nevertheless** for David's sake did the LORD his God give him a lamp in Jerusalem,
: 5	**Because** David did *that which was* right in the eyes of the LORD,

1 KINGS 15: 12	And he **took away** the sodomites out of the land, and **removed** all the idols that his father had made.

1 KINGS 15: 15	And he brought in the things **which** his father had dedicated, and the things **which** himself had dedicated,
2 Chron. 15: 18	And he brought into the house of God the things **that** his father had dedicated, and **that** he himself had dedicated,

1 KINGS 15: 17	And Ba-ash-a king of Israel went up against Judah, and built Ra-mah, that he **might not suffer any** to go out or come in to Asa king of Judah.
2 Chron. 16: 1	In the six and thirtieth year of the reign of Asa Ba-ash-a king of Israel came up against Judah, and built Ra-mah, to the intent that he might **let none go** out or come in to king king of Judah.

1 KINGS 15: 26	And he did evil in the sight of the LORD, and walked in the way of his father, and in his sin **wherewith** he made Israel to sin.
Zechariah 13: 6	Then he shall answer, *Those* **with which** I was wounded *in* the house of my friends.

1 KINGS 15: 27	**which** kept the the door of the king's house.
2 Chron. 12: 10	**that** kept the entrance of the king's house.

1 KINGS 15: 17	that he might not **suffer any** to go out or come in to Asa king of Judah.
2 Chron. 16: 1	and built Ra-mah, to the intent that he might **let none** go out or come in to king Asa of Judah.

1 KINGS 15: 19	*There is a* **league** between me and thee,
Isaiah 28: 15	We have made a **covenant** with death, and with hell we are at **agreement;**

1 KINGS 15: 22	and they took away the stones of Ra-mah, and the timber **thereof,**
7: 27	and four cubits the breadth **thereof,** and three cubits the height **of it.**

1 KINGS 15: 22	and the timber thereof, **wherewith** Ba-ash-a had builded;

| **1 KINGS 10: 7** | **Howbeit** I believed not the words, |
| 9: 24 | **But** Pharaoh's daughter came up out of the city of David... |

| **1 KINGS 10: 14** | Now the weight of gold that came to Solomon in one year was sixteen hundred three**score** and six talents of gold, |
| Lev. 27: 7 | And if *it be* from **sixty** years old, |

N.B. The underlined word is a numerical term meaning. To find the value of the 'score' number multiply 3x20=60+6=66.

| **1 KINGS 10: 15** | Beside *that he had* of the merchantmen, and of the **traffick** of the spice merchants, |
| Genesis 34: 10 | and the land shall be before you; dwell and **trade** ye therein, |

| **1 KINGS 10: 18** | **Moreover** the king made a great throne of ivory, |
| 1 Chron. 17: 10 | Moreover I will subdue all thine enemies. **Furthermore** I tell thee that the LORD will build thee an house. |

| **1 KINGS 10: 23** | So king Solomon **exceeded** all the kings of the earth for riches and for wisdom. |
| 2 Chron. 9: 22 | And king Solomon **passed** all the kings of the earth in riches and wisdom. |

| **1 KINGS 10: 27** | made he *to be* as the sycamore trees that *are* in the **vale,** |
| 2 Chron. 9: 27 | and cedar trees made he as the sycamore trees that *are* in the **low plains** in abundance. |

1 KINGS 11: 11	**Wherefore** the LORD said unto Solomon, Forasmch as this is done of thee,
: 12	**Notwithstanding** in thy days I will not do it for David thy father's sake: *but* I will rend it out of the hand of thy son.
: 13	**Howbeit** I wil l give one tribe to thy son for David my servant's sake,
: 22	Then Pharaoh said unto him, **But** what hast thou lacked with me,

| **1 KINGS 11: 15** | For it came to pass, David was in Edom, and Jo-ab the captain of the host was gone up to bury **the slain,** after he had smitten every male in Edom, |
| 1 Kings 3: 23 | Then said the king, The one saith, This *is* my son that liveth, and thy son *is* **the dead:** |

| **1 KINGS 11: 15** | For It came to pass, David was in Edom, and Jo-ab the captain of the captain of the host was gone up to bury the slain, after he **had smitten** every male in Edom, |
| 2 Chron. 25: 3 | that he slew his servants that **had killed** the king his father. |

1 KINGS 11: 18	which gave him an house, and appointed him **victuals,** and gave him land.
5 : 9	and thou shalt accomplish my desire, in giving **food** for my household.
1 KINGS 11: 22	Then Pharaoh said unto him, **But** what hast thou lacked with me, that, behold, thou seekest to go to thine own country? And he answered, Nothing: **howbeit** let me go in any wise.
1 KINGS 11: 24	and dwelt **therein,** and reigned in Damascus.
2 Kings 2: 21	and cast the salt **in there,**
7: 13	(behold, they *are* as all the multitude of Israel that are left **in it:** behold...)
1 KINGS 11: 25	and he **abhorred** Israel, and reigned over Syria.
2 Samuel 22: 18	*and* from them that **hated** me:
1 KINGS 11: 34	**Howbeit** I will not take the whole kingdom out of his hand: **but** I will make him prince all the days of his life for David my my servant's sake,
1 KINGS 12: 9	And he said unto them, **What counsel** give ye that we may answer this people,
2 Chron. 10: 9	And he said unto them, **What advice** give ye that we may return an answer to this people,
1 KINGS 12: 9	And he said unto them, What counsel give ye that we may answer this people, **who** have spoken to me saying, Make the yoke **which** thy father did put upon us lighter?
2 Chron. 10: 9	What advice give ye that we may return answer to this people **which** have spoken to me, saying, Ease somewhat the yoke **that** thy father put upon us?
1 KINGS 12: 10	Thus shalt thou **speak** unto this people that spake unto thee,
2 Chron. 10: 10	Thus shalt thou **answer** the people that spake unto thee,
1 KINGS 12: 14	My father made your yoke heavy, and I will add **to** your yoke:
1 Chron. 10: 14	My father made your yoke heavy, but I will add **thereto:**
2 Kings 18: 4	unto those days the children of Israeldid burn incense **to it:**
1 KINGS 12: 15	**Wherefore** the king hearkened not unto the people;
: 24	They hearkened **therefore** to the word of the LORD,
2 Chron. 10: 15	**So** the king hearkened not unto the people:
1 KINGS 12: 15	for the cause was from the LORD, **that** he might perform his saying, **which** the LORD spake by A-hi-jah the Shi-lo-nite
	unto Jer-o-bo-am the son of Nebat.

2 Chron. 11: 1	And when Re-ho-bo-am was come to Jerusalem, he **gathered** of the house of Judah...

1 KINGS 12: 21	with the tribe of Benjamin, an hundred and **fourscore** thousand men.
Genesis 5: 28	And La-mech lived an hundred **eighty** and two years,

N.B. The underlined word is a mathematical term meaning twenty. To find the value of the 'score' number multiply by 4x20=80.

1 KINGS 12: 25	Then Jer-o-bo-am built She-chem in mount E-phra-im, and dwelt **therein;**
2 Kings 2: 21	and cast the salt **in there,**
1 Chron. 16: 19	When ye were but few, even a few, and strangers **in it.**

1 KINGS 13: 6	And the king answered and said unto the man of God, **Intreat** now the face of the LORD thy God, and **pray for me,**

1 KINGS 13: 13	So they saddle him the ass: and he rode **thereon,**
Lev. 6: 12	and the priest shall burn wood **on it** every morning, and lay the burnt offering in order **upon it;** and he shall burn **thereon** the fat of the peace offerings.

1 KINGS 13: 21	**Forasmuch as** thou hast disobeyed the mouth of the LORD,

N.B. note the underlined word that gives the meaning of the whole word.

1 KINGS 14: 5	thus and thus shalt thou say unto her: for it shall be, when she cometh in, that she shall **feign herself** *to be* **another** *woman*.

1 KINGS 14: 7	Go, tell Jer-o-bo-am, Thus saith the LORD God of Israel, **Forasmuch** as I exalted thee from among the people,

N.B. note how the underlined word gives the meaning of the whole word.

1 KINGS 14: 10	**Therefore, behold,** I will bring evil upon thehouse of Jer-o-bo-am,

N.B. note how the two bold words mean the same thing.

1 KINGS 14: 14	**Moreover** the LORD shall raise him up a king over Israel,
2 Chron. 4: 9	**Furthermore** he made the court of the priests,

1 KINGS 14: 15	For the LORD **shall smite** Israel,
Job 20: 24	*and* the bow of steel **shall strike** him through.

1 KINGS 14: 26	And he **took away** the treasures of the house of the LORD,

2 Chron. 12: 9	he **carried away** also the shields of gold that Solomon had made.

| **I KINGS 14: 27** | And king Re-ho-bo-am made in their stead **brasen shields,** |
| 2 Chron. 12: 10 | Instead of which king Re-ho-bo-am made **shields of brass,** |

| **1 KINGS 14: 27** | which kept the **door** of the king's house. |
| 2 Chron. 12: 10 | that kept the **entrance** of the king's house. |

| **1 KINGS 15: 4** | **Nevertheless** for David's sake did the LORD his God give him a lamp in Jerusalem, |
| : 5 | **Because** David did *that which was* right in the eyes of the LORD, |

| **1 KINGS 15: 12** | And he **took away** the sodomites out of the land, and **removed** all the idols that his father had made. |

| **1 KINGS 15: 15** | And he brought in the things **which** his father had dedicated, and the things **which** himself had dedicated, |
| 2 Chron. 15: 18 | And he brought into the house of God the things **that** his father had dedicated, and **that** he himself had dedicated, |

| **1 KINGS 15: 17** | And Ba-ash-a king of Israel went up against Judah, and built Ra-mah, that he **might not suffer any** to go out or come in to Asa king of Judah. |
| 2 Chron. 16: 1 | In the six and thirtieth year of the reign of Asa Ba-ash-a king of Israel came up against Judah, and built Ra-mah, to the intent that he might **let none go** out or come in to king king of Judah. |

| **1 KINGS 15: 26** | And he did evil in the sight of the LORD, and walked in the way of his father, and in his sin **wherewith** he made Israel to sin. |
| Zechariah 13: 6 | Then he shall answer, *Those* **with which** I was wounded *in* the house of my friends. |

| **1 KINGS 15: 27** | **which** kept the the door of the king's house. |
| 2 Chron. 12: 10 | **that** kept the entrance of the king's house. |

| **1 KINGS 15: 17** | that he might not **suffer any** to go out or come in to Asa king of Judah. |
| 2 Chron. 16: 1 | and built Ra-mah, to the intent that he might **let none** go out or come in to king Asa of Judah. |

| **1 KINGS 15: 19** | *There is a* **league** between me and thee, |
| Isaiah 28: 15 | We have made a **covenant** with death, and with hell we are at **agreement;** |

| **1 KINGS 15: 22** | and they took away the stones of Ra-mah, and the timber **thereof,** |

| 7: 27 | and four cubits the breadth **thereof,** and three cubits the height **of it.** |

| **1 KINGS 15: 22** | and the timber thereof, **wherewith** Ba-ash-a had builded; |
| Genesis 26: 18 | and he called their names **by which** his father had called them. |

1 KINGS 16: 10	And Zimri went in and **smote, and killed** him.
: 11	as soon as he sat on throne, *that* he **slew** all the house of Ba-ash-a:
: 16	and hath also **slain** the king:

N.B. note how the underlined word separates words and phrases having the same meaning.

| **1 KINGS 16: 13** | in provoking the LORD God of Israel to anger with their **vanities.** |
| 15: 12 | and removed all the **idols** that his father had made. |

| **1 KINGS 16: 34** | and set up the gates **thereof** in his youngest *son* Se-gub, |
| 7: 27 | and four cubits the breadth **thereof,** and three cubits the height **of it.** |

| **1 KINGS 17: 3** | Get thee **hence,** and turn thee eastward, |
| : 9 | I have commanded a widow woman **there** to sustain thee. |

| **1 KINGS 17: 13** | but make me **thereof** a little cake first, |
| 7: 27 | and three cubits the height **of it.** |

1 KINGS 17: 17	and his sickness was so sore, **that there was no breath left in him.**
2 Kings 1: 17	So **he died** according to the word of the LORD which Elijah had spoken.
4: 32	And when Elisha was come into the house, behold, **the child was dead,**

| **1 KINGS 17: 18** | art thou come unto me to call my sin to remembrance, and **to lay** my son? |
| 2 Kings 5: 7 | and said, *Am* I God, **to kill** and to make alive, |

| **1 KINGS 17: 20** | hast thou also brought evil upon the widow with whom I sojourn, by **slaying** her son? |
| 2 Chron. 30: 17 | therefore the Levites had the charge of the **killing** of the passovers for every one *that was* not clean, |

| **1 KINGS 18: 4** | For it was *so,* when Jezebel **cut off** the prophets of the LORD, |
| : 13 | was it not told my lord what I did when Jezebel **slew** the prophets of the LORD, |

| **1 KINGS 18: 5** | and unto all brooks: **peradventure** we may find grass to save the horses, and mules alive, |

2 Kings 19: 4	**It may be** the LORD thy God will hear all the words of Rab-sha-keh,

1 KINGS 18: 9   there is no nation or kingdom, **whither** my lord hath not sent to seek thee:

    17: 19   and carried him up into a loft, **where** he abode,

1 KINGS 18: 23   and let them choose one bullock for themselves, and **cut it pieces**, and lay *it* on wood, and put no fire *under:* and I will **dress** the other bullock, **and lay***it* on wood,

I KINGS 18: 28   And they cried aloud, and cut themselves after their manner with **knives <u>and</u> lancets,**

N.B. note how the underlined word separates words and phrases having the same meaning.

1 KINGS 19: 9   And he came **thither** unto a cave, and lodged **there;**

1 KINGS 19: 10   and **slain** thy prophets with the sword;

    16: 7   and because he **killed** him.

1 KINGS 20: 3   Thy silver and thy gold *is* mine; thy wives also and thy children, *even* the **goodliest,** *are* mine.

    : 6   and it shall be, *that* **whatsoever is pleasant** in thine eyes, they shall put *it* in their hand, and take *it* away.

1 KINGS 20: 9   **Wherefore** he said unto the messengers of Ben-ha-dad,

    : 23   **therefore** they were stronger than we;

1 KINGS 20: 21   And the king of Israel went out, and **smote** the horses and chariots, and slew the Syrians with a great slaughter.

    16: 10   And Zimri went in and **smote him, <u>and</u>** killed him,

N.B. note how the underlined word separates words and phrases having the same meaning.

1 KINGS 20: 31   **peradventure** he will save thy life.

2 Kings 19: 4   **It may be** the LORD thy God will hear all the words of Rab-sha-keh,

1 KINGS 20: 35   And a certain man of the sons of the prophets said unto his neighbour in the word of the LORD, **Smite me,** I pray thee,

2 Kings 5: 11   and call upon the name of the LORD his God, and **strike** his hand over the place,

1 KINGS 20: 36   a lion **shall slay.** And as soon as he was departed from him,

     a lion found him, and **slew** him.

1 KINGS 21: 1	which *was* in Jez-rel, **hard by** the palace of Ahab king of Samaria.
: 2	because it *is* **near** unto my house:
1 KINGS 21: 10	And set two men, **sons of Belial,** before him,
2 Samuel 22: 5	the floods of **ungodly men** made me afraid.
1 KINGS 21: 18	*he is* in the vineyard of Naboth, **whither** he is gone down to possess it.
: 19	In the place **where** dogs licked the blood of Naboth shall dogs lick thy blood, even thine.
1 KINGS 21: 22	for the provocation **wherewith** thou hast provoked *me* to anger,
Zechariah 13: 6	Then he shall answer, *Those* **with which** I was wounded *in* the house of my friends.
1 KINGS 22: 9	Then the king of Israel called an officer, and said, **Hasten hither** Mi-cai-ah the son of Imlah.
2 Chron. 18: 8	And the king of Israel called for one *of his* officers, and said, **Fetch quickly** Mi-cai-ah the son of Imlah.
1 KINGS 22: 20	And the LORD said, Who shall **persuade** Ahab,
2 Chron. 18: 19	And the LORD said, Who shall **entice** Ahab king of Israel,
1 KINGS 22: 22	And the LORD said unto him, **Wherewith?**
21: 29	Seest thou **how** Ahab humbleth himself before me?
1 KINGS 22: 34	**wherefore** he said unto the driver of his chariot.
2 Chron. 18: 33	**therefore** he said to his chariot man.
1 KINGS 22: 34	wherefore he said unto **the driver of his chariot.**
2 Chron. 18: 33	therefore he said to **his chariot man.**

2 KINGS

2 KINGS 2: 2	And Elijah said unto Elisha, **Tarry** here, I pray thee;
6: 33	what should I **wait** for the LORD any longer?
2 Sam. 24: 16	It is enough: **stay** thine hand.
2 KINGS 2: 8	and **smote** the waters, and they were divided hither and thither,
2 Sam. 20: 10	and **struck** him not again; and he died.
2 KINGS 2: 8	and they were divided **hither and thither,**
4: 35	Then he returned, and walked in the house **to and fro;**
2 KINGS 2: 16	let them go, we pray thee, and seek thy master: lest **peradventure** the Spirit of the LORD hath taken him up,
19: 4	**It may be** the LORD thy God will hear all the words of Rab-sha-keh,

| **2 KINGS 2: 20** | And he said, Bring me a new cruse, and put salt **therein.** |
| : 21 | And he went forth unto the spring of the waters, and cast the salt **in there,** |

| **2 KINGS 2: 21** | Thus saith the LORD, I have healed these waters; **there** shall not be from **thence** any more death or barren *land.* |

| **2 KINGS 3: 2** | And he **wrought** evil in the sight of the LORD; |
| 1 Kings 22: 52 | And he **did** evil in the sight of the LORD, |

| **2 KINGS 3: 3** | he departed not **therefrom.** |
| 2 Chr. 20: 32 | and departed not **from it,** |

2 KINGS 3: 4	And Me-sha king of Moab was a sheepmaster, and **rendered** unto the king of Israel an hundred thousand lambs,
5: 1	because by him the LORD **had given** deliverance unto Syria:
10: 15	And he **gave** *him* his hand;

2 KINGS 3: 9	and the king of Edom: and they **fetched a compass** of seven days' journey:
9: 18	What hast thou to do with peace? **turn thee behind me.**
2 Chron.13: 13	But Jer-o-bo-am caused an ambushment to **come about behind them:**

| **2 KINGS 3: 19** | And ye shall **smite** every fenced city, |
| 5: 11 | and **strike** his hand over the place, |

| **2 KINGS 3: 25** | only in Kir-har-a-seth left they the stones **thereof;** |
| 12: 9 | and bored a hole in the lid **of it,** |

| **2 KINGS 4: 8** | And it fell on a day, that Elisha passed to Shu-nem, where *was* a great woman; and she **constrained** him to eat bread. |
| 5: 16 | And he **urged** him to take *it;* |

| **2 KINGS 4: 10** | and let us set for him **there** a bed, and a table, and a stool, and a candlestick: and it shall be, when he cometh to us, that he shall turn in **thither.** |

2 KINGS 4: 14	And Ge-ha-zi answered, **Verily** she hath no child,
5: 11	He will **surely** come out to me,
8: 10	Thou mayest **certainly** recover,

| **2 KINGS 4: 23** | And he said, **Wherefore** wilt thou go to him to day? |
| : 25 | And it came to pass, **when** the man of God saw her afar off, |

| **2 KINGS 4: 31** | **Wherefore** he went again to meet him, |

| : 33 | He went in **therefore,** and shut the door upon them twain, |
| 6: 32 | **But** Elisha sat in his house, |

2 KINGS 4: 33	and shut the door upon them **twain,**
2: 6	And they **two** went on.
2 KINGS 4: 38	And Elisha came again to Gilgal: and *there was* a **dearth** in the land;
6: 25	And there was a great **famine** in Samaria:
2 KINGS 4: 38	Set on the great pot, **seethe** pottage for the sons of the prophets.
Leviticus 8: 31	**Boil** the flesh *at* the door of the tabernacle of the congregation,
2 KINGS 4: 38	Set on the great pot, seethe **pottage** for the sons of the prophets.
Genesis 25: 34	Then Jacob gave Esau bread and pottage **of lentils;**
2 KINGS 4: 42	and full ears of corn in the husk **thereof.**
1 Kings 7: 27	and four cubits the breadth **thereof,** and three cubits the height **of it.**
2 KINGS 5: 5	and six thousand *pieces* of gold, and ten changes of **raiment.**
: 7	when the king of Israel had read the letter, that he rent his **clothes,**
: 22	give them, I pray thee, a talent of silver, and two changes of **garments.**
2 KINGS 5: 7	**wherefore** consider, I pray you, and see how he seeketh a quarrel against me.
: 15	now **therefore,** I pray thee, take a blessing of thy servant.
2 KINGS 5: 8	that he sent to the king saying, **Wherefore** hast thou rent thy clothes?
7: 3	and they said one to another, **Why** sit we here until we die?
2 KINGS 5: 11	But Na-a-man **was wroth,** and went away,
: 12	So he turned and went away **in a rage.**
2 KINGS 5: 17	for thy servant will **henceforth** offer neither burnt offering nor sacrifice unto other gods,
Psalm 113: 2	Blessed be the name of the LORD **from this time** forth and for evermore.
2 KINGS 5: 25	And Elisha said unto him, **Whence** *comest thou,* Ge-ha-zi? And he said, Thy servant went no **whither.**
4: 8	And it fell on a day, that Elisha passed to Shu-nem, **where** *was* a great woman,
2 KINGS 6: 1	Behold now, the place where we dwell with is **too strait** for us.

Numbers 22: 26	And the angel of the LORD went further, and stood in a **narrow** place,
Joshua 17: 15	if mount E-phra-im be **too narrow** for thee.
: 16	And the children of Joseph said, The hill is **not enough** for us:
2 KINGS 6: 2	Let us go, we pray thee, unto Jordan, and take **thence** every man a beam, and let us make us a place **there**, where we may dwell.
2 KINGS 6: 9	for **thither** the Syrians are come down.
: 10	and saved himself **there**, not once nor twice.
2 KINGS 6: 14	and they came by night, and **compassed the city about.**
: 24	and went up, and **besieged Samaria.**
2 KINGS 6: 25	until an ass's head was *sold* for **fourscore** *pieces* of silver,
Genesis 5: 28	And La-mech lived an hundred **eighty** and two years,

N.B. The underlined word is a numerical term meaning twenty. To find the value of the score number multiply the number by twenty 4x20=80.

2 KINGS 6: 27	And he said, If the LORD do not help thee, **whence** shall I help thee?
: 15	And his servant said unto him, Alas, my master! **how** shall we do?
2 KINGS 7: 2	And he said, Behold, thou shalt see *it* with thine eyes, but shalt not eat **thereof.**
12: 9	and bored a hole in the lid **of it,**
2 KINGS 7: 7	**Wherefore** they arose and fled in the twilight,
: 9	now **therefore** come, and that we go and tell the king's household.
2 KINGS 7: 8	and carried **thence** silver, and gold, and raiment,
24 :14	and he carried **away** all Jerusalem, and all the princes,
2 KINGS 7: 8	and carried hence silver, and gold, and **raiment,**
: 15	all the way *was* full of **garments**
Job 22: 6	and stripped the naked of their **clothing.**
2 KINGS 8: 7	The man of God is come **hither.**
7: 3	Why sit we **here** until we die.
2 KINGS 8: 10	Go, say unto him, Thou mayest **certainly** recover: howbeit
: 14	the LORD, hath shewed me that he shall **surely** die.
2 KINGS 8: 10	**howbeit** the LORD, hath shewed me that he shall surely die.
: 13	And Ha-za-el said, **But** what, *is* thy servant a dog,

2 KINGS 8: 19	**Yet** the LORD would not destroy Judah for David his servant's sake,
2 Chron. 21: 7	**Howbeit** the LORD would not destroy the house of David,
2 KINGS 8: 21	and smote the Edomites which **compassed him about,**
6: 24	and went up, and **besieged Samaria.**
Psalm 22: 12	strong *bulls* of Ba-shan **have beset me round.**
: 16	the assembly of the wicked **have inclosed me:**
2 KINGS 9: 2	And when thou comest **thither,**
6: 2	and let us make a way **there,** where we may dwell.
2 KINGS 9: 7	And thou shalt **smite** the house of Ahab thy master,
5: 11	and **strike** his hand over the place,
2 KINGS 9: 11	and *one* said unto him, *Is* all well? **wherefore** came this mad *fellow* to thee?
8: 12	And Ha-za-el said, **Why** weepeth my lord?
2 KINGS 9: 26	and I will **requite** thee in this plat,
Job 21: 31	and who shall **repay** him *what* he hath done?
2 KINGS 9: 26	And I will requite thee in this **plat,** saith the LORD.
: 36	In the **portion** of Jez-reel shall dogs eat the flesh of Jezebel:
2 KINGS 9: 36	**Wherefore** they came again, and told him.
: 26	Now **therefore** take *and* cast him into the plat *of ground,*
2 KINGS 10: 3	Look even out the **best and meetest** of your master's sons,

N.B. note how the underlined word separates words and phrases having the same meaning.

2 KINGS 10: 9	I conspired against my master, and **slew** him:
15: 25	and he **killed** him, and reigned in his stead.
2 KINGS 10: 15	And when he was departed **thence,**
: 23	and look that **there** be here with you none of the servants of the LORD,
2 KINGS 10: 22	And he said unto them that *was* over the vestry, Bring forth **vestments** for all the worshippers of Ba-al.
7: 15	and, lo, all the way *was* full of **garments** and vessels,
Job 22: 6	and stripped the naked of their **clothing.**
2 KINGS 10: 24	Jehu appointed **fourscore** men without,
Genesis 5: 28	And La-mech lived an hundred **eighty** and two years,

N.B. The underlined word is a numerical term meaning twenty. To find the value of the score number multiply the number by twenty, 4x20=80.

<u>**2 KINGS 10: 29**</u>	**Howbeit** *from* the sins of Jer-o-bo-am the sons of Ne-bat,
: 31	**But** Jehu took no heed to walk in the law of the LORD God...

<u>**2 KINGS 11: 8**</u>   And ye shall **compass** the king **round about,**

N.B. A compass is round and thus describes the protection given by his supporters perfectly. Also compare v.v. 11-12 of the same chapter.

<u>**2 KINGS 12: 2**</u>	And Je-ho-ash did *that which was* right in the sight of the LORD all his days **wherein** Je-hoi-a-da the priest instructed him.
Job 3: 3	Let the day perish **wherein** I was born, and the night *in which* it was said, There was a man child conceived.

<u>**2 KINGS 12: 3**</u>	**But** the high places were not taken away:
14: 4	**Howbeit** the places were not taken away:
15: 4	**Save** that the high places were not removed:

<u>**2 KINGS 12: 3**</u>	But the high places **were not taken away:**
15: 4	Howbeit the high places **were not removed:**

<u>**2 KINGS 12: 9**</u>	and the priests that kept the door put **therein** all the money *that was* brought into the house of the LORD.
7 : 13	(behold, they *are* as all the multitude of Israel that are left **in it:...**)

<u>**2 KINGS 12: 10**</u>	and **told** the money that was found in the house of the LORD.
: 15	Moreover they **reckoned** not with the men.

<u>**2 KINGS 12: 11**</u>	and they laid it out to the carpenters and builders, that **wrought** upon the house of the LORD.
Nehemiah 4: 21	So we **laboured** in the work:

<u>**2 KINGS 12: 13**</u>   **Howbeit there** was not made for the house of the LORD bowls of silver,

<u>**2 KINGS 12: 14**</u>	But they gave that to the workmen, and repaired **therewith** the house of the LORD.
1 Sam. 6: 15	and the coffer that was **with it,**
1 Sam. 18: 11	for he said, I will smite David even to the wall *with it.*

<u>**2 KINGS 12: 15**</u>	**Moreover** they reckoned not with the men.
1 Chron. 17: 10	**Moreover** I will subdue all thine enemies. **Furthermore** I tell thee that the LORD will build thee an house.

<u>**2 KINGS 13: 2**</u>   and followed the sins of Je-o-bo-am the son of Ne-bat, which made Israel to sin; he departed not **therefrom.**

1 Kings 22: 43	And he walked in all the ways of Asa his father; he turned not aside **from it,**
2 KINGS 13: 5	and the children of Israel dwelt in their tents, as **before**time.
2 KINGS 13: 6	**Nevertheless** they departed not from the sins of the house of Jer-o-bo-am,
12: 13	**Howbeit** there were not made for the house of the LORD bowls of silver,
: 14	**But** they gave that to the workmen,
2 KINGS 13: 6	Nevertheless they departed not from the **sins** of the house Jer-o-bo-am, who made Israel sin, *but* walked **therein:**
5: 12	*Are* not Ab-a-na and Phar-par, rivers of Damascus, better than all the waters **in them?**
2 KINGS 13: 18	And he said unto the king of Israel, **Smite** upon the ground
5: 11	and **strike** his hand over the place,
2 KINGS 13: 18	Smite upon the ground. And he **smote** thrice, and stayed.
2 Chron. 13: 20	and the LORD **struck** him, and he died.
2 KINGS 13: 18	And he smote him **thrice,** and stayed.
: 25	**Three times** did Jo-ash beat him, and recovered the cities of Israel.
2 KINGS 13: 19	Thou shouldest have **smittened** five or six times;
2 Chron. 13: 20	and the lord **struck** him, and he died.
2 KINGS 14: 5	**And it came to pass, as soon as** the kingdom was **confirmed** in his hand, that he slew his servants which had slain the king his father.
2 Chron. 25: 3	**Now it came to pass, when** the kingdom was **established** in in his hand, that he slew his servants that had killed the king his father.
2 KINGS 14: 5	that he slew his servants **which** had slain the king his father.
2 Chron. 25: 5	that he slew his servants **that** had killed the king his father.
2 KINGS 14: 5	that he **slew** his servants which **had slain** the king his father.
2 Chron. 25: 5	that he slew his servants that **had killed** the king his father.
2 KINGS 14: 10	and **tarry** at home:
6: 33	what should I **wait** for the LORD any longer?
2 KINGS 14: 19	but they sent after him to La-chish, and **slew** him there.
15: 25	and he **killed** him, and ruled in his room.
2 KINGS 15: 16	Then Men-a-hem smote Tiphsah, and all that *were* **therein,**
7: 13	they *are* as all the multitude of Israel that are left **in it:**

N.B. reverse the syllables in the first bold reference and the meaning is clear.

2 KINGS 15: 16   and the coasts **thereof** from Tirzah:
       14: 7   and called the name **of it** Jok-theel unto this day.

2 KINGS 15: 22   and Pek-a-hi-ah his son reigned in his **stead.**
       : 25   and he killed him, and reigned in his **room.**

2 KINGS 15: 35   **Howbeit** the high places were not removed:
       : 4   **Save** that the high places were not removed:

2 KINGS 15: 36   Now the rest of the acts of Jo-tham, and all that he did, *are*
                         they not written in the **book** of the **chronicles** of the kings
                         of Judah?
2 Chron. 27: 7   Now the rest of the acts of Jo-tham, and all his wars, and his
                         ways, they *are* written in the **book** of the kings of Israel and
                         Judah.

2 KINGS 16: 10   and the pattern **of it,** according to all the workmanship **thereof.**

2 KINGS 16: 11   so U-ri-jah the priest made *it* **against** king Ahaz came from
                         Damascus.
       : 14   which *was* **before** the LORD,

2 KINGS 16: 12   and the king approached to the altar, and offered **thereon.**
       : 15   and their drink offerings; and sprinkle **upon it** all the blood
                         of the burnt offering,

2 KINGS 16: 18   And the **covert** for the sabbath that they had built in the house,

N.B. note the underlined letter, if it was omitted the meaning of the word is clear.

2 KINGS 17: 11   and **wrought** wicked things to provoke the LORD to anger:
       : 22   walked in all the sins of Jer-o=bo-am which he **did;**

2 KINGS 17: 12   For they served idols, **whereof** the LORD had said unto them,
                         Ye shall not do this thing,
       23: 27   and will cast off this city Jerusalem **which** I have chosen,
                         and the house **of which** I said,My name shall be there.

2 KINGS 17: 14   **Notwithstanding** they would not hear, **but** hardened their
                         necks,

2 KINGS 17: 26   **Wherefore** they spake to the king of Assyria, saying, The
                         nations which thou hast removed... **therefore** he hath sent

                         lions among them,

one of the priests whom ye brought from **thence;** and let them go and dwell **there,**

2 KINGS 17: 29 every nation in their cities **wherein** they dwelt.

Job 3: 3 Let the day perish **wherein** I was born, and the night *in which* it was said, There is a man child conceived.

2 KINGS 17: 40 **Howbeit** they did not hearken, **but** they did after their former manner.

2 KINGS 18: 3 And he did *that which was* right in the sight of the LORD, according to all that David his father **did.**

2 Chron. 29: 2 And he did *that which was* right in the sight of the LORD, according to all that David his father **had done.**

2 KINGS 18: 8 and the borders **thereof,**

16: 10 and the pattern **of it,** according to all the workmanship **thereof.**

2 KINGS 18: 19 Thus saith the great king, the king of Assyria, What confidence *is* this **wherein** thou trustest?

Job 3: 3 Let the day perish **wherein** I was born, and the night *in which* It was said, There is a man child conceived.

2 KINGS 19: 6 Be not afraid of the words **which** thou hast heard, **with which** the servants of the king of Assyria have blasphemed me.

Isaiah 37: 6 Be not afraid of the words **that** thou hast heard, **wherewith** the servants of the king of Assyria have blasphemed me.

2 KINGS 19: 19 Now therefore, O LORD our God, **I beseech thee,**

18: 23 Now therefore, **I pray thee,**

2 KINGS 19: 21 The virgin the daughter of Zion **hath despised thee, _and_ laughed thee to scorn;**

N.B. note how the underlined word separates words and phrases having the same meaning.

2 KINGS 19: 22 and against whom hast thou **exalted** *thy* voice, and **lifted up** thine eyes on high?

2 KINGS 19: 25 Hast thou not heard **long ago** *how* I have done it, *and* of **ancient times** that I have formed it?

2 KINGS 19: 26 they were **dismayed _and_ confounded;**

N.B. note how the underlined word separates words and phrases having the same meaning.

2 KINGS 19: 35 and smote in the camp of the Assyrians an hundred **fourscore** and five thousand.

Genesis 5: 28 And La-mech lived an hundred **eighty** and two years,

N.B. The underlined word is a numerical term meaning twenty. To find the value of the score number multiply the number by twenty, 4x20=80.

2 KINGS 20: 1	And the prophet Isaiah the son of Amoz **came to** him,
Isaiah 38: 1	And Isaiah the prophet the son of Amoz **came unto** him,
2 KINGS 20: 3	**I beseech thee,** O LORD,
18: 23	Now therefore **I pray thee,**
2 KINGS 20: 14	What said these men? and from **whence** came they unto thee?
18: 34	**Where** *are* the gods of Ha-math, and of Arpad?
2 KINGS 21: 3	For he **built up** again the high places which Hez-e-ki-ah his father had destroyed; and he **reared up** altars for Ba-al,
2 KINGS 21: 6	he **wrought** much wickedness in the sight of the LORD,
: 2	And he **did** *that which was* evil in the sight of the LORD,
2 KINGS 21: 16	**Moreover** Ma-nas-seh shed innocent blood very much,
1 Chron. 17: 10	**Moreover** I will subdue all thine enemies. **Furthermore** I tell thee that the LORD will build thee an house.
2 KINGS 21: 16	beside his sin **wherewith** he made Judah to sin,
19: 6	Be not afraid of the words which thou hast heard, **with which** the servants of the king of Assyria hath blasphemed me.
1 King's 16: 13	and the sins of E-lah, his son, **by which** they sinned,
2 KINGS 21: 23	and **slew** the king in his own house.
15: 25	and he **killed** him, and reigned in his room.
2 KINGS 22: 4	that he may **sum the silver** which is brought into the house of the LORD,
Job 31: 4	Doth not he see my ways, and **count** all my steps?
Ezekiel 44: 26	they shall **reckon** unto him seven days.
2 KINGS 22: 7	**Howbeit** there was no reckoning made with them of the money that was delivered into their hand,
12: 14	**But** they gave that to the workman,
2 KINGS 22: 16	Behold, I will bring evil upon this place, and upon the inhabitants **thereof,**
16: 10	and the pattern **of it,** according to all the workmanship **thereof**
2 KINGS 22: 17	that they might provoke to **anger** with all the works of their hands; therefore my **wrath** shall be kindled against this place,
2 KINGS 23: 4	and he burned them **without** Jerusalem in the fields of Ki-dron,
1 Kings 7: 9	and *so* on the **outside** toward the great court.

2 KINGS 23: 12	and brake *them* down from **thence,**
: 34	and he came to Egypt, and died **there.**
2 KINGS 23: 15	**Moreover** the altar that *was* at Beth-el,
1 Chron. 17: 10	**Furthermore** I tell that the LORD will build thee an house.
2 KINGS 23: 19	and **did** to them according to all the acts that he **had done** in Beth-el.
2 KINGS 23: 22	Surely there was not **holden** such a passover from the days of the judges that ruled Israel,
18: 36	But the people **held** their peace,
2 KINGS 23: 26	Notwithstanding the LORD turned not from the fierceness of his great **wrath,** wherewith his **anger** was kindled against Judah,
2 KINGS 23: 26	Notwithstanding the LORD turned not from the fierceness of his great wrath, **wherewith** his anger was kindled against Judah,
19: 6	Be not afraid of the words **with which** the servants of the king of Assyria have blasphemed me.
2 KINGS 24: 7	for the king of Babylon had taken from the river of Egypt unto the river Eu-phra-tes all that **pertained to** the king of Egypt.
Esther 2: 9	and he speedily gave her things for purification, with such things as **belonged to** her,
2 KINGS 24: 13	And he carried out **thence all** the treasures of the house of the LORD,
: 14	And he carried **away all** Jerusalem, and all the princes,
2 KINGS 25: 3	and there was no **bread** for the people of the land.
1 Kings 5: 11	And Solomon gave Hiram twenty thousand measures of wheat for **food** to his household.
2 KINGS 25: 14	and all the vessels of brass **wherewith** they ministered,
19: 6	**with which** the servants of the king of Assyria have blasphemed me.
2 KINGS 25: 17	The height of the one pillar *was* eighteen cubits, and the chapiter upon it *was* brass:
2 Chron. 3: 15	Also he made before the house two pillars of thirty and five cubits high and the **chapiter** that *was* **on the top of** each of them *was* five cubits.

N.B. The three underlined letters spell out the meaning of the whole word.

2 KINGS 25: 19	and **threescore** men of the people of the land *that were* found in the city.
Leviticus 27: 7	And if *it be* from **sixty** years old and above;

N.B. The underlined word is a mathematical term meaning twenty. To find the value of the ' score' number multiply 3x20=60.

2 KINGS 25: 30	And allowance *was* **a continual allowance** given him of the king, a daily rate for every day,
Jeremiah 52: 34	And *for* his diet, there was **a continual diet** given him of the king of Babylon, every day **a portion** until the day of his death.
2 Kings 25: 30	**a daily rate** for **every day,** all the days of his life.

1 CHRONICLES

1 CHRON. 5: 9	because their cattle were **multiplied** in the land of Gilead.
4: 38	and the house of their fathers **increased** greatly.

1 CHRON. 5: 22	For there fell down many **slain,** because the war *was* of God.
2 Kings 15: 25	and he **killed** him, and reigned in his stead.

1 CHRON. 5: 25	And they **transgressed** against the God of their fathers,
2 Kings 17: 7	that the children of Israel had **sinned** against the LORD their God,

1 CHRON. 6: 55	and the suburbs **thereof** round about it.
1 Kings 7: 27	and four cubits the breadth **thereof,** and three cubits the height **of it.**

1 CHRON. 7: 5	reckoned in all by their genealogies **fourscore** and seven thousand.
Genesis 5: 28	And La-mech lived an hundred **eighty** and two years,

N.B. The underlined word is a numerical term meaning twenty. To find the value of the score number multiply 4x20=80.

1 CHRON. 7: 24	who built Beth-hor-on the **nether** and the upper,
Isaiah 22: 9	and ye gathered together the waters of the **lower** pool.

1 CHRON. 9: 13	a thousand and seven and **threescore,**
Leviticus 27: 7	And if *it be* from **sixty** years old and above;

N.B. The underlined word is a numerical term meaning twenty. To find the value of the score number multiply 3x20=60.

1 CHRON. 9: 18	Who **hitherto** *waited* in the king's gate eastward:
Numbers 14: 19	and as thou hast forgiven this people, from Egypt even **until now.**

1 CHRON. 10: 6	And Saul died, and his three sons, and all his **house** died together.
1 Samuel 31: 6	And Saul died and his three sons, and his armourbearer, and all his **men,** that same day together.

1 CHRON. 10: 7	and that Saul and his sons were **dead,**
: 8	when the Philistines came to strip the **slain,**
19: 18	and **killed** Sho-phach the captain of the host.

1 CHRON. 10: 9	and sent into the land of the Philistines round about, **to carry tidings** unto their idols,
Prov. 25: 25	*As* cold waters to a thirsty soul, so *is* good **news** from a far country.
1 Samuel 31: 9	and sent into the land of the Philistines round about, **to publish** *it in* the house of their idols,

1 CHRON. 11: 2	And **moreover** in time past,
17: 10	**Moreover** I will subdue all thine enemies. **Furthermore** I tell thee that the LORD will build thee an house.
11: 10	These **also** *are* the chief of the mighty men whom David had,

1 CHRON. 11: 5	And the inhabitants of Je-bus said to David, Thou shalt not come **hither.**
29: 17	and now have I seen with joy thy people, which are present **here,**

1 CHRON. 11: 11	he lifted up his spear against three hundred **slain** *by him* at one time.
19: 18	and **killed** Sho-phach the captain of the host.

1 CHRON. 11: 13	and there the Philistines were gathered together to battle, where was **a parcel of ground** full of barley;
2 Samuel 23: 11	and the Philistines were gathered together into a troop, where was **a piece of ground** full of lentils:

1 CHRON. 12: 16	And there came of the children Benjamin and Judah to the **hold** unto David.
11: 5	Nevertheless David took the **castle** of Zion,

1 CHRON. 12: 19	for the lords of the Philistines upon **advise**ment sent him away,
21: 12	Now therefore **advise** thyself what word I shall bring again to him that sent me.
2 Chron. 10: 6	What **counsel** give ye *me* to return answer to this people?
Judges 20: 7	give here your **advice <u>and</u> counsel.**

N.B. note how the underlined word separates words and phrases having the same

meaning.

1 CHRON. 13: 6	to bring up **thence** the ark of God the LORD,
: 10	and **there** he died before God.

1 CHRON. 13: 8	and with harps, and with **psalteries,** and with timbrels,
Psalms 33: 2	sing unto him with the **psaltery** *and* **an instrument of ten strings.**

1 CHRON. 13: 10	And the anger of the LORD was kindled against Uzzah and he **smote** him, because he put his hand to the ark: and there he **died** before God.
2 Chron. 13: 20	and the LORD **struck** him, and he **died.**

1 CHRON. 14: 8	two hundred and **fourscore** thousand:
Genesis 5: 28	And La-mech lived an hundred **eighty** and two years,

N.B. The underlined word is a numerical term meaning twenty. To find the value of the 'score' number multiply 4x20=80.

1 CHRON. 15: 15	And the children of the Levites **bare** the ark of God upon their shoulders with the staves thereon,
13: 13	And they **carried** the ark of God in a new cart out of the house of A-bin-a-dab:

1 CHRON. 15: 15	And the children of the Levites **bare** the ark of God...
13: 13	And they **carried** the ark of God in a new cart...

1 CHRON. 15: 15	And the children of the Levites bare the ark of God upon their shoulderswith the staves **thereon,**
Lev. 6: 12	and the priest shall burn wood **on it** every morning, and lay the burnt offering in order upon it; and he shall burn **thereon** the fat of the peace offerings.

1 CHRON. 15: 27	And David *was* clothed with **a robe of fine linen,** and all the Levites that bare the ark, and the singers, and Chen-a-ni-ah the master of the song with the singers: David also *had* upon him **an ephod of linen.**

1 CHRON. 16: 32	Let the sea roar, and the fullness **thereof:** let the fields rejoice, and all that *is* therein.
1 Kings 7: 31	And the mouth **of it** within the chapter and above *was* a cubit:

1 CHRON. 16: 30	the world also shall **be stable, that it be not moved.**

N.B. note how the comma separates words and phrases having the same meaning.

1 CHRON. 16: 32	let the fields rejoice, and all that *is* **therein.**
10: 7	and fled: and the Philistines came and dwelt **in them.**

1 CHRON. 16: 38	And O-bed-e-dom with their brethren, **threescore** and eight;
Leviticus 27: 7	And if *it be* from **sixty** years old and above;

N.B. The underlined word is a numerical term meaning twenty. To find the value of the 'score' number multiply 3x20=60.

1 CHRON. 17: 7	Now **therefore thus** shalt thou say unto my servant David,

N.B. note the two bold words, they mean the same thing.

1 CHRON. 17: 7	**Also** I will ordain a place for my people Israel,
2 Samuel 17: 10	**Moreover** I will appoint a place for my people Israel,

1 CHRON. 17: 9	Also I will **ordain** a place for my people Israel,
2 Samuel 7: 10	Moreover I will **appoint** a place for my people Israel,

1 CHRON. 17: 10	**Moreover** I will subdue all thine enemies. **Furthermore** I tell thee that the LORD will build thee an house.

1 CHRON. 17: 16	and what *is* mine house, that thou hast brought me **hitherto**?
Numbers 23: 23	according **to this time.**

1 CHRON. 18: 1	Now after this it came to pass, that David **smote** the Philistines, and subdued them,
: 5	David **slew** of the Syrians two and twenty thousand men.
19: 18	and **killed** Sho-phach the captain of the host.
1 CHRON. 18: 8	brought David very much brass, **wherewith** Solomon made the brazen sea,
Deut. 16: 3	Thou shalt eat no unleavened bread **with it**; seven days shalt thou eat unleavened bread **therewith,**
2 King's 19: 6	Be not afraid of the words which thou hast heard, **with which** the servants of the king of Assyria have blasphemed me.

1 CHRON. 19: 3	**But** the princes of the children of Ammon said to Ha-nun,
2 Samuel 10: 3	**And** the princes of the children of Ammon said unto Ha-nun their lord,

1 CHRON. 19: 6	And when the children of Ammon saw that they had made themselves **odious** to David,
2 Samuel 10: 6	And when the children of Ammon saw that they **stank** before David,

1 CHRON. 19: 7	And the children of Ammon gathered themselves together from their cities, and **came to battle.**
: 9	And the children of Ammon came out and **put the battle in array** before the gate of the city:
: 10	Now when Jo-ab saw that the **battle was set against him before and behind,**

1 CHRON. 19: 18	and David **slew** of the Syrians seven thousand *men which fought in* chariots, and **killed** Sho-phach captain of the host.
1 CHRON. 20: 1 1 Kings 20: 38	But David **tarried** at Jerusalem. and **waited** for the king by the way.
1 CHRON. 20; 2 18: 8	and he brought also **exceeding much** spoil out of the city. brought David **very much** brass,
1 CHRON. 21: 4 2 Samuel 24: 4 : 24	**Nevertheless** the king's word prevailed against Jo-ab. **Notwithstanding** the king's word prevailed against Jo-ab, **Wherefore** Jo-ab departed, and went throughout all Israel, Nay; **but** I will verily buy it for the full price:
1 CHRON. 21: 5 Leviticus 27: 7	and Judah *was* four hundred **threescore** and ten thousand men that drew sword. And if it *be* from **sixty** years old and above;

N.B. The underlined word is a numerical term which means twenty. To find the value of the 'score' number multiply three by twenty, 3x20=60.

1 CHRON. 21: 8 : 17	because I have done this thing: but now, **I beseech thee,** let thine hand, **I pray thee,** O LORD my God,
1 CHRON. 21: 12 : 22	even the **pestilence,** in the land, that the **plague** may be stayed from the people.
1 CHRON. 21: 13 2 Samuel 1: 26 Psalm 69: 17	And David said unto Gad, I am in a **great strait:** I am **distressed** for thee, For I am in **trouble:**
1 CHRON. 21: 24 2 Kings 24: 3	Nay; but I will **verily** buy it for the full price: **Surely** at the commandment of the LORD came *this* upon Judah,
1 CHRON. 21: 27 23: 26	and he put up his sword again into the sheath **thereof.** nor any vessels **of it** for the service **thereof.**
1 CHRON. 22: 6 : 17	Then he called for Solomon his son, and **charged him** to build an house for the LORD God of Israel. David also **commanded** all the princes of Israel to help Solomon his son, *saying,*
1 CHRON. 22: 13	be strong, and of good courage: **dread not, nor be dismayed.**

N.B. note how the underlined word separates words and phrases having the same

meaning.

1 CHRON. 22: 14	timber also and stone have I prepared; and thou mayest add **thereto.**
2 Kings 18: 4	for unto those days the children of Israel did burn incense **to it:**

1 CHRON. 22: 15	and all manner of **cunning** men for every manner of work.
28: 21	and *there shall be* with thee for all manner of workmanship every willing **skilful** man,

1 CHRON. 23: 3	and their number by their **polls,** man by man,
29: 20	and bowed down their **heads,** worshipped the LORD,

1 CHRON. 23: 29	and for *that which is baked in* **the pan,** and for that which is **fried,**

1 CHRON. 25: 1	**Moreover** David and the captains of the host separated to the service of the sons of A-saph,
1 Chron. 17: 10	**Moreover** I will subdue all thine enemies. **Furthermore** I tell thee that the LORD will build thee an house.
26: 6	**Also** unto Shem-ai-ah his son were sons born,

1 CHRON. 25: 7	*even* all that were **cunning,**
28: 21	for all manner of workmanship every willing **skilful** man,

1 CHRON. 25: 7	*even* all that were cunning, was two hundred **fourscore** and eight.
Genesis 5: 28	And La-mech lived an hundred **eighty** and two years,

N.B. The underlined word is a numerical term meaning twenty. To find the value of the 'score' number multiply 4x20=80.

1 CHRON. 28: 4	**Howbeit** the LORD God of Israel chose me before all my house of my father to be king over Israel for ever:
21: 24	**Nay; but** I will verily buy it for the full price:

1 CHRON. 28: 11	Then David gave to Solomon his son the pattern of the porch, and of the houses **thereof,**
1 Kings 7: 31	and four cubits the breadth **thereof,** and three cubits the height **of it.**

1 CHRON. 29: 2	and of **divers** colours, and **all manner of** precious stones,

1 CHRON. 29: 5	and for all manner of work *to be made* by the hands of **artificers.**
4: 14	the father of the valley of Cha-ra-shim; for they were **craftsmen.**

1 CHRON. 29: 10	**Wherefore** David blessed the LORD before all the

congregation:

: 13   Now **therefore,** our God, we thank thee, and praise thy glorious name.

2 CHRONICLES

2 CHRON. 1: 5	**Moreover** the brazen altar, that Bez-a-leel the son of U-ri,
4: 9	**Furthermore** he made the court of the priests,
2: 8	Send me **also** cedar trees,

2 CHRON. 1: 6	And Solomon went up **thither** to the brazen altar before the LORD,
: 3	for **there** was the tabernacle of the congregation of God,

2 CHRON. 1: 10	Give me **wisdom <u>and</u> knowledge,** that I may go out and come in before this people:
2: 12	who hath given to David the king a wise son, endued with **prudence <u>and</u> understanding,**

2 CHRON. 1: 15	and cedar trees made he as the sycamore that *are* in the **vale** for abundance.
35: 22	and came to fight in the **valley** of Me-gid-do.

2 CHRON. 2: 2	And Solomon **told** out threescore and ten thousand men to bear burdens.
: 17	And Solomon **numbered** all that *were* in the land of Israel,
5: 6	which could not be **told <u>nor</u> numbered** for multitude.
1 Kings 3: 8	that cannot be **numbered <u>nor</u> counted** for multitude.1Chron.
1 Chron. 9:22	These were **reckoned** by their genealogy in their villages,

N.B. note how the underlined words separate words and phrases having the same meaning.

2 CHRON. 2: 2	And Solomon told out **three<u>score</u>** and ten thousand men to bear burdens.
Ezra 2: 13	The children of Ad-o-ni-kam, six hundred **sixty** and six.

N.B. The underlined word is a numerical term meaning twenty. To find the value of the 'score' number multiply 3x20=60.

2 CHRON. 2: 2	and **four<u>score</u>** thousand to hew in the mountain,
Genesis 5: 28	And La-mech lived an hundred **eighty** and two years,

N.B. The underlined word is a numerical term meaning twenty. To find the value of the 'score' number multiply 4x20=80.

2 CHRON. 2: 3	and didst send him cedars to build him an house to dwell therein,

2 CHRON. 2: 7	Send me now therefore a man **cunning** to work in gold,

| **2 CHRON. 2: 7** | Send me now therefore a man **cunning** to work in gold, |
| : 14 | and his father *was* a man of Tyre, **skilful** to work in gold, |

| **2 CHRON. 2: 18** | And he set **threescore** and ten thousand of them *to be* bearers of burdens, |
| Ezra 2: 13 | The children of Ad-o-ni-kam, six hundred **sixty** and six. |

N.B. The underlined word is a mathematical term meaning twenty. To find the value of the 'score' number multiply 3x20=60.

| **2 CHRON. 2: 18** | and **fourscore** thousand *to* be hewers in the mountain, |
| Genesis 5: 28 | And La-mech lived an hundred **eighty** and two years: |

N.B. The underlined word is a mathematical term meaning twenty. To find the value of the score number multiply 4x20=80.

| **2 CHRON. 3: 5** | And the greater house he ceiled with fir tree, which he **overlaid** with fine gold, |
| 1 Kings 6: 5 | and the walls of the ceiling: *and* he **covered** *them* on the inside with wood, |

| **2 CHRON. 3: 7** | the beams, the posts, and the walls **thereof,** |
| 1 Kings 7: 27 | and four cubits the breadth **thereof,** and three cubits the height **of it.** |

| **2 CHRON. 3: 14** | And he **made** the vail *of* blue, and purple, and crimson, and fine linen, and **wrought** cherubims thereon. |

| **2 CHRON. 3: 14** | and fine linen, and wrought cherubims **thereon.** |
| Leviticus 13: 26 | But if the priest look **on it,** and behold, |

| **2 CHRON. 3: 15** | Also he made before the house two pillars of thirty and five cubits high, and the cha<u>p</u>iter that *was* **on the top** of each of them *was* five cubits, |
| 4: 12 | *To wit,* the two pillars, and the pommels, and the **chapiters** *which were* **on top of the two pillars,** |

N.B. note the underlined letters which are written in order spell the word cap and gives the meaning of the whole word.

2 CHRON. 4: 1	**Moreover** he made an altar of brass,
: 9	**Furthermore** he made the court of the priests,
1 Chron. 17: 10	**Moreover** I will subdue all thine enemies. **Furthermore** I tell thee that the LORD will build thee an house.

| **2 CHRON. 4: 1** | twenty cubits the length **thereof,** |
| : 5 | And the thickness **of it** *was* an handbreadth, |

| **2 CHRON. 4: 3** | And under it *was* the **similitude** of oxen, |

Job 4: 15	but I could not discern the **form** thereof: an **image** *was* before mine eyes,
2 CHRON. 4: 6	He made also ten **lavers,** and put five on the right hand, and five on the left, **to wash in** them:
2 CHRON. 4: 12	and the <u>chapiter</u>s *which were* **on the top** of the two pillars,

N.B. note the underlined letters in order give the meaning of the whole word which is verified by the three bold words.

2 CHRON. 4: 19	and the tables **whereon** the showbread *was set;*
2 Kings 18: 21	*even* upon Egypt, **on which** if a man lean,
2 CHRON. 5: 1	**Thus** all the work that Solomon made for the house of the LORD was finished:
1 Kings 7: 51	**So was ended** all the work that king Solomon made for the the house of the LORD.
2 CHRON. 5: 3	**Wherefore** all the men assembled themselves unto the king in the feast which *was* in the seventh month.
6: 10	The LORD **therefore** hath performed his word that he hath spoken.
2 CHRON. 5: 6	which could not **be told <u>nor</u> numbered** for multitude.

N.B. note how the underlined word separates words and phrases having the same meaning.

2 CHRON. 5: 7	to the **oracle of the house,** into **the most holy** *place,*
2 CHRON. 5: 8	and the cherubims covered the ark and the staves **thereof** above.
4: 5	And the thickness **of it** *was* an handbreadth,
2 CHRON. 5: 12	*being* arrayed in white linen, having cymbals and **psalteries and harps,**
Psalm 33: 2	Praise the LORD with **harp:** sing with the **psaltery <u>*and*</u> an instrument of ten strings.**
108: 2	Awake, **psaltery <u>and</u> harp:**
1 Chron. 13: 8	and with **harps, <u>and</u> with psalteries,**

N.B. note how the underlined words separate words and phrases having the same meaning.

2 CHRON. 6: 3	And the king turned his face, and blessed the **whole** congregation of Israel: and **all** the congregation of Israel stood.

2 CHRON. 6: 8	But the LORD said to David my father, **Forasmuch as** it was in thine heart to build an house for mine name,
: 9	**Notwithstanding** thou shalt not build the house;
1 Chron. 5: 1	(for he *was* the firstborn, **but, forasmuch, as** he had defiled his father's bed...)
2 CHRON. 6: 9	**Notwithstanding** thou shalt not build the house;
Genesis 26: 9	Behold, **of a surety** she *is* thy wife:
29: 14	**Surely** thou *art* my brother my bone and my flesh.
Leviticus 11: 4	**Nevertheless** these shall ye not eat of them that chew the cud,
1 Kings 1: 30	**Assuredly** Solomon thy son shall reign after me, and he shall sit upon my throne in my stead; even so will I **certainly** do this day.
2 CHRON. 6: 11	And **in it** have I put the ark, wherein *is* the covenant of the LORD,
Exodus 40: 3	And thou shalt put **therein** the ark of the testimony,
2 CHRON. 6: 11	And in it have I put the ark, **wherein** *is* the covenant of the **LORD,**
Job 3: 3	Let the day perish **wherein** I was born, and the night *in which* it was said, There is a man child conceived.
2 CHRON. 6: 17	Now then, O LORD God of Israel, let thy word be **verified,**
Genesis 42: 16	and ye shall be kept in prison, that your words may be **proved,**
2 CHRON. 6: 20	upon the place **whereof** thou hast said that thou wouldest put thy name there;
1 Kings 8: 29	*even* toward the place **of which** thou hast said, Thy name shall be there:
2 CHRON. 6: 22	If a man sin against his neighbour, and an oath be laid upon him **to make** him swear,
1 Kings 8: 31	If a man trespass against his neighbour, and an oath be laid upon him **to cause** him to swear,
2 CHRON. 6: 24	and shall return and confess thy name, and **pray and make supplication** before thee in this house;

N.B. note how the underlined word separates words and phrases having the same meaning.

2 CHRON. 6: 28	If there be dearth in the land, If there be pestilence,
1 Kings 8: 37	If there be in the land **famine,**
2 CHRON. 6: 28	If there be dearth in the land, if there be **pestilence,**
1 Kings 8: 37	whatsoever **plague,** whatsoever **sickness** *there be;*
2 Chron. 6: 28	whatsoever **sore** or whatsoever **sickness** *there be;*

173

1 CHRON. 6: 32	**Moreover** concerning the stranger,
1 Chron. 17: 10	**Moreover** I will subdue all thine enemies. **Furthermore** I tell thee that the LORD will build thee an house.
2 CHRON. 6: 34	If thy people go out **to war** against their enemies by the way that thou shalt send them,
1 Kings 8: 44	If thy people go out **to battle** against their enemy, whithersoever thou shalt send them,
2 CHRON. 6: 34	If thy people go out to war against their enemies **by the way that** thou shalt send them,
1 Kings 8: 44	If thy people go out to battle against their enemy **whithersoever** thou shalt send them,
2 CHRON. 6: 35	Then hear thou from the heavens **their prayer and supplication,** and maintain their cause.

N.B. note how the underlined word separates words and phrases having the same meaning.

2 CHRON. 6: 37	Yet if they **bethink** themselves in the land whither they are carried captive, **and turn and pray unto thee** in the land of their captivity,
1 Kings 8: 47	*Yet* if they **bethink** themselves in the land whither they were carried captives, **and repent, and make supplication unto thee** in the land of them that carried them captives,
2 CHRON. 6: 37	saying, **We have sinned, we have done amiss, and have dealt wickedly;**
2 CHRON. 6: 37	*Yet* if they bethink themselves in the land **whither** they are carried captive,
3: 1	**where** *the LORD* appeared unto David his father,
2 CHRON. 6: 40	Now, my God, let**, I beseech thee**, thine eyes be open,
2 Chron. 18: 4	Enquire, **I pray thee,** at the word of the LORD to day.
2 CHRON. 7: 7	Moreover Solomon **hallowed** the middle of the court that *was* before the house of the LORD:
29: 16	And the priests went into the inner part of the house of the LORD, **to cleanse** *it* **and brought out all the uncleanness** that they found in the temple of the LORD...
: 17	so **they sanctified the house of the LORD** in eight days;
2 CHRON. 7: 7	**Moreover** Solomon hallowed the middle of the court that *was* before the house of the LORD:
4: 9	**Furthermore** he made the court of the priests,
2 CHRON. 7: 15	Now mine eyes shall be open, and mine ears **attent** unto the

	prayer *that is made* in this place.
Nehemiah 1: 6	Let thine ear now be **attentive**, and thy eyes open,

2 CHRON. 7: 16	that my name may be there **for ever:** and mine eyes and mine heart shall be there **perpetually.**
2 CHRON. 8: 5	Also he built Beth-hor-on the upper, on the **nether,** fenced cities,
Nehemiah 4: 13	Therefore set I in the **lower** places behind the wall,

2 CHRON. 8: 1	And it came to pass at the end of twenty years, **wherein** Solomon had built the house of the LORD,
Job 3: 3	Let the day perish **wherein** I was born, and the night *in which* it was said, There is a man child conceived.

2 CHRON. 8: 16	and until it was **finished.** *So* the house of the LORD was **perfected.**

2 CHRON. 8: 18	and took **thence** four hundred and fifty talents of gold,
28: 8	and took away much spoil **from them,**

2 CHRON. 9: 1	And when the queen of Sheba heard of the fame of Solomon, she came to prove Solomon with hard questions at Jerusalem, **with a very great company,** and camels that bare spices, and gold in abundance,
1 Kings 10: 2	And she came to Jerusalem **with a very great train,** with camels, that bare spices, and very much gold,

2 CHRON. 9: 1	And when the queen of Sheba heard of the fame of Solomon, she came to prove Solomon with hard questions at Jerusalem, with a very great company, and camels that bare spices, and **gold in abundance,**
1 Kings 10: 2	And she came to Jerusalem with a very great train, with camels, that bare spices, and **very much gold,**

2 CHRON. 9: 4	his cupbearers also, and their **apparel;** and his ascent by which he went up into the house of the LORD;
1 Kings 10: 25	and vessels of gold, and **garments,** and armour,
21: 27	And it came to pass, when Ahab heard these words, that he rent his **clothes,**

2 CHRON. 9: 6	**Howbeit** I believed not their words,
8: 9	**But** of the children of Israel did Solomon make no servants for his work;

2 CHRON. 9: 11	and **harps and psalteries** for singers:
Psalms 33: 2	Praise the LORD with harp: sing unto him with the **psaltery and** an instrument of ten strings.

2 CHRON. 9: 14	Beside *that which* **chapmen and merchants** brought.

2 CHRON. 9: 19   And twelve lions stood there **on** the one side and on the other up**on** the six steps.

2 CHRON. 9: 24   and **raiment,** harness, and spices, horses, and mules,
1 Kings 10: 25   and **garments,** and armour, and spices, horses, and mules,

2 CHRON. 10: 2   And it came to pass, when Re-ho-bo-am the son of Ne-bat, who *was* in Egypt, **whither** he had fled from the presence of Solomon the king.
1 Kings 12: 2   And it came to pass, when Jer-o-bo-am the son of Ne-bat, who was yet in Egypt, heard *of it,* **(for** he was fled from the presence of king Solomon, and Jer-o-bo-am dwelt in Egypt;)
2 Chron. 3: 1   **where** *the* LORD appeared unto David his father,

2 CHRON. 10: 2   whither he **had** fled from the presence of Solomon the king.
1 Kings 12: 2   (for he **was** fled from the presence of king Solomon, and Jer-o-bo-am dwelt in Egypt;)

2 CHRON. 10: 6   What **counsel** give ye *me* to return answer to this people?
      : 9   What **advice** give ye that we may return answer to this people,

2 CHRON. 10: 14   My father made your yoke heavy, but I will add there**to:**
1 Kings 12: 14   My father made your yoke heavy, I will add **to** your yoke:

2 CHRON. 11: 1   And when Re-ho-bo-am was come to Jerusalem, he **gathered** of the house of Judah and Benjamin...
      5: 3   Wherefore all the men of Israel **assembled** unto the king in the feast which was in the seventh month.

2 CHRON. 11: 1   and Benjamin an hundred and **fourscore** thousand chosen *men,* which were warriors,
Genesis 5: 28   And La-mech lived an hundred **eighty** and two years,

N.B. The underlined word is a numerical term meaning twenty. To find the value of the 'score' number multiply 4x20=80.

2 CHRON. 11; 11   and put captains in them, and store of **victual,**
1 Kings 5: 9   and thou shalt accomplish my desire, in giving **food...**

2 CHRON. 12: 6   **Whereupon** the princes of Israel and the king humbled themselves;
Psalm 119: 49   Remember the word unto thy servant, **upon which** thou hast caused me to hope.

2 CHRON. 12: 10   Instead of which king Re-ho-bo-am made **shields of brass,**
1 Kings 14: 27   And king Re-ho-bo-am made in their stead **breasen shields,**

2 CHRON. 12: 10	**that** kept the entrance of the king's house.
1 Kings 14: 27	**which** kept the door of the king's house.

2 CHRON. 12: 10	that kept the **entrance** of the king's house.
1 Kings 14: 27	which kept the **door** of the king's house.

2 CHRON. 13: 7	And there are gathered unto him **vain men, the children of Belial,** and have strengthened themselves against Re-ho-bo-am the son of Solomon,

N.B. note how the comma separates words and phrases having the same meaning.

2 CHRON. 13: 11	and the candlestick of gold with the lamps **thereof,**
1 Kings 7: 31	And the mouth **of it** within the chapiter and above *was* a cubit:

2 CHRON. 13: 17	so there fell down **slain** of Israel five hundred thousand chosen men.
2 Chron. 18: 2	And Ahab **killed** sheep and oxen for him in abundance,

2 CHRON. 14: 8	And Asa had an army *of men* that bare **targets** and spears, out of Judah three hundred thousand; and out of Benjamin, that bare **shields,** and drew bows,

2 CHRON. 14: 8	two hundred and **fourscore** thousand; all these were mighty men of valour.
Genesis 5: 25	And Methuselah lived an hundred **eighty** and seven years,

N.B. The underlined word is a mathematical term meaning twenty. To find the value of the 'scoe' number multiply 4x20=80.

2 CHRON. 15: 17	**But** the high places were not taken away out of Israel: **Nevertheless** the heart of Asa was perfect all his days.

2 CHRON. 15: 17	But the high places were **not taken away** out of Israel:
1 Kings 15: 14	But the high places were **not removed:**

2 CHRON. 15: 18	And he brought into the house of God the things **that** his father had dedicated, and **that** he himself had dedicated,
1 Kings 15: 15	And he brought in the things **which** his father had dedicated, and the things **which** himself had dedicated,

2 CHRON. 16: 3	*There is* **a league** between me and thee,
Isaiah 28: 15	Because ye have said, We have made **covenant** with death, and with hell we are at **agreement;**

2 CHRON. 16: 6	and they carried away the stones of Ra-mah, and the timber **thereof,**
4: 5	And the thickness **of it** *was* an handbreadth,

2 CHRON. 16: 6	and the timber thereof, **wherewith** Ba-ash-a was building: and he built therewith Ge-ba and Mizpah.
2 Kings 19: 6	Be not afraid of the words **with which** the servants of the king of Assyria have blasphemed me.
2 CHRON. 16: 6	and he built **therewith** Ge-ba and Mizpah.
Deut. 16: 3	Thou shalt eat no leavened bread **with it**; seven days shalt thou eat unleavened **therewith,**
2 CHRON. 16: 9	**Herein** thou hast done foolishly: therefore henceforth thou shalt have wars.
Genesis 34: 15	But **in this** will we consent unto you:
2 CHRON. 16: 10	Then Asa **was wroth** with the seer, and put him in a prison house; for *he was* **in a rage** with him because of this *thing*.
2 CHRON. 16: 14	and laid him in the bed which was filled with sweet odours and **divers** kinds *of spices* prepared by the apothecaries, **art:**
2 CHRON. 17: 6	**moreover** he took away the high places and groves out of Judah.
2 Chron. 4: 9	**Furthermore** he made the court of the priests,
2 CHRON. 17: 15	And next to him *was* Je-ho-ha-nan the captain, and with him two hundred and **fourscore** thousand.
Genesis 5: 28	And La-mech lived an hundred **eighty** and two years.

N.B. The underlined word is a numerical term meaning twenty. To find the value of the 'score' number multiply 4x20=80.

2 CHRON. 18: 1	Now Je-hosh-a-phat had riches and honour in abundance, and **joined affinity** with Ahab.
21: 6	for he **had the daughter of Ahab to wife:**
2 CHRON. 18: 8	And the king of Israel called for one *of his* officers, and said, **Fetch quickly** Mi-cai-ah the son of Imlah.
1 Kings 22: 9	Then the king of Israel called an officer, **Hasten *hither*** Mi-cai-ah the son of Imlah.
2 CHRON. 18: 19	And the LORD said, Who shall **entice** Ahab king of Israel,
1 Kings 22: 20	And the LORD said, Who shall **persuade** Ahab,
2 CHRON. 18: 20	Then there came out a spirit, and stood before the LORD, and said, I will **entice** him. And the LORD said unto him, Wherewith?
2 CHRON. 18: 20	And the LORD said unto him, **Wherewith?**
: 15	And the king said to him, **How** many times...?

2 CHRON.18: 21	And *the LORD* said, Thou shalt **entice** *him,*
1 Kings 22: 21	And there came forth a spirit, and stood before the LORD, and said, I will **persuade** him.
2 CHRON. 18: 23	Then Zed-e-ki-ah the son of Chena-a-nah came near, and **smote** Mi-cai-ah upon the cheek,
13: 20	and the LORD **struck** him, and he died.
2 CHRON. 18: 31	It is the king of Israel. Therefore **compassed** about him to fight:
S.O.S. 4: 12	A garden **inclosed** *is* my sister,
2 CHRON. 18: 33	And a *certain* man drew a bow at a venture, and smote the king of Israel between the joints of the **harness:**
1 Kings 22: 38	and the dogs licked up his blood; and they washed his **armour;**
2 CHRON. 18: 33	therefore he said to his **chariot man,**
1 Kings 22: 34	wherefore he said unto the **driver of his chariot.**
2 CHRON. 19: 8	**Moreover** in Jerusalem did Je-hosh-a-phat set of the Levites,
4: 9	**Furthermore** he made the court of the priests,
2 CHRON. 20: 4	And Judah **gathered** themselves together,
: 26	And on the fourth day they **assembled** themselves in the valley Be-ra-chah,
2 CHRON. 20: 8	And they dwelt **therein,**

N.B. reverse the syllables and the meaning is clear.

2 CHRON. 20: 9	If, *when* evil cometh upon us, *as* the sword, judgment, or **pestilence,**
21: 14	Behold, with a great **plague** will the LORD smite thy people,
2 CHRON. 20: 27	Then they returned, every man of Judah and Jerusalem, and Je-hosh-a-phat in the **forefront** of them,

N.B. note that both syllables of the bold word mean the same thing, e.g forelegs of a horse refer to the front legs.

2 CHRON 20: 33	**Howbeit** the high places were not taken away:
25: 7	**But** there came a man of God came unto him,
2 CHRON. 21: 6	for he had the daughter of Ahab to wife: and he **wrought** *that which* was evil in the eyes of the LORD.
29: 2	And he **did** *that which was* right in the sight of the LORD, according to all that his father David **had done.**
2 Kings 18: 3	And he **did** *that which was* right in the sight of the LORD, according to all that his father David **did.**

2 CHRON. 21: 4	he strengthened himself, and **slew** all his brethren with the sword,
: 13	and also hast **slain** thy brethren of thy father's house,
25: 3	Now it came to pass, when the kingdom was established to him, that he **slew** his servants that had **killed** the king his father.
2 CHRON. 21: 18	And after all this the LORD **smote** him in his bowels with an incurable disease.
13: 20	and the LORD **struck** him, and he died.
2 CHRON. 22: 4	**Wherefore** he did evil in the sight of the LORD like the house of Ahab:
28: 11	Now me **therefore,** and deliver the captives again,
2 CHRON. 22: 8	and the sons of the brethren of A-ha-zi-ah, he **slew** them.
: 9	and when they **had slain** him,
25: 3	Now it came to pass, when the kingdom was established to him, that he **slew** his servants that **had killed** the king his father.
2 CHRON. 23: 9	**Moreover** Je-hoi-a-da the priest delivered to the captains of hundreds spears, and bucklers and shields,
4: 9	**Furthermore** he made the court of the priests,
23: 13	**also** the singers with instruments of musick,
2 CHRON. 23: 9	Moreover Je-hoi-a-da the priest delivered to the captains of hundreds spears, and **bucklers <u>and</u> shields,** that *had been* king David's,

N.B. note how the underlined word separates words and phrases having the same meaning.

2 CHRON. 24: 14	they brought the rest of the money before the king and Je-hoi-a-da, **whereof** were made vessels for the house of the LORD,
12: 10	Instead **of which** king Re-ho-bo-am made shields of brass,
Micah 2: 3	Behold, against this family do I devise an evil, **from which** ye shall not remove your necks;
2 CHRON. 24: 16	And they buried him in the city of David among the kings, because he **had done** good in Israel,
26: 4	And he **did** *that which was* right in the sight of the LORD,
2 CHRON. 24: 17	Now after the death of Je-hosh-a-phat came the princes of Judah, and **made obeisance** to the king.
1 Kings 1: 31	Then Bath-she-ba **bowed with** *her* **face to the earth, <u>and</u> did reverence** to the king,

2 CHRON. 24: 24	For the **army** of the Syrians came with a small company of men, and the LORD delivered a very great **host** into their hand,
2 CHRON. 25: 3	Now it came to pass, when the kingdom was established to him, that he slew his servants that had killed the king his father.
2 Kings 14: 5	And it came to pass, as soon as the kingdom was confirmed in his hand, that he slew his servants which had slain the king his father.
2 CHRON. 25: 3	Now it came to pass, when the kingdom was **established** to him, that he slew his servants that had killed the king his father.
2 Kings 14: 5	And it came to pass, when the kingdom was **confirmed** in in his hand, that he slew his servants which had killed his father.
2 CHRON. 25: 3	that he **slew** his servants that **had killed** the king his father.
2 Kings 14: 15	that he **slew** his servants which **had slain** the king his father.
2 CHRON. 25: 3	that he slew his servants **that** had killed the king his father.
2 Kings 14: 15	that he slew his servants **which** had killed the king his father.
2 CHRON. 25: 5	**Moreover** Am-a-zi-ah gathered Judah together,
4: 9	**Furthermore** he made the court of the priests,
: 24	the hostages **also,** and returned to Samaria.
31: 15	to give to their brethren by course, **as well** to the great and to the small:
2 CHRON. 26:14	and helmets, and **habergeons,** and bows,
1 Samuel 17: 5	and he *armed* with **a coat of mail:**
2 CHRON. 26: 15	And he made in Jerusalem engines, invented by **cunning** men,
2: 14	and his father *was* a man of Tyre, **skilful** to work in gold,
2 CHRON. 26: 17	And Az-a-ri-ah the priest went in after him, and with him **fourscore** priests of the LORD, *that were* valiant men:
Genesis 5: 28	And La-mech lived an hundred **eighty** and two years,

N.B. The underlined word is a mathematical term meaning twenty. To find the value of the 'score' number multiply 4x20=80.

2 CHRON. 26: 18	And they **withstood** Uz-zi-ah the king, and said unto him,
28: 12	and A-ma-sa the son of Had-la- i **stood against** them that came from the war,
2 CHRON. 26: 19	Then Uz-zi-ah **was wroth,** and had a censer in his hand to

	burn incense:
1 Kings 11: 9	And the LORD **was angry** with Solomon,
Daniel 2: 12	For this cause the king **was angry <u>and</u> very furious,**

N.B. note how the underlined word separates words and phrases having the same meaning.

<u>**2 CHRON. 26: 20**</u>	and they thrust him out from **thence;**
25: 27	but they sent to La-chish after him, and slew him **there.**

<u>**2 CHRON. 27: 4**</u>	**Moreover** he built cities in the mountains of Judah,
	His mother's name **also** *was* Je-ru-shah,
4: 9	**Furthermore** he made the court of the priests,

<u>**2 CHRON. 28: 5**</u>	**Wherefore** the LORD his God delivered him into the hand
	of the king of Syria;
: 11	Now hear me **therefore,**

<u>**2 CHRON. 28: 9**</u>	Behold, because the LORD God of your fathers **was wroth**
	with Judah, he hath delivered them into your hand, and ye have
	slain them **in a rage** *that* reacheth up into heaven.
: 11	and deliver the captives again, which ye have taken captive
	of your brethren: for the **fierce wrath** of the LORD *is*
	upon you.

<u>**2 CHRON. 28: 13**</u>	for **where<u>as</u>** we have offended against the LORD *already,*
: 6	**because** they had forsaken the LORD God of their fathers.
Genesis 2: 3	**because that** in it he had rested from all the work which God
	created and made.
22: 14	**as** it is said *to* this day,
26: 18	and he called their names after the names **by which** his father
	had called them.
Deut. 12: 12	**for<u>as</u>much as** he hath no part nor inheritance with you.
19: 6	**where<u>as</u>** he *was* not worthy of death, **in<u>as</u>much as** he hated
	him not in time past time.

<u>**2 CHRON. 28: 15**</u>	and with the spoil **clothed** all that were naked among them,
	and **arrayed** them,

<u>**2 CHRON. 28: 18**</u>	Gimzo also and the villages **thereof:**
1 Chron. 23: 26	they shall no *more* carry the tabernacle, nor any vessels **of it**
	for the service **thereof.**

<u>**2 CHRON. 29: 2**</u>	And he **did** *that which was* right in the sight the LORD,
	according to all that his father **had done.**

<u>**2 CHRON. 29: 8**</u>	**Wherefore** the wrath of the LORD was upon Judah and
	Jerusalem,
28: 11	Now hear **therefore,**

2 CHRON. 29: 22	So they killed the bullocks, and the priest received the blood, and sprinkled *it* on the altar: **likewise**; when they had killed the rams, they sprinkled the blood upon the altar: they killed **also** the lambs,
2 CHRON. 29: 24	And the priests killed them, and they made **reconciliation** with their blood upon the altar, to make an **atonement** for all Israel:
2 CHRON. 29: 32	which the congregation brought, was **threescore** and ten bullocks,
Ezra 2: 13	The children of Ad-o-ni-kam, six hundred **sixty** and six.

N.B. note the underlined word which is a numerical term meaning twenty. To find the value of the 'score' number multiply the number by twenty 3x20=60.

2 CHRON. 29: 35	So the service of the house of the LORD was **set in order**.
: 36	And Hez-e-ki-ah rejoiced, and all the people, that God had **prepared** the people:
2 CHRON. 30: 6	So **posts went with the letters** from the king and his princes throughout all Israel and Judah,
36: 16	But they mocked the **messengers** of God,
2 CHRON. 30: 10	but they **laughed them to scorn, and** mocked them.

N.B. note how the underlined word separates words and phrases having the same meaning.

2 CHRON. 30: 11	Nevertheless **divers** of Asher and Ma-nas-seh and of Ze-bu-lun humbled themselves,
: 13	And there assembled at Jerusalem **much people** to keep the feast of unleavened bread in the second month, **a very great congregation.**
: 18	For **a multitude** of the people, *even* **many** of E-phra-im,
2 CHRON. 31: 2	and for peace offerings, to minister, and **to give thanks, and to praise** in the gates of the tents of the LORD.

N.B. note how the underlined word separates words and phrases having the same meaning.

2 CHRON. 31: 14	And Kor-e the son of Imnah Levite, the porter toward the east, *was* over the free will **offerings** of God, to distribute the **oblations** of the LORD,
32: 23	And many brought **gifts** unto the LORD Jerusalem,
2 CHRON. 31: 20	And thus **did** Hez-e-ki-ah throughout all Judah, and **wrought** *that which was* good and right and truth before the LORD

his God.

2 CHRON. 32: 1	After these things, and the establishment **thereof,**
28: 15	and carried all the feeble **of them** upon asses

2 CHRON. 32: 3	which *were* **without** the city:
1 Kings 7: 9	and *so* on the **outside** toward the great court.

2 CHRON. 32: 9	After this did Sen-nach-er-ib king of Assyria send his servants to Jerusalem, (but he *himself laid siege* against La-chish, and **all his power** with him,)
2 Kings 18: 17	And the king of Assyria sent Tartan and Rab-sa-ris and Rab-sha-keh from La-chish to king Hez-e-ki-ah with **a great host** against Jerusalem.
Isaiah 36: 2	And the king of Assyria sent Rab-sha-keh from La-chish to Jerusalem unto king Hez-e-ki-ah with **a great army.**

2 CHON. 32: 17	He wrote also letters **to rail on the LORD God of Israel, and to speak against him** saying,

N.B. note how the underlined word separates words and phrases having the same meaning.

2 CHRON. 32: 18	Then they cried with a loud voice in the Jews' speech unto the people of Jerusalem that *were* on the wall, **to affright them, and to trouble them:**

2 CHRON. 32: 21	And when he was come into the house of his god, **they that came forth of his own bowels slew him** there with the sword.
2 Kings 19: 37	And it came to pass, as he was worshipping in the house of Nis-roch his god, that A-dram-me-lech and Sha-re-zer **his sons** smote him with the sword:

2 CHRON. 32: 23	And many brought **gifts** unto the LORD to Jerusalem, and **presents** to Hez-e-ki-ah king of Judah:

2 CHRON. 32: 23	so that he was magnified in the sight of all nations from **thenceforth.**
Isaiah 44: 8	have not I told thee **from that time,**

2 CHRON. 32: 25	But Hez-e-ki-ah rendered not again according to the benefit *done* unto him; for his heart wwas lifted up: **therefore** there was wrath upon him,
: 26	**Notwithstanding** Hez-e-ki-ah humbled himself for the pride of his heart,
: 31	**Howbeit** in *the business of* the ambassadors of the princes of Babylon,

2 CHRON. 32: 29	**Moreover** he provided him cities,

4: 9	**Furthermore** he made the court of the priests,
2 CHRON. 32: 31	**Howbeit** in *the business of* the ambassadors of the princes of Babylon,
: 25	**But** Hez-e-ki-ah rendered not again according to the benefit *done* unto him;
2 CHRON. 33: 4	Also he built altars in the house of the LORD, **whereof** the LORD had said, In Jerusalem shall my name be for ever.
2 Kings 21: 4	And he built altars in the house of the LORD, **of which** the LORD said, In Jerusalem will I put my name.
2 CHRON. 33: 6	And he **caused** his children to pass through the fire in the valley of the son of Hinnom:
2 Kings 21: 6	And he **made** his pass through the fire,
2 CHRON, 33: 6	he **wrought** much evil in the sight of the LORD, to provoke him to anger.
: 2	But **did** *that which was* evil in the sight of the LORD,
2 CHRON. 33: 6	he wrought much **evil** in the sight of the LORD,
2 Kings 21: 6	he wrought much **wickedness** in the sight of the LORD,
2 CHRON. 33: 7	And he set **a carved image,** the **idol** he had made,
2 CHRON. 33: 11	**Wherefore** the LORD brought upon them the captains of the host of the king of Assyria,
34: 25	**therefore** my wrath shall be poured out upon this place,
2 CHRON. 33: 12	And when he was in affliction, he **besought** the LORD his God,
: 13	And **prayed unto** him:
2 CHRON. 33: 14	Now after this he built a wall **without** the city of David,
1 Kings 7: 9	and *so* on the **outside** toward the great court.
2 CHRON. 33: 16	And he repaired the altar of the LORD, and sacrificed **thereon** peace offerings and thank offerings,
Exodus 30: 7	And Aaron shall burn **thereon** sweet incense every morning: when he dresseth the lamps, he shall burn incense **upon it.**
2 CHRON. 33: 19	His prayer also, and *how God* was intreated of him, and all **his sin, and his trespass,**

N.B. note how the underlined separates words and phrases having the same meaning.

2 CHRON. 33: 19	and the places **wherein** he built high places,

2 CHRON. 33: 24 But the people of the land **slew** all them that had conspired
against king Amon;

29: 22 So they **killed** the bullocks,

2 CHRON. 34: 2 And he did *that which was* right in the sight of the LORD,
and walked in the ways of David his father, and **declined**
neither to the right hand, nor to the left.

2 Kings 22: 2 And he did *which was* right in the sight of the LORD, and
walked in all the ways of David his father, and **turned not**
aside to the right hand, or the left.

2 Kings 15: 18 he **departed not** all the days from the sins of Jer-o-bo-am
the son of Ne-bat, who made Israel to sin.

2 CHRON. 34: 4 and made dust *of them,* and **strowed** *it* upon the graves of
them that had sacrificed unto them.

29: 22 and the priests **sprinkled** *it* on the altar:

2 CHRON. 34: 10 and they gave it to the workmen that **wrought** in the house of
the LORD, to repair and amend the house:

Nehemiah 4: 21 So we **laboured** in the work:

2 CHRON. 34: 11 Even to the **artificers** and builders gave they *it,*
Nehemiah 11: 35 Lod, and Ono, the valley of **craftsmen.**

2 CHRON. 34: 13 and *were* overseers of all that **wrought** the work in any
manner of service:

: 2 And he **did** *that which was* in the sight of the LORD,

2 CHRON. 34: 24 and upon the inhabitants **thereof,**
1 Kings 7: 27 and four cubits the breadth thereof, and three cubits the height
of it.

2 CHRON. 34: 25 that they might provoke me to **anger** with all the works of
their hands; therefore my **wrath** shall be poured out upon
this place, shall not be quenched.

2 CHRON. 34: 25 therefore my wrath shall be poured out upon this place,
shall not be **quenched.**

29: 7 Also they have shut up the doors of the porch, and **put out**
the lamps,

2 CHRON. 35: 1 **Moreover** Josiah kept a Passover unto the LORD in
Jerusalem:

35: 9 Co-na-ni-ah **also,** and Shem-ai-ah and Neth-a-neel,
1 Chron. 29: 1 **Furthermore** David the king said unto all the congregation,

2 CHRON. 35: 13 but the *other* holy *offerings* **sod** they in pots,
2 Kings 6: 29 So we **boiled** my son,

2 CHRON. 36: 15	And the LORD God of their fathers sent to them by his messengers, rising up **betimes,**
Genesis 28: 18	And Jacob rose up **early** in the morning,

2 CHRON. 36: 21	*for* as long as she desolate she kept sabbath, to fulfil **three-score** and ten years.
Ezra 2: 13	The children of Ad-o-ni-kam, six hundred **sixty** and six.

N.B. The underlined word is a mathematical term meaning twenty. To find the
value of the 'score' number multiply 3x20=60+10=70

2 CHRON. 36: 22	Now in the first year of Cyrus king of Persia, that the word of the LORD *spoken* by the mouth of Jeremiah might be **accomplished,**
Ezra 1: 1	Now in the first year of Cyrus king of Persia, that the word of the LORD by the mouth of Jeremiah might be **fulfilled,**

EZRA

EZRA 1: 1	Now in the first year of Cyrus king of Persia, that the word of the LORD by the mouth of Jeremiah might be **fulfilled,**
2 Chron. 36: 22	Now in the first year of Cyrus king of Persia, that the word of the LORD *spoken* by the mouth of Jeremiah might be **accomplished,**

EZRA 2: 9	The children of Zac-ca-i, seven hundred and **threescore.**
: 13	The children of Ad-o-ni-kam, six hundred **sixty** and six.

N.B. The underlined word is a mathematical word meaning twenty. To find the
value of the score number multiply 3x20=60.

EZRA 2: 63	And the **Tir-sha-tha** said unto them,
5: 3	At the same time came to them Tat-nai, **governor** on this side the river,

EZRA 3: 2	to offer burnt offerings **thereon** as *it is* written in the law of Moses the man of God.
Lev. 6: 12	and the priest shall burn wood **on it** every morning, and lay the burnt offering in order **upon it;** every morning and he shall burn **thereon** the fat of the peace offerings.

N.B. reverse the two syllables of the bold word in the first reference and the meaning
clear.

EZRA 3: 10	they set the priests in their **apparel** with trumpets,
2: 69	and one hundred priests' **garments.**
Neh. 4: 23	none of us put off our **clothes,**
Job 22: 6	and stripped the naked of their **clothing.**

EZRA 4: 2	and we do sacrifice unto him since the days of E-sar-had-don king of Assur, which brought us up **hither.**
Job 38: 11	and **here** shall thy proud waves be stayed?
EZRA 4: 14	and it **was not meet** for us to see the king's dishonour,
Jerem. 34: 15	And ye were now turned, and had done **right** in my sight,
EZRA 4: 14	therefore have we sent and **certified** the king;
8: 17	and I **told** them what they should say unto Iddo,
Daniel 9: 22	And he **informed** *me,*
EZRA 4: 16	and the walls **thereof** set up,
Psalm 80: 10	The hills were covered with the shadow **of it,** and the boughs **thereof** *were like* the goodly cedars.
EZRA 5: 10	We asked their names also, to **certify** thee,
2 Chr. 34: 23	Thus saith the LORD, God of Israel, **Tell** ye the man that sent you to me,
EZRA 6: 2	in the palace that *is* in the province of the Medes, a roll, and **therein** *was* a record thus written:
2 Chron. 6: 11	And **in it** have I put the ark, wherein *is* the covenant of the LORD,

N.B. Reverse the syllables of the bold word in the first reference and the meaning is clear.

EZRA 6: 3	*and* the breadth thereof **three**score cubits;
2: 13	The children of Ad-o-ni-kam, six hundred **sixty** and six.

N.B. The underlined word is a mathematical term meaning twenty. To find the value of the 'score' number multiply 3x20=60.

EZRA 6: 3	and let the foundations **thereof** be strongly laid;
1Chr. 23: 26	they shall no *more* carry the tabernacle, nor any vessels **of it** for the service **thereof.**
EZRA 6: 6	which *are* beyond the river, be ye far from **thence:**
2: 63	till **there** stood up a priest with U-rim and Thum-mim.
EZRA 6: 8	**Moreover** I make a decree what ye shall do to the elders of these Jews for the building of this house of God:
Job 34: 1	**Furthermore** E-li-hu answered and said,
EZRA 6: 8	**forthwith** expenses be given unto these men,
6: 8	I Dar-ri-us have made a decree; let it be **done with speed.**
: 13	according to that which Da-ri-us the king had sent, so they did **speedily.**
EZRA 6: 18	And they set the priests in their **divisions,** and the Levites in

	their **courses,**
EZRA 7: 20	**bestow** *it* out of the king's treasure house.
9: 8	and **give** us a little reviving in our bondage.
EZRA 7: 23	let it be **diligently** done for the house of the God of heaven:
Micah 1: 12	For the inhabitant of Mar-oth waited **carefully** for good:
EZRA 9: 3	and plucked off the hair of my head and off my beard, and sat down **astonied.**
Job 21: 5	Mark me, and be **astonished,**
32: 15	They were **amazed,**
EZRA 9: 14	Should we again break thy commandments, and **join in affinity** with the people of theses abominations?
Deut. 7: 3	Neither shalt thou **make marriages** with them;
1 Kings 3: 1	And Solomon **made affinity** with Pharaoh's daughter,
1 Kings 7: 8	Solomon made also an house for Pharaoh's daughter, whom he **had taken** *to wife,*

NEHEMIAH

NEH. 1: 3	and the gates thereof are **burned** with fire.
2: 3	and the gates thereof are **consumed** with fire?
NEH. 1: 11	O Lord, **I beseech thee,** let now thine ear be attentive to the prayer of thy servant, and to the prayer of your servants, who desire to fear thy name: and prosper, **I pray thee,** thy servant this day,
NEH. 1: 11	and grant him mercy in the sight of this man. For he was the king's **cupbearer.**
2: 1	in the twentieth year of Ar-ta-xerx-es the king, *that* **wine** *was* before him:
Genesis 40: 9	And the chief **butler** told his dream to Joseph,
NEH. 2: 1	Now I had not been *beforetime* sad in his presence.
1: 4	and prayed **before** the God of heaven,
2 Kings 13: 5	and the children of Israel dwelt in their **before**time.
NEH. 2: 2	**Wherefore** the king said unto me,
: 20	**therefore** we his servants will arise and build:
NEH. 3: 3	and set up the doors **thereof,**
: 1	and set up the doors **of it;**
NEH. 2: 7	**Moreover** I said unto the king,
: 18	as **also** the king's words that he had spoken unto me.
2 Chr. 4: 9	**Furthermore** he made the court of the priests,

<u>**NEH. 2: 15**</u>	and viewed the wall, and **turned backed,** and entered by the gate of the valley, and *so* **returned.**
<u>**NEH. 2: 16**</u> 13: 5	And the rulers knew not **whither** I went, or what I did; And he had prepared for him a great chamber, **where** afore-time they laid the meat offerings,
<u>**NEH. 2: 19**</u>	and Ge-shem the Arabian, heard *it*, **they laughed us to scorn, and despised us,**

N.B. note how the underlined word separates words and phrases having the same meaning.

<u>**NEH. 3: 3**</u> : 1	who *also* laid the beams **thereof,** and set up the doors, **thereof,** they sanctified it, and set up the doors **of it;**
<u>**NEH. 4: 9**</u> : 7	**Nevertheless** we made our prayer unto our God, **But** it came to pass,
<u>**NEH. 4: 15**</u> 5: 12	when our enemies heard that it was known unto us, and God had brought their counsel to **nought,** and will require **nothing** from them;
<u>**NEH. 4: 16**</u> 1 Sam. 17: 5 <u>**NEH. 4: 17**</u> : 21	and the bows, and the **habergeons;** and he *was* armed with **a coat of mail;** *every one* with one of his hands **wrought in the work,** So we **laboured in the work:**
<u>**NEH. 4: 20**</u> 5: 1	resort ye **thither** unto us: And **there** was a great cry of the people and of their wives...
<u>**NEH. 4: 22**</u> : 18 Deut. 22: 3	**Likewise** at the same time said I unto the people, as **also** the king's words that he had spoken unto me. **In like manner** shalt thou do with his ass;
<u>**NEH. 5: 3**</u> : 4	We have **mortgaged** our lands, We have **borrowed money** for the king's tribute,
<u>**NEH. 5: 3**</u> 2 Chr. 32: 11	that we might buy corn, because of the **dearth.** persuade you to give over yourselves to die by **famine** and by thirst,
<u>**NEH. 5: 6**</u> Num. 16: 15	And I was very **angry** when I heard their cry and these words. And Moses was very **wroth,**
<u>**NEH. 5: 7**</u> Prov. 28: 8	and said unto them, Ye exact **usury,** every one his brother. He that by usury and **unjust gain** increaseth his substance,

<u>**NEH. 5: 14**</u>	**Moreover** from the time that I was appointed to be their governor in the land of Judah,
: 16	Yea, **also** I continued in the work of this wall,
2 Chr. 4: 9	**Furthermore** he made the court of the priests,
<u>**NEH. 6: 1**</u>	and *that* there was no breach left **therein;**
9: 36	behold, we *are* servants **in it:**
<u>**NEH. 6: 6**</u>	**Wherein** *was* written,
Lev. 14: 40	take away the stones **in which** the plague *is,*
<u>**NEH. 6: 8**</u>	There are no things done as thou sayest, but **thou feignest them** out of thine own heart.
Job 35: 2	**Thinkest** thou this to be right,
<u>**NEH. 6: 10**</u>	Let us meet together in the house of God, **within** the temple,
1 Kings 6: 15	*and* he covered *them* on the **inside** with wood,
<u>**NEH. 6: 10**</u>	for they will come **to slay** thee;
Esther 3: 13	And the letters were sent by posts into all the king's provinces, **to destroy, to kill, <u>and</u> to cause to perish,**

N.B. note how the underlined word separates words and phrases having the same meaning.

<u>**NEH. 6: 16**</u>	for they perceived that this work was **wrought** of our God.
: 8	There are no such things **done** as thou sayest,
Isaiah 41: 4	Who hath **wrought <u>and</u> done** *it,*

N.B. note how the underlined word separates words and phrases having the same meaning.

<u>**NEH. 6: 17**</u>	**Moreover** in those days the nobles of Judah sent many letters unto To-bi-ah,
Job 34: 1	**Furthermore** E-li-hu answered and said,
<u>**NEH. 7: 4**</u>	Now the city *was* **large <u>and</u> great:**

N.B. note how the underlined word separates words and phrases having the same meaning.

<u>**NEH. 7: 4**</u>	but the people *were few* **therein,**
2 Chron. 6: 11	And **in it** have I put the ark,

N.B. Reverse the syllables of the first bold word and the meaning is clear.

<u>**NEH. 9: 26**</u>	**Nevertheless** they were disobedient,
: 27	**Therefore** thou deliveredst them into the hands of their enemies,

: 28	**But** after they had rest,
: 33	**Howbeit** thou *art* just in all that is brought upon us;

NEH. 7: 14	The children of Zac-ca-i, seven hundred and **threescore**.
Ezra 2: 13	The children of Ad-o-ni-kam, six hundred **sixty** and six.

N.B. The word score is a mathematical term meaning twenty. To find the value of the score number multiply 3x20=60.

NEH. 7: 26	The men of Beth-lehem and Ne-to-phah, an hundred **four-score** and eight.
Gen.5: 28	And La-mech lived an hundred **eighty** and two years.

N.B. The word score is a numerical term meaning twenty. To find the value of the 'score' number mutiply 4x20=80.

NEH. 7: 65	And the **Tir-sha-tha** said unto them,
8: 9	And **Nehemiah,** which is the **Tir-sha-tha,**
12: 26	and in the days of **Nehemiah the governor,**

NEH. 8: 15	And that they should **publish <u>and</u> proclaim** in all their cities,

N.B. note how the underlined word separates words and phrases having the same meaning.

NEH. 9: 6	the earth, and all *things* that *are* **therein,**
: 36	and the good thereof, behold we *are* servants **in it:**

N.B. reverse the the syllables of the bold word in thefirst reference nd the meaning is clear.

NEH. 9: 12	and in the night by a pillar of fire, to give them light in the way **wherein** they should go.
Job 3: 3	Let the day **wherein** I was born, and the night *in which* it was said, There is a man child conceived.
Isaiah 66: 4	but they did evil before mine eyes, and chose *that* **in which** I delighted not.

NEH. 9: 34	and thy testimonies, **wherewith** thou didst testify against them.
Zech. 13: 6	*Those* **with which** I was wounded *in* the house of my friends.

NEH. 10: 31	And *if* the people of the land **bring ware** or any victuals on the sabbath day to sell,
Ezek. 7: 13	For the seller shall not return to **that which is sold,**

NEH. 10: 31	And *if* the people of the land bring ware or any **victuals** on the sabbath day to sell,
Job 23: 12	I have esteemed the words of his mouth more than my necessary *food.*

NEH. 10: 37	and the **tithes** of our ground unto the Levites,
11: 1	to bring **one of ten** to dwell in Jerusalem the holy city,
Ezra 10: 16	and sat down in the first day of the **tenth** month to examine the matter.

NEH. 11: 6	All the sons of Pe-rez that dwelt at Jerusalem *were* four hundred **three<u>score</u>** and eight valiant men.
Num. 7: 88	the rams **sixty**, the he goats **sixty**,

N.B. The underlined word is a numerical term meaning twenty. To find the value of the 'score' number multiply 3x20=60.

NEH. 11: 18	All the Levites in the holy city *were* two hundred **four<u>score</u>** and four.
Gen. 5: 28	And La-mech lived an hundred **eighty** and two years,

N.B. The underlined word is a numerical term meaning twenty. To find the value of the 'score' number multiply 4x20=80.

NEH. 12: 8	**Moreover** the Levites:
: 29	**Also** from the house of Gilgal,
Job 34: 1	**Furthermore** E-li-hu answered and said,

NEH. 12: 25	*some* of the children of Judah dwelt at Kir-jath-ar-ba, and *in* the villages **thereof,**
3: 1	they sanctified it, and set up the doors **of it;**

NEH. 13: 5	where **aforetime** the laid the meat offerings,
: 4	And **before** this,
NEH. 13: 25	And I **contended** with them,
1 Sam. 25: 39	Blessed *be* the LORD, that hath **pleaded** the cause of my reproach from the hand of Na-bal,

ESTHER

ESTHER 1: 4	*even* an hundred and **four<u>score</u>** days.
Genesis 5: 28	And La-mech lived an hundred **eighty** and two years,

N.B. The underlined word is a numerical term meaning twenty. To find the value of the 'score' number multiply 4x20=80.

ESTHER 1: 5	And when these days **were expired,**
Deut. 31: 24	until they **were finished.**
34: 8	so the days of weeping *and* mourning for Moses **were ended.**

ESTHER 1: 12	therefore was the king **very wroth,** and his anger burned in him.
Nehemiah 5: 6	And I was **very angry** when I heard their cry and these words.

ESTHER 1: 12	therefore was the king very wroth, and his **anger** burned in him.
: 18	Thus *shall there arise* too much contempt and **wrath.**
ESTHER 1: 18	Thus *shall there arise* too much **contempt** and wrath.
3: 6	And he thought it **scorn** to lay hands on Mor-de-ca-I alone;
ESTHER 1: 22	into every province according to the writing **thereof,**
1 Chron. 23: 26	And also unto the Levites; they shall no *more* carry the tabernacle, nor any vessels **of it** for the service **thereof.**
ESTHER 2: 1	After these things, when the wrath of king A-has-u-e-rus was **appeased,**
7: 10	Then was the the king's wrath **pacified.**
Job 27: 14	and his offspring shall not be **satisfied** with bread.
ESTHER 2: 2	Let there be fair young **virgins** sought for the king:
: 8	and when many **maidens** were gathered together unto Shu-shan the palace,
ESTHER 2: 9	and he **preferred** her and her maids unto the best *place* of the house of the women.
5: 11	and all *the things* wherein the king had **promoted** him,
ESTHER 2: 10	Esther had not shewed her people not her **kin**dred:
8: 6	For how can I endure to see the evil that shall come to my **family?** or how can I endure to see the destruction of my **kindred?**
ESTHER 2: 17	and she obtained **grace <u>and</u> favour** in his sight more than all the virgins;

N.B. note how the underlined verse separates words and phrases having the same meaning.

ESTHER 2: 22	And the thing was known to Mor-de-ca-i, who **told** *it* unto Esther the queen; and Esther **certified** the king *thereof* in Mor-de-ca-i's name.
Daniel 9: 22	And he **informed** *me,* and talked with me,
ESTHER 3: 1	After these did king A-has-u-e-rus **promote** Ha-man the son of Ag-a-gite, and **advanced him,**
ESTHER 3: 5	And when Ha-man saw that Mor-de-ca-i **bowed not, <u>nor</u> did him reverence,** then was Ha-man full of wrath.

N.B. note how the underlined word separates words and phrases having the same meaning. Note also the comma that does the same thing.

ESTHER 3: 8 There is a certain people **scattered abroad and dispersed** among the people in all the provinces of thy kingdom;

N.B. note the underlined word which separates words and phrases having the same meaning.

ESTHER 3: 8 therefore it *is* not for the king's profit to **suffer** them.
    : 9 If it please the king, **let** it be written that they may be destroyed:

ESTHER 3: 13 And the letters were sent by posts into all the king's provinces, **to destroy, to kill, and to cause to perish,**

N.B. note the underlined word which separates words and phrases having the same meaning.

ESTHER 3: 6 **wherefore** Ha-man sought to destroy all the Jews...
    : 8 **therefore** it *is* not for the king's profit to suffer them.

ESTHER 3: 15 The **posts** went out, hastened by the king's commandment,
Nehemiah 6: 3 And I sent **messengers** unto them,

ESTHER 4: 3 And in every province, **whithersoever** the king's command-ment and his decree came,
    7: 5 Who is he, and **where** is he, that durst presume in his heart to do so?

ESTHER 4: 4 and she sent **raiment** to clothe Mor-de-ca-i,
    : 1 Mor-de-ca-i rent his **clothes,**
Job 22: 6 and stripped the naked of their **clothing.**
ESTHER 4: 16 I **also** and my maidens will fast **likewise;**
2 Chron. 31: 15 **as well** as to the great as to the small:

ESTHER 5: 6 What *is* thy **petition?** and it shall be granted thee: and what *is* thy **request?**

ESTHER 5: 11 and all *the things* **wherein** the king had promoted him,
Judges 4: 14 for this *is* the day **in which** the LORD hath delivered Sis-e-ra into thine hand:

ESTHER 5: 11 and all *the things* wherein the king **had promoted him, and how he had advanced him** above the princes and servants of the king.

ESTHER 5: 14 and to morrow speak thou unto the king that Mor-de-ca-i may be hanged **thereon:**
Lev. 6: 12 and the priest shall burn wood **on it** every morning, and lay the burnt offering in order **upon it;** and he shall burn **thereon** the fat of the peace offerings.

ESTHER 6: 8	Let the royal **apparel** be brought which the king *useth* to wear,
4: 1	Mor-de-ca-i rent his **clothes,**
: 4	and she sent **raiment** to clothe Mor-de-ca-i,
ESTHER 6: 9	that they may **array** the man *withal* whom the king delighteth to honour,
4: 4	and she sent raiment **to clothe** Mor-de-ca-i,
ESTHER 6: 13	And Ha-man told Ze-resh his wife and all his every *thing* that had **befallen** him.
4: 7	And Mor-de-ca-i told him of all that had **happened** unto him,
ESTHER 7: 4	although the enemy could **countervail** the king's damage.
8: 5	let it be written to **reverse** the letters devised by Ha-man the son of Ham-me-da-tha the Ag-a-gite,
ESTHER 7: 8	and Ha-man was fallen upon the bed **whereon** Esther *was.*
2 Kings 18: 21	*even* upon Egypt, **on which** if a man lean,
Psalm 119: 49	Remember thy word unto thy servant, **upon which** thou hast caused me to hope.
ESTHER 7: 9	Then the king said, Hang him **thereon.**
Leviticus 6: 12	and the priest shall burn wood **on it** every morning, and lay the burnt offering in order **upon it;** and he shall burn **thereon** the fat of the peace offerings.
ESTHER 7: 10	Then was the king's wrath **pacified.**
Job 27: 14	and his offspring shall not be **satisfied** with bread.
ESTHER 8: 3	and fell down at his feet, and **besought him** with tears to put away the mischief of Ha-man the Ag-a-gite,
Job 19: 16	I **intreated him** with my mouth.
ESTHER 8: 6	For how can I endure to see the evil that has come unto **my people?** or how can I endure to see the destruction of **my kin**dred?
ESTHER 8: 9	that *is,* the month Si-van, on the three and twentieth *day* **thereof,**
Neh. 3: 3	they sanctified it, and set up the doors **of it;**
ESTHER 8: 11	**Wherein** the king granted the Jews **which** *were* in every city to gather themselves together,
ESTHER 8: 14	*So* the **posts** that rode upon mules *and* camels went out,
2 Samuel 5: 11	And Hiram king of Tyre sent **messengers** to David,
ESTHER 8: 15	And Mor-de-ca-i went out from the presence of the king in royal **apparel** of blue and white,

Job 22: 6	and stripped the naked of their **clothing.**
ESTHER 8: 17	And in every province, and in every city, **whithersoever** the king's commandment and decree came,
7: 5	Who is he, and **where** is he, that durst presume in his heart to do so?
ESTHER 9: 2	and no man could **withstand** them;
Zechariah 3: 1	and Satan standing at his right hand to **resist** him.
ESTHER 9: 11	On that day the number of them that were **slain** in Shu-shan the palace was brought before the king.
Ezra 6: 20	and **killed** the passover for all the children of the captivity,
ESTHER 9: 16	and had rest from their **enemies,** and slew of their **foes** seventy and five thousand,
ESTHER 9: 20	*both* **nigh** and far,
5: 2	So Esther drew **near,**
ESTHER 9: 22	As the days **wherein** the Jews rested from their enemies,
Job 3: 3	Let the day perish **wherein** I was born, and the night *in which* it was said, There is a man child conceived.
ESTHER 9: 31	To confirm these days of Pu-rim in their times *appointed,* as Mor-de-ca-i the Jew and Esther the queen had **enjoined** them, and as they **decreed** for themselves and for their seed,
: 27	The Jews **ordained,** and took upon them,
Job 13: 18	Behold now, I have **ordered** *my* cause;

JOB

JOB 1: 1	and that man was **perfect and upright,** and one that feared God,
4: 7	or where were the **righteous** cut off ?

N.B. note how the underlined word separates words and phrases having the same meaning.

JOB. 1: 1	and one that feared God, and **eschewed** evil.
34: 27	Because they **turned back from** him,
2 Chron. 20: 10	but they **turned from** them,
25: 27	Now after the time that Am-a-zi-ah **did turn away from** following the LORD...
1 Samuel 16: 14	But the Spirit **departed from** Saul,
JOB 1: 9	Then Satan answered the LORD, and said, Doth Job fear God **for nought?**
6: 21	for now ye are **nothing;**

JOB 1: 17	and have carried them away, yea, and **slain** with the edge of the sword;
Ezra 6: 20	and **killed** the passover for all the captivity,
JOB 1: 19	and **smote** the four corners of the house,
2 Chron. 13: 20	and the LORD **struck** him, and he died.
JOB 1: 21	and naked shall I return **thither:**
: 13	And **there** was a day when his sons and his daughters...
JOB 2: 2	And the LORD said unto Satan, From **whence** comest thou?
4: 7	or **where** were the righteous cut off?
JOB 2: 3	a perfect man and an upright man, one that feareth God, and **escheweth** evil?
Isaiah 59: 15	and he *that* **departeth from** evil maketh himself a prey:
14: 25	then shall his yoke **depart from** off them,
JOB 2: 7	So went Satan forth from the presence of the LORD, **smote** Job with sore boils from the sole of his foot unto his crown.
2 Chron. 13: 20	and the LORD **struck** him, and he died.
Ezra 6: 20	and **killed** the passover for all the children of the captivity,
JOB 3: 3	Let the day perish **wherein** I was born, and the night *in which* it was said, There is a man child conceived.
Judges 4:14	And Deborah said unto Barak, Up; for this *is* the day **in which** the LORD hath delivered Sisera into thine hand:
JOB 3: 7	Lo, that night be solitary, let no joyful voice come **therein.**
6: 29	yea, return again, my righteousness *is* **in it.**
JOB 3: 9	Let the stars of the twilight **thereof** be dark;
1 Kings 7: 27	and four cubits the breadth **thereof,** and three cubits the height **of it.**
JOB 3: 17	There the wicked **cease** *from* troubling; and there the weary **be at rest.**
JOB 3: 20	**Wherefore** is light given to him that is in misery,
5: 17	**therefore** despise not the chastening of the Almighty:
JOB 4: 2	*If* we **assay** to communicate with thee,
7: 18	*and* **try** him every moment?
JOB 4: 7	Remember, I pray thee, who *ever* perished, being innocent? or where were the **righteous** were cut off?
: 6	and the **upright**ness of thy ways?
JOB 4: 12	and mine ear received a little **thereof.**
Neh. 3: 1	and set up the doors **of it;**

JOB 5: 2	For wrath **killeth** the foolish man, and envy **slayeth** the silly one.
JOB 5: 6	Although **affliction** cometh not forth of the dust, neither doth **trouble** spring out of the ground;
JOB 5: 13	and the counsel of the **froward** is carried headlong.
3: 17	There the **wicked** cease *from* troubling;
Deut. 32: 5	*they are* a **perverse and crooked** generation.

N.B. note how the underlined word separates words and phrases having the same meaning.

JOB 5: 25	Thou shalt know also that thy **seed** *shall be* great, and thine **offspring** as the grass of the earth.
JOB 5: 26	Thou shalt come to *thy* grave in a full age, like as a **shock** of corn.
Exod. 22: 6	If fire break out, and catch in thorns, so that the **stacks of corn,**
JOB 6: 4	For the arrows of the Almighty *are* within me, the poison **whereof** drinketh up my spirit.
2 Chron. 33: 7	in the house of God **of which** God had said to David and Solomon his son,
JOB 6: 15	My brethren have dealt deceitfully as a **brook,** *and* as the **stream** of brooks they pass away;
JOB 6: 16	Which are blackish **by reason of** the ice,
: 20	They were confounded **because** they had hoped;
JOB 6: 16	Which are blackish by reason of the ice, *and* **wherein** the snow is hid:
3: 3	and the night **in which** it was said, There is a man child conceived.
JOB 6: 20	they came **thither,** and were ashamed.
38: 11	and **here** shall thy waves be stayed?
JOB 6: 24	and cause me to understand **wherein** I have erred.
: 10	**In what** *therefore* ye hear the sound of the trumpet,
JOB. 7: 1	*are not* his days also like the days of an **hireling?**
: 2	As a **servant** earnestly desireth the shadow, and as an **hireling** looketh for *the reward of* his work.
JOB 7: 13	When I say, My **bed** shall comfort me, my **couch** shall ease my complaint;

JOB 8: 3　　　　　**Doth God pervert judgment? <u>or</u> doth the Almighty pervert justice?**

N.B. note how the underlined word separates words and phrases having the same meaning.

JOB 8: 5　　　　　If thou wouldest seek unto God **betimes,**
Psalm 63: 1　　　　O God, thou *art* my God; **early** will I seek thee:

JOB 8: 5　　　　　and make my **supplication** to the Almighty;
　　15: 4　　　　　and restraineth **prayer** before God.

JOB 8: 6　　　　　If thou *wert* **pure <u>and</u> upright;**
　　: 20　　　　　　Behold, God will not cast away a **perfect** *man,*

N.B. note how the underlined word separates words and phrases having the same meaning.

JOB 8: 10　　　　Shall not they teach thee, *and* **tell** thee, and **utter** words out of their heart?
　　: 2　　　　　　How long wilt thou **speak** these *things?*

JOB 8: 22　　　　and the dwelling place of the wicked shall come to **nought.**
　　6: 18　　　　　they go to **nothing,** and perish.

JOB 9: 3　　　　　If he will **contend** with him,
Ps. 43: 1　　　　　and **plead** my cause against an ungodly nation:

JOB 9: 6　　　　　Which shaketh the earth out of her place, and the pillars **thereof** tremble.
　　28: 5　　　　　*As for* the earth, out **of it** cometh bread:

JOB 9: 11　　　　Lo, he **goeth by** me, and I see *him* not: he **passeth on** also,

JOB 9: 11　　　　Lo, he goeth by me, and I **see** *him* not: he passeth on also, but I **perceive** him not.

JOB 9: 25　　　　Now my days are swifter than a **post:**
1 Sam. 5: 11　　　And Hiram king of Tyre sent **messengers** to David,
JOB 9: 33　　　　Neither is there any daysman **betwixt** us,
　　41: 16　　　　　that no air can come **between** them.

JOB 10: 2　　　　Do not condemn me; shew me **wherefore** thou contendest with me.
　　9: 29　　　　　*If* I be wicked, **why** then labour I in vain?

JOB 10: 8　　　　Thine hands have **made me <u>and</u> fashioned me** together round about;

N.B. note how the underlined word separates words and phrases having the same meaning.

JOB 10: 9	Remember, **I beseech thee,** that thou hast made me as the clay;
8: 8	For enquire, **I pray thee,** of the former age,
JOB 10: 10	**Wherefore** then hast thou brought me forth out of the womb?
9: 29	*If* I be wicked, **why** then labour I in vain:
JOB 12: 9	Who knoweth not in all these the hand of the LORD hath **wrought** this?
21: 31	and who shall repay him *what* he **hath done?**
28: 27	Then **did** he see it,
JOB 12: 20	He **removeth away** the speech of the trusty, and **taketh away** the understanding of the aged.
JOB 12: 21	He poureth **contempt** upon princes,
: 4	the just upright *man is* laughed to **scorn.**
JOB 13: 7	**Will ye speak wickedly for God? and talk deceitfully for him?**

N.B. note how the underlined word separates words and phrases having the same meaning.

JOB 13: 14	**Wherefore** do I take my flesh in my teeth, put my life in mine hand?
9: 29	*If* I be wicked, **why** then labour I in vain?
JOB 13: 17	Hear **diligently** my speech, and my **declaration** with your ears.
Deut. 15: 5	Only if thou **carefully** hearken unto the voice of the LORD thy God,
JOB 13: 23	How many *are* mine **iniquities and sins?** make me to know **my transgression and my sin.**

N.B. note how the underlined words separates words and phrases having the same meaning.

JOB 14: 7	that it will sprout again, and that the tender **branch** thereof will not cease.
: 9	*Yet* through the scent of water it will bud, and bring forth **boughs** like a plant.
JOB 14: 7	and that the tender branch **thereof** will not cease.
1 Kings 7: 27	and four cubits the breadth **thereof,** and three cubits the

height **of it.**

JOB 14: 18 And surely the mountain falling cometh to **nought,**
24: 25 and make my speech **nothing** worth?

JOB 15: 3 Should he reason with **unprofitable talk? or with speeches
wherewith he can do no good?**

N.B. note the underlined word which separates words and phrases having the same
meaning.

JOB 15: 3 Should he reason with unprofitable talk? or with speeches
wherewith he can do no good?
2 Kings 19: 6 Be not afraid of the words which thou hast heard, **with which**
the servants of the king of Assyria hath blasphemed me.

JOB 15: 6 Thine own mouth **condemneth** thee, and not I: yea, thine own
testify against thee.

JOB 15: 16 How much more **abominable and filthy** *is* man, which
drinketh iniquity like water?

N.B. note how the underlined word separates words and phrases having the same
meaning.

JOB 15: 20 The wicked man **travaileth** with **pain** all *his* days,
: 24 **Trouble and anguish** shall make him afraid;

N.B. note how the underlined word separates words and phrases having the same
meaning.

JOB 15: 26 He runneth upon him, *even* on *his* neck, upon the thick bosses
of his **bucklers:**
Psalm 35: 2 Take hold of **shield and buckler,** and stand up for mine help.

N.B. note how the underlined word separates words and phrases having the same
meaning.

JOB 15: 27 and maketh **collops** of fat on *his* flanks.
19: 2 and break me in **pieces** with words?
Esther 9: 22 and of sending **portions** one to another,

JOB 15: 31 Let not him that is deceived trust in vanity: for vanity shall be
his **recompence.**
6: 22 Did I say, Bring unto me? or, Give a **reward** for me of your
substance?

JOB 16: 3 Shall **vain words** have an end?

15: 3	Should he reason with **unprofitable talk?**
JOB 16: 6	Though I speak, my grief is not **asswaged:** and *though* I forbear, what am I **eased?**
Gen. 8: 5	And the waters were **decreased** continually until the tenth *month,*
JOB 16: 11	God hath delivered me to the **ungodly,** and turned me over into the **wicked.**
JOB 16: 12	I was at ease but he hath **broken me asunder:** he hath also taken *me* by my neck, and **shaken me to pieces,**
JOB 16: 13	His **archers** compass me around about,
Jerem 4: 29	The whole city shall flee for the noise of the horsemen and **bowmen,**
JOB 16: 13	His archers **compass me round about,** he cleaveth my reins asunder, and doth not spare;
19: 10	He hath destroyed me **on every side,** and I am gone:
JOB 16: 13	he poureth out my **gall** upon the ground.
13: 26	For thou writest **bitter things** against me,
JOB 17: 6	and **aforetime** I was as a tabret.
1 Chr. 11: 2	Moreover **in time past,** even when Saul was king,
JOB 17: 6	and aforetime I was as a **tabret.**
1 Sam. 10: 5	and a **tabret,** and a pipe, and a harp before them.

N.B. the bold word is in a group of musical instruments, therefore it is a musical instrument.

JOB 17: 8	**Upright** *men* shall be astonied at this,
: 9	The **righteous** also shall hold on his way,
JOB 17: 8	Upright *men* shall be **astonied** at this,
21: 5	Mark me, and be **astonished,**
32: 15	They were **amazed,** they answered no more:
JOB 18: 3	**Wherefore** are counted beasts,
9: 29	*If* I be wicked, **why** then labour I in vain?
JOB 18: 7	The steps of his strength shall be **straitened,**
Judg. 2: 15	and they were **greatly distressed.**
JOB 18: 8	For he is cast into a **net** by his own feet, and he walketh upon a **snare.**
: 9	The **gin** shall take *him* by the heel,

: 10	and a **trap** for him in the way.
JOB 18: 20	as they were **affrighted.**
: 11	Terrors shall make him **afraid** on every side,
JOB 19: 13	He hath put my brethren **far from** me, and my acquaintance are verily **estranged from** me.
19: 19	and they whom I loved are **turned against** me.
Neh. 13: 3	that they **separated from** Israel all the mixed multitude.
JOB 19: 13	and mine acquaintance are **verily** estranged from me.
18: 21	**Surely** such *are* the dwellings of the wicked,
36: 4	For **truly** my words *shall* not *be* false:
JOB 19: 15	count me for a **stranger:** I am an **alien** in their sight.
JOB 19: 19	All my inward friends **abhorred** me:
31: 29	If I rejoiced at the destruction of him that **hated** me,
JOB 20: 16	He shall suck the poison of **asps:** the **viper's** tongue shall slay him.
JOB 20: 18	according to *his* substance *shall* the restitution *be*, and he shall not rejoice *therein.*
22: 8	and the honourable man dwelt **in it.**
JOB 20: 22	In the fullness of his sufficiently he shall be **in straits:**
Genesis 32: 7	Then Jacob was **greatly afraid and distressed:**

N.B. note how the underlined word separates words and phrases having the same meaning.

JOB 21: 2	Hear **diligently** my speech, and let this be your consolations.
Deut. 15: 5	Only if thou **carefully** hearken unto the voice of the LORD thy God,
JOB 21: 2	Hear diligently my speech, and let this be your **consolations.**
Ps. 94: 19	In the multitude of my thoughts within me thy **comforts** delight my soul.
JOB 21: 7	**Wherefore** do the wicked live, become old, yea, are mighty in power?
: 4	**why** should not my spirit be troubled?
JOB 21: 17	How **oft** is the candle of the wicked put out!
Prov. 29: 1	He, that being **often** reproved hardeneth *his* neck,
JOB 21: 20	and he shall drink of the **wrath** of the Almighty.
: 17	*God* distributeth sorrows in his **anger.**

JOB 21: 33	as *there are* **innumerable** before him.
9: 10	yea, and wonders **without number.**
JOB 22: 6	For thou hast taken a pledge from thy brother for **nought,**
24: 25	and make my speech **nothing** worth?
JOB 22: 20	**Whereas** our substance is not cut down, **but** the remnant of them the fire consumeth.
Jud. 13: 16	**Though** thou detain me,
JOB 22: 21	Acquaint now thyself with him and be at peace, **thereby** good shall come unto thee.
28: 8	The lion's whelps have not trodden it, nor the fierce lion passed **by it.**
Ps. 41: 11	**By this** I know that thou favourest me,
JOB 24: 5	rising **betimes** for a prey:
Prov. 27: 14	rising **early** in the morning,
JOB 24: 7	They cause the **naked** to lodge **without clothing,** that *they have* **no covering** in the gold.
: 10	They cause *him* to go **naked without clothing,**
JOB 24: 13	they know not the ways **thereof,**
1 Kings 7: 27	and four cubits the breadth **thereof,** and three cubits the height **of it.**
JOB 24: 14	The murderer rising with the light killeth **the poor <u>and</u> needy,**

N.B. note the underlined word which separates words and phrases having the same meaning.

JOB 24: 23	*Though* it be given him *to be* in safety, **whereon** he resteth;
2 Kings 18: 21	*even* upon Egypt **on which** if a man lean, it will go into his hand,
JOB 26: 5	Dead *things* are formed from under the waters, and the inhabitants **thereof.**
28: 17	and the exchange **of it** *shall not be for* jewels of jewels of fine gold.
JOB 26: 6	Hell *is* **naked** before him, and destruction hath **no covering.**
JOB 26: 10	He hath **compassed** the waters with bounds,
Psalm 22: 16	the assembly of the wicked have **inclosed** me:
JOB 27: 1	**Moreover** Job continued his parable, and said,
34: 1	**Furthermore** E-li-hu answered and said,
JOB 27: 4	My lips shall not **speak wickedness,** nor my tongue **utter**

deceit.

JOB 27: 16	and prepare **raiment** as the clay;
31: 19	If I have seen any perish for want of **clothing,**
JOB 27: 20	Terrors take hold on him as waters, a **tempest** stealeth him away in the night.
: 21	and as a **storm** hurleth him out of his place.
JOB 28: 20	**Whence** then cometh wisdom? **and where** *is* the place of understanding?
JOB 30: 2	Yea, **whereto** *might* the strength of their hands *profit* me?
25: 4	**How** then can be justified with God?
JOB 30: 10	They **abhor** me, they flee far from me,
8: 22	They that **hate** thee shall be clothed with shame;
7: 16	I **loathe** *it;* I would not live always:
16: 20	My friends **scorn** me:
JOB 30: 13	They mar my path, they set forward my **calamity,**
: 16	the days of **affliction** have taken hold upon me.
: 25	Did not I weep for him that was in **trouble?**
JOB 30: 24	**Howbeit** he will not stretch out *his* hand to the grave,
: 1	**But** now *they that are* younger than I have me in derision,
32: 10	**Therefore** I said, Hearken to me;
Psalm 31: 22	**nevertheless** thou heardest the voice of my supplications when I cried unto thee.
JOB 30: 27	the days of affliction **prevented me.**
Psalm 95: 2	**come before** his presence with thanksgiving,
JOB 31: 3	*Is* not destruction to the **wicked?** and a strange *punishment* to the **workers of iniquity?**
JOB 31: 11	For this *is* an **heinous** crime;
28: 28	and to depart from **evil** *is* understanding.
27: 13	This *is* the portion of a **wicked** man with God,
JOB 31: 15	Did not he that made me in the womb **make** him? and did not one **fashion** us in the womb?
JOB 31: 17	and the fatherless hath not eaten **thereof;**
28: 17	and the exchange **of it** *shall not be for* jewels of fine gold.
JOB 31: 34	Did I fear a great multitude, or did the **contempt** of families terrify me..?
22: 19	and the innocent laugh them to **scorn.**

JOB 22: 20	**Whereas** our substance is not cut down, **but** the remnant of them the fire consumeth.
Jud. 13: 16	**Though** thou detain me,
JOB 22: 21	Acquaint now thyself with him and be at peace, **thereby** good shall come unto thee.
28: 8	The lion's whelps have not trodden it, nor the fierce lion passed **by it.**
Ps. 41: 11	**By this** I know that thou favourest me,
JOB 24: 5	rising **betimes** for a prey:
Prov. 27: 14	rising **early** in the morning,
JOB 24: 7	They cause the **naked** to lodge **without clothing,** that *they have* **no covering** in the gold.
: 10	They cause *him* to go **naked without clothing,**
JOB 24: 13	they know not the ways **thereof,**
1 Kings 7: 27	and four cubits the breadth **thereof,** and three cubits the height **of it.**
JOB 24: 14	The murderer rising with the light killeth **the poor <u>and</u> needy,**

N.B. note the underlined word which separates words and phrases having the same meaning.

JOB 24: 23	*Though* it be given him *to be* in safety, **whereon** he resteth;
2 Kings 18: 21	*even* upon Egypt **on which** if a man lean, it will go into his hand,
JOB 26: 5	Dead *things* are formed from under the waters, and the inhabitants **thereof.**
28: 17	and the exchange **of it** *shall not be for* jewels of jewels of fine gold.
JOB 26: 6	Hell *is* **naked** before him, and destruction hath **no covering.**
JOB 26: 10	He hath **compassed** the waters with bounds,
Psalm 22: 16	the assembly of the wicked have **inclosed** me:
JOB 27: 1	**Moreover** Job continued his parable, and said,
34: 1	**Furthermore** E-li-hu answered and said,
JOB 27: 4	My lips shall not **speak wickedness,** nor my tongue utter **deceit.**
JOB 27: 16	and prepare **raiment** as the clay;
31: 19	If I have seen any perish for want of **clothing,**
JOB 27: 20	Terrors take hold on him as waters, a **tempest** stealeth him

	away in the night.
: 21	and as a **storm** hurleth him out of his place.
JOB 28: 20	**Whence** then cometh wisdom? and **where** *is* the place of understanding?
JOB 30: 2	Yea, **whereto** *might* the strength of their hands *profit* me?
25: 4	**How** then can be justified with God?
JOB 30: 10	They **abhor** me, they flee far from me,
8: 22	They that **hate** thee shall be clothed with shame;
7: 16	I **loathe** *it;* I would not live always:
16: 20	My friends **scorn** me:
JOB 30: 13	They mar my path, they set forward my **calamity**,
: 16	the days of **affliction** have taken hold upon me.
: 25	Did not I weep for him that was in **trouble?**
JOB 30: 24	**Howbeit** he will not stretch out *his* hand to the grave,
: 1	**But** now *they that are* younger than I have me in derision,
32: 10	**Therefore** I said, Hearken to me;
Psalm 31: 22	**nevertheless** thou heardest the voice of my supplications when I cried unto thee.
JOB 30: 27	the days of affliction **prevented me.**
Psalm 95: 2	**come before** his presence with thanksgiving,
JOB 31: 3	*Is* not destruction to the **wicked?** and a strange *punishment* to the **workers of iniquity?**
JOB 31: 11	For this *is* an **heinous** crime;
28: 28	and to depart from **evil** *is* understanding.
27: 13	This *is* the portion of a **wicked** man with God,
JOB 31: 15	Did not he that made me in the womb **make** him? and did not one **fashion** us in the womb?
JOB 31: 17	and the fatherless hath not eaten **thereof;**
28: 17	and the exchange **of it** *shall not be for* jewels of fine gold.
JOB 31: 34	Did I fear a great multitude, or did the **contempt** of families terrify me..?
22: 19	and the innocent laugh them to **scorn.**
JOB 33: 1	**Wherefore,** Job, I pray thee,
32: 10	**Therefore** I said, Hearken to me;
JOB 33: 26	for he will render unto man his **righteousness.**
: 23	to shew unto man his **uprightness:**

JOB 34: 1	**Furthermore** E-li-hu answered and said,
27: 1	**Moreover** Job continued his parable, and said,
36: 10	He openeth **also** their ear to discipline,

JOB 34: 8   Which goeth in company with the **workers of iniquity**, and walketh with **evil men.**

JOB 34: 10   far be it from God, *that he should do* **wickedness**; and *from* the Almighty, *that he should commit* **iniquity.**

JOB 34: 31	Surely it is **meet** to be said unto God,
2 Kings 10: 3	Look out even the **best and meetest** of your master's sons,
Job 35: 2	Thinkest thou this to be **right,**

JOB 34: 33	*Should it be* according to thy mind? He will **recompense** it,
Psalm 15: 5	nor taketh **reward** against the innocent.

JOB 35: 1	E-li-hu also spake **moreover,** and said,
34: 1	**Furthermore** E-li-hu answered and said,

JOB 35: 13	**Surely** God will not hear vanity, neither will the Amighty regard it.
36: 4	For **truly** my words *shall* not *be* false:

JOB 36: 4	For **truly** my words *shall* not *be* false:
35: 13	**Surely** God will not hear vanity,

JOB 36: 16	Even so would he have removed thee out of the **strait** *into* a broad **place,**
Num. 22: 26	and stood in a **narrow place,**

JOB 36: 23	Who hath **enjoined** him his way?
13: 18	Behold now, I have **ordered** *my* cause;
Esther 9: 31	To confirm these days of Pu-rim in their times ***appointed,*** according as Mor-de-ca-I the Jew, and Esther the queen **had enjoined** them, and as they **had decreed** for themselves and for their seed, the matters of the fastings and their cry.
1: 8	for so the king **had appointed** to all the officers of his house,

JOB 36: 23	or who can say , Thou hast **wrought** iniquity?
Psalm 40: 5	*are* thy wonderful works *which* thou hast **done,**

JOB 36: 27	they pour down rain according to the vapour **thereof:**
38: 13	that the wicked may be shaken out **of it?**

JOB 36: 32	and commandeth it *not to shine* by *the cloud* that cometh **betwixt.**
41: 16	that no air can come **between** them.

<u>JOB 37: 6</u>	For he saith to the snow, Be thou on the earth; **likewise** to the small rain, and to the great rain of his strength.
: 1	As this **also** my heart trembleth,
<u>JOB 37: 10</u>	By the breath of God frost is given: and the breadth of the waters is **straitened.**
1 Kings 6: 4	And for the house he **made** windows of **narrow** lights.
<u>JOB 38: 6</u>	**Whereupon** are the foundations thereof fastened?
<u>JOB 38: 9</u>	When I made the cloud the garment **thereof,**
: 13	that the wicked might be shaken out **of it?**
<u>JOB 38: 11</u>	And said, **Hitherto** shalt thou come, but no further: and **here** shall thy proud waves be stayed?
<u>JOB 38: 26</u>	To cause it to rain on the earth, *where* no man *is; on* the wilderness, **where**in *there is* no man;
3: 3	Let the day perish **wherein** I was born, and the night *in which* it was said, There is a man child conceived.
<u>JOB 38: 27</u>	To satisfy the **desolate <u>and</u> waste** *ground;*

N.B. note how the underlined word separates words and phrases having the same meaning.

<u>JOB 38: 28</u>	Hath the rain a father? or who hath **begotten** the drops of dew?
: 29	and the hoary frost of heaven, who hath **gendered** it?
<u>JOB 38: 40</u>	When they couch in *their* dens, *and* abide in the **covert** to lie in wait?
<u>JOB 38: 40</u>	When they couch in *their* dens, *and* **abide** in their **covert lie in wait?**

N.B. Omit the underlined letter and the meaning of the word is clear.

<u>JOB 38: 41</u>	Who provideth for the raven his **food**? when his young ones cry unto God, they wander for lack of **meat.**
<u>JOB 39: 15</u>	And forgetteth that the foot may **crush** them, or that the wild beast may **break** them.
<u>JOB 39: 22</u>	**He mocketh at fear, <u>and</u> is not affrighted;** neither turneth he

	back from the sword.
: 20	Canst thou maketh him **afraid** as a grasshopper?

N.B. note how the underlined word separates words and phrases having the same meaning.

<u>JOB 40: 1</u>	**Moreover** the LORD answered Job, said,
: 8	Wilt thou **also** disannul my judgment?
34: 1	**Furthermore** E-li-hu answered and said,

<u>JOB 40: 2</u>	Shall he **contendeth** with the Almighty instruct *him*?
	he that **reproveth** God, let him answer it.

<u>JOB 40: 8</u>	Wilt thou also **disannul** my judgment?
Lev. 26: 15	so that ye will not do all my commandments, *but* that ye **break my covenant:**
Ps. 89: 39	Thou hast **made void** the covenant of thy servant.

<u>JOB 40: 11</u>	and **behold** every one *that is* proud, and abase him.
: 12	**Look on** every one *that is* proud, and bring him low;

<u>JOB 40: 11</u>	and behold every one *that is* proud, and **abase him.**
: 12	Look on every one *that is* proud, and **bring him low;**

<u>JOB 40: 21</u>	He lieth under the shady trees, in the **covert** of the reed,
: 22	The shady trees **cover** him *with* their shadow;

<u>JOB 41: 3</u>	Will he make many **supplications** unto thee?
22: 27	Thou shalt make thy **prayer** unto him,
1 Kings 9: 3	And the LORD said unto him, I have heard thy **prayer <u>and</u> supplication,** that thou hast made before me:

<u>JOB 41: 17</u>	they stick together, that they cannot be **sundered.**
38: 24	By what way is the light **parted,**
Neh. 4: 19	and we are **separated** upon the wall,
Ps. 68: 12	and she that tarried at home **divided** the spoil.

<u>JOB 41: 20</u>	Out of his nostrils goeth smoke, as *out* of **a seething pot <u>or</u> caldron.**
Job 41: 31	He maketh the deep **to boil like a pot:**

N.B. note how the underlined word separates words and phrases having the same meaning.

<u>JOB 40: 21</u>	He lieth under the shady trees, in the **covert** of the reed, and fens.
: 22	The shady trees **cover** him *with* their shadow;

<u>JOB 41: 24</u>	yea, as a piece of the **nether** *millstone.*

211

Neh. 4:13	Therefore set I in the **lower** places behind the wall,
JOB 41: 26	The sword of him that layeth at him cannot hold: the spear, the dart, nor the **habergeon.**
1 Sam. 17: 5	and he *was* armed with a **coat of mail;**
JOB 42: 4	Hear, **I beseech thee,** and I will speak:
33: 1	Wherefore **I pray thee,** hear my speeches,
JOB 42: 6	**Wherefore** I abhor *myself,*
: 8	**Therefore** take unto you now seven bullocks and seven rams,
JOB 42: 6	Wherefore I **abhor** *myself,* and repent in dust and ashes.
Psalm 21: 8	thy right hand shall find out those that **hate** thee.

PSALMS

PSALM 1: 1	**Blessed** *is* the man that walketh not in the counsel of the ungodly,
128: 2	**happy** *shalt* thou *be,*
PSALM 1: 3	his leaf shall not **whither;**
Jod 36: 14	They **die** in youth,
PSALM 1: 5	nor sinners in the congregation of the **righteous.**
Genesis 6: 9	Noah was a **just man *and* perfect** in his generations,
Deut. 9: 5	Not for thy **righteousness,** or for the **uprightness** of thine heart,
Ps. 17: 1	Hear the **right,** O LORD,
Prov. 11: 5	The righteousness of the **perfect** shall direct his way:
: 6	The righteousness of the **upright** shall deliver them:
PSALM 2: 3	Let us break their bands **asunder,**
: 9	thou shalt dash them **in pieces** like a potter's vessel.
4: 3	But know that the LORD hath set **apart** him that is godly for himself:
PSALM 2: 5	Then shall he speak unto them in his **wrath,** and vex them in his **hot displeasure.**
PSALM 3: 7	for thou hast **smitten** all mine enemies *upon* the cheek bone;
2 Chron. 13: 20	and the LORD **struck** him, and he died.
PSALM 4: 2	*how long* will ye love vanity, *and* seek after **leasing?**
31: 6	I have hated them that regard **lying** vanities:

: 3	My voice shalt thou **hear** of my cry,
Isaiah 49: 1	**Listen,** O isles, unto me; and **hearken,** ye people from afar;

PSALM 5: 4   For thou *art* not a God that hath pleasure in **wickedness:** neither shall **evil** dwell with thee.

| **PSALM 5: 6** | the LORD will **abhor** the bloody and deceitful man. |
| 21: 8 | thy right hand shall find out those that **hate** thee. |

PSALM 5: 12	with favour wilt thou **compass** him as a shield.
Judges 8: 34	who had delivered them out of the hands of all thine enemies **on every side.**
20: 43	*Thus* they **inclosed** the Benjamites **round about,**
1 Kings 4: 24	and he had peace on **all sides round about** him.

PSALM 6: 1   O LORD, **rebuke** me not in thine anger, neither **chasten** me in thy hot displeasure.

PSALM 6: 6   all the night make I my **bed** to swim; I water my **couch** with my tears.

| **PSALM 6: 8** | Depart from me, all ye **workers of iniquity;** |
| 119: 115 | Depart from me, ye **evildoers:** |

PSALM 6: 9   The LORD hath heard my **supplication;** the LORD will receive my **prayer.**

PSALM 7: 6   **Arise,** O LORD, in thine anger, **lift up** thyself because of the rage of mine enemies:

| **PSALM 7: 7** | So shall the congregation of the people **compass thee about:** |
| Job 19: 10 | He hath destroyed me **on every side,** |

PSALM 7: 9   but establish the **just:** for the **righteous** God trieth the hearts and reins.

PSALM 7: 10   My defence *is* of God, which saveth the **upright** in heart.

| **PSALM 7: 12** | If he turn not, he will **whet** his sword; |
| 1 Sam. 13: 20 | to **sharpen** every man his share, |

PSALM 7: 16	His mischief shall return **upon his own head,** and his violent dealing shall come down **upon his own pate.**
Isaiah 3: 17	Therefore the LORD will smite with a scab **the crown of the**
	head of the daughters of Zion.

PSALM 8: 6   Thou madest him to have **dominion** over the works of thy hands;

| 136: 9 | The moon and the stars **to rule** by night: |

PSALM 9: 2   I will be **glad and rejoice** in thee:

N.B. note how the underlined word separates words and phrases having the same
meaning.

PSALM 9: 6   O thou enemy, destructions are come to a **perpetual** end:
: 7   But the LORD shall **endure for ever:**
24: 7   and be ye lift up, ye **everlasting** doors;

PSALM 9: 8   And he shall judge in **righteousness,** he shall minister
judgment to the people in **uprightness.**

PSALM 10: 3   and blesseth the covetous, *whom* the LORD **abhorreth.**
9: 13   consider my trouble *which I suffer* of them that **hate** me,

PSALM 10: 7   His mouth is full of **cursing and deceit and fraud:**

N.B. note how the underlined words separate words and phrases having the same
meaning.

PSALM 10: 8   his eyes are **privily** set against the poor.
: 9   He lieth in wait **secretly** as a lion in his den:

PSALM 10: 12   **Arise,** O LORD; O God, **lift up** thine hand:

PSALM 10: 13   **Wherefore** doth the wicked contemn God?
: 1   **Why** standest thou afar off, O LORD?

PSALM 10: 13   Wherefore doth the wicked **contemn** God?
22: 7   All they that see me laugh me to **scorn:**
51: 17   O God, thou wilt not **despise.**

PSALM 10: 14   For thou beholdest mischief and spite, **to requite** *it* with thy
hand:
Job 41: 11   Who hath prevented me, that I should **repay** *him?*

PSALM 10: 15   Break thou the arm of **the wicked and the evil *man:***

N.B. note how the underlined word separates words and phrases having the same
meaning.
PSALM 11: 2   that they may privily shoot at the **upright** in heart.
: 3   If the foundations are destroyed what can the **righteous** do?

PSALM 11: 4   his eyes **behold,** his eyelids try, the children of men.
14: 2   to **see** if there were any that did understand,

PSALM 11: 7   For the **righteous** LORD loveth righteousness; his
countenance

doth behold the **upright.**

<u>PSALM 12: 7</u>	Thou shalt **keep** them, O LORD, thou shalt **preserve** them from this generation for ever.

<u>PSALM 14: 1</u>	They are corrupt, they have done **abominable** works,
10: 15	Break thou the arm of **the wicked <u>and</u> the evil *man:***
15: 4	In whose eyes a **vile** person is contemned;
Jerem. 16: 18	they have filled mine inheritance with the carcases of their **detestable <u>and</u> abominable** things.

N.B. note that the word 'evil' is an anagram of the word 'vile.' Also note how the underlined words separate words and phrases having the same meaning.

<u>PSALM 14: 5</u>	They were in **great fear:**
91: 5	Thou shalt not be afraid of the **terror;**

<u>PSALM 15: 4</u>	In whose eyes a vile person is **contemned;**
22: 24	For he hath not **despised <u>nor</u> abhorred...**

N.B. note how the underlined word separates words and phrases having the same meaning.

<u>PSALM 17: 1</u>	give ear unto my prayer, *that goeth* not of **feigned** lips.
31: 6	I have hated them that regard **lying** vanities:
35: 20	but they devise **deceitful** matters against *them that are* quiet in the land.

<u>PSALM 17: 3</u>	Thou hast **proved mine heart;** thou hast visited *me* in the night; thou hast **tried me,**

<u>PSALM 17: 7</u>	Shew thy marvellous **lovingkindness,**
18: 50	and sheweth **mercy** to his anointed,

<u>PSALM 17: 10</u>	They are **inclosed** in their own fat:
: 11	They have now **compassed** us in our steps:

<u>PSALM 17: 12</u>	**Like as** a lion *that* is greedy of his prey, and **as it were** a young lion lurking in secret places.

N.B. 'Like' and 'as' have the same meaning.

<u>PSALM 17: 15</u>	As for me, **I will** behold thy face in righteousness; **I shall** be satisfied when I awake with thy likeness.

<u>PSALM 18: 2</u>	my **buckler,** and the horn of my salvation,
: 35	Thou hast also given me the **shield** of thy salvation:

<u>PSALM 18: 4</u>	The sorrows of death **compassed me,**
17: 10	They are **inclosed** in their own fat:

PSALM 18: 5	the snares of death **prevented me.**
89: 15	mercy and truth shall **go before** thy face.
2 Kings 19: 32	nor **come before** it with shield.

PSALM 18: 7   Then **the earth shook and trembled; the foundations also**

                      of the hills moved and were shaken,

N.B. note how the underlined word separate words and phrases having the same meaning.

PSALM 18: 20   The LORD **rewarded me** according to my righteousness; according to the cleanness of my hands hath he **recompensed me.**

PSALM 18: 26	and with the **froward** thou wilt shew thyself froward.
17: 9	From the **wicked** that oppress me.
Job 9: 20	*if I say, I am* perfect, it shall also prove me **perverse.**

PSALM 18: 30	he *is* **buckler** to all those that trust in him.
: 35	Thou hast given me the **shield** of thy salvation.

PSALM 18: 35	and thy right hand hath **holden** me up,
39: 2	I was dumb with silence, I **held** my peace,

PSALM 18: 6	and there is nothing hid from the heat **thereof.**
Job 38: 13	that the wicked might be shaken out **of it?**

PSALM 19: 1	and the **firmament** sheweth his handywork.
Genesis 1: 8	And God called the firmament **Heaven.**

PSALM 19: 3   *There is* no **speech nor** language, *where* their voice is not heard.

PSALM 19: 6   and his circuit unto the ends **of it:** and there is nothing hid from the heat **thereof.**

PSALM 19: 11	**Moreover** by them is thy servant warned;
Job 34: 1	**Furthermore** E-li-hu answered and said,

PSALM 21: 2	and hast not **withholden** the request of his lips. Selah.
Genesis 39: 9	neither hath he **kept back** any thing from me but thee,
2 Sam. 18: 16	for Jo-ab **held back** the people.

PSALM 21: 9   Thou shalt make them as a fiery oven in the time of thine **anger:** the LORD shall swallow them up in his **wrath,**

PSALM 21: 11   For they **intended** evil against thee: they **imagined** a mischievous device, *which* they are not able *to perform.*

PSALM 22: 11   Be **not far** from me; for trouble *is* **near;**

PSALM 22: 12   Many bulls **have compassed me:** strong *bulls* of Bashan have **beset me round.**

           : 16   the assembly of the wicked **have inclosed me.**
Job 19: 10   He hath destroyed me **on every side,**

PSALM 22: 17   I may **tell all my bones:**
    139: 18   *If* I should **count them,** they are more in **number** than the sand.

PSALM 22: 18   They part my garments among them, and cast lots on my **vesture.**

PSALM 22: 24   For he hath not **despised <u>nor</u> abhorred** the affliction of the afflicted;

N.B. note how the underlined word separates words and phrases having the same meaning.

PSALM 23: 3   he leadeth me in the paths of **righteousness** for his name's sake.
    25: 21   Let integrity and **uprightness** preserve me:

PSALM 24: 1   The earth *is* the LORD'S, and the fullness **thereof;**
    19: 6   and his circuit unto the ends **of it:**

PSALM 24: 1   the world, and they that dwell **therein.**
    68: 14   When the Almighty scattered kings **in it,**

PSALM 24: 2   For he hath **founded it** upon the seas, and **established it** upon the floods.
PSALM 25 : 6   Remember, O LORD thy **tender mercies <u>and</u> thy tender lovingkindnesses;**

N.B. note how the underlined word separates words and phrases having the same meaning.

PSALM 25: 7   Remember not the **sins** of my youth, nor my **transgressions:**

PSALM 25: 21   Let integrity and **uprightness** preserve me;
    24: 5   and **righteousness** from the God of my salvation.

PSALM 26: 2   **Examine me,** O LORD, and **prove me; try my reins** and my heart.
PSALM 26: 4   I have not sat with vain persons, neither will I go with

dissemblers.
: 5   I have hated the congregation of **evil doers;**

PSALM 26: 7   That I may **publish** with the voice of thanksgiving, and **tell** of all thy wondrous works.

PSALM 27: 2   When the wicked, *even* mine **enemies and my foes,**

N.B. note how the underlined word separates words and phrases having the same meaning.

PSALM 27: 5   For in the time of trouble he shall hide me in his **pavilion:** in the secret of his **tabernacle** shall he hide me;
78: 60   So that he forsook the **tabernacle** of Shi-loh, the **tent** *which* he placed before men;

PSALM 27: 9   thou hast been my help; **leave me not, neither forsake me,** O God of my salvation.

N.B. note how the comma separates words and phrases having the same meaning.

PSALM 28: 3   Draw me not away with the **wicked,** and with the **workers of iniquity,**

PSALM 28: 4   **give** them after the work of their hands; **render** to them their desert.

PSALM 28: 6   Blessed *be* the LORD, because he hath heard the voice of my **supplications.**
2 Chron. 6: 39   then hear thou from heavens, *even* from thy dwelling place, their **prayer and their supplications,** and maintain their cause,

N.B. note how the underlined word separates words and phrases having the same meaning.

PSALM 30: 1   I will **extol thee,** O LORD; for thou hast lifted me up,
: 12   To the end that *my* glory may sing **praise** to thee,

PSALM 31: 4   Pull me out of the net that they have laid **privily** for me:
: 20   thou shalt keep them **secretly** in a pavilion from the strife of tongues.
PSALM 31: 6   I have hated them that regard lying **vanities:** but I trust in the LORD.
78: 58   For they provoked him to anger with their high places, and

moved him to jealousy with their **graven images.**
82: 1   God standeth in the congregation of the mighty; he judgeth among the the **gods.**

96: 5   For all the gods of the other nations *are* **idols:**

PSALM 31: 7   I will **be glad <u>and</u> rejoice** in thy mercy:

N.B. note how the underlined word separates words and phrases having the same

meaning.

PSALM 31: 7   for thou hast considered my trouble; thou hast known my
soul in **adversities;**

25: 17   The **troubles** of my heart are enlarged: *O* bring me out of
my **distresses.**

PSALM 31: 18   Let the lying lips be put to silence; which speak grievous
things **proudly <u>and</u> contemptuously** against the righteous.

N.B. note how the underlined word separates words and phrases having the same
meaning.

PSALM 32: 1   Blessed *is he whose* **transgression** *is* forgiven, *whose* **sin** *is*
covered.

: 2   Blessed *is* the man unto whom the LORD imputeth not
iniquity, and in whose spirit *there is* no guile.

PSALM 32: 2   Blessed *is* the man unto whom the LORD **imputeth** not
iniquity,

Job 19: 11   and he **counteth** me unto him as *one of* his enemies.

PSALM 32: 2   and in whose spirit *there is* no **guile.**

10: 7   His mouth is full of cursing and **deceit <u>and</u> fraud:**
deceit <u>and</u> guile depart not from her streets.

N.B. note how the underlined words separates words and phrases having the same
meaning.

PSALM 32: 5   I acknowledge my **sin** unto thee, and mine **iniquity** have
I not hid. I said, I will confess my **transgressions** unto the
LORD;

PSALM 32: 6   surely in the floods of great waters they shall not come **nigh**
unto him.

22: 11   Be **not far** from me; for trouble *is* **near:**

2 Sam. 22: 46 and they shall be afraid out of their **close** places.

PSALM 32: 8   **I will instruct thee <u>and</u> instruct thee** in the way which thou

shalt go:

N.B. note how the underlined word separates words and phrases having the same meaning.

<u>PSALM 32: 11</u>	**Be glad** in the LORD, and **rejoice,** ye righteous: **and shout for joy,** all ye upright in heart.
<u>PSALM 32: 11</u>	Be glad in the LORD, and rejoice, ye **righteous:** and shout for joy, all ye **upright** in heart.
<u>PSALM 33: 1</u>	Rejoice in the LORD, O ye **righteous:** *for* praise is comely for the **upright.**
<u>PSALM 33: 2</u>	Praise the LORD with harp: sing unto him with the **psaltery** <u>*and*</u> **an instrument of ten strings.**

N.B. note the underlined word how it separates words and phrases having the same meaning.

<u>PSALM 33: 4</u>	For the word of the LORD *is* **right;** and all his works are done in **truth.**
<u>PSALM 33: 8</u>	Let the earth **fear** the LORD: let all the inhabitants of the earth **stand in awe** of him.
<u>PSALM 33: 10</u>	The LORD bringeth the counsel of the heathen **to nought:** he maketh the devices of the people **of none effect.**
39: 5	and mine age *is* as **nothing** before thee:
<u>PSALM 33: 13</u>	The LORD **looketh** from heaven; he **beholdeth** all the sons of men.
<u>PSALM 34: 3</u>	O **magnify** the LORD with me, and let us **exalt** his name together.
<u>PSALM 34: 8</u>	O taste and see that the LORD *is* good: **blessed** *is* the man *that* trusteth in him.
127: 5	**Happy** *is* the man that hath his quiver full of them:
<u>PSALM 34: 13</u>	Keep thy tongue from evil, and thy lips from speaking **guile.**
40: 4	nor such as turn aside to **lies.**
<u>PSALM 34: 21</u>	Evil shall **slay** the wicked:
1 Kings 12: 27	and they shall **kill** me,
<u>PSALM 34: 18</u>	The LORD *is* **nigh** unto them that are of a broken heat;
22: 11	Be **not far** from me; for trouble *is* **near;**
Job 28: 21	and kept **close** from the fowls of the air.
<u>PSALM 34: 18</u>	and saveth such as be of **a contrite** spirit.
51: 17	The sacrifices of God *are* **a broken** spirit: and **a broken** <u>**and**</u> **a contrite heart,**

Isaiah 57: 15   I dwell in the high and holy *place,* with him also *that is* of a

      contrite **and** humble spirit, to revive the spirit of the
      humble, and to revive the heart of the contrite ones.

N.B. note how the underlined words separate words and phrases having the same
   meaning.

PSALM 35: 2   Take hold of **shield and buckler,** and stand up for mine help.

N.B. note how the underlined word separates words and phrases having the same
   meaning.

PSALM 35: 4   Let them be **confounded** and put to shame that seek after my
      soul: let them be turned back and **brought to confusion** that
      devise my hurt.

PSALM 35: 8   Let destruction come upon him **at unawares;**
    : 11   they laid to my charge *things* that I **knew not.**
Deut. 19: 4   Whoso killeth his neighbour **ignorantly,**

PSALM 35: 15   the **abjects** gathered themselves together against me,
    : 16   with **hypocritical mockers** in feasts,

PSALM 35: 26   let them be clothed with **shame and dishonour** that magnify
      themselves against me.

N.B. note how the underlined word separates words and phrases having the same
   meaning.

PSALM 36: 3   The words of his mouth *are* **iniquity and deceit:** he hath left
      off to be wise, *and* to do good.

N.B. note how the underlined word separates words and phrases having the same
   meaning.

PSALM 36: 5   **Thy mercy,** O LORD, *is* in the heavens;
    : 7   How excellent *is* **thy lovingkindness,** O God!

PSALM 36: 8   They shall be **abundantly satisfied** with the fatness of thy
      house;
Jerem. 31: 25   For I have **satiated** the weary soul,

PSALM 37: 1   Fret not thyself because of **evildoers,** neither be thou envious
      against the **workers of iniquity.**

PSALM 37: 3   *so* shalt thou dwell in the land, and **verily** thou shalt be fed.
   39: 6   **Surely** every man walketh in a vain shew:

62: 1	**Truly** my soul waiteth upon God:
PSALM 37: 8	Cease from **anger,** and forsake **wrath:**
PSALM 37: 10	thou shalt **diligently** consider his place,
Deut. 15: 5	Only if thou **carefully** hearken unto the voice of the LORD thy God,
PSALM 37: 14	The wicked have drawn out the sword, and have bent their bow, to cast down the **poor and needy,**

N.B. note how the underlined word separates words and phrases having the same meaning.

PSALM 37: 14	*and* to slay such as be of upright **conversation.**
1 Sam. 21: 5	and *the bread is* in a **manner** common,
PSALM 37: 16	A little that a **righteous** man hath *is* better than the riches of many wicked.
: 18	The LORD knoweth the days of the **upright:**
PSALM 37: 20	But the **wicked** shall perish, and **the enemies of the LORD** *shall be* as the fat of lambs:
PSALM 37: 29	The righteous shall inherit the land, and dwell **therein** for ever.
68: 14	When the Almighty scattered kings **in it,**
PSALM 37: 37	Mark the **perfect** *man,* and behold the **upright:**
PSALM 37: 40	And the LORD shall **help them, and** **deliver them:** he shall deliver them from the wicked, and **save them,**

N.B. notehow the underlined word separates words and phrases having the same meaning.

PSALM 38: 1	O LORD, **rebuke** me not in thy wrath: neither **chasten** me in thy hot displeasure.
50: 8	I will not **reprove** thee for thy sacrifices or thy burnt offerings,
PSALM 38: 1	O LORD, rebuke me not in thy **wrath:** neither chasten me in thy **hot displeasure.**
: 3	*There is* no soundness in my flesh because of thine **anger;**
PSALM 38: 11	My lovers and my friends **stand aloof** from my sore; and my kinsmen **stand afar off.**
PSALM 38:18	For I will declare mine iniquity; **I will be sorry for my sin.**
90 13	and let it **repent** thee concerning thy servants.

PSALM 39: 4   and the measure of my days, what it *is; that* I may know how
                       frail I *am.*
    38: 8   I am **feeble** and sore broken:
    6: 2   Have mercy upon me O LORD; for I *am* **weak:**

PSALM 39: 5   **verily** every man at his best state *is* altogether vanity. Se-lah.
    : 6   **Surely** every man walketh in a vain shew:

PSALM 40: 5   and thy thoughts *which are* to us-ward: they **cannot be**
                       reckoned in order unto thee: *if* I would declare and speak *of*
                       them, they are **more than can be numbered.**
    : 12   For **innumerable** evils have compassed me about:
Judges 6: 5   and they came as grasshoppers for **multitude;** *for* both and
                       their camels were **without number:**

PSALM 40: 10   I have **not hid** thy righteousness within mine heart; I have
                       declared thy faithfulness and thy salvation: I have **not**
                       concealed thy lovingkindness and thy truth from the great
                       congregation.

PSALM 40: 13   Be pleased, O LORD to **deliver me:** O LORD, make haste
                       to **help me.**

PSALM 40: 17   But I *am* **poor and needy;**

N.B.   note how the underlined word separates words and phrases having the same
       meaning.

PSALM 41: 3   The LORD will strengthen him upon the bed of **languishing:**
                       thou wilt make all his bed in his **sickness.**

PSALM 41: 10   and raise me up, that I may **requite** them.
Job 21: 31   and who shall **repay** him *what* he hath done?

PSALM 42: 1   As the hart **panteth** after the water brooks, so panteth my soul
                       after thee, O God.
    : 2   My soul **thirsteth** for God, for the living God:

PSALM 42: 5   and *why* art thou disquieted **in** me?
    : 11   and why art thou disquieted **within me?**
PSALM 42: 5   and *why* art thou **disquieted** in me? hope thou in God:
    77: 3   I remembered God, and was **troubled:**

PSALM 42: 8   *Yet* the LORD will command his **lovingkindness** in the
                       daytime,
    37: 21   but the righteous sheweth **mercy,** and giveth.

PSALM 43: 1   Judge me, O God, and **plead** my cause against an ungodly
                       nation:

Prov. 25: 9	**Debate** thy cause with thy neighbour *himself;*
Job 9: 3	If he will **contend** with him,

PSALM 43: 1	O deliver me from the **deceitful and unjust man.**

N.B. note how the underlined word separates words and phrases having the same meaning.

PSALM 44: 12	Thou sellest thy people for **nought,**
39: 5	and my age *is* as **nothing**

PSALM 44: 13	Thou makest a **reproach** to our neighbours, **a scorn and a**
	derision to them that are round about us.
: 14	Thou makest **a byword** among the heathen,

N.B. note how the underlined word separates words and phrases having the same meaning.

PSALM 44: 24	**Wherefore** hidest thou thy face..?
: 23	Awake, **why** sleepest thou O Lord?

PSALM 45: 2	**grace** is poured into thy lips:
: 12	*even* the rich among the people shall intreat thy **favour.**

PSALM 45: 8	**whereby** they have made thee glad.
2 Chron. 9: 4	and his ascent **by which** he went up into the house of the LORD;

PSALM 45: 10	**Hearken,** O daughter, and consider, and **incline thine ear;**
Isaiah 49: 1	**Listen,** O isles, unto me, and **hearken,** ye people, from far;

PSALM 45: 13	her **clothing** *is* of wrought gold.
: 14	She shall be brought unto the king in **raiment** of needlework:

PSALM 45: 13	her clothing *is* of **wrought gold.**
: 14	She shall be brought unto the king in raiment of **needlework:**

PSALM 45: 15	With **gladness and rejoicing** shall they be brought:

N.B. note the underlined word which separates words and phrases having the same meaning.

PSALM 46: 3	*Though* the waters **thereof** roar and be troubled,
Job 38: 13	that the wicked might be shaken out **of it?**

PSALM 46: 4	the streams **whereof** shall make glad the city of God,
44: 10	and they **which** hate us spoil for themselves.

PSALM 46: 9	he breaketh the bow, and cutteth the spear **in sunder;**
50: 23	Now consider this, ye that forget God, lest I tear *you* **in pieces,**

<u>PSALM 48: 9</u>	We have thought of thy **lovingkindness,**
52: 8	I trust in the **mercy** of God for ever and ever.
<u>PSALM 48: 12</u>	Walk about Zion rejoice, and go round about her: **tell** the
	towers thereof.
87: 6	The LORD shall **count,** when he writeth up the people,
<u>PSALM 48: 12</u>	Walk about Zion rejoice, and go round about her: tell the
	towers **thereof.**
80: 10	The hills were covered with the shadow **of it,** and the boughs
	thereof *were like* the goodly cedars.
<u>PSALM 49: 5</u>	**Wherefore** should I fear in the days of evil..?
52: 1	**Why** boastest thou thyself in mischief, O mighty man?
<u>PSALM 49: 10</u>	**likewise** the fool and the brutish person perish,
52: 6	The righteous **also** shall see,
<u>PSALM 49: 14</u>	and the **upright** shall have dominion over them in the morning;
52: 6	The **righteous** also shall see,
<u>PSALM 51: 8</u>	Make me to hear **joy <u>and</u> gladness;**
<u>PSALM 50: 3</u>	and it shall be very **tempestuous** round about him.
55: 8	I would hasten my escape from the **windy storm <u>*and*</u>**
	tempest.

N.B. note how the underlined word separates words and phrases having the same
meaning.

<u>PSALM 50: 12</u>	for the world *is* mine, and the fullness **thereof.**
55: 10	Day and night they go about it upon the walls **thereof:**
	mischief also and sorrow *are* in the midst **of it.**
<u>PSALM 50: 20</u>	Thou sittest *and* **speakest against** thy brother; thou **slanderest**
	thine own mother's son.
<u>PSALM 51: 1</u>	Have **mercy** upon me, O God, according to thy **lovingkind-**
	ness:
<u>PSALM 51: 2</u>	**Wash me thoroughly from mine iniqity, <u>and</u> cleanse me**
	from my sin.

N.B. note how the underlined word separates words and phrases having the same
meaning.

<u>PSALM 51: 3</u>	For I acknowledge **my transgressions:** and **my sin** is ever
	before me.

PSALM 51: 7   **Purge** me with hyssop, and I shall be **clean: wash** me, and I
Shall be whiter than snow.

PSALM 51: 8   Make me to hear **joy and gladness**,

N.B. note how the underlined word separates words and phrases having the same
meaning.

PSALM 51: 13   *Then* will I teach **transgressors** thy ways; and **sinners** shall
be converted unto thee.

PSALM 52: 5   God shall **likewise** destroy thee for ever,
      : 6   The righteous **also** shall see,

PSALM 52: 8   I trust in the **mercy** of God for ever and ever.
  107: 43   even they shall understand the **lovingkindness** of the LORD.

PSALM 53: 6   When God bringeth back the captivity of his people, **Jacob
shall rejoice, _and_ Israel shall be glad.**

PSALM 53: 6   **Jacob** shall rejoice, _**and**_ **Israel** shall be glad.

PSALM 53: 6   Jacob **shall rejoice, _and_** Israel **shall be glad.**

N.B. note how the underlined words separates words and phrases having the same
meaning.

PSALM 55: 1   **Give ear** to my prayer, O God;
      : 2   Attend unto me, and **hear me:**

PSALM 55: 5   **Fearfulness and trembling** are come upon me,

N.B. note how the underlined word separates word and phrases having the same
meaning.

PSALM 55: 8   I would hasten my escape from the **windy storm _and_
tempest.**

N.B. note how the underlined word separates words and phrases having the same
meaning.

PSALM 55: 9   for I have seen **violence and strife** in the city.

N.B. note how the underlined word separates words and phrases having the same
meaning.

PSALM 55: 10   Day and night they go about it upon the walls **thereof:**
mischief also and sorrow *are* in the midst **of it.**

PSALM 55: 11   Wickedness *is* in the midst thereof: **deceit and guile** depart not from her streets.

N.B.   note how the underlined word separates words and phrases having the same meaning.

PSALM 56: 5   Every day they **wrest** my words:
Prov. 17: 23   A wicked *man* taketh a gift out of the bosom **to pervert** the ways of judgment.
18: 5   **to overthrow** the righteous in judgment.
Isaiah 10: 2   **To turn aside** the needy from judgment,

PSALM 56: 12   **I will render** praises unto thee.
Proverbs 3: 28   and to morrow **I will give;**

PSALM 57: 6   they have digged a pit before me, into the midst **whereof** they are fallen *themselves.* Selah.
Isaiah 66: 4   but they did evil before mine eyes, and chose *that* **in which** I delighted not.

PSALM 57: 8   A wake up, my glory; awake, **psaltery and harp:**
92: 3   Upon **an instrument of ten strings, and** upon the psaltery;

N.B.   note how the underlined words separate words and phrases having the same meaning.

PSALM 58: 3   The wicked are **estranged** from the womb: they **go astray** as soon as they be born,

PSALM 58: 11   So that a man shall say, **Verily** *there is* a reward for the righteous:
62: 1   **Truly** my soul waiteth upon God:

PSALM 59: 10   The God of my mercy shall **prevent me:**
89: 14   mercy and truth shall **go before** thy face.

PSALM 60: 2   heal the breaches **thereof;** for it shaketh.
55: 10   mischief also and sorrow *are* in the midst **of it.**

PSALM 60: 6   I will **divide** She-chem, **and mete out** the valley of Suc-coth.

PSALM 61: 3   For thou hast been a **shelter** for me,
: 4   I will trust in the **covert** of thy wings. Selah.
62: 7   *and* my **refuge** *is* in God.

N.B.   in the second reference the meaning is in the word itself.

PSALM 61: 6   Thou wilt **prolong** the king's life:
1 King's 3: 14   then I will **lengthen** thy days.
PSALM 62: 1   **Truly** my soul waiteth upon God:

227

PSALM 62: 1	**Truly** my soul waiteth upon God:
: 9	**Surely** men of low degree *are* vanity,

PSALM 63: 1	my flesh longeth for thee in **a dry <u>and</u> thirsty <u>land</u>, where no water is;**

N.B. note how the underlined words separate words and phrases having the same meaning.

PSALM 63: 11	but the mouth of **them that speak lies** shall be stopped.
116: 11	I said in my haste, all men *are* **liars.**

PSALM 64: 4	That they may shoot **in secret** at the perfect:
: 5	they commune of laying snares **privily;**
Job 31: 27	And my heart hath been **secretly** enticed,

PSALM 64: 4	That they may shoot in secret at the **perfect:**
: 10	The **righteous** shall be glad in the LORD, and shall in him; and all the **upright** in heart shall glory.

PSALM 65: 3	**Iniquities** prevail against me: *as for* our **transgressions,**
Job 13: 23	How many *are* mine **iniquities <u>and</u> sins?**
Exodus 34: 7	for giving **iniquity <u>and</u> transgression <u>and</u> sin,**

N.B. note how the underlined words separate words and phrases having the same meaning.

PSALM 65: 10	Thou waterest the ridges **thereof** abundantly:
55: 10	mischief also and sorrow *are* in the midst **of it.**

PSALM 65: 13	The pastures are **clothed** with flocks; the valleys also are **clothed** over with corn;

PSALM 66: 10	For thou O **God, hast proved us: thou hast tried us,** as silver is tried.

N.B. note how the colon separates words and phrases meaning having the same meaning.

PSALM 66: 14	**Which my lips have uttered, <u>and</u> my mouth hath spoken,** when I was in trouble.

N.B. note how the underlined word separates words and phrases having the same meaning.

PSALM 67: 2	That thy way may be known upon earth, **thy saving health** among all nations.
69: 29	But I *am* poor and sorrowful: let **thy salvation,** O God,

PSALM 68: 4	Sing unto God, **sing praises** to his name: **extol him** that rideth

upon the heavens by his name JAH,

PSALM 68: 9	**whereby** thou didst confirm thine inheritance,
41: 11	**By this** I know thou favourest me,
2 Chron. 9: 4	and his ascent **by which** he went up into the house of the LORD;

PSALM 68: 10	Thy congregation hath dwelt **therein:**
: 14	When the Almighty scattered kings **in it,**
2 Kings 2: 21	and cast the salt **in there,**

PSALM 68: 12	and she that **tarried** at home divided the spoil.
63: 11	but the mouth of them that speak lies shall be **stopped.**
Eccl. 2: 9	also my wisdom **remained** with me.

PSALM 68: 12	kings of armies did **flee apace:**
Judges 4: 17	Howbeit Sis-e-ra **fled away** on his feet to he tent of Ja-el the wife of He-ber the Ke-nite:
Jeremiah 46: 21	*and* are **fled away** altogether:

PSALM 68: 13	although ye have **lien among the pots,**
Numbers 5: 19	if no man **hath lain** with thee,
Deut. 22: 22	*both* the the man that **lay** with the woman,

PSALM 68: 28	that which **thou hast wrought** for us.
52: 9	because **thou hast done** *it:*
1 Kings 2: 44	that **thou didst** to David my father:
14: 29	and all that **he did,**
15: 3	which **he had done** before him:

PSALM 68: 34	**Ascribe** ye strength unto God:
29: 1	**Give** unto the LORD,
60: 4	Thou hast **given** a banner to them that fear thee,
1 Samuel 18: 8	They have **ascribed** unto David ten thousands,

PSALM 69: 7	Because for thy sake I have borne **reproach; shame** hath covered my face.

N.B. note how the semi-colon separates words and phrases having the same meaning.

PSALM 69: 8	I am become a **stranger** unto my brethren, and an **alien** unto my mother's children.

PSALM 69: 16	Hear me, O LORD; for thy **lovingkindness** *is* good: turn unto me according to the multitude of thy **tender mercies.**

PSALM 69: 18	**Draw nigh** unto my soul,
107: 18	and they **draw near** unto the gates of death.

PSALM 69: 19   Thou hast known **my reproach, and** my shame, **and** my dishonour:

N.B. note how the underlined words separate words and phrases having the same meaning.

PSALM 69: 21   They gave me also gall for my **meat;**
78: 25   Man did eat angels' **food:** he sent them **meat** to the full.
: 27   He rained **flesh** also upon them as dust, and **feathered fowls** like as the sand of the sea:

PSALM 69: 30   I will **praise** the name of God with a song, and will **magnify** him with thanksgiving.

PSALM 69: 34   Let the heaven and earth praise him, the seas and every thing that moveth **therein.**
68: 14   When the Almighty scattered kings **in it,**

Psalm 69: 35   that they may **dwell there,** and have it in possession.
: 36   and they love his name shall **dwell therein.**

PSALM 70: 1   *Make haste,* O God, to **deliver me;** make haste to **help me,**

PSALM 70: 2   Let them be **ashamed and confounded** that seek after my soul: let them be turned backward, and **put to confusion,**

N.B. note how the underlined word separates words and phrases having the same meaning.

PSALM 70: 5   But I *am* **poor and** needy:

N.B. see comment on previous verse.

PSALM 70: 5   **make haste** unto me, O God: thou *art* my help and my deliverer; O LORD, make **no tarrying.**

PSALM 71: 6   By thee have I been **holden up** from the womb:
116: 6   I was brought low, and he **helped** me.
Isaiah 63: 5   And I looked, and *there was* **none to help:** and I wondered that *there was* **none to uphold:**

PSALM 71: 10   and they **that** lay wait for my soul take counsel together,
: 19   **who** hast done great things:
: 20   *Thou,* **which** hast shown me great and sore troubles,

PSALM 71: 13   let them be covered *with* **reproach and dishonour** that seek hurt.

PSALM 71: 17   and **hitherto** have I declared thy wondrous works.
2 Kings 8: 6   and all the fruits of the field since the day that she left the land,

	even **until now.**
2 Chron. 35: 25	and the singing women spake of Josiah in their lamentations
	to this day,
PSALM 71: 22	I will also praise thee with the **psaltery,**
144: 9	I will sing a new song unto thee, O God: upon a **psaltery** *and*
	an instrument of ten strings will I sing praises unto thee.
PSALM 72: 16	the fruit **thereof** shall shake like Lebanon:
73: 5	The earth and all the inhabitants **thereof** are dissolved: I bear up the pillars **of it.** Selah.
PSALM 72: 17	His name **shall endure for ever:** his name **shall be continued** as long as the sun:
PSALM 73: 1	**Truly** God is good to Israel, *even* to such as are of a clean heart.
: 13	**Verily** I have cleansed my heart *in* vain,
: 18	**Surely** thou didst thou didst set them in slippery places:
PSALM 73: 10	**Nevertheless** I *am* continually with thee:
: 28	**But** *it is* good for me to draw near to God:
PSALM 73: 10	Therefore his people return **hither:**
132: 14	This *is* my rest for ever: **here** will I dwell;
PSALM 73: 23	thou hast **holden** *me* by my right hand.
Isaiah 63: 5	and my fury, it **upheld** me.
PSALM 74: 2	Remember thy congregation, *which* thou hast **purchased** of old; the rod of thine inheritance, *which* thou hast **redeemed;**
PSALM 74: 2	this mount Zion, **where**in thou hast dwelt.
Job 3: 3	Let the day perish **wherein** I was born, and the night *in which* it was said,
PSALM 74: 6	But now they break down the carved work **thereof** at once with axes and hammers.
75: 3	The earth and all the inhabitants **thereof** are dissolved: I bear up the pillars **of it.** Selah.
PSALM 74: 15	**Thou didst cleave** the foundation and the flood:
Nehemiah 9: 11	**thou didst divide** the sea before them,
PSALM 74: 21	let the **poor and needy** praise thy name.

N.B. note how the underlined word separates words and phrases having the same meaning.

PSALM 75: 1	**Unto thee,** O God, do we give thanks, ***unto thee*** do we give thanks:
PSALM 75: 3	The earth and all the inhabitants **thereof** are dissolved: I bear up the pillars **of it.** Se-lah.
PSALM 76: 10 Isaiah 5: 25	Surely the **wrath** of man shall praise thee: Therefore the **anger** of the LORD kindled against his people,
PSALM 77: 18	the lightnings lightened the world: the earth **trembled <u>and</u> shook.**

N.B. note how the underlined word separates words and phrases having the same meaning.

PSALM 78: 5	For he **established a testimony in Jacob, <u>and</u> a appointed a law in Israel,**

N.B. note how the underlined word separates words and phrases having the same meaning.

PSALM 78: 8	a **stubborn <u>and</u> rebellious** generation; *that* set not their
: 10	heart aright, and whose spirit was **not stedfast** with God. They **kept not the covenant of God, <u>and</u> refused to walk in his law;**

N.B. note how the underlined words separate words and phrases having the same meaning.

PSALM 78: 18	And **they tempted God** in their heart by asking meat for their lust.
: 19	Yea, **they spake against God.**
PSALM 78: 20 2 Chron. 13: 20	Behold, he **smote** the rock, and the LORD **struck** him, and he died.
PSALM 78: 21 Daniel 2: 12	Therefore the LORD heard *this*, and **was wroth:** For this cause the king **was angry** and very furious,
PSALM 78: 25 : 27	Man did eat angels' **food:** he sent them **meat** to the full. He rained **flesh** also upon them as dust, and **feathered fowls** like as the sand of the sea:
105: 40	*The people* asked, and he brought **quails,**
PSALM 78: 29 : 30	for he gave them their own **desire;** They were not estranged from their **lust.**
PSALM 78: 34 44: 22	When **he slew** them, then they sought him: Yea, for thy sakes are we **killed** all the day long;

<u>**PSALM 78: 38**</u>	yea, many a time turned he **his anger** away, and did not stir
	up all **his wrath.**
<u>**PSALM 78: 43**</u>	How he **had wrought** his signs in Egypt,
106: 21	They forgat God their saviour, which **had done** great things in Egypt;
80: 9	and **didst** cause it to take root,
Isaiah 41: 4	Who **hath wrought and done** *it,*
10: 12	*that* when the LORD **hath performed** his work...

N.B. note how the underlined word separates words and phrases having the same meaning.

<u>**PSALM 78: 45**</u>	He sent **divers** sorts of flies among them,
: 38	yea, **many** a time turned he his anger away,
Daniel 7: 3	And four great beasts came up from the sea, **diverse** one from another.
<u>**PSALM 78: 49**</u>	He cast upon them the fierceness of his **anger, wrath, <u>and</u> indignation,** and trouble, by sending evil angels *among them.*
<u>**PSALM 78: 50**</u>	but gave their life over to the **pestilence;**
91: 10	neither shall any **plague** come nigh thy dwelling.
<u>**PSALM 78: 51**</u>	And **smote** all the firstborn in Egypt;
1 Kings 16: 10	And Zimri went in and **smote him, <u>and</u> killed him,**

N.B. note how the underlined word separates words and phrases having the same meaning.

<u>**PSALM 78: 56**</u>	Yet they **tempted <u>and</u> provoked** the most high God, and kept not his testimonies:
<u>**PSALM 78: 59**</u>	When God heard *this,* **he was wroth, <u>and</u> greatly abhorred** Israel:
<u>**PSALM 78: 59**</u>	When God heard *this,* he was **wroth,**
79: 5	wilt thou be **angry** for ever?
<u>**PSALM 78: 59**</u>	and greatly **abhorred** Israel:
55: 12	neither *was it* he that **hated** me...

N.B. note how the underlined word separates words and phrases having the same meaning.

<u>**PSALM 78: 60**</u>	So that he **forsook** the tabernacle of Shi-loh,
Jeremiah 17: 13	all that **forsake** thee shall be ashamed, *and* they that **depart from** me shall be written in the earth,

19: 4	Because they have **forsaken me and have estranged this place,**
23: 39	**and I will forsake you,**
Ezekiel 29: 5	**And I will leave thee...**

N.B. note how the underlined word separates words and phrases having the same meaning.

<u>**PSALM 78: 60**</u>	So that he forsook the **tabernacle** of Shi-loh, the **tent** *which* he placed among men;
<u>**PSALM 78: 66**</u>	he put them to a **perpetual** reproach.
: 69	like the earth which he hath established **for ever.**
<u>**PSALM 78: 67**</u>	**Moreover** he refused the tabernacle of Joseph,
: 14	In the daytime **also** he led them with a cloud,
Ezekiel 8: 6	He said **furthermore** unto me,
<u>**PSALM 79: 4**</u>	We are become **a reproach** to our neighbours, **a scorn and derision** to them that are round about us.

N.B. note how the underlined word separates words and phrases having the same meaning.

<u>**PSALM 79: 6**</u>	Pour out thy **wrath** upon the heathen that have not known thee,
78: 50	He made a way to his **anger;**
<u>**PSALM 79: 8**</u>	let thy tender mercies speedily **prevent us:**
: 11	let the sighing of the prisoner **come before** thee;
89: 14	mercy and truth shall **go before** thy face.
<u>**PSALM 79: 10**</u>	**Wherefore** should the heathen say, Where *is* thy God?
80: 12	**Why** hast thou *then* broken down her hedges,
<u>**PSALM 79: 12**</u>	**wherewith** they have reproached thee, O Lord.
Zechariah 13: 6	Then he shall answer, *Those* **with which** I was wounded *in* the house of my friends.
<u>**PSALM 80: 10**</u>	The hills were covered with the shadow **of it,** and the boughs **thereof** *were like* the goodly cedars.
<u>**PSALM 80: 11**</u>	She sent out her **boughs** unto the sea, and her **branches** unto the river.
<u>**PSALM 80: 13**</u>	The **boar** out of the wood doth waste it, and the **wild beast** of the field doth devour it.
<u>**PSALM 80: 14**</u>	Return, we **beseech** thee, O God of hosts:
Jonah 1: 8	Then said they unto him, Tell us we **pray** thee,

| PSALM 80: 16 | they perish at the rebuke of thy **countenance.** |
| : 3 | Turn us again, O God, and cause thy **face** to shine; |

| PSALM 81: 2 | Take a psalm, and bring **hither** the timbrel, |
| 132: 14 | This *is* my rest for ever: **here** will I dwell; |

| PSALM 81: 2 | the pleasant harp with the **psaltery.** |
| 92: 3 | Upon **an instrument of ten strings,** and upon **the psaltery;** |

| PSALM 81: 3 | Blow up the trumpet in the new moon, in the time **appointed,** |
| : 5 | This he **ordained** in Joseph *for* a testimony, |

| PSALM 81: 8 | **Hear,** O my people, and I will testify unto thee: O Israel, if thou wilt **hearken** unto me; |
| Isaiah 49: 1 | **Listen,** O isles, unto me; and **hearken,** ye people, from far; |

PSALM 81: 14	I should soon have subdued **their enemies,** and turned my hand against **their adversaries.**
Esther 9: 16	and had rest from **their enemies, and slew of their foes** seventy and five thousand,
Esther 9: 16	and **slew** of their foes seventy and five thousand,
1Kings 16: 10	and **killed** him, in the twenty and seventh year of Asa king of Judah,

N.B. note how the underlined word separates words and phrases having the same meaning.

| PSALM 82: 3 | Defend the poor and fatherless: do justice to the **afflicted and needy.** |
| : 4 | Deliver the **poor and needy:** |

N.B. note how the underlined words separate words and phrases having the same meaning.

| PSALM 83: 8 | they have **holpen** the children of Lot. Selah. |
| 116: 6 | I was brought low, and he **helped** me. |

| PSALM 83: 5 | For they have **consulted together with one consent: they are confederate against** thee: |

N.B. note how the colon separates words and phrases having the same meaning.

| PSALM 83: 8 | they have **holpen** the children of Lot. Se-lah. |
| 116: 6 | I was brought low, and he **helped** me. |

| PSALM 83: 15 | So persecute them with thy **tempest,** and make them afraid with thy **storm.** |

PSALM 83: 17	Let them be **confounded <u>and</u> troubled** for ever; yea, **let them be put to shame,**

N.B. note how the underlined word separates words and phrase having the same meaning.

PSALM 85: 3	Thou hast taken away all thy **wrath**: thou hast turned *thyself* from the fierceness of thine **anger.**
PSALM 85: 9	Surely his salvation *is* **nigh** them that fear him;
75: 1	for *that* thy name is **near** thy wondrous works declare.
PSALM 86: 1	Bow down thine ear, O LORD, hear me: for I am **poor <u>and</u> needy.**

N.B. note how the underlined word separates words and phrases having the same meaning.

PSALM 86: 15	and gracious, **longsuffering,** and plenteous in mercy and truth.
Eccl. 7: 8	*and* the **patient** in spirit *is* better than the proud in spirit.
PSALM 86: 17	because thou, LORD, hast **holpen** me,
116: 6	I was brought low, and he **helped** me.
PSALM 88: 11	Shall my **lovingkindness** be declared in the grave?
89: 2	For I have said, **Mercy** shall be built up for ever:
PSALM 88: 13	But unto thee have I cried, O LORD; and in he morning shall My prayer **prevent** thee.
: 2	Let my prayer **come before** thee:
PSALM 88: 17	They **came round about** me daily like water; they **compassed me about** together.
22: 16	the assembly of the wicked **inclosed me:**
PSALM 89: 6	For who in the heaven **can be compared** unto the LORD? *who* among the sons of the mighty **can be likened** unto the LORD?
PSALM 89: 7	God is greatly **to be feared** in the assembly of the saints, and **to be had in reverence** of all *them that are* about him.
PSALM 89: 9	when the waves **thereof** arise,
55: 10	Day and night they go about it upon the walls **thereof:** mischief also and sorrow *are* in the midst **of it.**
PSALM 89: 33	Nevertheless my **lovingkindness** will I notutterly take
	from him,
: 28	My **mercy** will I keep for him for evermore,

PSALM 89: 42	Thou hast set up the right hand of his **adversaries;** thou hast made all his **enemies** to rejoice.
PSALM 89: 47	**wherefore** hast thou made all men in vain?
88: 14	LORD, **why** casteth thou off my soul?
PSALM 89: 51	**Wherewith** thine enemies have reproached, O Lord;
91: 14	**Because** he hath set his love upon thee,
PSALM 90: 7	For we are consumed by thine **anger, and by thy wrath** we are troubled.

N.B. note how the underlined word separates words and phrases having the same meaning.

PSALM 90: 10	The days of our days *are* **threescore** years and ten;
Genesis 5: 27	And all the days of Methuselah were nine hundred **sixty** and nine years:

N.B. The underlined word is a numerical term which means twenty. To find the value of the 'score' number multiply the number, 3x20=60.

PSALM 90: 15	Make us glad according to the days *wherein* thou hast afflicted us, *and* the years *wherein* we have seen evil.
Job 3: 3	Let the day perish **wherein** I was born, and the night *in which* it was said, There is a man child conceived.
PSALM 91: 3	Surely he shall deliver thee from the snare of the fowler, *and* from the **noisome** pestilence.
: 10	There shall no **evil** befall thee,
PSALM 91: 3	*and* from the noisome **pestilence.**
: 10	neither shall any **plague** come nigh thy dwelling.
PSALM 91: 7	*but* it shall not **come nigh** thee.
75: 1	for *that* thy name is **near** thy wondrous works declare.
Num. 4: 19	when **they approach unto** the most holy things:
Exodus 28: 43	or when **they come near unto** the altar...
Daniel 8: 7	And I saw him **come close unto** the ram,
PSALM 91: 8	Only with thine eyes shalt thou **behold and see** the reward of the wicked.

N.B. note how the underlined word separates words and phrases having the same meaning.

PSALM 91: 13	Thou shalt **tread** upon the lion and adder: the young lion and the dragon shalt thou **trample** under feet.

PSALM 92: 3   Upon **an instrument of ten strings, and** upon **the psaltery;**

N.B. note how the underlined word separates words and phrases having the same
    meaning.

PSALM 92: 7   When the **wicked** spring as the grass, and when all **the
                    workers of iniquity** do flourish; *it is* that they shall be
                    destroyed for ever:

PSALM 92: 8   But thou, LORD, *art most* high for **evermore.**
    93: 2   thou *art* from **everlasting.**
        : 5   holiness becometh thine house, O LORD, **for ever.**

PSALM 94: 2   **render** a reward to the proud.
        : 7   **Give** unto the LORD,

PSALM 94: 4   *How long* shall they utter **_and_ speak** hard things?

N.B. note how the underlined word separates words and phrases having the same
    meaning.

PSALM 94: 6   They **slay** the widow and the stranger, and **murder** the
                    fatherless.

PSALM 94: 15   and all the **upright** in heart shall follow it.
        : 21   They gather themselves together against the soul of the
                    righteous,
PSALM 94: 23   And he shall bring upon them **their own iniquity,** and shall
                    cut them off in **their own wickedness;**

PSALM 95: 5   The sea *is* his, and he **made it:** and his hands **formed** the
                    dry *land.*

PSALM 95: 8   Harden not your heart, as in the **provocation,** *and* as *in* the
                    day of **temptation** in the wilderness:
        : 9   When your fathers **tempted me, proved me,** and saw my
                    work.

N.B. note how the comma separates words and phrases having the same meaning.

PSALM 95: 9   When your fathers **tempted me, proved me,** and saw my
                    work.

N.B. note the comma which separates words and phrases having the same meaning.

PSALM 96: 2   **shew** forth his salvation from day to day.

        : 3   **Declare** his glory among all people.

PSALM 96: 11	let the sea roar, and the fullness **thereof.**
80: 10	The hills were covered with the shadow **of it,** and the boughs **thereof** *were like* the goodly cedars.
PSALM 96: 12	Let the field be joyful, and all that *is* **therein:**
105: 12	yea, very few, and strangers **in it.**
PSALM 97: 7	Confounded are they that serve **graven images,** that boast themselves of **idols:**
PSALM 97: 9	For thou, *art* **high above** all the earth: thou art **exalted** far above all gods.
PSALM 97: 11	Light is sown for the **righteous,** and gladness for the **upright** in heart.
PSALM 98: 7	Let the sea roar, and the fullness **thereof:**
55: 10	mischief also and sorrow in the midst **of it.**
PSALM 98: 7	and they that dwell **therein.**
2 Chron. 6: 11	And **in it** have I put the ark,
PSALM 98: 9	**with righteousness** he judge the world, and the people **with equity.**
119: 7	I will praise thee **with uprightness** of heart,
PSALM 100: 1	Make a **joyful noise** unto the LORD, all ye lands.
: 2	come before his presence with **singing.**
PSALM 101: 4	A **forward** heart shall depart from me: I will not know a a **wicked** *person.*
PSALM 101: 5	Whoso **privily** slandereth his neighbour,
31: 20	thou shalt keep them **secretly** in a pavilion from the strife of tongues.
PSALM 101: 7	He that worketh deceit **shall not dwell** within my house: he that lies **shall not tarry** in my sight.
PSALM 101: 7	He that worketh deceit shall not dwell **within** my house: he that lies shall not tarry **in** my my sight.
PSALM 102: 6	I am like a pelican of the **wilderness:** I am like an owl of the **desert.**
PSALM 102: 10	Because of thine **indignation and** thy **wrath:**

N.B. note how the underlined word separates words and phrases having the same

meaning.

PSALM 102: 13	Thou shalt arise, *and* have **mercy** upon Zion: for the time to **favour** her,
PSALM 102: 14	and favour the stones **thereof.**
55: 10	mischief also and sorrow *are* in the midst **of it.**
PSALM 102: 17	He will regard the prayer of **the destitute,**
Ezekiel 36: 34	And **the desolate** land shall be tilled,
PSALM 102: 26	all of them shall wax old **like** a **garment; as** a **vesture** shalt thou change them,

N.B. note how the semi-colon separates words and phrases having the same meaning.

PSALM 103: 1	and all that is **within** me, *bless* his holy name.
: 22	Bless the LORD, all his works **in** all places of his dominion;
1 Kings 6: 15	And he built the walls of the house **within** with boards of cedar, both the floor of the house, and the walls of the cieling: *and* he covered *them* on the **inside** with wood,
PSALM 103: 4	who redeemeth thy life from destruction, who crowneth thee with **lovingkindness and** tender mercies;

N.B. note how the underlined word separates words and phrases having the same meaning.

PSALM. 103: 8	The LORD *is* merciful and gracious, **slow to anger,**
Eccl. 7: 8	*and* the **patient** in spirit *is* better than the proud in spirit.
PSALM 103: 9	He will not always **chide:** neither will he keep *his anger* for ever.
104: 7	At thy **rebuke** they fled;
74: 22	Arise, O God, **plead** thine own cause:
Isaiah 27: 8	thou wilt **debate** with it:
Job 9: 3	if he will **contend** with him,
PSALM 103: 10	He hath not dealt with us after **our sins,** nor rewarded us according to **our iniquities.**
: 12	*so* far hath he removed **our transgressions** from us.
PSALM 103: 16	and the place **thereof** shall know it no more.
55: 10	mischief also and sorrow *are* in the midst **of it.**

PSALM 104: 7	At thy rebuke they **fled**; at the voice of the thunder they **hasted away.**
Judges 9: 21	And Jo-tham **ran away, <u>and</u> fled,** and went to Beer,
1 Samuel 19: 18	So David **fled, <u>and</u> escaped,**

N.B. note how the underlined word separates words and phrases having the same meaning.

PSALM 104: 11	the wild asses **quench** their thirst.
91: 16	With long life will I **satisfy** him,

PSALM 104: 14	that he may bring forth **food** out of the earth;
: 15	and **bread** *which* strengtheth man's heart.
: 21	and seek their **meat** from God.

PSALM 104: 20	**where**in all the beasts of the forest do creep *forth.*
: 17	**Where** the birds make their nests:
Isaiah 66: 4	but they did evil before mine eyes, and chose *that* **in which** I delighted not.

PSALM 104: 24	O LORD, **how mani**fold are thy works!
93: 4	The LORD on high *is* mightier than the noise of **many** waters,
PSALM 104: 25	**where**in *are* things creeping innumerable,
Isaiah 66: 4	and chose *that* **in which** I delighted not.

PSALM 104: 25	*So is* this great and wide sea, wherein *are* things creeping **innumerable,**
105: 34	He spake, and the locusts came, and caterpillars, and that **without number.**

PSALM 104: 26	**There** go the ships: *there is* that leviathan, *whom* thou hast made to play **therein.**
Jeremiah 8: 16	and all that is **in it**; the city, and those that dwell **therein.**

N.B. The meaning of the word 'therein' can also be found by reversing the syllables.

PSALM 104: 35	**Let the sinners be consumed out of the earth, <u>and</u> let the wicked be no more.**

N.B. note how the underlined word separates words and phrases having the same meaning.

PSALM 105: 2	Sing unto him, sing psalms unto him: talk ye of all his **wondrous works.**
: 5	Remember his **marvellous works** that he hath done;

PSALM 105: 16	**Moreover** he called for a famine upon the land:
105: 23	Israel **also** came into Egypt;
52: 5	God shall **likewise** destroy thee for ever,

2 Chron. 4: 9	**Furthermore** he made the court of the priests,
PSALM 105: 23	Israel also came into **Egypt;** and Jacob sojourned in the **land of Ham.**
PSALM 105: 24 107: 38	And he **increased his people** greatly; so that **they are multiplied** greatly;
PSALM 105: 25 52: 2	to deal **subtilly** with his servants. like a sharp razor, working **deceitfully.**
PSALM 105: 29 44: 22	He turned their water into blood, and **slew** their fish. Yea, for thy sake are we **killed** all the day long;
PSALM 105: 31 104: 43	He spake, and there came **divers** sorts of flies, **Many** times did he deliver them;
PSALM 105: 35	And **did eat up** all the herbs in their land, and **devoured** the fruit of their ground.
PSALM 106: 6	**We have sinned** with our fathers, **we have committed iniquity, we have done wickedly.**
PSALM 106: 14 109: 30	But lusted **exceedingly** in the wilderness, I will **greatly** praise the LORD with my mouth;
PSALM 106: 14 : 24	But lusted exceedingly in the wilderness, and **tempted God** in the desert. they despised the pleasant land, **they believed not his word:**
PSALM 106: 40 : 41	insomuch that he **abhorred** his own inheritance. and they that **hated** them ruled over them.
PSALM 106: 40	insomuch **that** he abhorred his own inheritance.
PSALM 106: 42	Their enemies also **oppressed** them, and they were **brought into subjection** under their hand.
PSALM 107: 1 : 43	O give thanks unto the LORD, for *he is* good: for his **mercy** endureth for ever. even they shall understand the **lovingkindness** of the LORD.
PSALM 107: 11 106: 24	and **contemned** the counsel of the most High: Yea, they **despised** the pleasant land,
PSALM 107: 16	For he hath broken the gates of brass, and cut the bars of iron **in sunder.**
94: 5	They **break in pieces** thy people,

PSALM 107: 25	which lifted up the waves **thereof.**
80: 10	The hills were covered with the shadow **of it**, and the boughs **thereof** *were like* the goodly cedars.
PSALM 107: 32	Let them exalt him also in the **congregation** of the people, and praise him in the **assembly** of the elders.
PSALM 107: 34	for the wickedness of them that dwell **therein.**
Jeremiah 8: 16	and all that is **in it;** the city, and those that dwell **therein.**
PSALM 107: 43	Whoso *is* wise, and will observe these *things,* even they shall understand the **lovingkindness** of the LORD.
: 1	for his **mercy** *endureth* for ever.
PSALM 108: 2	Awake, **psaltery** and harp:
92: 3	Upon **an instrument of ten strings,**
PSALM 108: 7	God hath spoken in his holiness, I will rejoice, I will **divide** She-chem, and **mete** out the valley of Suc-coth.
PSALM 108: 11	and wilt not thou, O God, **go forth** with our hosts?
60: 10	and *thou* O God, *which* didst not **go out** with our **armies?**
PSALM 109: 14	Let the **iniquity** of his fathers be remembered with the LORD; and let not the **sin** of his mother be blotted out.
PSALM 109: 16	but persecuted the **poor <u>and</u> needy** man,

N.B. note how the underlined word separates words and phrases having the same meaning.

PSALM 109: 19	and for a girdle **wherewith** he is girded continually.
2 Kings 19: 6	Be not afraid of the words which thou hast heard, **with which** the servants of the king of Assyria have blasphemed me.
PSALM 109: 20	*Let* this *be* the reward of mine **adversaries** from the LORD, And of **them that speak evil** against my soul.
PSALM 111: 1	I will praise the LORD with *my* whole heart, in the **assembly** of the upright, and *in* the **congregation.**
107: 32	Let them exalt him also in the **congregation** of the people, and praise him in the **assembly** of the elders.
PSALM 111: 2	The works of the LORD *are* great, sought out of all that have pleasure **therein.**
115: 8	They that make them are like unto them; *so is* every one that trusteth **in them.**
PSALM 111: 5	He hath given **meat** unto them that fear him:
78: 25	Man did eat angel's **food:** he sent them **meat** to the full.

| PSALM 111: 7 | The works of his hands *are* **verity** and judgment; |
| : 8 | *and are* done in **truth** and uprightness. |

| PSALM 111: 8 | *and are* done in truth and **uprightness.** |
| : 3 | and his **righteousness** endureth for ever. |

| PSALM 112: 3 | **Wealth <u>and</u> riches** *shall be* in his house. |

N.B. note how the underlined word separates words and phrases having the same meaning.

| PSALM 112 : 4 | Unto the **upright** there ariseth light in the darkness: *he is* gracious, and full of compassion, and **righteous.** |

| PSALM 112: 7 | **his heart is fixed,** trusting in the LORD. |
| : 8 | **His heart** *is* **established,** he shall not be afraid, |

| PSALM 112: 9 | He hath **dispersed,** he hath **given** to the poor; |

PSALM 115: 2	**Wherefore should** the heathen say, Where is thy God?
88: 14	LORD, **Why** castest thou off my soul?
S of S 1: 7	for **why should** I be as one that turneth aside by the flocks of thy companions?

| PSALM 116: 3 | The sorrows of death **compassed me,** |
| 22: 16 | the assembly of the wicked have **inclosed me:** |

| PSALM 118: 1 | O give thanks unto the LORD, for *he is* good: **because** his mercy *endureth* for ever. |
| : 29 | O give thanks unto the LORD, for *he is* good: **for** his mercy *endureth* for ever. |

| PSALM 118: 10 | **All nations** compassed me about: |
| : 11 | **They** compassed me about; |

| PSALM 118: 25 | Save now, **I beseech thee,** O LORD: |
| Isaiah 29: 11 | saying, Read this, **I pray thee:** |

| PSALM 118: 28 | Thou *art* my God, and **I will praise thee:** *thou art my* God, **I will exalt thee.** |

| PSALM 119: 1 | Blessed *are* the **undefiled** in the way, |
| Job 1: 8 | that *there* is none like him in the earth, a **perfect <u>and</u> upright** man, that feareth God, |

N.B. note how the underlined word separates words and phrases having the same meaning.

| PSALM 119: 4 | Thou hast commanded *us* to keep thy precepts **diligently.** |
| Micah 1: 12 | For the inhabitant of Mar-oth waited **carefully** for good: |

PSALM 119: 9	**Wherewithal** shall a young man cleanse his way?
: 84	**How** many *are* the days of thy servant?

PSALM 119: 15	I will **meditate** in thy precepts,
143: 5	**I remember** the days of old; **I meditate** on all thy works;
	I muse on the work of thy hands.
Proverbs 15: 28	The righteous **studieth** to answer:

PSALM 119: 21	Thou hast rebuked the proud *that are* cursed, which **do err**
	from thy commandments.
: 10	O let me not **wander from** thy commandments.

PSALM 119: 22	Remove from me **reproach <u>and</u> contempt;**

N.B. note how the underlined word separates words and phrases having the same meaning.

PSALM 119: 25	**quicken** thou me according to thy word.
Numbers 31: 18	**keep alive** for yourselves.
Nehemiah 4: 2	will they **revive** the stones out of the heaps...?

PSALM 119: 35	Make me to go in the path of thy commandments; for **therein**
	do I delight.
118: 24	This *is* the day *which* the LORD hath made; we will reoice
	and be glad **in it.**
PSALM 119: 42	So shall I have **wherewith** to answer him that reproacheth
	me: for I trust in thy word.
I Samuel 20: 26	**Something** hath befallen him, he *is* not clean;

PSALM 119: 58	I **intreated** thy favour with *my* whole heart:
1 Samuel 25: 39	Blessed *be* the LORD, that hath **pleaded** the cause of my
	reproach from the hand of Nabal

PSALM 119: 60	I **made haste, <u>and</u> delayed not** to keep thy commandments.

N.B. note how the underlined word separates words and phrases having the same meaning.

PSALM 119: 73	Thy hands **have made me <u>and</u> fashioned me:**

N.B. note how the underlined word separates words and phrases having the same meaning.

PSALM 119: 78	for they dealt **perversely** with me without a cause:
2 Samuel 24: 17	I have sinned, and have done **wickedly:**
2 Chron. 6: 37	We have sinned, and have done **amiss,**

PSALM 119: 108	Accept, **I beseech thee,** the freewill offerings of my mouth,
Isaiah 29: 11	Read this, **I pray thee:**

PSALM 119: 126	*It is* time for *thee*, LORD to work: *for* they have **made void** thy law.
Numbers 30: 5	and the LORD shall forgive her, because her father **disallowed** her.
: 8	wherewith she bound her soul, **of none effect:**

PSALM 119: 130	The entrance of thy words giveth light; it giveth understanding to the **simple.**
73: 22	So **foolish** *was* **I, and ignorant:**
Deut. 32: 6	Do ye thus requite the LORD, O **foolish people and unwise?**
Lam. 2: 14	Thy prophets have seen **vain and foolish** things for thee:

N.B. note how the underlined words separates words and phrases having the same meaning.

PSALM 119: 137	**Righteous** *art* thou, O LORD, and **upright** *are* thy judgments.

PSALM 119: 143	**Trouble and anguish** have taken hold on me:

N.B. note how the underlined word separates words and phrases having the same meaning.

PSALM 119: 148	Mine eyes **prevent** the *night* watches,
: 170	Let my supplication **come before** thee:

PSALM 119: 163	**I hate and abhor** lying: *but* thy law do I love.

N.B. note how the underlined word separates words and phrases having the same meaning.

PSALM 119: 167	My soul hath kept thy testimonies; and I love them **exceedingly;**
Genesis 7: 18	And the waters prevailed, and were **increased greatly** upon earth,
: 19	And the waters prevailed **exceedingly** upon the earth;

PSALM 120: 2	Deliver my soul, O LORD, from **lying** lips, *and* from a **deceit-ful** tongue.
: 3	or what shall be done unto thee, thou **false** tongue?

PSALM 120: 5	Woe is me, that I **sojourn** in Me-sech, *that* I **dwell** in the tents of Ke-dar!

PSALM 121: 1	I will lift up mine eyes unto the hills, from **whence** cometh my help.
122: 5	For **there** are set thrones of judgment,

PSALM 121: 4	Behold, he that keepeth Israel shall neither **slumber nor sleep.**

N.B. note how the underlined word separates words and phrases having the same meaning.

<u>PSALM 121: 6</u>	The sun shall not **smite** thee by day, nor the moon by night.
110: 5	The LORD at thy right hand shall **strike** through kings...

<u>PSALM 121: 7</u>	The LORD shall **preserve thee** from all evil:
: 3	he that **keepeth** will not slumber.

<u>PSALM 122: 4</u>	**Whither** the tribes go up,
: 5	For **there** are set thrones of judgment,
115: 2	**Where** *is* thy God?

<u>PSALM 122: 2</u>	Our feet shall stand **within** thy gates, O Jerusalem.
1 Kings 6: 15	*and* he covered them on the **inside** with wood,

<u>PSALM 123: 3</u>	for we are **exceedingly** filled with contempt.
119: 51	The proud have had me **greatly** in derision:

<u>PSALM 123: 3</u>	for we are exceedingly filled with **contempt.**
119: 51	The proud have had me greatly in **derision:**
123: 4	Our soul is exceedingly filled with **the scorning of those that are at ease, *and* with contempt of the proud.**

N.B. note how the underlined word separates words and phrases having the same meaning.

<u>PSALM 124: 3</u>	Then they had swallowed us up **quick,**
41: 2	The LORD will preserve him, and keep him **alive;**

<u>PSALM 124: 4</u>	Then the waters **had overwhelmed us,** the stream **had gone over us,**

<u>PSALM 125: 2</u>	so the LORD *is* round about his people **from henceforth** even for ever.
121: 8	and thy coming in **from this time forth,** and even for evermore.

<u>PSALM 125: 2</u>	from henceforth **even for ever.**
121: 8	from this time forth, and **even for evermore.**

<u>PSALM 125: 3</u>	For the rod of the wicked shall not rest upon the lot **of the righteous;**
111: 1	ın the assembly **of the upright,**

<u>PSALM 126: 3</u>	The lord hath done great things for us; *whereof* we are glad.
Jeremiah 43: 1	**for which** the LORD their God had sent him to them,

<u>PSALM 128: 1</u>	**Blessed** *is* **every one that** feareth the LORD;

| | : 2 | **happy** *shalt* thou *be*, and *it shall be* well with thee. |

PSALM 129: 4 The LORD *is* righteous: he hath **cut asunder** the cords of
the wicked.

Leviticus 1: 17 *but* shall not **divide** *it* **asunder:**

1 Kings 2: 11 and **parted them** both **asunder;**

2 Chron. 28: 24 and **cut in pieces** the vessels of the house of God,

Genesis 15: 10 And he took unto him all these, and **divided them** in the
midst,

Exodus 8: 22 And I will **sever** in that day the land of Goshen,

: 23 And I will **put a division** between my people and thy people:

PSALM 129: 7 **Wherewith** the mower filleth not his hand;

Zechariah 13: 6 Then he shall answer, *Those* **with which** I was wounded *in*
the house of my friends.

PSALM 131: 1 LORD, my heart is not **haughty**, nor mine eyes **lofty:** neither
do I exercise myself in great matters, or in things **too high** for
me.

123: 4 *and* with **the contempt of the proud.**

1 Samuel 2: 3 Talk no more so **exceeding proudly**; let *not* **arrogancy** come
out of thy mouth:

Proverbs 8: 13 The fear of the LORD *is* to hate evil: **pride, <u>and</u> arrogancy,**

Jerem. 48: 29 We have heard the **pride** of Moab, (he is **exceeding proud**)
his **loftiness, <u>and</u>** his **arrogancy, <u>and</u>** his **pride, <u>and</u>** the
haughtiness of his heart.

N.B. note how the underlined words separate words and phrases having the same
meaning.

PSALM 131: 3 Let Israel hope in the LORD **from henceforth** and for ever.

121: 8 The LORD shall preserve thy going out and thy coming in
from this time forth, and even for evermore.

PSALM 132: 3 **Surely** I will not come into the tabernacle of my house, nor
go up into my bed;

: 11 The LORD hath sworn *in* **truth** unto David;

PSALM 132: 4 **I will not give sleep to mine eyes, <u>or</u> slumber to my eyelids,**

N.B. note how the underlined word separates words and phrases having the same
meaning.

PSALM 132: 9 Let thy priests be clothed **with righteousness;**

119: 7 I will praise thee **with uprightness** of heart,

PSALM 132: 15 I will satisfy her poor with **bread.**

136: 25 Who giveth **food** to all flesh:

PSALM 132: 17 I have **ordained** a lamp for mine anointed.

135: 4	For the LORD hath **chosen** Jacob unto himself,
PSALM 135: 4	For the LORD hath chosen Jacob unto himself, *and* Israel for his **peculiar** treasure.
Deut. 7: 6	the LORD thy God hath chosen thee to be a **special** people unto himself,
PSALM 135: 8	Who **smote** the firstborn of Egypt,
44: 22	Yea, for thy sake are we **killed** all the day long;
136: 18	And **slew** famous kings:
PSALM 136: 10	To him that **smote** Egypt in their firstborn:
: 18	And **slew** famous kings:
PSALM 137: 2	We hanged our harps upon the willows in the midst **thereof.**
80: 10	The hills were covered with the shadow **of it,** and the boughs **thereof** *were like* goodly cedars.
PSALM 137: 5	If **I forget** thee, O Jerusalem, let my right hand forget *her* cunning.
: 6	If I **do not remember** thee,
PSALM 137: 7	who said, **Rase it, rase it,** *even* to the foundation thereof.
Daniel 7: 26	to consume and to **destroy it,**
Amos 9: 8	and I will **destroy it** from off the face of the earth;
PSALM 139: 3	Thou **compassest** my path and my lying down,
: 5	Thou hast **beset me behind and before,**
Psalm 22: 16	the assembly of the wicked have **inclosed me:**
PSALM 139: 7	**Wither** shall I go from thy spirit?
115: 2	**Where** *is* now their God?
PSALM 139: 8	If I **ascend up** into heaven, thou *art* there:
132: 3	nor **go up** into my bed;
PSALM 139: 15	My substance was not hid from thee, when I **was made in secret, _and_ curiously wrought** in the lowest parts of the earth.
: 14	for I am fearfully *and* **wonderfully made:**
: 16	*which* in continuance **were fashioned,** when *as there was* none of them.

N.B. note how the underlined word separates words and phrases having the same meaning.

PSALM 140: 4	Keep me, O LORD, from the hands of the wicked; **preserve me** from the violent man;

PSALM 140: 5	The proud have hid a **snare** for me, and cords they have spread a **net** by the wayside; they have set **gins** for me. Se-lah.
141: 10	Let the wicked fall into their own **nets**.

PSALM 140: 9	*As for* the head of those that **compass me about,**
1 Samuel 7: 16	And he went from year to year in **circuit** to Beth-el,

Job 22: 14	and he walked in the **circuit** of heaven.
Isaiah 23: 16	Take a harp, **go about** the city,
40: 22	*It is* he that sitteth upon the **circle** of the earth,
Ezekiel 37: 21	and will gather them on **every side,**
40: 5	And behold a wall on the **outside** of the **house round about,**

PSALM 140: 4	**Keep me,** O LORD, from the hands of the wicked; **preserve me** from the violent man,

PSALM 140: 5	The proud have hid a **snare** for me, and cords; they have spread a **net** by the wayside; they have set **gins** for me. Selah.
PSALM 140: 13	Surely the **right**eous shall give thanks unto thy name: the up**right** shall dwell in thy presence.

PSALM 142: 3	In the way **wherein** I walked have they privily laid a snare for me.
Job 3: 3	Let the day perish **wherein** I was born, and the night *in which* it was said, There is a man child conceived.

PSALM 142: 7	the righteous shall **compass me about;**
22: 16	the assembly of the wicked have **enclosed me:**

PSALM 143: 1	**Hear** my prayer, O LORD, **give ear** to my supplications:

PSALM 143: 1	Hear my **prayer,** O LORD, give ear to my **supplications:**

PSALM 143: 5	**I remember** the days of old; **I meditate** on all thy works; **I muse** on the works of thy hands.

PSALM 143: 12	And of thy **mercy** cut off mine enemies,

: 8	Cause me to hear thy **lovingkindness** in the morning;

PSALM 144: 1	**Blessed** *be* the LORD my strength,
: 15	**Happy** *is that* people, that is in such a case:

PSALM 144: 9	upon a **psaltery _and_ an instrument of ten strings** will I sing praises unto thee.

N.B. note how the underlined word separates words and phrases having the same meaning.

| **PSALM 144: 12** | *that* our daughters *may be* as corner stones, polished *after* the **similitude** of a palace: |
| 17:15 | I shall be satisfied, when I awake, with thy **likeness.** |

| **PSALM 144: 13** | *That* our **garners** *may be* full, |
| Proverbs 3:10 | So shall thy **barns** be filled with plenty, |

| **PSALM 145: 1** | I will **extol** thee, my God, |
| : 2 | and I will **praise** thy name for ever and ever. |

| **PSALM 145: 11** | They shall **speak** of the glory of thy kingdom, and **talk** of thy power: |

| **PSALM 145: 15** | and thou givest them their **meat** in due season. |
| 146: 7 | which giveth **food** to the hungry. |

| **PSALM 145: 18** | The LORD *is* **nigh** unto all them that call upon him, |
| 148: 14 | *even* of the children of Israel, a people **near** unto him. |

PROVERBS

PROV. 1: 3	To receive the instruction of wisdom, justice, and judgment, and **equity;**
Psalm 96: 13	**he shall judge the world with righteousness, <u>and</u> the people with his truth.**
98: 9	**with righteousness shall he judge the world, <u>and</u> the people with equity.**
99: 4	thou dost establish **equity,** thou executest judgment and **righteousness** in Jacob.

PROV. 1: 4	To give **subtilty** to the simple,
: 2	To know **wisdom** and instruction;
9: 13	*she is* **simple, <u>and</u> knoweth nothing.**
Psalm 73: 22	So **foolish** *was* I, <u>and</u> ignorant:
Deut. 32: 6	Do ye thus requite the LORD, **foolish people <u>and</u> unwise?**

N.B. note how the underlined word separates words and phrases having the same meaning.

| **PROV. 1: 4** | To give subtilty to the **simple,** |
| Psalm 73: 22 | So foolish *was* I, and **ignorant:** |

| **PROV. 1: 9** | For they *shall be* an ornament of **grace** unto thy head, |
| 3: 4 | So shalt thou find **favour** and good understanding in the sight of God and man. |

| **PROV. 1: 10** | My son, if sinners **entice** thee consent thou not. |
| 1 Kings 22: 20 | And the LORD said, Who shall **persuade** Ahab, |

| **PROV. 1: 11** | let us lurk **privily** for the innocent without cause: |

Psalm 31: 20	thou shalt keep keep them **secretly** in a pavilion from the strife of tongues.
PROV. 1: 19	*which* taketh away the life of the owners **thereof.**
2: 22	and the transgressors shall be rooted out **of it.**
PROV. 1: 22	How long will ye love **simplicity?**
Num. 15: 24	Then it shall be, if *ought* be committed by **ignorance without he knowledge** of the congregation,

N.B. note in the second reference that the second third and fourth words means the same as the first bold word.

PROV. 1: 25	But ye have set at **nought** all my counsel,
9: 13	A foolish woman *is* clamorous: *she* is simple and knoweth **nothing.**
PROV. 1: 26	I also will laugh at your **calamity;**
: 27	when **distress <u>and</u> anguish** cometh upon you.

N.B. note how the underlined word separates words and phrases having the same meaning.

PROV. 2: 7	He layeth up sound wisdom for the **righteous:** *he is* a buckler to **them that walk uprightly.**
PROV. 2: 9	Then shalt thou understand **righteousness,** and judgment, and **equity:**
PROV. 2: 11	Discretion shall **preserve** thee, understanding shall **keep** thee:
PROV. 2: 12	To deliver thee from the way of the **evil** *man,* from the man that speaketh **froward** things;
: 14	Who rejoice to do **evil,** *and* delight in the forwardness of the **wicked:**
: 15	whose ways *are* **crooked,** *they* **froward** in their paths:
PROV. 2: 20	That thou mayest walk in the way of good *men,* and keep the paths of the **righteous.**
: 21	For the **upright** shall dwell in the land, and the **perfect** shall remain in it.
PROV. 3: 11	My son, despise not the **chastening** of the LORD; neither be weary of his **correction:**
PROV. 3: 14	and the gain **thereof** thine fine gold.
2: 22	and the transgressors shall be rooted out **of it.**
PROV. 3: 19	The LORD by wisdom hath **founded** the earth; by

understanding hath he hath he **established** the heavens.

PROV. 3: 34	Surely he scorneth the scorners: but he giveth **grace** unto the lowly.
: 4	So shalt thou find **favour** and good understanding in the sight of God and man.

PROV. 4: 4	He taught me also, and said unto me, Let thine heart **retain** my words: **keep** my commandments, and live.
: 6	Forsake her not, and she shall **preserve** thee.

PROV. 4: 12	When thou goest, thy steps shall not be **straitened;**
1 Sam. 22: 2	And every one *that was* **in distress,**

PROV. 4: 15 **Avoid it,** pass not by it, **turn from it,** and pass away.

PROV. 4: 24 Put away from thee **froward** mouth, and **perverse** lips put far from thee.

PROV. 4: 25 Let thine eyes **look right on,** and let thine eyelids **look straight** before thee.

PROV. 4: 26	**Ponder** the path of thy feet,
6: 6	Go to the ant thou sluggard; **consider** her ways, and be wise:

PROV. 5: 8	Remove thy way far from her, and come not **nigh** the door of her house:
10: 14	but the mouth of the foolis *is* **near** destruction.

PROV. 5: 14 I was almost in all evil in the midst of the **congregation and assembly.**

N.B. note how the underlined word separates words and phrases having the same meaning.

PROV. 6: 2 Thou art **snared** with the words of thy mouth, thou art **taken** with the words of thy mouth.

PROV. 6: 4 **Give not sleep to thine eyes, nor slumber to thine eyelids.**

N.B. note how the underlined word separates words and phrases having the same meaning.

PROV. 6: 8 Provideth her **meat** in summer *and* gathereth her **food** in the harvest.

PROV. 6: 10 *Yet* **a little sleep, a little slumber,** a little folding of the hands to sleep:

N.B. note how the comma separates words and phrases having the same meaning.

PROV. 6: 12   A **naughty** person, a **wicked** man, walketh with a **froward** mouth,

PROV. 6: 24   To keep thee from the **evil woman,** from the flattery of the tongue of a **strange woman.**

: 26   For by means of a **whorish woman** *a man is brought* to a piece of bread: and the **adulteress** will hunt for the precious life.

7 : 10   there met him a woman *with* the attire of an **harlot,**

PROV. 7: 7   And beheld among the **simple ones,** I discerned among the youths, a young man **void of understanding,**

PROV. 7: 9   In the twilight, in the evening, in the **black and dark night:**

N.B. note how the underlined word separates words and phrases having the same meaning.

PROV. 7: 19   For the **goodman** *is* not at home,

12: 4   A virtuous woman *is* a crown to her **husband:**

PROV. 8: 8   All the words of my mouth *are* in righteous; *there is* nothing **froward or perverse** in them.

N.B. note how the underlined word separates words and phrases having the same meaning.

PROV. 8: 29   When he gave to the sea **his decree,** that the waters should not pass **his commandment:**

PROV. 9: 2   She hath killed her beasts; she hath **mingled** her wine;

23: 30   they that go to seek **mixed** wine.

PROV. 9: 4   Whoso *is* simple, let him turn in **hither:**

Psalm 132: 14   **here** will I dwell;

PROV. 9: 4   Whoso *is* **simple,** let him turn in hither:
as for him that **wanteth understanding,**

PROV. 9: 5   Come, eat of my **bread,**

6: 8   *and* gathereth her **food** in the harvest.

PROV. 9: 5   and drink of the wine *which* I have **mingled.**

23: 30   they that go to seek **mixed** wine.

PROV. 9: 7   He that **reproveth** a scorner getteth to himself shame: and he **rebuketh** a wicked *man getteth* himself a blot.

and he will love thee.

<u>PROV. 9: 13</u>	A foolish woman *is* clamorous: *she is* simple, <u>and</u> knoweth nothing.

N.B. note how the underlined word separates words and phrases having the same meaning.

<u>PROV. 9: 15</u>	To call **passengers** who go right on their ways:
Judges 5: 6	and the **travellers** walked through byways.

<u>PROV. 10: 3</u>	The LORD will not suffer the soul of the righteous to **famish:**
19: 15	and an idle soul shall suffer **hunger.**

<u>PROV. 10: 28</u>	The **hope** of the righteous *shall be* gladness: but the **expectation** of the wicked shall perish.
11: 7	When a wicked man dieth, *his* **expectation** shall perish: and the **hope** of unjust *men* perisheth.
<u>PROV. 10: 29</u>	but destruction *shall be* to **the workers of iniquity.**
: 30	but **the wicked** shall not inhabit the earth.

<u>PROV. 11: 5</u>	The righteousness of the **perfect** shall direct his way:
: 6	The righteousness of the **upright** shall deliver them:
: 8	The **righteous** is delivered out of trouble,
12: 13	but the **just** shall come out of trouble.

<u>PROV. 11: 7</u>	When a wicked man dieth, *his* **expectation** shall perish: and the **hope** of unjust *men* perisheth.

<u>PROV. 11: 12</u>	He that is **void of wisdom** despiseth his neighbour:
9: 16	and *as for* him that **wanteth understanding,**

<u>PROV. 11: 24</u>	and *there is* that which holdeth **more than is meet,**
12: 5	The thoughts of the righteous *are* **right:**

<u>PROV. 11: 31</u>	Behold, the righteous shall be **recompensed** in the earth:
13: 13	but he that feareth the commandment shall be **rewarded.**

<u>PROV. 12: 6</u>	The words of the wicked *are* to lie in wait for blood: but the mouth of the **upright** shall deliver them.
: 7	The wicked are overthrown, **and** *are* not: but the house of the **righteous** shall stand.

<u>PROV. 13: 24</u>	but he that loveth chasteneth him **betimes.**
27: 14	rising **early** in the morning,

<u>PROV. 14: 2</u>	He that walketh in his **uprightness** feareth the LORD:
13: 6	**Righteousness** keepeth *him that is* upright in the way:

<u>**PROV. 14: 9**</u>	Fools make a mock at sin: but among the **righteous** *there is* favour.
: 11	but the tabernacle of the **upright** shall flourish.
<u>**PROV. 14: 12**</u>	There is a way which seemeth right unto a man, but the end **thereof** *are* the ways of death.
Psalm 55: 10	mischief also and sorrow *are* in the midst **of it.**
<u>**PSALM 14: 13**</u>	Even in **laughter** the heart is sorrowful; and the end of that **mirth** *is* heaviness.
<u>**PROV. 14: 23**</u>	but the talk of the lips *tendeth* only to **penury.**
6: 11	So shall thy **poverty** as one that travelleth, and thy **want** as an armed man.
<u>**PROV. 15: 4**</u>	A wholesome tongue *is* a tree of life: but perverseness **therein** *is* a breach in the spirit.
Eccl. 3: 10	I have seen the travail, which God hath given to the sons of men to be exercised **in it.**
<u>**PROV. 15: 5**</u>	but he that regardeth reproof is **prudent.**
: 2	The tongue of the **wise** useth knowledge aright:
<u>**PROV. 15: 6**</u>	In the house of the **righteous** *is* much treasure:
: 8	but the prayer of the **upright** *is* his delight.
<u>**PROV. 15: 16**</u>	Better *is* little with the fear of the LORD than great treasure and trouble **therewith.**
Deut. 16: 3	Thou shalt eat no leavened bread **with it;** seven days shalt eat unleavened bread **therewith,**
<u>**PROV. 15: 19**</u>	The way of the **slothful** *man is* as an hedge of thorns:
: 15	and an **idle** soul shall suffer hunger.
<u>**PROV. 16: 13**</u>	**Righteous** lips *are* the delight of kings; and they love him that speaketh **right.**
<u>**ROV. 16: 21**</u>	The **wise** in heart shall be called **prudent:**
<u>**PROV. 16: 25**</u>	There is a way that seemeth right unto a man, but the way **thereof** *are* the ways of death.
Psalm 80: 10	The hills were covered with the shadow **of it,** and the boughs **thereof** *were like* the godly cedars.
<u>**PROV. 16: 28**</u>	A **froward** man soweth strife:
: 27	An **ungodly** man diggeth up evil:
17 : 4	A **wicked** doer giveth heed to false lips; *and* a liar giveth ear to a **naughty** tongue.
: 20	and he that hath a **perverse** tongue falleth into mischief.
<u>**PROV. 17: 1**</u>	Better *is* a dry morsel, and quietness **therewith,** than an

256

Deut. 16: 3	house full of sacrifices *with* strife.
	Thou shalt eat no leavened **with it;** seven days shalt thou eat unleavened bread **therewith,**
PROV. 17: 18	A man **void of understanding** striketh hands,
: 24	but the eyes of **a fool** *are* in the ends of the earth.
PROV. 17: 20	He that hath a **forward** heart findeth no good: and he that hath a **perverse** togue falleth into mischief.
: 23	A wicked *man* taketh a gift out of the bosom to pervert the ways of judgment.
PROV. 17: 26	Also to punish the just *is* not good, *nor* to strike princes for **equity.**
Psalm 96: 13	he shall judge the world with **righteousness,** and the people with his truth.
PROV. 18: 3	When the wicked cometh, *then* cometh also **contempt, and with ignominy reproach.**

N.B. note how the underlined word separates words and phrases that have the same meaning.

PROV. 18: 9	He also that is **slothful** in his work is brother to him that is a great waster.
19: 15	Slothfulness casteth into a deep sleep; and an **idle** soul shall suffer hunger.
PROV. 18: 15	The heart of the **prudent** getteth knowledge, and the ear of the **wise** seeketh knowledge.
PROV. 18: 21	Death and life *are* in the power of the tongue: and they that love it shall eat the fruit **thereof.**
4: 23	Keep thy heart with all diligence; for out **of it,** *are* the issues of life.
PROV. 19: 17	He that pity upon the poor lendeth unto th LORD; and that which he hath given will he **pay him again.**
Job 41: 11	Who hath prevented me, that I should **repay** *him?*
PROV. 19: 28	An **ungodly** witness scorneth judgment: and the mouth of the **wicked** devoureth iniquity.
PROV. 20: 1	Wine *is* a mocker, strong drink *is* raging, and whosoever is deceived **thereby** is not wise.
26: 28	A lying tongue hateth *those that are* afflicted **by it;**
PROV. 20: 16	Take his garment that is **surety** *for* a stranger: and take a **pledge** of him for a strange woman.

PROV. 20: 22	Say not thou, I will **recompense** evil;
25: 22	and the LORD shall **reward** thee.

PROV. 21: 18	The wicked *shall be* a ransom for the **righteous**, and the
	and the transgressor for the **upright**.

PROV. 21: 22	and casteth down the strength **thereof.**
	mischief also and sorrow *are* in the midst **of it.**

PROV. 21: 25	The desire of the **slothful** killeth him; for his hands **refuse to labour.**

PROV. 22: 3	A prudent *man* forseeth the **evil,** and hideth himself:
: 5	Thorns *and* snares *are* in the way of the **froward:**

PROV. 22: 3	A **prudent** *man* forseeth the evil,
: 17	Bow down thine ear, and hear the words of the **wise,**

PROV. 22: 10	Cast out the scorner, and **contention** shall go out; yea, **strife and reproach** shall cease.

N.B. note how the underlined word separates words and phrases having the same meaning.

PROV. 22: 14	The mouth of strange women *is* a deep pit: he that is
	abhorred of the LORD shall fall **therein,**
Eccl. 3: 10	I have seen the travail, which God hath given to the sons of
	men to be exercised **in it.**
2 Kings 2: 21	And he went forth unto the spring of the waters and cast the
	in there,

N.B. reverse the syllables in the first bold word in the first reference and the meaning is clear.

PROV. 22: 24	Make no friendship with an **angry** man, and with a **furious** man thou shalt not go.

PROV. 23: 20	Be not among **winebibbers;** among riotous eaters of flesh:
: 21	For the **drunkard** and the glutton shall come to poverty:

PROV. 23: 27	For a **whore** *is* a deep ditch; and a **strange woman** *is* a narrow pit.

PROV. 23: 32	At the last it biteth like a **serpent,** and stingeth like an **adder.**

PROV. 24: 31	*and* nettles had covered the face **thereof.**
S. of S. 3: 10.	the bottom **thereof** *of* gold, the covering **of it** *of* purple,

PROV. 24: 33	*Yet* **a little sleep, a little slumber,**

N.B. note how the comma separates words and phrases having the same meaning.

PROV. 25: 7	For better *it is* that it be said unto thee, Come up **hither;**
Psalm 132: 14	This *is* my rest for ever: **here** will I dwell;

PROV. 25: 7	than that thou shouldest **be put lower** in the presence...
Isaiah 2: 11	The lofty looks shall be **humbled,**

PROV. 25: 9	Go not hastily to strive, lest *thou no not* what to do in the end **thereof,**
S. of S. 3: 10	He made the pillars **thereof** *of* silver, thew bottom **thereof** of gold, the covering **of it** *of* purple,

PROV. 25: 15	By **long forbearing** is a prince is a prince persuaded,
Psalm 86: 15	and gracious, **longsuffering,** and plenteous in mercy
103: 8	and gracious, **slow to anger,** and plenteous in mercy.
Eccl. 7: 8	*and* the **patient** in spirit *is* better than the proud in spirit.

PROV. 25: 16	Hast thou found honey? eat so much as is sufficient for thee, lest thou be filled **therewith,** and vomit it.
Deut. 16: 3	Thou shalt eat no leavened bread **with it;** seven days shalt thou eat unleavened bread **therewith,**

PROV. 26: 1	and as rain in harvest, so honour is **not seemly** for a fool.
25: 27	*It is* **not good** to eat much honey:
20: 1	and whosoever is deceived thereby is **not wise.**
Hosea 13: 13	he *is* an **unwise** son;

PROV. 26: 24	He that hateth **dissembleth** with his lips, and **layeth up deceit** within him.

PROV. 26: 27	Whoso diggeth a pit shall fall **therein:**
Eccl. 3: 10	I have seen the travail, which God hath given to the sons of men to exercised **in it.**
2 Kings 2: 21	And he went forth unto the spring of the waters, and cast the salt **in there,**

N.B. reverse the the syllables in the first refence and the meaning is clear.

PROV. 27: 4	**Wrath** *is* cruel, and **anger** *is* outrageous;

PROV. 27: 13	Take his garment that is **surety** for a stranger, and take a **pledge** of him for a strange woman.

PROV. 27: 18	Whoso keepeth the fig tree shall eat the fruit **thereof:**
Psalm 80: 10	The hills were covered with the shadow **of it,** and the boughs **thereof** *were like* the goodly cedars.

PROV. 27: 23	Be thou **diligent** to know the state of thy flocks,

: 12	A **prudent** *man* foreseeth the evil,
28: 11	The rich man *is* **wise** in his own conceit:
1 Kings 4: 13	Behold, thou hast been **careful** for us with all this care;

PROV. 28: 8   He that by **usury and unjust gain** increaseth his substance,

N.B.   note how the underlined word separates words and phrases having the same meaning.

PROV. 28; 10   Whoso causeth the **righteous** to stray in an evil way, he shall fall himself into his own pit: but the **upright** shall have good *things* in possession.

PROV. 29: 22   An **angry** man stirreth up strife, and a **furious** man aboundeth in transgression.

PROV. 30: 2   Surely I *am* more **brutish** than *any* man, and **have not the understanding of a man.**

PROV. 31: 14   She is like the merchants, ships; she bringeth her **food** from afar.
  : 15   She riseth also while it is yet night, and giveth **meat** to her household,

PROV. 31; 20   She **stretcheth out** her hand to the poor; yea, she **reacheth forth** her hands to the needy.

PROV. 31: 20   She stretcheth out her hand to the **poor**; yea, she reacheth forth her hands to the **needy.**

ECCLESIASTES

ECCL. 1: 7   unto the place from **whence** the rivers come, thither they return again.
  : 5   and hasteth to his place **where** he arose.

ECCL, 1: 7   **thither** they return again.
  : 11   neither shall **there** be *any* remembrance of *things*...

ECCL. 1: 10   Is there *any* thing **whereof** it may be said, See, this *is* new?
Genesis 3: 17   and hast eaten of the tree, **of which** I commanded thee,

ECCL. 1: 13   And I gave my heart to **seek and search** out by wisdom concerning all *things* that are done under heaven:

N.B.   note how the underlined word separates words and phrases having the same meaning.

ECCL. 1: 13   this sore **travail** hath God given to the sons of man...

2: 25	For all his days *are* sorrows, and his **travail, grief;**

Judges 10: 16	and his soul was grieved for the **misery** of Israel.
Neh. 9: 27	and in the time of their **trouble,**
Psalm 25: 18	Look upon mine **affliction and pain;**
Deut. 2: 25	and shall tremble, and be in **anguish** because of thee.

N.B. note how in the second reference the comma between the bold words separate two words having the same meaning.

<u>ECCL. 1: 17</u>	And I gave my heart to know wisdom, and to know **madness, and folly:**

N.B. note how the underlined word separates words and phrases having the same meaning.

<u>ECCL. 2: 2</u>	I said of **laughter,** *It is* mad: and of **mirth,** what doeth it?

<u>ECCL. 2: 6</u>	I made me pools of water, to water **therewith** the wood that bringeth forth trees:
Zech. 13: 6	*Those* **with which** I was wounded *in* the house of my friends.

<u>ECCL. 2: 8</u>	I gathered me also silver and gold, and the **peculiar** treasure of kings and the provinces:
Deut. 7: 6	the LORD thy God hath chosen thee to be a **special** people unto himself,

<u>ECCL. 2: 11</u>	Then I looked on all the works that my hands **had wrought,** and on the labour that I **had laboured** to do:
2: 4	I **made** me great works;

2 Sam. 21: 11	the concubine of Saul **had done.**
Isaiah 41: 4	Who hath **wrought and done** *it,*

N.B. note how the underlined word separates words and phrases having the same meaning.

<u>ECCL. 2: 12</u>	And I turned myself to behold wisdom, and **madness and folly:**

N.B. note how the underlined word separates words and phrases having the same meaning.

<u>ECCL. 2: 19</u>	yet shall he rule over all my labour **wherein** I have laboured,
Job 3: 3	Let the day perish **wherein** I was born, and thenight *in which* it was said, There is a man child conceived.

<u>ECCL. 2: 21</u>	For there is a man whose labour *is* in wisdom, and in knowledge, and in **equity;**
3: 16	and the place of **righteousness,**

| ECCL. 2: 21 | yet to a man that hath not laboured **therein** shall he leave *for* his portion. |
| 3: 10 | I have seen the travail, which God hath given to the sons of men to be exercised **in it.** |

| ECCL. 3: 22 | **Wherefore** I perceive that *there is* nothing better, |
| 5: 2 | **therefore** let thy words be few. |

| ECCL. 5: 6 | **Suffer not** thy mouth to cause thy flesh to sin; |
| : 2 | and **let not** thine heart be hasty to utter *any* thing before God: |

| ECCL. 5: 6 | **wherefore** should God be angry at thy voice? |
| 2: 15 | and **why** was I then more wise? |

| ECCL. 5: 11 | and what good *is there* to the owners **thereof,** |
| Psalm 55: 10 | mischief also and sorrow *are* in the midst **of it.** |

| ECCL. 5: 19 | Every man also to whom God hath given **riches <u>and</u> wealth,** |

N.B. note how the underlined word separates words and phrases having the same meaning.

ECCL. 7: 14	In the day of prosperity be joyful, but in the day of **adversity** consider:
1 Kings 1: 29	*As* the LORD liveth, who hath redeemed my soul out of all **distress,**
Prov. 1: 27	and your destruction cometh as a whirlwind; when **distress <u>and</u> anguish** cometh upon you.
Jerem. 14: 8	the saviour thereof in time of **trouble,**
15: 11	in the time of evil and in the time of **affliction.**

N.B. note how the underlined word separates words and phrases having the same meaning.

| ECCL. 7: 25 | and to know the wickedness of **foolishness <u>*and*</u> madness:** |

N.B. note how the underlined word separates words and phrases having the same meaning.

| ECCL. 8: 9 | *there is* a time **wherein** one man ruleth over another to his own hurt. |
| Job 3: 3 | Let the day perish **wherein** I was born, and the night *in which* it was said, There is a man child conceived. |

| ECCL. 8: 15 | Then I commended **mirth,** because a man hath no better thing Under the sun, than to eat, and to drink, and **to be merry:** |

men.

| S.O.S. 4: 12 | A garden **inclosed** *is* my sister, *my* spouse; a spring **shut up**, |

a fountain **sealed**.

| S.O.S. 6: 8 | There are **threescore** queens, and fourscore concubines, and virgins without number. |
| Num. 7: 88 | the rams **sixty**, the he goats **sixty**, the lambs of the first **sixty**, |

N.B. The underlined word is a mathematical term meaning twenty. To find the value of the ' score' number multiply 3x20=60.

| S.O.S. 6: 8 | There are threescore queens, and **fourscore** concubines, |
| Gen. 5: 25 | And Methuselah lived an hundred **eighty** and seven years, |

N.B. The underlined word is a mathematical term meaning twenty. To find the value of the 'score' number multiply 4x20=80.

| S.O.S. 6: 8 | There are threescore queens, and fourscore **concubines,** |
| Jerem. 3:1 | but thou hast played the harlot with many **lovers;** |

| S.O.S. 7: 1 | the work of the hands of a **cunning** workman. |
| 1 Chron. 5: 18 | and to shoot with bow, and **skilful** in war, |

| S.O.S. 8: 7 | if a man would give all his substance of his house for love, it would utterly be **contemned.** |
| : 1 | I would kiss thee; yea, I should not be **despised.** |

ISAIAH

| ISAIAH 1: 4 | they have provoked the Holy One of Israel unto anger, **they are gone away backward.** |
| : 2 | and **they have rebelled against me.** |

ISAIAH 1: 13	Bring no more vain **oblations;**
: 11	I am full of the burnt **offerings** of rams,
: 23	every one loveth **gifts,**

ISAIAH 1: 13	Bring no more **vain** oblations;
30: 7	For the Egyptians shall **in vain, and to no purpose:**
Exodus 20: 16	Thou shalt not bear **false** witness against thy neighbour.

N.B. note how the underlined word separates words and phrases having the same meaning.

| ISAIAH 1: 13 | the new moons and sabbaths, the calling of the assemblies **I cannot away with;** |
| : 14 | **they are a trouble unto me; I am weary to bear** *them.* |

| ISAIAH 1: 15 | **And when ye spread forth your hands, I will hide mine** |

ECCL. 9: 11	that the race *is* not to the swift, nor the battle to the strong, neither yet **bread** to the wise,
Prov. 31: 14	She is like the merchants' ships; she bringeth her **food** to her household.
ECCL. 10: 9 8: 12	Whoso moveth stones shall be hurt **therewith,** yet surely I know that it will be well **with them** that fear God.
ECCL. 10: 9 Isaiah 28: 18	*and* he that cleaveth the wood shall be endangered **thereby.** then ye shall be trodden down **by it.**
ECCL. 10: 18	By much **slothfulness** the building decayeth; and through **idleness** of the hands the house droppeth through.

SONG OF SOLOMON

S.O.S. 1: 12 3: 10	my spikenard sendeth forth the smell **thereof.** the bottom **thereof** *of* gold, the covering **of it** *of* purple,
S.O.S. 1: 13	A bundle of myrrh *is* my wellbeloved unto me; he shall lie all night **betwixt** my breasts.
Prov. 18: 18	The lot causeth contentions to cease, and parteth **between** the mighty.
S.O.S. 3: 7	Behold his bed, which *is* Solomon's ; **threescore** valiant men *are* about it,
Lev. 27: 7	And if *it be* from **sixty** years old and above;

N.B. The underlined word is mathematical term meaning twenty. To find the

value of the whole number multiply the number by twenty, 3x20=60.

S.O.S. 3: 10	He made the pillars **thereof** *of* silver, the bottom **thereof** *of* gold, the covering **of it** *of* purple,
S.O.S. 3: 11	and behold king Solomon with the crown **wherewith** his mother crowned him in the dy of his espousals,
Zech. 13: 6	Then he shall answer, *Those* **with which** I was wounded *in* the house of my friends.
S.O.S. 4: 2	**whereof** every one bear twins, and none *is* barren among them.
2 Chr. 33: 7	**of which** God had said to David and to Solomon his son,
S.O.S. 4: 4	**whereon** there hang a thousand bucklers, all shields of mighty men.
Ps. 119: 49	Remember the word unto thy servant, **upon which** thou hast caused me to hope.
S.O.S. 4: 4	whereon there hang a thousand **bucklers, all shields** of mighty

eyes from you: **yea, when ye make many prayers,** I will not hear:

ISAIAH 1: 18   thou your sins shall be **as** scarlet, they shall be **as** white **as**

snow; though they be red **like** crimson,

ISAIAH 1: 20   But if ye **refuse and rebel,**

N.B. note how the underlined word separates words and phrases having the same meaning.

ISAIAH 1: 24   the mighty One of Israel, Ah, **I will ease me of mine adversaries, and avenge me of mine enemies:**

N.B. note how the underlined word separates words and phrases having the same meaning.

ISAIAH 1: 25   And I will turn my hand upon thee, and **purely purge away** thy dross, and **take away** all thy tin:
: 16   **Wash you, make you clean;**

ISAIAH 1: 26   **And I will restore thy judges as at the first, and thy councillors as at the beginning:**

N.B. note how the underlined word separates words and phrases having the same meaning.

ISAIAH 1: 28   And the destruction **of the transgressors and of the sinners** *shall be* **together,**

N.B. note how the underlined word separates words and phrases having the same meaning.

ISAIAH 2: 3   for out of Zion shall go forth **the law, and the word of the** LORD from Jerusalem.

N.B. note how the underlined word separates words and phrases having the same meaning.

ISAIAH 2: 9   And the **mean** boweth down,
3: 5   and the **base** against the honourable.
ISAIAH 2: 11   The lofty looks of man shall be **humbled,** and the haughtiness of men shall be **bowed down,**
: 12   and upon every *one that is* lifted up; and he shall be **brought low:**

ISAIAH 3: 3   and the **cunning** artificer,
2 Chron. 2: 14   and his father *was* a man of Tyre, **skilful** to work in gold,

<u>ISAIAH 3: 3</u>	and the cunning **artificer,**
Deut. 27: 15	the work of the hands of the **craftsman,**

<u>ISAIAH 3: 14</u>	and the princes **thereof:**
5: 2	and gathered out the stones **thereof,** and planted it with the choicest vine, and built a tower in the midst **of it,**

<u>ISAIAH 3: 16</u>	**Moreover,** the LORD saith,
Ezekiel 8: 6	He said **furthermore** unto me,

<u>ISAIAH 3: 17</u>	Therefore the LORD will **smite** with a scab the crown of the head of the daughters of Zion,
Prov. 22: 26	Be not thou *one* of them that **strike** hands,

<u>ISAIAH 3: 22</u>	The changeable suits of **apparel, <u>and</u> the mantles, <u>and</u> the wimples, <u>and</u>** the crisping pins,
36: 22	to Hez-e-ki-ah with *their* **clothes** rent,
52: 1	put on thy beautiful **garments,** O Jerusalem, the holy city:

N.B. note how the underlined words separate words and phrases having the same meaning.

<u>ISAIAH 3: 26</u>	And her gates shall **lament <u>and</u> mourn;**

N.B. note how the underlined word separates words and phrases having the same meaning.

<u>ISAIAH 4: 4</u>	When the Lord **shall have washed away** the filth of the daughters of Zion and **shall have purged** the blood of Jerusalem from the midst thereof by the spirit of judgment,

<u>ISAIAH 4: 6</u>	and for a place of **refuge,** and for a **covert** from storm and from rain.

N.B. note the word 'cover' in 'covert' which gives the meaning of the whole word.

<u>ISAIAH 5: 2</u>	And he fenced it, and gathered out the stones **thereof,** and planted it with the joicest vine, and built a tower in the midst **of it,**

<u>ISAIAH 5: 3</u>	And now inhabitants of Jerusalem, and men of Judah, judge I pray you, **betwixt** me and my vineyard.
22: 11	Ye made also a ditch **between** the two walls for the water...

<u>ISAIAH 5: 2</u>	and also made a winepress **therein:**
: 4	What could have been done to my vineyard, that I have not done **in it?**

<u>ISAIAH 5: 4</u>	**wherefore,** when I looked that it should bring forth grapes, brought it forth wild grapes?

1: 5	**Why** should ye be stricken any more?
ISAIAH 5: 9	In mine ears *said* the LORD of hosts, **Of a truth** many houses shall be desolate,
6: 9	Hear ye **indeed,** but understand not;
7: 9	If ye will not believe, **surely** ye shall not be established.
Eccl. 11: 7	**Truly** the light *is* sweet,
ISAIAH 5: 9	Of a truth many houses shall be **desolate,** *even* great and fair, **without inhabitant.**
ISAIAH 5: 12	but they **regard not** the work of the LORD, **neither consider** the operation of his hands.
ISAIAH 5: 14	and their pomp, and he that rejoiceth, shall **descend into** it.
Prov. 26: 22	and they **go down** into the innermost parts of the belly.
ISAIAH 5: 15	And the mean man **shall be brought down, <u>and</u> the mighty man shall be humbled:**

N.B. note how the underlined word separates words and phrases having the same meaning.

ISAIAH 5: 19	That say, Let him **make speed, <u>*and*</u> hasten** his work,
: 26	and, behold, they shall **come with speed speedily:**

N.B. note how the underlined word separates words and phrases having the same meaning.

ISAIAH 5: 19	and let the counsel of the Holy One of Israel draw **nigh** and come,
13: 22	and her time *is* **near** to come,
Jerem. 42: 16	shall follow **close** after you there in Egypt;
ISAIAH 5: 14	and their pomp, and he that rejoiceth, shall **descend into** it.
Prov. 26: 22	and they **go down into** the innermost parts of the belly.
ISAIAH 5: 21	Woe unto *them that are* **wise in their own eyes, <u>and</u> prudent in their own sight!**

N.B. note how the underlined word separates words and phrases having the same meaning

ISAIAH 5: 26	And he will lift up an **ensign** to the nations from far,
13: 2	Lift ye up **a banner** upon the high mountain,
ISAIAH 5: 27	None shall be weary nor stumble among them; none shall **slumber <u>nor</u> sleep;**

N.B. note how the underlined word separates words and phrases having the same

meaning.

| ISAIAH 5: 30 | and the light is darkened in the heavens **thereof.** |
| : 2 | and built a tower in the midst **of it,** |

| ISAIAH 6: 2 | each one had six wings; with **twain** he covered his face, |
| 7: 4 | for the **two** tails of these smoking firebrands, |

| ISAIAH 6: 7 | and **thine iniquity is taken away, and thy sin purged.** |

N.B. note how the underlined word separates words and phrases having the same meaning.

| ISAIAH 6: 11 | And he answered, Until the cities be **wasted without inhabitant, and the houses without man, and the land be utterly desolate.** |

N.B. note how the underlined words separate words and phrases having the same meaning.

| ISAIAH 6: 13 | as a **teil tree, and an oak,** |

N.B. note how the underlined word separates words and phrases having the same meaning.

| ISAIAH 7: 4 | Take heed, and be quiet; **fear not, neither be faint - hearted** for the two tails of these smoking firebrands, |

N.B. note how the comma separates words and phrases having the same meaning.

| ISAIAH 7: 6 | and let us make a breach **therein** for us, |
| 6: 13 | But yet **in it** *shall be* a tenth, |

| ISAIAH 7: 8 | and within three**score** and five years shall E-phra-im shall be broken, |
| Lev. 27: 7 | And if *it be* from **sixty** years and above, |

N.B. note the underlined word is a numerical term meaning twenty. To find the value of the 'score' number multiply 3x20=60.

| ISAIAH 7: 10 | **Moreover** the LORD spake again unto Ahaz, saying, |
| Ezek. 8: 6 | He said **furthermore** unto me, |

| ISAIAH 7: 24 | With arrows and with bows shall *men* come **thither;** |
| 21: 9 | And, behold, **here** cometh a chariot of men, |

| ISAIAH 8: 1 | **Moreover** the LORD said unto me, |
| Ezekiel 8: 6 | He said **furthermore** unto me, |

| ISAIAH 8: 6 | **Forasmuch as** this people refuseth the waters of Shi-lo-ah |

N.B. note that the underlined word gives the meaning of the whole word.

<u>ISAIAH 8: 8</u> he shall **overflow <u>and</u>** **go over,** and he shall reach *even* to the neck,

N.B. note how the underlined word separates words and phrases having the same meaning.

<u>ISAIAH 8: 10</u> Take counsel together, and it shall **come to nought;** speak the word, and it **shall not stand:**
  34: 12 but none *shall be* there, and all her princes shall **be nothing.**

<u>ISAIAH 8: 14</u> and for a rock of offence to both the houses of Israel, **for a gin <u>and</u> for a snare** to the inhabitants of Jerusalem.

N.B. note how the underlined word separates words and phrases having the same meaning.

<u>ISAIAH 8: 16</u> **Bind up the testimony, seal the law** among my disciples.
  : 20 **To the law <u>and</u> to the testimony:**

N.B. note how the comma separates words and phrases having the same meaning, likewise the underlined word.

<u>ISAIAH 9: 7</u> and to establish it with justice and with justice from **hence-forth** even for ever.

  48: 6 I have shewed thee new things **from this time,** even hidden things, and thou didst not know them.

<u>ISAIAH 9: 11</u> Therefore the LORD shall set up the **adversaries** of Re-zin him, and join his **enemies** together;

<u>ISAIAH 10: 7</u> but *it is* in his heart to destroy and cut off nations **not a few.**
  8: 15 And **many** among them shall stumble,

<u>ISAIAH 10: 10</u> and whose **graven images** did excel them of Jerusalem and of Samaria;
  : 11 as I have done unto Samaria and her **idols,**

<u>ISAIAH 10: 12</u> **Wherefore** it shall come to pass,
  : 16 **Therefore** shall the LORD,

<u>ISAIAH 10: 15</u> Shall the axe boast itself against him that heweth **therewith?**
  27: 8 In measure, when it shooteth forth, thou will debate **with it:**

<u>ISAIAH 10: 24</u> he shall **smite** with a rod,
Job 20: 24 and the bow of steel shall **strike** him through.

269

ISAIAH 10: 33	and the high ones of stature *shall be* **hewn down,**
: 34	And he shall **cut down** the thickets of the forest with iron.
ISAIAH 11: 4	But with **righteousness** shall he judge the poor, and reprove with **equity** for the meek of the earth:
ISAIAH 11: 8	And the sucking child shall play on the hole of the **asp,** and the weaned child shall put his hand on the **cockatrice'** den.
14: 29	for out of the serpent's root shall come forth a **cockatrice,** and his fruit *shall be* a fiery flying **serpent.**
ISAIAH 11: 12	shall **assemble** the outcasts of Israel and **gather together** the dispersed of Judah from the four corners of the earth.
ISAIAH 11: 16	from Assyria; **like as** it was to Israel in the day that he came up out of the land of Egypt.
ISAIAH 12: 4	Praise the LORD, call upon his name, **declare his doings** among the people, **make mention** that his name is exalted.
ISAIAH 13: 2	**Lift ye up** a banner upon the high mountain, **exalt** the voice unto them,
ISAIAH 13: 3	I have commanded my **sanctified ones,**
Proverbs 2: 8	He keepeth the way of his **saints.**
ISAIAH 13: 9	to lay the land desolate: and he shall destroy the sinners **thereof** out **of it.**
ISAIAH 13: 11	and I will cause the **arrogancy** of the proud to cease, and will lay low the **haughtiness** of the terrible.
ISAIAH 13: 13	and the earth shall **remove** out of her place,
18: 5	and **take away** *and* cut down the branches.
ISAIAH 13: 15	Every one that is found shall be **thrust through;** and every one that is joined *unto them* shall **fall by the sword.**
ISAIAH 14: 3	and from the hard from the hard bondage **wherein** thou wast made to serve.
66: 4	but they did evil before mine eyes, and chose *that* **in which** I delighted not.
ISAIAH 14: 6	He who **smote** the people in wrath with a continual stroke,
2 Chron. 13: 20	and the LORD **struck** him, and he died.
ISAIAH 14: 6	He who smote the people in **wrath** with a continual stroke, he that ruled the nations in **anger,** is persecuteth,
ISAIAH 14: 10	All they shall **speak** **and** say unto thee,

N.B. note how the underlined word separates words and phrases having the same meaning.

<u>ISAIAH 14: 23</u>   and I will **sweep** it with the **besom** of destruction,

N.B. The word besom is a noun only mentioned here in the K.J.V. The other bold word is a verb and describes the action of the noun. Thus the meaning of the noun is clear.

<u>ISAIAH 14: 24</u>   The LORD of hosts hath sworn, saying, **Surely as I have thought, so shall it come to pass; <u>and</u> as I have purposed, *so* shall it stand:**

N.B. note how the underlined word separates words and phrases having the same meaning.

<u>ISAIAH 14: 30</u>   and I will **kill** thy root with famine, and he shall **slay** thy remnant.

<u>ISAIAH 15: 5</u>   his fugitives *shall flee* unto Zo-ar, **an heifer of three years old:**
    11: 6   and the **calf** and the young lion and the fatling together;

<u>ISAIAH 16: 3</u>   hide the outcasts; **bewray** not him that wandereth.

1 Chron. 12: 17   but if *ye be come* to **betray** me to my enemies,

<u>ISAIAH 16: 6</u>   We have heard of the **pride** of Moab; *he is* **very proud:** *even* of his **haughtiness, <u>and</u> his pride,**

N.B. note how the underlined word separates words and phrases having the same meaning.

<u>ISAIAH 16: 10</u>   And **gladness** is taken away, and **joy** out of the plentiful field;

<u>ISAIAH 16: 11</u>   Wherefore **my bowels** shall sound like an harp for Moab, and **mine inward parts** for Kir-har-esh.

<u>ISAIAH 16: 14</u>   and the glory of Moab shall be **contemned,**
    5: 24   and **despised** the word of the Holy One of Israel.

<u>ISAIAH 18: 5</u>   For **afore** the harvest, when the bud is perfect,
    17: 13   and shall be chased as the chaff of the mountains **before** the wind,

<u>ISAIAH 17: 9</u>   In that day shall his strong cities be as a **forsaken** bough, and an uppermost branch, which they **left** because of the children of Israel:

ISAIAH 17: 9	In that day shall his strong cities be as a forsaken **bough**, and an uppermost **branch,**
ISAIAH 17: 10	therefore shalt thou plant pleasant plants, and shalt set it with **strange slips:**
Nahum 2: 2	for the emptiers have empted them out, and marred their **vine branches.**
ISAIAH 17: 12	Woe to the **multitude** of **many** people,
ISAIAH 17: 14	And behold at **evening**tide trouble; *and* before the morning he *is* not.
ISAIAH 18: 2	Go, ye swift messengers, **to a nation** scattered and peeled, **to a people** to terrible from their beginning hitherto;
ISAIAH 18: 2	to a people terrible from their beginning **hitherto;**
44: 8	have not I told thee **from that time,**
Ezra 5: 16	and **since that time** even until now hath it been in building,
ISAIAH 18: 2	a nation **meted out** and trodden down,
40: 12	Who hath **measured** the waters in the hollow of his hand, and meted out heaven with the span,
ISAIAH 18: 2	a nation meted out and **trodden down,**
: 7	a nation meted out and **trodden underfoot,**
ISAIAH 18: 5	For **afore** the harvest,
17: 13	as the chaff of the mountains **before** the wind,
ISAIAH 19: 3	And the spirit of Egypt shall fail in the midst **thereof;**
: 1	And the heart of Egypt shall melt in the midst **of it.**
ISAIAH 19: 8	**The fishers** also shall mourn, and all they that **cast angle** into the brooks shall lament, and they that **spread nets** upon the waters shall languish.
ISAIAH 19: 11	the counsel of the wise councillors of Pharaoh is **become brutish:**
: 13	The princes of Zo-an are **become fools,**
ISAIAH 19: 12	and let them know what the LORD of hosts hath **purposed** upon Egypt.
: 17	because of the counsel of the LORD of hosts, which he hath **determined** against it.
ISAIAH 19: 13	they have also seduced Egypt, *even they that are* the stay of the tribes **thereof.**
13: 9	and he shall destroy the sinners **thereof** out **of it.**
ISAIAH 19: 21	and shall do sacrifice and **oblation;**

40: 16	nor the beasts sufficient for a burnt **offering.**
ISAIAH 20: 6	Behold, such *is* our expectation, **whither** we flee for help to be delivered from the king of Assyria:
19: 12	**where** *are* thy wise *men?*
ISAIAH 21: 3	**I was bowed down** at the hearing *of it;* **I was dismayed** at the seeing *of it.*
ISAIAH 21: 4	My heart panted, fearfulness **affrighted me:**
Deut. 7: 21	**Thou shalt not be affrighted** at them:
: 18	**Thou shalt not be afraid** of them:
ISAIAH 21: 7	and he hearkened **diligently with much heed:**
Micah 1: 12	For the inhabitant of Mar-oth waited **carefully** for good:
ISAIAH 21: 14	they **prevented** with their bread him that fled.
Psalm 68: 25	The singers **went before,**
ISAIAH 22: 13	And behold joy **and gladness,**

N.B. note how the underlined word separates words and phrases having the same meaning.

ISAIAH 23: 3	and she is a **mart** of nations.
Ezekiel 27: 17	they traded in thy **market** wheat of Minnith,
ISAIAH 23: 7	her own feet shall carry her afar off **to sojourn.**
40: 22	and spreadeth them out as a tent **to dwell** in.
ISAIAH 23: 11	to destroy the strong holds **thereof.**
19: 1	and the heart of Egypt shall melt in the midst **of it.**
ISAIAH 24: 6	and they that dwell **therein** are desolate:
30: 21	This *is* the way, walk ye **in it,**
2 Kings 2: 21	and cast the salt **in there,**
ISAIAH 24: 13	When thus it shall be **in the midst** of the land **among** the people,
ISAIAH 25: 6	a feast of wines on the **lees,**
Psalm 75: 8	but the **dregs** thereof,
ISAIAH 26: 10	Let favour be shewed to the wicked, *yet* will he not learn **righteousness:** in the land of **uprightness** will he deal justly,
ISAIAH 26: 14	*They are dead,* they shall not live; *they are* **deceased,** they shall not rise:

ISAIAH 27: 9	in chalkstones that are beaten **in sunder,**
Daniel 2: 5	ye shall be cut **in pieces,**

ISAIAH 27: 10   *and* the habitation **forsaken, and left like a wilderness:**

N.B. note how the underlined word separates words and phrases having the same meaning.

ISAIAH 27: 10	and there shall he lie down, and consume the branches **thereof.**
42: 5	and that which cometh forth **out of it,**

ISAIAH 28: 2   *which* **as a tempest of hail *and* a destroying storm,**

N.B. note how the underlined word separates words and phrases having the same meaning.

ISAIAH 28: 7   **But they also have erred through wine, and through strong drink are out of the way;**

N.B. note how the underlined word separates words and phrases having the same meaning.

ISAIAH 28: 14	**Wherefore** hear the word of the Lord, ye scornful men,
: 16	**Therefore** thus saith the Lord GOD,
ISAIAH 28: 15	We have made a **covenant** with death, and with hell are we at **agreement;**

ISAIAH 28: 15   **for we have made lies our refuge, and under falsehood have we hid our selves:**

N.B. note how the underlined word separates words and phrases having the same meaning.

ISAIAH 28: 18   And your **covenant** with death shall be disannulled, and your **agreement** with hell shall not stand;

ISAIAH 28: 18   And your covenant with death shall be **disannulled,** and your agreement with hell **shall not stand;**

ISAIAH 28: 25   doth he not **cast abroad** the fitches, and **scatter** the cumin,

ISAIAH 28: 26   For his God doth **instruct** him to discretion, *and* doth **teach** him.

ISAIAH 28: 27   but the fitches are beaten out with a **staff,** and the cummin with a **rod.**

ISAIAH 29: 2   Yet I will distress Ariel, and there shall be **heaviness and sorrow:**

ISAIAH 29: 6   with **storm and tempest,** and the flame of devouring fire.

N.B. note how the underlined word separates words and phrases having the same meaning.

ISAIAH 29: 7   even all that fight against her **munition;**
     : 3   and I will raise **forts** against thee.

ISAIAH 29: 13   **Wherefore** the Lord said, **Forasmuch as** this people draw near me with their mouth,
     : 14   **Therefore,** behold, I will proceed to do a marvellous work among this people,

ISAIAH 30: 7   For the Egyptians shall help **in vain, and to no purpose:**

N.B. note how the underlined word separates words and phrases having the same meaning.

ISAIAH 30: 23   Then shall he give the rain of thy seed, that thou shalt **sow the ground** withal;
     : 24   The oxen likewise and the young asses that **ear the ground** shall eat clean provender,

ISAIAH 30: 26   **Moreover** the light of the moon shall be as the light of the sun,
Ezekiel 8: 6   He said **furthermore** unto me,

ISAIAH 30: 33   For To-phet *is* **ordained** of old; yea, for the king it is **prepared;**

ISAIAH 30: 33   the pile **thereof** *is* fire and much wood;
    44: 19   I have burned part **of it** in the fire;

ISAIAH 31: 3   both he that helpeth shall fall, and he that is **holpen** shall fall down,
    41: 6   They **helped** every one his neighbour;

ISAIAH 32: 2   And a man shall be as an **hiding place** from the wind, and a **covert** from the tempest;

N.B. If the meaning of the third bold word is not clear then omit the last letter and this gives another word meaning the same thing.

ISAIAH 32: 4   The heart of the **rash** shall understand knowledge,
     : 9   hear my voice, **ye careless** daughters;

ISAIAH 32: 11   **strip you, and make you bare,** and gird *sackcloth* upon *your* loins.

N.B. note how the underlined word separates words and phrases having the same meaning.

<u>**ISAIAH 32: 18**</u>	And my people shall dwell in a **peaceable** habitation, and in sure dwellings, and in **quiet** resting places.
<u>**ISAIAH 33: 1**</u>	when thou **shalt cease** to spoil, thou shalt be spoiled; *and* when thou **shalt make an end** to deal treacherously with thee.
<u>**ISAIAH 33: 3**</u>	At the **noise** of the **tumult** the people fled;
<u>**ISAIAH 33: 15**</u>	He that walketh **righteously,** and speaketh **uprightly;**
<u>**ISAIAH 33: 15**</u>	he that despiseth **the gain of oppressions,** that shaketh his hands from holding of **bribes,**
<u>**ISAIAH 33: 20**</u> 34: 1	not one of the stakes **thereof** shall ever be removed, the world, and all things that come forth **of it.**
<u>**ISAIAH 34: 1**</u> : 11	let the earth hear, and all that is **therein;** the owl also and the raven shall dwell **in it:**
<u>**ISAIAH 34: 3**</u> : 4	and the mountains shall be **melted** with their blood. And all the host of heaven shall be **dissolved,**
<u>**ISAIAH 34: 8**</u> Daniel 5: 17	For *it is* the day of the LORD'S vengeance, *and* the year of **recompences** for the controversy of Zion. Let thy gifts be to thyself, and give thy **rewards** to another;
<u>**ISAIAH 34: 9**</u> : 1	And the streams **thereof** shall be turned into pitch, the world, and all things that come forth **of it.**
<u>**ISAIAH 34: 17**</u>	And he hath **cast the lot** for them, and hi hand **hath divided** it unto them line by line:
<u>**ISAIAH 34: 17**</u> : 11	from generation to generation shall dwell **therein.** the owl also and the raven shall dewll **in it:**
<u>**ISAIAH 35: 4**</u> 40: 10	*even* God *with* a **recompence;** behold, his **reward** *is* with him,
<u>**ISAIAH 35: 7**</u> 32: 2	And the **parched** ground shall become a pool, and the **thirsty** land springs of water: as rivers in a **dry** place,
<u>**ISAIAH 35: 7**</u>	where each lay, *shall be* grass with **reeds <u>*and*</u> rushes.**

N.B. note how the underlined word separates words and phrases that have the same meaning.

ISAIAH 35: 9	nor *any* ravenous beast shall go up **thereon,**
Lev. 6: 12	and the priest shall burn wood **on it** every morning, and lay the burnt offering in order **upon it;** and he shall burn **thereon** the fat of the burnt offerings.
ISAIAH 35: 9	nor *any* **ravenous** beast shall go thereon,
32: 6	to make empty the soul of the **hungry,**
ISAIAH 35: 10	they shall obtain **joy <u>and</u> gladness,** and **sorrow <u>and</u> sighing** shall flee away.

N.B. note how the underlined words separate words and phrases having the same meaning.

ISAIAH 36: 1	Now it came to pass in the fourteenth year of king Hez-e-ki-ah, *that* Sen-nach-er-ib king of Assyria **came up against** all the defenced cities of Judah, and took them.
2 Chron. 32: 1	Sen-nach-er-ib king of Assyria came, and **encamped against** the fenced cities,
ISAIAH 36: 1	Sen-nach-er-ib king of Assyria came up against all the **defenced** cities,
2 Chron. 32: 1	and entered into Judah, and encamped against the **fenced** cities,

N.B. note that the word 'fenced' appears in the bold word in the first reference.

ISAIAH 36: 4	Thus saith the great king, the king of Assyria, What confidence *is* this **wherein** thou trustest?
66: 4	but they did evil before mine eyes, and chose *that* **in which** I delighted not.
ISAIAH 36: 6	Lo, thou trustest in the staff of this broken reed, on Egypt; **whereon** if a man lean, it will go into his hand,
36: 5	I say, *sayest thou,* (but *they are but* vain words) *I have* counsel and strength for war: now **on whom** doest thou trust,
ISAIAH 36: 6	**Lo,** thou trustest in the staff of this broken reed,
2 Kings 18: 21	Now, **behold,** thou trustest upon the staff of this bruised reed,
ISAIAH 36: 6	Lo, thou trustest in the staff of this broken reed, on Egypt; **whereon** if a man lean, it will go into his hand and pierce it:
2 Kings 18: 21	Now, behold, thou trustest upon the staff of this bruised reed, *even* Egypt, **on which** if a man lean, it will go into his hand and pierce it:
ISAIAH 36: 6	whereon if a man lean, **it will go into his hand <u>and</u> pierce it:**

N.B. note how the underlined word separates words and phrases having the same meaning.

ISAIAH 37: 3	This day *is* a day of trouble, and of **rebuke**, and of blasphemy:
: 4	It may be the LORD thy God will hear the words Rab-sha-keh,
	whom the king of Assyria his master hath sent to **reproach**
	the living God, and will **reprove** the words which the LORD
	thy God hath heard:

ISAIAH 37: 4	**wherefore** lift up *thy* prayer for the remnant that is left.
: 20	Now **therefore,** O lord our God, save us from his hand,

ISAIAH 37: 6	Be not afraid of the words that thou hast heard, **wherewith**
	the servants of the king of Assyria have blasphemed me.
2 Kings 19: 6	Be not afraid of the words which thou hast heard, **with which**
	the servants of the king of Assyria have blasphemed me.

ISAIAH 37: 21	Thus saith the LORD God of Israel, **Where<u>as</u>** thou hast
	prayed to me against Sen-nach-er-ib king of Assryria:
2 Kings 19: 20	Thus saith the LORD God of Israel, ***That* which** thou hast
	prayed to me,

N.B. note how the underlined word gives the meaning of the entire word.

ISAIAH 37: 22	The virgin, the daughter of Zion, **hath despised thee, _and_**
	laughed thee to scorn;

N.B. note how the underlined word separates words and phrases having the same meaning.

ISAIAH 37: 23	and against whom hast thou **exalted** *thy* voice, and **lifted up**
	thine eyes on high?

ISAIAH 37: 24	to the sides of Lebanon; and I will cut down the tall cedars
	thereof,
34: 1	and all things that come forth **of it.**

ISAIAH 37: 26	Hast thou not heard **long ago,** *how* I have done it; *and* of
	ancient times, that I have formed it?

ISAIAH 37: 27	Therefore their inhabitants *were* of small power, **they were**
	dismayed <u>and</u> confounded:

N.B. note how the underlined word separates words and phrases having the same meaning.

ISAIAH 37: 36	and **smote** in the camp of the Assyrians a hundred and
	fourscore and five thousand:
2 Chron. 13:20	and the LORD **struck** him, and he died.

fourscore and five thousand:

Genesis 5: 28   And La-mech lived an hundred **eighty** and two years,

N.B. The underlined word is a numerical term meaning twenty. To find the value of the ' score' number multiply the number by twenty 4x20=80.

ISAIAH 38: 1   And Isaiah the son of Amoz came **unto** him,
2 Kings 20: 1   And the prophet Isaiah the son of Amoz came **to** him,

ISAIAH 38: 3   And said, Remember now, O LORD, **I beseech thee,**
    36: 8   Now therefore give pledges, **I pray thee,**

ISAIAH 39: 3   and from **whence** came they unto thee?
    37: 13   **Where** *is* the king of Ha-math,

ISAIAH 40: 12   Who hath **measured** the waters in the hollow of his hand,
                       and **meted** out heaven with the span,

ISAIAH 40: 16   nor the beasts **thereof** sufficient for a burnt offering.
    34: 1   the world, and all things that come forth **of it.**

ISAIAH 40: 16   nor the beasts thereof **sufficient** for a burnt offering.
    56: 11   Yea, *they are* greedy dogs *which* can never have **enough,**

ISAIAH 40: 18   To whom then will ye **liken** God? or what likeness will ye
                       compare unto him?

ISAIAH 40: 20   He that *is* so **impoverished** that he hath **no oblation...**
        : 16   nor the beasts thereof sufficient for a burnt **offering.**

ISAIAH 40: 20   he seeketh unto him a **cunning** workman to prepare a graven
                       image,
2 Chron 2: 14   his father *was* a man of Tyre, **skilful** to work in gold,

ISAIAH 40: 22   that **stretcheth** out the heavens as a curtain, and **spreadeth**
                       them out as a tent to dwell in:

ISAIAH 41: 4   Who hath **wrought and done** *it,*

N.B. note the underlined word which separates words and phrases having the same meaning.

ISAIAH 41: 5   The isles saw *it,* and **feared;** the ends of the earth **were afraid,**

ISAIAH 41: 9   and called thee from the chief men **thereof**
    44: 19   I have burned part **of it** in the fire;

ISAIAH 41: 12   *even* them that **contended with thee: they that war against
                       thee:**

ISAIAH 41: 12	they that war against thee shall be as **nothing,** and as a thing of **nought.**
ISAIAH 41: 17	*When* the **poor and** needy seek water,

N.B. note how the underlined word separates words and phrases having the same meaning.

ISAIAH 41: 29	Behold, they *are* all **vanity;** their works *are* **nothing:**
ISAIAH 42: 5	he that giveth breath unto the people upon it, and spirit to them that walk **therein:**
34: 11	the owl also and the raven shall dwell **in it:**
ISAIAH 42: 10	the isles, and the inhabitants **thereof.**
: 5	and that which cometh out **of it;**
ISAIAH 42: 14	I have long time **holden** my peace;
36: 21	But they **held** their peace,
ISAIAH 42: 23	Who among you will **give ear** to this? *who* will **hearken and hear** for the time to come?

N.B. note how the underlined word separates words and phrases having the same meaning.

ISAIAH 43: 1	But now thus saith the LORD that **created** thee, O Jacob, and he that **formed** thee,
: 7	*Even* every one that is called by my name: for I have **created** him for my glory, I have **formed** him; yea, I have **made** him.
ISAIAH 43: 9	Let all the nations be **gathered together, and let the people be assembled:**

N.B. note how the underlined word separates words and phrases having the same meaning.

ISAIAH 43: 13	I will work, and who shall **let it?**
Psalm 35: 3	Draw out also the spear, and **stop** *the way* against them that persecute me:
ISAIAH 43: 17	they are extinct, they are quenched as **tow.**
42: 3	and the **smoking flax** shall he not quench:
ISAIAH 43: 18	Remember ye not the former things, neither consider the things of old.

N.B. note how the comma separates words and phrases having the same meaning,

| ISAIAH 44: 2 | Thus saith the LORD **that made thee, and formed thee** from the womb, |

N.B. note how the underlined word separates words and phrases having the same meaning.

| ISAIAH 44: 7 | And who, as I, shall call, and shall declare it, and **set it in order** for me, since I **appointed** the ancient? |

| ISAIAH 44: 12 | The smith with the tongs both **worketh** in the coals, and **fashioneth** it with hammers, |

| ISAIAH 44: 15 | he maketh it a graven image, and falleth down **thereto.** |
| 2 Kings 18: 4 | for unto those days the children of Israel did burn incense **to it:** |

| ISAIAH 44: 19 | I have burned part **of it** in the fire; yea, also I have baked coals **thereof;** |

ISAIAH 44: 23	break forth into singing, ye mountains, O forest, and every tree **therein:**
34: 11	the owl also and the raven shall dwell **in it:**
2 Kings 2: 21	and cast the salt **in there,**

N.B. reverse the two syllables of the first bold word and the meaning is clear.

| ISAIAH 45: 2 | I will **break in pieces** the gates of brass, and **cut in sunder** the bars of iron: |

| ISAIAH 45: 7 | I **form** the light, and **create** the darkness: I **make** peace, |

| ISAIAH 45: 15 | **Verily** thou *art* a God that hidest thyself O God of Israel, the Saviour. |
| : 24 | **Surely,** shall *one* say, in the LORD have I righteousness and strength: |

| ISAIAH 46: 1 | your carriages *were* **heavy loaden** *they are* a burden to the weary *beast.* |

N.B. The underlined letters of the first bold word spell out another word meaning the ame thing.

| ISAIAH 46: 5 | To whom will ye **liken me,** and make *me* equal, and **compare me,** that we may like? |

| ISAIAH 46: 7 | They **bear him** upon the shoulder, they **carry him,** and set him in his place, |

| ISAIAH 46: 8 | **Remember this,** and shew yourselves men: **bring** *it* **again** |

to mind,

ISAIAH 47: 2	Take the millstones, and grind meal: **uncover** thigh locks, **make bare** leg,

ISAIAH 47: 6	I was **wroth** with my people,
12: 1	though thou wast **angry** with me,

ISAIAH 47: 11	thou shalt not know from **whence** it riseth:
49: 21	Behold, I was left alone; these, **where** *had* they *been?*

ISAIAH 47: 12	and with the multitude of thy sorceries, **wherein** thou hast
	laboured from thy youth;
66: 4	but they did evil before mine eyes, and chose *that* **in which** I delighted not.

ISAIAH 48: 5	lest thou shouldest, say, **Mine idol** hath done them, and **my graven image,** and my **molten image,** hath commanded them.

ISAIAH 48: 19	and the offspring of thy bowels like the gravel **thereof;**
44: 19	I have burned part **of it** in the fire;

ISAIAH 48: 22	*There is* no peace, saith the **LORD, unto** the wicked.
57: 21	*There is* no peace, saith **my God, to** the wicked.

ISAIAH 49: 4	I have spent my strength **for nought, and in vain:**

N.B. note how the underlined word separates words and phrases having the same meaning.

ISAIAH 49: 19	shall even now be **too narrow** by reason of the inhabitants,
: 20	The place *is* **too strait** for me:

ISAIAH 50: 2	**Wherefore,** when I came, *was there* no man?
63: 17	O LORD, **why** hast thou made us to err from thy ways,

ISAIAH 51: 3	**joy and gladness** shall be found therein,

N.B. note how the underlined word separates words and phrases having the same meaning.

ISAIAH 51: 3	joy and gladness shall be found **therein,**
2 Kings 2: 21	and cast the salt **in there,**

N.B. reverse the two syllables of the first bold word and the meaning is clear.

ISAIAH 51: 11	they shall obtain **gladness and joy;** *and* **sorrow and mourning** shall flee away.

N.B. note how the underlined word separates words and phrases having the same meaning.

<u>ISAIAH 52: 1</u>	for **henceforth** there shall no more come into thee the uncircumcised and the unclean.
48: 6	I have shewed thee new things **from this time,**

<u>ISAIAH 52: 3</u>	Ye have sold yourselves for **nought;**
Jerem. 10: 24	lest thou bring me to **nothing.**

<u>ISAIAH 52: 12</u>	and the God of Israel *will be* your **rereward.**
Joshua 6: 9	and the **rereward came after** the ark of the LORD,

<u>ISAIAH 53: 3</u>	He is **despised <u>and</u> rejected** of men;

N.B. note how the underlined word separates words and phrases having the same meaning.

<u>ISAIAH 53: 2</u>	**he hath no form nor comeliness;** and when we see him, *there is* **no beauty** that we should desire him.

<u>ISAIAH 53: 4</u>	Surely he hath **borne** our griefs, and **carried** our sorrows;

<u>ISAIAH 55: 2</u>	**Wherefore** do ye spend money for *that which is* not bread?
63: 17	O LORD, **why** hast thou made us to err from thy ways?

<u>ISAIAH 55: 2</u>	**hearken** diligently unto me, eat ye *that which is* good,
: 3	**hear,** and your soul shall live;
49: 1	**Listen,** O isles, unto me; and **hearken,** ye people,

<u>ISAIAH 55: 2</u>	hearken **diligently** unto me, eat ye that which is good,
Deut. 15: 5	Only if thou **carefully** hearken unto the voice of the LORD my God,

<u>ISAIAH 55: 10</u>	For as the rain cometh down, and the snow from heaven, and returneth not **thither,**
57: 10	*yet* saidst thou not, **There** is no hope:

<u>ISAIAH 55: 11</u>	and it shall prosper *in the thing* **whereto** I sent it.
Jeremiah 43: 1	**for which** the LORD their God had sent him to them, *even* all these words.

<u>ISAIAH 57: 7</u>	Upon a **lofty <u>and</u> high** mountain hast thou set thy bed:

N.B. note how the underlined word separates words and phrases having the same meaning.

<u>ISAIAH 57: 11</u>	And of whom hast thou been **afraid <u>nor</u> feared,**

<u>ISAIAH 57: 17</u>	and he went on **frowardly in the way of his heart.**
Jerem. 17: 9	**The heart** *is* **deceitful above all** *things*, **and desperately wicked who can know it?**

<u>ISAIAH 58: 3</u>	**Wherefore** have we fasted, *say they,* and thou seest not?
63: 17	O LORD, **Why** hast thou made us to err from thy ways, *and* hardened our heart from thy fear?

<u>ISAIAH 58: 6</u>	*Is* not this that I have chosen? **To loose** the bands of wickedness, **to undo** the heavy burdens,

<u>ISAIAH 59: 3</u>	your lips have spoken **lies,** your tongue hath muttered **perverseness.**

<u>ISAIAH 59: 13</u>	In transgressing and **lying** against the LORD...**falsehood.**

<u>ISAIAH 59: 5</u>	They hatch **cockatrice'** eggs, and weave the spider's web: he that eateth of their eggs dieth, and that which is crushed breaketh out into a **viper.**

<u>ISAIAH 59: 8</u>	whosoever goeth goeth **therein** shall not know peace.

N.B. reverse the two syllables of the bold word and the meaning is clear.

<u>ISAIAH 59: 12</u>	and our **sins** testify against us for our **transgressions** *are* with us; and *as for* our **iniquities,** we know them;

<u>ISAIAH 59: 18</u>	accordingly he will **repay,** fury to his adversaries, **recompence** to his enemies;
Exodus 22: 12	And if it be stolen from him, he shall **make restitution** unto the owner thereof.

<u>ISAIAH 59: 21</u>	**from henceforth** and for ever.
48: 6	I have shewed thee new things **from this time,**
Psalm 121: 8	The LORD shall preserve thy going out and thy coming in **from this time forth,** and even for evermore.

<u>ISAIAH 60: 6</u>	The multitude of **camels** shall cover thee, the **dromedaries** of Midian and Ephah;

<u>ISAIAH 60: 12</u>	For the **nation <u>and</u> kingdom** that will not serve thee shall perish;

<u>ISAIAH 60: 12</u>	For the nation and kingdom that will not serve thee shall

perish; yea *those* nations shall be **utterly wasted.**

<u>**ISAIAH 61: 9**</u> : 11	And their seed shall be known among the **Gentiles,** and praise to spring forth before all the **nations.**
<u>**ISAIAH 62: 1**</u> 44: 19	until the righteousness **thereof** go forth as brightness, I have burned part **of it** in the fire;
<u>**ISAIAH 63: 1**</u>	Who *is* this that cometh from Edom, with dyed **garments** from Bozrah? this *that is* glorious in his **apparel,**
<u>**ISAIAH 63: 2**</u> : 17	**Wherefore** *art thou* red in thine apparel...? O LORD **why** hast thou made us to err from thy ways..?
<u>**ISAIAH 63: 3**</u>	for I will **tread them in my anger, <u>and</u> trample them in my fury;**

N.B. note how the underlined word separates words and phrases having the same meaning.

<u>**ISAIAH 63: 7**</u>	which he hath bestowed on them according to his **mercies,** and according to the multitude of his **lovingkindnesses.**
<u>**ISAIAH 64: 9**</u> Jonah 1: 8	behold, see, **we beseech thee,** we are all thy people. Then said they unto him, Tell us, **we pray thee,**
<u>**ISAIAH 65: 12**</u> 66: 4 Numbers 6: 5	but did evil before mine eyes, and did choose *that* **wherein** I delighted not. but they did evil before mine eyes, and chose *that* **in which** I delighted not. until the days be fulfilled, **in the which** he separateth *himself* unto the LORD,
<u>**ISAIAH 65: 16**</u> : 17	because the former troubles are **forgotten,** and because they are hid from mine eyes. and the former shall **not be remembered, nor come into mind.**

N.B. note how the comma separates words and phrases having the same meaning.

<u>**ISAIAH 65: 20**</u> : 9	There shall be no more **thence** an infant of days, and my servant shall dwell **there.**
<u>**ISAIAH 66: 3**</u> : 20	he that offereth an **oblation,** *as if he offered* swine's blood; as the children of Israel bring an **offering** unto the LORD...

JEREMIAH

JER. 1: 11	**Moreover** the word of the LORD came unto me,
Ezek. 8: 6	He said **furthermore** unto me,

JER. 1: 13	And I said, I see a seething pot; and a face **thereof** *is* toward the north.
Isaiah 44: 19	I have burned part **of it** in the fire;

JER. 2: 9	**Wherefore** I will yet plead with you, saith the LORD,

1: 17	Thou **therefore** gird up thy loins,

JER. 2: 19	**Thine own wickedness shall correct thee, <u>and</u> thy backslidings shall reprove thee:**

N.B. note how the underlined word separates words and phrases having the same meaning.

JER. 2: 23	*thou art* a swift **dromedary** traversing her ways;
Isaiah 60: 6	The multitude of **camels** shall cover thee, the **dromedaries** of Midian and Ephah;

JER. 2: 29	**Wherefore** will ye plead with me?
: 33	**Why** trimmest thou thy way to seek love?

JER. 2: 33	Why **trimmest** thou thy way to seek love?
7: 3	**Amend your ways** and your doings,

JER. 2: 36	**Why gaddest thou about** so much to change thy way?
5: 1	**Run ye to and fro** through the streets of Jerusalem,

JER. 3:2	Lift up thine eyes unto the high places, and see where thou hast not been **lien with.**
Deut. 22: 22	If a man be found **lying with** a woman married to an husband,

JER. 3: 8	when all the causes **whereby** backsliding Israel committed adultery I had her put away,
Isaiah 3: 8	So the sun returned ten degrees, **by which** degrees it had gone down.

JER. 3: 10	Judah hath not turned unto me with her whole heart, but **feignedly,** saith the LORD.
Lev. 6: 3	and sweareth **falsely;**
Gen. 34: 13	And the sons of Jacob answered She-chem and Ha-mor his father **deceitfully,**

JER. 3: 16	The ark of the covenant of the LORD: **neither shall it come to mind: neither shall they remember it;**

286

N.B. note how the colon separates words and phrases having the same meaning.

JER. 3: 20	**Surely** *as* a wife treacherously departeth from her husband,
: 23	**Truly** in *vain is salvation hoped for* from the hills,

JER. 4: 16	**Make ye mention** to the nations; behold **publish** against Jerusalem, *that* watchers come from a far country, and **give out** their voices against the cities of Judah.

JER. 4: 22	For my people *is* **foolish,** they have not known me; they *are* **sottish children, and they have none understanding:**

N.B. note how the underlined word separates words and phrases having the same meaning.

JER. 4: 26	and all the cities **thereof** were broken down at the presence of the LORD,
Isaiah 44: 19	I have burned part **of it** in the fire;

JER. 5: 4	**Therefore** I said, Surely these *are* poor;
: 6	**Wherefore** a lion out of the forest shall slay them,
: 18	**Nevertheless** in those days, saith the LORD,

JER. 5: 12	They have **belied** the LORD, and said, *It is* not he;
Job 31: 28	for I should have **denied** the God *that is* above.

JER. 5: 17	they shall impoverish thy fenced cities, **wherein** thou trustedst,
Isaiah 66: 4	and chose *thin* **in which** I delighted not.

JER. 5: 19	**Wherefore** doeth the LORD our God all these *things* unto us?
2: 36	**Why** gaddest thou about so much to change thy way?

JER. 5: 23	But this people hath **a revolting and a rebellious heart;**

N.B. note how the underlined word separates words and phrases having the same meaning.

JER. 5: 25	Your **iniquities** have turned away these *things*, and your **sins** have withholden good *things* from you.

JER. 6: 8	Be thou instructed, Jerusalem, lest my soul depart from thee; lest I make thee **desolate, a land not inhabited.**

N.B. note how the comma separates words and phrases having the same meaning.

JER. 6: 23	They shall lay hold on bow and spear; they *are* **cruel, and have no mercy:**

N.B. note how the underlined word separates words and phrases having the same meaning.

JER. 6: 26   make thee **mourning,** *as for* an only son, **most bitter lamentation:**

JER. 7: 5   Thus saith the LORD of hosts, the God of Israel, **Amend**

your ways and your doings, and I will cause you to dwell in this place.

JER. 7: 14   Therefore will I do unto *this* house, which is called by my name, **wherein** ye trust,

Isaiah 66: 4   but they did evil before mine eyes, and chose *that* **in which** I delighted not.

JER. 7: 20   Therefore thus saith the Lord GOD; Behold **mine anger and my fury** shall be poured out upon this place,

N.B. note how the underlined word separates words and phrases having the same meaning.

JER. 7: 33   and for the beasts of the earth, and none shall **fray** *them* away.

Isaiah 17: 2   which shall lie down, and none shall **make them afraid.**

JER. 8: 5   Why *then* is this people of Jerusalem **slidden back** by a perpetual **backsliding?**

JER. 8: 16   and all that is **in it;** the city, and those that dwell **therein.**

JER. 8: 17   For, behold, I will send **serpents, cockatrices,** among you,

N.B. note how the third   comma separates words and phrases having the same meaning.

JER. 8: 19   Why have they provoked me to anger with their **graven images, _and_ with strange vanities?**

N.B. note how the underlined word separates words and phrases having the same meanjng.

JER. 9: 5   And they will **deceive** every one his neighbour, and **will not speak the truth:** they have taught their tongue to **speak lies,**

JER. 9: 10   For the mountains will I take up a **weeping _and_ wailing,** and

for the habitations of the wilderness **a lamentation,**

N.B. note how the underlined word separates words and phrases having the same

meaning.

JER. 9: 11   and I will make the cities of Judah **desolate, without an inhabitant.**

N.B. note how the first bold word means the same as the following three bold words. Also how the last three bold words mean the same as the first bold word.

JER. 9: 13   And the LORD saith, Because they have **forsaken** my law which I have set among them, and have **not obeyed** my voice,

JER. 9: 17   and send for **cunning** *women*, that they may come:
2 Chron. 2:14   and his father *was* a man of Tyre, **skilful** to work in gold,

JER. 9: 22   and as the handful after the **harvestman,** and none shall gather *them.*
Amos 9: 13   that the plowman shall overtake the **reaper,**

JER. 10: 6   Forasmuch **as** *there is* like unto thee, O LORD;

N.B. note how the underlined word gives the meaning of the whole word.

JER. 10: 20   My **tabernacle** is spoiled, and all my cords are broken: my children are gone forth of me, and they *are* not: *there is* none to stretch forth my **tent** any more,

JER. 10: 22   Behold, **the noise** of the bruit is come, and a great commotion out of the north country,
2 Kings 19: 7   and he shall a **rumour,** and shall return to his own land;
1 Sam. 2: 24   for *it is* no good **report** that I hear:
4: 19   and when she heard the **tidings** that ark of God was taken,

JER. 10: 22   and a **great commotion** out of the north country,
Isaiah 9: 5   For every battle of the warrior *is* with **confused noise,**

JER. 11: 15   *seeing* she hath wrought **lewdness** with many,
12: 4   for the **wickedness** of them that dwell therein...?
Isaiah 28: 8   For all the tables are full of vomit *and* **filthiness,**

JER. 11: 19   Let us destroy the the tree with the fruit **thereof,**
Isaiah 44 19   I have burned part **of it** in the fire;

JER. 12: 1   **Wherefore** doth the way of the wicked prosper?
14: 8   **why** shouldest thou be as a stranger in the land,

JER. 12: 4   How long shall the land mourn, and the herbs of every field whither, for the wickedness of them that dwell **therein?**
8: 16   and all that is **in it;** the city, and those that dwell **therein.**

JER. 12: 7	I have **forsaken** mine house, I have **left** mine heritage;
JER. 12: 16	And it shall come to pass, if they will **diligently** learn the ways of my people,
Micah 1: 12	For the inhabitant of Mar-oth waited **carefully** for good:
JER. 13: 6	Arise, go to Eu-phra-tes, and take the girdle from **thence**,
	which I commanded thee to hide **there.**
JER. 13: 7	and, behold, the girdle was **marred, it was profitable for nothing.**
: 10	shall even be as this girdle, which is **good for nothing.**

N.B.   note the first bold word before the comma means the same as the five following bold words.

JER.13: 14	even the fathers and the sons together, saith the LORD: **I will not pity, nor spare, nor have mercy, but destroy them.**

N.B.   note how the underlined words separates words and phrases having the same meaning.

JER. 13: 21	for thou hast taught them *to be* **captains and as chiefs over thee:**

N.B.   note how the underlined word separates words and phrases having the same meaning.

JER. 14: 1	The word of the LORD that came to Jeremiah concerning the **dearth.**
: 14	but I will consume them by the sword, and by the **famine,**
JER. 14: 9	Why shouldest thou be as a man **astonied,**
19: 8	every one that passeth thereby shall be **astonished...**
JER. 14: 12	and when they offer burnt **offering and oblation,** I will not accept them:
JER. 14: 14	and a thing of **nought,** and the deceit of their heart.
32: 17	*and* there is **nothing** too hard for thee:
JER. 14: 22	Are there *any* among the **vanities** of the Gentiles that can cause rain?
16: 13	and there shall ye serve other **gods** day and night;
JER 15: 2	if they say unto thee, **Whither** shall we go forth?
13: 20	**where** *is* the flock *that* that was given thee..?

JER 15: 10 that thou hast borne me **a man of strife and a man of contention** to the whole earth?

N.B. note how the underlined word separates words and phrases having the same meaning.

JER. 15: 11 The LORD said, **Verily** it shall be well with thy remnant;

16: 19 **Surely** our fathers have inherited lies, vanity,
10: 19 but I said, **Truly** this *is* a grief, and I must bear it.

JER. 15: 18 and my wound **incurable, *which* refuseth to be healed?**

N.B. note how the underlined word separates words and phrases having the same meaning.

JER. 16: 9 and in your days, **the voice of mirth, and the voice of gladness,**

N.B. note how the underlined word separates words and phrases having the same meaning.

JER. 16: 5 for I have taken away my peace from this people, saith the LORD, *even* **lovingkindness and mercies.**

N.B. note how the underlined word separates words and phrases having the same meaning.

JER. 16: 15 and from all the lands **whither** he had driven them.
: 13 and there shall ye serve other gods day and night; **where** I will not shew you favour.

JER. 16: 18 And first I will **recompense** their iniquity and their sin double;
Isaiah 62: 11 behold, his **reward** *is* with him, and his work before him.

JER. 16: 18 they have filled mine inheritance with the carcases of their **destestable and abominable** things.

N.B. note how the underlined word separates words and phrases having the same meaning.

JER. 16: 19 Surely our fathers have inherited lies, vanity, and *things* **wherein** *there is* no profit.
Isaiah 66: 4 but they did evil before mine eyes, and chose *that* **in which** I delighted not.

JER. 17: 13 O LORD, the hope of Israel, all that **forsake thee** shall be

ashamed, *and* they that **depart from me** shall be written in the earth,

JER. 17: 19	Go and stand in the gate of the children of the people, **where**by the kings of Judah come in, and **by the which** they go out,
Isaiah 37: 29	and I will turn thee back by the way **by which** thou camest.

JER. 17: 19	whereby the kings of Judah **come in,** and by the which they go out,
: 20	and all the inhabitants of Jerusalem, that **enter in** by these gates:

JER. 17: 24	but hallow the sabbath day, to do no work **therein;**
19: 4	and have burned incense **in it** unto other gods,

JER. 18: 3	Then I went down to the potter's house, and, behold, he **wrought** a work on the wheels.
: 4	And the vessel that he had **made** of clay was marred in the hand of the potter:

JER. 18: 10	then I will repent of the good, **wherewith** I said I would benefit them.
Zech. 13: 6	*Those* **with which** I was wounded *in* the house of my friends.

JER. 18: 16	every one that passeth there**by** shall be astonished,
49: 17	every one that goeth **by it** shall be astonished,
22: 8	And many nations shall pass **by this** city,

JER. 18: 20	Shall evil be **recompensed** for good?
31: 16	for thy works shall be **rewarded,** saith the LORD;

JER. 19: 9	and they that seek their lives, shall **straiten** them.
10: 18	and will **distress** them, that they may find *it so.*

JER. 19: 12	and to the inhabitants **thereof,** and *even* make this city as To-phet:
Isaiah 44: 19	I have burned part **of it** in the fire;

JER. 19: 14	Then came Jeremiah from To-phet, **whither** the LORD had sent him to prophesy;
22: 26	into another country, **where** ye were not born;

JER. 20: 5	**Moreover** I will deliver all the strength of this city,
Ezek. 8: 6	He said **furthermore** unto me,

JER. 20: 7	I am in **derision** daily, every one **mocketh** me.
: 8	the word of the LORD was made a **reproach** unto me, and a **derision,** daily.

JER. 20: 10	**Peradventure** he will be enticed,

36: 3	**It may be** that the houseof Judah will hear all the evil which I purpose to do unto them;
JER. 20: 14 Isaiah 66: 4	Cursed *be* the day **wherein** I was born: but they did evil before mine eyes, and chose *that* **in which** I delighted not.
JER. 20: 18 19: 6	**Wherefore** came I forth out of the womb...? **Therefore**, behold, the days come,
JER. 21: 4 Ezek. 40: 5	which besiege you **without** the walls, And behold a wall on the **outside** of the house round about.
JER. 21: 5	And I myself will fight against you with an outstretched hand and with a strong arm, even **in anger, <u>and</u> in fury, <u>and</u> in great wrath.**

N.B. note how the underlined word separates words and phrases having the same meaning.

JER. 21: 7	he shall not spare them, **neither have pity, <u>nor</u> have mercy.**

N.B. note how the underlined word separates words and phrases having the same meaning.

JER. 21: 14 Isaiah 44: 19	and I will kindle a fire in the forest **thereof,** I have burned part **of it** in the fire;
JER. 22: 8 26: 9	and they shall say every man to his neighbour, **Wherefore** hath the LORD done thus unto this great city? **Why** hast thou prophesied in the name of the LORD,
JER. 22: 11 Ezekiel 8: 6	which went forth out of this place; He shall not return **thither** any more. *even* the great abominations that the house of Israel hath committeth **here,**
JER. 22: 12 : 26	But he shall die in the place **whither** they have led him captive, and shall see this land no more. into another country, **where** ye were not born;
JER. 22: 13	Woe unto him that buildeth his house **by unrighteousness,** and his chambers **by wrong;**
JER. 22: 14 1 Kings 6 15	and *it is* **ceiled** with cedar, and painted with vermilion. *and* he **covered** *them* on the inside with wood,
JER. 22: 16	He judged the cause of the **poor <u>and</u> needy;**

N.B. note how the underlined word separates words and phrases having the same

meaning.

JER. 22: 27	But to the land whereunto they desire to return, **thither** shall they not return.
: 1	Go down to the house of the king of Judah, and speak **there** this word,

JER. 22: 28	*is he* a vessel **wherein** *is no pleasure*?
Isaiah 66: 4	and chose *that* **in which** I delighted not.

JER. 23: 2	Therefore thus saith the LORD God of Israel against the **pastors** that feed my people;
: 4	And I will set up **shepherds** over them which shall feed them:

JER. 23: 3	And I will gather the remnant of my flock out of all countries **whither** I have driven them,
22: 26	into another country, **where** ye were not born;

JER. 23: 6	and this *is* his name **whereby** he shall be called,
Isa. 37: 29	and I will turn thee back by the way **by which** thou camest.
JER. 23: 8	and from all countries **whither** I had driven them;
22: 26	**where** ye were not born;

JER. 23: 12	and fall **therein**: for I will bring evil upon them,
8: 16	and all that is **in it**; the city, and those that dwell **therein**.

JER. 23: 19	Behold, a whirlwind of the LORD is gone forth in **fury**,
: 20	The **anger** of the LORD shall not return,

JER. 23: 40	**And I will bring an everlasting reproach upon you, and a perpetual shame,**

N.B. note how the underlined word separates words and phrases having the same meaning.

JER. 24: 2	and the other basket *had* very **naughty** figs, which could **not be eaten, they were so bad.**

JER. 24: 9	in all places **whither** I shall drive them.
22: 26	**where** you were not born;

JER. 24: 14	and I will **recompense** them according to their deeds,
40: 5	So the captain of the guard gave him victuals and a **reward**,

JER. 25; 38	He hath forsaken his **covert**, as the lion:

N.B. The meaning of the whole world is in the first five letters.

JER. 26: 14	As for me, behold, I *am* in your hand: do with me as **seemeth good and meet** unto you.

| JER. 26: 14 | do with me as seemeth good and **meet** unto you. |
| 34: 15 | And ye were now turned, and had done **right** in my sight, |

| JER. 26: 15 | ye shall **surely** bring innocent upon yourselves, and upon this |
| | city and upon the inhabitants thereof: for **of a truth** the LORD hath sent me unto you... |

| JER. 26: 15 | and upon the inhabitants **thereof:** |
| Isaiah 44: 19 | I have burned part **of it** in the fire; |

| JER. 27: 11 | those will I let remain still in their own land, saith the LORD; and they shall till it, and dwell **therein.** |
| 8: 16 | and all that is **in it**; the city, and those that dwell **therein.** |

| JER. 27: 17 | **wherefore** should this city be laid waste? |
| 26: 9 | **Why** hast thou prophesied in the name of the LORD..? |

| JER. 29: 7 | And seek the peace of the city **whither** I have caused you to carried away captives, |
| 22: 26 | **where** ye were not born; |

| JER. 29: 14 | and from all the places **whither** I have driven you, saith the LORD; and I will bring you again into the place **whence** I caused to be carried away captive. |
| 35: 7 | that ye may live many days in the land **where** ye *be* strangers. |

| JER. 30: 6 | **wherefore** do I see every man with his hands on his loins, |
| 29: 27 | Now therefore **why** hast thou not reproved Jeremiah of An-a-thoh, |

| JER. 30: 17 | For **I will restore health unto thee, <u>and</u> I will heal thee of thy wounds,** |

N.B. note how the underlined word separates words and phrases having the same meaning.

| JER. 30: 20 | Their children also shall be as **aforetime,** and their congregation shall be established **before** me, |

| JER. 30: 21 | and I will cause him to **draw near, <u>and</u> he shall approach** unto me: |

N.B. note how the underlined word separates words and phrases having the same meaning.

| JER. 31: 2 | The people *which were* left of the sword found **grace** in the wilderness; |

16: 13	where I will not shew you **favour.**
JER. 31: 8	and her that travail with child together: a great company shall return **thither.**
Ezek. 8: 6	*even* the great abominations that the house of Israel committeth **here,**
JER. 31: 9	**wherein** they shall not stumble: for I am a father to Israel,
Isaiah 66: 44	but they did evil before my eyes, and chose *that* **in which** I delighted not.
JER. 31: 11	For the LORD hath **redeemed** Jacob, and **ransomed** him from the hand of *him that was* stronger than he.
JER. 31: 14	And I will **satiate** the soul of the priests with fatness,
Prov. 5: 19	let her breasts **satisfy** thee at all times;
JER. 31: 20	therefore **my bowels** are troubled for him;
: 33	I will put my law in their **inward parts,**
JER. 31: 25	For I have **satiated** the weary soul,
: 14	and my people shall be **satisfied** with my goodness,
JER. 31: 35	which divideth the sea when the waves **thereof** roar;
Isaiah 44: 19	I have burned part **of it** in the fire;
JER. 32: 3	For Zed-e-ki-ah king of Judah shut him up, saying, **Wherefore** dost thou prophesy..?
26: 9	**Why** hast thou prophesied in the name of the LORD..?
JER. 32: 36	concerning this city, **whereof** ye say,
2 Chr. 12: 10	In stead **of which** king Re-ho-bo-am made shields of brass,
JER. 32: 37	Behold, I will gather them out of all countries, **whither** I have driven them in mine anger, and in my fury, and in great wrath;
36: 9	that ye may live many days in the land **where** ye *be* strangers.
JER. 32: 37	whither I have driven them **in mine anger, and** in my fury, and in great wrath;**

N.B. note how the underlined words separates words and phrases having the same meaning.

JER. 33: 5	whom I have slain **in mine anger and in my fury,**

N.B. note how the underlined verse separates words and phrases having the same meaning.

JER. 33: 10	which ye say *shall be* **desolate without man and without beast,**

N.B. see comment on last verse.

| JER. 33: 8 | whereby they have sinned, <u>and</u> whereby they have transgressed against me. |

N.B. note how the underlined word separates words and phrases having the same meaning.

| JER. 33: 8 | whereby they have sinned, |
| Isa. 38: 8 | by which degrees it was gone down. |

| JER. 33: 16 | and this *is the name* wherewith she shall be called, |
| Ezek. 40: 2 | by which *was* as the frame of a city on the south. |

JER. 34: 18	when they cut the calf in twain,
33: 24	The two families which the LORD hath chosen,
JER. 35: 14	notwithstanding I have spoken unto you,
: 17	Therefore thus saith the LORD God of hosts,

| JER. 36: 2 | Take thee a roll of a book, and write therein all the words that I have spoken unto thee against Israel, |
| : 28 | Take thee again another roll, and write in it all the former words that were in the first roll, |

| JER. 36: 14 | Take in thine hand the roll wherein thou hast read in the ears of the people, |
| Job 3: 3 | Let the day perish wherein I was born, and the night *in which* it was said, There is a man child conceived. |

| JER. 38: 4 | Therefore the princes said unto the king, We beseech thee, |
| 2 Kings 6: 2 | Let us go, we pray thee, unto Jordan, |

| JER. 38: 10 | Take from hence thirty men with thee, |
| Ezek. 8: 6 | the great abominations that the house of Israel committeth here, |

| JER. 38: 11 | and took thence old cast clouts <u>and</u> old rotten rags, |

N.B. note how the underlined word separates words and phrases having the same meaning.

| JER. 38: 20 | Obey, I beseech thee, the voice of the LORD, |
| 37: 20 | Therefore hear now, I pray thee, |

| JER. 39: 4 | by the gate betwixt the two walls: |
| 34: 18 | and passed between the parts thereof. |

| JER. 39: 7 | Moreover he put out Zed-e-ki-ah's eyes, |
| Ezek. 8: 6 | He said furthermore unto me, |

JER. 39: 9	Then Neb-u-zar-ad-an the captain of the guard carried away captive into Babylon the **remnant** of the people that remained in the city...with **the rest of the people** that remained.

JER. 40: 4	**whither** it seemeth good and convenient for thee to go, thither go.
35: 7	that ye may live many days in the land **where** ye *be* strangers.

JER. 40: 4	whither it seemeth good and convenient for thee to go, **thither** go.
41: 3	and the Chal-de-ans that were found **there,**

JER. 40: 5	So the captain of the guard gave him **victuals** and a reward,
Prov. 31: 14	she bringeth her **food** from afar.

JER. 40: 12	Even all the Jews returned out of all places **whither** they were driven,
35: 7	that ye might live in the land **where** ye *be* strangers.

JER. 40: 15	**wherefore** should he slay thee,
46: 15	**Why** are thy gallant *men* swept away?

JER. 41: 5	and from Samaria, *even* **fourscore** men,
Gen. 5: 28	And La-mech lived an hundred **eighty** and two years:

N.B. the underlined word is a numerical term meaning twenty. To find the value of the 'score' number multiply by twenty 4x20=80.

JER. 41: 9	Now the pit **wherein** Ish-ma-el had cast all the dead bodies of the men,
Isaiah 66: 4	and chose *that* **in which** I delighted not.

N.B. note the underlined word gives the meaning of the whole word.

| JER. 42: 2 | Let, **we beseech thee,** our supplication be accepted before thee, and **pray** for us unto the LORD thy God, *even* for all

this remnant; (for we are *but* a few of many, as thine eyes do behold...) |
|---|---|

JER. 42: 2	*even* for all this **remnant;** (for we are left *but* **a few of many,** as thine eyes do behold us:)

JER. 42: 3	That the LORD thy God may shew us the way **wherein** we may walk,
Isa. 66: 4	but they did evil before mine eyes, and chose *that* **in which** I delighted not.

JER. 42: 10	If ye will still **abide** in this land,
: 13	But if ye say, We will not **dwell** in this land,
: 15	and go to **sojourn** there;

| **JER. 42: 16** | and the famine, **whereof** ye were afraid, |
| 2 Chr. 12: 10 | Instead **of which** king Re-ho-bo-am made shields of brass, |

| **JER. 42: 18** | and ye shall be **an execration, and an astonishment and a curse, and a reproach;** |

N.B. note how the underlined word separates words and phrases having the same meaning.

| **JER. 42: 20** | For ye **dissembled** in your hearts, |
| Isaiah 57: 11 | that thou hast **lied**, and hast not remembered me, |

| **JER. 43: 5** | **whither** they had been driven, to dwell in the land of Judah: |
| 35: 7 | that ye may live many days in the land **where** ye *be* strangers. |

| **JER. 44: 2** | this day they *are* a desolation, and no man dwelleth **therein**, |
| 8: 16 | and all that is **in it**; the city, and those that dwell **therein**. |

N.B. reverse the two syllables of the bold word and the meaning is clear.

JER. 44: 4	**Howbeit** I sent unto you all my servants the prophets,
: 7	**Therefore** now saith the LORD, the God of hosts,
36: 25	**Nevertheless** El-na-than Del-ai-ah and Gem-a-ri-ah...
38: 13	**So** they drew up Jeremiah with cords,

| **JER. 44: 6** | Wherefore **my fury and mine anger** was poured forth, |
| : 8 | In that ye provoke me unto **wrath** with the works of your hands, |

| **JER. 44: 7** | **Wherefore** commit ye *this* great evil against your souls, |
| 46: 15 | **Why** are thy valiant *men* swept away? |

| **JER. 44: 25** | ye will **surely accomplish your vows, and surely perform your vows.** |

N.B. note how the underlined word separates words and phrases having the same meaning.

| **JER. 44: 28** | Yet a **small number** that escape the sword shall return out of the land of Egypt into the land of Judah, and all the **remnant** of Judah, |

| **JER. 45: 5** | but thy life will I give unto thee for a prey in all **whither** thou goest. |
| 42: 14 | but we will go into the land of Egypt, **where** we will see no |

war,

JER. 46: 8   I will destroy the city and the inhabitants **thereof.**
    30: 7   even the time of Jacob's trouble; but he shall be saved out **of it.**

JER. 46: 3   Order ye the **buckler and shield,** and draw near to battle.

N.B. note how the underlined word separates words and phrases having the same meaning.

JER. 46: 4   **furbish** spears, *and* put on the brigadines.
    51: 11   **Make bright** the arrows;

JER. 46: 4   furbish the spears, *and* put on the **brigandines.**
   1 Sam. 17: 5   and he *was* armed with a **coat of mail;**
JER. 46: 5   **Wherefore** have I seen them dismayed *and* turned away back?
    : 15   **Why** are thy valiant *men* swept away?

JER. 46: 19   for Noph shall be **waste and desolate without an inhabitant.**

N.B. note how the underlined word separates words and phrases having the same meaning.

JER. 46: 20   Egypt *is like* a very fair **heifer,**
   Isaiah 7: 21   *that* a man shall nourish **a young cow,**
    15: 5   his fugitives *shall flee* unto Zoar, **an heifer of three years old:**

JER. 46: 28   for I will make a full end of all the nations **whither** I have driven thee:
    42: 14   nor have hunger of bread; and **there** will we dwell:

JER. 47: 2   and all that is **therein;** the city, and them that dwell **therein:**
    49: 18   neither shall a son of mine dwell **in it.**

JER. 48: 1   Misgab is **confounded and dismayed.**

N.B. note how the underlined word separates words and phrases having the same meaning.

JER. 48: 8   the valley also shall **perish,** and the plain shall be **destroyed,**

JER. 48: 9   for the cities **thereof** shall be desolate, without any to dwell therein.

   Isaiah 44: 19   I have burned part **of it** in the fire;

JER. 48: 9   for the cities thereof shall be **desolate, without any to dwell**

N.B. note how the comma separates words and phrases having the same meaning.

| JER. 48: 11 | Moab hath been at ease from his youth, and he hath settled on his **lees,** |
| Psalm 75: 7 | and he poureth out of the same: but the **dregs** thereof, |

| JER. 48: 29 | We have heard the pride of Moab, (he is exceeding **proud)** his **loftiness, <u>and</u> arrogancy, <u>and</u> his pride, <u>and</u>** the **haughtiness** of his heart. |
| **JER. 48: 31** | **Therefore will I howl for Moab, <u>and</u> I will cry out for all Moab;** |

N.B. note how the underlined word separates words and phrases having the same meaning.

| JER. 49: 4 | **Wherefore** gloriest thou in the valley..? |
| : 1 | **why** *then* doth their king inherit God..? |

| JER. 49: 10 | But I have made Esau **bare,** I have **uncovered** his secret places, |

| JER. 49: 16 | I will bring thee down from **thence,** saith the LORD. |
| 50: 3 | For out of the north **there** cometh up a nation against her, |

| JER. 49: 18 | no man shall **abide** there, neither shall a son of mine **dwell** in it. |

| JER. 49: 24 | and fear hath seized on *her:* **anguish <u>and</u> sorrows** have her, as a woman in travail. |

| JER. 50: 9 | from **thence** she shall be taken: |
| : 3 | For out of the north **there** cometh up a nation against her, |

JER. 50: 23	How is the hammer of the whole earth **cut asunder** and
	broken!
51: 21	And with thee will I **break in pieces** the horse and his rider;

| JER. 50: 29 | **recompense** her according to her work; |
| Hosea 4: 9 | and **reward** them their doings. |

| JER. 50: 42 | They shall hold the bow and the lance: they *are* **cruel, <u>and</u> will not shew mercy:** |

N.B. note the underlined word that separates words and phrases having the same meaning.

| JER. 50: 23 | How is the hammer of the whole earth **cut asunder** and |

	broken!
51: 21	And with thee will I **break in pieces** the horse and his rider;

| **JER. 50: 39** | and the owls shall dwell **therein:** |
| 49: 18 | neither shall a son of mine dwell **in it.** |

| **JER. 50: 40** | As God overthrew Sodom and Gomorrah and the neighbour *cities* **thereof,** saith the LORD; |
| Isaiah 44: 19 | I have burned part **of it** in the fire; |

| **JER. 50: 42** | they *are* **cruel, and will not shew mercy:** |

N. B. note how the underlined word separates words and phrases having the same meaning.

| **JER. 51: 3** | and against *him that* that lifteth himself up in his **brigandine:** |
| 1 Sam. 17: 5 | and he *was* armed with **a coat of mail;** |

| **JER. 51: 6** | he will render unto her a **recompence.** |
| 40: 5 | So the captain of the guard gave him victuals and a **reward,** |

JER. 51: 30	The mighty men of Babylon have **forborn** to fight,
44: 18	But since we **left off** to burn incense to the queen of heaven,
Lam. 5: 14	The elders have **ceased** from the gate,

| **JER. 51: 31** | **One post** shall run to meet another, and **one messenger** to meet another, |

| **JER. 51: 32** | and the men of war are **affrighted.** |
| Ezek. 2: 6 | And thou, son of man, be not **afraid** of them, |

| **JER. 51: 42** | she is covered with the multitude of the waves **thereof.** |
| Ezek. 11: 7 | Your slain whom ye have laid in the midst **of it,** |

| **JER. 51: 43** | a land **wherein** no man dwelleth, |
| Isa. 66: 4 | but they did evil before mine eyes, and chose *that* **in which** I delighted not. |

| **JER. 51: 43** | a land wherein no man dwelleth, neither doth *any* son of man pass **thereby.** |
| 49: 17 | every one that goeth **by it** shall be astonished, |

| **JER. 51: 52** | **Wherefore,** behold, the days come, saith the LORD, |
| : 47 | **Therefore,** behold, the days come, |

| **JER. 51: 56** | for the LORD God of **recompences** shall surely requite. |
| Daniel 5: 17 | Let thy **gifts** be to thyself, and thy **rewards** to another; |

| **JER. 51: 56** | for the LORD God of recompenses shall surely **requite.** |
| Isaiah 59: 18 | According to *their* deeds, accordingly he will **repay,** |

JER. 52: 15	and the **residue** of the people that remained in the city,
42: 2	*even* for all this **remnant;**

JER. 52: 18	and all the vessels of brass **wherewith** they ministered,
Zech. 13: 6	*Those* **with which** I was wounded *in* the house of my friends.

JER. 52: 22	And a <u>chapiter</u> of brass *was* **upon it;**

N.B. The underlined letters spelt out will give the meaning of the whole word. This is confirmed by the bold word.

JER. 52: 25	and **three<u>score</u>** men of te people of the land,
Gen. 5: 15	And Ma-hal-a-leel lived **sixty** and five years,

N.B. The underlined word is a numerical term meaning twenty. To find the value of the whole word multiply 3x20=60.

LAMENTATIONS

LAM. 1: 3	Judah is gone into **captivity** because of affliction, and because of great **servitude:**

LAM. 1: 5	Her **adversaries** are the chief, her **enemies** prosper;

LAM. 1: 6	her princes are become like **harts** that find no pasture,
1 Kings 4: 23	beside **harts, and roebucks, and fallowdeer,**

LAM. 1: 7	Jerusalem remembered in the days **of her affliction <u>and</u> her miseries** all her pleasant things that she had in the days of old,

N.B. note how the underlined word separates words and phrases having the same meaning.

LAM. 1: 9	O LORD, behold my affliction: for the **enemy** hath magnified *himself.*
: 10	The **adversary** hath spread out his hand upon all her pleasant things:

LAM. 1: 11	All her people sigh, they seek **bread;** they have given their pleasant things for **meat** to relieve the soul:
Ezek. 48: 18	and the increase thereof shall be for **food** unto them that serve the city.

LAM. 1: 12	**which** is done unto me, **wherewith** the LORD hath afflicted *me* in the day of his fierce anger.
Zech. 13: 6	Then he shall answer, *Those* **with which** I was wounded *in* the house of my friends.

LAM. 2: 1	How hath the Lord covered the daughter of Zion with a cloud in his **anger,**
: 2	he hath thrown in his **wrath** the strong holds of the daughter of Judah;
: 4	he poured out his **fury** like fire.
LAM. 2: 2	he hath polluted the kingdom and the princes **thereof.**
Psalm 55: 10	Day and night they go about it upon the walls **thereof:** Mischief also and sorrow *are* in the midst **of it.**
LAM. 2: 5	and hath increased in the daughter of Judah **mourning and lamentation.**

N.B. note how the underlined word separates words and phrases having the same meaning.

LAM. 2: 7	The Lord hath cast off his altar, he hath **abhorred** his sanctuary,
Ezek. 16: 37	with all *them* that thou hast **hated;**
: 45	which **lothed** their husbands and their children:
LAM. 2: 14	Thy prophets have seen **vain and foolish** things for thee:

N.B. note how the underlined word separates words and phrases having the same meaning.

LAM. 2: 21	thou hast **slain** *them* in the day of thine anger: thou hast **killed,** *and* not pitied.
LAM. 3: 5	and **compassed** *me* with gall and travail.
: 7	He hath **hedged me about,**
: 9	He hath **inclosed** my ways with hewn stone,
LAM. 3: 21	This I **recalled to my mind,** therefore have I hope.
5: 1	**Remember,** O LORD, what is come upon us:
LAM. 3: 39	**Wherefore** doth a living man complain, a man for the punishment of his sins?
Jer. 49: 1	**why** *then* doth their king inherit Gad..?
LAM. 4: 10	The hands of the pitiful women have **sodden** their own
	children: they were their meat in the destruction of the daughter of my people.
2 Kings 6: 29	So we **boiled** my son, and did eat him:
LAM. 4: 10	they were their **meat** in the destruction of the daughters of my people.
Prov. 31: 14	she bringeth her **food** from afar.

<u>**LAM. 4: 11**</u>	The LORD hath accomplished his **fury**: he hath poured out his fierce **anger**.
<u>**LAM. 4: 13**</u>	For the **sins** of her prophets, *and* the **iniquities** of her priests,
<u>**LAM. 4: 14**</u> : 15	they have **polluted** themselves with blood, They cried unto them, Depart ye; *it is* **unclean**;
<u>**LAM. 4: 21**</u>	**Rejoice <u>and</u> be glad,** O daughter of Edom,

N.B. note how the underlined word separates words and phrases having the same meaning.

<u>**LAM. 5: 2**</u>	Our inheritance is turned to **strangers,** our houses to **aliens.**

EZEKIEL

<u>**EZEK. 1: 4**</u> 11: 7	and out of the midst **thereof** as the colour of amber, but I will bring you forth out of the midst **of it.**
<u>**EZEK. 1: 7**</u> 21: 15 Daniel 10: 6	and they sparkled like the colour of **burnished** brass. ah! *it is* **made bright,** *it is* wrapped up for the slaughter. and his arms and his feet like in colour to **polished** brass,
<u>**EZEK. 1: 12**</u> 3: 15	**whither** the spirit was to go, they went; and I sat **where** they sat,
<u>**EZEK. 1: 20**</u> : 3	they went, **thither** *was their* spirit to go; and the hand of the LORD was **there** upon him.
<u>**EZEK. 1: 22**</u>	And the likeness of the **firmament** upon the heads of the living creature *was* as the colour of the terrible crystal, stretched forth **over their heads above.**
Genesis 1: 8	And God called the firmament **Heaven.**
<u>**EZEK. 2: 9**</u> Jer. 49: 18	and, lo, a roll of a book *was* **therein;** neither shall a son of mine dwell **in it.**
<u>**EZEK. 2: 10**</u>	and *there was* written therein **lamentations, <u>and</u> mourning, <u>and</u> woe.**

N.B. note the underlined word that separates words and phrases having the same meaning.

<u>**EZEK. 3: 1**</u> 8: 6	**Moreover** he said unto me Son of man, He said **furthermore** unto me,
<u>**EZEK. 5: 2**</u>	and thou shalt take a third part, *and* **smite** about it with a

	knife:
Hab. 3: 14	Thou didst **strike** through with his staves like the head of his villages.

EZEK. 5: 3	Thou also take **thereof** of a few in number,
S.O.S. 3: 10	the bottom **thereof** *of* gold, the covering **of it** *of* purple,
Psalm 55: 10	Day and night they go about it upon the walls **thereof:** mischief also and sorrow *are* in the midst **of it.**

EZEK. 5: 11	**Wherefore,** *as* I live, saith the Lord GOD; Surely because thou hast defiled my sanctuary with all thy detestable things, and with all thine abominations, **therefore** will I diminish *thee;*

EZEK. 5: 14	**Moreover** I will make thee waste,
8: 6	He said **furthermore** unto me,

EZEK. 5: 15	So it shall be **a reproach and a taunt, an instruction and an astonishment** unto the nations that *are* round about thee, when I shall execute judgments in thee **in anger and in fury and in furious rebukes.**

N.B. note how the underlined words separate words and phrases having the same meaning.

EZEK. 6: 4	and your **images** shall be broken: and I will cast down your slain *men* before your **idols.**

EZEK. 7: 1	**Moreover** the word of the LORD came unto me, saying,
8: 6	He said **furthermore** unto me,

EZEK. 7: 3	and will **recompense** upon thee all thine abominations.
Isaiah 59: 18	According to their deeds, accordingly he will **repay,**

EZEK. 7: 8	Now will I shortly pour out my **fury** upon thee, and accomplish mine **anger** upon thee: and I will judge thee according to thy ways, and will recompense thee for all thine abominations.
: 12	for **wrath** *is* upon all the multitude thereof.

EZEK. 7: 12	for wrath *is* upon all the multitude **thereof.**
S.O.S. 3: 10	the covering **of it** *of* purple, the midst **thereof** being paved *with* love,

EZEK. 7: 18	They shall also **gird** *themselves* with sackcloth, and horror shall **cover them;**

EZEK. 7: 20	**but they made the images of their abominations _and_ of their detestable things** therein:

N.B. note how the underlined word separates words and phrases having the same meaning.

<u>EZEK. 7: 22</u>	and they shall **pollute** my secret *place:* for the robbers shall enter into it, and **defile** it.

<u>EZEK. 9: 5</u>	Go ye after him through the city, and **smite:**
: 6	**Slay** utterly old *and* young,

<u>EZEK. 10: 11</u>	but to the place **whither** the head looked they followed it;
11: 17	and assemble you out of the countries **where** ye have been scattered,

<u>EZEK. 10: 21</u>	Every one had four faces **apiece,**
4: 6	I have appointed thee **each** day for a year.

<u>EZEK. 11: 7</u>	but I will bring you forth out of the midst **of it.**
: 9	And I will bring you out of the midst **thereof,**

<u>EZEK. 12: 15</u>	when I shall **scatter** them among the nations, and **disperse** them in the countries.

<u>EZEK. 12: 16</u>	that they may declare all their abominations among the heathen **whither** they come;
11: 16	yet will I be to them as a little sanctuary in the countries **where** ye have been scattered,

<u>EZEK. 12: 17</u>	**Moreover** the word of the LORD came to me, saying,
8: 6	He said **furthermore** unto me,

<u>EZEK. 12: 19</u>	that her land may be desolate from all that is **therein,**
14: 23	and ye shall know that I have done without cause all that I have done **in it.**

N.B. reverse the syllables of the first bold word and the meaning is clear.

<u>EZEK. 13: 12</u>	Where *is* the daubing **wherewith** ye have daubed *it?*
Zech. 13: 6	*Those* **with which** I was wounded *in* the house of my friends.

<u>EZEK. 13: 14</u>	and ye shall be consumed in the midst **thereof:**
15: 4	the fire devoureth both the ends of it, and the midst **of it** is burned.

<u>EZEK. 13: 20</u>	**Wherefore** thus saith the Lord GOD;
: 23	**Therefore** ye shall see no more vanity,

<u>EZEK. 14: 13</u>	then will I stretch out mine hand upon it, **and will break the staff of the bread thereof, <u>and</u> will send famine upon it,**

N.B. note how the underlined word separates words and phrases having the same meaning.

<u>EZEK. 14: 15</u>	If I cause **noisome** beasts to pass through the land,
: 22	and ye shall be comforted concerning the **evil**...

<u>EZEK. 14: 22</u>	Yet, behold, **therein** shall be left a remnant that shall be brought forth,
: 23	I have not done without cause all that I have done **in it,**

<u>EZEK. 15: 3</u>	Shall wood be taken **thereof** to do any work?
14: 21	...and the pestilence, to cut off **from it** man and beast?

<u>EZEK. 15: 3</u>	or will *men* take a pin of it to hang any vessel **thereon?**
13: 9	And mine hand shall be **upon** the prophets that see vanity,

<u>EZEK. 15: 5</u>	Behold, when it was whole, it was **meet** for no work:
18: 18	and did *that* which is not **good** among his people,

<u>EZEK. 16: 3</u>	Thus saith the Lord GOD unto Jerusalem; **Thy birth and thy nativity** *is* of the land of Canaan;

<u>EZEK. 16: 7</u>	whereas thou *wast* **naked <u>and</u> bare.**

N.B. note how the underlined word separates words and phrases having the same meaning.

<u>EZEK. 16: 10</u>	I **clothed** thee also with broidered work, and shod thee with badgers' skin, and girded thee about with fine linen, and I **covered** thee with silk.

<u>EZEK. 16: 13</u>	and thy **raiment** *was of* fine linen,
: 16	And of thy **garments** thou didst take,

<u>EZEK. 16: 14</u>	And thy **renown** went forth among the heathen for thy beauty:
Zeph. 3: 19	and I will get them **praise <u>and</u> fame** in every land where they have been put to shame.

<u>EZEK. 16: 16</u>	and deckedst thy high places with **divers** colours,
17: 7	and **many** feathers:

<u>EZEK. 16: 20</u>	**Moreover** thou hast taken thy sons and daughters,
8: 6	He said **furthermore** unto me,

<u>EZEK. 16: 22</u>	when thou wast **naked <u>and</u> bare,**

N.B. note the underlined word how it separates words and phrases having the same meaning.

<u>**EZEK. 16: 24**</u>	*That* thou hast also built unto thee **an eminent place, and** **Hast made the an high place** in every street.
<u>**EZEK. 16: 25**</u> : 37	and hast made thy beauty to be **abhorred,** with all *them* that thou hast **hated;**
<u>**EZEK. 16: 28**</u> : 29	because thou wast **unsatiable;** and yet thou wast **not satisfied** herewith.
<u>**EZEK. 16: 29**</u> 1 Sam. 30: 23	and yet thou wast not satisfied **herewith.** Ye shall not do so, my brethren , **with that** which the LORD hath given us,
<u>**EZEK. 16: 35**</u> : 37 : 60	**Wherefore,** O harlot, hear the word of the LORD: Behold, **therefore** I will gather all thy lovers, **Nevertheless** I will remember my covenant with thee...
<u>**EZEK. 16: 49**</u>	neither did she strengthen the hand of the **poor <u>and</u> needy.**

N.B. note how the underlined word separateswords and phrases having the same
meaning.

<u>**EZEK. 17: 4**</u>	and carried it into **a land of traffick;** he set it in **a city of** **merchants.**
<u>**EZEK. 17: 6**</u> 15: 4	and the roots **thereof** were under him: the fire devoureth both the ends **of it,**
<u>**EZEK. 17: 11**</u> 23: 40	**Moreover** the word of the LORD came unto me, And **furthermore,** that ye have sent for men to come from far,
<u>**EZEK. 17: 14**</u> : 24	That the kingdom **might be base,** the LORD have **brought down** the high tree,
<u>**EZEK. 17: 19**</u> Isaiah 59: 18	even it will I **recompense** upon his own head. accordingly he will **repay,**
<u>**EZEK. 18: 5**</u>	But if a man be **just,** and do that which is **lawful <u>and</u> right,**

N.B. note how the underlined word separates words and phrases having the same
meaning.

<u>**EZEK. 18: 13**</u>	Hath **given forth upon usury, <u>and</u> hath taken increase:**

N.B. see comment on previous verse.

house of Israel: Is not my way equal? Are not your ways **unequal?**

N.B. note the underlined word and letters that they mean the same thing. The two underlined letters are called a prefix and are placed at the beginning of a word. It will be noticed that they mean the opposite of the word itself. Many more words can thus be made.

EZEK. 18: 31	Cast away from you all your trangressions, **whereby** ye have transgressed;
Zech. 13: 6	Then he shall answer, *Those* **with which** I was wounded *in* the house of my friends.
EZEK. 19: 2	she lay down among lions, she nourished her **whelps** among **young lions.**
EZEK. 19: 11	and her **stature** was exalted among the thick branches, and she in her **height** with the multitude of her branches.
EZEK. 19: 12	and the east wind **dried up** her fruit: her strong rods were broken and **withered;**
EZEK. 20: 9	But I **wrought** for my name's sake,
Eccl. 2: 11	Then I looked on all the works that my hands had **wrought,** and on the labour that I had **laboured** to do:
EZEK. 20: 10	**Wherefore** I caused them to go forth out of the land of Egypt,
: 17	**Nevertheless** mine eye spared them from destroying them,
: 18	**But** I said unto their children in the wilderness,
: 21	**Notwithstanding** the children rebelled against me:
: 27	**Therefore,** son of man, speak unto the house of Israel,
EZEK. 20: 17	**Nevertheless** mine high spared them from destroying them,
: 18	**But** I said unto their children in the wilderness,
: 21	**Notwithstanding** the chidren rebelled against me:
EZEK. 20: 23	that I would **scatter** them among the heathen, and **disperse** them through the countries;
EZEK. 20: 25	**Wherefore** I gave them also statutes *that were* not good,
: 27	**Therefore,** son of man, speak unto the house Israel,
EZEK. 20: 25	and judgments **whereby** they should not live;
40: 2	and set me upon a very high mountain, **by which** *was* as the frame of a city on the south.
EZEK. 20: 29	Then I said unto them, What *is* the high place **whereunto** ye go?
EZEK. 20: 29	And the name **thereof** is called Bamah unto this day.

15: 4	the fire devoureth both ends **of it,**
EZEK. 20: 31	For when ye offer your **gifts,** when ye make your sons…
: 40	and there will I require your **offerings,** and the firstfruits of of your **oblations,**
EZEK. 20: 34	and will gather you out of the countries **wherein** ye are scattered,
Isaiah 66: 4	but they did evil before mine eyes, and chose *that* **in which** I delighted not.
EZEK. 20: 36	**Like as** I pleaded with your fathers in the wilderness of the land of Egypt.
EZEK. 20: 44	not according to your **wicked** ways, nor according to your **corrupt** doings,
EZEK. 20: 45	**Moreover** the word of the LORD came unto me,
23: 40	And **furthermore,** that ye have sent for men to come from afar,
EZEK. 21: 10	It is **sharpened** to make a sore slaughter; it is **furbished** that it may glitter:
: 15	ah! *it is* **made bright,** *it is* wrapped up for the slaughter.
EZEK. 21: 12	**smite** therefore upon *thy* thigh.
Hab. 3: 14	Thou didst **strike** through…
EZEK. 21: 13	Because *it is* a trial, and what if *the sword* **contemn** even the rod?
23: 32	thou shalt be laughed to **scorn and** had in derision;
Isaiah 30: 12	Because ye **despise** this word,

N.B. note how the underlined word separates words and phrases having the same meaning.

EZEK. 21: 19	**both twain** shall come forth out of one land:
: 21	at the head of **two** ways,
EZEK. 22: 1	**Moreover** the word of the LORD came unto me,
8: 6	He said **furthermore** unto me,
EZEK. 22: 4	therefore have I made thee **a reproach** unto the heathen, and **a mocking** to all countries.
EZEK. 22: 9	in the midst of thee they commit **lewdness.**
: 15	and will consume thy **filthiness** out of thee.
EZEK. 22: 12	thou hast taken **usury and** increase, thou hast **greedily**

: 13	**gained** of thy neighbours by **extortion,** and hast forgotten me, therefore I have smitten mine hand at thy **dishonest gain** which thou hast made,
EZEK. 22: 21	and ye shall be melted in the midst **thereof.**
24: 11	Then set it empty upon the coals **thereof,** that the brass **of it** may be hot,
EZEK. 23: 11	she was more corrupt in her **inordinate love** than she,
: 12	She **doted upon** the Assyrians *her* neighbours,
EZEK. 23: 19	**wherein** she had played the harlot in the land of Egypt.
Isaiah 66: 4	and chose *that* **in which** I delighted not.
EZEK. 23: 20	For she doted upon their **paramours,**
: 9	Wherefore I have delivered her into the hand of her **lovers,**
EZEK. 23: 24	*which* shall set against thee **buckler and shield** and helmet round about:

N.B. note how the underlined word separates words and phrases having the same meaning.

EZEK. 23: 25	and thy **remnant** shall fall by the sword: they shall take thy sons and thy daughters; and thy **residue** shall be devoured by the fire.
EZEK. 23: 29	and shall leave thee **naked and bare:** and the nakedness of thy whoredoms shall be discovered, both **thy lewdness and thy whoredoms.**

N.B. note how the underlined words separate words and phrases having the same meanjng.

EZEK. 23: 32	Thou shalt drink of thy sister's cup deep and large: thou shalt be **laughed to scorn and had in derision;**
EZEK. 23: 36	The LORD said **moreover** unto me;
: 40	And **furthermore,** that ye have sent for men from far,
EZEK. 23: 38	**Moreover** this they have done unto me:
: 40	And **furthermore,** that ye have sent for men to come from far,
EZEK. 23: 41	And satest upon a stately bed, **whereupon** thou hast set mine incense and mine oil.
Lev. 11: 35	And every *thing* **whereupon** *any part* of their carcase falleth shall be unclean;
16: 9	And Aaron shall bring the goat **upon which** the LORD'S lot fell,

EZEK. 23: 44	so went they in unto A-ho-lah and unto A-hol-i-bah, the **lewd women.**
: 45	because they *are* **adulteresses,**

EZEK. 23: 47	And the company shall stone them with stones, and **dispatch them** with their swords; the shall **slay** their sons and their daughters,

N.B. note how the underlined word separates words and phrases having the same meaning.

EZEK. 23: 49	And they shall **recompense** your lewdness upon you,
Isaiah 59: 18	accordingly he will **repay,**

EZEK. 24: 4	Gather the pieces **thereof** into it,
: 5	and let them seethe the bones **of it** therein.

EZEK. 24: 5	*and* make it **boil** well, and let them **seethe** the bones of it therein.

EZEK. 24: 5	and let them seethe the bones of it **therein.**
: 11	and *that* the filthiness of it may be molten **in it,**

N.B. note also the syllables in the first reference which can be reversed and a further is clear.

EZEK. 24: 13	In thy **filthiness *is* lewdness:**

N.B. note how the underlined word separates words and phrases having the same meaning.

EZEK. 24: 13	In thy **filthiness** *is* **lewdness:**

EZEK. 24: 25	the joy of their glory, **the desire of their eyes, and that whereupon they set their minds,**

N.B. note how the underlined word separates words and phrases having the same meaning.

EZEK. 25: 5	and the Ammonites **a couchingplace** for flocks:
Zeph. 2: 15	**a place for beasts to lie down in!**

EZEK. 25: 12	Edom hath dealt against the house of Judah by **taking vengeance,** and hath greatly offended, and **revenged himself** upon them;

EZEK. 25: 14	and they shall do in Edom **according to mine anger and according to my fury;**

N.B. note how the underlined word separates words and phrases having the same meaning.

<u>**EZEK. 26: 2**</u>	I shall **be replenished,** *now* she is late waste:
23: 33	Thou shalt **be filled** with drunkenness and sorrow,
<u>**EZEK. 26: 8**</u>	and cast a mount against thee, and lift up the **buckler** against thee.
27: 10	they hanged the **shield** and helmet in thee,
<u>**EZEK. 26: 10**</u>	as men enter into a city **wherein** is made a breach.
Job 3: 3	Let the day perish **wherein** I was born, and the night *in which* it was said, There is a man child conceived.
Isaiah 66: 4	and chose *that* **in which** I delighted not.
<u>**EZEK. 26: 19**</u>	When I shall make thee a **desolate city,** like the cities that are **not inhabited:**
<u>**EZEK. 27: 9**</u>	The ancients of Ge-bal and the wise *men* **thereof** were in thee calkers:
24: 11	and *that* the scum **of it** may be consumed.
<u>**EZEK. 27: 9**</u>	all the ships of the sea with their mariners were in thee to **occupy their merchandise.**
30: 12	and **sell** the land into the hand of the wicked:
Jer. 32: 44	Men shall buy fields for money,
Gen. 34: 21	therefore let them dwell in the land, and **trade** therein;
<u>**EZEK. 27: 10**</u>	they set forth thy **comeliness.**
: 11	they have made thy **beauty** perfect.
<u>**EZEK. 27: 16**</u>	they **occupied** in thy fairs with emeralds,
: 12	they **traded** in thy fairs.
<u>**EZEK. 27: 27**</u>	and thy pilots, thy calkers, and the **occupiers** of thy merchandise,
: 15	The men of De-dan *were* thy **merchants;** many isles *were* the merchandise of thine hand:

N.B. note the words of the Lord Jesus in Luke 19: 13, 15

<u>**EZEK. 28: 11**</u>	**Moreover** the word of the LORD came unto me saying,
23: 40	And **furthermore,** that ye have sent for men from far,
<u>**EZEK. 28: 18**</u>	Thou hast defiled thy sanctuaries by the multitude of thine iniquities, by the iniquity of thy **traffick;**
Genesis 46: 34	That ye shall say, Thy servants' **trade** hath been about cattle

314

From our youth until now,

EZEK. 28: 26   And they shall dwell safely **therein,** and build houses,
2 Kings 2: 21   And he went forth unto the spring of the waters, and cast the
the salt **in there,**

EZEK. 29: 2   Son of man, set thy face against **pharaoh king of Egypt,**

N.B. note that the second and third bold words give the meaning of the first bold
word.

EZEK. 29: 9   And the land of Egypt shall be **desolate <u>and</u> waste;**

N.B. note how the underlined word separates words and phrases having the same
meaning.

EZEK. 29: 12   and **I will scatter the Egyptians among the nations, <u>and</u>
will disperse them through the countries.**

N.B. note how the underlined word separates words and phrases havingthe same
meaning.

EZEK. 30: 12   and I will make the land waste, and all that is **therein,**
    : 6   from the tower of Sy-e-ne shall they fall **in it** by the sword,

EZEK. 30: 13   Thus saith the Lord GOD; I will also destroy the **idols,** and I
will cause *their* **images** to cease out of Noph;

EZEK. 30: 16   and No shall be rent **asunder,** and Noph *shall have* distresses
daily.
   22: 10   they humbled her that was set **apart** for pollution.

EZEK. 30: 23   And I **will scatter the Egyptians among the nations, <u>and</u>
will disperse them through the countries.**

N.B. note how the underlined word separates words and phrases having the same
meaning.

EZEK. 31: 3   Behold, Assyrian was a cedar in Lebanon with fair **branches,**
and with a shadowing shroud, and of an high stature; and his
top was among the thick **boughs.**

    : 6   All the fowls of heaven made their nests in his **boughs,** and
under his **branches** did all the beasts of the field bring forth
their young,

EZEK. 31: 14   to the **nether** parts of the earth,
   40: 19   from the forefront of the **lower** gate...

EZEK. 31: 15   and I **restrained** the floods thereof, and the great waters were stayed:

| EZEK. 31: 15 | and I restrained the floods **thereof,** |
| 24: 11 | *that* the scum **of it** may be consumed. |

| EZEK. 31: 16 | and all the trees of Eden, the **choice and best** of Lebanon, |

N.B. note how the underlined word separates words and phrases having the same meaning.

| EZEK. 32: 1 | After these things, and the establishment **thereof,** |
| 28: 15 | and carried all the feeble **of them** upon asses. |

| EZEK. 32: 6 | I will also water with thy blood the land **wherein** thou swimmest, |
| Isaiah 66: 4 | and chose *that* **in which** I delighted not. |

| EZEK. 32: 12 | and all the multitude **thereof** shall be destroyed. |
| 24: 11 | *that* the scum **of it** may be consumed. |

| EZEK. 32: 15 | When I shall make the land of Egypt **desolate,** and the country shall be **destitute** of that whereof it was full, |

| EZEK. 32: 15 | and the country shall be destitute of that **whereof** it was full, |
| 2 Kings 23: 27 | And the LORD said, I will remove Judah out of my sight, as I removed Israel, and will cast off this city Jerusalem **which** I have chosen, and the house **of which** I said, My name shall be there. |

| EZEK. 32: 15 | when I shall smite all them that dwell **therein,** |
| 30: 6 | from the tower of Syene shall they fall **in it** by the sword, |

N.B. Reverse the two syllables of the first bold word and the meaning is clear.

| EZEK. 32: 16 | This the lamentation **wherewith** they shall lament her: |
| Zech. 13: 6 | Then he shall answer, *Those* **with which** I was wounded *in* the house of my friends. |

| EZEK. 32: 18 | unto the **nether** parts of the earth, with them that **go down** into the pit. |
| 40: 19 | Then he measured the breadth from the forefront of the **lower** gate... |

EZEK. 33: 6	**But** if the watchman see the sword come,
: 9	**Nevertheless,** if thou warn the wicked of his way to turn from it;
: 10	**Therefore,** O thou son of man, speak unto the house of Israel;

| EZEK. 33: 18 | When the righteous turneth from his righteousness, and |

316

	committeth iniquity, he shall even die **thereby.**
39: 15	then shall he set up a sign **by it,**

EZEK. 33: 22   **afore** he that was escaped came;
: 31   and they sit **before** thee *as* my people,

EZEK. 34: 4   **The diseased** have ye not strengthened, neither have ye healed **that which was sick,**

EZEK. 34: 8   *As* I live saith the Lord GOD, surely **because my flock became a prey, and my flock became meat to every beast of the field,** because *there was* no shepherd,

N.B.   note how the underlined word separates words and phrases having the same meaning.

EZEK. 35: 1   **Moreover** the word of the LORD came unto me,
8: 6   He said **furthermore** unto me,

EZEK. 35: 4   I will lay thy cities **waste,** and thou shalt be **desolate,**

EZEK. 35: 6   and blood shall pursue thee: **sith** thou hast not hated blood, even blood shall pursue thee.
Daniel 12: 1   such as never was **since** there was a nation *even* to that same time:

EZEK. 35: 10   **Because** thou hast said, These two nations and these two countries shall be mine, and we will possess it; **whereas** the LORD was there:

EZEK. 35: 10   Because thou hast said, **These two nations and these two countries** shall be mine,

N.B.   note how the underlined word separates words and phrases having the same meaning.

EZEK. 36: 20   And when they entered unto the heathen, **whither** they went,
34: 12   and will deliver them out of all places **where** they have been scattered in the cloudy and dark day.

EZEK. 36: 31   Then shall ye remember **your own evil ways, and** your **doings that** *were* **not good,**

N.B.   note how the underlined word separates words and phrases having the same meaning.

EZEK. 37: 20   And the sticks **whereon** thou writest shall be in thine hand before their eyes.
Psalm 119: 49   Remember the word unto thy servant, **upon which** thou hast

caused me to hope.

EZEK. 37: 21	Behold, I will take children of Israel from among the heathen, **whither** they be gone,
34: 12	and will deliver them out of all places **where** they have been scattered in the cloudy and dark day.

EZEK. 37: 23	**wherein** they have sinned,
Isaiah 66: 4	and chose *that* **in which** I delighted not.

EZEK. 37: 25	wherein your fathers have dwelt; and they shall dwell **therein,**
24: 11	and *that* the filthiness of it may be molten **in it.**

EZEK. 37: 26	**Moreover** I will make a covenant of peace with them;
8: 6	He said **furthermore** unto me,

EZEK. 38: 4	*even* a great company *with* **bucklers and shields,**

N.B. note how the underlined word separates words and phrases having the same meaning..

EZEK. 38: 9	Thou shalt **ascend** and come like a storm,
: 11	I will **go up** to the land of unwalled villages;

EZEK. 38: 13	with all the young lions **thereof,**
39: 24	and hid my face **from them.**

EZEK. 39: 8	This *is* the day **whereof** I have spoken.
2 Kings 23: 27	and the house **of which** I said,

EZEK. 39: 9	and shall set on fire and burn the weapons, both the **shields and bucklers,**

EZEK. 39: 26	and all their trespasses **whereby** they have trespassed against me,
40: 2	**by which** *was* as the frame of a city on the south.

EZEK. 40: 1	in the selfsame day the hand of the LORD was upon me, and brought me **thither.**
Hosea 7: 9	gray hairs are **here** and there upon him,

EZEK. 40: 5	so he measured the **breadth** of the building,
: 6	*which was* one reed, **broad;**

EZEK. 40: 6	and went up the stairs **thereof,**
43: 20	and put *it* on the four horns **of it,**

EZEK. 40: 14	He made also posts of **threescore** cubits,
Lev. 27: 7	And if *it be* from **sixty** years and above;

N.B. The word 'score' is a mathematical term meaning twenty. To find the value of the 'score' number multiply the number by twenty, 3x20=60

<u>EZEK. 40: 33</u>	and *there were* windows **therein** and in the arches thereof round about:
: 29	and *there were* windows **in it** and in the arches thereof round about:

<u>EZEK. 40: 39</u>	and two tables on that side, to slay **thereon** the burnt offering and the sin offering and the trespass offering.

N.B. Reverse the two syllables and the meaning is clear.

<u>EZEK. 40: 41</u>	by the side of the gate; eight tables, **whereupon** they slew *their sacrifices.*
2 Kings 18: 21	*even* upon Egypt **on which** if a man lean it will go into his hand,

<u>EZEK. 40: 42</u>	whereupon also they laid the instruments **wherewith** they
	slew the burnt offering and the sacrifice.
Zech. 13: 6	*Those* **with which** I was wounded *in* the house of my friends

<u>EZEK. 40: 49</u>	and *he brought me* by the steps **whereby** they went up to it:
: 2	**by which** *was* as the frame of a city on the south.

<u>EZEK. 41: 2</u>	and he measured the length **thereof,** forty cubits:
43: 20	and put *it* on the four horns **of it,**

<u>EZEK. 41: 9</u>	The thickness of the wall, which *was* for the side chamber
	without,
40: 5	And behold a wall on the **outside** of the house round about,

<u>EZEK. 41: 9</u>	and *that* which *was* left *was* the place of the side chambers that *were* **within.**
1 Kings 6: 15	*and* he covered *them* on the **inside** with wood,

<u>EZEK. 41: 10</u>	And between the chambers *was* the **wideness** of twenty cubits round about the house on every side.
: 11	and the **breadth** of the place that *was* five cubits round about.
<u>EZEK. 42: 6</u>	therefore *the building* was **straitened** more than the lowest
	and the middlemost from the ground.
41: 26	And *there were* **narrow** windows and palm trees on the one side and on the other side,

<u>EZEK. 42: 6</u>	therefore *the building* was straitened more than the lowest and the **middlemost** from the ground.

EZEK. 42: 14	When the priests enter **therein,** then shall they not go out of the holy *place* into the utter court, but **there** they shall their garments wherein they minister;

N.B. reverse the syllables in the first bold word and the meaning is clear.

EZEK. 42: 14	but there they shall lay their garments **wherein** they minister;
Isaiah 66: 4	and chose *that* **in which** I delighted not.
	was troubled,
Zech. 13: 6	Then he shall answer, *Those* **with which** I was wounded *in* the house of my friends.

DANIEL 2: 5	if ye will not make known unto me the dream, with the interpretation **thereof,**
: 7	and we will shew the interpretation **of it.**

DANIEL 2: 9	for ye have prepared **lying <u>and</u> corrupt** words to speak before me,

DANIEL 2: 12	For this cause the king was **angry <u>and</u> very furious,**

N.B. note how the underlined word separates words and phrases having the same meaning.

DANIEL 2: 34	which **smote** the image upon his feet *that were* of iron and clay,
2 Chron.13: 20	and the LORD **struck** him and he died.

DANIEL 2: 38	And **where**soever the children of men dwell,

DANIEL 2: 41	And **where<u>as</u>** thou sawest the feet and toes, part of potters' clay, and part of iron, the kingdom shall be divided; but there shall be in it of the strength of the iron, **for<u>a</u>smuch** as thou sawest the iron mixed with miry clay.

N.B. note how the underlined words separate words and phrases having the same meaning.

DANIEL 2: 43	And whereas thou sawest iron **mixed** with miry clay, they shall **mingle** themselves with the seed of men:

DANIEL 2: 45	**For<u>a</u>smuch <u>as</u>** thou sawest that the stone was cut out of the mountain without hands,

DANIEL 2: 47	The king answered unto Daniel, **Of a truth** *it is,* that your God *is* a God of Gods,
3: 24	They answered and said unto the king, **True,** O king.
Micah 3: 8	But **truly** I am full of power by the spirit of the LORD,

DANIEL 2: 46	and commanded that they should offer an **oblation** and sweet odours unto him.
Ezek. 48: 8	shall be the **offering** which ye shall offer

DANIEL 3: 1	Neb-u-chad-nez-zar the king made an image of gold, whose height *was* **threescore** cubits,
Lev. 27: 7	And if *it be* from **sixty** years old and above;

N.B. The underlined word is a numerical term meaning twenty. To find the value of the whole number multiply, 3x20=60.

DANIEL 3: 13	Then Neb-u-chad-nez-zar in *his* **rage <u>and</u> fury** commanded to bring Sha-drach, Me-shach, and A-bed-ne-go.

N.B. note how the underlined word separates words and phrases having the same meaning.

DANIEL 3: 19	and the form of his **visage** was changed against Sha-drach, Me-shach, and A-bed-ne-go.
2: 46	Then the king N=u-chad-nez-zar fell upon his **face,**

DANIEL 3: 19	that they should heat the furnace one seven times more than it was **wont** to be heated.
Jer. 13: 23	*then* may ye also do good, that are **accustomed** to do evil.

DANIEL 3: 24	Then Neb-u-chad-nez-zar the king was **astonied,**
8: 27	and I was **astonished** at the vision,

DANIEL 3: 29	Therefore I make a decree, That every people, nation, and language, which speak any thing **amiss against** the God of Sha-drach, Me-shach, and A-bed-ne-go, shall be cut in pieces, and their houses made a dunghill,

DANIEL 4: 2	I thought it good to shew the signs and wonders that the high God hath **wrought** toward me.
Hosea 2: 5	she that conceived them hath **done** shamefully:

DANIEL 4: 12	The leaves **thereof** *were* fair, and the fruit thereof much,
2: 7	Let the king tell his servants the dream, and we wil shew the interpretation **of it.**

DANIEL 4: 12	and the fowls of the heaven dwelt in the boughs **thereof,** and all flesh was fed of it.
Hosea 10: 5	for the glory **thereof,** because it is departed **from it.**

DANIEL 4: 12	and the fowls of the heaven dwelt in the **boughs** thereof,
: 14	Hew down the tree, and cut off his **branches,**

DANIEL 4: 15	**Nevertheless** leave the stump of his roots in the earth,
: 8	**But** at the last Daniel came in before me,

DANIEL 4: 18   for<u>as</u>much **as** all the wise *men* of my kingdom are not able to make known unto me the interpretation:

N.B. note how the underlined word gives the meaning of the whole word.

DANIEL 4: 27   **Wherefore,** O king, let my counsel be acceptable unto thee,

: 6   **Therefore** made I a decree to bring in all the wise *men* of Babylon before me,

DANIEL 4: 37   Now I Neb-u-chad-nez-zar **praise <u>and</u> extol <u>and</u> honour** the king of heaven,

N.B. note how the underlined words separate words and phrases having the same meaning.

DANIEL 5: 2   that the king, and his princes, his wives, and his **concubines,** might drink therein.
Hosea 2: 5   for she said, I will go after my **lovers,**

DANIEL 5: 2   that the king, and his concubines, might drink **therein.**
: 3   and the king, and his princes, his wives, and his concubines, drank **in them.**

DANIEL 5: 6   Then the king's **countenance** was changed,
2: 46   Then the king Neb-u-chad-nez-zar fell upon his **face,**

DANIEL 5: 7   Whosoever shall read this writing, and shew the **interpretation thereof,** shall be clothed with scarlet,
2: 7   Let the king tell his servants the dream, and we will shew the **interpretation of it.**

DANIEL 5: 31   And Da-ri-us Median took the kingdom, being about **three score** and two years old.
Leviticus 27: 7   And if *it be* from **sixty** years old above;

N.B. The underlined word is a mathematical term meaning twenty. To find the value of the underlined word multiply the number by three, 3x20=60.

DANIEL 6: 3   Then this Daniel was **preferred above** the presidents and princes,
3: 30   Then the king **promoted** Sha-drach, Me-shach, and A-bed-ne-go, in the province of Babylon.

DANIEL 6: 4   forasmuch as he was faithful, neither was there any **error <u>or</u> fault** found in him.

N.B. note how the underlined word separates words and phrases having the same meaning.

DANIEL 6: 10	and prayed, and gave thanks **before** his God as he did **aforetime.**
DANIEL 6: 15	That no **decree** <u>**nor**</u> **decree** which the king establisheth
	may be changed.

N.B. note how the underlined word separates words and phrases having the same meaning.

| **DANIEL 7: 4** | I beheld till the wings **thereof** were plucked, |
| : 5 | and *it had* three ribs in the mouth **of it** between the teeth of it, |

| **DANIEL 7: 28** | **Hitherto** *is* the end of the matter. |
| 4: 24 | **This** *is* the interpretation, O king, |

| **DANIEL 7: 28** | As for me Daniel, my **cogitations,** much troubled me, |
| 2: 30 | and that thou mightest know the **thoughts** of thy heart. |

| **DANIEL 8: 23** | a king of fierce **countenance,** and understanding dark sentences shall stand up. |
| : 17 | I was afraid, and fell upon my **face:** |

| **DANIEL 8: 26** | **wherefore** shut thou up the vision; for it *shall be* for many days. |
| 9: 4 | **Therefore** hath the LORD watched upon the evil, |

| **DANIEL 9: 7** | through all the countries **whither** thou hast driven them, |
| 8: 17 | So he came near **where** I stood: |

| **DANIEL 9: 15** | and hast gotten thee renown, as at this day; **we have sinned, we have done wickedly.** |

N.B. note how the comma separates words and phrases having the same meaning.

| **DANIEL 9: 16** | O Lord, according to all thy righteousness, **I beseech thee,** |
| Jonah 4: 2 | And he prayed unto the LORD, and said, **I pray thee,** |

| **DANIEL 9: 26** | And after **threescore** and two weeks shall Messiah be cut off, |
| Leviticus 27: 7 | And if *it be* from **sixty** years old and above; |

N.B. The underlined word is a numerical term meaning twenty. To find the value of the 'score' number multiply 3x20=60.

| **DANIEL 9: 26** | and the end **thereof** *shall be* with a flood, |
| 7: 6 | which had on the back **of it** four wings of a fowl; |

| **DANIEL 9: 27** | and in the midst of the week he shall the sacrifice and **oblation** to cease, |
| Zeph. 3: 10 | *even* the daughter of my dispersed, shall bring mine **offering.** |

DANIEL 10: 20	Then said he, Knowest thou **wherefore** I come unto thee?
2: 15	**Why** *is* the decree *so* hasty from the king?

DANIEL 11: 11	And the king of the south shall be **moved with choler,**
9: 16	I beseech thee, let thine **anger <u>and</u> thy fury** be turned away
	from thy city Jerusalem,

N.B. note how the underlined word separates words and phrases having the same meaning.

DANIEL 11: 22	and shall be broken; yea, also the prince of the **covenant.**
: 23	And after the **league** *made* with him he shall work deceitfully:
: 6	for the king's daughter of the south shall come to the king of the king to make an **agreement:**

DANIEL 11: 34	Now when they shall fall, they shall be **holpen** with a little help:
2 Chron. 28: 21	and gave *it* unto the king of Assyria: but he **helped** them not.

DANIEL 11: 36	and **he shall exalt himself, <u>and</u> magnify himself above every god,**

N.B. note how the underlined word separates words and phrases having the same meaning.

HOSEA

HOSEA 1: 10	Yet the number of the children of Israel shall be as the sand of sea, which cannot be **measured <u>nor</u> numbered;**

N.B. note how the underlined word separates words and phrases having the same meaning.

HOSEA 2: 2	let therefore put away her **whoredoms** out of her sight, and her **adulteries** from between her breasts,
: 10	and now will I discover her **lewdness** in the sight of her lovers, and the **wickedness** of Samaria:

HOSEA 2: 5	For she said, I will go after my lovers, that give *me* my **bread** and my water,
Ezekiel 48: 11	and the increase thereof shall be for **food,**

HOSEA 2: 9	and take away my corn in the time **thereof,**
Daniel 7: 5	and *it had* three ribs between the teeth **of it:**

HOSEA 2: 10	And now I will discover her **lewdness** in the sightof her lovers,
: 2	let her therefore put away her **whoredoms** out of her sight,

And her **adulteries** from between her breasts;

HOSEA 2: 12	And I will destroy her vines and her fig trees, **whereof** she said,
2 Chron. 33: 7	And he set a carved image, **which** he had made in the house of God, **of which** God had said to David and to Solomon his son...
HOSEA 2: 13	And I will visit upon her the days of Ba-a-lim, **wherein** she burned incense to them,
Isaiah 66: 4	but they did evil before mine eyes, and cose that **in which** I delighted not.
HOSEA 2: 15	And I will give her her vineyards from **thence,** and the valley of A-chor for a door of hope: and she shall sing **there,**
HOSEA 2: 19	I will betroth thee unto me in **righteousness,**
Isaiah 57: 2	they shall rest in their beds, *each one* walking in his **uprightness.**
HOSEA 2: 19	and in **lovingkindness and mercies.**

N.B. note how the underlined word separates words and phrases having the same meaning.

HOSEA 3: 4	and without a sacrifice, and without an **image,** and without an ephod, and *without* **teraphim:**
8: 4	of their silver and their gold have they made them **idols,**
HOSEA 4: 3	and every one that dwelleth **therein** shall languish,
Amos 5: 20	even very dark, and no brightness **in it?**
HOSEA 4: 9	and I will punish them for their ways, and **reward** them their doings.
Isaiah 59: 18	Accordingly to *their* deeds, accordingly he will **repay,**
HOSEA 4: 12	My people ask counsel at their **stocks,**
: 17	E-phra-im *is* joined to **idols:**
HOSEA 4: 13	under oaks and poplars and elms, because the shadow **thereof** *is* good:
Ezekiel 48: 8	and the sanctuary shall be in the midst **of it.**
HOSEA 5: 4	for the spirit of whoredoms *is* **in the midst of** them,
: 9	**among** the tribes of Israel have I made known that which shall surely be.
HOSEA 5: 8	Blow ye the **cornet** in Gib-e-ah, *and* the **trumpet** in Ra-mah:

N.B. The cornet is a smaller version of the trumpet.

HOSEA 6: 8	for they commit **lewdness.**
7: 1	and the **wickedness** of Samaria:

2: 2	let her therefore put away here **whoredoms** out of her sight, and her **adulteries** from between her breasts;
HOSEA 7: 2	now their own doings have **beset them about;**
Psalm 22: 16	the assembly of the wicked have **inclosed me:**
HOSEA 7: 13	yet **they have spoken** lies against me.
13: 1	When E-phra-im **spake** ttrmbling,
HOSEA 8: 8	now shall they be among the Gentiles as a vessel **wherein** *is* no pleasure.
Isaiah 66: 4	and chose *that* **in which** I delighted not.
HOSEA 8: 9	For they are gone up to Assyria, a wild ass **alone by himself:**

N.B. note the underlined words mean the same thing.

HOSEA 9: 7	The days of visitation are come, the days of **recompence** are come;
: 1	thou hast loved a **reward** upon every cornfloor.
HOSEA 10: 11	And E-phra-im *is as* an **heifer** *that is* taught,
Isaiah 11: 7	And the **cow** and the bear shall feed;
15: 5	an heifer of **three years old:**
HOSEA 11: 9	for I *am* God, and not man; the Holy One **in the midst of thee:**
8: 8	now shall they be **among** the Gentiles as a vessel wherein *is* no pleasure.
HOSEA 11: 12	E-phra-im **compasseth me about** with lies,
Psalm 22: 16	the assembly of the wicked have **inclosed me:**
HOSEA 12: 2	according to his doings will he **recompense** him.
Isaiah 59: 18	accordingly he will **repay,**
HOSEA 13: 8	and will **rend** the caul of their heart, and there will devour them like a lion: the wild beast shall **tear** them.
HOSEA 13: 11	I gave thee a king in mine **anger,** and took him away in my **wrath.**
HOSEA 13: 14	**I will ransom them** from the power of the grave; **I will redeem them** from death:
HOSEA 14: 7	the scent **thereof** *shall be* as the wine of Lebanon.
Joel 1: 3	Tell ye your children **of it,**
HOSEA 14: 9	and the just shall walk **in them:** but the transgressors shall fall therein.

HOSEA 14: 9   but the transgressors shall fall **therein.**

N.B. reverse the two syllables of the bold word and the meaning is clear.

JOEL

JOEL 1: 7   the branches **thereof** are made white.
  3: 1   Tell ye your children **of it,**

JOEL 1: 12   The vine is **dried up,** and the fig tree languisheth; the pomegranate tree, the palm tree also, and the apple tree also, *even* all the trees of the field, are **withered;**

JOEL 1: 16   Is not meat cut off before our eyes, *yea,* **joy and gladness** from the house of our God?

N.B. note how the underlined word separates words and phrases having the same meaning.

JOEL 1: 17   The seed is rotten under their clods, the **garners** are laid desolate, the **barns** are broken down,

JOEL 2: 10   The earth shall **quake** before them; the heavens shall **tremble:**

JOEL 2: 16   **Gather** the people, sanctify the congregation, **assemble** the elders,

JOEL 2: 17   **wherefore** should they say among the people, Where *is* their God?
Jonah 1: 10   **Why** hast thou done this?

JOEL 2: 19   and ye shall be satisfied **therewith:**
Deut. 16: 3   Thou shalt eat no leavened bread **with it;** seven days shalt thou eat unleavened bread **therewith,**

JOEL 2: 20   and his hinder part toward the utmost sea, and **his stink shall come up, and his ill savour shall come up,**

N.B. note how the underlined word separates words and phrases having the same meaning.

JOEL 3: 4   will ye render me a **recompence?** and if ye **recompense** me,
Hosea 9: 1   thou hast loved a **reward** upon every cornfloor.
JOEL 3: 4   and if ye **recompense** me,
Hosea 4: 9   and **reward** them their doings.

N. B. note the underlined letters form different words. The first word is a noun and the second word is a verb. The modern word, compensation originates from the second word.

JOEL 3: 4   and if ye recompense me, **swiftly _and_ speedily...**

N.B. note how the underlined word separates words and phrases having the same meaning.

JOEL 3: 5   Can a bird fall in a **snare** upon the earth, where no **gin** _is_ for him?

JOEL 3: 7   Behold, I will raise them out of the place **whither** ye have sold them,

Amos 3: 5   Can a bird fall in a snare upon the earth, **where** no gin _is_ for him?

JOEL 3: 11   **thither** cause thy mighty ones to come down, O LORD.

: 17   and **there** shall no strangers pass through her any more.

AMOS

AMOS 1: 3   I will not turn away _the punishment_ **thereof;**

Joel 1: 3   Tell ye your children **of it,**

AMOS 1: 11   and **his anger did tear perpetually, _and_ he kept his wrath for ever:**

N.B. note how the underlined word separates words and phrases having the same meaning.

AMOS 3: 15   And I will **smite** the winter house with the summer house;

Hab. 3: 14   Thou didst **strike** through with his staves the head of his villages:

AMOS 4: 1   Hear this word, ye **kine** of Ba-shan,

N.B. The word 'kine' refers to the female of a herd of cattle. Cattle is the collective name for a herd of both male and female animals.

AMOS 4: 7   one piece was rained upon, and the piece **where**upon it ranied not withered.

Psalm 119: 49   Remember the word unto thy servant, **upon which** thou hast caused me to hope.

AMOS 4: 9   I have **smitten** you with blasting and mildew:

2 Chron. 13: 20   and the LORD **struck** him, and he died.

AMOS 4: 13   For, lo, he that **formeth** the mountains, and **created** the wind,

AMOS 5: 7   and leave off **righteousness** in the earth,

Isaiah 57: 2   _each one_ walking in his **uprightness.**

AMOS 5: 10   They **hate** them that rebuketh in the gate, and they **abhor** him that speaketh uprightly.

AMOS 5: 11   **Forasmuch therefore as** your treading *is* upon the poor,

N.B. Each of the three bold words are called synonyms, words having the same meaning.

AMOS 5: 21   I **hate,** I **despise** your feast days,

AMOS 5: 24   and **righteousness** as a mighty stream.
Isaiah 57: 2   *each one* walking *in* his **uprightness.**

AMOS 6: 2   and from **thence** go ye down to Ha-math the great:
  : 9   if **there** remain ten men in one house,

AMOS 6: 8   therefore will I deliver up the city with all that is **therein.**
  5: 20   even very dark, and no brightness **in it?**

N.B. The bold word in the reference if the two syllables are reversed the meaning is clear.

AMOS 6: 13   Ye which rejoice in a thing of **nought,**
  3: 5   shall *one* take up a snarefrom the earth, and have taken **nothing** at all?

AMOS 7: 9   And the high places of Isaac shall be **desolate,** and the sanctuaries of Israel shall be **laid waste;**

AMOS 7: 12   then I said, O Lord GOD, forgive, **I beseech thee:**
Jonah 4: 2   and said, **I pray thee,** O LORD,

AMOS 8: 10   And I will turn your feasts into **mourning,** and all your songs into **lamentation;**

AMOS 8: 10   and I will make it as the mourning of an only *son* and the end **thereof** as a bitter day.
Hab. 2: 19   and *there is* n o breath at all in the midst **of it.**

AMOS 9: 1   I saw the Lord standing upon the altar: and he said, **Smite** the lintel of the door,
Hab. 3: 14   Thou didst **strike** through with his staves the head of his villages;

AMOS 9: 1   Smite the **lintel** of the door,
Exodus 12: 7   and strike *it* on the two side posts and on the **upper door post** of the houses,

AMOS 9: 2   Though they dig into hell, **thence** shall mine hand take them;

329

| 7: 12 | and **there** eat bread, and prophesy there. |

OBADIAH

| **OBAD. 4** | and though thou set thy nest among the stars, **thence** will I bring thee down, saith the LORD. |

OBAD. 12	neither shouldest thou have spoken proudly in the day of **distress.**
13	yea, thou shouldest not have looked on their **affliction** in the
14	day of their **calamity,**

JONAH

| **JONAH 1: 3** | so he paid the fare **thereof,** and went down into it |
| Hab. 2: 19 | and *there is* no breath at all in the midst **of it.** |

| **JONAH 1: 4** | But the LORD sent out **a great wind** into the sea, and there was **a mighty tempest** in the sea, |
| Nahum 1: 3 | the LORD *hath* his way in the whirlwind and in the **storm,** |

| **JONAH 2: 3** | and the **floods** compassed me about, |
| : 5 | The **waters** compassed me about, |

| **JONAH 2: 5** | The waters **compassed** me about, *even* to the soul: the depths **closed me round about,** the weeds were **wrapped about my head.** |
| Psalm 22: 16 | the assembly of the wicked have **inclosed me:** |

| **JONAH 4: 3** | Therefore now, O LORD, take, **I beseech thee,** my life from me, |

JONAH 4: 2	And he prayed unto the LORD, and said, **I pray thee,** O
LORD,	
: 3	Therefore now, O LORD, **I beseech thee,** my life from me;

| **JONAH 4: 11** | And should I not spare Nin-e-veh, that great city, **wherein** are more than sixscore thousand persons that cannot discern between their right hand and there left hand; |
| Isaiah 66: 4 | and chose *that* **in which** I delighted not. |

| **JONAH 4: 11** | wherein are more than **sixscore** thousand persons... |
| Leviticus 27: 7 | And if *it be* from **sixty** years old and above; |

N.B. The underlined word is a mathematical term meaning twenty. To find the value of the 'score' number multiply 6x20=120

MICAH

MICAH 1: 2   hearken, O earth, and all that **therein** is:

N.B. reverse the syllables of the bold word and the meaning is clear.

MICAH 1: 6   and I will pour down the stones **thereof** into the valley,
Hab. 2: 19   and *there is* no breath at all in the midst **of it.**

MICAH 1: 8   Therefore I will **wail <u>and</u> howl,** I will go **stripped <u>and</u> naked:**

N.B. note how the underlined word separates words and phrases having the same
        meaning.

MICAH 2: 12   **I will surely assemble, O Jacob, all of thee; I will surely
                 gather the remnant of Israel;**

N.B. note how the semi-colon separates words and phrases having the same
        meaning.

MICAH 3: 8   and of judgment, and of might, **to declare unto Jacob
                 his transgression, <u>and</u> to Israel his sin.**

N.B. note how the underlined word separates words and phrases having the same
        meaning.

MICAH 4: 7   and the LORD shall reign over them in mount Zion from
                 henceforth, even for ever.
Jerem. 3: 4   Wilt thou not **from this time** cry unto me, My father, thou *art*
                 the guide of my youth?

MICAH 5: 1   they shall **smite** the judge of Israel with a rod upon the cheek.
Hab. 3: 14   Thou didst **strike** through with his staves the head of his
                 villages:

MICAH 6: 3   O my people, what have I done unto thee? and **wherein** have I
                 wearied thee?
   2: 4   **how** hath he removed *it* from me!

MICAH 6: 6   **Wherewith** shall I come before the LORD,
Exod. 10: 26   and we know not **with what** we must serve the LORD,

MICAH 6: 10   and the **scant** measure *that is* abominable?
   : 11   Shall I count *them* pure with the **wicked** balances, and with the
                 bag of **deceitful** weights?

MICAH 6: 12   For the rich man **thereof** are full of violence,
Hab. 2: 19   nd *there is* no breath at all in the midst **of it.**

| MICAH 7: 13 | the land shall be desolate because of them that dwell **therein,** |
| Amos 5: 20 | even very dark, and no brightness **in it?** |

NAHUM

| NAHUM 1: 2 | God *is* jealous, and the LORD **revengeth;** and *is* furious; |
| | the LORD **will take vengeance** on his adversaries, |

| NAHUM 1: 13 | and will burst thy bonds **in sunder.** |
| Zech. 12: 12 | every family **apart;** |

NAHUM 2: 1	keep the **munition,** watch the way,
3: 12	All thy **strong holds** *shall be like* fig trees with the firstripe
	figs:

| NAHUM 2: 10 | She is **empty, and void, and waste:** |

N.B. note how the underlined words separate words and phrases having the same
meaning.

| NAHUM 3: 3 | and *there is* a **multitude** of slain, and a **great number** of |
| | carcases; |

| NAHUM 3: 7 | **Whence** shall I seek comforters for thee? |
| Zech. 1: 5 | Your fathers, **where** *are* they? |

| NAHUM 3: 19 | all that hear the **bruit** of thee shall clap thy hands over thee: |
| 2 Kings 19: 7 | he shall hear a **rumour,** and shall return to his own land; |

HABAKKUK

| HAB. 1: 3 | and there are *that* raise up **strife and contention.** |

N.B. note how the underlined word separates words and phrases having the same
meaning.

| HAB. 1: 7 | They *are* **terrible and dreadful:** |

N.B. see comment on previous verse.

| HAB. 1: 10 | And they shall **scoff** at the kings, and the princes shall be a |
| | **scorn** unto them: they shall **deride** every strong hold; |

| HAB. 1: 13 | **wherefore** lookest thou upon them that deal treacherously...? |
| Micah 4: 9 | Now **why** dost thou cry out aloud? |

| HAB. 1: 15 | They take up all of them with the **angle,** they catch them in |
| | their **net,** and gather them in their **drag:** |

HAB. 2: 3	though it **tarry, wait** for it:
HAB. 2: 7	and thou shalt be for **booties** unto them?
: 17	and the **spoil** of beasts,
HAB. 2: 8	and of all that dwell **therein.**
Amos 5: 20	even very dark, and no brightness **in it?**

N.B. reverse the two syllables in the first bold word and the meaning is clear.

HAB. 2: 18	What profiteth the graven image that the maker **thereof** hath graven it;
: 19	and *there is* no breath at all in the midst **of it.**
HAB. 3: 1	A prayer of Habakkuk the prophet upon **Shg-i-o-noth.**
: 19	To the chief singer on my **stringed instruments,**
HAB. 3: 6	and drove **asunder** the nations;
Zech. 12: 12	And the land shall mourn, every family **apart;**

ZEPHANIAH

ZEPH. 1: 8	and all such as are clothed with strange **apparel.**
Amos 2: 8	And they lay *themselves* down upon **clothes** laid to pledge...
Jer. 10: 9	blue and purple *is* their **clothing:**
ZEPH. 2: 8	and the revilings of the children of Ammon, **whereby** they have reproached my people,
Ezek. 40: 2	**by which** *was* as the frame of a city on the south.
ZEPH. 2: 13	and will make Nin-e-veh **a desolation, _and_ dry like a wilderness.**
ZEPH. 2: 14	both the cormorant shall lodge in the **upper lintels** of it;
Exodus 12: 7	and strike *it* on the two side posts and on the **upper door post** of the houses,
ZEPH. 3: 5	The just LORD *is* in the midst **thereof:**
: 18	*to whom* the reproach **of it** *was* a burden.
ZEPH. 3: 11	**wherein** thou hast transgressed against me:
Isaiah 66: 4	and chose *that* **in which** I delighted not.
ZEPH. 3: 19	and I will save her that **halteth,**
2 Sam. 19: 26	because thy servant *is* **lame.**

HAGGAI

HAGGAI 1: 4	*Is it* time for you, O ye, to dwell in your **cieled** houses,
1 Kings 7: 3	And *it was* **covered** with cedar above upon the beams,

333

HAGGAI 2: 2	and to **the residue of the people;**
1: 14	and the spirit of all **the remnant of the people;**
HAGGAI 2: 17	I **smote** you with blasting and with mildew and with hail...
2 Chron. 13: 20	and the LORD **struck** him, and he died.

ZECHARIAH

ZECH. 1: 12	against which thou hast indignation these **threescore** and ten years?
Genesis 5: 27	And all the days of Methuselah were nine hundred **sixty** and nine years:

N.B. The underlined word is a numerical term meaning twenty. To find the value of the 'score' number multiply 3x20=60.

ZECH. 1: 21	but these are **come to fray** them,
Ezek. 34: 28	and none shall **make *them* afraid.**
ZECH. 2: 2	Then said I, **Whither** goest thou?
1: 5	Your fathers, **where** *are* they?
ZECH. 3: 3	Now Joshua was clothed with filthy **garments,** and stood before the angel.
: 4	and I will clothe thee with a change of **raiment.**
ZECH. 3: 9	behold, I will engrave the graving **thereof,**
4: 2	with a bowl upon the top **of it,**
ZECH. 4: 2	and his seven lamps **thereon,**
Haggai 1: 9	I did blow **upon it.**
ZECH. 4: 8	**Moreover** the word of the LORD came unto me,
Ezek. 23: 40	And **furthermore,** that ye sent for two men to come from far,
ZECH. 4: 10	and shall see the **plummet** in the hand of Ze-rub-ba-bel *with* those seven;
2: 1	and behold a man with a **measuring line** in his hand.
ZECH. 5: 10	Then said I to the angel that talked with me, **Whither** do these bear the ephah?
1: 5	Your fathers, **where** *are* they?
ZECH. 6: 3	and in the fourth chariot **grisled <u>and</u> bay.**
Gen. 30: 32	and the **speckled <u>and</u> spotted** among the goats:
ZECH. 6: 6	The black horses which *are* **therein** go forth into the north country;

N.B. reverse the syllables and the meaning is clear.

ZECH. 6: 7	and he said, **Get you hence,** walk to and fro through the earth.
Ezek. 3: 22	Arise, **go forth** into the plain,

ZECH. 8: 19	and the fast of the tenth, shall be to the house of Judah **joy** **and** gladness,

N.B. note the underlined word how it separates words and phrases having the same meaning.

ZECH. 9: 4	and he will **smite** her power in the sea;
Hab. 3: 14	Thou didst **strike** through with his staves the head of his villages:

ZECH. 9: 11	by the blood of the covenant I have sent forth thy prisoners out of the pit **wherein** *is* no water.

ZECH. 10: 11	and shall **smite** the waves in the sea,
Hab. 3: 14	Thou didst **strike** through with his staves the head of his villages:

ZECH. 11: 4	Thus saith the LORD my God: Feed the flock of the **slaughter;**
: 5	Whose possessors **slay** them,

ZECH. 11: 8	and my soul **lothed** them, and their soul also **abhorred** me.

ZECH. 11: 10	And I took my staff, *even* Beauty, and **cut it asunder,**
12: 3	all that burden themselves with it shall be **cut in pieces,**

ZECH. 14: 12	And this shall be the plague **wherewith** the LORD will smite all the people that have fought against Jerusalem;
13: 14	*Those* **with which** I was wounded *in* the house of my friends.

MALACHI

MAL. 1: 2	Yet ye say, **Wherein** hast thou loved us?
Hag. 2: 3	and **how** do ye see it now?

MAL. 1: 4	**Whereas** Edom saith, We are impoverished,

N.B. note how the underlined word gives the meaning of the whole word.

MAL. 1: 4	Whereas Edom saith, We are **impoverished,**
Ezek. 22: 29	and have vexed the **poor and needy,**
32: 15	When I shall make the land of Egypt **destitute,**

N.B. note how the underlined word separates words and phrases having the same

meaning.

MAL. 1: 9	And now, I **pray** you, **beseech**, God he will be gracious unto us:

N.B. Of the two bold words either one or the other can be omitted without changing the meaning of the phrase. Therefore both words have been kept for emphasis.

MAL. 1: 10	neither do ye kindle *fire* on mine altar for **nought.**
Hag. 2: 3	*is it* not in your eyes in comparison of it **nothing?**

MAL. 1: 12	and the fruit **thereof,**
Hag. 2: 3	*is it* not in your eyes in comparison **of it** as nothing?

MAL. 2: 5	and I gave them to him *for* the **wherewith** he feared me,
Zech. 13: 6	Then he shall answer, *Those* **with which** I was wounded *in* the house of my friends.

MAL. 2: 6	he walked with me in peace and **equity.**
3: 3	that they may offer unto the LORD an offering in **righteousness.**

MAL. 2: 9	Therefore have I also made you **contemptible and base.**

N.B. note how the underlined word separates words and phrases having the same meaning.

MAL. 2: 13	and with crying out, **insomuch that** he regardeth not the offering any more,

N.B. note how the two underlined words separate words and phrases having the same meaning.

MAL. 2: 14	Yet ye say, **Wherefore?** Because the LORD hath been witness between thee and the wife of thy youth,
: 10	**why** do we deal treacherously every man against his brother,

MAL. 2: 15	And **wherefore** one? That he might seek a godly seed. **Therefore** take heed to your spirit,

MAL. 2: 17	Yet ye say, **Wherein** have we wearied *him?*
Zech. 1: 12	**how** long wilt thou not have mercy on Jerusalem and the cities of Judah...?

MAL. 3: 3	And he shall sit *as* **a refiner and purifier of silver:**

N.B. note how the underlined word separates words and phrases having the same meaning.

<u>**MAL. 3: 4**</u>	Then shall the offering of Judah and Jerusalem be pleasant unto the LORD, **as in the days of old, <u>and</u> as in former years.**

N.B. see comment on previous verse.

<u>**MAL. 3: 10**</u>	that there may be meat in my house, and prove me now **here**with, saith the LORD of hosts,

<u>**MAL. 4: 6**</u>	lest I come and **smite** the earth with a curse.
Hab. 3: 14	Thou didst **strike** through with his staves the head of his villages:

MATTHEW

<u>**MATT. 1: 18**</u>	When as his mother Mary was **espoused** to Joseph,
Deut. 20: 7	And what man *is there* that hath **betrothed** a wife,

N.B. remove the first and last letters in the first reference and the word 'spouse' is shown which applies to either sex in marriage today.

<u>**MATT. 1: 19**</u>	and not willing to make her a publick example, was minded to put her away **privily.**
Luke 10: 23	And he turned him unto *his* disciples, and said **privately,**
John 11: 28	and called Mary her sister **secretly,**

<u>**MATT. 2: 8**</u>	And he sent them to Bethlehem, and said, Go and search **diligently** for the young child;
Phil. 2: 28	I sent him therefore the **more carefully,**

<u>**MATT. 2: 16**</u>	when he saw that he was mocked by the wise men, was exceeding **wroth,**
Daniel 2: 12	For this cause the king **was angry <u>and</u> very furious,**

N.B. note how the underlined word separates words and phrases having the same meaning.

<u>**MATT. 2: 16**</u>	and **slew** all the children that were in Bethlehem,
16: 21	and be **killed,** and be raised again the third day.

<u>**MATT. 2: 16**</u>	and in all the coasts **thereof,**
7: 27	and great was the fall **of it.**

<u>**MATT. 2: 22**</u>	But when he heard that Ar-che-la-us did reign in Judaea in the room of his father Herod, he was afraid to go thither: **notwithstanding,**
<u>**MATT. 2: 22**</u>	he was afraid to go **thither:**
: 1	**there** came wise men from the east to Jerusalem.

<u>**MATT. 3: 4**</u>	And the same John had his **raiment** of camel's hair,

7: 15	which come to you in sheep's **clothing,**
9: 16	No man putteth a piece of new unto an old **garment,**
MATT. 3: 4	And the same John had his raiment of camel's hair, and a **leathern girdle** about his loins;
Mark 1: 6	And John was clothed with camel's hair, and with a **girdle of a skin** about his loins,
MATT. 3: 8	Bring forth therefore fruits **meet** for repentance:
Luke 3: 8	Bring forth therefore fruits **worthy** of repentance,
MATT. 3: 10	therefore every tree which bringeth not forth good is **hewn down,** and cast into the fire.
21: 8	others **cut down** branches from the trees,
MATT. 3: 12	and he will throughly purge his floor, and gather his wheat into the **garner;**
13: 30	and bind them in bundles to burn them: but gather the wheat into my **barn.**
MATT. 3: 15	And Jesus answering said unto him, **Suffer** *it to be so* now:
5 : 8	**let** him have *thy* cloke also.
MATT. 4: 2	And when he had fasted forty days and forty nights, he was afterward **an hungred.**
Mark 11: 12	And on the morrow, when they were come from Bethany, he **was hungry:**
MATT. 4: 8	Again, the devil taketh him up into an **exceeding** high mountain,
10: 30	But the **very** hairs of your head are all numbered.
MATT. 4: 10	Then saith Jesus unto him, Get thee **hence,** Satan: for it is written;
5: 31	It hath been said, Whosoever shall put **away** his wife,
Zephan.1: 4	and I will cut off the remnant of Ba-al **from this place,**
MATT. 4: 20	And they **straightway** left their *their nets,* and followed him.
: 22	And they **immediately** left the ship and their father,
MATT. 4: 23	And Jesus went about all Galilee, teaching in their synagogues, and **preaching the gospel** of the kingdom,
Acts 8: 4	Therefore they were scattered abroad went every where **preaching the word.**
: 25	And they, and when they had testified and **preached the word of the Lord,** returned to Jrusalem, and **preached the gospel** in many villages of the Samaritans.
10: 36	The **word** which *God* sent unto the children of Israel, preaching peace by **Jesus Christ:**
13: 5	And when they were at Salamis, they **preached the word of**

	God in the synagogues of the Jews:
John 1: 1	In the beginning was **the Word,** and the Word was with God, and **the Word** was God.
Heb.4: 2	For unto us was the **gospel preached,** as well unto them: but the **word preached** did not profit them,
Rev. 19: 13	And he *was* clothed with a vesture dipped in blood: and his name is called **The Word of God.**

<u>MATT. 4: 24</u>	and they brought unto him all sick people that were taken with **divers** diseases and torments,
: 23	and healing **all manner of** disease among the people.

<u>MATT. 5: 13</u>	Ye are the salt of the earth: but if the salt hath lost his **savour,**
16: 28	There be some standing here, which shall not **taste** of death,

<u>MATT. 5: 13</u>	Ye are the salt of the earth: but if the salt hath lost his savour, **wherewith** shall it be salted?
7: 4	Or **how** wilt thou say to thy brother,

<u>MATT. 5: 18</u>	For **verily** I say unto you,
3: 11	I **indeed** baptize you with water unto repentance:
26: 73	**Surely** thou art *one* of them;
Mark 14: 38	the spirit **truly** *is* ready, but the flesh *is* weak.
Luke 9: 27	But I tell you **of a truth,**
23: 47	**Certainly** this was a righteous man.

<u>MATT. 5: 21</u>	Ye have heard that it was said by them of old time, Thou shalt **not kill;** and whosoever shall kill shall be in danger of the judgment:
19: 18	Jesus said, Thou shalt do **no murder,** Thou shalt not commit adultery,

<u>MATT. 5: 23</u>	and there rememberest that thy brother hath **ought** against thee;
Mark 9: 22	but if thou canst do **any thing,** have compassion on us,

<u>MATT. 5: 26</u>	Thou shalt by no means come out **thence,** till thou hast paid the uttermost farthing.
Mark 6: 10	there abide till ye depart **from that place.**

<u>MATT. 5: 26</u>	till thou hast paid the **uttermost** farthing.
Luke 12: 59	till thou hast paid the **very last** mite.

<u>MATT. 5: 33</u>	Again, ye have heard that it hath been said by them of old time, **Thou shalt not forswear thyself,** but shalt perform unto the Lord thine oaths:
Deut. 23: 23	**That which hath gone out of thy lips thou shalt perform;**

<u>MATT. 5: 37</u>	But let your **communication be,** Yea, yea; Nay, nay:
Acts 20: 7	and continued his **speech** until midnight.

MATT. 5: 39	but whosover shall **smite** thee on thy right cheek,
Mark 14: 65	and the servants did **strike** him with the palms of their hands.
MATT. 5: 41	And whosoever shall compel thee to go a mile, go with him **twain.**
4: 18	And Jesus, walking by the seaof Galilee, saw **two** brethren,
MATT. 6: 1	Take heed that ye do not your **alms** before men,
5: 16	that they may see your **good works,**
MATT. 6: 2	**Verily,** I say unto you, They have their reward.
9: 37	The harvest **truly** *is* plenteous, but the labourers *are* few;
MATT. 6: 16	**Moreover** when ye fast,
2 Cor. 2: 12	**Furthermore,** when I came to Tro-as to *preach* Christ's gospel,
MATT. 6: 25	Therefore I say unto you, **Take no thought** for your life, what ye shall eat, or what ye shall drink;
1 Sam. 9: 20	**set not thy mind on them;**
MATT. 6: 25	Is not the life more than meat, and the body than **raiment?**
7: 15	Beware of false prophets, which cometo you in sheep's **clothing,**
MATT. 6: 27	Which of you by taking thought can add one cubit unto his **stature?**
Rom. 8:39	Nor **height,** nor depth,
MATT. 6: 29	That even Solomon in all his glory was not **arrayed** like one of these.
11: 8	But what went ye out for to see? A man **clothed** in soft raiment?
MATT. 6: 30	**Wherefore,** if God so clothe the grass of the field,
: 31	**Therefore** take no thought,
MATT. 6: 31	What shall we eat? or, **Wherewith**al shall we be clothed?
5: 13	but if the salt have lost his savour, **wherewith** shall it be salted?
12: 29	Or **how** can one enter into a strong man's house...?
7: 2	and **with what** measure ye mete,
MATT. 6: 34	Sufficient unto the day the evil **thereof.**
7: 27	and it fell: and great was the fall **of it.**
MATT. 7: 13	Enter ye in at the **strait gate:**
: 14	and **narrow** *is* the way,
MATT. 7: 13	for **wide** *is* the gate, and **broad** *is* the way, that leadeth to

destruction,

MATT. 7: 13	and many **there** be which go in **there**at:
MATT. 7: 20	**Wherefore** by their fruits ye shall know them.
: 24	**Therefore** whosoever heareth these sayings of mine,
MATT. 7: 25	And the rain **descended,** and the winds blew, and beat upon that house; and it **fell** not:
MATT. 8: 5	there came unto him a centurion, **beseeching** him,
Mark 11: 25	And when ye stand **praying,**
MATT. 8: 10	**Verily** I say unto you,
3: 11	I **indeed** baptize you with water unto repentance:
9: 37	The harvest **truly** *is* plenteous,
Luke 9: 27	But I tell you **of a truth,**
MATT. 8: 14	he saw his **wife's mother** laid, and sick of a fever.
10: 35	and the daughter in law against her **mother in law.**
MATT. 8: 16	When the **even** was come,
14: 15	And when it was **evening,**
MATT. 8: 21	Lord, **suffer me** first to go and bury my father.
: 22	Follow me; and **let** the dead bury their dead.
1 Cor. 16: 7	but I trust to tarry a while with you, if the Lord **permit.**
MATT. 8: 24	And, behold, there arose **a great tempest** in the sea,
Mark 4: 37	And there arose **a great storm** of wind,
MATT. 8: 24	insomuch **that** the ship was covered with waves:
: 28	exceeding fierce, **so that** no man might pass by that way.
Mark 4: 37	and the waves beat into the ship, **so that** it was now full.
MATT. 8: 28	there met him two possessed with devils, coming out of the tombs, **exceeding** fierce,
10: 30	But the **very** hairs of your head are all numbered.
MATT. 8: 29	art thou come **hither** to torment us before the time?
12: 41	and, behold, a greater than Jonas *is* **here.**
MATT. 9: 4	And Jesus knowing their thoughts said, **Wherefore think ye** evil in your hearts?
Mark 2: 8	**Why reason ye** these things in your hearts?
MATT. 9: 6	But that ye may know that the Son of man hath **power** on earth to forgive sins,
Luke 4: 36	What a word *is* this! for with **power and authority** he commandeth the unclean spirits, and they come out.

N.R. note how the underlined word separates words and phrases having the same meaning.

<u>MATT. 9: 9</u>	And as Jesus passed by **thence,**
8: 30	And **there** was a good way off from them and herd of many swine feeding.
<u>MATT. 9: 14</u>	Why do we and the Pharisees fast **oft,** but thy disciples fast not?
Luke 5: 33	Why do the disciples of John fast **often...?**
<u>MATT. 9: 26</u>	And the fame **hereof** went abroad into all that land.
13: 22	and the care **of this** world,
21: 34	that they may receive the fruits **of it.**
<u>MATT. 9: 35</u>	teaching in their synagogues, and preaching **the gospel** of the kingdom,
Luke 5: 1	as the people pressed upon him to hear **the word of God,**
1 Peter 1: 25	And this **the word** which by **the gospel** is preached unto you.
John 1: 1	In the beginning was **the Word,**
Rev. 1: 2	Who bare record of **the word of God,** and the testimony of **Jesus Christ,**
<u>MATT. 9: 37</u>	The harvest truly *is* **plenteous,**
Luke 10: 2	The harvest truly *is* **great,**
<u>MATT. 9: 30</u>	and Jesus **straitly charged** them, saying
10: 5	These twelve Jesus sent forth, and **commanded** them,
<u>MATT. 10: 10</u>	Nor **scrip** for your journey,
1 Sam. 17: 40	and put them in **a shepherd's bag** which he had, even in **a scrip;**
<u>MATT. 10: 11</u>	and there **abide** till ye go from thence.
Luke 10: 7	And in the same house **remain,**
Hosea 13: 13	for he should not **stay** in *the place of* the breaking forth of children.
<u>MATT. 10: 11</u>	And into whatsoever city or town ye shall enter, enquire who in it is worthy; and **there** abide till ye go from **thence.**
Mark 6: 10	In what place soever ye enter into an house, there abide till ye depart **from that place.**
<u>MATT. 10: 11</u>	and there abide till ye **go from** thence.
Mark 6: 10	there abide till ye **depart from** that place.
<u>MATT. 10: 15</u>	**Verily,** I say unto you,
9: 37	The harvest **truly** *is* plenteous,
<u>MATT. 10: 16</u>	Behold, I send you forth as sheep **in the midst of** wolves:
Luke 10: 3	behold, I send you forth as lambs **among** wolves.

<u>**MATT. 10: 26**</u>	for there is nothing **covered,** that shall not be revealed; and **hid,**
<u>**MATT. 10: 26**</u>	that shall not be **revealed;** and hid, that shall not be **known.**
<u>**MATT. 10: 35**</u>	For I am come to set a man **at variance against** his father,
Luke 12: 53	The father shall be **divided against** the son,
<u>**MATT. 11: 1**</u>	he departed **thence** to teach and to preach in their cities.
Mark 6: 10	there abide till ye depart **from that place.**
<u>**MATT. 11: 5**</u>	the dead are raised up, and the poor have **the gospel** preached to them.
John 1: 1	In the beginning was **the Word,**
Luke 8: 21	My mother and my brethren are these which hear **the word of God,** anddo it.
Acts 8: 25	And they, when they had testified and preached **the word of the Lord,** returned to Jerusalem, and preached **the gospel** in many of the villages of the Samaritans.
<u>**MATT. 11: 8**</u>	A man clothed in soft **raiment?** behold, they that wear soft *clothing* are in king's houses.
<u>**MATT. 11: 11**</u>	**notwithstanding** he that is least in the kingdom of heaven is greater than he.
: 16	**But** whereunto shall I liken this generation?
<u>**MATT. 11: 16**</u>	But **whereunto** shall I liken this generation?
Luke 13: 18	Then said said he, **Unto what** is the kingdom of God like? and **whereunto** shall I resemble it?
<u>**MATT. 11: 16**</u>	But whereunto shall I **liken** this generation?
Luke 13: 18	and whereunto shall I **resemble** it?
<u>**MATT. 11: 20**</u>	Then began he to upbraid the cities **wherein** most of his mighty works were done,
Luke 13: 14	There are six days **in which** men ought to work:
<u>**MATT. 11: 25**</u>	because thou hast hid these things from the **wise <u>and</u> prudent,**

N.B. note how the underlined word separates words and phrases having the same meaning.

<u>**MATT. 12: 5**</u>	how that on the sabbath days the priests in the temple profane the sabbath, and are **blameless?**
: 7	ye would not have condemned the **guiltless.**
27: 54	I am **innocent** of the bloodof this just person:

MATT. 12: 12	**Wherefore** it is lawful to do well on the sabbath days.
Mark 2: 28	**Therefore** the Son of man is Lord also of the sabbath.
MATT. 12: 22	and he healed him, insomuch **that** the blind and dumb both spake and saw.
8: 28	**so that** no man might pass by that way.
MATT. 12: 36	they shall give account **thereof** in the day of judgment.
21: 34	that they might receive the fruits **of it.**
MATT. 12: 44	I will return into my house from **whence** I came out;
13: 5	**where** they had not much earth:
MATT. 12: 46	While he yet **talked** to the people,
13: 3	And he **spake** many things unto them in parables,
MATT. 12: 46	While he yet talked with the people, behold *his* mother and his brethren stood **without,** desiring to speak with him,
MATT. 12: 46	and his brethren stood **without,** desiring to speak with him,
23: 25	for ye make clean the **outside** of the cup and the platter,
MATT. 13: 4	and the **fowls** came and devoured them up:
: 32	so that the **birds** of the air come and lodge in the branches thereof.
MATT. 13: 4	so that the birds of the air come and lodge in the branches **thereof.**
John 7: 7	The world cannot hate you; but it hateth me, because I testify **of it,** that the works **thereof** are evil.
MATT. 13: 5	and **forthwith** they sprung up, because they had no deepness of earth:
: 20	and **anon** with joy receiveth it;
Mark 4: 5	and it **immediately** it sprang up,
Luke 8: 6	and **as soon as** it was sprung up,
MATT. 13: 5	Some fell upon stony places, where they had **not much earth:** and forthwith they sprung up, because they had **no deepness of earth:**
Mark 4: 5	because it had **no depth of earth:**
MATT. 13: 17	For **verily** I say unto you,
: 32	Which **indeed** is the least of all seeds:
17: 11	Elias **truly** shall first come,
MATT. 13: 27	from **whence** hath it tares?
Luke 8: 25	And he said unto them, **Where** is your faith?
MATT. 13: 32	so that the birds of the air come and lodge in the branches

thereof.

John 7: 7	but me it hateth, because I testify **of it,** that the works **thereof** are evil.
MATT. 13: 35	I will **utter** things which have been kept secret from the foundation of the world.
: 13	Therefore **speak** I to them in parables:
MATT. 13: 49	the angels shall come forth, and **sever** the wicked from among the just.
25: 32	and he shall **separate** them one from another,
Luke 12: 13	Master, speak to my brother, that he **divide** the inheritance with me.
MATT. 13: 53	And it came to pass, *that* when Jesus had finished these parables, he departed **thence.**
Mark 6: 10	there abide till ye depart **from that place.**
MATT. 13: 54	he taught them in their synagogue, insomuch **that** they were astonished,
: 32	and cometh a tree, **so that** the birds of the air come and lodge in the branches thereof.
MATT. 13: 57	A prophet is not without honour, **save** in his own country,
Mark 6: 4	A prophet is not without honour, **but** in his own country,
Matt. 12: 29	**except** he first bind the strong man?
MATT. 14: 9	**nevertheless** for the oath's sake, and them which sat with him at meat,
: 6	**But** when Herod's birthday was kept,
MATT. 14: 11	and given to the **damsel:** and she brought *it* to her mother.
1: 23	Behold, a **virgin** shall be with child,
9: 24	Give place: for the **maid** is not dead, but sleepeth.
MATT. 14: 13	When Jesus **heard** *of it,* he departed thence by ship into a desert place apart: and when the people **heard** *thereof,*
MATT. 14: 15	send the multitude away, that they may go into the villages, and buy themselves **victuals.**
1 Tim. 6: 8	And having **food** and raiment let us be therewith content.
MATT. 14: 22	And **straightway** Jesus constrained his disciples to get into a ship,
: 31	And **immediately** Jesus stretched forth *his* hand,
MATT. 14: 22	And straightway Jesus **constrained** his disciples to get into a ship,

Acts 26: 11	and **compelled** *them* to blaspheme;
2 Kings 5: 23	And he **urged** him, and bound two talents of silver in two bags,
MATT. 14: 24	But the ship was now in the **midst** of the sea,
25: 6	And at **mid**night there was a cry made,
Acts 26: 13	At **mid**day, O king, I saw in the way a light from heaven,
Exodus 28: 38	And the **middle** bar in the **midst** of the boards shall reach from end to end.
MATT. 14: 31	O thou of little faith, **wherefore** didst thou doubt?
15: 2	**Why** do thy disciples transgress the tradition of the elders?
MATT. 14: 36	And **besought** him that theymight only touch the hem of his garment:
: 39	And he went a little farther, and fell on his face, and he **prayed,**
MATT. 15: 8	This people draweth **nigh** unto me with their mouth,
Isaiah 29: 13	Forasmuch as this people draw **near** *me* with ther mouth,
MATT. 15: 18	But those things which **proceed out of** the mouth **come forth from** the heart; and they defile the man.
MATT. 15: 21	Then Jesus went **thence,**
Mark 6: 10	there abide till you depart **from that place.**
MATT. 15: 26	It is not **meet** to take the children's bread, and cast *it* to the dogs.
11: 26	Even so, Father: for so it seemed **good** in thy sight.
20: 4	and whatsoever is **right** I will give you.
MATT. 15: 31	Insomuch **that** the multitude wondered,
MATT. 15: 33	**Whence** should we have so much bread in the wilderness, as to fill so great a multitude?
Mark 8: 4	**From whence** can a man satisfy these *men* with bread here in the wilderness?
Matt. 26: 17	**Where** wilt thou that we prepare for thee to eat the passover?
MATT. 16: 4	but the sign of the prophet Jonas. **And he left them and departed.**

N.B. note how the underlined word separates words and phrases having the same meaning.

MATT. 16: 6	Then Jesus said unto them, **Take heed and beware** of the leaven of the Pharisees and of the Sad-du-cees.

N.B. note how the underlined word separates words and phrases having the same meaning.

<u>**MATT. 16: 28**</u>	**Verily** I say unto you,
17: 11	Elias **truly** shall first come,
<u>**MATT. 17: 2**</u>	And was **transfigured** before them:
Luke 9: 29	the fashion of his countenance was **altered,**
Acts 28: 6	and saw no harm come to him, they **changed** their minds,
<u>**MATT. 17: 2**</u>	and his face did shine as the sun, and his **raiment** was white as the light.
Mark 12: 38	Beware of the scribes, which love to go in long **clothing,**
<u>**MATT. 17: 9**</u>	And as they came down from the mountain, Jesus **charged them,**
Mark 6: 8	And **commanded them** that they should take nothing for *their* journey,
<u>**MATT. 17: 12**</u>	That Elias is come already, and they knew him not, but have done unto him whatsoever they **listed.**
Mark 15: 16	Now at *that* feast he released unto them one prisoner, whomsoever they **desired.**
John 2: 3	And when they **wanted** wine,
<u>**MATT. 17: 12**</u>	**Likewise** shall **also** the Son of man suffer of them.
<u>**MATT. 17: 15**</u>	for he is lunatick, and **sore vexed:**
2 Kings 6: 11	Therefore the heart of the king of Syria was **sore troubled** for this thing;
Daniel 5: 9	Then was king Belshazzar **greatly troubled,**
<u>**MATT. 17: 15**</u>	for **oft**entimes he falleth into the fire, and **oft** into the water.
<u>**MATT. 17: 17**</u>	how long shall I suffer you? bring him **hither** to me.
: 4	Lord, it is good for us to be **here:**
<u>**MATT. 17:17**</u>	how long shall I **suffer you?**
18: 26	Lord, **have patience** with me,
<u>**MATT. 17: 21**</u>	**Howbeit** this kind goeth not out **but** by prayer and fasting.
<u>**MATT. 17: 27**</u>	**Notwithstanding, lest** we should offend them,
<u>**MATT. 18: 2**</u>	And Jesus called a little child unto him, and set him **in the midst of** them.
13: 7	And some fell fell **among** thorns;
<u>**MATT. 18: 3**</u>	And said, **Verily** I say unto you, except ye be converted,
3: 11	I **indeed** baptize you with water unto repentance:

17: 11	Elias **truly** shall first come,
<u>MATT. 18: 3</u> 1 Cor. 15: 2	And said, Verily I say unto you, **except** ye be converted, **unless** ye have believed in vain.
<u>MATT. 18: 8</u> 　　: 4 Mark 9: 43	**Wherefore if** thy hand or thy foot offend thee, Whosoever **therefore** shall humble himself as this little child, And **if** thy hand offend thee,
<u>MATT. 18: 8</u> 15: 30	it is better for thee to enter into life **halt** or maimed, having with them *those that were* **lame,** blind,
<u>MATT. 18: 10</u> Phil. 4: 6	**Take heed** that ye depise not one of these little ones; **Be careful** for nothing;
<u>MATT. 18: 11</u> 　　: 12	For the Son of man is come to save that which **was lost.** and seeketh that which was **gone astray?**
<u>MATT. 18: 15</u> 　　: 33 2 Cor. 2: 12	**Moreover** if thy brother shall trespass against thee, Shouldest not **also** have had compassion on thy fellow- servant,…? **Furthermore,** when I came to Tro-as to *preach* Christ's gospel,
<u>MATT. 18: 15</u> 　　: 21	Moreover if thy brother shall **trespass** thee, Lord how oft shall my brother **sin** against me and I forgive him?
<u>MATT. 18: 19</u> Phil. 3: 20	That if two of you shall agree on earth as **touching** any thing that they shall ask, Because for the work of Christ he was nigh unto death not **regarding** his life,
<u>MATT. 18: 21</u> 23: 37	Lord how **oft** shall my brother sin against me and I forgive him? how **often** would I have gathered thy children together,
<u>MATT. 18: 25</u> 13: 13	But **forasmuch as** he had not to pay, because they **seeing** see not;
<u>MATT. 18: 33</u> 5: 7	Shouldest not thou also have had **compassion** on thy fellow- servant, even as I had **pity** on thee? Blessed are the merciful: for they shall obtain **mercy.**
<u>MATT. 18: 34</u> 5: 22	And his lord was **wroth,** That whosoever is **angry** with his brother without a cause shall be in danger of the judgment:
<u>MATT. 18: 35</u>	So **likewise** shall my heavenly father do **also** unto you,

<u>MATT. 19: 6</u>	**Wherefore** they are no more twain, but one flesh. What **therefore** God hath joined together, let no man put asunder.
<u>MATT. 19: 6</u> 18: 19	Wherefore they are no more **twain,** but one flesh. That if **two** of you shall agree on earth as touching any thing that they shall ask,
<u>MATT. 19: 6</u> 25: 32	What there God hath joined together, let not man **put asunder.** and he shall **separate** them from one another, as a shepherd **divideth** *his* sheep from the goats:
<u>MATT. 19: 14</u> : 6	But Jesus said, **Suffer** little children, and forbid them not, What therefore God hath joined together, **let** not man put asunder.
<u>MATT. 19: 15</u> Mark 6: 10	And he laid *his* hands on them, and departed **thence.** there abide till ye depart **from that place.**
<u>MATT. 19: 16</u> 18: 8	Good Master, what good thing must I do, that I may have **eternal** life? rather than having two or two feet to be cast into **everlasting** fire.
<u>MATT. 19: 23</u> 17: 11 20: 23 26: 73	Then said Jesus unto his disciples, **Verily** I say unto you, And Jesus answered and said unto them, E-li-as **truly** shall first come, And he saith unto them, Ye shall **indeed** drink of my cup, and said to Peter, **Surely** thou also art *one* of them;
<u>MATT. 19: 25</u> 7: 28	When his disciples heard *it,* they were **exceedingly amazed,** the people were **astonished** at his doctrine:
<u>MATT. 20: 5</u> : 7	Again he went out about the sixth and ninth hour, and did **likewise.** Go ye **also** into the vineyard;
<u>MATT. 20: 11</u> : 1 Luke 13: 25	And when they had received *it,* they murmured against the **goodman** of the house. For the kingdom of heaven is like unto a man *that is* an **householder,** When once the **master** of the house is risen up,
<u>MATT. 20: 12</u> 25: 40	Saying, These last **have wrought** *but* one hour, Inasmuch as ye **have done** *it* unto one of the least of these of these my brethren, ye have done *it* unto me.
<u>MATT. 20: 25</u>	Ye know that the princes of the Gentiles **exercise dominion**

over them, and they that are great **exercise authority** upon them.

<u>MATT. 21: 1</u>	And when they **drew nigh** unto Jerusalem,
: 34	And when the time of the fruit **drew near,**

<u>MATT. 21: 2</u>	and **straightway** ye shall find an ass tied,
20: 34	and **immediately** their eyes received sight,

<u>MATT. 21: 7</u>	and put on them their clothes, and they set *him* **thereon.**
Mark 11: 7	and cast their garments **upon him;** and he sat on him.

<u>MATT. 21: 8</u>   And a very great multitude **spread** their garments in the way; others cut down branches from the trees, and **strawed** *them* in the way.

<u>MATT. 21: 9</u>	Blessed *is* he that cometh in the name of the Lord; **Hosanna** in the highest.
Luke 2: 14	**Glory to God** in the highest,
<u>MATT. 21: 31</u>	**Whether** of them twain did the will of *his* father?
19: 18	He saith unto him, **Which?**

<u>MATT. 21: 31</u>	Whether of them **twain** did the will of *his* father?
: 28	A *certain* man had **two** sons;

<u>MATT. 21: 33</u>	and let it out to **husbandmen,** and went into a far country:
John 15: 1	I am the true **vine,** and my Father is the **husbandman.**
Jer. 51: 23	and with thee will I break in pieces the **husbandman** and his **yoke of oxen;**
Zech. 13: 5	But he shall say, I *am* no prophet, I am a **husbandman;** for man taught me to keep **cattle** from my youth.
Genesis 4: 2	And Abel was a keeper of sheep, but Cain was **a tiller of the ground.**
9: 20	And Noah began *to be* **an husbandman,** and he **planted a vineyard:**
2 Kings 25: 12	But the captain of the guard left of the poor of the land *to be* **vine-dressers and husbandmen.**

<u>MATT. 21: 43</u>	and given to a nation bringing forth the fruits **thereof.**
: 34	that they might receive the fruits **of it.**

<u>MATT. 22: 6</u>	And the remnant took his servants and en**treated** *them* spitefully, and **slew** *them.*
23: 31	that ye are the children of them which **killed** the prophets.

<u>MATT. 22: 7</u>	But when the king heard *thereof,* he was **wroth:**
5: 22	That whosoever is **angry** with his brother without a cause

	shall be in danger of the judgment:
MATT. 22: 12	Friend, how camest thou in **hither** not having a wedding garment?
20: 6	Why stand ye **here** all the day idle?
MATT. 22: 21	Then saith he unto them, **Render** therefore unto Caesar the things which are Caesar's;
: 17	Is it lawful **to give** tribute unto Caesar, or not?
MATT. 22: 25	when he had married a wife, **deceased,**
: 27	And last of all the woman **died** also.
MATT. 22: 26	**Likewise** the second **also,** and the third, unto the seventh.
MATT. 23: 5	they **make broad** their phylacteries, and **enlarge** the borders of their garments,
MATT. 23: 6	And love the **uppermost** rooms at feasts, and the **chief** seats in the synagogues,
MATT. 23: 7	And greetings in the markets, and to be called of men, **Rabbi, Rabbi.**
: 8	But be not ye called **Rabbi :** for one is your **Master,**
MATT. 23: 12	And whosoever shall exalt himself shall be **abased:**
Phil. 2: 8	And being found in fashion as a man, he **humbled** himself,
MATT. 23: 17	for **whether** is greater, the gold, or the temple that sanctifieth the gold?
: 24	*Ye* blind guides, **which** strain at a gnat, and swallow a camel.
MATT. 23: 20	Whoso therefore shall swear by the altar, sweareth by it, and by all things **thereon.**
: 18	but whosoever sweareth by the gift that is **upon it,**
MATT. 23: 21	And whoso shall swear by it, and by him that dwelleth **therein.**
21: 33	and hedged it round about, and digged a winepress **in it,**
MATT. 23: 29	because ye build the **tombs** of the prophets, and garnish the **sepulchres** of the righteous,
MATT. 23: 36	**Verily** I say unto you,
27: 54	**Truly** this was the Son of God.
23: 41	And we **indeed** justly;
MATT. 24: 7	and there shall be famines, and pestilences, and earthquakes, in **divers** places.
: 10	And then **many** be offended,
MATT. 24: 14	And this **gospel** of the kingdom shall be preached in all the world for witness unto all nations,

Acts 8: 4	Therefore they that were scattered abroad went every where preaching **the word.**
: 14	Now when the apostles which were at Jerusalem heard that Samaria had received **the word of God.**
: 25	when they had testified and preached **the word of the Lord,**
10: 36	**The word** which *God* sent unto the childrenof Israel, preaching peace by **Jesus Christ:**
John 1: 1	In the beginning was **the Word,**
1 John 5: 7	For there are three that bare record in heaven, the Father, **the Word,** and the Holy Ghost:
Rev. 1: 2	Who bare record of **the word of God,** and of the testimony of **Jesus Christ,**

<u>MATT. 24: 24</u>	insomuch **that,** if *it were* possible, they shall deceive the very elect.
13: 2	**so that** he went into a ship, and sat,

<u>MATT. 24: 32</u>	and putteth forth leaves, ye know that summer *is* **nigh:**
: 33	when ye shall see all these things, know that it is **near,**

<u>MATT. 24: 49</u>	And shall begin to **smite** *his* fellowservants,
Mark 14: 65	and the servants did **strike** him with the palms of their hands.

<u>MATT. 25: 5</u>	While the bridegroom tarried, they all **slumbered** <u>**and**</u> **slept.**

N.B. note how the underlined word separates words and phrases having the same meaning.

<u>MATT. 25: 12</u>	But he answered and said, **Verily** I say unto you, I know you not.
26: 73	**Surely** thou also art *one* of them;
27: 54	**Truly** this was the Son of God.

<u>MATT. 25: 13</u>	Watch therefore, for ye know neither the day nor the hour **wherein** the Son of man cometh.
Luke 13: 14	there six days **in which** men ought to work:

<u>MATT. 25: 15</u>	to every man according to his several abilty; and **straightway** took his journey.
24: 29	**immediately** after the tribulation of those days shall the sun be darkened,

<u>MATT. 25: 17</u>	And **likewise** he that *had received* two, he **also** gained other two.

<u>MATT. 25: 24</u>	and gathering where thou hast not **strawed:**
26: 31	and the sheep of the flock shall be **scattered** abroad.

MATT. 25: 26	*Thou* wicked and **slothful** servant,
20: 3	and saw others standing **idle** in the marketplace.
MATT. 25: 46	And these shall go away into **everlasting** punishment: but the righteous into life **eternal.**
MATT. 26: 10	Why trouble ye the woman? For she **hath wrought** a good work upon me.
: 13	*there* shall also this, that this woman **hath done,**
MATT. 26: 20	Now when the **even** was come, he sat down with the twelve.
Mark 14: 17	And in the **evening** he cometh with the twelve.
MATT. 26: 31	I will **smite** the shepherd, and the sheep of the flock shall scattered abroad.
Mark 14: 65	and the servants did **strike** him with the palms of their hands.
MATT. 26: 35	**Likewise also** said the disciples.
MATT. 26: 38	**tarry** ye here, and watch with me.
Luke 12: 36	And ye yourselves like unto men that **wait** for their lord,
MATT. 26: 39	let this cup pass from me: **nevertheless** not as I will, **but** as thou *wilt.*
MATT. 26: 41	the spirit **indeed** *is* willing, but the flesh *is* weak.
Mark 14: 38	The spirit **truly** *is* ready, but the flesh *is* weak.
MATT. 26: 41	the spirit indeed *is* **willing,**
Mark 14: 38	The spirit indeed *is* **ready.**
MATT. 26: 49	And **forthwith** he came to Jesus,
: 74	And **immediately** the cock crew.
MATT. 26: 63	**I adjure thee** by the living God,
: 72	And again he denied **with an oath,**
Gen. 50: 25	And Joseph **took an oath** of the children of Israel,
MATT. 26: 69	Now Peter sat without in the palace: and a **damsel** came unto him,
Mark 14: 69	And a **maid** saw him again,
MATT. 27: 14	And he answered him to never a word; insomuch **that** the governor marvelled greatly.
MATT. 27: 15	Now at *that* feast the governor **was wont to** release unto the people a prisoner, whom they would.
Luke 4: 16	And he came to Nazareth, where he had been brought up: and **as his custom was,**
MATT. 27: 21	**Whether** of the twain will ye that I release unto you?

: 22	What shall I do then with Jesus **which** is called Christ?
MATT. 27: 21	Whether of the **twain** will ye that I release unto you?
: 38	Then were there **two** thieves crucified with him?
MATT. 27: 30	And they spit upon him, and took the reed, and **smote** him on the head.
26: 51	and **struck** a servant of the high priest's, and **smote** off his ear.
MATT. 27: 31	and put his own **raiment** on him, and led him away to crucify *him.*
: 35	They parted my **garments** among them, and upon my **vesture** did they cast lots.
MATT. 27: 34	They gave him vinegar to drink **mingled with** gall:
Hebrews 4: 2	not being **mixed with** faith in them that heard *it.*
MATT. 27: 41	**Likewise also** the chief priests mocking *him,*
MATT. 27: 48	And **straightway** one of them ran, and took a spunge,
26: 74	And **immediately** the cock crew.
MATT. 27: 57	When the **even** was come,
16: 2	When it is **evening,**
MATT. 27: 60	And laid it in his own new **tomb,** which he had hewn out in the rock: and he rolled a great stone to the door of the **sepulchre,** and departed.
John 11: 17	he found that he had *lain* in the **grave** four days already.
MATT. 28: 3	His **countenance** was like lightning, and his raiment white as snow:
17: 2	and his **face** did shine as the sun,
MATT. 28: 3	and his **raiment** white as snow:
27: 35	and they crucified him, and parted his **garments,**

MARK

MARK 1: 1	The beginning of the **gospel** of Jesus Christ,
Luke 5: 1	as the people pressed upon him to hear **the word of God,**
John 1: 1	In the beginning was **the Word,**
Acts 8: 25	And they, when they had testified and preached **the word of the Lord,** returned to Jerusalem, and preached **the gospel** in many villages of the Samaritans.
MARK 1: 6	And John was clothed with camel's hair, and with **a girdle of**

	a skin about his loins;
Matt. 3: 4	And the same John had his raiment of camel's hair, and a leathern girdle about his loins;

MARK 1: 10	And straightway coming up out of the water,
: 12	And immediately Spirit driveth him into the wilderness.
: 29	And forthwith, when they were come out of the synagogue,
: 30	But Simon's wife's mother lay sick of a fever, and anon they tell him of her.
: 42	And as soon as he had spoken, immediately the leprosy departed from him,

MARK 1: 19	And when he had gone a little further thence,
: 13	And he was there in the wilderness forty days,

MARK 1: 21	And they went into Ca-per-na-um; and straightway on the sabbath day he entered into the synagogue, and taught.

MARK 1: 27	And they were all amazed, insomuch that they questioned among themselves,
3: 20	And the multitude cometh together again, so that they could not so much as eat bread.

MARK 1: 30	But Simon's wife's mother lay sick of a fever,
Matt. 10: 35	and the daughter against her mother, and the daughter in law against her mother in law.

MARK 1: 32	And at even, when the sun did set,
14: 17	And in the evening he cometh with the twelve,

MARK 1: 34	And he healed many that were sick of divers diseases,

MARK 1: 41	And Jesus, moved with compassion, put forth *his* hand,
Matt. 18: 33	Shouldest not thou also have had compassion on thy fellowservant, even as I had pity on thee?

MARK 1: 42	And as soon as he had spoken, immediately the leprosy departed from him,

MARK 1: 43	And he straitly charged him,
Acts 5: 28	Saying, Did not we straitly command you that ye should not teach jn this name?

MARK 1: 45	But he went out, began to publish *it* much, and to blaze abroad the matter,

N.B. note how the underlined word separates words and phrases having the same meaning.

MARK 2: 2	And **straightway** many were gathered together,
: 12	And he **immediately** he arose,
MARK 2: 12	in**somuch that** they were all amazed,
3: 20	**so that** they could not so much as eat bread.
MARK 3: 12	And he **straitly charged** them that they should not make him known.
5 : 43	And he **charged them straitly** that no man should know it; and **commanded** that something should be given her to eat.
MARK 3: 28	**Verily** I say unto you, all shall be forgiven unto the sons of men,
14: 38	The spirit **truly** *is* ready but the flesh *is* weak.
: 70	**Surely** thou art *one* of them:
MARK 3: 28	and blasphemies **wherewith** soever they shall blaspheme:
4: 24	Take heed what ye hear: **with what** measure ye mete,
MARK 4: 16	And these are they **likewise** which are sown on stony ground;
2: 26	and gave **also** to them which were with him?
MARK 4: 22	For there is nothing **hid,** which shall not be manifested; neither was any thing **kept secret,**
MARK 4: 30	And he said, **Whereunto** shall we liken the kingdom of God? **with what** comparison shall we compare it?
Luke 13: 18	Then said he, **Unto what** is the kingdom of God like?
MARK 4: 30	And he said, Whereunto shall we **liken** the kingdom of God? with what comparison shall we **compare** it?
Luke 13: 18	and whereunto shall I **resemble** it?
MARK 4: 37	And there arose **a great storm of wind,**
Matt. 8: 24	And behold, there arose **a great tempest** in the sea,
MARK 5: 4	and the chains had been **plucked asunder** by him, and the fetters **broken in pieces:**
MARK 5: 7	What have I to do with thee, Jesus, *thou* Son of the most high God? I **adjure thee** by God,
Matt. 26: 72	And again he **denied with an oath,** .
Gen. 50: 25	And Joseph **took an oath** of the children of Israel,
MARK 5: 10	And he **besought him much** that he would not send them away out of the country.
: 9	And he **asked** him,
Matt. 27: 58	He went to Pilate, and **begged** the body of Jesus.

<u>**MARK 5: 11**</u>	Now there was there **nigh** unto the mountains a great herd of swine feeding.
13: 28	and putteth forth leaves, ye know that summer is **near:**
<u>**MARK 5: 13**</u>	And **forthwith** Jesus gave them leave.
: 2	**immediately** there met him out of the tombs a man with an unclean spirit,
<u>**MARK 5: 16**</u>	And they that saw *it* told them how it **befell** to him that was possessed with the devil,
Esther 4: 7	And Mor-de-ca-i told him of all that **had happened** unto him,
<u>**MARK 5: 19**</u>	**Howbeit** Jesus suffered him not,
: 6	**But** when he saw Jesus afar off,
<u>**MARK 5: 19**</u>	Howbeit Jesus **suffered** him not,
Acts 26: 1	Thou art **permitted** to speak for thyself,
<u>**MARK 5: 23**</u>	and the keepers standing **without** before the doors:
Matt. 23: 25	for ye make clean the **outside** of the cup and of the platter,
<u>**MARK 5: 29**</u>	And **straightway** the fountain of her blood was dried up;
: 30	And Jesus, **immediately** knowing in himself that virtue had gone out of him,
<u>**MARK 5: 31**</u>	Thou seest the **multitude** thee, and sayest thou who touched me?
: 21	**much people** gathered unto him:
<u>**MARK 5: 36**</u>	**As soon as** Jesus heard the word that was spoken,
: 30	And Jesus, **immediately** knowing that virtue had gone out out of him,
Mark 5: 42	And **straightway** the damsel arose,
<u>**MARK 5: 43**</u>	And he **charged** them **straitly** that no man should know it; and **commanded** that something should be given her to eat.
<u>**MARK 6: 1**</u>	And he went out from **thence,**
: 5	And he could **there** do no mighty work,
<u>**MARK 6: 2**</u>	that even such mighty works are **wrought** by his hands?
5: 14	And they went out to see whatit was that was **done.**
<u>**MARK 6: 4**</u>	But Jesus said unto them, A prophet is not without honour, **but** in his own country,
Matt. 13: 57	**But** Jesus said unto them, A prophet is not without honour, **save** in his own country,
Mark 7: 3	For the Pharisees, and all the Jews, **except** they wash *their* hands oft, eat not,
<u>**MARK 6: 8**</u>	no **scrip,** no bread, no money in *their* purse:

John 12: 6	but because he was a thief, and had the **bag**,
MARK 6: 11	and whosoever shall not receive you, nor hear you, when ye depart **thence**,
: 10	In what place soever ye enter into an house, there abide till ye depart **from that place.**
MARK 6: 11	**Verily** I say unto you,
14: 38	The spirit **truly** *is* ready, but the flesh *is* weak.
MARK 6: 22	and pleased Herod and them that sat with him, the king said unto the **damsel,**
Matt.9: 25	and took her by the hand, and the **maid** arose.
MARK 6: 25	And she came in **straightway with haste,** unto the king,
	and asked, I will that thou give me **by and by** in a charger the head of John the Baptist.
: 27	And **immediately** the king sent an executioner,
MARK 6: 33	and many knew him, and ran **afoot** thither out of all cities,
Matt. 14: 13	they followed him **on foot** out of the cities.
MARK 6: 35	And when the day was now **far spent,** his disciples came unto him, and said, This a desert place, and now the time *is* **far passed:**
MARK 6: 45	And **straightway** he constrained his disciples to get into the ship,
: 50	And **immediately** he talked with them,
MARK 6: 45	And straightway he **constrained** his disciples to get into the ship,
Acts 26: 11	And I punished them oft in every synagogue, and **compelled** *them* to blaspheme;
MARK 7: 2	And when they saw some of his disciples eat bread with **defiled,** that is to **say,** with **unwashen** hands,
MARK 7: 3	except they wash *their* hands **oft**, eat not,
5: 4	Because that he had been **often** bound with fetters and chains,
MARK 7: 7	**Howbeit** in vain do they worship me, teaching *for* doctrines the commandments of men.
Matt. 15: 9	**But** in vain do they worship me, teaching *for* doctrines the commandments of men,
MARK 7: 12	And ye **suffer** him no more to do ought for his father or his mother;
Luke 11: 48	Truly ye bear witness that ye *allow* the deeds of your fathers:

1 Cor. 16: 7	but I trust to tarry a while with you, if the Lord **permit**.
MARK 7: 22	Thefts, covetousness, wickedness, deceit, **lasciviousness,**
1 Peter 2: 11	abstain from **fleshly lusts,**

| **MARK 7: 24** | And from **thence** he arose, |
| 6: 5 | And he could **there** no mighty work, |

| **MARK 7: 26** | and she **besought him** that he would cast forth the devil out of her daughter. |
| : 5 | Then the Pharisees and the scribes **asked him,** |

MARK 7: 27	for it is not **meet** to take the children's bread,
9: 5	Master, it is **good** for us to be here:
Matt. 20: 7	and whatsoever is **right,** *that* ye shall receive.

| **MARK 7: 35** | And **straightway** his ears were opened, |
| 6: 27 | And **immediately** the king sent an executioner, |

| **MARK 7: 36** | but the more he charged them, **so much the more a great deal** they published *it* ; |

N.B. note how the first four bold words mean the same as the last three bold words.

| **MARK 8: 1** | In those days **the multitude being very great,** |

| **MARK 8: 3** | they will faint by the way: for **divers** of them came from far. |
| : 31 | that the Son of man must suffer **many** things, |

| **MARK 8: 12** | **verily** I say unto you, |
| 15: 39 | **Truly** this man was the Son of God. |

| **MARK 8: 23** | and put his hands upon him, he asked him if he saw **ought.** |
| 9: 22 | but if thou canst do **any thing,** have compassion on us, |

| **MARK 8: 30** | And he **charged them** that they should tell no man of him. |
| 6: 8 | And **commanded them** that they should take nothing for *their* journey, |

| **MARK 9: 3** | And his **raiment** became shining, |
| 14: 63 | Then the high priest rent his **clothes,** |

| **MARK 9: 6** | For he **wist** not what to say; |
| 8: 17 | And when Jesus **knew** *it,* |

| **MARK 9: 9** | he **charged** them that they should tell no man what things they had seen, |
| 5: 43 | and **commanded** that something should be given her to eat. |

: 13	But I say unto you, That Elias is **indeed** come,
MARK 9: 12	that he must suffer many things, and be set at **nought**.
: 9	This kind can come forth by **nothing**,
MARK 9: 13	and they have done unto him whatsoever they have **listed**,
15: 6	Now at *that* feast he released unto them one prisoner,
	whomsoever they **desired**.
John 2: 3	And when they **wanted** wine,
MARK 9: 22	And **oftimes** it hath cast him into the fire,
Luke 5: 33	And they said unto him, Why do the disciples of John fast
	often,
MARK 9: 26	and he was as one dead; insomuch **that** many said, He is dead.
4: 32	**so that** the fowls of the air may lodge under the shadow of it.
MARK 9: 45	it is better for thee to enter **halt** into life,
Matt. 15: 30	having with them *those that were* **lame**,
MARK 9: 50	Salt *is* good: but if the salt have lost his **saltness**, wherewith
	will ye season it?
Luke 14: 24	That none of those men which were bidden shall **taste** of
	my supper.
MARK 9: 50	**wherewith** will ye season it?
: 19	**how** long shall I be with you?
4: 24	**with what** measure ye mete,
MARK 10: 1	and the people resort unto him again; and as he **was wont**
	he taught them again.
Luke 4: 16	and, **as his custom was,** he went into the synagogue on the
	sabbath day,
MARK 10: 8	And they **twain** shall be one flesh:
9: 43	than having **two** hands to go into hell,
MARK 10: 9	What therefore God hath joined together, let not man put
	asunder.
Matt. 25: 32	and he shall **separate** them one from another,
MARK 10: 14	and said unto them, **Suffer** the little children to come unto me,
7: 27	But Jesus said unto her, **Let** the little children first be filled:
MARK 10: 15	**Verily** I say unto you, Whosoever shall not receive...
: 39	Ye shall **indeed** drink of the cup that I drink of;
15: 39	**Truly** this man was the Son of God.
MARK 10: 15	Whosoever shall not receive the kingdom of God as a child,
	he shall not enter therein.
MARK 10: 39	and with the baptism that I am baptized **withal**...

: 38	and be baptized with the baptism that I am baptized **with?**
MARK 10: 48	And many **charged** him that he should hold his peace:
: 49	And Jesus stood still, and **commanded** him to be called.
MARK 11: 3	And if any man say unto you, Why do ye do this? say ye that the Lord hath need of him, and **straightway** he will him hither.
: 2	and **as soon as** ye be entered into it,
10: 52	And **immediately** he received his sight,
MARK 11: 8	And many **spread** their garments in the way: and others cut down branches off the trees, and **strawed** *them* in the way.
MARK 11: 10	Blessed *be* the kingdom of our father David, that cometh in the name of the Lord: **Hosanna in the highest.**
Luke 2: 14	**Glory to God in the highest,**
MARK 11: 11	and now the **eventide** was come,
14: 17	And in the **evening** he cometh with the twelve.
MARK 11: 13	And seeing a fig tree afar off having leaves, **if haply he might** find any thing thereon:
Acts 8: 22	and pray God, **if perhaps** the thought of thine heart may be forgiven thee.

N.B. note that the first two bold numbers mean the same as the third and fourth bold numbers in the first verse.

MARK 11: 13	And seeing a fig tree afar off having leaves, if haply he might find any thing **thereon:**
Matt. 28: 2	and sat **upon it.**
MARK 11: 16	And would not **suffer** that any man should carry *any* vessel through the temple.
1 Cor. 16: 7	but I trust to tarry a while with you, if the Lord **permit.**
MARK 11: 21	Master, behold, the fig tree which thou cursedst is **withered** away.
: 20	as they passed by, they saw the fig tree **dried up** from the roots.
MARK 12: 1	A *certain* man planted a vineyard, and set an hedge about *it,* and digged *a place for* the **winefat,**
Matt. 21: 33	There was a certain householder, which planted a vineyard, and hedged it round about, and digged a **winepress** in it,
MARK 12: 17	**Render** to Caesar the things that are Caesar's,
: 14	Is it lawful to **give** tribute to Caesar, or not?

MARK 12: 15	But he, knowing their **hypocrisy**, said unto them,
: 40	and for a **pretence** make long prayers:
MARK 12: 21	neither left he any seed: and the third **likewise**.
: 22	and left no seed: last of all the woman died **also**.
MARK 12: 30	and with all thy soul, and with all thy **mind**,
: 33	and with all the **understanding**,
MARK 12: 37	David therefore calleth him Lord; and **whence** is he *then* his son?
: 35	**How** say the scribes that Christ is the son of David?
MARK 12: 43	**Verily** I say unto you,
15: 39	**Truly** this man was the Son of God.
Luke 21: 3	**Of a truth** I say unto you,
MARK 12: 39	And the **chief** seats in the synagogues, and the **uppermost** rooms at feasts:
MARK 13: 8	and there shall be earthquakes in **divers** places,
: 6	For **many** shall come in my name,
MARK 13: 10	And **the gospel** must be published among all nations.
7: 13	Making **the word of God** of none effect through your tradition,
Acts 8: 25	And they, when they had testified and preached **the word of the Lord,**
Acts 10: 36	**The word** which *God* sent unto the children of Israel, preaching peace by **Jesus Christ:**
Heb. 4: 2	For unto us was **the gospel** preached, as well unto them: but **the word** preached did not profit them,
Rev. 1: 2	Who bare record of **the word of God,** and of the testimony of **Jesus Christ,**
MARK 13: 29	know that it is **nigh,** *even* at the doors.
: 28	ye know that summer is **near:**
MARK 14: 6	Let her alone; why trouble ye her? she **hath wrought** a good on me.
: 9	*this* also that she **hath done** shall be spoken of for a memorial of her.
MARK 14: 14	And wheresoever he shall go in, say ye to **the goodman of house,**
: 35	Watch therefore: for ye know not when **the master of the house** cometh,
MARK 14: 18	**Verily** I say unto you, One of you which eateth with me

	shall betray me.
: 21	The Son of man **indeed** goeth, as it is written of him:
15: 39	**Truly** this was the Son of God.

| **MARK 14: 27** | for it is written, I will **smite** the shepherd and the sheep will be scattered. |
| : 65 | and the servants did **strike** with the palms of their hands. |

MARK 14: 31	But he spake the **more vehemently,**
15: 14	And they cried out the **more exceedingly,**
Luke 23: 23	And they were instant **with loud voices,**

| **MARK 14: 31** | I will not deny thee in any wise. **Likewise also** said they all. |

MARK 14: 34	**tarry** ye here, and watch.
6: 10	there **abide** till ye depart from that place.
Luke 12: 36	And ye yourselves like unto men that **wait** for their Lord,

| **MARK 14: 36** | take away this cup from me: **nevertheless** not what I will, **but** what thou wilt. |

| **MARK 14: 40** | he found them asleep again, (for their eyes were heavy,) neither **wist** they what to answer him. |
| 15: 45 | And when he **knew** *it* of the centurion, |

| **MARK 14: 45** | And **as soon as** he was come, he goeth **straightway** to him, and saith, Master, master; and kissed him. |
| : 43 | And **immediately, while he yet spake,** |

| **MARK 14: 65** | and to cover his face, and to **buffet him,** and to say unto him, Prophesy: and the servants did **strike him** with the palms of their hands. |

| **MARK 14: 72** | And when he thought **thereon,** he wept. |
| Luke 10: 6 | And if the son of peace be there, your peace shall rest **upon it,** |

| **MARK 15: 19** | And they **smote** on the head with a reed, |
| Luke 22: 64 | they **struck** him on the face, |

| **MARK 15: 23** | And they gave him to drink wine **mingled** with myrrh: |
| Hebrews 4: 2 | not being **mixed** with faith in them that heard *it*. |

| **MARK 15: 38** | And the veil of the temple was rent in **twain** from the top to the bottom. |

| 16: 12 | After that he appeared in another form unto **two** of them, |

| **MARK 15: 43** | and went in boldly unto Pilate, and **craved** the body of Jesus. |
| Matt. 27: 58 | He went to Pilate, and **begged** the body of Jesus. |

MARK 16: 5	and they **were affrighted.**
: 8	for they **were afraid.**

MARK 16: 10	*And* she went and told them that had been with him, as they **mourned and wept.**

N.B. note how the underlined word separates words and phrases having the same meaning.

MARK 16: 15	And he said unto them, Go ye into all the world, and preach **the gospel** to every creature.
Acts 10: 36	**The word** which *God* sent unto the children of Israel, preaching peace by **Jesus Christ:**

LUKE

LUKE 1: 1	**Forasmuch as many** have taken in hand to set forth in order a declaration of those things which are most surely believed among us,

N.B. note that the first bold word means the same as the second and third bold word.

LUKE 1: 2	which **from the beginning** were eyewitnesses,
: 3	having had perfect understanding of all things **from the very first,** to write unto thee in order,

LUKE 1: 6	walking in all the **commandments and ordinances** of the Lord blameless.

N.B. note how the underlined word separates words and phrases having the same meaning.

LUKE 1: 7	And they had **no child,** because that Elisabeth was **barren,** and they both were *now* well stricken in years.

LUKE 1: 13	And thou shalt have **joy and gladness;** and many shall reoice at his birth.

N.B. note how the underlined word separates words and phrases having the same meaning.

LUKE 1: 18	And Zacherias said unto the angel, **Whereby** shall I know this?
: 34	Then said Mary unto the angel, **How** shall this be, seeing I know not a man?

LUKE 1: 20	And, behold, thou shalt be **dumb, and not able to speak,** until the day that these things shall be performed, because thou believest not my words,
: 22	And when he came out, he **could not speak** unto them: and

they perceived that he had seen a vision in the temple: for he beckoned unto them, and **remained speechless.**

LUKE 1: 25 Thus hath the Lord dealt with me in the days **wherein** he looked on *me,*

13: 14 There are six days **in which** men ought to work:

LUKE 1: 27 To a virgin **espoused** to a man named Joseph,

N.B. The word is used today and refers to either husband or wife.

LUKE 1: 39 And Mary arose in those days, and went into the hill country **with haste,**

14: 21 Go out **quickly** into the streets and lanes of the city,

LUKE 1: 39 And Mary arose in those days, and **went into** the hill country with haste, into a city of Juda:

: 40 And **entered into** the house of Zacharias, and saluted Elisabeth.

LUKE 1: 43 And **whence** *is* this to me, that the mother of my Lord should come to me?

: 66 **What** manner of child shall this be!

LUKE 1: 54 He hath **holpen** his servant Israel,

Acts 18: 27 who, when he was come, **helped** them much which had believed through grace:

LUKE 1: 61 There is none of thy **kin**dred that is called by this name.

LUKE 1: 78 **whereby** the dayspring on high hath visited us,

Acts 6:10 And they were not able to resist the wisdom and the spirit **by which** he spake.

LUKE 2: 20 And the shepherds returned, **glorifying and praising** God for all the things that they had seen and heard,

N.B. note how the underlined words separate words and phrases havng the same meaning.

LUKE 2: 40 And the child **grew, and waxed strong** in spirit, filled with wisdom:

LUKE 2: 40 And the child grew, and waxed stronge in spirit, filled with wisdom: and the **grace** of God was upon him.

: 52 And Jesus increased in wisdom and stature, and in **favour** with God and man.

LUKE 2: 43 as they returned, the child Jesus **tarried** behind in Jerusalem;

1: 22 for he beckoned unto them, and **remained** speechless.

Acts 19: 22	but he himself **stayed** in Asia for a season.
LUKE 2: 44	and they sought him among *their* **kins**folk and acquaintance.
LUKE 2: 49	How is it that ye sought me? **wist ye not** that I must be about my Father's business?
1 Cor. 6: 3	**Know ye not** that we shall judge angels?
LUKE 3: 11	He that hath two coats, let him **impart** to him that hath none:
6: 3	**Give,** and it shall be given unto you;
LUKE 3: 11	and he that hath **meat,** let him do likewise.
1 Tim. 6: 8	And having **food** and raiment let us be therewith content.
LUKE 3: 11	and he that hath meat, let him do **likewise.**
: 12	Then came **also** publicans to be baptized,
LUKE 3: 17	and will gather the wheat into his **garner;**
12: 24	which neither have storehouse or **barn.**
LUKE 4: 9	If thou be the Son of God, cast thyself down from **hence:**
: 23	do also **here** in thy country.
: 14	and there went out a **fame** of him through all the region round about.
Acts 6: 3	look ye out among you seven men of honest **report,**
LUKE 4: 18	The Spirit of the Lord *is* upon me, because he hath anointed me to preach **the gospel** to the poor;
John 1: 1	In the beginning was **the Word,**
Acts 8: 4	Thereforth they that were scattered abroad went every where preaching **the word.**
8: 25	and preached **the word of the Lord,**
10: 36	**The word** which *God* sent unto the children of Israel, preaching peace by **Jesus Christ:**
LUKE 4: 23	And he said unto them, Ye will **surely** say unto me this proverb, Physician, heal thyself: whatsoever we have heard done in Ca-per-na-um, do also here in thy country.
: 24	And he said, **Verily** I say unto you, No prophet is accepted in his own country.
: 25	But I tell you **of a truth,** many widows were in Israel in the days of Elias,
LUKE 4: 29	and led him unto the brow of the hill **whereon** their city was built, that they might cast him down headlong.
Rev.17: 9	The seven heads are seven mountains, **on which** the woman sitteth.

LUKE 4: 36   What a word *is* this! for with **authority and** **power** he
                       commandeth the unclean spirits,

N.B. note how the underlined word separates words and phrases having the same
        meaning.

LUKE 4: 38   And **Simon's wife's mother** was taken with a great fever;
Matt. 10: 35   and the daughter against her **mother in law.**

LUKE 4: 40   Now when the sun was setting, all they that had any sick
                       with **divers** diseases brought them unto him;
        : 41   And devils also came out of **many,**

LUKE 5: 25   And immediately he rose up before them, and took up that
                       whereon he lay,
Rev. 17: 9   The seven heads are seven mountains, **on which** the woman
                       sitteth.

LUKE 5: 39   No man also having drunk old *wine* **straightway** desireth
                       new:
        : 25   And **immediately** he arose up before them,

LUKE 6: 13   And when it was day, he called *unto him* his **disciples:** and
                       of them he chose twelve, whom he also called **apostles;**

LUKE 6: 29   And unto him that **smiteth** thee on the *one* cheek offer also
                       the other;

Rev. 9: 5   and their torment *was* as the torment of a scorpion, when he
                       striketh a man.

LUKE 6: 31   And as you would that men should do to you, do ye **also** to
                       them **likewise.**

LUKE 6: 38   For with the same **measure** that ye **mete with**al it shall be
                       measured to you again.

LUKE 7: 12   Now when he came **nigh** to the gate of the city,
        15: 1   Then drew **near** unto him all the publicans and sinners for
                       to hear him.

LUKE 7: 17   And this **rumour** of him went forth throughout all Judaea,
Acts 6: 3   look ye out among you seven men of honest **report,**

LUKE 7: 25   But what went ye out for to see? A man clothed in soft
                       raiment?
        8: 27   which had devils long time, and ware no **clothes,**

LUKE 7: 25   But what went ye out for to see? A man **clothed** in soft
                       raiment? Behold, they which are gorgeously **apparelled,**

LUKE 7: 31	And the Lord said, **Whereunto** then shall I liken the men of this generation? and **to what** are they like?
LUKE 7: 47	**Wherefore** I say unto thee,
: 28	**For** I say unto you,
: 42	Tell me **therefore,** which of them will love him most?
LUKE 8: 6	And some fell upon a rock; and **as soon as** it was sprung up,
Mark 4: 5	and **immediately** it sprang up,
LUKE 8: 23	and there a great storm of wind on the lake; and they were filled *with water,* and were **in jeopardy.**
Matt. 5: 21	and whosoever shall shall **in danger** of the judgment.
LUKE 8: 32	and they besought that he would **suffer** them to enter into them.
11: 48	Truly ye bear witness that ye **allow** the deeds of your fathers:
1 Cor. 16: 7	but I trust to tarry a while with you, if the Lord **permit.**
LUKE 8: 32	And he **suffered them.**
Mark 5: 13	And forthwith Jesus **gave them leave.**
LUKE 8: 44	and **immediately** her issue of blood **stanched.**
Mark 5: 29	and **straightway** the fountain of her blood **was dried up;**
LUKE 9: 1	Then he called his twelve disciples together, and gave them **power and authority** over all devils, and to cure diseases.

N.B. note how the underlined word separates words and phrases having the same meaning.

LUKE 9: 3	Take nothing for *your* journey, neither staves, nor **scrip,**
John 12: 6	and had the **bag,** and bear what was put therein.
LUKE 9: 3	neither money; neither have two coats **apiece.**
13: 15	*Thou* hypocrite, doth not **each** one of you on the sabbath day Loose his ox or *his* ass from the stall,
LUKE 9: 4	And whatsoever house ye enter into, there **abide,**
: 12	and **lodge,** and get victuals:
LUKE 9: 6	and went through the towns, preaching **the gospel,**
Acts 13: 7	Sergius Paulus, a prudent man; who called for Barnabas and Saul, and desired to hear **the word of God.**
8: 4	Therefore they that were scattered went every where preaching **the word.**
10: 36	**The word** which *God* sent unto the children of Israel, preaching peace by **Jesus Christ:**

LUKE 9: 12	that they may go into the towns and country round about, and lodge and get **victuals:**
1 Tim. 6: 8	And having **food** and raiment let us be therewith content.
LUKE 9: 21	And he **straitly charged them, and commanded _them_** to tell no man.

N.B. note how the underlined word separates words and phrases having the same meaning.

LUKE 9: 22	and be rejected of the elders and chief priests and scribes, and be **slain,**
11: 47	Woe unto you! for ye build the sepulchres of the prophets, and your fathers **killed** them,
LUKE 9: 27	But I tell you **of a truth,**
10: 2	The harvest **truly** _is_ great,
LUKE 9: 38	Master, **I beseech thee,** look upon my son:
14: 18	**I pray thee** have me excused,
LUKE 9: 41	how long shall I be with you, and suffer you? Bring thy son **hither.**
: 33	Master, it is good for us to be **here:**
LUKE 9: 59	But he said, Lord, **suffer me** first to go and bury my father.
: 61	but **let me** first go bid them farewell,
LUKE 10: 1	**whither** he himself would come.
: 33	as he journeyed, came **where** he was:
LUKE 10: 9	And heal the sick that are **therein,**
Matt. 10: 11	enquire who **in it** is worthy;
LUKE 10: 9	say unto them, The kingdom of God is come **nigh** unto you.
15: 1	Then drew **near** unto him all the publicans and sinners for to hear him.
LUKE 10: 11	**notwithstanding** be ye sure of this,
: 12	**But** I say unto you,
LUKE 10: 21	that thou hast hid these things from the **wise and prudent,**

N.B. note how the underlined word separates words and phrases having the same meaning.

LUKE 10: 30	and fell among thieves, which stripped him of his **raiment,**
8: 27	which had devils long time, and ware no **clothes,**
19: 35	and they cast their **garments** upon the colt,

Mark 12: 38	which love to go in long **clothing,**

LUKE 10: 33	and when he saw him, he had **compassion** *on him,*
: 37	And he said, He that shewed **mercy** on him,
Matt. 18: 33	Shouldest not thou also have had **comassion** on thy fellow-servant, even as I had **pity** on thee?

LUKE 10: 37	Then said Jesus unto him, Go, and do **likewise.**
: 1	After these things the Lord appointed other seventy **also,**

LUKE 10: 40	But Martha was **cumbered about** much serving,
: 41	Martha, Martha, thou art **careful** <u>and</u> **troubled about many things:**

N.B. note how the underlined word separates words and phrases having the same meaning.

LUKE 11: 2	Our Father which art in heaven, **hallowed** be thy name.
1: 49	For he that is mighty hath to me great things; and **holy** *is* his name.

LUKE 11: 22	he taketh from him all his armour **wherein** he trusted,
13: 14	There are six days **in which** men ought to work:

LUKE 11: 47	Woe unto you! for ye build the **sepulchres** of the prophets,
: 44	for ye are as **graves** which appear not,

LUKE 11: 51	**verily** I say unto you,
: 48	**Truly** ye bear witness that ye allow the deeds of your fathers: for they **indeed** killed them,

LUKE 12: 1	In the mean time, when there were gathered together an **innumerable multitude** of people,

N.B. The two bold words have the same meaning.

LUKE 12: 15	And he said unto them, **Take heed,** <u>and</u> **beware** of covetousness:

N.B. note how the underlined word separates words and phrases having the same meaning.

LUKE 12: 23	The life is more than **meat,** and the body *is more* than raiment.
1 Tim. 6: 8	And having **food** and raiment let us be therewith content.

LUKE 12: 23	The life is more than meat, and the body more than **raiment.**
Mark 12: 38	Beware of the scribes, which love to go in long **clothing,**

LUKE 12: 24	which neither have **storehouse** <u>nor</u> **barn;**

N.B. note how the underlined word separates words and phrases having the same meaning.

<u>LUKE 12: 25</u>	And which of you with taking thought can add to his **stature** one cubit?
Romans 8: 39	Nor **height**, nor depth, nor any other creature,
<u>LUKE 12: 27</u>	that Solomon in all his glory was not **arrayed** like one of these.
16: 19	which was **clothed** in purple and fine linen,
<u>LUKE 12: 37</u>	**verily** I say unto you,
: 44	**Of a truth** I say unto you,
<u>LUKE 12: 39</u>	And this know, that if the **goodman of the house** had known what hour the thief would come,
13: 25	When once the **master of the house** is risen up,
<u>LUKE 12: 39</u>	and not **suffered** his house to be broken through.
13: 8	Lord, **let** it alone this year,
<u>LUKE 12: 50</u>	and how am I **straitened** till it be accomplished!
2 Cor. 4: 8	*We are* **troubled** on every side,
<u>LUKE 12: 54</u>	When ye see a cloud rise out of the west, **straightway** ye say,
13: 13	And he laid *his* hands on her: and **immediately** she was made straight,
<u>LUKE 12: 58</u>	lest he **hail thee** to the judge, and the judge **deliver thee** to to the officer,
<u>LUKE 13: 2</u>	**Suppose ye** that these Galilaeans, were sinners above all the Galilaeans,
: 4	**think ye** that they were sinners above all men that dwelt in Jerusalem.
<u>LUKE 13: 6</u>	and he came and sought fruit **thereon,**
10: 6	your peace shall rest up**on it:**
Matt. 12: 11	will he not lay hold **on it,** and lift *it* out?
<u>LUKE 13: 7</u>	cut it down; why **cumbereth** the ground?
Mark 14: 4	and why was this **waste** of the ointment made?
<u>LUKE 13: 18</u>	Then said he, Unto what is the kingdom of God **like?** and whereunto shall I **resemble** it?
<u>LUKE 13: 24</u>	Strive to enter in at the **strait** gate:
Matt. 7: 14	Because strait *is* the gate, and **narrow** *is* the way,
<u>LUKE 13: 33</u>	**Nevertheless** I must walk to day, and to morrow,
: 27	**But** he shall say, I tell you,

LUKE 13: 35	and **verily** I say unto you,
11: 48	**Truly** ye bear witness that ye allow the deeds of your fathers: for they **indeed** killed them,
LUKE 14: 5	and will not **straightway** pull him out on the sabbath day?
13: 13	and **immediately** she was made straight, and glorified God.
LUKE 14: 12	lest they also bid thee again, and a **recompence** be made thee.
23: 41	for we receive the due **reward** of our deeds:
LUKE 14: 13	But when thou makest a feast, call the poor, the maimed, the **lame,** the blind:
: 21	and bring in hither the poor, and the maimed, and the **halt,** and the blind.
LUKE 14: 14	And thou shalt be blessed; for they cannot **recompense** thee:
10: 35	and whatsoever thou spendest more, I will **repay** thee.
LUKE 14: 29	**Lest haply,** after he hath laid the foundation,
20: 13	**it may be** that they will reverence *him* when they see him.
LUKE 14: 32	Or else, while the other is yet a great way off, he sendeth an **ambass**age, and desireth conditions of peace.
2 Cor. 5: 20	Now then we are **ambassadors** for Christ,
LUKE 14: 33	So **likewise,** whosoever he be of you that forsake all that he hath, cannot be my disciple.
: 12	Then said he **also** to him that bade him,
LUKE 14: 34	but if the salt have lost his savour, **wherewith** shall it be seasoned?
16: 2	How is it that I hear this of thee?
Mark 4: 30	or **with what** comparison shall we compare it?
LUKE 14: 34	but if the salt have lost his **savour,**
: 24	That none of those men which were bidden shall **taste** of my supper.
LUKE 15: 7	I say unto you, that **likewise** joy shall be in heaven over one sinner that repenteth,
14: 12	The said he **also** to him that bade him,
LUKE 15: 8	and sweep the house, and seek **diligently** till she find *it?*
Phil. 2: 28	I sent him therefore the **more carefully,**
LUKE 15: 10	**Likewise,** I say unto you,
14: 12	Then said he **also** to him that bade him,
LUKE 15: 23	And bring **hither** the fatted calf,

17: 21	Neither shall they say, Lo **here!**
LUKE 15: 25	and as he came and drew **nigh** to the house,
: 1	Then drew **near** unto him all the publicans and sinners for to hear him.
LUKE 15: 32	It was **meet** that we should make merry,
14: 34	Salt *is* **good:**
Matt. 20: 4	and whatsoever is **right** I will give you.
Acts 15: 5	That it was **needful** to circumcise them,
Heb. 9: 23	*It was* therefore **necessary** that the pattern of these...
LUKE 16: 21	**moreover** the dogs came and licked his sores.
2 Cor. 2: 12	**Furthermore,** when I came to Tro-as to *preach* Christ's gospel,
LUKE 16: 26	so that they which would pass from **hence** to you cannot;
17: 21	Neither shall they say, Lo **here!**
LUKE 16: 26	neither can they pass to us, that would come from **thence.**
17: 21	Lo here! or, lo **there!**
LUKE 17: 8	Make ready **where**with I may sup,
LUKE 17: 9	Doth he thank that servant be he did the things that were
	commanded him? I **trow** not.
13: 2	**Suppose** ye that these Galilaeans were sinners above all the Galilaeans.
: 4	**think** ye that they were sinners above all men that dwelt in Jerusalem?
LUKE 17: 28	**Likewise, also** as it was in the day of Lot;
LUKE 18: 16	**suffer** little children to come unto me, and forbid them not:
17: 31	**let** him likewise not to return back.
1Cor. 16: 7	but I trust to tarry a while with you, if the Lord **permit.**
LUKE 18: 17	**Verily** I say unto you,
21: 3	And we **indeed** justly;
23: 47	**Certainly** this was a righteous man.
LUKE 18: 20	Do not **kill,**
19: 20	Thou shalt do no **murder,**
LUKE 18: 22	sell all that thou hast, and **distribute** unto the poor,
Matt. 19: 21	go *and* sell that thou hast, and **give** to the poor,
LUKE 18: 30	Who shall not receive **manifold more** in this present time,

: 39	but he cried so **much the more,**
Matt. 10: 25	how **much more** *shall they call* them of his household?

LUKE 18: 35 And it came to pass, that as he **was come nigh** unto Jericho, and when he **was come near,**

LUKE 19: 21 I feared thee, because thou art an **austere** man:
Matt. 25: 24 Lord, I know thee that thou art an **hard** man,

LUKE 19: 30 **whereon** yet never man sat: loose him, and bring *him hither.*
Rev. 17: 9 The seven heads are seven mountains, **on which** the woman sitteth.

LUKE 19: 23 **Wheefore** then gavest not thou my money into the bank.
: 31 And if any man ask you, **Why** do ye loose *him*?

LUKE 19: 29 when he was come **nigh** to Beth-pha-ge and Bethany,
: 41 And when he was come **near,**

LUKE 19: 43 and **compass thee round, and** keep thee in on every side,

N.B. note how the underlined word separates words and phrases having the same meaning.

LUKE 19: 45 and began to cast out them that sold **therein,**

LUKE 20: 11 and en**treated** *him* shamefully, and sent *him* away empty.

LUKE 20: 13 I will send my beloved son: it may be they will **reverence** when they see him.
18: 20 **Honour** thy father and thy mother.
Rom. 2: 11 For there is no **respect** of persons with God.

LUKE 20: 20 so that they might deliver him unto the **power and authority** of the governor.

LUKE 20: 25 **Render** therefore unto Caesar the things that be Caesar's,
: 22 Is it lawful for us to **give** tribute unto Caesar, or no?

LUKE 20: 29 and the first took a wife, and died **without children.**
: 30 and the second took her to wife, and he died **childless.**
: 31 and they left **no children,** and died.

LUKE 21: 2 And he saw also a certain poor widow casting in **thither** two mites.
: 6 in the which **there** shall not be left one stone upon another,

LUKE 21: 4 but she of her **penury** hath cast in all the living that she had.
Mark 12: 44 but she of her **want** did cast in all that she had,

LUKE 21: 9	for these things must first come to pass; but the end *is* **not by and by.**
19: 40	if these should hold their peace, the stones would **immediately** cry out.
Matt. 24: 6	for all *these things* must come to pass, but the end is **not yet.**

| LUKE 21: 11 | And great earthquakes shall be in **divers** places, |
| 11: 42 | for ye tithe mint and rue and **all manner of** herbs, |

| LUKE 21: 15 | which all your adversaries shall be able to **gainsay nor resist.** |

N.B. note how the underlined word separates words and phrases having the same meaning.

| LUKE 21: 20 | then know that the desolation **thereof** is nigh. |
| : 21 | and let them which are in the midst **of it** depart out; |

| LUKE 21: 21 | and let not them that are in the countries enter **thereinto.** |
| 8: 32 | and they besought him that he would suffer them **to enter into them.** |

| LUKE 22: 1 | Now the feast of unleavened bread drew **nigh** which is called the Passover. |
| 24: 15 | Jesus himself drew **near,** and went with them. |

LUKE 22: 4	And he went his way, and **communed** with the chief priests and captains,
: 60	And immediately, while he yet **spake,** the cock crew.
24: 14	And they **talked** together of all these things which had happened.

| LUKE 22: 5 | And ye shall unto the **goodman** of the house, |
| 13: 25 | When the **master** of the house is risen up, |

| LUKE 22: 16 | For I say unto you, I wil not any more eat **thereof,** |
| 21: 21 | and let them which are in the midst **of it** depart out; |

| LUKE 22: 20 | **Likewise also** the cup after supper, |

| LUKE 22: 39 | And he came out, and went, **as he was wont** , to the mount of Olives; |
| 4: 16 | and, **as his custom was,** he went into the synagogue on the sabbath day, |

| LUKE 22: 42 | if thou be willing, **remove** this cup from me: |
| Mark 14: 36 | all things *are* possible unto thee; **take away** this cup from me: |

| LUKE 22: 42 | if thou be willing, remove this cup from me: **nevertheless** |

not my will, **but** thine, be done.

LUKE 22: 64   they **struck** him on the face, and asked him, saying, Prophesy, who is it that **smote** thee?

LUKE 23: 7   And as soon as he knew that he belonged under Herod's **jurisdiction,**

20: 20   that so they might deliver him unto the **power and authority** of the governor.

LUKE 23: 11   and **arrayed** him in a gorgeous robe,

16: 19   There was a certain rich man, which was **clothed** in and fine linen,

LUKE 23: 14   have found no fault in this man touching those things **whereof** ye accuse:

: 27   **which** also bewailed and lamented him.

LUKE 23: 16   I will therefore chastise him, and **release *him.***

: 22   I will therefore chastise him, and **let *him*** go.

LUKE 23: 27   And there followed him a great company of people, and of women, which also **bewailed and lamented** him.

N.B. note how the underlined word separates words and phrases having the same meaning.

LUKE 23: 34   And they parted his **raiment,** and cast lots.
Mark 12: 38   Beware of the scribes, which love to go in long **clothing,**

LUKE 23: 41   for we receive the due reward of our deeds: but this man hath done nothing **amiss.**
Matt. 20: 13   Friend, I do thee no **wrong:**

LUKE 23: 43   And Jesus said unto him, **Verily** I say unto thee,

: 41   And we **indeed** justly;

: 47   **Certainly** this was a righteous man.

21: 3   And he said, **Of a truth** I say unto you,

22: 22   And **truly** the Son of man goeth,

LUKE 23: 53   and lad it in a sepulchre that was hewn in stone, **wherein** never man before was laid.

LUKE 24: 4   behold, two men stood by them in shining **garments:**

: 12   he beheld the linen **clothes** laid by themselves,

LUKE 24: 5   And has they were **afraid,** and bowed down *their* faces to the earth,

: 37   But they were **terrified and affrighted,**

N.B. note how the underlined word separates words and phrases having the same meaning.

<u>**LUKE 24: 13**</u>	two of them went that same day to a village called Emmaus, which was from Jerusalem *about* threescore furlongs.
: 14	And they **talked** together of all these things which had happened.
: 15	And it came to pass, that, while they **communed** *together* and reasoned,
<u>**LUKE 24: 27**</u>	he **expounded** unto them in all the scriptures the things concerning himself.
: 45	Then **opened he their understanding,** that they might understand the scriptures,
<u>**LUKE 24: 46**</u>	and thus it **behoved** Christ to suffer,
23: 17	(For **of necessity** he must one unto them at the feast.)

JOHN

<u>**JOHN 1: 14**</u>	And the Word was made flesh, and dwelt among us, (and we beheld his glory, the glory as of the only begotten of the Father,) full of **grace** and truth.
Luke 2: 52	And Jesus increased in wisdom and stature, and in **favour** with God and man.
<u>**JOHN 1: 47**</u>	Jesus saw Nathanael coming to him, and saith of him, Behold an Israelite indeed, in whom is no **guile!**
Rom. 1: 29	full of envy, murder, debate, **deceit,** malignity;
<u>**JOHN 1: 48**</u>	Nathanael said unto him, **Whence** knowest thou me?
3: 4	Nicodemus saith unto him, **How** can a man be born when he is old?
<u>**JOHN 1: 51**</u>	And he saith unto him, **Verily, verily,** I say unto you,
: 47	Behold an Israelite **indeed,** in whom is no guile!
4: 18	in that saidst thou **truly.**
<u>**JOHN 2: 6**</u>	after the manner of the Jews, containing two or three firkins **apiece.**
Acts 2: 3	and it sat upon **each** of them.
<u>**JOHN 3: 5**</u>	**Verily, verily,** I say unto thee,
4: 18	in that saidst thou **truly.**
1: 47	Behold an Israelite **indeed** in whom is no guile!
Luke 22: 48	**Certainly** this was a righteous man.

JOHN 3: 8	The wind bloweth where it **listeth,**
4: 34	My meat is to do the **will** of him that sent me,
JOHN 3: 8	and thou hearest the sound **thereof,** but canst not whence it cometh,
7: 7	but me it hateth, because I testify **of it,** that the works **thereof** are evil.
JOHN 3: 15	That whosoever believeth in him should not perish, but have **eternal** life.
: 16	that whosoever believeth in him should not perish, but have **everlasting** life.
JOHN 4: 11	from **whence** then hast thou thatliving water?
: 20	that in Jerusalem is the place **where** men ought to wworship.
JOHN 4: 16	Jesus saith unto her, Go, call thy husband, and come **hither.**
: 9	There is a lad **here,** which hath five barley loaves, and two small fishes:
JOHN 4: 37	And **herein** is that saying true,
: 20	Our fathers worshipped **in this** mountain;
JOHN 4: 43	Now after two days he departed **thence,**
: 6	Now Jacob's well was **there.**
JOHN 4: 49	Sir, come down **ere** my child die.
5: 8	another steppeth down **before** me
JOHN 5: 3	In these lay a great multitude of **impotent** folk, of blind, halt, **withered,** waiting for the moving of the water.
Acts 20: 35	how that so labouring ye ought to support the **weak,**
JOHN 5: 3	of blind, **halt,** withered, waiting for the moving of the water.
Luke 14: 13	call the poor, the maimed, the **lame,** the blind:
JOHN 5: 13	And he that was healed **wist not** who it was:
2: 25	for he **knew** what was in man.
JOHN 5: 16	And therefore did the Jews persecute Jesus, and sought **to slay him,**
: 18	Therefore the Jews sought the more **to kill him,**
JOHN 5: 17	My Father worketh **hitherto,** and I work.
2: 10	*but* thou hast kept the good **until now.**
JOHN 5: 19	**Verily,** verily, I say unto you,
4: 18	in that saidst thou **truly.**

<u>**JOHN 5: 19**</u>	for what things soever he doeth, these **also** doeth the Son **likewise.**
<u>**JOHN 6: 2**</u>	And **a great multitude** followed him,
: 5	and saw **a great company** come unto him,
<u>**JOHN 6: 4**</u>	And the passover of the Jews was **nigh.**
4: 5	**near** to the parcel of ground that Jacob gave to his son Joseph.
<u>**JOHN 6: 5**</u>	he saith unto Philip, **Whence** shall we buy bread, that these may eat?
: 62	*What* and if ye shall see the Son of man ascend up **where** he was before?
<u>**JOHN 6: 16**</u>	And when **even** was *now* come,
Luke 24: 29	Abide with us: for it is toward **evening,**
<u>**JOHN 6: 19**</u>	they see Jesus walking on the sea, and drawing **nigh** unto the ship:
4: 5	**near** the parcel of ground that Jacob gave to his son Joseph.
<u>**JOHN 6: 21**</u>	and immediately the ship was at the land **whither** they went.
4: 19	and ye say, that in Jerusalem is the place **where** men ought to worship.
<u>**JOHN 6: 22**</u>	save that one **whereinto** his disciples were entered.
Luke 13: 14	There are six days **in which** men ought to work:
<u>**JOHN 6: 25**</u>	Rabbi, when camest thou **hither?**
: 9	There is a lad **here,** which hath five barley loaves,
<u>**JOHN 6: 26**</u>	Jesus answered them and said, **Verily, verily,**
Luke 22: 22	And **truly** the Son of man goeth, as it was determined:
<u>**JOHN 7: 7**</u>	The world cannot hate you; but me it hateth, because I testify **of it,** that the works **thereof** are evil.
<u>**JOHN 7: 10**</u>	then went he also up unto the feast, **not openly,** but as it were **in secret.**
<u>**JOHN 7: 13**</u>	**Howbeit** no man spake openly of him **for** fear of the Jews.
: 10	**But** when his brethren were gone up,
<u>**JOHN 7: 23**</u>	are ye angry at me, because I have made a man **every wit** whole on the Sabbath day?
9: 34	Though wast **altogether** born in sins,
<u>**JOHN 7: 52**</u>	Art thou also of Galilee? **Search <u>and</u> look:**

N.B. note how the underlined word separates words and phrases having the same meaning.

JOHN 8: 21	and ye shall seek me, and shall die in your sins: **whither** I go, ye cannot come.
: 19	Then said they unto him, **Where** is thy Father?

JOHN 8: 43	for I **proceeded forth and** came from God;

N.B. note how the underlined word separates words and phrases having the same meaning,

JOHN 8: 51	**Verily, verily,** I say unto you,
4: 18	in that thou saidst **truly.**

JOHN 9: 13	They brought to the Pharisees him that **aforetime was** blind.
: 8	The neighbours therefore, and they **which before** had seen him that he was blind,
Gal.1: 13	For ye have heard of my conversation **in time past,**

N.B. note that the second bold word in the first reference means the same as the second bold word.

JOHN 9: 30	The man answered and said unto them, Why **herein** is a marvellous thing,

JOHN 11: 4	This sickness is not unto death, but for the glory of God, that the Son of God might be glorified **thereby.**
12: 25	He that loveth his life shall lose it; and he that hateth his **in this** shall keep it unto life eternal.
13: 35	**By this** shall all *men* that ye are my disciples,

JOHN 11: 8	the Jews of late sought to stone thee, and goest thou **thither** again?
: 10	But if a man walk in the night, because **there** is no light in him.

JOHN 11: 13	**Howbeit** Jesus spoke of his death: **but** they thought that he had spoken of taking of rest in sleep.

JOHN 11: 31	when they saw Mary, that rose up **hastily,**
: 29	As soon as she heard *that*, she arose **quickly**, and came unto him.

JOHN 11: 50	Nor consider it is **expedient** for us, that one man should die for the people,
Acts 13: 46	and said, It was **necessary** that the word of God should first have been spoken to you,

JOHN 11: 54	Jesus therefore walked no more openly among the Jews; but went **thence** unto a country near to the wilderness,

12: 26	and where I am, **there** also my servant be:
JOHN 11: 55	And the Jews passover was **nigh at hand:**
: 54	but went thence unto a country **near** to the wilderness,

N.B. The second and third bold words in the first reference mean the same as the first word. All three words mean the same as the bold word in the second reference.

JOHN 12: 6	but because he was a thief, and had the bag, and bare what was put **therein.**
Acts 7: 5	And gave none inheritance **in it,**
JOHN 12: 13	and went forth to meet him, and cried **Hosanna:**
Luke 2: 14	**Glory to God** in the highest,
JOHN 12: 14	And Jesus, when he had found a young ass, sat **thereon;**
Matt. 23: 18	but whosoever sweareth by the gift that is **upon it,** he is guilty.
JOHN 12: 24	**Verily, verily,** I say unto you,
20: 30	And many other signs **truly** did Jesus in the presence of his disciples,
JOHN 13: 5	and to wipe *them* with the towel **wherewith** he was girded.
Rev. 19: 20	**with which** he deceived them that had received the mark of the beast,
JOHN 13: 7	What I do thou knowest not now; but thou shalt know here-**after.**
JOHN 13: 32	God shall glorify him in himself, and shall **straightway** shall glorify him.
: 30	He then having received the sop went **immediately** out:
JOHN 13: 33	and as I said unto the Jews, **Whither** I go, ye cannot come;
12: 1	**where** Lazarus was which had been dead,
JOHN 15: 8	**Herein** is my Father glorified, that ye bear much fruit;
12: 25	and he that hateth his life **in this** world shall keep it unto life eternal.
JOHN 16: 7	Nevertheless I tell you the truth; It is **expedient** for you that I go away:
Acts 13: 46	and said, **It was necessary** that the word of God should first have been spoken to you:
Jude 3	**it was needful** for me to write unto you,
JOHN 16: 13	**Howbeit** when he, the Spirit of truth is come,
: 22	**but** I will see you again,

JOHN 17: 26	that the love **wherewith** thou hast loved me may be in them,
Rev. 19: 20	**with which** he deceived them that had received the mark of the beast,

JOHN 17: 26	that the love **wherewith** thou hast loved me may be in them,
Rev. 19: 20	**with which** he deceived them that had received the mark of the beast,

JOHN 18: 2	for Jesus **oftimes** resorted thither with his disciples.
Luke 13: 34	how **often** would I have gathered thy children together,

JOHN 18: 2	for Jesus oftimes resorted **thither** with his disciples.
: 18	And the servants and officers stood **there,**
JOHN 18: 10	Then Simon Peter having a sword drew, and **smote** the high priest's servant and cut off his right ear.
: 22	one of the officers which stood by **struck** Jesus with the palm of his hand,

JOHN 18: 17	Then saith the **damsel** that kept the door unto the door,
Mark 14: 69	And a **maid** saw him again,

JOHN 18: 20	I ever taught in the synagogue, and in the temple, **whither** the Jews always resort;
: 1	he went forth with his disciples over the brook Ce-dron, **where** was a garden,

JOHN 18: 23	but if well, why **smitest** thou me?
Mark 14: 65	and the servants did **strike** him with the palms of their hands.

JOHN 19: 20	for the place where Jesus was crucified was **nigh to** the city:
: 42	for the sepulchre was **nigh at hand.**
21: 8	(for they were **not far** from land...)
Acts 7: 31	and as he drew **near to** behold *it,*
9: 3	And as he journeyed, he **came near** Damascus:

JOHN 19: 24	They parted my **raiment** among them, and for my **vesture** they did cast lots.
: 23	when they had crucified Jesus, took his **garments,**
20: 5	*and looking in,* saw the linen **clothes** lying;

JOHN 19: 34	But one of the soldiers with a spear pierced his side, and **forthwith** came there out blood and water.
21: 3	They went forth, and entered into a ship **immediately;**

JOHN 20: 15	Sir, if thou have **borne** him hence,
Acts 5: 6	And the young arose, wound him up, and **carried** *him* out,

JOHN 20: 15	Sir, if thou have borne him **hence,** tell me where thou hast
	laid him, and I will take him **away.**

JOHN 20: 23	Whose sover sins ye **remit,** they are **remitted** unto them;
Luke 23: 34	Then said Jesus, Father **forgive** them;
Acts 8: 22	if perhaps the thought of thine heart may be **forgiven** thee.
JOHN 20: 27	and behold my hands; and reach **hither** thy hand,
Acts 4: 10	*even* by him doth this man stand **here** before you whole.
JOHN 21: 18	**Verily, verily,** I say unto thee,
20: 30	And many other signs **truly** did Jesus in the presence of his disciples,
JOHN 21: 22	Jesus saith unto him, If I will that he **tarry** till I come,
Acts 1: 4	but **wait** for the promise of the Father,
JOHN 21: 9	they saw a fire of coals there, and fish laid **thereon,**
11: 38	It was a cave, and a stone laid **upon it.**

ACTS

ACTS 1: 3	and speaking of things **pertaining** to the kingdom of God:
Luke 9: 10	and went aside privately into a desert **belonging** to the city called Beth-sa-i-da.
ACTS 1: 5	but ye shall be baptized with the Holy Ghost not many days **hence.**
3: 26	sent him to bless you, in turning **away** every one of you from his iniquities.
ACTS 1: 10	behold, two men stood by them in white **apparel;**
10: 30	and behold, a man stood before me in bright **clothing.**
John 20: 5	And he stooping down, *and looking in,* saw the linen **clothes** lying; yet went he not in.
ACTS 1: 21	**Wherefore** of these men which have companied with us all the time that the Lord Jesus went in and out among us,
2: 26	**Therefore** did my heart reoice, and my tongue was glad;
ACTS 1:22	must one be **ordained** to be a witness with us of his resurrection.
: 23	And they **appointed** two,
: 24	shew whether of these two thou hast **chosen.**
ACTS 2: 8	And how hear we every man in our own tongue, **wherein** we were born?
1: 2	Until the day **in which** he was taken up,
ACTS 2: 22	a man approved of God among you by **miracles and**
	wonders and signs, which God did by him in the midst of

you,

N.B. note how the underlined word separates words and phrases having the same meaning.

<u>ACTS 2: 23</u>	Him, being delivered by the **determinate counsel and foreknowledge** of God.

N.B. see comment on previous verse.

<u>ACTS 2: 23</u>	and by wicked hands have crucified and **slain:**
3: 15	And **killed** the Prince of life,

<u>ACTS 2: 26</u>	and my tongue was glad; **moreover also** my flesh shal hope:

N.B. The two bold words mean the same as each other.

<u>ACTS 2: 32</u>	This Jesus hath God raised up, **whereof** we are all witnesses.
Heb. 7: 13	For he of whom these things are spoken pertaineth to
	another tribe, **of which** no man gave attendance at the altar.

<u>ACTS 2: 36</u>	Therefore let all the house of Israel know **assuredly,**
1: 5	For John **truly** baptized with water;

<u>ACTS 2: 38</u>	and be baptized every one of you in the name of Jesus Christ
	for the **remission of sins,**
5: 31	for to give repentance to Israel, and **forgiveness of sins.**

<u>ACTS 2: 40</u>	Save yourselves from this **froward** generation.
: 23	ye have taken, and by **wicked** hands have crucified and slain:

Phil. 2: 15	without rebuke, in the midst of a **crooked and** perverse
	nation,

N.B. note how the underlined word separates words and phrses having the same meaning.

<u>ACTS 3: 17</u>	brethren, I **wot** that through ignorance ye did *it*,
: 16	whom ye see and **know:**

<u>ACTS 4: 3</u>	and put *them* in hold unto the next day: for it was **eventide.**
John 20: 19	Then the same day at **evening,**

<u>ACTS 4: 6</u>	and as many as were of the **kin**dred of the high priest,
Eph. 3: 15	Of whom the whole family in heaven and earth is named,

<u>ACTS 4: 9</u>	If we this day be examined of the good deed done to the
	impotent man,
20: 35	how that so labouring ye ought to support the **weak,**

| ACTS 4: 11 | This the stone which was set at **nought** of you builders, |
| : 21 | they let them go, finding **nothing** how they might punish them, |

| ACTS 4: 12 | for there is none other name under heaven given among men, **whereby** we must be saved. |
| 6: 10 | And they were not able to resist the wisdom and the spirit **by which** he spake. |

| ACTS 5: 10 | Then fell she down **straightway** at his feet, |
| 3: 7 | and **immediately** his feet and ankle bones received strength. |

| ACTS 5: 12 | And by the hands of the apostles were many signs and wonders **wrought** among the people; |
| 4: 16 | for that indeed a notable miracle hath been **done** by them *is* manifest to all them that dwell in Jerusalem; |

| ACTS 5: 15 | Insomuch **that** they brought forth the sick into the streets, |
| 16: 26 | And suddenly there was a great earthquake, **so that** the foundations of the prison were shaken: |

| ACTS 5: 21 | and called the **council** together, and all the **senate** of the children of Israel, |

| ACTS 5: 39 | **lest haply** ye be found even to fight against God. |
| 8: 22 | and pray God, **if perhaps** the thought of thine heart may be forgiven thee. |

| ACTS 6: 3 | **Wherefore**, brethren, look ye out among you seven men of honest report, |
| 8: 4 | **Therefore** they that were scattered abroad went every where preaching the word. |

| ACTS 6: 7 | And the word of God **increased**; and the number of the disciples **multiplied** in Jerusalem greatly; |

| ACTS 6: 11 | Then they **suborned** men, |
| : 13 | And **set up false witnesses,** |

| ACTS 7: 4 | and dwelt in Char-ran, and from **thence,** |
| : 11 | Now **there** came a dearth over all the land of Egypt and Cha-na-an, |

| ACTS 7: 4 | he removed him into this land, **wherein** ye now dwell. |
| : 20 | **In which** time Moses was born, |

| ACTS 7: 6 | That his seed should **sojourn** in a strange land; |
| : 4 | he removed him into this land, wherein ye now **dwell.** |

| ACTS 7: 34 | I have seen the **affliction** of my people which is in Egypt. |

: 6	and that they should bring into **bondage,**
ACTS 7: 40	for *as for* this Moses, which brought us out of the land of Egypt, we **wot not** what has become of him.
Matt. 26: 74	the began to curse and to swear, *saying* I **know not** the man,
ACTS 8: 9	But there was a certain man, called Simon, which **before**time in the same city used sorcery,
ACTS 8: 25	when they had testified and preached **the word of the Lord,** returned to Jerusalem, and preached **the gospel** in many villages of the Samaritans.
: 14	Now when the apostles heard that the Samaritans had received **the word of God,**
: 5	Then Philip went down to the city of Samaria, and preached **Christ** unto them.
: 4	Therefore they that were scattered abroad went every where preaching **the word.**
ACTS 8: 30	And Philip ran **thither** to *him,*
: 8	And **there** was great joy in that city.
ACTS 9: 19	And when he had received **meat,** he was strengthened.
14: 17	and fruitful seasons, filling our hearts with **food** and gladness.
ACTS 9: 20	And **straightway** he preached Christ in the synagogues,
: 18	And **immediately** there fell from his eyes as it had been scales: And he received sight **forthwith,**
ACTS 9: 21	and came **hither** for that intent,
: 14	And **here** he hath authority from the chief priests to bind all that call on thy name.
ACTS 9: 29	but they went about **to slay him:**
: 23	the Jews took council **to kill him:**
ACTS 9: 36	this woman was full of **good works and almsdeeds** which she did.

N.B. note how the underlined word separates words and phrases having the same meaning.

ACTS 9: 38	And **forasmuch as** Lydda was nigh to Joppa,

N.B. The two bold words have the same meaning.

ACTS 9: 38	And forasmuch as Lydda was **nigh** to Joppa,
: 3	And as he journeyed, he came **near** Damascus:

<u>**ACTS 9: 39**</u>	and showing the coats and **garments** which Dorcas,
7: 58	and the witnesses laid down their **clothes** at a young man's feet whose name was Saul.
<u>**ACTS 9: 43**</u>	And it came to pass, that he **tarried** many days in Joppa with one Simon a tanner.
12: 19	And he went down from Judaea to Caesarea, and *there* **abode.**
27: 41	and the forepart stuck fast, and **remained** immoveable,
<u>**ACTS 10: 2**</u>	*A* devout *man,* <u>**and**</u> one that feared God with all his house,

N.B. note how the underlined word separates words and phrases having the same meaning.

<u>**ACTS 10: 4**</u>	Thy prayers and thine alms are come up for a **memorial** before God.
: 31	and thine alms are had in **remembrance** in the sight of God.
<u>**ACTS 10: 12**</u>	**Wherein** were all manner of fourfooted beasts of the earth,
1: 2	Unto the day **in which** he was taken up,
<u>**ACTS 10: 16**</u>	This was done **thrice:**
11: 10	And this was done **three times:**
<u>**ACTS 10: 24**</u>	and had called together his **kins**men and near friends.
<u>**ACTS 10: 29**</u>	Therefore came I *unto you* without gainsaying, **as soon as** I was sent for:
: 33	**immediately** therefore I sent to thee;
<u>**ACTS 10: 32**</u>	Send therefore to Joppa, and call **hither** Simon,
: 33	Now therefore are we all **here** present before God,
<u>**ACTS 10: 39**</u>	whom they **slew** and hanged on a tree:
12: 2	And he **killed** James the brother of John with the sword.
<u>**ACTS 11: 5**</u>	A certain vessel **descend,** as it had been a great sheet, **let down** from heaven by four corners;
<u>**ACTS 11: 7**</u>	And I heard a voice saying unto me, Arise, Peter; **slay** and eat.
10: 13	And there came a voice to him, Rise, Peter; **kill,** and eat.
<u>**ACTS 11: 14**</u>	Who shall tell thee words, **whereby** thou and all thy house shall be saved.
6: 10	And they were not able to resist the wisdom and the spirit **by which** he spake.
<u>**ACTS 11: 28**</u>	and signified by the Spirit that there should be great **dearth** throughout all the world:

| Luke 15: 14 | there arose a mighty **famine** in that land; |

ACTS 12: 7   and he **smote** Peter on the side,
John 18: 22   one of the officers which stood by **struck** Jesus with the palm of his hand,

ACTS 12: 9   and **wist not** that it was true which was done by the angel;
John 21: 4   but they **knew not** thait was Jesus.

ACTS 12: 10   and **forthwith** the angel departed from him.
: 23   and **immediately** the angel of the Lord smote him,

ACTS 12: 11   Now I know **of a surety**, that the Lord hath sent his angel,
10: 34   Then Peter opened *his* mouth, and said, **Of a truth** I perceive that God is no respecter of persons:

ACTS 12: 13   a **damsel** came to hearken, named Rhoda.
Luke 22: 56   But a certain **maid** beheld him as he sat by the fire,

ACTS 12: 21   And upon a set day Herod, arrayed in royal **apparel**,
10: 30   and, behold, a man stood before me in bright **clothing**,

ACTS 13: 2   Separate me Barnabas and Saul for the work **whereunto** I have called them.
26: 7   **For which** hope's sake, I am accused by the Jews.

ACTS 13: 4   and from **thence** they sailed to Cyprus.
: 1   Now **there** were in the church that was at Antioch certain prophets and teachers;

ACTS 13: 28   yet desired they Pilate that he should be **slain**.
12: 2   And he **killed** James the brother of John with the sword.

ACTS 14: 6   They were **ware** of *it*,
Luke 12: 46   and at an hour when he is not **aware**,

ACTS 14: 8   And there sat a certain man at Lystra, **impotent in his feet**, **being a cripple** from his mother's womb, who **never had walked**:

ACTS 14: 15   We also are men of like passions with you, and preach unto you that ye should turn from these **vanities** to the living God,
Rom. 2: 22   dost thou commit adultery? Thou that abhorrest **idols**,

ACTS 14: 15   and the sea, and all things that are **therein**:
7: 5   And he gave him noninheritance **in it**,

ACTS 14: 20   **Howbeit**, as the disciples round about him, he rose up,

: 5   **But** the Jews which believed not, moved with envy,
17: 20   **Nevertheless** he left not himself without witness,

<u>ACTS 14: 26</u>	And **thence** sailed to Antioch,
: 7	And **there** they preached the gospel.
<u>ACTS 14: 26</u>	from **whence** they had been recommended for the grace...
	and visit our brethren in every city **where** we have preached...
<u>ACTS 14: 27</u>	they **rehearsed** all that God had done with them,
15: 4	and they **declared** all things God had done with them.
16: 36	And the keeper of the prison **told** this saying to Paul,
<u>ACTS 15: 2</u>	When therefore Paul and Barnabas had no small **dissension**
	and disputation with them,

N.B. note how the underlined word separates words and phrases having the same meaning.

<u>ACTS 15: 12</u>	declaring what miracles and wonders God **had wrought**
	among the Gentiles by them.
14: 27	they rehearsed all that God **had done** by them.
<u>ACTS 15: 16</u>	and I will build again the ruins **thereof,**
13: 17	and with an high arm he brought them out **of it.**
<u>ACTS 15: 19</u>	**Wherefore** my sentence is,
: 10	Now **therefore** why tempt ye God,
<u>ACTS 15: 24</u>	Forasmuch **as** we have heard,

N.B. The bold word means the same as the first word in the phrase.

<u>ACTS 15: 28</u>	to lay upon you no greater than these **necessary** things;
: 5	That it was **needful** to circumcise them,
<u>ACTS 15: 30</u>	and when they had gathered the multitude together, they
	delivered the **epistle:**
23: 25	And he wrote a **letter** after this manner:
<u>ACTS 15: 33</u>	And after they had **tarried** *there* a space,
17: 14	but Silas and Timotheus **abode** there still.
19: 10	so that all they which **dwelt** in Asia heard the word of the
	Lord Jesus,
: 22	but he himself **stayed** in Asia for a season.
<u>ACTS 16: 10</u>	assuredly gathering that the Lord had called us for to
	preach **the gospel** unto them.
8: 25	And they, when they had testified and preached **the word**
	of the Lord,
11: 1	And the apostles and the brethren that were in Judaea
	heard that the Gentiles had also received **the word of God.**
2 Tim. 2: 8	Remember that **Jesus Christ** of the seed of David was

Rev. 1: 2	raised from the dead according to my **gospel:** Who bare record of **the word of God,** and of the testimony of **Jesus Christ,**
ACTS 16: 12 18: 11	And from **thence** to Philippi, And he continued *there* a year and six months,
ACTS 16: 15 26: 11	And she **constrained** us. and **compelled** *them* to blaspheme;
ACTS 16: 16 Luke 22: 56	a certain **damsel** possessed with a spirit of divination met us, But a certain **maid** beheld him as he sat by the fire,
ACTS 16: 33 : 26	and was baptized, he and all his, **straightway.** and **immediately** all the doors were opened,
ACTS 16: 37 John 11: 28	and now do they thrust us out **privily?** and called Mary her sister **secretly,**
ACTS 16: 37 5: 23	nay **verily;** but let them come themselves and fetch us out. Saying, The prison **truly** found we shut up with all safety,
ACTS 17: 6 16: 28	These that have turned the world upside down are come **hither** also; Do thyself no harm: we are all **here.**
ACTS 17: 19 Heb. 7: 13	May we know what this new doctrine, **whereof** thou speakest, *is?* **of which** no man gave attendance at the altar.
ACTS 17: 24 7: 5	God that made and all things **therein,** And he gave him none inheritance **in it,**
ACTS 17: 27 8: 22	**if haply** they might feel after him, and pray God, **if perhaps** the thought of thine heart be forgiven thee.
ACTS 18: 4	And he **reasoned** in the synagogue every sabbath, and **persuaded** the Jews and the Greeks.
ACTS 18: 6 16: 22	and blasphemedm he shook *his* **raiment,** and the magistrates rent off their **clothes,**
ACTS 18: 25 Phil. 2: 28	he spake and taught **diligently** the things of the Lord. I sent him therefore the more **carefully,**
ACTS 18: 26 21: 19	and **expounded** unto him the way of God more perfectly. he **declared** particularly what things God had wrought among the Gentiles by his ministry.

<u>ACTS 19: 4</u>	Then said Paul, John **verily** baptized with the baptism of repentance,
<u>ACTS 19: 9</u>	But when **divers** were hardened,
: 18	And **many** that believed came and confessed,
<u>ACTS 19: 11</u>	And God **wrought** special miracles by the hands of Paul:
: 14	And there were seven sons of *one* Sce-va, a Jew, *and* chief of the priests, which **did** so.
<u>ACTS 19: 26</u>	**Moreover** ye see and hear, that not alone at Ephesus,
2 Cor. 2: 12	**Furthermore,** when I came to Tro-as to *preach* Christ's Christ's gospel.
<u>ACTS 19: 27</u>	So that not only this our craft is in danger to be set at **nought;**
: 36	ye ought to be quiet, and to do **nothing** rashly.
<u>ACTS 19: 30</u>	And when Paul would have entered in unto the people disciples **suffered** him not.
26: 1	Then Agrippa said unto Paul, Thou art **permitted** to speak for thyself.
<u>ACTS 19: 31</u>	desiring *him* that he would not ad**venture** himself into the theatre.
<u>ACTS 19: 32</u>	for the assembly was confused; and the more part knew not **wherefore** they were come together.
John 9: 30	**Why** herein is a marvellous thing,
<u>ACTS 19: 38</u>	**Wherefore if** De-me-tri-us, and the craftsmen which are with him,
: 32	Some **therefore** cried one thing, and some another:
<u>ACTS 19: 40</u>	there being no cause **whereby** we may give an account of this concourse.
26: 7	**For which** hope's sake, king Agrippa, I am accused of the Jews.
<u>ACTS 19: 40</u>	there being no cause whereby we may give an account of this **concourse.**
: 41	And when he had thus spoken, he dismissed the **assembly.**
<u>ACTS 20: 5</u>	These going before **tarried** for us at Tro-as.
: 6	Where we **abode** seven days.
17: 16	Now while Paul **waited** for them at Athens,
<u>ACTS 20: 33</u>	I have coveted no man's silver, or gold, or **apparel.**
10: 30	and, behold, a man stood before in bright **clothing,**

ACTS 21: 24	and all may know that those things, **whereof** they were concerning thee, are nothing;
Heb. 7: 13	**of which** no man gave attendance at the altar.
ACTS 21: 30	and **forthwith** the doors were shut.
: 32	Who **immediately** took soldiers and centurions,
ACTS 21: 34	and when he could know the certainty for the **tumult,**
Titus 1: 6	having faithful children not accused of **riot** and unruly.
ACTS 21: 35	so it was, that he **was borne** of the soldiers for the violence of the people.
: 34	he commanded him to be **carried** into the castle.
ACTS 21: 39	a citizen of no mean city: and, **I beseech thee,** suffer me to speak to the people.
24: 4	**I pray thee** that thou wouldest hear us of thy clemency a few words.
ACTS 21: 39	and, I beseech thee, **suffer me to** speak unto the people.
23: 15	which they themselves **allow,**
ACTS 22: 3	I am **verily** a man *which am* a Jew, born in Tarsus,
: 9	And they that were with me saw **indeed** the light,
ACTS 22: 20	and consenting unto his death, and kept the **raiment** of them slew him.
: 9	And as they cried out, and cast off *their* **clothes,**
ACTS 22: 29	Then **straightway** they departed from him which should have examined him:
21: 32	Who **immediately** took soldiers and centurions,
ACTS 23: 2	And the high priest An-a-ni-as commanded them that stood by him to **smite** him on the mouth.
Mark 14: 65	Prophesy: and the servants did **strike** him with the palms of their hands.
ACTS 23: 5	Then said Paul, I **wist not,** brethren,
19: 32	and the more part **knew not** wherefore they were come together.
ACTS 23: 7	there arose **a dissension** between Pharisees and the Sad-du-cees:
John 10: 19	There was **a divison** therefore again among the Jews for these sayings.
ACTS 23: 33	and delivered the **epistle** to the governor,
: 25	And he wrote a **letter** after this manner:

ACTS 24: 4	**Notwithstanding,** that I be not further tedious unto thee,
: 7	**But** the chief captain Lys-i-as came *upon us,*
ACTS 24: 8	by examining of whom thyself mayest take knowledge of all these things, **whereof** we accuse him.
Heb. 7: 13	**of which** no man gave attendance at the altar.
ACTS 24: 9	And these Jews also **assented,**
23: 20	And he said, The Jews have **agreed** to desire thee...
ACTS 24: 26	wherefore he sent for him the oftener, and **communed with** him.
10: 27	And as he **talked with** him, he went in,
19: 6	and they **spake with** tongues,
ACTS 25: 6	And when he had **tarried** among them more than ten days,
19: 22	but he himself **stayed** in Asia for a season.
22: 12	having a good report of all the Jews which **dwelt** *there,*
21: 8	which was *one* of the seven;
ACTS 25: 11	but if there be none of these things **whereof** these accuse me,
Heb. 7: 13	**of which** no man gave attendance at the altar.
ACTS 25: 17	Therefore, when they were come **hither,**
: 24	And Festus said, King Agrippa, and all men which are **here** presence with us,
ACTS 25: 27	For it seemeth to me unreasonable to send a prisoner, and not **withal** to signify the crimes *laid* against him.
26: 29	but also all that hear me this day, were both almost, and **altogether** such as I am,
ACTS 26: 2	because I shall answer for myself this day before thee touching all the things **whereof** I am accused of the Jews:
Heb. 7: 13	**of which** no man gave attendance at the altar.
ACTS 26: 3	**wherefore** I beseech thee to hear me patiently.
25: 17	**Therefore,** when they come hither,
ACTS 26: 3	wherefore **I beseech thee** to hear me patiently.
24: 4	**I pray thee** that thou wouldest hear us of thy clemency a few words.
ACTS 26: 9	I **verily** thought with myself,
22: 9	And they that were with me **indeed** the light,
ACTS 26: 20	that they should repent and turn to God, and do works **meet** for repentance.
: 31	This man doeth nothing **worthy** of death or of bonds.
ACTS 27: 6	And there the centurion found a ship of Alexandria sailing

	into Italy; and he put us **therein.**
7: 5	and he gave him no inheritance **in it,**
ACTS 27: 8	**nigh** whereunto was the city *of* La-se-a.
23: 15	and we, or ever he come **near,**
ACTS 27: 8	nigh **where**unto was the city *of* La-se-a.
ACTS 27: 11	**Nevertheless** the centurion believed the master and the owner,
: 14	**But** not long after there arose against it a tempestuous wind,
: 27	**Howbeit** we must be cast upon a certain island.
ACTS 27: 17	fearing lest they should fall into the quicksands, **strake** sail,
John 18: 22	one of the officers which stood by **struck** Jesus...
ACTS 28: 14	Where we found brethren, and were desired to **tarry** with them
	seven days:
27: 31	Except these **abide** in the ship,
ACTS 28: 19	I was **constrained** to appeal unto Caesar;
26: 11	and **compelled** *them* to blaspheme;

ROMANS

ROMANS 1: 2	(Which he had promised **afore** by his prophets in the holy
	scriptures,)
Glatians 1: 13	For ye have heard of my conversation **in time past time** in
	the Jews' religion,
ROMANS 1: 5	By whom we have received **grace** and apostleship,
Acts 7: 46	Who found **favour** before God,
ROMANS 1: 13	Now I would not have you ignorant brethren, that **often**times
	I purposed to come unto you,
ROMANS 1: 13	that oftentimes I purposed to come unto you, (but was **let**
	hitherto,)
15: 22	For which cause also I have been **much hindered** from
	coming to you.
ROMANS 1: 13	that oftentimes I purposed to come unto you, (but was let
	hitherto,)
8: 22	For we know that the whole creation groaneth and travaileth
	until now.
ROMANS. 1: 15	I am ready to preach **the gospel** to you that are at Rome also.
Acts 16: 6	Now when they had gone throughout Phryg-i-a and the
	region of Galatia, and were forbidden of the Holy Ghost to
	preach **the word** in Asia,

Acts 13: 5	And when they were at Salamis, they preached **the word of God** in the synagogues of the Jews:
Rom. 15: 16	ministering the **the gospel of God,**
Rev. 1: 2	Who bare record of **the word of God,** and of the testimony of **Jesus Christ,**
19: 13	and his name is called **The Word of God.**

ROMANS 1: 16 For I am not ashamed of the gospel of Christ: for it is the power of God unto salvation to **every one** that believeth;

: 7 To **all** that be in Rome, beloved of God,

ROMANS 1: 17 For **therein** is the righteousness of God revealed from faith to faith:

ROMANS 1: 24 **Wherefore** God also gave them up to uncleanness through the lusts of their own hearts,

: 26 **For this cause** God gave them up unto vile affections:

2: 1 **Therefore** thou art inexcusable,

ROMANS 1: 27 And **likewise also** the men leaving the natural use of the woman, burned in their lust one toward another;

ROMANS 1: 27 and receiving in themselves that **recompence** of their error which was meet.

4: 4 Now to him that worketh is the **reward** not reckoned of grace, but of debt.

ROMANS 1: 27 and receiving in themselves that recompence of their error which was **meet.**

3: 26 that he might be **just** and justifier of him which believeth in Jesus.

ROMANS 2: 1	for **wherein** thou judgest another, thou condemnest thyself;
Mark 6: 10	And he said unto them, **in what** place soever ye enter into an house,

ROMANS 2: 4 Or despiseth thou the riches of his goodness, and **forbearance and longsuffering;**

5: 3 but we glory in tribulations also: knowing that tribulation worketh **patience;**

N.B. note how the underlined word separates words and phrases having the same meaning. Note also that the three bold words in the first reference means the same as the word 'patience' and vice-versa.

ROMANS 2: 18	And knowest *his* will, and approvest the things that are **more excellent,**
Hebrews 1: 4	Being made **so much better** han the angels,

ROMANS 2: 25 For circumcision **verily** profiteth, if thou keep the law:

Acts 5: 23	Saying, The prison **truly** found we shut with all safety,
ROMANS 3: 1	What **advantage** then hath the Jew? Or what **profit** *is there* of circumcision?
ROMANS 3: 3	For what if some did not believe shall their unbelief make the faith of God **without effect?**
4: 14	For if they which are of the law *be* heirs, faith is **made void,** And the promise **of none effect:**
ROMANS 3: 24	Being justified freely by his grace through the **redemption** that is in Christ Jesus:
Acts 28: 28	Be it known therefore unto you, that the **salvation** of God **is** sent unto the Gentiles,
ROMANS 3: 24	Being **justified** freely by his grace through the redemption that is in Christ Jesus:
: 25	**to declare** his **righteous**ness for the remission of sins that are past,
ROMANS 3: 25	Whom God set forth *to be* a **propitiation** through faith in his blood,
5: 11	by whom we have received **the atonement.**
2 Cor. 5: 18	And all things *are* of God, who hath reconciled us to himself By Jesus Christ, and hath given to us the ministry of **reconciliation;**
ROMANS 3: 25	to declare his righteousness for the **remisson** of sins that are past,
Acts 5: 31	for to give repentance to Israel, and **forgiveness** of sins.
ROMANS 3: 25	through the **forbearance** of God;
5: 33	knowing that tribulation worketh **patience;**
ROMANS 4: 1	What shall we say then that Abraham our father, as **pertaining** To the flesh, hath found?
Luke 9: 10	and went aside privately into a desert place **belonging** to the city called Beth-sa-i-da.
ROMANS 4: 3	and it was **counted** unto him for righteousness.
: 9	for we say that faith was **reckoned** to Abraham for righteousness.
: 11	that righteousness might be **imputed** unto them also:
ROMANS 4: 10	How was it then reckoned? when he was in circumcision, or in **uncircumcision? Not** in circumcision,

N.B. note that the bold word and parts of a word mean the same.

ROMANS 4: 19	And being **not weak** in faith,

: 20	but was **strong** in faith, giving glory to God;
ROMANS 5: 2	By whom also we have access by faith into this grace **wherein** we stand,
1 Cor. 11: 23	That the Lord Jesus the *same* night **in which** he was betrayed took bread:
ROMANS 5: 7	yet **peradventure** for a good man some would even dare to die.
2 Cor. 2: 7	lest **perhaps** such a one should be swallowed up with over-much sorrow.
ROMANS 5: 12	**Wherefore,** as by one man sin entered into the world,
: 18	**Therefore** as by the offence of one *judgment came* upon all men to condemnation:
ROMANS 5: 20	**Moreover** the law entered, that the offence might abound.
2 Cor. 2: 12	**Furthermore,** when I came to Tro-as to *preach* Christ's gospel,
ROMANS 6: 2	How shall we, that are dead to sin live any longer **therein?**
Acts 7: 5	and he gave him none inheritance **in it,**
ROMANS 6: 6	that **henceforth** we should not serve sin.
: 19	even so **now** yield your members servants to righteousness unto holiness.
ROMANS 6: 11	**Likewise** reckon ye **also** yourselves to be dead indeed unto sin,
ROMANS 6: 12	Let not sin therefore reign in your mortal body, that ye should obey it in the lusts **thereof.**
John 7: 7	but me it hateth, because I testify **of it,** that the works **thereof** are evil.
ROMANS 6: 14	For sin shall not **have dominion** over you:
: 12	Let not sin therefore **reign** in your mortal body,
ROMANS 6: 21	What fruit had ye then in those things **whereof** ye are now ashamed?
Hebrews 7: 13	**of which** no man gave attendance at the altar.
ROMANS 7: 6	that being dead **wherein** we were held;
1 Cor. 11: 23	Then the night **in which** he was betrayed took bread:
ROMANS 7: 8	wrought in me all manner of **concupiscence.**
1 Peter 2: 11	abstain from **fleshly lusts,** which war against the soul;
Ephesians 2: 3	Among whom also we all had our conversation in times past in **the lusts of our flesh,** fulfilling **the desires of the flesh and of the mind;**

ROMANS 8: 13	but if ye through the Spirit do **mortify** the deeds of the body,
7: 4	Wherefore, my brethren, ye also are **become dead** to the law by the body of Christ;
ROMANS 9: 22	endured with much **longsuffering** the vessels of wrath fitted to destruction:
8: 25	But if we hope for that which we see not, *then* do we with **patience** wait for *it.*
ROMANS 10: 4	For Christ *is* the end of the law for righteousness to **every one**
: 12	fot the same Lord over all is rich unto **all** that call upon him.
: 13	For **whosoever** shall call upon the name of the Lord shall be saved.
ROMANS 10: 8	The word is **nigh** thee, *even* in thy mouth,
Acts 27: 27	about midnight the shipmen deemed that they drew **near** some country;
ROMANS 10: 18	Yes **verily** their sound went into all the earth,
John 17: 8	and have **surely** that I came out from thee,
2 Cor. 12: 12	**Truly** the signs of an apostle were wrought among you in all patience,
ROMANS 11: 2	**Wot ye not** what the scripture saith of Elias?
1 Cor. 6: 15	**Know ye not** that your bodies are the members of Christ?
ROMANS 11: 9	And David saith, Let their table be made **a snare, and a trap, and a stumblingblock,**

N.B. note how the underlined words separate words and phrases having the same meaning.

ROMANS 11: 14	If by any means I may provoke to **emulation** *them which are* my flesh,
: 11	for to provoke them to **jealousy.**
ROMANS 12: 1	**I beseech you** therefore, brethren, by the mercies of God,
Acts 27: 34	Wherefore **I pray you** to take *some* meat:
ROMANS 12: 11	Not **slothful** in business;
Matt. 20: 3	And saw others standing **idle** in the marketplace,
ROMANS 12: 17	**Recompense** to no man evil for evil.
: 19	I will **repay**, saith the Lord.
ROMANS 13: 1	For there is no power but of God: the powers that be are **ordained** of God.
1 Cor. 4: 9	For I think that God hath set forth us the apostles last, as it were **appointed** to death:

ROMANS 13: 7	**Render** therefore to all their dues:
14: 12	So then every one of us shall **give** an account of himself to God.
ROMANS 13: 9	and if *there be* any other commandment, it is briefly **comprehended** in this saying, Thou shalt love thy neighbour as thyself.
1 Cor. 13: 11	I **understood** as a child,
ROMANS 14: 10	But why dost thou set at **nought** thy brother?
: 14	that *there is* **nothing** unclean of itself:
ROMANS 15: 4	For whatsoever things were written **aforetime** were written for our learning,
Acts 8: 9	But there was a certain man, Simon, which **beforetime** in the same city used sorcery,
ROMANS 15: 11	And again, **Praise the Lord,** all ye Gentiles; and **laud him,**
ROMANS 15: 14	filled with all knowledge, able also to **admonish** one another.
1 Cor. 4: 14	I write not these things to shame you, but as my beloved sons I **warn** *you.*
ROMANS 15: 16	ministering **the gospel of God,**
Acts 13: 44	And the next sabbbath day came almost the whole city together to hear **the word of God.**
8: 25	when they had testified and preached **the word of the Lord,** returned to Jerusalem, preached **the gospel** in many villages of the Smaritans.
10: 36	**The word** which *God* sent unto the children of Israel,
	preaching peace by **Jesus Christ:**
2 Tim. 2: 8	Remember that **Jesus Christ** of the seed of David was raised from the dead according to my **gospel:**
Rev. 1: 2	Who bare record of **the word of God,** and the testimony of **Jesus Christ,**
19: 13	And his name is called **The Word of God.**
John 1: 1	In the beginning was **the Word,**
ROMANS 15: 17	I have therefore **whereof** I may glory through Jesus Christ in those things which pertain to God.
Hebrews 7:13	**of which** no man gave attendance at the altar.
ROMANS 15: 18	For I wil not dare to speak of those things which Christ hath not **wrought** by me,
1 Cor. 5: 2	...hath **done** this deed might be taken away from among you.
ROMANS 16: 2	for she hath been **a succourer** of many,
: 9	Salute Ur-bane, our **helper** in Christ,

1 COR. 1: 2	to them that are **sanctified** in Christ Jesus,
1 Cor. 6: 11	but ye are **washed,** but ye were **sanctified,**
Acts 11: 9	What God hath **cleansed,** *that* call not thou common.
1 COR. 1: 3	**Grace** *be* unto you, and peace,
Acts 2: 47	Praising God, and having **favour** with all the people.
1 COR. 1: 8	*that ye may be* **blameless** in the day of our Lord Jesus Christ.
2: 6	Howbeit we speak wisdom among them that are **perfect:**
1 COR. 1:10	Now **I beseech you,** brethren, by the name of our Lord Jesus Christ,
Acts 27: 34	Wherefore **I pray you** to take *some* meat:
1 COR. 1: 11	that there are **contentions** among you.
: 10	and *that* there be no **divisions** among you;
3: 3	and **strife,** and divisions,
1 COR. 1: 17	For Christ sent me not to baptize, but to preach **the gospel:**
: 23	But we preach **Christ** crucified,
Mark 7:13	Making **the word of God** of none effect through your tradition,
1 COR. 1: 28	and things which are not, to **bring to nought** things that are:
: 19	and will **bring to nothing** the understanding of the prudent.
1 COR. 2: 6	**Howbeit** we speak wisdom among them that are perfect:
: 7	**But** we speak the wisdom of God in a mystery,
1 COR. 2: 7	which God **ordained** before the world unto our glory:
4: 9	as it were **appointed** to death:
1 COR. 3: 2	for **hitherto** ye were unable *to bear it,*
Phil. 1: 5	For your fellowship in the gospel **until now;**
1 COR. 3: 10	and another buildeth **thereon.**
Rev. 20: 11	And I saw a great white throne, and him that sat **on it,**
1 COR. 3: 13	Every man's work shall be **made manifest:** for the day shall declare it, because it shall be **revealed** by fire;
4: 5	who both will **bring to light** the hidden things of the darkness,
1 COR. 4: 2	**Moreover** it is required in stewards, that a man be found faithful.
2 Cor. 2: 12	**Furthermore,** when I came to Tro-as *preach* Christ's gospel,
1 COR. 4: 15	for in **Christ Jesus** I have begotten you through **the gospel.**

1 COR. 4: 15	for in **Christ Jesus** I have begotten you through **the gospel.**
John 1: 1	In the beginning was **the Word,**
Luke 8: 11	Now the parable is this: The seed is **word of God.**
1 Peter 1: 25	And this is **the word** which by **the gospel** is preached unto you.
Acts 8: 25	And they, when they had testified and preached **the word of the Lord,**
1 COR. 5: 3	For I **verily,** as absent in the body, but present in the spirit,
2 Cor. 12: 12	**Truly** the signs of an apostle were wrought among you with all patience,
1 COR. 5: 8	Therefore let us keep the feast, not with the old leaven, neither with the leaven of **malice <u>and</u> wickedness;**

N.B. note how the underlined word separates words and phrases having the same meaning.

1 COR. 6: 3	Know ye not that we shall judge angels? how much more things that **pertain** to this life?
7: 32	He that is unmarried careth for the things that **belong** to the Lord,
1 COR. 6: 9	Be not deceived: neither fornicators, nor idolators, nor
	adulterers, **nor effeminate, nor abusers of themselves with mankind,**
Rom. 1: 27	**men with men working that which is unseemly,**
Eph. 5: 5	that **no whoremonger, nor unclean person,**
Rev. 22: 15	For without *are* **dogs,** and sorcerers, and **whoremongers,**
1 COR. 7: 3	and **likewise also** the wife unto the husband.

N.B. The two bold words mean the same.

1 COR. 7: 20	Let every man abide in the same calling **wherein** he was called.
11: 23	That the Lord Jesus the *same* night **in which** he was betrayed took bread:
1 COR. 8: 1	Knowledge puffeth up, but **charity** edifieth.
: 3	But if any man **love** God, the same is known of him.
1 COR 8: 7	**Howbeit** *there is* not in every man that knowledge:
7: 28	**Nevertheless** such shall have trouble in the flesh:
: 29	**But** this I say, brethren the time *is* short:
1 COR. 9: 2	If I be not an apostle unto others, yet **doubtless** I am to you:
: 10	For our sakes, **no doubt,** *this* is written:
1 COR. 9: 12	but suffer all things, lest we should hinder **the gospel of Christ.**

Acts 8: 25	when they had testified and preach **the word of the Lord,** returned to Jerusalem, and preached **the gospel** in many villages of the Samaritans.
Rev. 1: 2	Who bare record of **the word of God,** and of the testimony of **Jesus Christ,**
1 COR. 9: 15	for *it were* better for me to die, than that any man should make my glorying **void.**
1: 17	lest the cross of Christ should be **made of none effect.**
1 COR. 9: 17	but if against my will, a **dispensation** *of the gospel* is committed unto me.
Luke 16: 2	give an account of your **stewardship;**
1 COR. 9: 23	that I might be a partaker **thereof** with *you.*
Acts 13: 17	and with an high arm brought them out **of it.**
1 COR. 10: 1	**Moreover,** brethren, I would not that ye should be ignorant,
2 Cor. 2: 12	**Furthermore** I call God for a record upon my soul,
1 COR. 10: 11	and they are written for our **admonition,**
4: 14	but as my beloved sons I **warn** *you.*
1 COR. 10: 23	All things are lawful for me, but all things are not **expedient:**
12: 22	Nay, much more those members of the body, which seem to be more feeble, are **necessary:**
1 COR. 10: 28	for the earth *is* the Lord's, and the fullness **thereof:**
2 Cor. 8: 11	Now therefore perform the doing *of it;*
1 COR. 11: 11	**Nevertheless** neither is the man without the woman,
: 15	**But** if a woman have long hair, it is a glory to her:
: 20	When ye come together **therefore** into one place,
1 COR. 11: 25	this do ye, as **oft** as ye drink *it,* in remembrance of me.
: 26	for as **often** as ye eat this bread,
1 COR. 12: 4	Now there are **diversities** of gifts, but the same Spirit.
: 5	And there are **differences** of administrations,
1 COR. 12: 10	to another *divers* kinds of tongues;
: 12	For as the body is one, and have **many** members,
1 COR. 12: 25	That there should be no **schism** in the body;
11: 18	I hear that there be **divisions** among you;
1 COR. 13: 4	charity **vaunteth not itself, is not puffed up.**

N.B. note how the comma separates words and phrases having the same meaning.

<u>1 COR. 14: 2</u>	**howbeit** in the spirit he speaketh mysteries.
: 3	**But** he that prophesieth speaketh unto men *to* edification,

<u>1 COR. 14: 9</u>	So **likewise** ye,
: 15	and I will pray with the understanding **also:**

<u>1 COR. 14: 17</u>	For thou **verily** givest thanks well,
9: 2	yet **doubtless** I am to you:
1 Thess. 2: 13	ye received *it* not *as* the word of men, but as it is **in truth,**

<u>1 COR. 15: 1</u>	**Moreover,** brethren, I declare unto the gospel which I preached unto you,
2 Cor. 2: 12	**Furthermore,** when I came to Tro-as to *preach* Christ's gospel,

<u>1 COR. 15: 24</u>	when he shall put all **authority <u>and</u> power.**

N.B. note how the underlined word separates words and phrases having the same meaning.

<u>1 COR. 15: 30</u>	And why stand we **in jeopardy** every hour?
Acts 19: 40	For we are **in danger** to be called in question for this day's uproar,

<u>1 COR. 16: 4</u>	And if it be **meet** that I go also,
1 Thess. 3: 1	we thought it **good** to be left at Athens alone;

<u>1 COR. 16: 7</u>	but I trust to **tarry** a while with you,
: 6	And it may be that I will **abide,**

<u>1 COR. 16: 15</u>	**I beseech you,** brethren,
Acts 27: 34	Wherefore **I pray you** to take *some* meat:

2 CORINTHIANS

<u>2 COR. 1: 4</u>	by the comfort **wherewith** weourselves are comforted of God.
Rev. 19: 20	**with which** he deceived them that had received the mark of the beast,

<u>2 COR. 1: 8</u>	above strength insomuch **that** we despairing even of life:
2: 7	**So that** contrariwise ye *ought* rather to forgive *him,*

<u>2 COR. 1: 12</u>	we have had our **conversation** in the world,
2 Tim. 3: 10	But thou hast known my doctrine, **manner of life,**

<u>2 COR. 1: 12</u>	and more abundantly to **you-ward.**
: 18	But *as* God *is* true, our word **toward you** was not yea, and nay.

<u>2 COR. 2: 7</u>	and comfort *him,* **lest perhaps** such a one should be swallowed

up with overmuch sorrow.

2 COR. 3: 1 as some *others*, **epistles** recommendation to you, or *letters* of commendation from you?

2 COR. 4: 3 But if our **gospel** be hid, it is hid to them that are lost:
Heb. 4: 2 For unto us was **the gospel** preached, as well as unto them: but **the word** preached did not profit them,
Acts 13: 44 And the next sabbath day came almost the whole city together to hear **the word of God.**
Rev. 1: 2 Who bare record of **word of God**, and the testimony of **Jesus Christ,**
Acts 8: 25 And they, when they had testified and preached **the word of the Lord,**

2 COR. 4: 8 *We are* **troubled** on every side, yet not **distressed**; *we are* **perplexed**, but not in despair;

2 COR. 5: 18 and hath given to us the ministry of **reconciliation;**
Rom. 5: 11 by whom we have now the **atonement;**

2 COR. 5: 19 **To wit,** that God was in Christ, reconciling the world unto himself,

1 Cor. 2: 2 For I determined not **to know** any thing among you,
Rom. 13: 9 it is briefly comprehended in this saying, **namely,** Thou shalt love thy neighbour as thyself.
2 COR. 5: 20 as though God did **beseech** *you* by us: we **pray** *you* in Christ's stead,

2 COR. 6: 2 and in the day of salvation have I **succoured** thee:
Rev. 12: 16 And the earth **helped** the woman,

2 COR. 6: 6 By pureness, by knowledge, by **longsuffering**, by kindness,
 : 4 in **much patience,** in afflictions,

2 COR. 6: 6 by the Holy Ghost, by love **unfeigned.**
James 3: 17 without partiality, and **without hypocrisy.**

2 COR. 6: 15 or what part hath he that believeth with an **infidel?**
 : 14 Be not unequally yoked together with **unbelievers:**

2 COR. 6: 15 And what **concord** hath Christ with Belial?
 : 16 And what **agreement** hath the temple of God with idols?

2 COR. 6: 17 **Wherefore** come out from among them, and be ye separate,
7: 1 Having **therefore** these promises,

2 COR. 7: 9 but that ye sorrowed to repentance: for ye were **made sorry after a godly manner,**

2 COR. 8: 1	Moreover, brethren, we **do you to wit** of the grace of God bestowed on the churches of Macedonia;
: 9	For **ye know** the grace of our Lord Jesus Christ,
2 COR. 8: 6	Insomuch **that** we desired Titus,
7: 7	**so that** I rejoiced the more.
2 COR. 8: 10	And **herein** I give *my* advice: for this is expedient for you,
5: 2	For **in this** we groan,
2 COR. 8: 10	for this is **expedient** for you,
9: 5	Therefore I thought it **necessary** to exhort the brethren,
2 COR. 9: 4	**Lest haply if** they of Macedonia come with me,
2: 7	**Lest perhaps** such a one should be swallowed up with over-much sorrow.
2 COR. 9: 5	and make up beforehand your bounty, **whereof** ye had notice before.
Heb. 7: 13	**of which** no man gave attendance at the altar.
2 COR. 9: 10	(... and **multiply** your seed sown, and **increase** the fruits of your righteousness;)
2 COR. 10: 1	Now I Paul myself **beseech** you by the meekness and gentle-ness of Christ,
5: 20	as though God did **beseech** *you* by us: we **pray** *you* in Christ's stead,
2 COR. 10: 16	To preach **the gospel** in the *regions* beyond you,
: 14	for we are come as far as you also in *preaching* **the gospel of Christ:**
Hebrews 4: 2	For unto us was **the gospel** preached, as wellas unto them: but **the word** preached did not profit them,
Acts 10: 36	**The word** which *God* sent unto the children of Israel, preaching peace by **Jesus Christ;**
Rev. 1: 2	Who bare record of **the word of God,** and of the testimony of **Jesus Christ,**
2 COR. 11: 5	For I suppose I was **not a whit** behind the very chiefest apostles.
12: 11	for I ought to have been commended of you: for **in nothing** am I behind the very chiefest apostles,
2 COR. 11: 11	**Wherefore?** because I love you not? God knoweth.
1 Cor. 6: 7	**Why** do ye not rather take wrong?
2 COR. 11: 12	that **wherein** they glory, they may be found even as we.
Hebrews 6: 18	That by two immutable things, **in which** *it was* impossible

for God to lie,

2 COR. 12: 1	It is not **expedient** for me doubtless to glory.
9: 5	Therefore I thought it **necessary** to exhort the brethren,

2 COR. 12: 6	for I will say the truth: but *now* I **forbear,**
11: 10	no man shall **stop** me of this boasting in the regions of A-chai-a.
Col. 1: 9	do not **cease** to pray for you,

2 COR. 12: 9	My grace is sufficient for thee: for my strength is made perfect in **weakness.** Most gladly therefore will I rather glory in my **infirmities,** that the power of Christ may rest upon me.

2 COR. 12: 12	Truly the signs of an apostle were **wrought** among you in all patience,
5: 10	according to that he hath **done,** whether *it be* good or bad.

2 COR. 12: 13	For what is it **wherein** ye were inferior to other churches,
1 Cor. 11: 23	That the Lord Jesus the *same* night **in which** he was betrayed took bread:

2 COR. 13: 2	and being absent now I write to them which **heretofore** have sinned,
Gal. 1: 13	For ye have heard of my conversation **in time past** in the Jews' religion,

2 COR. 13: 5	Know ye not your own selves, how that Jesus Christ is in you, except ye be **reprobates?**
6: 14	Be not unequally yoked together with **unbelievers:**
: 15	or what part hath he that believeth with **an infidel?**

GALATIANS

GAL. 1: 7	but there be some that trouble you, and would **pervert** the gospel of Christ.
2 Cor. 2: 17	For we are not as many, which **corrupt** the word of God:

GAL. 1: 7	but there be some that trouble you, and would pervert **the gospel of Christ.**
2 Cor. 2: 17	For we are not as many, which corrupt **the word of God:**
Acts 8: 25	And they, when they had testified and preached **the word of the Lord,** returned to Jerusalem, and preached **the gospel** in many villages of the Samaritans.
Rev. 1: 2	Who bare record of **the word of God,** and the testimony of **Jesus Christ,**

GAL. 1: 11	But I **certify** you, brethren,

Eph. 1: 9	Having **made known** unto us the mystery of his will,
GAL. 1: 13	For ye have heard of my **conversation** in time past in the Jews' religion,
2 Tim. 3: 10	But thou hast fully known my doctrine, **manner of life,**
GAL. 1: 16	immediately I **conferred** not with flesh and blood:
John 12: 10	But the chief priests **consulted** that they might put Lazarus also to death;
GAL. 2: 13	And the other Jews **dissembled** likewise with him; insomuch that Barnabas also was carried away with their dissimulation.
: 12	but when they were come, he **withdrew <u>and</u> separated** himself,

N.B. note how the underlined word separates words and phrases having the same meaning.

GAL. 2: 13	And the other Jews dissembled **likewise** with him; insomuch that Barnabas **also** was carried away with their dissimulation.
GAL. 2; 13	insomuch **that** Barnabas also was carried away with their dissimulation.
2 Cor. 7: 7	**so that** I rejoiced the more.
GAL. 2: 13	insomuch that Barnabas also was carried away with their **dissimulation.**
1 Tim. 4: 2	Speaking lies in **hypocrisy;**
GAL. 3: 15	yet *if it be* confirmed, no man disannulleth, or **add**eth thereto.
GAL. 3: 19	**Wherefore** then *serveth* the law?
2: 14	**why** compellest thou the Gentiles to live as do the Jews?
GAL. 3: 24	**Wherefore** the law was our schoolmaster *to bring us* unto Christ,
: 7	Know you **therefore** that they which are of faith,
GAL. 4: 5	To **redeem** them that were under the law,
1 Tim. 3: 13	For they that have used the office of a deacon well **purchase** to themselves a good degree,
James 4: 13	and **buy** and sell, and get gain:
GAL.4: 12	Brethren, **I beseech you,** be as I *am;*
Acts 27: 34	Wherefore **I pray you** to take *some* meat:
GAL. 5: 1	Stand fast therefore in the liberty **wherewith** Christ hath made us free,
Rev. 19: 20	and with him the false prophet that wrought miracles before

him,

GAL. 5: 19	Adultery, fornication, uncleanness, **lasciviousness,**
2 Pet. 2: 18	they allure through the **lusts of the flesh,**
GAL. 5: 20	Idolatry, witchcraft, hatred, variance, **emulations,**
: 21	**Envyings,** murders, drunkenness,
GAL. 6: 12	As many as desire to make a fair shew in the flesh, they **constrain** you to be circumcised;
Luke 14: 23	and **compel** *them* to come in, that my house may be filled.
11: 53	the scribes and the Pharisees began to **urge** *him* vehemently,

EPHESIANS

EPH. 1: 5	Having **predestinated** us unto the adoption of children by Jesus Christ to himself,
: 4	According has he hath **chosen** us in him before the foundation of the world,
EPH. 1: 6	To the praise of the glory of his grace, **wherein** he hath hath made us accepted in the beloved.
1 Cor. 15: 2	**By which** also ye are saved,
EPH. 1: 13	In whom ye also *trusted,* after that ye heard **the word of truth, the gospel** of your salvation:
John 10: 35	If he called them god, unto whom **the word of God** came,
Acts 10: 36	**The word** which *God* sent unto the children of Israel, preaching peace by **Jesus Christ:**
EPH. 2: 2	And you *hath he quickened,* who were dead in **trespasses and sins;**

N.B. note how the underlined word separates words and phrases having the same meaning.

EPH. 2: 3	Among whom also we all had our **conversation** in times past in the lusts of our flesh,
2 Tim. 3: 10	But thou hast fully known my doctrine, **manner of life,**
EPH. 2: 4	But God, who is rich in mercy, for his great love **wherewith** he loved us,
Rev. 19: 20	**with which** he deceived them that had received the mark of the beast,
EPH. 2: 12	That at that time ye were without Christ, being **aliens** from the commonwealth of Israel, and **strangers** from the covenants of promise,
: 19	Now therefore ye are no more **strangers and** foreigners,

N.B. note how the underlined word separates words and phrases having the same meaning.

<u>EPH. 2: 15</u>	for to make in himself of **twain** one new man, *so* making peace;
2: 16	And that he might reconcile **both** unto God in one body by the cross,
5: 31	and they **two** shall be one flesh.
<u>EPH. 2: 16</u>	having slain the enmity **thereby:**
Heb. 11: 4	And **by it** he being dead yet speaketh.
<u>EPH. 2: 21</u>	In whom all the building fitly **framed together** groweth unto an holy temple of the Lord:
: 22	In whom ye also are **builded together** for an habitarion of God through the Spirit.
<u>EPH. 3: 2</u>	If ye have heard of the **dispensation** of the grace of God which is given me to you-ward:
Luke 16: 2	give an account of thy **stewardship;**
<u>EPH. 3: 4</u>	(...**Whereby,** when ye read, you may understand my knowledge in the mystery of Christ)
Heb. 11: 2	For **by it** the elders obtained a good report.
<u>EPH. 3: 6</u>	That the Gentiles should be fellowheirs, and of the same body, and partakers of his promise in **Christ** by the **gospel:**
Acts 8: 4	Therefore they that were scattered abroad went evey where preaching **the word.**
Acts 10: 36	**The word** which *God* sent unto the children of Israel, preaching peace by **Jesus Christ:**
2 Tim. 2: 9	Wherein I suffer trouble, as an evil doer, *even* unto bonds; but **the word of God** is not bound.
<u>EPH. 3: 7</u>	**Whereof** I was made a minister.
Heb. 7: 13	**of which** no man gave attendance at the altar.
<u>EPH. 3: 18</u>	May be able to **comprehend** with all saints what *is* the breadth,
: 4	(...Whereby, when ye read, ye may **understand** my knowledge in the mystery of Christ)
<u>EPH. 4: 1</u>	I therefore, the prisoner of the Lord, **beseech you** that ye walk worthy of the vocation wherewith ye are called,
2 Cor. 5: 20	as though God did **beseech *you*** by us: we **pray *you*** in Christ's stead, be ye reconciled to God.
<u>EPH. 4: 1</u>	beseech you that ye walk worthy of the **vocation** wherewith ye are called,

: 4	even as ye are called in one hope of your **calling:**
EPH. 4: 1	beseech you that ye walk worthy of the vocation **wherewith** ye are called,
Heb. 11: 4	**by which** he obtained witness that he was righteous,
EPH. 4: 2	With all **lowliness and meekness,** with longsuffering,

N.B. note how the underlined word separates words and phrases having the same meaning.

EPH. 4: 2	with **longsuffering,** forbearing one another in love;
Col. 1: 11	unto all **patience and longsuffering** with joyfulness;

N.B. note how the underlined word separates words and phrases having the same meaning.

EPH. 4: 14	and carried about with every wind of doctrine by the **sleight of men, _and_ cunning craftiness,** whereby they lie in wait to deceive;

N.B. note how the underlined word separates words and phrases having the same meaning.

EPH. 4: 19	Who being past feeling have given themselves over unto **lasciviousness,** to work all **uncleanness** with greediness.
5: 5	For this ye know, that no **whoremonger, nor unclean person,**
Rom. 1: 26	For this cause God gave them up unto **vile affections:** for even their women did change the natural use into that which is against nature:
: 27	And likewise also the men, leaving the natural use of the woman, **burned in their lust one toward another, men with men working that which is unseemly,**
: 31	Without understanding, covenantbreakers, **without natural affection,**

N.B. note how the underlined words separates words and phrases having the same meaning.

EPH. 4: 29	Let no **corrupt communication** proceed out of your mouth,
5: 4	**Neither filthiness, nor foolish talking, nor jesting,**

N.B. note how the underlined words separates words and phrases having the same meaing.

EPH. 4: 30	And grieve not the holy Spirit of God, **whereby** ye are sealed unto the day of redemption.
Rev. 19: 20	**with which** he deceived them that had received the mark of the beast,

EPH. 5: 15	See then that ye walk **circumspectly,**
Phil. 2: 28	I sent him therefore the **more carefully,**
EPH. 5: 18	And be not drunk with wine, **wherein** is excess;
Heb. 6: 18	**in which** *it was* impossible for God to lie,
EPH. 6: 13	that ye may be able to **withstand** in the evil day,
: 11	that ye may be able to **stand against** the wiles of the devil.

PHILIPPIANS

PHIL. 1: 7	Even as it is **meet** for me to think this of you all,
Eph. 6: 1	Children, obey your parents in the Lord: for this is **right.**
PHIL. 1: 8	For God is my record, how greatly I long after you all in the **bowels of Jesus Christ.**
Luke 15: 20	and had **compassion,** and ran,
2 Cor. 7: 15	And his **inward affection** is more abundant toward you,
PHIL. 1: 17	knowing that I am set for the defence of **the gospel.**
Acts 10: 36	**The word** which *God* sent unto the children of Israel, preaching peace by **Jesus Christ:**
8: 25	And they, when they had testified and preached **the word of the Lord,**
PHIL. 1: 18	and I **therein** do rejoice, yea, and I will rejoice.
Gal. 5: 14	For all the law is fulfilled in one word, *even* **in this:**
PHIL. 1: 22	yet what I shall choose **I wot not.**
1 Cor. 14: 11	Therefore if **I know not** the meaning of the voice,
PHIL. 1: 27	Only let your **conversation** be as it becometh the gospel of Christ:
2 Tim. 3: 10	But thou hast fully known my doctrine, **manner of life,**
PHIL. 1: 17	Only let your conversation be as it becometh **the gospel of Christ:**
Acts 14: 25	And when they had preached **the word** in Perga,
10: 36	**The word** which *God* sent unto the children of Israel, preaching peace by **Jesus Christ:**
Rev. 1: 2	Who bare record of **the word of God,** and the testimony of **Jesus Christ,**
PHIL. 3: 4	If any other man thinketh that he hath **whereof** he might trust the flesh, I more:
Heb. 7: 13	**of which** no man gave attendance at the altar.
PHIL. 4: 2	I **beseech** Eu-o-di-as, and beseech Syn-ty-che, that they be of

411

the same mind in the Lord.

: 3	And I **intreat** thee also, true yokefellow,
2 Thess. 3: 1	Finally, brethren, **pray for** us,

COLOSSIANS

COL. 1: 5	**whereof** ye heard before in the word of the truth of the gospel;
Heb. 7: 13	**of which** no man gave attendance at the altar.

COL. 1: 5	For the hope which is laid up for you in heaven, whereof ye heard before in **the word of the truth** of **the gospel;**
John 14: 6	Jesus saith unto him, I am the way, **the truth** and the life:
1 Thess. 1: 8	For you sounded out **the word of the Lord** not only in Macedonia and A-chai-a,

2: 2	we were bold in our God to speak unto you **the gospel of God** with much contention.
Rev. 1: 2	Who bare record of **the word of God,** and the testimony of **Jesus Christ,**

COL. 1: 11	unto all **patience and longsuffering** with joyfulness;

N.B. note how the underlined word separates words and phrases having the same meaning.

COL. 1: 12	Giving thanks unto the Father, which hath made us **meet** to be partakers of the inheritance of the saints in light:
: 10	that ye might walk **worthy** of the Lord unto all pleasing,

3: 18	Wives, submit yourselves unto your own husbands, as it is **fit** in the Lord.

COL. 1: 13	Who hath **delivered us** from the power of darkness,
Gal. 3: 13	Christ hath **redeemed us** from the curse of the law,

COL. 1: 21	And you that were sometime **alienated** and enemies in *your* mind by wicked works,
Eph. 2: 13	But now in Christ Jesus ye who sometime were **far off** are made nigh by the blood of Christ.

COL. 1: 22	to present you **holy and unblameable and unreproveable** in his sight:

N.B. note how the underlined words separate words and phrases having the same meaning.

COL. 1: 23	If ye continue in the faith **grounded and** settled,
2: 7	**Rooted and** built up in him,

<u>COL. 1: 25</u>	**Whereof** I am made a minister, according to the dispensation of God which is given to me for you,
Heb. 7: 13	**Of which** no man gave attendance at the altar.

<u>COL. 1: 25</u>	according to the **dispensation** of God which is given to me for you,
Luke 16: 2	give an account of thy **stewardship:**

<u>COL. 1: 28</u>	that we may present every man **perfect** in Christ Jesus:
2: 10	And ye are **complete** in him,

<u>COL. 1: 29</u>	**Whereunto** I also labour,
Heb. 6: 18	**in which** *it was* impossible for God to lie,

<u>COL. 2: 4</u>	And this I say, lest any man should **beguile you** with enticing words.
2 Thess. 2: 3	Let no man **deceive you** by any means:

<u>COL. 2: 8</u>	Beware lest any man spoil you through **philosophy <u>and</u> vain deceit,** after the **tradition of men,**

N.B. note how the underlined word separates words and phrases having the same meaning.

<u>COL. 2: 12</u>	Buried with him in baptism, **wherein** also ye are risen with *him* through the faith of the operation of God,
: 19	**from which** all the body by joints and bands having nourishment ministered,

<u>COL. 3: 5</u>	fornication, uncleanness, **inordinate affection, evil concupiscence,**
Rom. 1: 26	For this cause God gave them up unto **vile affections:**

<u>COL. 3: 12</u>	Put on therefore, as the elect of God, holy and beloved, **bowels of mercies,** kindness, humbleness of mind, meekness, longsuffering;
Heb. 5: 2	Who can have **compassion** on the ignorant,

<u>COL. 4: 12</u>	Ep a phras, who is *one* of you, a servant of Christ, saluteth you, always labouring fervently for you in prayers that ye may stand **perfect <u>and</u> complete** in all the will of God.
Heb. 5: 14	But strong meat belongeth to them that are of **full age,**

N.B. note how the underlined word separates words and phrases having the same meaning.

1 THESSALONIANS

1 THESS. 1: 8	For from you sounded out of you **the word of the Lord** not only in Macedonia and A-chai-a,
2: 2	we were bold in our God to speak unto you **the gospel of God** with much contention.
: 13	when ye received **the word of God** which ye heard of us,
3: 2	and our fellowlabourer in **the gospel of Christ,**

1 THESS. 2: 3   For our exhortation was *not* of **deceit,** nor of uncleanness, nor in **guile:**

1 THESS. 2: 9   For ye remember, brethren, our **labour <u>and</u> travail:**

N.B. note how the underlined word separates words and phrases having the same meaning.

1 THESS. 3: 1	**Wherefore when** we could no longer forbear,
: 5	**For this cause, when** I could no longer forbear,
: 7	**Therefore,** brethren,

1 THESS. 3: 1	Wherefore when we could no longer **forbear,**
Matt. 18: 26	Lord **have patience** with me, and I will pay thee all.

1 THESS. 3: 4	For **verily,** when we were with you,
Heb. 7: 23	And they **truly** were many priests,

1 THESS. 3: 7   we were comforted over you all in our **affliction <u>and</u> distress** by your faith:

N.B. note how the underlined word separates words and phrases having the same meaning.

1 THESS. 3: 9	for all the joy **wherewith** we joy for your sakes before our God;
Heb. 6: 18	**in which** *it was* impossible for God to lie,

1 THESS. 4: 1	Furthermore then **we beseech you,**
2 Cor. 5: 20	as though God did **beseech** *you* by us: **we pray** *you* in Christ's stead, be ye reconciled to God.

1 THESS. 4: 5	Not in the lust of **concupiscence,** even as the Gentiles which know not God:
1 Peter 2: 11	abstain from **fleshly lusts,** which war against the soul;

1 THESS. 4: 15	that we which are alive *and* remain unto the coming of the Lord shall not **prevent** them which are asleep.
5: 4	But ye, brethren, are not in darkness, that the day should **overtake** you as a thief.

1 THESS. 5: 3	then sudden destruction cometh upon them, as **travail** upon a woman with child;
: 12	to know them which **labour** among you,

2 THESSALONIANS

2 THESS. 1: 3	We are bound to thank God always for you, brethren, as it is **meet**, because that your faith growth exceedingly,
Col. 4: 1	give unto *your* servants that which is **just** and equal;
Acts 8: 21	for thy heart is not **right** in the sight of God.
2 THESS. 1: 6	Seeing *it is* a righteous thing with God to **recompense** tribulation to them that trouble you;
Rom. 12: 19	Vengeance *is* mine; I will **repay**, saith the Lord.

1 TIMOTHY

1 TIM. 1: 5	Now the end of the commandment is **charity** out of a pure heart,
: 14	And the grace of our Lord was exceeding abundant with faith and **love** which is in Christ Jesus.
1 TIM. 1: 5	and *of* a good conscience, and *of* faith **unfeigned:**
James 3: 17	without partiality, and **without hypocrisy.**
1 TIM. 1: 7	understanding neither **what** they say, and **whereof** they affirm.
1 TIM. 1: 9	Knowing this, that the law is not made for a righteous man, But for the **lawless <u>and</u> disobedient,** for the **ungodly <u>and</u>**
	for unholy <u>and</u> profane,

N.B. note howthe underlined words separate words and phrases having the same meaning.

1 TIM. 1: 10	For **<u>whoremongers,</u>** them that **defile themselves with man-kind,**
Rom. 1: 26	For this cause God gave them unto **vile affections:** for even their **women did change their natural use** into that which is **against nature:**
: 27	**men with men working that which is unseemly,**

N.B. The underlined word refers to both men and women.

1 TIM. 1: 16	**Howbeit for this cause** I obtained mercy,

N.B. The first bold word means the same as the second, third, and fourth words. Also the second, third, and fourth word means the same as the first.

1 TIM. 2: 7	**Whereunto** I am ordained a preacher,
Acts 26: 7	**For which** hope's sake, king Agrippa,

1 TIM. 2: 7	(I speak the **truth** in Christ, *and* lie not;) ateacher of the Gentiles in faith and **verity.**

1 TIM. 2: 9	that women adorn themselves in modest **apparel,** with shamefacedness and sobriety; not with broidered hair, or gold, or costly **array;**
James 2: 3	And ye have respect to him that weareth the gay **clothing,**
5: 2	Your riches are corrupted, and your **garments** are moth-eaten.

1 TIM. 2: 12	But I **suffer** not a woman to teach,
Heb. 6: 3	And this will we do, if God **permit.**

1 TIM. 4: 6	and of good doctrine, **whereunto** thou hast attained.
Acts 26: 7	**Unto which** *promise* our twelve tribes, instantly serving God day and night, hope to come.

1 TIM. 4: 12	but be thou an example of the believers, in word, **in conversation,** in charity, in spirit, in spirit, in faith, in purity.
2 Tim. 3: 10	But thou hast fully known my doctrine, **manner of life,**

1 TIM. 5: 4	let them learn first **piety** at home,
4: 7	and exercise thyself *rather* unto **godliness.**

1 TIM. 5: 4	and to **requite** their parents: for that is good and acceptable before God.
Philemon v19	I Paul have written *it* with my own hand, I will **repay** *it:*

1 TIM. 5: 5	and desolate, trusteth in God, and continueth in **supplications and prayers** night and day.

N.B. note how the underlined word separates words and phrases having the same meaning.

1 TIM. 5: 21	that thou observe these things **without preferring one before another, doing nothing by patiality.**

N.B. note how the comma separates words and phrases having the same meaning.

1 TIM. 5: 25	**Likewise also** the good works *of some* are manifest beforehand;

N.B. Note that the first and second words mean the same.

1 TIM. 6: 8	And having food and **raiment** let us therewith be content.
James 2: 3	And ye have respect to him who weareth the gay **clothing,**

1 TIM. 6: 10	For the love of money is the root of all evil: which while some have coveted after, they have **erred from** the faith,
1: 6	From which some **having swerved have turned aside** unto vain jangling;
1 TIM. 6: 12	Fight the good fight of faith, lay hold on eternal life, **whereunto** thou art also called,
Heb. 1: 13	But **to which** of the angels said he at any time,

2 TIMOTHY

2 TIM. 1: 5	When I call to remembrance the **unfeigned** faith that is in thee,
Phil. 1: 10	that ye may be **sincere** and without offence till the day of Christ;
James 3: 17	**without partiality, <u>and</u> without hypocrisy.**
2 TIM. 1: 11	**Whereunto** I am appointed a preacher,
Eph. 6: 20	**For which** I am an ambassador in bonds:
2 TIM. 1: 17	he sought me out very **diligently,**
Heb. 12: 17	though he sought it **carefully** with tears.
2 TIM. 1: 6	**Wherefore** I put thee in remembrance that thou stir up the gift of God,
: 8	Be not thou **therefore** ashamed of the testimony of our Lord,
2 TIM. 1: 8	but be thou partaker of the **afflictions** of the gospel according to the power of God;
Mark 13: 8	and there shall be famines and **troubles:**
2 TIM. 1: 11	**Whereunto** I am appointed a preacher, and an apostle,
Eph. 6: 20	**For which** I am an ambassador in bonds:
2 TIM. 1: 17	But, when he was in Rome, he sought me out very **diligently,** and found *me*.
Heb. 12: 17	though he sought it **carefully** with tears.
2 TIM. 2: 9	**Wherein** I suffer trouble, as an evil doer,
Heb. 6: 18	That by two immutable things, **in which** *it was* impossible for God to lie,
2 TIM. 2: 21	he shall be a vessel unto honour, sanctified, and **meet** for the master's use,
1 Tim. 5: 18	And, the The labourer *is* **worthy** of his reward.
2 TIM. 2: 25	if God **peradventure** will give them repentance to the acknowledging the truth;
1 Cor. 16: 6	And **it may be** that I will abide,

Philemon 15	For **perhaps** he therefore departed for a season,
2 TIM. 3: 5	Having a form of godliness, but denying the power **thereof:**
James 5: 11	and the grace of the fashion **of it** perisheth:
2 TIM. 3: 6	and lead captive silly women laden with sins, led away with **divers** lusts,
James 3: 7	For **every kind of** beasts,
Luke 11: 42	for ye tithe mint and rue and **all manner of** herbs,
2 TIM. 3: 8	Now as Jan-nes and Jam-bres **withstood** Moses, so do these also **resist** the truth:
2 TIM. 3: 10	But thou hast fully known my doctrine, manner of life, purpose, **longsuffering,** charity, **patience,**
2 TIM. 4: 1	I charge *thee* therefore before God, and the Lord Jesus Christ, Who shall judge the **quick** and the dead at his appearing and his kingdom;
1 Tim. 6: 17	nor trust in uncertain riches, but in the **living** God,
2 TIM. 4: 2	**reprove, rebuke,** exhort with all longsuffering and doctrine.

N.B. note how the comma separates the two bold words having the same meaning.

2 TIM. 4: 9	Do thy **diligence** to come shortly unto me:
Luke 11: 31	for she came from the **utmost** parts of the earth to hear the wisdom of Solomon;
1 Cor. 12: 31	But covet earnestly the **best** gifts:
2 TIM. 4: 15	Of whom **be** thou **ware** also;
2 Peter 3: 17	**beware** lest ye also,

TITUS

TITUS 1: 3	But hath in due times **manifested** his word through preaching,
2 Thess. 2: 8	And then shall that Wicked be **revealed.**
TITUS 1: 6	having faithful children not accused of **riot or unruly.**

N.B. not how the underlined word separates words and phrases having the same meaning.

TITUS 1: 7	not selfwilled, **not soon angry,** not given to wine,
2 Tim. 2: 24	but be gentle unto all *men,* apt to teach, **patient,**
TITUS 1: 8	But a lover of hospitality, a lover of good men, **sober,** just, holy, **temperate;**
2: 5	*To be* **discreet,** chaste,
3: 8	that they which have believed in God might **be careful** to

maintain good works,

TITUS 1: 16	being **abominable, <u>and</u> disobedient,** and unto every good work **reprobate.**
Heb. 3: 13	lest any of you be **hardened** through deceitfulness of sin.

N.B.   note how the underlined word separates words and phrases having the same meaning.

TITUS 2: 10	Not **purloining,** but shewing all good fidelity;
Acts 5: 3	why hath Satan filled thine heart to lie to the Holy Ghost, and **to keep back** *part* of the price of the land?

TITUS 3: 3	serving **divers** lusts and pleasures, living in malice and envy,
James 3: 7	For **every kind** of beasts,
Luke 11: 42	for ye tithe mint and rue and **all manner of** herbs,

PHILEMON

PHIL'M v 10	**I beseech thee** for my son O-nes-i-mus,
Acts 24: 4	**I pray thee** that thou wouldst hear us of thy clemency a few words.

PHIL'M v19	**albeit** I do not say to thee how owest unto me even thine own self besides.
v 22	**but** withal prepare me also a lodging:

v 22	but **withal** prepare me also a lodging:
1 Thess. 5: 10	we should live **together** with him.

HEBREWS

HEB. 1: 11	and they all shall **wax** old as doth a garment;
2 Pet. 2: 2	desire the sincere milk of the that ye may **grow** thereby:

HEB. 2: 2	and every transgression and disobedience received a just **recompence** of **reward;**

HEB. 2: 4	and with **divers** miracles,
: 10	in bringing **many** sons unto glory,
James 3: 7	For **every kind** of beasts,
Luke 11: 42	for ye tithe mint and rue and **all manner of** herbs,

HEB. 2: 5	For unto the angels hath he not put in subjection the world to come, **whereof** we speak.
7: 13	**of which** no man gave attendance at the altar.

HEB. 2: 16	For **verily** he took not on *the nature of* angels;
7: 23	And they **truly** were many priests,

<u>**HEB. 2: 18**</u>	he is able **to succour** them that are tempted,
4: 16	and find grace **to help** in in time of need.

<u>**HEB. 4: 6**</u>	Seeing therefore it remaineth that some must enter **therein,**

N.B. reverse the two syllables in the bold word and the meaning is clear.

<u>**HEB. 4: 12**</u>	For the word of God *is* **quick,** and powerful,
3: 12	in departing from the **living** God.
1 Thess. 4: 17	Then we which are **alive** *and* remain shall be caught up together with them in the clouds,

<u>**HEB. 4: 12**</u>	piercing even to the dividing **asunder** of soul and spirit,
James 1: 21	Wherefore lay **apart** all filthiness and superfluity of naughtiness,

<u>**HEB. 4: 12**</u>	Neither is there any that is not **manifest** in his sight:
1 Peter 1: 5	Who are kept by the power of God unto salvation ready to be **revealed** in the last time.

<u>**HEB. 5: 1**</u>	For every high priest taken from among men is **ordained** for men in things *pertaining* to God,
1 Thess. 3: 3	for yourselves know that we are **appointed** thereunto.

<u>**HEB. 5: 3**</u>	And by reason **hereof** he ought, as for the people,
Matt.13: 22	and the care **of this** of this world,

<u>**HEB. 5: 9**</u>	And being made **perfect,**
: 14	But strong meat belongeth to them that are of **full age,**

<u>**HEB. 6: 7**</u>	and bringeth forth herbs **meet** for them by whom it is dressed,
13: 10	whereof they have no **right** to eat which serve the tabernacle.

<u>**HEB. 6: 12**</u>	That ye be not **slothful** ,
1 Tim. 6: 11	and not only **idle,**

<u>**HEB. 6: 17**</u>	**Wherein** God, willing more abundantly to shew unto the heirs of promise the immutability of his counsel,
:18	**in which** *it was* impossible for God to lie,

<u>**HEB. 6: 20**</u>	**Whither** the forerunner is for us entered,
9: 16	For **where** a testament *is,*

<u>**HEB. 7: 5**</u>	And **verily** they that are of the sons of Levi,
: 23	And they **truly** were many priests,

<u>**HEB. 7: 5**</u>	have a commandment to take **tithes** of the people according to the law,
: 2	To whom also Abraham gave **a tenth part** of all;

<u>HEB. 7: 19</u>	For the law made nothing **perfect,**
8: 7	For if that first *covenant* had been **fault,**
<u>HEB. 7: 19</u>	by the which we **draw nigh** unto God.
10: 22	Let us **draw near** with a true heart in full assurance of faith,
<u>HEB. 7: 25</u>	**Wherefore** he is able also to save to the uttermost that come unto God by him.
4: 1	Let us **therefore** fear,
<u>HEB. 9: 1</u>	Then **verily** the first *covenant* had also ordinances of divine service,
7: 23	And they **truly** were many priests,
<u>HEB. 9: 2</u>	For there was a tabernacle made; the first, **wherein** *was* the candlestick,
10: 32	But call to remembrance the former days, **in which,** ye were illuminated,
<u>HEB. 9: 6</u>	Now when these things were thus **ordained,**
: 27	And as it is **appointed** unto men once to die,
<u>HEB. 9: 10</u>	*Which stood* only in meats and drinks, and **divers** washings,
12: 15	and thereby **many** be defiled;
<u>HEB. 9: 21</u>	**Moreover** he sprinkled with blood both thetabernacle,
12: 9	**Furthermore** we have had fathers of our flesh which corrected *us,*
<u>HEB. 9: 22</u>	and without shedding of blood there is no **remission.**
Col. 1: 14	*even* the **forgiveness** of sins:
<u>HEB. 10: 11</u>	And every priest standeth daily ministering and offering **often**times the same sacrifices, which can never take away sins:
<u>HEB. 10: 13</u>	From **henceforth** expecting till his enemies be made his footstool.
Matt. 26: 16	And **from that time** he sought opportunity to betray him.
<u>HEB. 10: 17</u>	And their **sins <u>and</u> iniquities** will I remember no more.

N.B. note how the underlined word separates words and phrases having the same meaning.

<u>HEB. 10: 29</u>	and hath counted the the blood of the covenant, **wherewith** he was sanctified, an unholy thing,
: 10	**By** the **which** will we are sanctified through the offering of the body of Jesus Christ once *for all.*

11: 4	**by which** he obtained witness that he was righteous,
HEB. 10: 30	Vengeance *belongeth* unto me, I will **recompense**, saith the Lord.
Phile. v 19	I Paul have written *it* with mine own hand, I will **repay** *it:*
HEB. 10: 32	But call to rembrance the former days, in which, after ye were **illuminated,** ye endured a great fight of afflictions;
6: 4	For *it is* impossible for those who were once **enlightened,**
Job 38: 36	or who hath **given understanding** to the heart?
HEB. 11: 9	By faith he **sojourned** in the land of promise,
2 Tim. 4: 20	E-ras-tus **abode** at Corinth:
Acts 28: 30	And Paul **dwelt** two years in his own hired house,
HEB. 11: 12	and as the sand which is by the sea which is by the sea shore **innumerable.**
Luke 12:1	when there were gathered together **an innumerable multitude** of people,
John 6: 2	And **a great multitude** followed him,
: 5	and saw **a great company** come unto him,
Acts 11: 24	and **much people** was added unto the Lord.
HEB. 11: 36	yea, **moreover** of bonds and imprisonment:
12: 9	**Furthermore** we have had fathers in the flesh which corrected *us,*
HEB. 12: 8	**whereof** all are partakers, then are ye bastards,
9: 5	**of which** we cannot now speak particularly.
HEB. 12: 11	nevertheless afterward it yieldeth the peaceable fruit of righteousness unto them which are exercised **thereby.**
11: 2	For **by it** the elders received a good report.
HEB. 12: 15	Looking **diligently** lest any man fail of the grace of God;
: 17	though he sought **carefully** with tears.
HEB. 12: 18	and that burned with fire, nor unto **blackness and darkness,**

N.B. note how the underlined word separates words and phrases having the same meaning.

HEB. 12: 28	whereby we may serve God acceptably with **reverence and godly fear:**

N.B. note comment on previous verse.

HEB. 13: 4	but **whoremongers** and adulterers God will judge.
Rom. 1: 26	for even their **women did change the natural into that**

	which is against nature:
: 27	men with men working that which is unseemly,

HEB. 13: 19	But **I beseech** *you* the rather to do this,
: 18	**Pray** for us:

HEB. 13: 20	through the blood of the **everlasting** covenant,
: 21	to whom *be* glory for **ever and ever.** Amen.

JAMES

JAMES 1: 2	My brethren, count it all joy when ye fall into **divers** temptations;
3: 7	For **every kind** of beasts,
Luke 11: 42	for ye tithe mint and rue and **all manner of** herbs,

JAMES 1: 4	But let patience have *her* work, that ye may be **perfect and entire, wanting nothing.**

N.B. note how the underlined word separates words and phrases having the same meaning.

JAMES 1: 11	and the flower **thereof** falleth, and the grace of the fashion **of it** perisheth:

JAMES 1: 14	But every man is tempted, when he is **drawn away** of his own lust, and **enticed.**

JAMES 1: 21	Wherefore lay apart all filthness and **superfluity** of naughtiness,
2 Cor. 8: 2	How that in a great trial of affliction the **abundance** of their joy and their deep poverty...

JAMES 1: 24	and **straightway** forgetteth what manner of man he was.
Rev. 4: 2	And **immediately** I was in the spirit:

JAMES 2: 2	For if there come unto your assembly with a gold ring, in **apparel,** and there come in also a poor man in vile **raiment;**
: 3	And ye have respect to him that weareth the gay **clothing.**
5: 2	Your riches are corrupted, and your **garments** are motheaten.

JAMES 2: 11	For he that said, Do not commit adultery, said also, Do not **kill.**
Matt. 19: 18	Jesus said, Thou shalt do no **murder.**

JAMES 2: 25	**Likewise also** was not Rahab the harlot justified by works,

N.B. note how both bold words mean the same thing.

JAMES 3: 9	**Therewith** bless we God, even the Father;

Rev. 19: 15	that **with it** he should smite the nations:
JAMES 3: 9	and therewith curse we men, which are made after the **similitude** of God.
Phili. 2:7	and was made in the **likeness** of men:
Heb. 10: 1	*and* not the very **image** of the things,
JAMES 3: 13	let him shew out of a good **conversation** his works with meek-ness of wisdom.
2 Tim. 3: 10	But thou hast fully known my doctrine, **manner of life,**
JAMES 4: 1	From **whence** *come* wars and fightings among you?
3: 16	For **where** envying and strife *is,*

1 PETER

1 PETER 1: 6	**Wherein** ye greatly rejoice,
2 Peter 3: 16	speaking in them of these things; **in which** are some things hard to be understood,
1 PETER 1: 6	you are in heaviness through **manifold** temptations:
James 3: 2	For in **many** things we offend all.
1 PETER 1: 10	Of which salvation the prophets have inquired and searched **diligently,**
Heb. 12: 17	though he sought it **carefully** with tears.
1 PETER 1: 13	**Wherefore** gird up the loins of your mind,
2: 7	Unto you **therefore** which believe *he is* precious:
1 PETER 1: 18	as of a lamb **without blemish** <u>and</u> **without spot:**

N.B. note how the underlined word separates words and phrases having the same meaning.

1 PETER 1: 20	Who **verily** foreordained before the foundation of the world,
Heb. 11: 15	And **truly,** if they had been mindful...
1 PETER 1: 22	Seeing you have purified your souls in obeying the truth through the Spirit unto **unfeigned love** of the brethren,
Jmes 3: 17	full of mercy and good fruits, without partiality, and **without hypocrisy.**
1 PETER 1: 24	The grass withereth, and the flower **thereof** falleth away:
James 1: 11	and the grace of the fashion **of it** perisheth:
1 PETER 1: 25	But **the word of the Lord** endureth for ever. And this is **the word** which by **the gospel** is preached unto you.
Rev. 1: 2	Who bare record of **the word of God,** and of the testimony

of **Jesus Christ,**

1 PETER 2: 8	being disobedient: **whereunto** also they were appointed.
Heb. 1: 13	But **to which** of the angels said he at any time,

1 PETER 2: 8	being disobedient: whereunto also they were **appointed.**
: 9	But ye *are* a **chosen** generation,

1 PETER 2: 11	Dearly beloved, **I beseech *you*** as strangers and pilgrims,
Heb. 13: 18	**Pray** for us: for we trust we have a good conscience,

1 PETER 2: 12	Having your **conversation** honest among the Gentiles:
2 Timothy 3: 10	But thou hast fully known my doctrine, **manner of life,**

1 PETER 2: 18	not only to the good and gentle, but also to **the forward.**
2 Peter 2: 7	vexed with the filthy conversation of **the wicked:**

1 PETER 2: 21	For **hereunto** were ye called: because Christ also suffered for us,
1 John 3: 8	**for this purpose** the Son of God was manifested,

1 PETER 2: 22	Who did no sin, neither was **guile** found in his mouth,
1 Thess. 2: 23	For our exhortation *was* not of **deceit,**

1 PETER 3: 1	**Likewise,** ye wives, *be* in subjection to your own husbands;
: 5	For after this manner in the old time the holy women **also,**

1 PETER 3: 11	Let him **eschew** evil, and do good;
Titus 3: 9	But **avoid** foolish questions,

1 PETER 3: 11	Let him eschew evil, and do good; let him seek peace and **ensue it.**
Rom. 14: 19	Let us therefore **follow after** the things which make for peace,

1 PETER 3: 20	while the ark was preparing, **wherein** few, that is, eight souls were saved by water.
2 Peter 3: 16	**in which** are some things hard to be understood,

1 PETER 3: 21	The like figure **whereunto** *even* baptism doth **also** now save us (not the putting away of the filth of the flesh...)

1 PETER 4: 3	For the time past of *our* past may suffice us to have **wrought** the will of the Gentiles,
Heb. 10: 36	after ye have **done** the will of God, ye might receive the promise.

1 PETER 4: 3	For the time past of *our* past may **suffice** us to have wrought the will of the Gentiles,
Mark 8: 4	From whence can a man **satisfy** these *men* with bread here

In the wilderness?

1 PETER 4: 3	when we walked in **lasciviousness, lusts,**
2 Cor. 12: 21	and have not repented of the **uncleanness <u>and</u> fornication <u>and</u>** which they have committed.
Galatians 5: 19	Now **the works of the flesh** are *these;*

1 PETER 4: 5	Who shall give account to him that is ready to judge the **quick** and the dead.
1 Peter 2: 4	To whom coming, *as unto* a **living** stone,

2 PETER

2 PETER 1: 4	**Whereby** are given us exceeding great and precious promises:
1 Peter 3: 19	**By which** also he went and unto the spirits in prison;

2 PETER 1: 8	they make *you that shall* neither *be* **barren <u>nor</u> unfruitful** In the knowledge of our Lord Jesus Christ.

N.B. note how the underlined word separates words and phrases having the same meaning.

2 PETER 1: 13	Yea, I think it **meet,** as long as I am in this tabernacle,
1 Thess. 3: 1	we thought it **good** to be left at Athens alone;
Acts 4: 19	Whether it be **right** in the sight of God to hearken unto more than unto God, judge ye.

2 PETER 2: 1	who **privily** shall bring in damnable heresies,
John 19: 38	being a disciple of Jesus, but **secretly** for fear of the Jews,
Acts 23: 19	and went *with him* aside **privately,**

2 PETER 2: 2	And many shall follow their **pernicious ways;** by reason of whom the way of truth shall be **evil** spoken of.
: 3	And through covetousness shall they with **feigned** words make merchandise of you:
3 John v10	prating against us with **malicious** words:

2 PETER 3: 6	**Whereby** the world that then was,
1 Peter 3: 19	**By which** also he went and preached to the spirits in prison.

1 JOHN

1 JOHN 1: 8	If we say that we have no sin, we deceive ourselves, and **the truth** is not in us.
: 10	If we say that we have not sinned, we make him a liar, and **his word** is not in us.
John 14: 6	Jesus said unto him, I am the way, **the truth,** and the life:
Rev. 19: 13	and his name is called **THE WORD OF GOD.**

1 JOHN 2: 2	And he is the **propitiation** for our sins:
Romans 5: 11	by whom we have received the **atonement.**
Heb. 2: 17	to make **reconciliation** for the sins of the people.
10: 12	But this man, after he had offered one **sacrifice** for sins
forever,	
: 14	For by one **offering** he hath perfected for ever them that are sanctified.
1 JOHN 2: 5	But whoso keepeth his word, in him **verily** is the love of God perfected:
1: 3	and **truly** our fellowship *is* with the Father, and with his Son Jesus Christ.
1 JOHN 2: 5	**hereby** know we that we are in him.
5: 2	**By this** we know that we love the children of God,
1 JOHN 2: 17	And the world passeth away, and the lust **thereof:**
James 1: 11	and the flower **thereof** falleth, and the grace of the fashion **of it** perisheth:
1 JOHN 2: 18	even now are there many antichrists: **whereby** we know that it is the last time.
5: 2	**By this** we know that we love the children of God,
1 JOHN 2: 20	But ye have an **unction** from the Holy One,
: 27	But the **anointing** which ye have received of him abideth in you,
1 JOHN 2: 24	Let that therefore **abide** in you, which ye have heard from the beginning. If that which ye have heard from the beginning shall **remain** in you,
1 JOHN 3: 12	And **wherefore** slew he him? Because his own works were evil,
Col. 2: 20	**Wherefore** if ye be dead with Christ from the rudiments of the world, **why,** as though living in the world,
1 JOHN 4: 3	and this is that *spirit* of antichrist, **whereof** ye have heard that it should come;
1 Peter 1: 10	**Of which** salvation the prophets have enquired and searched diligently,

2 JOHN

2 JOHN v 5	And now I **beseech** thee,
1 John 5: 16	I do not say that he shall **pray** for it.
2 JOHNv 8	Look to yourselves, that we lose not those things which we have **wrought,**

Heb. 10: 36	For ye have need of patience, that, after ye have **done** the will of God, ye might receive the promise.

3 JOHN

3 JOHN v 6	Which have borne witness of thy **charity** before the church:
Jude v 2	Mercy unto you, and peace, and **love** be multiplied.

3 JOHN v 10	**Wherefore, if** I come, I will remember his deeds which he doeth,
v 8	We **therefore** ought to receive such,

N.B. note the two bold in the first reference mean the same thing.

JUDE

JUDE v 4	turning the grace of God into **lasciviousness,**
v 7	giving themselves over to **fornication,** and going after **strange flesh,**

JUDE v 8	**Likewise also** these *filthy* dreamers defile the flesh,

N.B. note that the two bold words mean the same thing.

JUDE v 4	For there are certain men crept in unawares, who were before of old ordained to this condemnation, **ungodly** men, turning the grace of our God into **lasciviousness,**

Romans 1: 26	For this cause God gave them up unto **vile affections:**
: 29	**Being filled with all unrighteousness, fornication, wickedness, covetousness, maliciousness;**
: 31	**without natural affection,**

REVELATION

REV. 1: 3	and keep those things which are written **therein:**
20: 13	And the sea gave up the dead which were **in it;**

REV. 1: 15	And his feet **like** unto fine brass, **as** if they burned in a furnace;

REV. 1: 16	and out of his mouth went **a sharp twoedged sword:**
2: 2	These things saith he which hath **the sword with the two edges;**

REV. 1: 19	and the things which are, and the things which shall be here-**after;**

REV. 2: 4	**Nevertheless** I have *somewhat* against thee,
: 14	**But** I have a few things against thee,

: 20	**Notwithstanding** I have a few things against thee,
<u>REV. 2: 4</u>	Nevertheless I have ***somewhat*** against thee,
: 14	But I have **a few things** against thee,
<u>REV. 2: 13</u>	even in those days **wherein** An-ti-pas *was* my faithful martyr,
2 Peter 3: 16	**in which** are some things hard to be understood,
<u>REV. 3: 3</u>	If therefore thou shalt not watch, I will come **on** thee as a thief,
	And thou shalt not know what hour I will come **upon** thee.
<u>REV. 3: 16</u>	So then because thou art **lukewarm, <u>and</u> neither cold or hot,**
	I will spue thee out of my mouth.

N.B. note how the underlined word separates words and phrases having the same meaning.

<u>REV. 4: 1</u>	Come up **hither,** and I will shew thee things which must be hereafter.
13: 10	**Here** is the patience and the faith of the saints.
<u>REV. 4: 4</u>	clothed in white **raiment;**
6: 11	And white **robes** were given unto every one of them;
Jas. 2: 3	and ye have respect to him that weareth gay **clothing,**
<u>REV. 5: 2</u>	Who is worthy to open the book, and loose the seals **thereof?**
John 7: 7	because I testify **of it,** that the works **thereof** are evil.
<u>REV. 5: 3</u>	neither under the earth, was able to open the book, neither to look **thereon.**
Heb.6: 7	Fort the earth which drinketh in the rain that cometh oft **upon it,**
<u>REV. 8: 4</u>	And the smoke of the incense, *which came* with the prayers saints, **ascended up** before God out of the **angel's** hand.
Acts 1: 10	And while they looked stedfastly toward heaven as he **went up,**
<u>REV. 11: 1</u>	Rise, and measure the temple of God, and the altar, and them that worship **therein.**

N.B. reverse the syllables of the bold word and the meaning is clear.

<u>REV. 11: 13</u>	and the remnant were **affrighted,** and gave glory to the God of heaven.
Mark 16: 8	neither said they any thing to any *man;* for they were **afraid.**
<u>REV. 12: 2</u>	And she being with child cried, **travailing in birth, <u>and</u> pained to be delivered.**

REV. 13: 2   and the dragon gave him **power,** and his seat, and great **authority.**

REV. 13: 12   and causeth the earth and them which dwell **therein** to worship the first beast,

21: 23   And the city had no need of the sun, neither of the moon, to shine **in it:**

REV. 16: 2   and there fell a **noisome** <u>**and**</u> **grievous sore** upon the men which had the mark of the beast,

N.B.   note how the underlined word separates words andphrases having the same meaning.

REV. 16: 12   and the water **thereof** was dried up,

21: 22   for the Lord God Almighty and the Lamb are the temple **of it.**

REV. 18: 5   For her **sins** have reached unto heaven, and God hath remembered her **iniquities.**

REV. 18: 9   and lived deliciously with her, **shall bewail her** <u>**and**</u> **lament for her,** when they shall see the smoke of her burning.

: 15   shall stand afar off for the fear of her torment, **weeping** <u>**and**</u> **wailing,**

N.B.   note how the underlined word separates words and phrases having the same meaning.

REV. 18: 17   For in one hour so great riches is come to **nought.**

3: 17   Because thou sayest, I am rich, and increased with goods, and have need of **nothing;**

REV. 19: 20   And the beast was taken, and with him the false prophet that **wrought** miracles before him,

: 2   for he hath judged the great whore, which **did** corrupt the earth with her fornication,

2 Cor. 7: 12   *I did it* not for this cause that **had done** the wrong,

REV. 20: 7   And when the thousand years are **expired,**

Acts 21: 27   And when the seven days were almost **ended,**

REV. 20: 9   And they went up on the breadth of the earth and **compassed** the camp of the saints about,

Luke 19: 43   that thine enemies shall cast a trench about thee, and **compass thee round,** <u>**and**</u> **keep thee in on every side,**

N.B.   note how the underlined word separates words and phrases having the same meaning.

<u>**REV. 21: 12**</u>	and at the gates twelve angels, and names written **thereon,**
20: 4	And I saw thrones, and they sat **upon them,**
<u>**REV. 21: 15**</u>	And he that talked with me had a golden reed to measure the
	city, and the gates **thereof,**
: 18	And the building of the wall **of it** was *of* jasper:
<u>**REV. 21: 22**</u>	And I saw no temple **therein:**
22: 3	but the throne of God and of the Lamb shall be **in it;**
<u>**REV. 22: 15**</u>	For without *are* **dogs,** and sorcerers, and **whoremongers,**
1 Tim. 1: 10	For **whoremongers, for them that defile themselves with mankind,**

THE END

ATALOGUE ·

"Every word of God is pure:"
— Proverbs 30:5

King James Bibles

We have searched for King James Bibles that avoid the misleading marginal notes and careless spelling seen in some.

Cambridge Large Print	**$85.95**
Genuine Leather, gilt edge, ribbon, black	
Hardback	**$39.95**
Cambridge Windsor (Standard Print)	**$39.95**
Calfskin leather, gilt edge, ribbon, black or burgundy	
Hardback	**$12.95**
New Testament paperback	**$1.65**
Case of 40 Paperbacks (includes shipping)	**$85.00**
Holy Bible	**$6.50**
Black vinyl with gold foil stamped title	
Paperback	**$5.95**
Case of 20 Paperbacks (includes shipping)	**$140.00**
Photographic Reproduction of KJV 1611	
New Testament *Vinyl cover*	**$29.95**
CD-ROM Photographic Reproduction of entire 1611 King James Bible	**$9.95**

THE LANGUAGE OF THE KING JAMES BIBLE
by Gail Riplinger

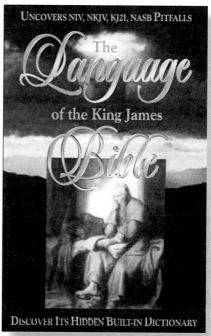

UNCOVERS NIV, NKJV, KJ21, NASB PITFALLS

The *Language* of the King James *Bible*

DISCOVER ITS HIDDEN BUILT-IN DICTIONARY

THE BOOK $12.95
*Demonstrates the precision
and power of the KJV*

30% discount off 5 or more   ($9.07)

30% discount off 5 or more   ($7.77)

THE DVDs $19.95
*Many charts shown and included in
Xerox format   2 Hrs*

THE POWERPOINT $19.95
(PDF also)

THE AUDIO (Radio interviews and lectures CDs)
The Language of the KJV $5.95

More Language of the KJV $5.95

**Language & Corrupt Lexicons:
Roots of the New Versions $5.95**

*Shows how to answer those who say,
'But the Greek says.' Answers the
toughest critics.*

AUDIO CD SET $9.95
Set includes both:

- The Language of the KJV
- Language & Corrupt Lexicons

Tracts

NIV, NASV Verse Comparison   20¢

Compares 78 critical NIV, ESV, HCSB, or NASV verses, which clearly shows their substitution of liberal and New Age teachings for the historical Christian doctrines seen in the KJV.

NKJV Death Certificate   33¢

Compares over 200 verses with the KJV. Shows 21 verses in which the NKJV demotes Jesus Christ, several dozen where it follows the Jehovah Witness Version and dozens and dozens where the NKJV supports New Age philosophy. A comparison of 138 words proves the KJV is easier to read than the NKJV. Folds out to 11 x 17 poster.

New Living Translation: A Critique   50¢

Compares over 100 verses with the KJV. This translation says the "number of the beast" should be called the "number of humanity"! Millions of unwary Christians are watching Pat Robertson promote this new corrupt 'bible' which he calls 'The Book'.

Book

NEW AGE BIBLE VERSIONS

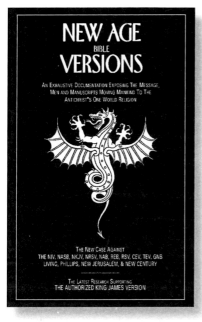

by G.A. Riplinger   **$16.95**

OVER 250,000 COPIES SOLD
BESTSELLER
EVER ON KJB ISSUE

- Over 2,500 verses compared
- 1,480 referenced footnotes
- 700 pages, 42 chapters

30% discount off 5 or more ($11.87 ea.)

40% discount off case of 14 ($160.00

includes shipping)

New!   Word and Name Index to New Age Bible Versions $3.00

New!   Scripture Location Index for New Age Bible Versions $2.00

New!   PowerPoint Presentation $19.95

New Book!
**The Only Authorized Picture
of Christ:**   **$7.95**
is the Holy Bible
by Russ & Riplinger
Critiques the movie, 'The Passion.'

Folios   by Riplinger

New!   Subliminal Embeds Exposed $2.50

New!   Collation of Corruptions in Holman's Christian Standard Bible $3.50

New!   Old Scofield Bible vs New Scofield $1.50

In Awe of Thy Word

Understanding the King James Bible
Its Mystery & History
Letter by Letter
by Gail Riplinger $29.95
1200 Page Hardcover, color-coded

*C*HIS BOOK is the first and only *documented* history of *the words* of the Holy Bible.

- It is based on word-for-word and letter-by-letter analysis of a vault of ancient, rare and valuable Bibles. Ten thousand hours of collation rescued echoes from these documents almost dissolved by time.

- See for yourself the unbroken preservation of the pure holy scriptures, from the first century to today's beloved King James Bible. Watch the English language and its Holy Bible unfold before your very eyes.

- Examine the letters and sounds, shown in red, which bind the words of each successive Bible from the Gothic, Anglo-Saxon, pre-Wycliffe, Tyndale, Coverdale, Great, Geneva, and Bishops' to the King James Bible.

- Uncover time-buried eyewitness reports, views and Bible study secrets of history's great translators and martyrs.

- See word-for-word collations, aided by the KJV translators' newly discovered notes, revealing exactly *how* the KJV translators polished the sword of the Spirit.

- Watch in horror as the destroyer, through the NIV, TNIV, HCSB, NKJV, NASB and ESV, teams up with Jehovah Witness and Catholic versions to silence the utterances of the Holy Ghost. History's Bibles and their champions defeat their challengers, as they meet on this book's pages.

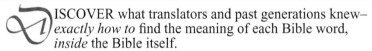

*D*ISCOVER what translators and past generations knew– *exactly how to* find the meaning of each Bible word, *inside* the Bible itself.

- Understand also what translators, such as Erasmus and Coverdale, meant when they spoke of the vernacular Bible's "holy letters" and "syllables."

- See how these God-set alphabet building blocks build a word's meaning and automatically define words for faithful readers of the King James Bible—which alone brings forward the fountainhead of letter meanings discovered by computational linguists from the world's leading universities.

- Learn about the latest research tools from the University of Toronto (EMEDD) and Edinburgh University, which prove the purity of the KJV and the depravity of the new versions.

- Find out how only the King James Bible teaches and comforts through its "miraculous" mathematically ordered sounds..

- Meet the KJV's build-in English teacher, ministering to children and over a billion people around the globe.

- Journey around the world and see that only the KJV matches the pure scriptures preserved "to all generations" including the Greek, Hebrew, Old Italia, Italian, Danish, German, French, Spanish and others.

CD-ROMs

$\mathcal{J}$N AWE of THY $\mathcal{W}$ORD

The book is also *searchable* on

3 CD-ROMS

$39.95

These include:

- **The King James Bible** searchable by words, letter groups and phrases.

- **In Awe of Thy Word** by G.A. Riplinger (searchable!). Plus exact photographic facsimiles of three complete documents used in the book's research:

- **The Nuremberg Polyglot** (A.D. 1599) containing the Gospels of the New Testament in 12 languages, as they appeared *before* the King James Bible (approx. 1100 pages). The Greek, Hebrew, Syriac, Latin, French, Spanish, Italian, German, English, Bohemian, Polish and Danish match the KJV precisely and prove the TNIV, NIV, NKJV, NASB, HCSB and ESV in error. This documents verse comparisons in *In Awe of Thy Word*, chapter 28.

- **The Tome of the Paraphrase of Erasmus Upon the New Testament** (1548-1549) Vol. 1 and Vol. 2 Erasmus' commentary on the New Testament (the original English translation), valued at over $30,000 today, has never before been made available to everyone. It is about 1880 pages, accompanied by the English New Testament of the Great Bible of 1540. It provides an addition to chapter 27 of *In Awe of Thy Word*.

- **The Acts and Monuments** by John Foxe This is the rare *entire* 8 volumes of Foxe's *Book of Martyrs*, nearing 6000 pages long. It was originally written in 1563; this is the 1837-49 printing. Reading this is a spiritual experience of a lifetime. It documents quotes in chapters 15 - 28 of *In Awe of Thy Word*. Print a page a day for 16 years of devotionals.

In Awe of Thy Word
Audio CDs
by Gail Riplinger
$21.95
5 CDs / 4 Hours
Hear Riplinger discuss the research and discoveries in
In Awe of Thy Word.

King James and His Translators
by Gail Riplinger   **$5.95**

THIS BOOK is an entire chaper drawn from the 1,200 page classic, *In Awe of Thy Word*, by G. A. Riplinger.

THE CHAPTER herein documents that King James I of England was a linguist and a scholar, but more importantly he was a Christian king and a godly man who sought the salvation of his family and subjects and authorized the Bible which has come to be called the King James Bible. Like many who seek to promote the word of God, James has been unfairly represented by "false accusers."

This chapter brings primary sources to bear which vindicate his character and retraces the steps which brought about the Authorized Version. The special qualities of each of the King's translators are presented. The myth of any subsequent revisions of the text of the King James Bible is put to rest. The Apocrypha is shown to be merely historical and pseudographic, as it was understood to be in 1611.

Tract

Why Only The KJB?
A Summary of *In Awe of Thy Word*   40¢

Share with others over 100 comparisons from the book proving why only the King James Bible is the pure word of God for English speakers. Help them learn how to understand the words in the Bible.

Folds into an envelope, then opens into a 16" x 26" poster, which demonstrates errors in the NIV, TNIV, NKJV, NASB, ESV, New Living Translation, and Holman Christian Standard Bible, which often match the Jehovah Witness and Catholic versions. Demonstrates 12 reasons why 'Only the King James Bible' is pure.

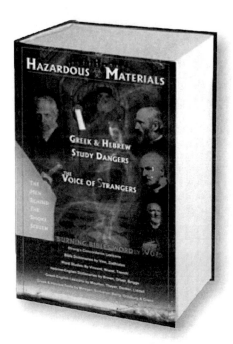

HAZARDOUS 🕱 MATERIALS

SAMPLES FROM THE TABLE OF CONTENTS

PART I

PROBLEMS WITH ALL GREEK LEXICONS & GRAMMARS

"Confessions of a Lexicographer" sounds warnings by professional lexicon and Bible dictionary makers themselves.

2 "Lexicon Death Certificates — Signed by the Doctors" Professional insider's secrets...58

3 "The 7 Deadly Sins: How Bible Dictionaries Are Made" Plagiarizing the past and paying penance today for the Liddell-Scott *Greek-English Lexicon* 71

4 "The Battle: The Spirit vs. The Desires of the Flesh & of the Mind" Secularizing words...97

5 "Mortal Sins: Living Verbs Wounded in Grammars" exposes the fallacies of current New Testament Greek grammar books and new version renderings 121

6 "Metzger's Lexical Aids and Greek Text Are Deadly" Nuggets From the Greek or Fools Gold?..136

PART II

ALL GREEK LEXICONS ARE FAULTY: *WHO'S WHO*

Greek Lexicons by Members of the Corrupt Westcott-Hort *Revised Version* Committee of 1881: Strong, Thayer and Scott

7 "Strong Delusion" James Strong's dangerous definitions in the back of his *Strong's Concordance*...........................157

8 "Logos Bible Software's Liddell–Scott *Greek-English Lexicon*" Did Henry Liddell protect 'Jack the Ripper' suspect, *Alice in Wonderland*'s Lewis Carroll (a.k.a. Charles Dodgson)? 203

Appendix:

Liddell-Scott *Greek-English Lexicon* editor Dean Henry (Humpty) Liddell & His Best Fiend* *Alice in Wonderland*'s Charles Dodgson...276

9 "Thayer's *Greek-English Lexicon*" reflects his Unitarianism; ASV words used as definitions 328

The Early Corrupters of New Testament Lexicons

10 "R. C. Trench: *Synonyms of the New Testament*" exposes this author, who uses the Luciferian serpent logo 358

Lexicons Defending Their Father's Westcott-Hort *Revised Version*:

11 "Moulton & Milligan's *Vocabulary of the Greek New Testament*" was co-authored by an editor who thinks pagan Zoroastrianism was a forerunner for Christianity; H.K. Moulton's *Analytical Greek Lexicon* exposed 402

Copycats

12 "Vine's *Expository Dictionary*" defines words with RV and ASV words and now has NIV editors. Vine denies that the blood saves 417

PART III

All AVAILABLE GREEK NEW TESTAMENT TEXTS ARE FAULTY

The following chapters will document problems relating to the printed editions of Greek texts, not covered in *New Age Bible Versions*. (Also see chapter 6 for problems relating to Metzger's UBS and NA text.)

17 "The Textual Heresies of F.H.A. Scrivener" He was a Bible critic and *Revised Version* Committee member, working under Westcott and Hort. He wanted to omit many crucial parts of the New Testament 578

18 "The Trinitarian Bible Society's Little Leaven: Scrivener's Greek *Textus Receptus*" Chapter exposes this text and Frederick Scrivener, who back-translated the KJB into Greek and also made some unwarranted changes to this *Textus Receptus*, now published as a so-called edition of Beza; exposes Green's *Interlinear* 629

19 "Very Wary of George Ricker Berry" demonstrates the problems with his *Greek-English Interlinear* New Testament which wrongly omits words, a whole verse, and is accompanied by a faulty English interlinear 695

20 "The Wobble Unorthodox Greek Orthodox Crutch" shows the heresies and textual errors that plague the Greek text preserved by the Orthodox church and wrongly presented as the 'Majority text' by Zodhiates, Hodges-Farstad, and Pierpoint-Robinson. Exposes origin and heresy of the 'Divine Intimacy' 730

21 "Zodhiates' Byzantine Empire Strikes Back" discloses his corrupt lexicon, which plagiarized NIV editors. Shows his use of a corrupt Greek text 797

22 "Child Molester on New Version Committee" This and the following chapter reveal for the first time that B.F. Westcott, the editor of the Greek text underlying new versions such as the TNIV, NIV, NRSV, NASB, ESV, and HCSB, opened the door for his old homosexual and pedophile compatriot, C. J. Vaughan, to work closely with him on his RV Committee. These men's RV English word choices are echoed in *Vine's Expository Dictionary*, other lexicons, and all new versions 825

Hebrew Lexicon by Member of the Corrupt Westcott-Hort *Revised Version* Committee of 1881

25 "Brown, Driver, and Briggs *Hebrew-English Lexicon*" was taken from Gesenius; Briggs's secret meeting with the Catholic hierarchy in Rome (recently revealed by a Harvard University journal) and his trial for heresy are brought to light. Their words are seen in the NIV and all new versions today 918

28 "Hebrew Masoretic Old Testament Non-Authoritative Texts" shockingly reveals that C. Ginsburg, editor of the only currently available printed edition of the good Bomberg (so-called Ben Chayim) Rabbinic Bible and published by the Trinitarian Bible Society, was a follower of the wicked Kabbala and Luciferian Madame Helena P. Blavatsky; also exposes Jay P. Green's *Interlinear* 1005

30 "The Scriptures to All Nations": Translating Yesterday and Today...1093

31 "Seven Proofs of the King James Bible's Inspiration" 1131

Answering The Skeptics

Blind Guides   2007 Update   **$8.95**
25% discount off 5 or more ($6.70 ea.)

*Riplinger's detailed and scholarly responses—
unanswerable by skeptics like James White, Hunt,
Cloud, Hanagraaff, House, Morey and Passantino.*

Answers Minton I: **$3.95**
NIV, ESV, HCSB, NASB, NKJV errors

*Riplinger answers KJV critic Ron Minton, providing
support for the unwisely criticized KJV reading in
Titus 2:13, II Peter 1:1 and Psalm 12:6,7. Includes
Harvard professor's concurrence regarding B. F.
Westcott's denial of the creed. Adds data about the
earliest papyri and the NKJV's faulty* **Hodges-Farstad**
so-called **Majority Text.**

Answers Minton II: NKJV Errors   **$3.95**
Proves KJV superior to NKJV at every point.

*Riplinger's defence of the use of the KJV's words 'God'
and 'blood'—omitted numerous times by the NKJV.
Proves conclusively that the NKJV ignores the Hebrew
text, uses weaker renderings, paraphrase and new age
buzz words.*

PowerPoint: 490 Slides To The Plummet From the Summit
*Riplinger's original research answering hundreds of
common myths and false charges against the KJB.*
CD-ROM (PDF also)   **$19.95**

The Collected Works of Dr. Alan O'Reilly
*Britain's brightest professor defends the KJB against the
attacks of James White, Kirk DiVietro, and others. An
encyclopedia of original and scriptural research.*
CD-ROM (PDF)   **$19.95**

Book of Bible Problems
by Gerardus Bouw Ph.D.   **$16.95**
*Answers every question. A classic book!
Proves KJV error free!*

Books, Audio CDs, and CD-ROMs

New Release!
WHICH BIBLE IS GOD'S WORD?
2007 EXPANDED UPDATES

by G.A. Riplinger **$12.95**

Transcript of the series of interviews with G.A. Riplinger by Noah Hutchings of the nationally syndicated program Southwest Radio Church. Answers these and many other common questions concerning bible versions.

- *How do new versions change the gospel?*
- *How do the NIV, ESV, HCSB and NASB support New Age philosophy?*
- *What about the NKJV, KJ²¹, and others which say they merely update the KJV?*
- *Where was the bible before the KJV 1611?*
- *What errors are the KJV critics making?*

30% discount off 5 or more ($9.07 ea.)
40% discount off case of 14 ($120.00 includes shipping)

The Audios 2 CD Audio transcript of *Which Bible*: $9.95

The best CDs available on the KJV issue. Thoroughly exposes the corrupt NKJV as well as the NIV, ESV, HCSB and NASB.

The Classics

The Revision Revised by John Burgon (CD-ROM)	**$9.95**
The Last Twelve Verses of Mark (CD-ROM)	**$9.95**
The Traditional Text of the Holy Gospels (CD-ROM)	**$9.95**
The Causes of Corruption of the Traditional Text (CD-ROM)	**$9.95**
Which Bible? edited by D.O. Fuller (paperback book)	**$13.95**

The classic defense of the KJV which led Dr. S. Franklin Logsdon, who had set forth the guidelines for the NASB, to renounce his own NASB and all new versions.

The King James Defended   by Edward F. Hills   (paperback)   **$18.95**
The author, a graduate of Yale University and Westminister Theological Seminary, with a Th.M. from Columbia Seminary and Th.D from Harvard presents overwhelming evidence for the historical accuracy of the KJV.

Video DVDs and Audio CDs

RESEARCH UPDATE
by G. A. Riplinger

2 DVDs	**$24.95**
3 Audio CDs	**$9.95**

INFORMATION OVER-LOAD! Over three hours of lectures are presented on these two videos. They begin with a half hour overview presenting problems in the NKJV, followed by nearly an hour update and overview of errors in the NIV, ESV, HCSB, NASB and other new versions. Listeners will learn that 1) Rupert Murdoch, owner of the Bart Simpson television program, now owns the NIV's printing rights, 2) Roman Catholic Cardinal Carlo Maria Martini, the man Time magazine said is most likely to be the next pope, now edits the Greek text underlying the NIV and NASV, 3) Martin Woudstra, a supporter of the homosexual movement, was the NIV's Old Testament chairman!

DVD TWO IS A 2 HOUR PUBLIC QUESTION AND ANSWER SESSION. The following are just a few of the many questions answered: What is the origin of the Catholic edition? Why do "good men" unknowingly use corrupt versions? Why is "Easter" the correct rendering in Acts 12:4? How is the KJV's own self-contained dictionary superior to definitions given in Greek and Hebrew lexicons written by unsaved liberals like Thayer and Briggs? Why is "Lucifer" etymologically the correct rendering in Isaiah 14:12? What are the Satanic parallels to NKJV's logo? Why is the KJ²¹ more difficult to read than the real KJV? Why are the so-called "literal" translations in Berry's, Green's, and Kohlenburger's Interlinears in error? What are the parallels between the Jehovah Witness version and the NKJV?

Riplinger also discusses many other subjects such as: 1) The KJV's use of cognitive scaffolding which makes it a perfect tool for teaching "little folks" to read, 2) the dangerous Dead Sea Scrolls 3) the recent discovery by the world's pre-eminent mathematicians of names imbedded in the KJV's Hebrew text. (Nothing could be found when they tried their statistical analysis with the texts underlying the NKJV, NIV, ESV, HCSB, and NASB) and 4) Lucis Trust (Lucifer Publishing Co.) documents discussing their planned infiltration of the church.

These lectures were televised on Scripps Howard cable network and WPMC-TV. They were taped at Temple Baptist Church.

Video DVDs

TRANSPARENT TRANSLATIONS & TRANSLATORS

DVD	$25.00
PowerPoint	$19.95
Handout Master	$14.95
Summary of Version Issue (12 *Xerox pages*)	$1.50

Thousands of participants in nearly a dozen of the major U.S. cities viewed this presentation filmed at a TV station in Kansas City or heard it aired on radio. Dr. Riplinger lectured 2½ hours, presenting on a huge screen, nearly 100 actual pictures and charts documenting the new age and occult influence in the counterfeit new versions. The audience often gasped in shock, seeing such things as the NKJV's 666 logo—now on the forehead of the latest smart card owners. This "picture show" is one-of-a-kind.

*This is the **best** video to share with friends who need a thorough analysis of the thousands of errors in the NIV, ESV, HCSB, NASB & NKJV.*

NKJV LOGO EXPOSED   DVD $14.95

Participants flew from France, Australia, and Canada and watched this pictorial history of the NKJV logo as Dr. Riplinger traced it from its origin in Baal worship and through its migration to the Druids, the church of Rome, the Masons, and the Satanists.

Video DVDs and Audio CDs

OVERVIEW by G. A. Riplinger

Single DVD $16.95
Audio 3 CDs $9.95

This single two hour video clearly presents the differences between the corrupt new versions and our beloved King James Bible. It presents the history of the Bible chronologically—its inspiration and perfect preservation by God—as well as attempted corruptions, past, present, and planned.

The material is presented simply and slowly for viewers who would like an overview and introduction to the subject. It is excellent for beginning a discussion with Sunday School classes, youth groups or precious friends who unknowingly use new corrupt versions like the ESV, HCSB, NIV, NKJV, NASV, NRSV, CEV, TEV, REB, KJ²¹, RV, NAB, Good News, New Living, Phillips, New Jerusalem, Message or New Century versions.

These lectures of Dr. Riplinger's were televised over WBFX and aired over WPIP radio from The Berean Baptist Church.

OVERVIEW
2 HOURS

INTERVIEWS

Nationally syndicated Christian programs in which host interviews G. A. Riplinger about the book *New Age Bible Versions*. Discussions thoroughly cover the contents and topics in the book.

DVD

Niteline $19.95
This video has gone all around the world converting many precious souls to the KJV. 90 min.

Action Sixties $24.95
Used successfully in scores of churches as a teaching series to educate members regarding the errors in corrupt new versions. One pastor commented that his most hardened new version fan "melted like a popsicle in a microwave" after viewing these 4 programs. (4 hours)

Video DVDs and Audio CDs

New Age Bible Versions Album $35.95
30 interviews with the author by talk show hosts across the nation. Lots of ideas for answering tough questions. 16 audio CDs

KNIS Radio Interview   **$5.95**
with Riplinger/Feltner (audio CD)

DETAILED UPDATE
Audio 2 CDs $9.95

Hundreds of pastors gathered to hear Dr. Riplinger's very detailed and convincing answers to the excuses given by new version users; includes important textual alerts for pastors and students. NKJV is thoroughly discussed. 2 hours

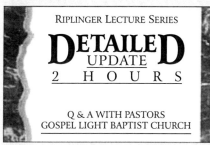

RIPLINGER LECTURE SERIES
DETAILED
UPDATE
2   H O U R S

Q & A WITH PASTORS
GOSPEL LIGHT BAPTIST CHURCH

Testimony & Lecture: Riplinger in the Lion's Den (DVD or CD)   **$14.95**

From NASB to KJV, Dr. S. Franklin Logsdon (audio CD)   **$5.95**

Ridiculous Bible Versions of the New Age, Bryan Denlinger   **$19.95**
(Fabulous production and research) DVD

The Real Bible Version Issue Exposed, Bryan Denlinger   **$19.95**
(Show your friends!) DVD

Hush, You Don't Speak Greek   **$14.95**
Gutsy sermon preached by Dr. Norris Belcher **DVD**

New Book

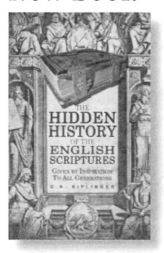

Hidden History of the English Scriptures

by G. A. Riplinger **$7.95**

5 or more copies $3.97 each

The definitive treatise on the history of our English Bible from Acts 2 to the KJB, distilled like DNA molecules and tightly packed with dynamic facts. Proves conclusively, using direct quotes from the 1500s and linguistic experts, that 'the originals' were not written in Greek alone.

Hidden History of the English Scriptures DVD **$12.95**
This pictoral history of the English Bible comes alive with Riplinger's son-in-law, Stephen Shutt, its author and presenter.

Hidden History PowerPoint CD-ROM **$19.95**
Presented by Stephen Shutt across the U.S. for the 400th anniversary of the KJB, this PowerPoint blessed and enlightened thousands.

KJB Inspiration Defended

King James Bible Inspiration: DVD **$19.95**
Join the congregation for over 4 hours of lectures. Using our Inspiration PowerPoint, Stephen Shutt eloquently explains from primary historical sources and the scriptures why the KJB is inspired. Hear Sam Gipp, Rick Sowell and others, too.

KJV Inspiration PowerPoint CD-ROM **$19.95**
Riplinger's powerful 439 slide PowerPoint demonstrates the dangers of Greek & Hebrew study tools and proves the inspiration of the KJB. This exhaustive and detailed presentation of primary sources is a must!

Further Thoughts on the Word of God
by John M. Asquith **$7.95**
Defends KJB inspiration.

Hath God Said?
by Dan Goodwin **$10.95**
Defends KJB inspiration.

Recent Scholarship

The Answer Book by Samuel Gipp Th.D. **$6.95**
Answers the 62 questions most frequently asked by the cynics. Includes answers to false arguments about King James, Erasmus, the word "Easter" etc.

New! **A Testimony Founded Forever: The King James Bible Defended In Faith and History** by Dr. James Sightler
Riplinger said this is "the most exhaustively researched book on the KJV issue in the last 100 years!" Focuses on the sinister beliefs of B. F. Westcott, the chief editor of the corrupt Greek text-type underlying the NIV and NASB. Other books by Sightler below. **$18.95**

Westcott's New Bibles
$7.95

Silver Words and Pure
Questions & Answers
$5.95

Lively Oracles
Defends KJV Inspiration
$4.95

A Closer Look: Early Manuscripts and the A.V.
by Jack Moorman **$15.95**
Great tool! Examines the papyri, uncials, cursives, as well as the Latin, Syriac, Coptic, Gothic, Armenian, and Ethiopic versions, and the church 'Fathers', in light of their agreement with the KJV.

Missing in Modern Bibles:
An Analysis of the NIV by Jack Moorman **$12.95**
Contains a collation of important changed passages and a discussion of the poor theories and manuscripts underlying them.

When the KJV Departs From The Majority
by Jack Moorman **$15.95**
The NKJV footnotes erroneously point to the 'Majority' text, when they are in fact only referring to the faulty Greek Text According to the Majority (1982) by Hodge and Farstad. It falls far short of a full collation of manuscripts since it is based primarily on Von Soden's collation of only 414 of the over 5000 manuscripts.

Early Church Fathers and the A.V. by Jack Moorman **$8.95**
Documentation proving that the early church 'fathers' were quoting a KJV text type.

By Divine Order   **$12.95**
The King James Code   **$14.95**
By Michael Hoggard
*Two books by Hoggard explore the
miraculous number patterns in
the KJV.*

The Word: God Will Keep It   **$16.95**
by Joey Faust   *Best researched book of the
21st century!! Includes 335 pages of direct
quotations from the 1600s to the present,
demonstrating that men have always believed
that the KJB is inspired and not in need of
"defining" via questionable Greek sources.*

Easy To Read

If the Foundations Be Destroyed by Chick Salliby   **$5.95**
*An easy to read and beautifully written comparison of the NIV
and KJV text, proving the bankruptcy of the NIV.*

Things That are Different by Dr. Mickey Carter   **$6.95**
Helped NKJV editor switch.

Let's Weigh The Evidence by Barry Burton   **$5.95**

Did the Roman Catholic Church Give Us the Bible?   **$9.95**
by David Daniels
Chick publications make learning fun & easy. A classic!

Look What's Missing! A must!! by David W. Daniels   **$12.95**

Words in the Word: KJB Bible Definitions & Grammar

By Definition by James Knox   **$10.95**
Interesting KJV word studies.

The King James Bible's Built-In Dictionary
by Barry Goddard **(Book and CD-ROM)**   **$29.95**
*Set includes both the soft-cover book, as well as the
new 2012 675-page searchable CD-ROM edition,
which is 37% bigger and allows you to find all of the
ways words are defined throughout the Bible.*

How to Find the KJB's Built-In Dictionary

Narrated by British trained Dan Woolridge. $49.95

Sit back and watch these 14 DVDs with nearly 11 hours of training,
and see the KJB's built-in dictionary come to life.

American Dictionary of the English Language

edited 1828 by Noah Webster $69.95

A must for every home. Defines words as they were used during the writing
of the KJV 1611. Contains scripture references, etymologies from 28 languages
and pronunciations. Modern dictionaries reflect cultural corruptions; consider and
compare definitions for words such as sin, marriage, truth, spirit, and Jesus Christ.

Also available on CD-Rom **$29.95**

Understand things you've never understood before with these three books.

English for Bible Readers	**$12.95**
by Paul Scott	
Diagramming the Scriptures	**$21.95**
by Shirley Forsen	
Archaic Words	**$29.95**
630 page hardback KJB dictionary	
by Laurence Vance	

Notecards (12)

Plan of Salvation on the back. KJV only

Scriptures (a)	**$6.95**
Messiah (b)	**$6.95**
Parables of Jesus (c)	**$6.95**
Name of the Lord (d)	**$6.95**

(a) (b) (c) (d)

Music CDs and Book

God Hath Done All Things Well (Music CD): Bryn Riplinger Shutt **$14.95** *A voice like an angel!*

Ask for the Old Paths (Music CD): Bryn Riplinger Shutt **$14.95** *Pure conservative music*

Take Heed What Ye Hear by Bryn Riplinger Shutt **$6.95** *How to select scriptural music*

TO ORDER

"please call or see avpublications.com for price updates"

BY PHONE: **1-800-435-4535** (credit card only)

BY FAX: 1-276-251-1734

(other callers 1-276-251-1734)

BY MAIL: Send check or Money Order or VISA,
MasterCard, American Express, or Discover Card Number
and Expiration Date to: **A.V. Publications**
P.O. Box 280
Ararat, VA 24053 USA

SHIPPING:	$1.01-$4.00 add $3.00	$30.01-$40.00 add $10.00
	$4.01-$20.00 add $8.00	$40.01-$70.00 add $11.00
	$20.01-$30.00 add $9.00	$70.01 and over add 15%

CANADIAN SHIPPING:	$1.00-$20.00 add $12.00	$70.01-$90.00 add $43.00
	$20.01-$30.00 add $22.00	$91.00 and over add 50%
	$30.01-$70.00 add $30.00	

FOREIGN SHIPPING:	$1.00-$20.00 add $20.00	$80.01-$100.00 add $52.00
	$20.01-$50.00 add $32.00	$100.01 and over add 50%
	$50.01-$80.00 add $50.00	We will discount foreign and Canadian shipping for light DVDs and CDs.

FOREIGN and CANADIAN ORDERS: Credit Card Only

VA RESIDENTS: Add 5% sales tax

BOOKSTORES: Call for discounts.

VISIT OUR WEBSITE
www.avpublications.com

- View complete and updated catalogue of KJV Bibles and books, videos, and tracts supporting the KJV.
- Place secure credit card orders
- Download verse comparison tract; see research updates.

"Finally, brethren, pray for us, that the word of the Lord may have free course, and be glorified, even as it is with you:" II Thess. 3:1